The **Rough Guide** to

Belize

written and researched by

Peter Eltringham

with additional contributions by

Daniel C. Chang, Nadine Pedoe and AnneLise Sorensen

NEW YORK • LONDON • DELHI

www.roughguides.com

Contents

Colour section 1–16

Introduction 6
Where to go 9
When to go 11
Things not to miss 12

Basics 17–58

Getting there 19
Arrival 26
Getting around 26
Accommodation 31
Food and drink 34
Health 36
The media 41
Festivals 42
Sports and outdoor activities 43
Culture and etiquette 44
Shopping 45
Travelling with children 46
Travel essentials 47

Guide 59–302

1. Belize City 61
2. The north 91
3. The northern cayes and atolls 123
4. Cayo and the west 159
5. Tikal and Flores 209
6. The south 233

Contexts 303–376

History 305
Chronology of the Maya 325
Chronology of Belize 327
The Maya achievement 329
Archeology 335
Landscape and wildlife 338
Conservation 345
Human rights and democracy 354
Ethnic Belize 356
Music 358
Dance 365
Books 366

Language 377–384

Kriol 379
Spanish 381

Travel store 385–400

Small print & Index 401–416

The Maya world colour section following p.112

Belize's reef and cayes colour section following p.224

◀◀ Sunset over the Caribbean Sea ◀ Glover's Reef

Cancún
0
50 km
N
MEXICO
Chetumal
Santa Elena
Consejo
Santa Rita
Corozal
Sarteneja
Cerros
Kinichná
Río Bec
Kohunlich
MEXICO
Río Hondo
Shipstern Lagoon
Progresso Lagoon
Xcalak
Bacalar Chico
Reef Point
Deer Caye
Orange Walk
COROZAL DISTRICT
Ambergris Caye
Barrier Reef
Blackadore Caye
San Pedro
La Unión
Blue Creek
Blue Creek
San Felipe
New River
NORTHERN HIGHWAY
OLD NORTHERN HIGHWAY
Maskall
CARIBBEAN SEA
La Milpa
Río Bravo
Lamanai
Indian Church
Crooked Tree
Altun Ha
Río Azul
Caye Caulker
Hick's Caye
New River Lagoon
BELIZE DISTRICT
Caye Chapel
Sand Hill
ORANGE WALK DISTRICT
Burrell Boom
Bermudian Landing
Long Caye
Mauger Caye
Chan Chich
Ladyville
Gallon Jug
International airport
Hattieville
Belize City
St George's Caye
Belize Zoo
Sibun River
English Caye
Northern Caye
Turneffe Islands
Blue Hole
Central Lagoon
Belize River
Northern Lagoon
Uaxactún
El Pilar
Spanish Lookout
WESTERN HIGHWAY
La Democracia
Middle Long Caye
Lighthouse Reef
Tikal
BELMOPAN
Southern Lagoon
Gales Point
Bluefield Range
Georgeville
Half Moon Caye

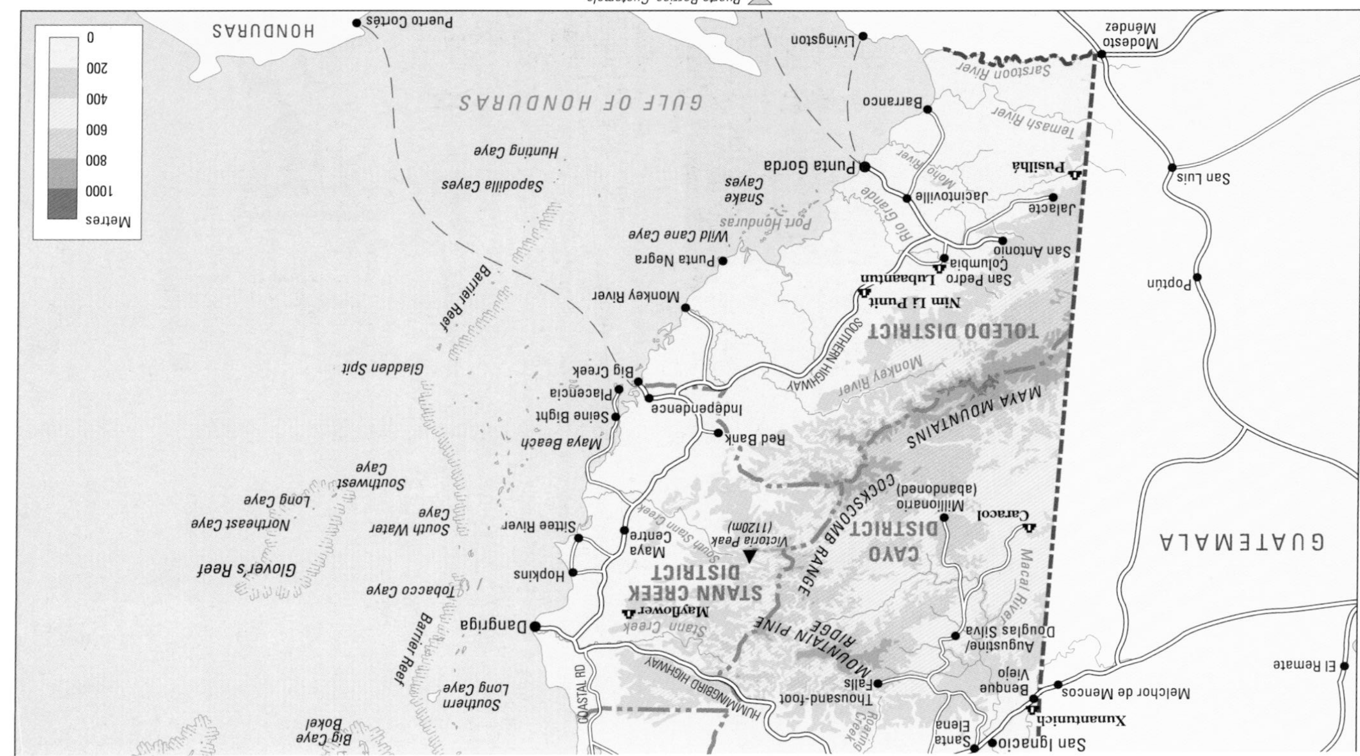
Metres
1000
800
600
400
200
0
HONDURAS
GULF OF HONDURAS
GUATEMALA
Puerto Barrios, Guatemala
Flores
Flores
Puerto Cortés
Livingston
Modesto Méndez
Sarstoon River
Temash River
Barranco
Hunting Caye
Sapodilla Cayes
Punta Gorda
Snake Cayes
Port Honduras
Rio Grande
Moho River
Jacintoville
Pusilhá
Jalacte
San Luis
San Antonio
San Pedro Columbia
Lubaantun
Nim Li Punit
Wild Cane Caye
Punta Negra
Monkey River
Barrier Reef
TOLEDO DISTRICT
SOUTHERN HIGHWAY
Monkey River
Poptún
Gladden Spit
Big Creek
Placencia
Independence
Seine Bight
Red Bank
Maya Beach
MAYA MOUNTAINS
Southwest Caye
Long Caye
Northeast Caye
Glover's Reef
South Water Caye
Sittee River
Maya Centre
South Stann Creek
Victoria Peak (1120m)
COCKSCOMB RANGE
Millionario (abandoned)
CAYO DISTRICT
Caracol
Macal River
Hopkins
STANN CREEK DISTRICT
Mayflower
Tobacco Caye
Dangriga
Barrier Reef
Stann Creek
MOUNTAIN PINE RIDGE
Augustine/ Douglas Silva
Southern Long Caye
COASTAL RD
HUMMINGBIRD HIGHWAY
Thousand-foot Falls
Roaring Creek
Benque Viejo
Melchor de Mencos
El Remate
Big Caye Bokel
Santa Elena
San Ignacio
Xunantunich

Introduction to

Belize

Wedged into the northeastern corner of Central America, Belize offers some of the most breathtaking coastal scenery – both above and below water – in the Caribbean. Throw in magnificent landscapes, vast archeological sites and wildlife to rival that of any destination in the region, and it's easy to see why the number of visitors to this tiny country increases every year.

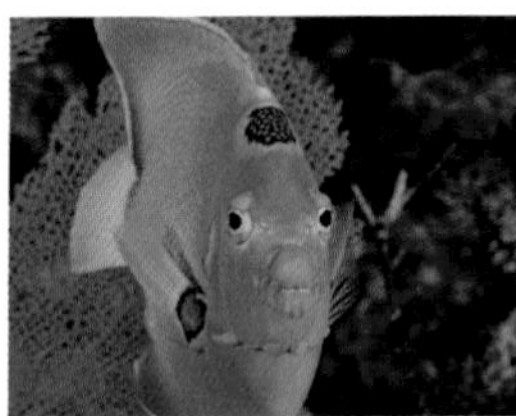

Belizean territory comprises marginally more sea than land, and for most visitors the sea is the main attraction. Lying just offshore is one of the country's, and the continent's, most astonishing natural wonders – the dazzling turquoise shallows and cobalt depths of the longest **barrier reef** in the Americas. Beneath the surface, a brilliant technicolour world of fish and corals awaits divers and snorkellers, while a chain of islands known as **cayes**, scattered along the entire reef, protects the mainland from the ocean swell and holds more than a hint of tropical paradise. Beyond the reef lie the real jewels in Belize's natural crown – three of only four **coral atolls** in the Caribbean. These reefs and islands, among the most diverse marine ecosystems on the planet, are increasingly under threat; Belize, however, is developing effective protection for the entire coastal zone, which for visitors means a chance to explore some of the best **marine reserves** in the world.

In fact, Belizeans' recognition of the importance of their natural heritage means that the country now has the greatest proportion of protected land (over 40 percent) in the hemisphere. As a result, the densely **forested interior** remains relatively untouched. The rich tropical forests support a tremendous range of **wildlife**, including howler and spider

▲ Maya pottery

monkeys, tapirs and pumas, jabiru storks and scarlet macaws. Although it's the only Central American country without a volcano, Belize does have some rugged uplands – the **Maya Mountains**, situated in the south-central region and rising to over 1100m. The country's main rivers start here, flowing north and east to the Caribbean, and forming some of the largest **cave systems** in the Americas along the way.

In addition to these natural attractions, Belize boasts a wealth of archeological remains. Rising mysteriously out of the forests are the ruins of the **ancient cities** of the **Maya**, the civilization that dominated the area from around 2000 BC until the arrival of the Spanish. Although only a few sites in Belize have been as extensively restored as the great Maya cities of Mexico's Yucatán Pensinsula, many are at least as large, and in their forest settings you'll see more wildlife and fewer tour buses.

Culturally, Belize is as Caribbean as it is Latin

Fact file

- Belize shares a border with Mexico to the north and Guatemala to the west and south; to the east is the Caribbean Sea. Belize's 22,806 square kilometres of land is roughly equal to that of Massachusetts or Wales, and it has a slightly greater area of territorial sea. Tourism is now the mainstay of the economy, but agriculture and fishing still play important roles.
- Belize has a bicameral **National Assembly**, consisting of a House of Representatives with 29 members and a 12-member Senate. The government is headed by the **Prime Minister** but, as Belize is a **constitutional monarchy**, the head of state is Queen Elizabeth II, represented in Belize by the Governor-General, who is always a Belizean.
- As of July 2007, Belize's **population** was estimated at just under 295,000, with an average age of 20 years. Average life expectancy is 68 years.
- Belize's **national anthem** is "Land of the Free by the Carib Sea", and a recording by schoolchildren is broadcast every morning at 6am on Love FM. The national **animal** is the Baird's tapir, the national **bird** is the keel-billed toucan, the national **flower** is the black orchid and the national **tree** is the mahogany tree; you can see all of these at the Belize Zoo (see p.79).

Belizean art

The Belizean **art scene** becomes more self-assured every year. Locally born and naturalized artists abound in this visually inspirational country, and as generations grow up under their influence and develop their own political, environmental and social awareness, techniques and subjects become ever more sophisticated.

Whether you prefer classic watercolours of Caribbean shores, Picasso-esque abstracts, traditional Maya wood carvings or provocative installations, Belize's innumerable **galleries** are bound to have something to suit your tastes. Don't miss the excellent **Image Factory** in Belize City (see p.72), where conceptual artists demonstrate their own brands of politically and socially charged work, and monthly exhibitions showcase pieces from around the country. Set in dramatic forest near the Guatemalan border, the astonishing Land-Sculpture Park of Poustinia (see p.206) features absorbing, environmentally and historically themed installations. And Belizeans from every corner of the country display their latest work at the Sidewalk Arts Festival in Placencia each February.

Culturally, Belize is as much a Caribbean nation as a Latin one, but with plenty of distinctively Central American features – above all, a blend of races and cultures that includes Maya, mestizo, African and European. English is the official language – Belize only gained full independence from Britain in 1981 – and Spanish is equally common, but it's the rich, lilting **Creole**, based on English but essentially Caribbean, that's spoken and understood by almost every Belizean.

▲ Pier on Ambergris Caye

Where to go

Belize is an ideal place to explore independently; even on a short visit you'll be able to take in both the cayes and the heartland of the ancient Maya. Almost every visitor will have to spend at least some time in chaotic **Belize City**, even if only passing through, as it's the hub of the country's transport system. Nearby, the **Belize Zoo** is easily the best in Central America and well worth making a special effort to visit.

Northern Belize is relatively flat and often swampy, with a large proportion of agricultural land. **Lamanai**, near Orange Walk, is one of the most impressive Maya sites in Belize, while the lagoons at **Shipstern Nature Reserve** on the northeast coast and inland at **Crooked Tree** provide superb protected habitats for the country's abundant wildlife, particularly birds. In the northwest, adjacent to the Guatemalan border, is the vast **Rio Bravo Conservation and Management Area**, where hunting has been banned for over a decade, allowing the possibility of close encounters with the wildlife.

Belize offers everything the eco-tourist could want

The mainland coast is almost entirely low-lying marsh – wonderful for wildlife, but for swimming and underwater activities you'll need to visit the **cayes**. The largest of these, **Ambergris Caye**, draws over half of all Belize's tourists, with the tiny resort town of **San Pedro** their main destination; **Caye Caulker**, to the south, is the most popular island for independent travellers. Organized diving and snorkelling day-trips are available to the wonderful atolls of the **Turneffe Islands** and **Lighthouse Reef**.

In the west of the country, **San Ignacio** and its environs offer everything the eco-tourist could want: Maya ruins and rainforest, rivers and caves and excellent, low-impact accommodation in every price range. **Caracol**, the largest Maya site in Belize, is now a routine day-trip from here,

▲ Scarlet macaws

while the magnificent ruins of **Xunantunich** lie en route to the Guatemalan border. Cross the border and a few hours later you can be in **Tikal**, one of the greatest of all Maya cities.

Dangriga, the main town of the south-central region, is a jumping-off point for visitors to the central cayes and **Glover's Reef**, Belize's most remote atoll. Further south, on the coast, the quiet Garifuna village of **Hopkins** sees more visitors every year, while the delightful, relaxed fishing village of **Placencia**, at the tip of a long, curving peninsula, has some of the country's best **beaches**. Inland, at the village of **Maya Centre**, is the road to **Cockscomb Basin Wildlife Sanctuary** (the **Jaguar Reserve**) and the trailhead to **Victoria Peak**, Belize's most majestic mountain. The majority of visitors to the coastal community of **Punta Gorda**, the main town of Toledo District, are on their way by boat to or from Puerto Barrios in Guatemala. Venture inland, however, and you'll come across the villages of the **Mopan** and **Kekchí Maya**, set in stunning countryside and surrounded by the country's only true **rainforest**. Here are yet more caves, rivers and Maya sites, including **Lubaantun**, source of the enigmatic Crystal Skull.

The Garifuna

One of Belize's most fascinating ethnic groups is the **Garifuna** (or **Garinagu**), descendents of escaped African slaves and indigenous Caribbean islanders. Today they thrive along the southern coast, particularly in the villages of Dangriga, Hopkins, Seine Bight, Punta Gorda and Barranco. Most carry out a subsistence lifestyle, with women working the farms and preparing meals, men heading to sea before daybreak to fish and children helping with family chores.

Their culture is exuberantly displayed on November 19, **Garifuna Settlement Day**, a national holiday celebrating their historic arrival in Belize in the early nineteenth century. Many Garifuna re-enact their migration in dories loaded with drums, cassava, banana leaves, palm fronds and flags of yellow, white and black. Equally festive are **rituals** surrounding the deceased: the *beluria* is a nine-day devotional ceremony for the dead, and the *dugu* is a sacred rite involving ancestral spirit worship.

When to go

▲ Caye Caulker

Due to Belize's **sub-tropical** latitude, the weather is always warm by European standards, and often hot and very humid. The climate in any one place is largely determined by **altitude**: evenings in the forests of the Mountain Pine Ridge are generally pleasantly cool, while the lowland jungle is always steamy and humid. On the cayes, the sun's heat is tempered by near-constant ocean breezes.

Although Belize has its dry and rainy seasons, you'll find that the sun shines most of the year, and while rain can fall in any month, it's rarely persistent enough to ruin a holiday. The **dry season** runs roughly from February to May, and the last couple of months before the rains come can be stiflingly hot. During the **rainy season**, from around June to November, mornings are generally clear while afternoons can be drenched by an hour or two of downpours. During especially heavy rains, rural roads may be flooded and journeys delayed, particularly in the **south**. The worst of the rains fall in September and October, which is also the height of the **hurricane season**, though most severe storms follow a track well to the north of Belize. If you're out on the cayes or near the coast you'll need to leave, but rest assured that Belize has an efficient warning system and a network of shelters. The rain can continue into December, a time when **cold fronts**, known locally as "**northers**", sometimes lower temperatures to 10°C for a couple of days.

With all this in mind, the **best time of year** to visit Belize is from late December to March, when the vegetation is still lush and the skies are generally clear. This is also the main tourist season and therefore the priciest time to visit. Plenty of people visit during the summer months, too – a period that's appropriately promoted by the tourism industry as the "**green season**".

Average temperatures in Belize City

	Jan	Feb	Mar	Apr	May	June	July	Aug	Sept	Oct	Nov	Dec	Average
Belize City													
max °C	29	29	30	31	31	31	32	32	32	31	28	28	30
min °C	19	20	21	24	24	23	23	22	22	22	20	20	22
max °F	84	84	86	88	88	88	90	90	90	88	82	82	87
min °F	66	68	70	75	75	73	73	72	72	72	68	68	71

things not to miss

It's not possible to see everything that Belize has to offer in one trip – and we don't suggest you try. What follows is a selective and subjective taste of the country's highlights: outstanding natural features, underwater wonders, Maya ruins and distinctive cultural traditions. They're arranged in five colour-coded categories to help you find the very best to see, do and experience. All entries have a page reference to take you straight into the Guide, where you can find out more.

01 **Ambergris Caye** Page **129** • On Belize's largest and most popular island, take a well-deserved break from the hectic day- and night-time activities in and around San Pedro.

02 The Mountain Pine Ridge Page **179** • Hike the hills, peaks and gorges of this vast forest reserve, taking in the majesty of the tallest waterfall in Central America and perhaps staying in a luxurious riverside lodge.

03 Caracol Page **183** • The greatest of Belize's ancient Maya cities is gradually revealing its history and becoming more accessible every year.

04 Turtles Page **156** • The Half Moon Caye Natural Monument allows you to observe these ancient wanderers of the sea, as they return to the beaches to lay their eggs in the sand.

05 Carnival Page **363** • The electrifying energy of Carnival in Belize City is the highlight of the "September Celebrations", which commemorate Independence Day and the Battle of St George's Caye.

06 The Belize Barrier Reef Page **125** • For spellbinding natural beauty it's hard to beat a snorkelling or diving trip to the Belize Barrier Reef, the longest in the western hemisphere.

07 Lamanai Page **108** • More than two thousand years ago Lamanai was the largest city anywhere in the Maya world; today, climbing its massive temples is a daunting, though rewarding, experience.

08 Garifuna drumming Page **252** • Listen to the rhythms of Africa pulsing through the Caribbean as the drumbeats of the Garifuna proclaim their unique cultural heritage.

09 Toucans Page **256** • The unmistakable keel-billed toucan is the national bird of Belize and, though found almost anywhere, is best seen in the village of Sittee River.

10 The Blue Hole Page **156** • On Lighthouse Reef, dive the inky depths of the coral-encrusted Blue Hole, an enormous circular cavern 300m across – or fly over it in a light plane or helicopter.

11 The Museum of Belize Page **75** • This museum boasts excellent collections of painted Maya ceramics and jade jewellery, and a visit here is one of Belize City's highlights.

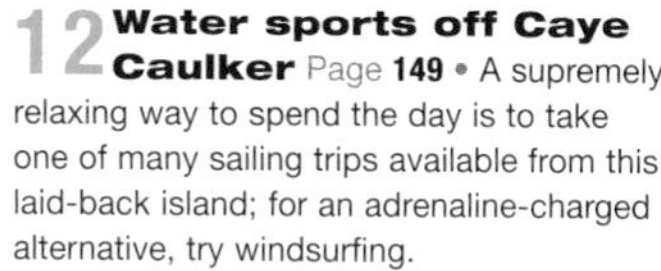

12 Water sports off Caye Caulker Page **149** • A supremely relaxing way to spend the day is to take one of many sailing trips available from this laid-back island; for an adrenaline-charged alternative, try windsurfing.

13 Caves Page **174** • Belize boasts countless spectacular caves, among them those at Barton Creek and Río Frio. Many are partly filled with water and hold Maya artifacts that haven't seen daylight for centuries.

14 The Belize Zoo Page **79** • Enjoy very close encounters with the animals and birds of Central America at this charming and well-run little zoo.

15 San Ignacio Page **186** • San Ignacio, the adventure centre of western Belize, also has the best market in the country.

16 Sea kayaking Page **258** • For a real "away from it all" adventure, take a sea kayaking trip to the pristine waters of Belize's southern cayes and atolls.

17 Tikal Page **218** • Across the Guatemalan border is the truly monumental Maya city of Tikal, set in a magnificent protected rainforest.

18 Placencia Page **267** • This relaxed, southern fishing village, home to the narrowest street in the world, is renowned for the unmatched beauty of its beaches.

19 Lobster-Fest Page **145** • Placencia and Caye Caulker celebrate the opening of the lobster season in June and July, respectively, with a weekend-long festival featuring music and dancing – and of course sampling the catch.

Basics

Basics

Getting there ... 19

Arrival ... 26

Getting around ... 26

Accommodation ... 31

Food and drink ... 34

Health ... 36

The media ... 41

Festivals ... 42

Sports and outdoor activities ... 43

Culture and etiquette ... 44

Shopping ... 45

Travelling with children ... 46

Travel essentials ... 47

Getting there

Although most visitors arrive by air at the international airport outside Belize City, it's also possible to reach Belize by bus or boat from neighbouring countries (see p.28). There's no national airline as of yet, but a pair of domestic companies facilitate transport around the country once you arrive.

Airfare prices from the US rise during the **high season** (December to early April, especially around Christmas and Easter) and also in July and August for flights originating in Europe. At these times seat availability can be a problem: flying mid-week and booking ahead are good ideas. If you plan to travel around the region, you should consider buying an open-jaw ticket, enabling you to fly into one city and out of another. You might also consider combining this with an **airpass** from Aeroméxico, Mexicana or TACA; contact the airlines for details (see p.22 & p.23).

Flights from North America

Four US airlines fly **nonstop** directly to Belize: American Airlines from Miami and Dallas, Continental from Houston and Newark, Delta from Atlanta and Los Angeles and US Airways from Charlotte, North Carolina. El Salvador-based TACA also has daily, nonstop flights from Houston. Together, depending on the day of the week, these cities have between six and seven daily, direct flights to Belize International Airport; from elsewhere in the US, you'll probably have to fly to one of these hubs first. There are no direct flights from anywhere in Canada yet, but you can get same- or next-day connections to the hubs above from Vancouver, Toronto and Montréal.

Typical **prices from the US** are around US$530 (low season)/$550–830 (high season) from New York; US$540/$900–1200 from Seattle; and US$450/$800–900 from Houston. Taxes can add about US$90. **From Canada** (Toronto, Montréal and Ottawa) expect to pay around Can$930 (low season)/$1100 (high season) and from Vancouver, Can$850/$940–1600. Flight taxes are about Can$100–120, depending on departure airport and routing.

Flights from the UK and Ireland

Visitors from the UK and Ireland have two options for getting to Belize, neither of which involves a direct flight (though this may soon change when a new, large runway is completed at Belize International Airport). The first option is to fly to one of the US hubs and then take a connecting flight. Unfortunately, this invariably means passing through the officious **US immigration system** and staying overnight in the US – at your own expense – as flight times do not match up. You must have a machine-readable passport and leave ample time to obtain a US visa if you need one (see p.49).

Although **flying from London** gives you the widest choice of flights to the US and onwards to Belize, you can often get flights from Manchester, Birmingham, Glasgow and other UK airports for the same price. A scheduled return flight to Belize City on American, Delta, Continental, US Airways or Virgin (in conjunction with TACA) will cost around £500–550 in the low season (Feb & Nov to mid-Dec), £550–580 in the shoulder season (May, June, Sept & Oct) and £700–1000 in the high season (July, Aug, mid-Dec to Jan & Easter). These prices do not include taxes of around £90. Most tickets allow a stay of between three and six months, sometimes up to one year (though you will pay more for this flexibility); some work out cheaper if you're away for fewer than thirty days.

The second, and increasingly popular, option is to fly to Mexico and continue **overland** (see p.21). Several European airlines fly directly to Mexico City or

Cancún, often a considerably cheaper route than flying through the US, and also avoiding US immigration. Many US airlines operating from the UK also have well-priced flights to Mexico via a US hub, not requiring an overnight stay. From a flight specialist or discount agent you can sometimes get airfare to Cancún for around £400 or less. These are usually for only a two-week stay, though you may find them for longer. From Mexico City, you can fly directly to Chetumal daily with Click Airways (ⓣ52/55 5322 6262, ⓦwww.clickmx.com), for around £100, and continue by bus to Belize from there.

From Ireland, Continental and American Airlines fly direct from Belfast and Dublin to Houston, Newark or another US city requiring transit to one of the US hubs. You can also get flights from Belfast or Dublin to London and then connect with one of the transatlantic flights. Fares from Belfast to Belize (via the US) are similar to or sometimes lower than those from London, around £520 (low season)/£800 (high season). From Dublin to Belize you can expect to pay around €770/€1200, plus roughly €140 in taxes. Alternatively, you can fly **direct from Ireland to Mexico** and continue overland; discount fares from Belfast to Cancún range

Fly less – stay longer! Travel and climate change

Climate change is the single biggest issue facing our planet. It is caused by a build-up in the atmosphere of carbon dioxide and other greenhouse gases, which are emitted by many sources – including planes. Already, flights account for around 3–4 percent of human-induced global warming: that figure may sound small, but it is rising year on year and threatens to counteract the progress made by reducing greenhouse emissions in other areas.

Rough Guides regard travel, overall, as a global benefit, and feel strongly that the advantages to developing economies are important, as are the opportunities for greater contact and awareness among peoples. But we all have a responsibility to limit our personal "carbon footprint". That means giving thought to how often we fly and what we can do to redress the harm that our trips create.

Flying and climate change

Pretty much every form of motorized travel generates CO_2, but planes are particularly bad offenders, releasing large volumes of greenhouse gases at altitudes where their impact is far more harmful. Flying also allows us to travel much further than we would contemplate doing by road or rail, so the emissions attributable to each passenger become truly shocking. For example, one person taking a return flight between Europe and California produces the equivalent impact of 2.5 tonnes of CO_2 – similar to the yearly output of the average UK car.

Less harmful planes may evolve but it will be decades before they replace the current fleet – which could be too late for avoiding climate chaos. In the meantime, there are limited options for concerned travellers: to reduce the amount we travel by air (take fewer trips, stay longer!), to avoid night flights (when plane contrails trap heat from Earth but can't reflect sunlight back to space), and to make the trips we do take "climate neutral" via a carbon offset scheme.

Carbon offset schemes

Offset schemes run by **climatecare.org, carbonneutral.com** and others allow you to "neutralize" the greenhouse gases that you are responsible for releasing. Their websites have simple calculators that let you work out the impact of any flight. Once that's done, you can pay to fund projects that will reduce future carbon emissions by an equivalent amount (such as the distribution of low-energy light bulbs and cooking stoves in developing countries). Please take the time to visit our website and make your trip climate neutral.

www.roughguides.com/climatechange

from £490 to £680 with return. The same airlines also often have good deals on flights from Dublin to Cancún from €700 plus around €100 tax.

Flights from Australia, New Zealand and South Africa

With no direct flights from Australasia to Belize, you've got little choice but to fly to the US first, generally and least expensively to Los Angeles. Flights via Asia are longer and cost more, but you do get a subsidized overnight in the carrier's home city. For most Australasian airlines, low season is mid-January to the end of February and October to the end of November; high season is mid-May to the end of August and December to mid-January. Seat availability on some flights out of Australia and New Zealand can be limited, so it's best to book several weeks ahead.

From Australia, the cheapest fares (from Sydney and most of the eastern state capitals) via Los Angeles to Belize City (on Qantas and Delta, TACA via San Salvador or Continental via Houston) start at Aus$2810 (low season) and Aus$3640 (high season), plus about Aus$180 taxes. Departing from Perth or Darwin can be Aus$400–650 higher. **From New Zealand** (Auckland) the cheapest flights to Belize City are via Los Angeles (on Air Tahiti Nui or Air New Zealand and Delta), around NZ$2700/$3400 with about NZ$200 in taxes. Expect to pay an extra NZ$210 for Christchurch or Wellington departures. Flying to Cancún or Mexico City from any of these cities is hundreds of dollars **cheaper** than flying into Belize.

From South Africa, you can fly to the US or to the UK and continue your journey from there. Flights from Johannesburg to Belize City (via Atlanta on Delta or South African Airways) start around R13770 in the low season and R21540 in the high season.

Overland from Mexico

Flying into Cancún or Mexico City from a non-US origin is an attractive option for travellers who don't want to tangle with US immigration. Unfortunately, there are currently **no direct flights** between Mexico and Belize, though Click Airways (Ⓣ52/55 5322 6262, Ⓦwww.clickmx.com) runs **daily flights** from Mexico City to Chetumal, just north of the Belizean border. Aside from this option, buses are the most practical mode of transport between the two countries.

Buses in Mexico are fast and offer high levels of comfort. From every Mexican city, there are constant buses to the capital and good connections from there to the town of **Chetumal** (around 22hr), close to the Belizean border. From Chetumal, several Belizean and Guatemalan bus companies leave from either the ADO bus terminal or the central market for Orange Walk and onward to Belize City. Departures begin at 4am and continue throughout the morning, with fewer in the afternoon. Unlike at other bus terminals in Belize and Mexico, buses from Chetumal's central market are not regulated, and open competition can be a little fierce. If you've spent fewer than three days in Mexico, you shouldn't have to pay the roughly £12/US$20 **exit fee**; if you do need to pay it, do so only at a bank in Mexico, not at the border itself.

Travelling **overland from the US** through Mexico is a long, two- to three-day haul, but allows you to see some of the country on the way. Greyhound buses (Ⓣ1-800/229-9424, Ⓦwww.greyhound.com) run regularly to all major US-Mexico border crossings, and some even take you over the frontier and into the Mexican bus station. You can buy tickets and a discount "Discovery Pass" on the company's website.

Heading south **by car** gives you more freedom but entails a good deal of bureaucracy. You'll need a credit card to pay a bond to ensure you don't sell the car in Mexico, and separate **insurance** to cover your drive through the country; purchase it from Sanborns (Ⓣ1-800/222-0158) at the US-Mexico border for about US$10 per day. The agency has a 24-hour emergency hotline and provides legal assistance, road maps and guides. Crossing the Belizean border with a car can entail large **customs charges** (payable in cash only), particularly if you plan to leave your vehicle in the country.

US, Canadian, EU, Australian and New Zealand driving licences are valid in Mexico and Belize, but it's a good idea to arm yourself with an **International Driving**

Licence as well; contact your local driving authority to obtain one. If you run into problems with the traffic police for any reason, show that first, and if they disappear with it you at least still have your own licence. If you belong to a motoring organization at home, you may find they'll arrange for advice, maps and even help from reciprocal organizations in Mexico. Unleaded petrol is widely available in Mexico and Belize. For details on driving in Belize, see p.29.

Airlines, agents and operators

Online booking

ⓦ **www.expedia.co.uk** (in UK), ⓦ **www.expedia.com** (in US), ⓦ **www.expedia.ca** (in Canada)
ⓦ **www.lastminute.com** (in UK)
ⓦ **www.opodo.co.uk** (in UK)
ⓦ **www.orbitz.com** (in US)
ⓦ **www.travelocity.co.uk** (in UK), ⓦ **www.travelocity.com** (in US), ⓦ **www.travelocity.ca** (in Canada)
ⓦ **www.zuji.com.au** (in Australia), ⓦ **www.zuji.co.nz** (in New Zealand)

Airlines in North America

Aeroméxico ⓣ1-800/237-6639, ⓦwww.aeromexico.com. Direct flights from many US gateways to Mexico City and Cancún. Tickets can be linked to the "Mexipass" for connections throughout Mexico, and onwards to Central and South America.
American Airlines ⓣ1-800/433-7300, ⓦwww.aa.com. Two daily nonstops from Miami and one from Dallas to Belize City.
Continental ⓣ1-800/231-0856, ⓦwww.continental.com. Two daily nonstops from Houston and a direct flight from Newark on Saturdays to Belize City, and many flights to Mexico and all Central American capitals. Alliance with Copa (which has an airpass) of Panama means good prices flying on connections with Central and South America.
Delta ⓣ1-800/221-1212, ⓦwww.delta.com. Daily flights from Atlanta, and weekly from Los Angeles.
Mexicana ⓣ1-800/531-7921, ⓦwww.mexicana.com. Frequent flights from Chicago, Denver, LA, New York, San Francisco, Montréal and Toronto to many destinations in Mexico. Tickets can be linked to the "Mexipass" airpass.
TACA US ⓣ1-800/535-8780, Canada ⓣ1-888/261-3269, ⓦwww.taca.com. Handles reservations for four of the national airlines of Central America: Aviateca (Guatemala), NICA (Nicaragua), Lacsa (Costa Rica) and TACA (El Salvador). TACA has daily flights from Houston and Miami to Belize City, as well as from many other cities in North America to all Central American capitals. Tickets can be linked to the "TACA Airpass".
US Airways ⓣ1-800/622-1015, ⓦwww.usairways.com. Direct flights at weekends (and daily in busy season) to Belize City from Charlotte, North Carolina, with good connections throughout the US.

Flight and travel specialists in North America

Air Courier Association ⓣ1-877/303-4258, ⓦwww.aircourier.org. Courier flights and other good airfare and travel deals for members.
Air-tech ⓣ212/219-7000, ⓦwww.airtech.com. Standby seat broker and courier flights. Very good deals on their website, if you're prepared to be flexible.
eXito ⓣ1-800/655-4053, ⓦwww.exitotravel.com. North America's top specialists for flights and tours to Belize and Latin America. Website has a particularly useful fare-finder and there's a candid comparison of the merits of various airpasses.
Flightcentre US ⓣ1-866/WORLD-51, ⓦwww.flightcentre.us, Canada ⓣ1-888/WORLD-55, ⓦwww.flightcentre.ca. Rock-bottom fares worldwide.
Now Voyager ⓣ212/459-1616, ⓦwww.nowvoyagertravel.com. Courier flight broker. Check the excellent website first, then call for flight prices, though usually only flights to Mexico, not Belize, are offered.
STA Travel US ⓣ1-800/781-4040, Canada ⓣ1-888/427-5639, ⓦwww.sta.com. Worldwide discount travel specialists in student/youth fares and all travel-related services. Offices throughout US, Canada and worldwide.
Travel Cuts ⓣ1-800/359-2887 or 1-866/416-2887, ⓦwww.travelcuts.com. Foremost Canadian specialists in student/youth fares, IDs, insurance and other travel services. Dozens of branches throughout Canada, mainly on college campuses.

Tour operators in North America

Adventure Life ⓣ1-800/344-6118, ⓦwww.adventure-life.com. Specialists in small-group travel and customized itineraries to wilderness areas and nature reserves in Latin America, using the best local and international guides. On the eleven-day "Ultimate Adventure" trip (US$1998), you spend a few days on Glover's Reef, then head inland to the jungle, rivers and caves of Cayo District. Or, for US$1200, you get six days' sea kayaking from islands and beaches in southern Belize.

Close Encounters ⓣ1-888/875-1822, ⓦwww.belizecloseencounters.com. Small company, very experienced in arranging individual itineraries for all budgets to Belize.

Elderhostel ⓣ1-800/454-5768, ⓦwww.elderhostel.org. A nonprofit organization offering upmarket educational programmes for over-55s (companions can be younger). A week studying bottlenose dolphins on the Belize atolls is around US$2000; a fifteen-day visit to Maya sites in Honduras, Belize and Guatemala costs US$2700.

Gap Adventures ⓣ1-800/708-7761, ⓦwww.gapadventures.com. Canadian company offering a wide range of group trips (some camping) with diving and kayaking in Yucatán, Belize and throughout Central America. Around US$1600 plus US$300 local payment for 22 days in Belize and Tikal, including sea kayaking and jungle trips in Belize.

International Expeditions ⓣ1-800/633-4734, ⓦwww.internationalexpeditions.com. Superbly led natural history tours and individual itineraries throughout Latin America, including Belize and Tikal. A ten-day "Reefs, Rainforests and Ruins" trip to Belize and Tikal costs around US$3400.

Island Expeditions ⓣ1-800/667-1630 ⓦwww.islandexpeditions.com. Vancouver-based company, one of the best going to Belize, running expertly led and superbly equipped sea and river kayaking expeditions in remote destinations. The ten-night "Ultimate Adventure", from the Maya Mountains to Glover's Reef, is US$2000; the eight-night "Coral Islands" kayak expedition takes in 50km of the southern Barrier Reef for US$1390. Both include flights within Belize.

Journeys International ⓣ1-800/255-8735, ⓦwww.journeys.travel. Award-winning nature- and culture-oriented tours to Belize and the rest of Central America, some for women only. US$1550–3250 for a week.

Latin American Escapes ⓣ1-800/510-5999, ⓦwww.latinamericanescapes.com. Adventure and diving holidays in Belize. Eight days inland for around US$1470; four days' diving on Ambergris Caye for US$635.

The Moorings ⓣ1-800/888-8420, ⓦwww.moorings.com. Luxurious, fully equipped catamaran charters based in Placencia, enabling guests to explore the pristine southern cayes. Prices depend on size of yacht and time of year; insurance is extra.

Peter Hughes Diving ⓣ1-800/932-6237, ⓦwww.peterhughes.com. Luxurious, all-inclusive trips on live-aboard dive boats based in Belize, departing Saturdays. Around US$2300 per week; advanced dive instruction and underwater photography courses available.

Sea Kunga ⓣ1-800/781-2269, ⓦwww.seakunga.com. Friendly, experienced Canadian company leading good-value, small-group sailing, sea kayaking and jungle trips, mainly in southern Belize: eight days' sea kayaking US$1300; ten days' rivers, caves and sea kayaking US$1800.

Slickrock Adventures ⓣ1-800/390-5715, ⓦwww.slickrock.com. One of the very best adventure companies, offering sea kayaking and jungle and river (some whitewater) expeditions in Belize: US$2275 for eight-day adventure "week" with caving, jungle hiking and sea and river kayaking; US$1975 for a week of kayaking and snorkelling from their base at Long Caye on Glover's Reef.

TMM Bareboat Charters ⓣ1-800/633-0155, ⓦwww.sailtmm.com. Superb catamaran charters in San Pedro, Ambergris Caye and Placencia, from a very experienced company. The fully equipped boats (some have a/c) range in size from 35ft to over 46ft, and sleep six to twelve. Prices, from US$2500 to $8000 per week (plus $30/day insurance), vary according to size and season, and you'll usually need to book well in advance.

Victor Emanuel Nature Tours ⓣ1-800/328-8368, ⓦwww.ventbird.com. The best small-group birding tours you can get, led by dedicated professionals. US$5100 for ten days at *Chan Chich* and Crooked Tree; price includes internal flights.

Wildside Tours ⓣ1-888/875-9453, www.wildsidetoursinc.com. Excellent birding and nature trips, with emphasis on photography; US$2600 for eight days, including Crooked Tree and Cockscomb Basin.

Airlines in the UK and Ireland

American Airlines UK ⓣ08457/789 789, Dublin ⓣ01/602 0550, ⓦwww.aa.com. Daily from Heathrow to Miami or Dallas, then next day to Belize.

British Airways UK ⓣ0870/850 9850, Dublin ⓣ01800/626 747, ⓦwww.ba.com. Daily to Miami and three flights a week to Mexico City.

Continental ⓣ08456/076 760, ⓦwww.continental.com. Daily flights from Gatwick to Houston and Newark, then to Belize City next day.

Groupo TACA ⓣ0870/241 0340, ⓦwww.taca.com. Agents for several Central American airlines and their airpasses.

Mexicana ⓣ020/8492 0000, ⓔsales@mextours.co.uk. Information and reservations only; no Mexicana flights from UK, but they do sell the "Mexipass" airpass.

Flight and travel specialists in the UK and Ireland

Journey Latin America London ⓣ020/8747 3108, ⓦwww.journeylatinamerica.co.uk,

Manchester ⓣ0161/832 1441, ⓔman@journeylatinamerica.co.uk. The industry leaders for airfares and tours to Latin America, with some of the best prices on high-season flights.

Maxwell's Travel Dublin ⓣ01/677 9479, ⓕ679 3948. Very experienced in travel to Latin America, and Ireland's representatives for many of the specialist tour operators in the UK.

North South Travel ⓣ01245/608291, ⓦwww.northsouthtravel.co.uk. Small, friendly and competitive agency offering worldwide discounted fares. Profits are used to support development projects in Africa, Asia and Latin America.

South American Experience ⓣ020/7976 5511, ⓦwww.southamericanexperience.co.uk. Flight and tailor-made itinerary specialists, with very good airfare prices and high-quality, good-value tours to Belize.

STA Travel ⓣ0870/160 6070, ⓦwww.statravel.co.uk. Student/youth travel specialists with 250 offices worldwide, offering flights, tours, accommodation and many travel-related services, including a help desk if you have problems while abroad.

Trailfinders London ⓣ020/7938 3939, Manchester ⓣ0161/839 6969, Glasgow ⓣ0141/353 2224, Birmingham ⓣ0121/236 1234, Bristol ⓣ0117/929 9000, Dublin ⓣ01/677 7888, UK ⓦwww.trailfinders.co.uk, Ireland ⓦwww.trailfinders.ie. Airfare and package specialists for independent travellers. Offices throughout the UK and an excellent travel health clinic in the London Kensington High Street branch.

Usit Dublin ⓣ0818/200 020, Belfast ⓣ028/9032 4073, ⓦwww.usit.ie. All-Ireland student travel experts with eighteen offices, mainly on campuses; very useful website.

Tour operators in the UK and Ireland

Explore ⓣ01252/760 000, ⓦwww.explore.co.uk. Wide range of two- to three-week hotel-based tours to Central America and Mexico. Most tours run year-round. Around £1550, including airfare, for fifteen days in Belize, with a trip to Tikal.

Global Travel Club ⓣ01268/541 363, ⓦwww.global-travel.co.uk. Small company specializing in individually arranged diving, adventure and cultural tours to Belize, Mexico and all of Central America.

Imaginative Traveller ⓣ0800/316 2717, ⓦwww.imaginative-traveller.com. A range of good budget trips through Mexico and Central America, staying at hotels and using public transport; 15-day "Mayan Explorer" for £565.

Journey Latin America ⓣ020/8747 8315, ⓦwww.journeylatinamerica.co.uk. Wide range

of high-standard group tours and tailor-made itineraries from the acknowledged experts. Their three-week "Quetzal Journey" through Guatemala, Chiapas, Yucatán and Belize costs around £1000.

Naturetrek ⓣ01962/733 051, ⓦwww.naturetrek.co.uk. Superb birding trips led by expert naturalists, staying at very comfortable jungle and beach lodges in Belize, with a visit to Tikal; £2900 for fifteen days.

Reef and Rainforest Tours ⓣ01803/866 965, ⓦwww.reefandrainforest.co.uk. Individual itineraries and family holidays from a very experienced company, focusing on nature reserves, research projects and diving in Belize, Honduras and Costa Rica.

Scuba Safaris ⓣ01342/851 196, ⓦwww.scuba-safaris.com. A knowledgeable, well-organized company, specializing in fully inclusive dive packages. Around £1350 for a week on a live-aboard boat in Belize; extra for airfare and overnight accommodation in the US.

Trips Worldwide ⓣ0117/311 4400, ⓦwww.tripsworldwide.co.uk. Friendly, experienced company with an inspired range of high-quality, tailor-made itineraries and tours to Belize, Mexico and all of Central America. Does a fourteen-day "Belize Highlights" trip, taking in Cayo, Orange Walk and Placencia, for £12700, including airfare.

Airlines in Australia, New Zealand and South Africa

Air New Zealand Australia ⓣ1800/803 298, New Zealand ⓣ0800/737 000, ⓦwww.airnz.com. Daily to Los Angeles from Auckland, either direct or via Honolulu/Tonga/Fiji/Papeete.

Air Tahiti Nui Australia ⓣ02/9244 2899, New Zealand ⓣ09/308 3360, ⓦwww.airtahitinui-usa.com. Daily from Auckland to Los Angeles via Papeete; code-share with Qantas from Australia.

Delta South Africa ⓣ2721/425 7446 or 2711/482 4582, ⓦwww.delta.com. Flights from Johannesburg to Belize City via Atlanta.

JAL Australia ⓣ02/9272 1111, New Zealand ⓣ09/379 9906, ⓦwww.japanair.com. Several flights a week to Los Angeles and Mexico City from Sydney and other major Australian cities and from Auckland; an overnight stopover in Tokyo is included in the fare.

Korean Airlines Australia ⓣ02/9262 6000, New Zealand ⓣ09/914 2000, ⓦwww.koreanair.com. Several flights a week from Sydney, Brisbane and Auckland to Los Angeles, with an overnight in Seoul included in the fare.

Qantas Australia ⓣ13 13 13 or 02/9700 7890, New Zealand ⓣ0800/808 767, ⓦwww.qantas.com. Daily to Los Angeles from major Australian cities, either nonstop or via Honolulu, and daily from Auckland via Sydney.

United Airlines Australia ⓣ02/9292 4111, New Zealand ⓣ09/379 3800, ⓦwww.ual.com. Daily to Los Angeles and San Francisco from Sydney, Melbourne and Auckland, either direct or via Honolulu.

Flight and travel specialists in Australia, New Zealand and South Africa

Flight Centre Australia ⓣ133 133, ⓦwww.flightcentre.com.au, New Zealand ⓣ0800/243 544, ⓦwww.flightcentre.co.nz, South Africa ⓣ0860/400 727, ⓦwww.flightcentre.co.za. Competitive discounts on airfares, plus a wide range of package holidays and adventure tours.

STA Travel Australia ⓣ1300/733 035, ⓦwww.statravel.com.au, New Zealand ⓣ0508/782 782, ⓦwww.statravel.co.nz, South Africa ⓣ0861/781 781, ⓦwww.statravel.co.za. Discount fares for students and under-26s, as well as visas, student cards and travel insurance; good website and branches throughout all three countries.

Trailfinders ⓣ1300/780 122, ⓦwww.trailfinders.co.au. Discount flights from superb independent travel specialists.

Travel.com.au ⓣ1300/130 482, ⓦwww.travel.com.au. Great prices from online fare-finder and all travel services.

Tour operators in Australia, New Zealand and South Africa

Adventure Associates Australia ⓣ1800/222 141, ⓦwww.adventureassociates.com. Jungle, archeological and cultural tours to Mexico and Belize.

Contours Australia ⓣ03/8670 9670, ⓦwww.contourstravel.com.au. Specialists in cultural and archeological tours in Central America, ranging from short stays in Belize to multi-day expeditions throughout the region.

Intrepid Travel Australia ⓣ1300/364 512 or 03/9473 2626, ⓦwww.intrepidtravel.com. Small-group tours throughout Belize and the Maya region, with an emphasis on cross-cultural contact and low-impact tourism.

Arrival

Most people will arrive in Belize City at Philip Goldson International Airport, about a twenty-minute drive from the centre. Those arriving by bus will pull in either at the Marine Terminal or the main bus terminal on Canal Street, where taxis are plentiful. Points of arrival in other towns are bus terminals and ports, from where it's simple to find your way around in a taxi or otherwise.

By air

From the international airport, you have three options for getting into town: walking to the Northern Highway (around 25min), where you can flag down a local bus into the city; catching an onward flight to another Belizean destination (see opposite); or, as many people do, paying the Bz$50 **taxi** fare to the centre. Drivers with large cars will try to fill them before departing, and will charge each group of people separately, so **getting together** with other travellers before leaving the terminal saves money.

By bus

All the Belizean companies arriving in Belize City will drop you at the main bus terminal on Canal Street. It's fairly central but in a not-so-desirable part of the city, so getting a taxi to or from here is a good idea. The **fare** to pretty much anywhere in town is around Bz$7. If you arrive with a Guatemalan bus company, such as San Juan or Linea Dorada from Chetumal or Flores, you'll pull into the **Marine Terminal**, where you can catch a water taxi to the Northern Cayes (see p.123).

By car

There are only two land routes into Belize from outside the country, one from Mexico and the other from Guatemala. These points of entry merge, respectively, with the Northern and Western highways. If you arrive in the south by boat and rent a car in one of the southern towns, you'll travel north along the Southern Highway before turning onto the Western Highway for Belize City (east) or Belmopan and beyond (west). If you intend to bring your own car to Belize, watch out for heavy import taxes, which are payable in cash only.

Getting around

Belize has a good public transport network and all main roads are now paved, save for a few kilometres of the Southern Highway. Buses on the three main highways (the Northern, Western and Southern) are cheap, generally frequent and fairly fast. The south has fewer buses but scheduled services are improving all the time.

If you visit the cayes during your visit, you'll surely do some travelling by **boat**; water journeys to Guatemala and Honduras are also possible. River transport is popular in Belize, too – it's the most convenient way to reach some Maya ruins and isolated field stations.

Flying between Belizean destinations is the fastest way to get around, though it's not cheap and by no means environmentally sensitive. In the south, however, where bus transport can be patchy, a short hop on a small plane can give superb views of the hills and the clear, blue sea. **Car rental** in Belize is not inexpensive, either: it generally runs US$60–120/day, but it does enable you to visit more places in a shorter time than you could by bus. Cars and four-wheel-drive trucks are readily available from several rental companies in Belize City.

By air

The main towns and tourist destinations in Belize are linked by domestic flights operated by two main carriers: Maya Island Air (Ⓣ223-1140, Ⓦwww.mayaairways.com) and Tropic Air (Ⓣ226-2012, Ⓦwww.tropicair.com). There are also several **charter airlines**. Together, Maya Island and Tropic Air provide up to eight or nine daily flights on each of the main routes – Belize City to Dangriga (Bz$75), Placencia (Bz$144) and Punta Gorda (Bz$185) – and dozens to San Pedro and Caye Caulker (both Bz$63). There are no direct flights from Belize City to Corozal – though you can fly there from San Pedro (Bz$86) – and there are currently no flights to Belmopan and San Ignacio. The prices quoted above are one-way, including tax, from Belize Municipal Airport (a few kilometres north of the city centre). All scheduled domestic flights also connect with Belize International Airport; you'll pay around Bz$50 more to depart from there.

Flying is also the most convenient way to make **side trips** out of Belize to neighbouring countries. Domestic airlines operate international flights to Flores (for Tikal; Bz$207 plus tax), and TACA flies daily from Belize City to its main hub in San Salvador for connections throughout Central America. Atlantic Airlines (Ⓣ225-2163, Ⓦwww.atlanticairlinesint.com) flies three times a week from Belize City to San Pedro Sula, Honduras.

By bus

The vast majority of buses in Belize are of the US school bus variety, brightly painted and managed by several different companies. They are well maintained and removed from service when they get too old, but still aren't comfortable for lengthy journeys or long limbs. The faster **"express"** buses are occasionally the luxury coach type; they operate along all main highways, stopping only in terminals in the towns. The more common non-express or "regular" buses will stop anywhere a passenger requests along their route. Tell the driver or conductor where you're headed and they'll usually know where to let you off.

Services usually begin in the very early morning and finish sometime in the evening – there are **no overnight buses**. On Sundays and holidays, some services are reduced or, in the case of smaller, local ones, often non-existent. For details of the bus routes from Belize City, see p.86.

Over half of the buses that ply the Northern Highway cross the Mexican border to serve

Distances from Belize City

Distances are based on transportation routes, not as the crow flies.

Belize City to...	Distance
Belmopan	84 km (52 miles)
Caye Caulker	34 km (21 miles)
Chetumal, Mexico	149 km (93 miles)
Corozal	135 km (84 miles)
Dangriga	171 km (106 miles)
Guatemalan border	130 km (81 miles)
Orange Walk	87 km (54 miles)
Placencia	259 km (161 miles)
Punta Gorda	343 km (213 miles)
San Ignacio	116 km (72 miles)
San Pedro	51 km (32 miles)
Tikal, Guatemala	240 km (149 miles)

the town of Chetumal. Others terminate in Corozal town, 14km south of the border. On the Western Highway, all buses now terminate in Benque Viejo —you'll need to take a *colectivo* (shared) taxi the remaining 2km to the **Guatemalan border**. Services along the Southern Highway are less frequent, particularly beyond Dangriga, although there are still several daily routes.

Heading away from the main highways, you'll rely mostly on **local buses** operated by small agencies, which rarely have backup plans when breakdowns occur. Travelling this way is a fairly slow business, as it caters primarily to the needs of villagers – taking produce to market, transporting building materials and so on – but it has its rewards: you're sharing a ride with people who know the area well, and by the time your ride's over you'll have made friends eager to show you around.

Fares are a bargain compared to the cost of most things in Belize, though they may soon rise slightly to reflect the recent increase in petrol prices. Currently, regular buses cost Bz$7 from Belize City to San Ignacio, Bz$14 to Chetumal and Bz$22 to Punta Gorda (the longest bus ride in the country). Tickets for express buses are just a few dollars more. Bus terminals don't have ticket offices; you pay the conductor, who will remember your destination whether or not he's issued you an actual ticket.

Buses can be very **crowded**, though you should get a seat if you board at the station a half-hour before departure; get on at a later stop and you may have to stand. **Holidays** are especially busy, so opt for express buses at these times. Luggage is generally stacked in the back of the bus, though some regular and most express services have compartments underneath. **Theft**, while not common, does occur on buses and usually from side pockets, so it pays to lock your bag and try to watch your belongings as people come and go. On long journeys you might insist on using a bicycle lock to secure your bag to one of the back seats.

By boat

Your first experience of water transport in Belize will likely be aboard one of the fast skiffs that ferry passengers (around 25–40 at a time) from Belize City and other mainland destinations out to the **cayes**. Many now have half- or full cabins, though some are still open-deck and may not have padded seats. They provide a quick (if sometimes bumpy), reliable and safe service. If you're going in an open boat, check the weather, since the combination of rain and high speeds isn't very pleasant.

Transport to the cayes and other popular **coastal destinations** leaves daily from the Marine Terminal, next to the Swing Bridge in Belize City, and the Courthouse Wharf, a few minutes' walk away. Services to Caye Caulker and San Pedro on Ambergris Caye operate approximately every ninety minutes, with most boats making both stops; see p.86, p.130 & p.145 for more information. Some of the boats on the Caye Caulker/San Pedro run will also call at St George's Caye on request, although only at certain times.

There are **no advance bookings** for these water journeys and seats are not reserved, though tickets for early-morning departures from the cayes can be purchased the night before. It's wise to show up at least 15min prior to departure; at busy times, one or two extra boats will be on hand for overflow, so it's extremely unlikely you won't find space, though you may end up on a different boat than your luggage.

Many **tours** include boat transport in their itineraries, often to destinations, such as outlying cayes and atolls, that public routes don't serve. Placencia is a popular base for boat tours of the Monkey River (see p.276), as is Orange Walk for the New River and the Maya site of Lamanai (see p.108). For a more personal experience, you could **charter** a boat and choose which rivers and islands you want to explore; San Ignacio, near the confluence of the Macal and Mopan rivers, is an ideal base for this, with canoes readily available for an hour's or week's rental. You can also rent canoes in Bermudian Landing, Placencia, Punta Gorda and a growing number of other locations.

The only **international boat services** are skiffs from Punta Gorda to Puerto Barrios, Guatemala (daily), Punta Gorda to Lívingston, Guatemala (weekly) and Dangriga and Placencia to Puerto Cortés, Honduras (twice weekly; see p.249 & p.269). It's best to book

Tour operators in Belize

In addition to the overseas tour operators listed in Getting there (pp.19–25), several Belizean agencies can expertly plan and book itineraries throughout the country. Being local, their staff are informed about sites and activities, current availability and travel conditions. Many more specialist tour companies, often associated with hotels or resorts, are covered individually throughout this Guide.

Adventures in Belize ⓣ822-2800, ⓦwww.adventuresinbelize.com. Based at *Caves Branch Jungle Lodge* (see p.241) and offering everything from wilderness survival to luxury tours, all with outstanding guides.

Belize Trips ⓣ223-0376 or 610-1923, in the USA ⓣ1-561/210-7015, ⓦwww.belize-trips.com. Run by the very knowledgeable Katie Valk, able to connect you with any tour in Belize.

IBTM ⓣ614-2080, ⓔinfo@ibtm.net. Specializing in southern Belize, Bruno Kuppinger can organize hard-to-find services all over the country.

Maya Travel Services ⓣ223-1623, ⓦwww.mayatravelservices.com. Great for advice on international flights and very knowledgeable about tours and hotels in Belize.

Travel & Tour Belize ⓣ226-2031, ⓦwww.traveltourbelize.com. Able to plan almost any aspect of your visit to Belize, with specialities in Ambergris Caye and even wedding arrangements.

ahead for international departures by contacting the boat operator or their agents at least one day before.

By car

Although Belize has only four **paved highways**, driving is a popular option among visitors, and these roads offer relatively easy motoring and generally smooth surfaces; if you plan to conduct further exploration, you'll need high clearance and probably four-wheel drive. Main roads, and even most unpaved side roads, are typically well maintained and passable except in the very worst rainstorms, though mud, dust and the occasional massive pothole can be a problem at any time. Under Belize's seatbelt law, you'll be fined Bz$25 for not buckling up, and the speed limit outside towns is 55mph/88kph. Distances in Belize are measured in miles (though throughout the book they're given in kilometres), with some addresses reading "Mile 29, Western Highway", for example. At press time, **fuel** prices were Bz$9.53 per US gallon (which is how it's sold) for super/premium unleaded, Bz$9.23 for regular and Bz$7.00 for diesel; when planning your journey, bear in mind that petrol stations are scarce outside towns.

Traffic is generally light outside Belize City, but driving standards everywhere are abysmal and **fatal accidents** are high relative to traffic density. The busiest stretch of road is on the Western Highway between Belize City and Belmopan. Road signs are becoming more noticeable along the main highways, but you'll have to watch out for **speed bumps** of variable height; these are occasionally signed, but every new driver in Belize is bound to be caught unaware at least once – with potentially disastrous consequences. Look for them on entering and leaving any settlement along the highways, as well as shortly before bus stops.

The best guide to Belize's roads is Emory King's *Driver's Guide to Beautiful Belize*, updated annually and sold at hotels and petrol stations throughout the country. The slim volume contains recommendations that are little more than advertisements, but the **sketch maps** and distances are accurate and it offers a characteristically Belizean account of the road network. You'll also need a copy of the *International Travel Map* (see p.53).

If you've succeeded in transporting your own car to Belize (see p.26), any further problems you might face are likely to seem fairly minor; the traffic police operate regular roadside checkpoints, though, so keep your licence and other documents handy.

Insurance is available for a few US dollars per day from agents just inside both of the land border crossings and in Belize City. Note that some spare car parts can be difficult to get hold of.

Car rental

All the main rental companies offer cars, trucks and vans, including **four-wheel drive** options, for US$70–125/day, plus nine percent sales tax and another US$13–15/day for insurance, depending on the class of vehicle; renting for a week may be more economical than for a few days. All companies have offices at the international airport and in Belize City.

Avis, Budget, Hertz and Thrifty all have franchises in Belize and, along with local firm Crystal (which offers some of the best rental prices and is the only company that allows you to take its vehicles to Tikal), accept advance bookings; there are also other local companies. **Reserving ahead** of time can save money and guarantees that a car will be waiting for you on arrival. One-way rentals typically aren't available, but your rental company can provide a pickup or drop-off at your Belize City hotel or the airport. See Listings on p.88 for details of car rental companies in Belize City.

In most cases you'll need to be 25 to rent a vehicle (between 21 and 25 you may be required to pay a premium), and you'll probably have to leave a credit card imprint as a damage deposit when you pick up the car. Before you belt up and drive off into the sunset, check exactly what the **insurance** covers, examine the car carefully for signs of existing damage (making sure it's marked on the rental contract) and check what spares and equipment are included. A good **spare wheel** (and the tools to put it on) is essential – you'll get an average of one puncture a week from heavy driving on Belize's roads.

Taxis

All taxis in Belize are licensed and easily identifiable by their green licence plates. Drivers operate from ranks in the centres of towns and bus stations and, particularly in Belize City, will call out to anyone they suspect is a foreigner. There are **no meters**, so you'll need to establish a rate in advance, though within the towns a fixed fare of Bz$6–7 for one or two people usually applies. You can negotiate **out-of-town fares** with the driver. Designated airport taxis from the international airport charge Bz$50 to Belize City; taxis will almost certainly be waiting for all scheduled domestic flights at Belize Municipal Airport, and at all bus stations. Some drivers (such as those at the Marine Terminal in Belize City) are also **licensed tour guides** and have been through tourism training. It is very common to share taxis in Belize, so your driver may stop to pick up another fare during your journey.

Hitchhiking

In the more remote parts of Belize, bus services will likely operate only once a day, if at all, so unless you have your own transport, **hitching** is the only other option. Although locals, including women and children, regularly hitch rides in rural areas, women travellers may prefer to do so with a friend; hitching in Belize is generally safer than at home or in neighbouring countries, but attacks have occurred, and the practice should never be considered entirely safe. Apart from this, the main drawback is the **lack of traffic**, but if cars or, more likely, pickup trucks do pass, the driver will usually offer you a lift, though occasionally you may be expected to donate some money for the ride. On the plus side, seeing the countryside from the back of a pickup is a wonderful experience – provided you sit on some sort of padding, and are fully inside the flatbed.

Cycling

Touring Belize by bike is fairly straightforward, particularly in the north and west where the roads are well surfaced, and marvellous along the Hummingbird Highway – if you can manage the hills. Some locals will be surprised to see you using this form of transport, but don't assume that you're always noticed – **stay alert** to traffic. Biking on the highways after dark is not recommended.

Cycling is a popular sport in Belize: citizens compete internationally, and several annual races, in which visitors are welcome to take part, are heavily attended. You'll find cycle

Addresses

Addresses in Belize appear in a few different ways. The familiar "number, street name" format is prevalent in most towns; along the highways, addresses often refer to the nearest mile marker. In smaller settlements or villages, well-known landmarks are used to describe the location of establishments. Since there is no postal service in many parts of the country, PO Boxes are the dominant form of receiving mail. Should you need to send mail to a person or business for which you don't have a PO Box number, simply write "General Delivery", followed by the village, under the recipient's name.

repair shops in all towns. Mountain or beach bikes are available for rent at an increasing number of shops and resorts (sometimes free for guests). Inspect rental bikes carefully since they deteriorate quickly in coastal climes, and if you intend to cycle a lot, bring or buy your own lock, lights and a helmet, which can be difficult to find. Two of the **best places** to rent a bike are San Ignacio, where you can ride along the forest roads in the Mountain Pine Ridge, and Placencia, whose smooth, sandy resort road makes for an enjoyable day's riding. Renting a mountain bike in Punta Gorda will give you the freedom to explore the Maya villages and hills of Toledo.

Bikes can only rarely be carried on top of buses; few Belizean buses have the **roof racks** so common in Guatemala. If you're lucky – and if there's room – the driver may let you put your bike in the back of the bus.

If you've cycled into Belize from Mexico or Guatemala, there's usually no problem bringing your bike over the **border**, though it may be recorded in your passport and you might then have difficulty leaving the country without it. In the UK, membership of the Cyclists' Touring Club (Ⓣ0870/873-0060, Ⓦwww.ctc.org.uk) enables you to access information and recent trip reports from cyclists who've taken bikes to Belize and around the region.

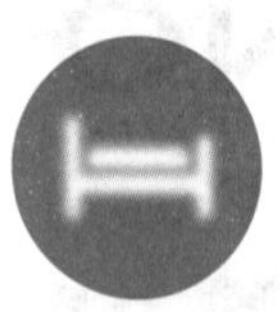

Accommodation

Accommodation in Belize ranges from world-renowned resorts to cheap, clapboard hotels. In each category between, there's a wide range of prices and it's fairly easy to find somewhere both comfortable and affordable to stay.

Towns in Belize are so small that you can usually walk to the majority of hotels from the bus stop to see what's on offer; even in Belize City, most places are within 1.5km of the Swing Bridge. For much of the year occupancy rates are very low, and you should have little difficulty finding a room even in the high season. The few exceptions are Christmas, New Year and Easter, when you'll almost certainly need to **book ahead** in resort areas – something you should also do if you have your heart set on somewhere specific.

The cost of accommodation in Belize is notably higher than in surrounding countries, but a little investigation can often turn up good bargains. Many of the mid-range and upmarket hotels give **discounts** to visitors using *Rough Guides*, especially in the low season, and may offer cheaper rates for **booking direct** rather than through an agent. Toucan Trail, a consortium of small, affordable

Accommodation price codes

All accommodation listed in the Guide has been given a price code according to the following scale. The prices refer to the cost of a **double room in high season** (generally December to Easter) in Belize dollars, but, unless otherwise stated in the text, do not include the government hotel tax of nine percent. Note that some establishments, particularly higher-end resorts, also add a service charge of around ten percent. To get the equivalent price in US$, simply divide by two.

1 under Bz$30
2 Bz$30–40
3 Bz$40–60
4 Bz$60–90
5 Bz$90–120
6 Bz$120–150
7 Bz$150–200
8 Bz$200–250
9 over Bz$250

hotels that have met the association's standards of social and environmental sustainability, recommends places to stay on its website (ⓦwww.toucantrail.com).

Arriving early at your destination gives you time to look around for the best room in your budget. A good idea, especially in cheaper places, is to ask to see the room before you accept it; check that the light and fan work, and if you've been told there's hot water, see just what that means. In towns, it's sometimes better to get a room at the back, away from the street noise, although people-watching from the front balcony can be fascinating; an upstairs room means you're more likely to benefit from a breeze. Although there's no official rating system in Belize, all hotels are inspected by the Belize Tourism Board to verify that they meet **minimum standards** applicable to their class. If you have a complaint that the hotel owner or manager doesn't deal with satisfactorily, you can take it to the BTB (see box, p.56) or the Belize Tourism Industry Association (BTIA), PO Box 62, 10 North Park St, Belize City (ⓣ227-5717, ⓔbtia@btl.net).

Budget and mid-range hotels

Most small hotels are family-run, and owners generally take pride in the **cleanliness** of the rooms. Check-in is typically informal – you'll

usually have to pay on arrival and sign the register. There may be a place to hand-wash clothes, but ask first before you use it.

Budget hotels (①–③; see box, opposite) run the gamut. As a rule, a basic room will have a bed, light and fan, and all but the most rock-bottom of places will supply a towel, soap and toilet paper. You'll often have the option of a **private bathroom**, which can be worth paying a little extra for. In most places a fan will be more desirable than hot water, though nowadays even budget hotels have hot water most of the time (reviews in the Guide indicate where it's not available).

In Belize City, most simple double rooms cost roughly Bz$50, with around Bz$10 added for a private bathroom. Oddly enough, budget rooms in the popular tourist areas of Caye Caulker, San Ignacio and Placencia are usually less expensive, though you'll pay much more in San Pedro. Rooms in **mid-range** hotels vary from Bz$50 to Bz$200; they'll almost certainly have a private bathroom and likely a balcony, and many also have the option of **air-conditioning**. In the countryside, especially in Cayo District, you can occasionally get a private cabaña for as little as Bz$100 out of season.

Resorts and lodges

With more money to spend, you could stay in a very comfortable **private cabaña** at one of the island resorts, which have spectacular beach or atoll locations. Alternatively, head inland to one of the beautiful **jungle lodges**, often in or near national parks and offering private, thatched cabañas with balconies overlooking a forest or river. These options may be expensive, but the extra dollars will soon be forgotten as you watch the sun rise over the reef or hear the rainforest's dawn chorus. Specialist diving, adventure and nature tours (see p.138, p.150 & p.188) often use resorts and lodges as bases, sometimes taking only paying guests on **trips** that include transport, meals and activities. Several places offer spa and massage services, perfect for unwinding after a day spent hiking or on horseback.

Rates may start at as little as US$75/night for a double room, but can reach over

US$200 per person. Watch out for a possible **service charge** (see p.47), which, combined with the nine percent hotel tax, can raise the price considerably.

Hostels

There are very few dormitory-style cheap hostels in Belize, although you will find some in Caye Caulker and San Ignacio.

Camping

Formal **camping facilities** are few and far between in Belize, and the few trailer parks that exist are small and fairly basic in comparison with anything in the US or Canada, although they are getting better. Specialist camping **supplies** are scarce or unobtainable, so don't expect to find gas canisters or Coleman fuel, though kerosene is widely available; in most cases cooking will be done over a wood fire. You can only camp in forest reserves and national parks if you obtain **special permission** from the Forest Department in Belmopan. Two notable exceptions (where you can just turn up and pay the fee) are the Jaguar Reserve and the forestry village of Augustine/Douglas Silva in the Mountain Pine Ridge (see p.263 & p.180, respectively).

Generally, a **tent** is useful mainly if you plan to hike off the beaten track, usually with a guide who will lead you to places where you can set up camp. You might also want to take a tent if you're hiking around the Maya villages in southern Toledo, though many of these will have a simple guest house. Some of the rural resorts in Cayo and villages throughout Belize (particularly Crooked Tree) have **camping areas**, but these are rare on Ambergris Caye or Caye Caulker.

Food and drink

Belizean food is a distinctive mix of Latin American and Caribbean influences, with Creole "rice and beans" cuisine dominating the scene but plenty of other dishes playing important roles. At its best, Creole food is delicious, taking fresh ingredients from the sea and mixing them with the smooth taste of coconut – a favourite ingredient – and lively spices. The range of international cuisines on offer increases every year, and you can find authentic delicacies from as far afield as Lebanon and Thailand.

You'll soon become accustomed to the **lunch hour** (noon to 1pm), observed with almost religious devotion. Abandon all hope of getting anything else done and find a seat with the locals. This is often the main meal of the day and, though most places naturally also serve dinner, **dining late** is not a Belizean custom; generally, planning to get to your table by 8pm will give you a good range of options, and possibly better service. Many places will be closed by nine or earlier, even in tourist areas.

Typical cuisine

There are few surprises waiting at **breakfast**: you're likely to be offered eggs with ham or sausage, usually accompanied by bread (sometimes toasted) or flour tortillas and stewed or refried red beans, though in tourist areas you'll almost always be offered fresh fruit and pancakes, often served with yoghurt or locally produced honey. One exciting and delicious breakfast treat is **fry jacks**, fluffy, fried dough usually eaten with sweet jam. Except at upscale hotels, breakfast shouldn't cost more than US$4–5.

The other daily meals (mostly US$4–8) are generally variations on **rice and beans**, Creole mainstays that feature heavily in most restaurants. The white rice and red beans are cooked together in coconut oil and flavoured with *recado* (a mild, ground red spice) – often with a chunk of salted pork thrown in for extra taste – and usually served with fried fish or stewed chicken or beef. In **stewed beans and rice**, the beans are stewed, sometimes with spices, and ladled on top of the boiled white rice. If you like your flavours full on, there'll always be a bottle of hot sauce on the table for extra kick. Despite the proximity of Mexico, its cuisine has had only a superficial effect on Belizean restaurant food; however, you will see *tamales* and *escabeche* (a spicy onion soup with chicken), though perhaps without the usual accompaniment of corn tortillas.

Adventurous eaters may want to try agouti, a peculiarly Belizean delicacy also known as **gibnut**: in the wild, it's a large, nocturnal rodent; on the plate it's said to taste like pork. On the other end of the dietary spectrum, **vegetables** are scarce in Creole food, but on the side you'll often get a portion of potato salad, coleslaw and/or green salad, and sometimes fried plantain or flour tortillas.

Seafood is almost always excellent. Grouper and red snapper are invariably fantastic, and you might also try a barracuda steak, conch fritters or a plate of fresh (though usually farmed) shrimp. On San Pedro and Caye Caulker the food can be exceptional, with **lobster** served in an amazing range of dishes: in addition to grilled or barbecued lobster, you'll see pasta with lobster sauce, lobster and scrambled eggs, and even lobster chow mein or curry. Watch out for lobster served during the off-season from mid-February to mid-June, though; it's most likely been illegally poached. **Turtle** is only on the menu in a very few places, in theory only during the short open season, but all species are protected – avoid trying it, or indeed any exotic animal taken from the wild.

Belize has many **Chinese restaurants**, varying enormously in quality. Chinese food will probably feature more in your trip than you anticipated, as it's often the only food available on Sundays, or late evenings in smaller places. Other Belizean ethnic minorities are now starting to break into the restaurant trade; many places serve **Garifuna dishes**, and there are Indian restaurants in Belize City and San Ignacio (where there's also a Sri Lankan restaurant), serving superb curries.

Street food

Central American-style, streetside **snack bars**, often run by former refugees from El Salvador or Honduras, are now found all over the country, and provide cheap and delicious fast food. You'll find tasty *tamales* (a savoury cornmeal "pudding", usually with chicken cooked in a lightly spiced sauce inside, wrapped in a banana leaf and steamed), tacos, *empanadas* (similar to tacos but the tortilla is folded in half after filling, then deep fried) and other Latin staples, adding variety to the range of cuisine on offer. Travelling, you'll find that these snacks, as well as the usual Belizean standby of "ham" burgers (literally a slice of canned ham in a bun), are sometimes hawked to waiting **bus passengers**, although the practice isn't nearly as common as elsewhere in Central America.

Vegetarian and vegan diets

Vegetarians will find the pickings in Belize slim, and there are few specifically vegetarian restaurants. Within the resort areas, you should find at least a couple of vegetarian dishes on the menu, and the staff should understand the concept. Note that in some traditional Belizean restaurants, if you say you don't eat meat you're likely to be offered chicken or ham (white meat is often not considered "meat" in the true sense). The fruit is good and there are some excellent locally produced vegetables (thanks mainly to the Mennonites and Central American refugees), but these are rarely served in local restaurants. Your best bet outside the main tourist areas is to try a Chinese restaurant.

Dairy products are easier to avoid, although if you're ordering any kind of potatoes or tacos, be sure to specify your preference, as they often have cheese or cream melted into them.

Drinks

The most basic drinks to accompany food are water, beer and the oversweetened, but familiar, soft drinks. Belikin, the only brewery in Belize, produces almost all the **beer** consumed here. Belikin beer comes in several varieties: regular, a tasty, lager-type bottled and draught beer; bottled stout (a rich, dark beer); and Premium and Lighthouse, more expensive bottled beers and often all that upmarket hotels and restaurants offer. If you simply ask for a beer at the average bar, you'll usually be served a bottled (regular) Belikin. All varieties are **overpriced**, with even regular at more than US$1.40 for a small bottle (higher on the cayes); imported European and American beers cost twice this much. Bottled Guinness, brewed under licence by Belikin, is also available, but Mexican and Guatemalan beer is virtually unobtainable. The legal age for drinking alcohol in Belize is 18.

Cashew nut and berry **wines**, rich and full-bodied, are bottled and sold in some villages, and you can also get hold of imported wine, though it's far from cheap. On Ambergris Caye, *Rendezvous Restaurant and Winery* (see p.144) produces several varieties of red and white wine from imported grape juice, fermented and bottled at the restaurant; the wine is available at local supermarkets and the airport duty-free shops. Local **rum**, in both dark and clear varieties, is the best deal in Belizean alcohol (about Bz$8 per bottle) and there's plenty to choose from. The locally produced gin, brandy and vodka, however, are poor imitations – cheap and fairly nasty.

Nonalcoholic drinks include a predictable range of **soft drinks** including Sprite, Fanta, Coke and Pepsi. Despite the number of citrus plantations, fresh fruit juices are not always available, though you can generally get orange, lime and watermelon juices, and sometimes pineapple. *Licuados*, the thirst-quenching blended fruit drinks, ubiquitous throughout Mexico and the rest of Central America, are only rarely served in Belize. **Tap water** in towns, though safe, is highly chlorinated, and many villages (with the exception of Caye Caulker) now have a potable water system. Filtered, bottled water and mineral water are sold almost everywhere, and pure rainwater is usually available in the countryside and on the cayes.

Coffee, except in the best establishments, will generally be instant. Tea, due to the British influence, is a popular hot drink, as are Milo and Ovaltine (malted, milky drinks). One last drink that deserves a mention is **seaweed**, a strange blend of actual seaweed, milk, cinnamon, sugar and cream. If you see someone selling this on a street corner, give it a try.

Health

Belize has a high standard of public health, and most visitors leave without suffering so much as a dose of diarrhoea. Tap water in all towns and many villages (though not in Caye Caulker) is safe to drink, though heavily chlorinated. Rainwater is collected in rural areas; it's usually safe, but you might want to treat it, especially for children (see box, p.38). Restaurants are subject to stringent hygiene regulations, so ice in drinks will almost certainly be shop-bought or made from treated water. Bottled water is also widely available.

Still, it's essential to get the best **health advice** you can before you set off; always schedule a visit with your doctor or a travel clinic (see p.40). Many clinics also sell travel-related medical supplies, such as malaria tablets, mosquito nets and water filters. Regardless of how well prepared you are, **medical insurance** is also essential (see p.50). You might also want to take a travel medical kit, which range from a box of Band-Aids/plasters to a complete set of syringes and sutures; both are usually available from clinics, pharmacies and specialist suppliers (see p.89).

If you're **pregnant** or taking an oral contraceptive, you'll need to mention this when seeking health advice on travel medicine, as some vaccines and drugs can have harmful interactions or side effects. Travel health specialists and bookshops stock a number of books on health precautions and disease prevention.

Vaccinations

The only obligatory inoculation for Belize is against yellow fever, and that's only if you're arriving from a "high-risk" area (northern South America and equatorial Africa); carry your **vaccination certificate** as proof. However, there are several other inoculations that you should have anyway, particularly if you intend to spend time in remote, rural areas. At least eight weeks before you leave (longer if you plan to be away for more than six months and need several immunizations), check that you're up to date with diphtheria, polio and tetanus jabs, and arrange for typhoid and hepatitis A inoculations. Both typhoid and hepatitis A are transmitted through **contaminated food and water**. The former is very rare in Belize, but the hepatitis A virus is common throughout Central America and can lay a victim low for several months with exhaustion, fever, diarrhoea and possible liver damage. One dose of vaccine will give protection for up to a year; a further shot, six to twelve months later, gives up to ten years' protection. Although the risk of contracting hepatitis B is low unless you receive unscreened blood products or have unprotected sex, travel clinics often recommend inoculation; a joint hepatitis A and B vaccine is now available from GPs and travel clinics. A course of three injections takes five weeks and gives up to five years' protection.

Rabies exists in Belize, and vaccination (a course of three shots over a month) is recommended for anyone travelling to Latin America for over thirty days. If you're here for less time but intend to travel for days in rural areas, you should also get the vaccine. The best advice is, as usual, prevention; give dogs a wide berth, and don't play with any animals at all, no matter how cuddly they look. Treat **any mammal bite** as suspect: wash the wound immediately with soap or detergent, and apply alcohol or iodine if possible. Act immediately to get treatment – rabies is fatal once symptoms appear.

North Americans will have to pay for inoculations, available at any immunization centre or at most local clinics. Many GPs in the UK have a travel surgery where you can get advice and certain vaccines on prescription, though they may not administer some of the less common immunizations; most now charge for the service. **Travel clinics** tend to be cheaper and give vaccinations almost immediately. In Australasia too, travel clinics tend to be less expensive than doctors' surgeries.

Malaria and dengue fever

Malaria is endemic to many parts of Central America, especially the rural lowlands. Though it poses no great threat in Belize's tourist areas – due to an effective nationwide control programme – several thousand cases do occur each year, so you should still take all the recommended precautions. The recommended malaria prophylactic in Belize is **chloroquine**; you need to start taking the tablets one week before arrival and continue for four weeks after leaving the area. This drug can cause adverse reactions such as nausea, so ask your travel clinic about using doxycycline or Malarone as an alternative. Avoiding bites in the first place is the best prevention: sleep in screened rooms or under nets, burn mosquito coils containing permethrin, cover up arms and legs (especially around dawn and dusk when mosquitoes are most active) and use repellent containing over 35 percent DEET (15 percent for children). Belizeans use smouldering **coconut husks** or cohune nuts to ward off biting insects, to very good effect.

Keeping mosquitoes at bay is doubly important in the case of **dengue fever** – a viral infection transmitted by mosquitoes active both day and night – for which there is no vaccine or specific treatment. The first symptom is a fever, accompanied by severe joint and muscle pains, which subsides, only to recur a few days later, this time with a rash likely to spread all over the body. After this second outbreak, the fever and rash recede and recovery is usually complete. Epidemic outbreaks of dengue fever are frequent in Belize during the wetter seasons.

Intestinal troubles

A bout of **diarrhoea** is the medical problem you're most likely to encounter in Belize, generally caused by the change of diet and exposure to unfamiliar bacteria. Following a few simple precautions should help keep you healthy: be sure to drink clean water (any bottled drinks, including beer and soft drinks, are already purified; for more advice on water, see box, below), steer clear of raw shellfish and don't eat anywhere that's obviously dirty. If you do go down with a dose, the best cure is also the simplest: take it easy for a day or two, eat only the blandest of foods – **papaya** is good for soothing the stomach and is also packed with vitamins – and, most importantly, ensure that you replace lost fluids and salts by drinking lots of bottled water and taking **rehydration salts**. If you can't get hold of these, half a teaspoon of salt and three of sugar in a litre of water will do the trick. If diarrhoea lasts more than three or four days or is accompanied by a fever or blood in your stools, seek immediate medical help.

If you're spending any time in rural areas, you may also pick up **parasitic infections**: protozoa – amoeba and giardia – and intestinal worms. These sound (and can be) hideous, but they're treatable once detected. If you suspect you may have an infestation, take a stool sample to a pathology laboratory and go to a doctor or pharmacist with the results. More serious is **amoebic dysentery**, endemic to many parts of the region. The symptoms are more or less the same as a bad dose of diarrhoea, but include bleeding. On the whole, a course of Flagyl (metronidazole or tinidozole) will cure it. If you plan to visit the far-flung corners of Central America, it's worth carrying this just in case – but get advice on its usage from a medical professional before you go.

Finally, if you're using the **Pill** – or any other orally administered drug – bear in mind that severe diarrhoea can reduce its efficacy.

Heat and dehydration

Another common cause of discomfort – and even illness – is **the sun**. The best advice is to build up exposure gradually, use a strong sunscreen and, if you're walking around during the day, wear a hat and stay in the shade. Be aware that overheating can cause **heatstroke**, which is potentially fatal. Signs are a very high body temperature without a feeling of fever, accompanied by headaches and disorientation. Lowering body temperature (with a tepid shower, cool drinks or a fan, for example) is the first step in treatment. **Avoid dehydration** by taking plenty of fluids, especially water. If you know you're going to be hiking in the

Water purification

Contaminated water is a major cause of illness amongst travellers in Central America, due to the presence of pathogenic organisms: bacteria, viruses and cysts. In Belize, however, water in most hotels and resorts is treated, and bottled water is available pretty much everywhere; you will only need to consider treating water if you travel to remote areas. Bottled water is also easy to find in Flores and Tikal in Guatemala. While boiling water for ten minutes kills most micro-organisms, it's not the most convenient method. Chemical sterilization with either chlorine or **iodine tablets** or a tincture of iodine liquid is effective (except in preventing amoebic dysentery or giardiasis), but the resulting liquid doesn't taste very pleasant, though it can be masked with lemon or lime juice. Iodine is unsafe for pregnant women, babies and people with thyroid complaints. Purification, involving both sterilization and filtration, gives the most complete treatment, and travel clinics and good outdoor equipment shops stock a wide range of portable water purifiers.

jungle for days, you may want to bring oral rehydration tablets or powder, though you'll need pure water to reconstitute them.

Bites and stings

Aside from malaria-carrying mosquitoes, there are several other biting insects (and other animals) whose nips could leave you in varying degrees of discomfort. **Sandflies**, often present on beaches, are tiny, but their bites, usually on feet and ankles, itch like hell and last for days. Head or body **lice** can be picked up from people or bedding and are best treated with medicated soap or shampoo. **Ticks**, which you're likely to attract if you pass through wooded or agricultural areas, need careful removal with tweezers – those in a Swiss Army knife are ideal.

Scorpions are common but mostly nocturnal, avoiding the daytime heat under rocks and in crevices. Species in Belize can cause a painful sting but are rarely fatal. You're unlikely to be stung, but if you camp or sleep in a rustic cabaña, shake out your shoes before putting them on and avoid wandering around barefoot. Stings hurt at first, but the pain usually goes away fairly quickly – though some people experience a severe **allergic reaction**. If the pain seems significantly worse than a bee sting, seek medical treatment.

You're even less likely to be bitten by a **spider** (tarantulas won't bite unless severely provoked, and even if you're bitten the pain soon dies down), but the advice is the same as for scorpions – seek **medical treatment** if the pain persists or increases, or if the bite becomes infected. You're unlikely to see many snakes and most are harmless in any case; if you're walking through undergrowth, wearing boots and long trousers and treading heavily to announce your presence will go a long way towards preventing a bite. If you are bitten, remember what the snake looked like, immobilize the bitten limb as far as possible and seek medical help: **antivenin** is available in most hospitals.

Swimming and snorkelling might bring you into contact with some potentially dangerous or venomous sea creatures. Shark attacks have been virtually unknown in Belize; **stingrays** are generally very gentle creatures, but if you step on one (they rest in the sand) it will give a very painful sting. Shuffling your feet in shallow water gives them warning that you are approaching. The Portuguese man-o'-war **jellyfish**, with its purple, bag-like sail, has very long tentacles with stinging cells that inflict raw, red welts; equally painful is a brush against **fire coral**. In both cases, clean the wound with vinegar or iodine and seek medical help if the pain persists or infection develops. For advice on mammal bites, see the information on rabies on p.37.

Getting medical help

Doctors in Belize have received training abroad, usually in the US, Mexico or Cuba, and are generally informed of current treatments. Your embassy keeps a list of recommended specialists. A visit to a **local clinic** is usually by donation; around Bz$20 is suggested, which doesn't cover possibly expensive treatment and medications. **Private doctors** set their own fees, which can be considerably more costly. However, if you suspect all is not well with your insides, it might be worth heading straight for the local **pathology lab** (all the main towns have them) before seeing a doctor, as he or she will probably send you there anyway. Pharmacists are knowledgeable and helpful, and sometimes provide drugs only available by prescription at home. **Herbal remedies** are also quite popular in Belize, and if you have confidence in alternative medicine (or are willing to try it), you could seek advice from a number of respected practitioners – see p.202 for details of the Ix Chel Wellness Center.

Many rural communities have a **health centre** where care is free, although there may be only a nurse or health worker available. Should you need an injection, make sure that the equipment is sterile (it might be worth bringing a sterile kit from home) and ensure any blood you receive is screened. For anything serious you should go to the best hospital you can reach.

Medical resources for travellers

Whether you're a frequent traveller or this is your first trip to the tropics, check the listings below to find the latest travel health advice from the most reliable providers. By far the best source for a comprehensive assessment of health risks is the website of the **Centers for Disease Control** in the US; no matter where you live, check here first.

In North America

Many state and local health departments throughout the US provide travel immunizations; if one doesn't, they can usually tell you who in the area does. Visit the website of the **International Society for Travel Medicine** (Ⓦwww.istm.org) for a full list of travel clinics.

Canadian Society for International Health 1 Nicholas St, Suite 1105, Ottawa, K1N 7B7 Ⓣ613/241-5785, Ⓦwww.csih.org. Nongovernmental organization for the promotion of health in the developing world. Distributes a free pamphlet – *Health Information for Canadian Travellers* – containing an extensive list of travel health centres in Canada. Excellent website with very good links.

Centers for Disease Control Ⓦwww.cdc.gov/travel/camerica.htm. The best travel health website in the world, with current country- and area-specific health information; check here first if you can. Latest information on health risks and precautions, plus links to travel health clinics.

Health Canada Ⓦwww.travelhealth.gc.ca. Accurate, informative website in English and French, produced by the Canadian government; lists travel health clinics throughout Canada, along with lots of other useful links.

Travel Medicine 351 Pleasant St, Suite 312, Northampton, MA 01060 Ⓣ1-800/872-8633. Sells first aid kits, mosquito netting, water filters and other health-related travel products.

In the UK and Ireland

British travellers should pick up a copy of the excellent free booklet *Health Advice for Travellers*, published by the Department of Health and available from GPs' surgeries, many chemists and most of the agencies listed below.

British Airways Travel Clinic Two in central London: 213 Piccadilly and 101 Cheapside Ⓣ0845/600 2236, Ⓦwww.britishairways.com/travel/healthclinintro. All travel vaccinations (walk-in service available) and a comprehensive range of travel health items.

Hospital for Tropical Diseases Travel Clinic Mortimer Market Building, Capper St, London WC1E 6AU Ⓣ020/7388 9600, Ⓦwww.thehtd.org. Healthline message service on Ⓣ09061/337 733 (50p/min) with hints on hygiene, illness prevention and appropriate immunizations (after the brief introduction, key in "68" for Belize). All travel vaccinations (usually by appointment only) and travel health products; a visit to a tropical medicine consultant costs £15, which is waived if you have vaccinations at HTD. Open Mon–Fri 9am–5pm.

MASTA (Medical Advisory Service for Travellers Abroad) Ⓣ09068/224 100, Ⓦwww.masta.org. Extremely informative and organized website with plenty of practical advice on staying healthy abroad, plus information on diseases you might encounter and travel health products. All travel vaccinations available at MASTA-affiliated clinics throughout the country.

Nomad Travel Store and Medical Centre 40 Bernard St, Russell Square, London WC1N 1LJ Ⓣ020/7833 4114, Ⓦwww.nomadtravel.co.uk; plus other locations in London and Bristol (see website). The Nomad Travel Health Line (60p/min; Ⓣ09068/633 414) lets you speak to a health professional, or you can leave a message and someone will call you back free of charge. One of the most experienced travel equipment suppliers in the UK, with mail and online ordering services. The clinics have some of the most competitive prices for vaccinations, so it's best to call ahead for an appointment.

Trailfinders Travel Clinic 194 Kensington High St, London W8 6BD Ⓣ020/7938 3999. Expert medical advice and a full range of vaccines and travel medical supplies; no appointments necessary and discounts for Trailfinders clients.

Travel Medicine Services PO Box 254, 16 College St, Belfast 1 Ⓣ028/9031 5220. Operates a travel clinic (Mon 9–11am & Wed 2–4pm, only call during these times) that gives inoculations after referral from a GP.

Tropical Medical Bureau Grafton St Medical Centre, Dublin 2 Ⓣ01/671 9200, Ⓦwww.tmb.ie. Eight specialist travel medicine clinics in the Republic of Ireland; call Ⓣ1850/487 674 for the nearest to you.

In Australia and New Zealand

The **International Association for Medical Assistance to Travellers** (Ⓦwww.iamat.org) is a nonprofit organization open to all; there's no charge for membership, although a donation is requested to help support its work. Membership brings a number of benefits, including climate charts, leaflets on various diseases and inoculations and a list of English-speaking doctors in Central America.

Travellers Medical and Vaccination Centre Ⓣ1300/658 844, Ⓦwww.tmvc.com.au. Excellent information on travel health; you can also subscribe to the online *Travel Doctor*. Twenty-five TMVC clinics across Australia, with others in New Zealand, South Africa and Southeast Asia.

The media

Although Belize, with its English-language media, can come as a welcome break in a region of Spanish-speakers, it's not always easy to keep in touch with what's happening in the rest of the world. News sources, particularly the press but also radio and television, report in a very nationalistic manner, often prioritizing relatively trivial local stories over important international ones. Your best bet for keeping abreast of world news is cable TV or the Internet, both widely available in towns and resort locales.

Newspapers and magazines

The five **national newspapers** – *The Amandala*, *The Belize Times*, *The Guardian* (no relation to the UK broadsheet), *The Reporter* and *The Independent* – are all published on Friday with a dateline of the following Sunday, though *The Amandala* also produces a slim, mid-week edition. The first two exhibit racist and xenophobic tones that would make a British tabloid wince, and it helps to have an understanding of which newspaper follows which party line: *The Belize Times* is the propaganda organ of the ruling People's United Party (PUP), which *The Amandala* also generally supports, while *The Guardian* is the mouthpiece of the opposition United Democratic Party (UDP); *The Reporter* and *The Independent* try their best to be objective and impartial. Allegiances aside, they all make **entertaining reading**, and you'll find some interesting articles in each edition. For online magazines covering Belize, see the list of recommended websites on p.56.

In Belize City, Belmopan, San Pedro and occasionally some other towns, you should be able to get hold of some **foreign newspapers and magazines**, including *Time*, *Newsweek* and the Caribbean edition of *The Miami Herald*, usually the day after publication (though the top hotels in Belize City get them the same day on incoming afternoon flights). **The Book Center**, at 4 Church Street in Belize City, has the largest selection of magazines in the country.

Radio

All **radio** stations in Belize are commercial and privately owned. Love FM (89.9, 95.1 and other frequencies around the country), offering easy listening, news and current affairs, has the most extensive network and also runs sister stations Estero Amor (in Spanish) and More FM (youth-oriented). Another major station is KREM (91.1 and 96.5FM), with an emphasis on talk, reggae and **punta rock**. Belize City's other stations are WAVE FM (105.9) and FM 2000 (90.5), and each major district town has its own local station. There's also a **British forces** station, BFBS (93.1FM), and Mexican stations come through in the north, Honduran and Guatemalan ones in the south and west.

Television

There are two more-or-less national **television** stations. Channel 5 is the country's best broadcaster, producing superb news and factual programmes (you can access their daily news output on the Internet at Ⓦwww.channel5belize.com), although they don't transmit everywhere in the country. Channel 7, on the other hand, shows mostly **American programming** from various satellite channels, mixed in with some local news and rambling political discussion programmes. Both show some educational programming and broadcast their main news stories at 6.30pm. But it's cable TV (mostly pirated from satellite by local companies) that gets most of the nation's viewers, with its saturation coverage of American soaps, talk shows, sports, movies and CNN.

Film and video

There's only one **cinema** in Belize (in Belize City's *Princess Hotel*) and, unsurprisingly, no local film industry, though the country has been the location for a few renowned films: *The Dogs of War*, *The Mosquito Coast*, *Heart of Darkness* and *After the Storm*. However, the success of the **Belize Film Festival**, established in 2003, has introduced foreign filmmakers to local talent and resulted in several film proposals; for more on this event, visit Ⓦwww.belizefilmfestival.com.

Great Belize Productions, 17 Regent St, Belize City (Ⓣ227-3146, Ⓦwww.channel5belize.com), produces an excellent series of locally made **videos**, which can make great souvenirs. These include *The Best of Belize All Over*, showing slices of local life to the accompaniment of great Belizean music, and *From Invasion to Nation – A History of Belize*, presented by Belizean historian Assad Shoman and diplomat Robert Leslie. Both are available in North American (NTSC) and European (PAL) formats. The company also produces several marvellous nature documentaries, the daily Channel 5 news programmes and an annual video anthology of news relevant to Belize.

Festivals

Festivals are popular in Belize and often involve entire communities. They range from full-on Carnival to local school fundraisers, all celebrated with flair and exuberance. Some welcome visitors while others are mostly for schoolchildren or sports-team diehards. The following list is just a sample of what's on when and where; check locally for exact dates and venues.

New Year's Day Horse racing in Burrell Boom village; Cycling Classic from Corozal to Belize City.
February Sidewalk Arts Festival in Placencia; end-of-season Lobster-Fest in Caye Caulker.
March La Ruta Maya canoe race from San Ignacio to Belize City (see p.190), on the Baron Bliss Day weekend.
April Regattas in Caye Caulker and Sarteneja; Easter Fair in San Ignacio and other Easter celebrations throughout the country.
May Cashew Festival in Crooked Tree village; National Agriculture Show in Belmopan.
June Día de San Pedro in San Pedro; Lobster-Fest in Placencia.
July Benque Viejo Fiesta in Cayo District; Lobster-Fest in Caye Caulker.
August International Costa Maya Festival in San Pedro; Deer Dance Festival in San Antonio, Toledo District.
September Independence Day celebrations nationwide; St George's Caye Day; Carnival in Belize City.
October Pan American Day: fiestas in mestizo areas.
November Garifuna Settlement Day in Dangriga, Hopkins and other Garifuna communities.
December Boxing Day: parties, dances, cycle race in Belize City and horse races in Burrell Boom.

Sports and outdoor activities

The main spectator sports in Belize are football (soccer) and baseball, which rank equally as national games and receive avid reporting in the press. Softball is also popular, as is track and field, and televised American football and baseball have devoted followings. As elsewhere in Central America, cycling is closely followed and there are frequent races all over Belize. Finally, there are a number of horse races around Christmas and New Year.

Many of the sports that visitors to Belize can participate in are connected to the water in some way, with sailing, windsurfing, diving and snorkelling all extremely popular. **Diving courses**, for beginners or experts, are run from Belize City, San Pedro, Placencia, Caye Caulker and many other cayes. Sea and river kayaking, too, are becoming ever more popular, and a number of outfits organize trips. **Fly-fishing** for bonefish on a catch-and-release basis has long attracted dedicated anglers to the shallow, sandy "flats" off Belize's cayes and atolls. Several lodges, specialist operators, and local guides can arrange this as well as fishing for permit, tarpon and other sportfish.

Away from the coast, **canoeing**, **rafting** and **tubing** – floating along rivers in a giant inner tube – are extremely popular, particularly in Cayo District, where plenty of people are eager to arrange this for you. Many of the same tour operators can arrange **jungle hiking**: anything from a guided walk along a medicinal plant trail to very demanding, multi-day jungle survival courses. Beneath the jungle, Belize's amazing subterranean landscape is becoming ever more accessible, with motivated, very competent **caving** guides leading tours and organizing specialist expeditions. *Caves Branch Jungle Lodge* (see p.241), owned by a founding member of the Belize Cave and Wilderness Rescue Team, makes safety a prime feature of its caving trips; they also offer rappelling and rock climbing.

Horseback riding and mountain biking are other possibilities in Cayo and indeed anywhere in rural Belize, with some superb routes through forested hills to Maya sites. Organizers of the above activities are listed on p.138, p.175 & p.188, and in relevant places throughout the Guide.

On most guided trips you'll be led by enthusiastic and highly qualified tour guides. In order to earn a **tour guide licence**, these men and women have successfully completed numerous courses in everything from archeology and history to geology, biology and presentation skills; all guides must also renew their first aid and CPR training biannually. Licensed guides will have a **photo ID** (often stating their main field of expertise), which must be displayed when they're conducting a tour, but it's not a bad idea to research the reputations of different companies, as quality can sometimes vary.

Culture and etiquette

On the whole, Belize is friendly and welcoming to outsiders, and, being a popular vacation destination, is relatively accustomed to visitors' sometimes peculiar habits. At heart, however, it's a very traditional and religious country, something that you should respect while here.

Due to Belize's warm climate, clothing is mostly very casual; businesspeople often dress smartly, but full suits are uncommon. Locals will outwardly tolerate visitors who make a habit of walking about in **skimpy swimwear**, especially in the cayes, but may think of them in less-than-generous terms.

Before asking questions of a stranger, you should first extend a polite greeting; many locals greet each other simply in passing, and you'll usually be expected to return such niceties. **Solo female travellers** may have a hard time differentiating between a friendly greeting and a romantic overture; Belize shares Central America's **culture of machismo**, and local men can be boldly persistent, particularly in Belize City and tourist areas. Replying to them with a short greeting and moving on quickly will usually convey your lack of interest without being insulting.

Though Belizeans rarely **tip** unless they receive exceptional service, foreigners are expected to do so in most situations. An average practice is to tip **ten percent** for food and drink, but significantly more for specialized, personal service (eg an exceptional tour guide). It's customary to leave a tip for hotel cleaning staff, but check whether this is already factored into your bill as a service charge – and if they actually receive it.

Public toilets are quite rare in Belize, though the Marine Terminal and bus stations in Belize City do have them. Facilities are basic but usually very clean. In most parts of the country (except high-end resorts), sewage disposal can only handle human waste. If there's a basket beside the toilet, you should put used toilet paper, sanitary napkins, tampons and other such waste in it. **Toilet paper** is usually provided, but you may want to carry your own to be sure.

Shopping

Compared to its neighbours, Belize has less to offer in terms of traditional crafts or local markets, the latter being primarily for food. Proper craft and gift shops are found throughout the country, but you'll often get better prices from the artisans themselves, when you can find them on the street or in villages.

If time is short, the National Handicraft Center in Belize City (see p.74) is the best place to buy souvenirs, with a wide range of good-quality, genuine Belizean crafts, including paintings, prints and music. The craftspeople are paid fair prices for their work, with the added bonus of no longer having to hawk it on the street. Established Belizean artists often exhibit here too, though the best place for contemporary **Belizean art** is The Image Factory in Belize City (Ⓦwww.imagefactory.org; see p.72). Unlike in nearby countries, haggling or **bargaining** is not common practice in Belize and although it's sometimes worth proposing a cheaper price, you risk upsetting shopkeepers by persisting when they refuse.

Wood carvings, common throughout the country, make beautiful and unusual souvenirs. Carvers often sell their wares in Belize City and at Maya sites; their exquisite renderings of dolphins, jaguars, ships and more are made from *zericote*, a two-toned wood that grows only in Belize and surrounding areas. The best wood is **kiln-dried**, though the items you see on the street may not be. **Slate carvers**, also common at Maya sites, create high-quality reproductions of gods, glyphs and stelae. Belizean ceramics generally aren't as attractive as wood and slate carvings, but the art is becoming more refined. In the Maya villages in southern Belize, you'll also come across beautiful **embroidery**, though the quality of both the cloth and the work is better in Guatemala. Maya, Garifuna and Creole villages produce good basketware and superb drums; Dangriga, Hopkins, Gales Point and the Toledo villages are the places to shop for these.

For superb **video programmes** on Belizean wildlife, culture or history, have a look at the series produced by Great Belize Productions, which can be purchased from gift shops or the company's office (see p.42). Visitors with a philatelic bent might appreciate a set of wildly colourful Belize **stamps**; relatively cheap and certainly easy to post home, they often feature the exotic animals and plants of the country. You can find many of them in post offices around the country, but the one in Belize City has a dedicated Philatelic Department. One tasty souvenir that everyone seems to want to take home

Suspect souvenirs

Some souvenirs you'll see are dependent on the destruction of Belize's reef and wildlife. They include black coral, often made into jewellery, turtle shells, which look far better on their rightful owners, and most other marine curios. The sale of corals in any form is prohibited, and many of the animal and plant souvenirs you may be offered are **illegal** in Belize and may also be listed in Appendix 1 to **CITES** (The Convention on International Trade in Endangered Species; Ⓦwww.cites.org). If you're caught trying to bring these items into the US, Canada or Europe, you could face a hefty fine.

Even more insidious black-market goods are **archeological artifacts** or remains; all such items belong to Belize, and their theft and trade is strictly prohibited. Anyone attempting to smuggle them out of the country could end up in jail at home or in Belize.

is a bottle (or three) of Marie Sharp's Pepper Sauce, made from Belizean *habañero peppers* in strengths ranging from "mild" to "fiery hot". This spicy accompaniment to rice and beans graces every restaurant table in the country, and visits to the factory near Dangriga can be arranged.

For **everyday shopping** – basic clothing, food items, toiletries – you'll find some kind of shop in every village in Belize, and Belize City has a department store and several supermarkets. If you have the time to hunt around, most things you'd find in North America or Europe are also available in Belize – at a price. Luxury items, such as electronic goods, cameras and really anything imported, tend to be very expensive. **Film** is more expensive than at home, but easy to get hold of – make sure to check the expiry dates, though.

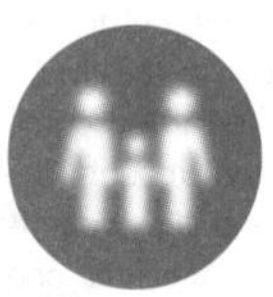

Travelling with children

Belize is a very child-friendly destination, perhaps because it's so young: nearly half of the population is under 18. There is plenty to keep active and inquisitive children occupied, and most Belizeans are patient and helpful, having grown up in large families themselves. Few hotels and resorts prohibit children, though it's worth asking before you book.

All community stores carry supplies of baby formula and nappies (diapers), and most restaurants have high chairs. Some women do breast-feed in public, though usually very discreetly, perhaps beneath a scarf or shawl. The dearth of public toilets means **changing facilities** are rare. Larger resorts may have them, but for the most part babies are changed when necessary, in public or otherwise.

Children tend to prefer seeing Belize's **wildlife**, particularly the underwater variety (if they're old enough to snorkel), over Maya ruins. While this certainly shouldn't rule out trips to the ruins, their interest is likely to wane long before yours. Highlights for older children include caving activities in Cayo and kayaking on the rivers.

Childcare facilities do exist in larger resorts, and you can usually find a well-known local to watch your children by asking around on arrival. While many Belizean women take their children to work, there are just as many who leave them with family or a professional.

Travel essentials

Costs

Though Belize may be the cheapest country in the Caribbean, it has the fully deserved reputation of being the **most expensive** country in Central America; if you've been travelling cheaply through the region to get here, many prices are going to come as a shock. Even on a tight budget, you'll spend at least forty percent more than you would in, say, Guatemala. Aside from some park and reserve entry fees, however, you'll be paying the same prices as locals.

Prices in Belize are generally lower than in North America and Europe, though not by much. What you will spend depends on when, where and how you travel. **Peak tourist seasons**, such as Christmas and around Easter, tend to push hotel prices up, and certain tourist centres – notably San Pedro – are more expensive than others. A **sales tax** of ten percent increases costs, but the rate of inflation remains relatively low.

As a general rule, a **solo budget traveller** will spend around US$25/day on basics (accommodation, food and transport); trips such as snorkelling or canoeing will add to this. Travelling in a couple will reduce per-person costs slightly, but to enjoy a reasonable level of comfort and the best of Belize's natural attractions, you should allow at least US$40/day per person.

Taxes

Hotel rooms in Belize are subject to a nine percent tax, sometimes included in the quoted price, and separate from the ten percent service charge that some higher-end places impose. A ten percent **general sales tax (GST)**, which applies to most goods and services (including meals in restaurants, though not to drinks), should not apply to hotel rooms; some package operators may try to slap it on anyway, so check carefully to see what you're paying for. To leave Belize by air, you'll pay a US$35 **exit tax** (payable in US dollars) at the international airport, although some tickets include all or part of the taxes. Land borders levy a Bz$30 **border tax** (payable in either Belize or US currency), plus a PACT conservation fee of Bz$7.50 (see p.212). If you'll be returning to Belize within thirty days, hold on to your receipt to get a discount on the next exit tax.

Illegal Drugs

Belize has long been an important link in the chain of supply between producers in South and Central America and users in North America, with minor players often being paid in product, creating a deluge of illegal drugs in the country. Marijuana, cocaine and crack are all readily available in Belize, and whether you like it or not you'll receive regular offers, particularly in San Pedro, Caye Caulker and Placencia. All such substances are **illegal**, and despite the fact that dope is smoked openly in the streets, the police do arrest people for possession of marijuana; they particularly enjoy catching tourists. If you're caught you'll probably end up spending a couple days in jail and paying a **fine** of several hundred US dollars. Practically every year foreigners are incarcerated for drug offences – the pusher may have a sideline reporting clients to the police, and catching "international drug smugglers" gives the country brownie points with the US Drug Enforcement Agency. Expect little sympathy from your embassy – they'll probably send someone to visit you, and maybe find an English-speaking lawyer, but certainly won't break you out of jail.

Crime and personal safety

While Belize has a relatively high **crime** rate, it has a great safety record for tourists, and despite the sometimes intimidating character of Belize City, you're very unlikely to experience any crime during your visit. Most locals are honest and forthright, and if you accidentally leave an item somewhere, often someone will chase you down the street to return it.

That said, it pays to be aware of the dangers. If you've got valuables, **insure** them properly (see p.50), keep them close to you (preferably in a concealed moneybelt) and always store **photocopies** of your passport and insurance documents in a secure place. Trousers with zippered pockets are also good pickpocket-deterrents. Looking generally "respectable" without appearing affluent will go some way in avoiding unwanted attention.

The best and most accurate overview of the possible dangers of visiting Belize and Central America is on the UK Foreign Office **Travel Advice Unit** website, ⓦwww.fco.gov.uk. The unit also produces a helpful leaflet for independent travellers, explaining what a consul can and cannot do for you while you're abroad. The US equivalent is the State Department's **Consular Information Service** (ⓦtravel.state.gov), which also publishes consular information sheets and lists the current dangers to US citizens. It can take some time for these sites to be updated, so local knowledge should also be sought out.

Break-ins at hotels are one of the most common types of petty theft – something you should bear in mind when selecting a room. Make sure the lock on your door works, from the inside as well as out. In some budget hotels, the lock will be a small padlock on the outside; for extra safety, it's a good idea to supply your own so you're the only one with keys. Many hotels will have a **safe** for valuables. It's up to you whether you use it; most of the time it will be fine, but make sure whatever you put in is securely wrapped – a lockable moneybelt does the job. In the UK, Catch 22 (ⓦwww.catch22products.co.uk) produces an excellent range of travel security products, available from most travel equipment suppliers (see p.40).

Solo women travellers, in addition to exercising the usual precautions, should be especially careful when talking to new male acquaintances in restaurants and bars, particularly in the cayes and Belize City. As in many other parts of the world, drugs intended to make women susceptible to **date rape** and other violent crimes are occasionally slipped into food or drinks. Though most victims of such acts have been local women, it's still never a good idea to accept food or drinks from anyone you don't know well.

If you follow a few simple precautions, you shouldn't experience any trouble at **border crossings**; the presence of armed officials generally discourages thieves in the immediate area of the immigration post. Nevertheless, it's still advisable to do any transactions with moneychangers out of sight of other people and, once away from the post, be on your guard. Watch out especially for people "helping" you find a bus and offering to carry your luggage; most of the time they'll just be after a tip, but it's easy to get distracted – never let your belongings out of sight unless you're confident they're in a safe place.

Finally, don't let anyone without the official credentials talk you into accepting them as your "guide" – all legal tour guides in Belize are licensed and will have a **photo ID**. If you have doubts about using a certain guide, trust your instinct and report the incident to the authorities.

Police emergency numbers

The police emergency number in Belize is ⓣ90 or 911; to contact the tourism police or to report a crime in Belize City, call ⓣ227-2210 or 227-2222.

Tourism police and reporting a crime

In addition to its regular police force, Belize has special **tourism police**, operating from local police stations. Easily identified by their shirts and caps emblazoned with "Tourism Police", they patrol Belize City, San Pedro,

Caye Caulker, Placencia and many other tourist destinations around the country. Police in Belize are poorly paid and, despite an ongoing campaign against criminals who prey on tourists, it's often difficult to convince them to do any more than simply fill out a report – if you can get them to do even that. Tourism police are specially trained to assist visitors and will likely prove more helpful than regular police, so it's best to track them down first if you have a problem.

If you're a victim of any crime, you should also report it to your **embassy** if you can – doing so helps the consular staff support their case for better tourist protection. This is not to say that crime against tourists is taken lightly in Belize; if criminals are caught, they're brought into court the next day, much more quickly than in other countries in the region.

Electricity

The main supply is 110 volts AC, with American-style, two- or three-pin sockets. Any electrical equipment made for the US or Canada should function properly, but anything from Britain will need a plug adapter and possibly a transformer. The electricity supply is generally pretty dependable, but **power cuts** do occur; if you're bringing any delicate equipment, like a laptop, you'll need a good surge protector. In small villages where electricity is supplied by local generators, voltage will often be lower and less dependable. Some lodges and resorts in remote areas aren't on the grid – in which case they'll have their own generators – and electricity may not be available all night.

Entry requirements

Citizens of the US, Canada, the EU, Australia, New Zealand and South Africa do not need **visas** to enter Belize as tourists. Swiss, Japanese and Israeli citizens, as well as most other nationalities, do need a visa (US$50), for which they have to apply at a **Belizean embassy** or consulate in advance, as visas are not officially obtainable at the border. There is no charge to enter Belize – just fill out the immigration form on the plane or at the border. Even if you don't require a visa, keep your **passport** or a photocopy with you at all times in Belize, as you may be asked to show it at police checkpoints.

Non-US citizens passing through the US en route to Belize will need a **machine-readable passport** and possibly a US visa. It's essential you confirm before you travel that your current passport will permit you to enter the US; allow at least two months if you need to obtain a US visa. For more on this, check the latest information on the US Department of Homeland Security website (ⓦwww.dhs.gov/us-visit).

All visitors to Belize are generally allowed a maximum stay of **thirty days**, but entry stamps can be renewed for up to a year: Bz$50/month for the first six months and Bz$100/month for the remainder, though you will likely raise the interest of the authorities if you stay this long. If you're flying in on a one-way ticket (in the unlikely event the airline lets you board), be prepared to prove your intention to leave the country, typically by showing a return air ticket to your home country, and to show "sufficient funds" for your stay – estimated at US$35 per day – though these conditions are rarely, if ever, enforced upon arrival.

The vast majority of foreign **embassies and consulates** are still in Belize City, though the US embassy has moved to Belmopan, which is also the location of the British High Commission. All current contact numbers are under the Diplomatic Listings in the green pages of the Belize telephone directory.

Belize embassies and consulates

These are just a few of the Belizean embassies and consulates around the world. In **New Zealand** and **South Africa**, contact the British High Commission, which represents Belize in these countries.

Australia (Honorary Consul) 5/1 Oliver Rd, Roseville, NSW ⓣ02/9905 8144, ⓔoutcast@acon.com.au.

Canada (Honorary Consuls) Suite 3800, South Tower, Royal Bank Plaza, Toronto M5J 2JP ⓣ416/865-7000, ⓔmpeterson@mcbinch.com; in Québec ⓣ514/288-1687; in Vancouver ⓣ604/730-1224.

El Salvador Calle El Bosque Norte, Block P Casa, Col La Cima IV, San Salvador ⓣ503/248-1423, ⓔembassyofbelizeinelsal@yahoo.com.

Guatemala (also accredited to **Costa Rica**, **Honduras**, **Nicaragua** and **Panama**) Av La Reforma 1–50, Zona 9, Edificio El Reformador Suite 801 & 802, Guatemala City ⓣ502/334-5531, ⓔembelguat@guate.net.
Mexico 215 Calle Bernado de Gálves, Col Lomas de Chapultepec, México DF 11000 ⓣ555/520-1274, ⓔembelize@prodigy.net.mx; there are also Belize consulates in Chetumal (the border town with Belize) on Armada de México 91 ⓣ983-21803, ⓔbzeconsulate@prodigy.net.mx, and in Cancún on Av Náder 34, 1st Floor ⓣ988-78417, ⓔnelbel@prodigy.net.mx.
Switzerland 7 Rue du Mont-Blanc, CH140, Geneva ⓣ22/906-8420, ⓔmission.belize@ties.itu.int.
UK (also accredited to **Spain** and **Italy**) Belize High Commission, Third Floor, 45 Crawford Place, London W1H 4LP ⓣ020/7723 3603, ⓦwww.bzhc-lon.co.uk.
USA 2535 Massachusetts Ave NW, Washington DC 20008 ⓣ202/332-9636, ⓦwww.embassyofbelize.org; also 5825 Sunset Blvd, Suite 206, Hollywood, CA 90028 ⓣ323/469-7343.

Gay and lesbian travellers

Belize overall is not a gay-friendly country, and local homosexuals often keep their orientation a secret. Few people will make their disapproval obvious to foreigners, however, and many openly welcome the gay cruises that visit the country. San Pedro and Caye Caulker are probably your best bets for a hassle-free time. There are no specifically gay venues in the country.

Insurance

Travel insurance is essential for a trip to Belize; your coverage should include emergency treatment and provision for repatriation by air ambulance, with medical cover of US$2,000,000. Although there is a modern, private hospital in Belize City, in emergencies you may well need treatment in a US hospital, so ensure that your policy provides you with a 24-hour emergency contact number.

Consider also taking out coverage for **loss or theft** of personal possessions, as petty theft is fairly common in Belize; for more on this and how to avoid it, see p.48. If you plan to participate in what insurance companies define as "hazardous activities", such as scuba diving, kayaking, rafting, rappelling or caving using ropes and specialized equipment – all possible in Belize – you may have to pay a premium.

Before shopping around for a policy, check first to see what coverage you already have. **Household insurance policies** may cover theft or loss of documents, money or valuables while overseas. Bank, credit and charge cards often have certain levels of medical or other insurance included, especially if you use them to pay for your trip. While this can be quite comprehensive, it should still be considered **supplementary** to full travel insurance; the medical coverage, in particular, is usually insufficient for North and Central America. Canadian provincial health plans typically provide some overseas medical coverage, although they are unlikely to pick up the full tab in the event of a mishap. Holders of official student/teacher/youth cards are entitled to **accident coverage** and hospital in-patient benefits – annual membership to the issuing organization is far less than the cost of buying comparable insurance on your own. **Students** may also find that their student health coverage extends through vacations and for one term beyond the date of last enrolment; if you need extra coverage, check with the student travel specialists STA or Travel Cuts (see p.22, p.24 & p.25), though policies sold by travel agents are rarely the best value. It's also worth asking if you can extend your coverage if you stay abroad longer than planned.

Policies vary: some are comprehensive while others cover only certain risks, such as accidents, illnesses, delayed or lost luggage, cancelled flights, etc. Most North American travel policies only cover items lost, stolen or damaged while in the custody of an identifiable, responsible **third party** – hotel porter, airline, luggage consignment, etc. In particular, ask whether the policy pays medical costs up front or reimburses you later, and whether it provides for **medical evacuation** to your home country. For any policy, make sure you know the claims procedure and the **emergency helpline number**. Note also that very few insurers will arrange on-the-spot payments in the event of a major expense or loss; you will usually be reimbursed only after going home. In all cases of loss or theft of goods, you will have to visit the local police station to have a report made out (make sure you get a copy) so that your insurer can process the claim.

Rough Guides has teamed up with Columbus Direct to offer you **travel insurance** that can be tailored to suit your needs. Products include a low-cost **backpacker** option for long stays, a **short break** option for city getaways, an **adventure** option for high-risk activities and others. There are also annual **multi-trip** policies for those who travel regularly.

See our website (Ⓦwww.roughguides.com/website/shop) for eligibility and purchasing options. Alternatively, UK residents should call Ⓣ0870/033 9988, Australians Ⓣ1300/669 999 and New Zealanders Ⓣ0800/55 9911. All other nationalities should call Ⓣ+44 870/890 2843.

Internet

Belizean businesses and individuals are avid users of **email** and the **Internet**, and the number of places visitors can get online increases all the time, although the price, speed and reliability of the service varies enormously. In the cayes and other tourist centres, you can expect good connections and prices around Bz$4 for 15 minutes. Rates generally decrease for longer usage, and you may be able to buy time in advance for less if you plan to be in a specific area for a while.

Laundry

Most high-end hotels offer a **laundry service** starting at around Bz$2 per item. Most towns and villages also have a drop-off laundry service, and many have a coin-operated one, with prices around Bz$4 per load to wash and the same to dry.

Living in Belize

Living in Belize is very different from visiting it. Poor infrastructure, hefty import taxes and the high cost of living in reasonable comfort are challenges that dissuade some, though others persevere and find Belize a very rewarding place to call home.

Because any company hiring a foreigner must first prove that no Belizean could do the job, most work opportunities for foreigners are in the **volunteer sector**. Work permits, available only on yearly bases, are required for any job, paid or not. Anyone planning to stay must also apply for **permanent residency**, a lengthy and costly process that prohibits you from leaving the country for more than fourteen days in your first year. After five years of residency (or a year of marriage to a Belizean) you can apply for **citizenship**.

Voluntary work and study

There are plenty of opportunities for **volunteer work** – mainly as a fee-paying member of a conservation expedition – or study at a field study centre or archeological field school. These options generally mean raising a considerable sum for the privilege and committing yourself to weeks (or months) of hard but rewarding work, often in difficult conditions. Many of the expeditions are aimed at students taking time off between school and university, and arrange work on **rural infrastructure projects** such as schools, health centres and the like, or on trails and visitor centres in nature reserves. These organizations will usually take expedition members from any country; they also sometimes need experienced technical and administrative staff whose stays may be subsidized, even if the work is still unpaid.

At least twenty academic **archeological groups** undertake research in Belize each year, and many of them invite paying volunteers; for details, see the box on p.336 in Contexts. There is also a growing number of **field study centres** in Belize, aimed primarily at college students on a degree course, though there are opportunities for nonstudents to learn about the ecology and environment of Belize; for more information, look under "field study centres" in the index. If you want to learn **Spanish** relatively cheaply, you could extend a trip to Tikal by studying at one of the language schools in and around Flores, Guatemala.

If the cost of joining a volunteer expedition deters you, there are a handful of organizations that don't collect fees (see p.52), as well as opportunities to volunteer independently; the **conservation organizations** in Contexts (see box, p.350) all have volunteer programmes. If you want to work with children, the **YWCA** accepts volunteers to help teach and organize sports and arts activities in the school they run in Belize City; contact the YWCA Education Director (Ⓣ203-4971, Ⓔywca@btl.net). For any of these options you'll need to be self-motivated and self-supporting – no funding will be available, though you'll probably get food and accommodation.

The **Internet** is a great resource for learning about opportunities abroad: try Ⓦwww.gapyear.com (UK-based, free membership), which holds a vast amount of general information on volunteering, and a huge, invaluable database on travel and living abroad. Also worth looking at is the comprehensive range of books and information published by Vacation Work (Ⓣ01865/241 978, Ⓦwww.vacationwork.co.uk). Titles include *Directory of Summer Jobs Abroad*, *Taking a Gap Year*, *Green Volunteers* and *Work Your Way Around the World*, among many others.

Free volunteer organizations

Ecologic Development Fund US Ⓣ617/441-6300, Ⓦwww.ecologic.org. Ecologic is a highly respected organization with a great deal of experience in Central America. It aims to conserve endangered habitats by using community-based development and resource management in partnership with local organizations. Internship programmes for volunteers could include training communities in sustainable agriculture or helping local organizations develop environmental advocacy and protected-area management skills.

The Peace Corps US Ⓣ1-800/424-8580, Ⓦwww.peacecorps.gov. Since 1962, the Peace Corps has been sending American volunteers to Belize to teach in rural areas, work in agricultural and environmental education and computer and business-training centres, and assist with women's groups, youth and community outreach and health awareness programmes.

Fee-based volunteer organizations

Cornerstone Foundation PO Box 242, 90 Burns Ave, San Ignacio, Cayo District, Belize Ⓣ824-2373, Ⓦwww.peacecorner.org/cornerstone.htm. A Belize-based grassroots organization, offering volunteer placements in areas such as women's development, disabilities, literacy, HIV/AIDS outreach, the environment and youth education. A three-month stay (which can be extended) costs around US$1155, including accommodation and one daily meal. You can also learn about indigenous natural healing methods in a three-week programme for US$699, or AIDS education in two weeks for US$599.

Earthwatch US Ⓣ1-800/776-0188, UK Ⓣ01865 318838, Ⓦwww.earthwatch.org. Earthwatch matches paying volunteers from around the world with scientists working on marine conservation projects in southern Belize. Current projects focus on studies of manatees and archeological and reef ecology investigations. The cost for a two-week stint is currently US$2249/£1195.

Trekforce Worldwide The Granary, Way-to-Wooler, Northumberland, NE71 6AQ Ⓣ0845 241 3085, Ⓦwww.trekforceworldwide.com Under new management, Trekforce runs projects ranging from surveys of remote Maya sites to infrastructure development in national parks and village communities. Expeditions last from two to five months, starting from £2800. The longer programmes also involve learning Spanish in Guatemala and teaching in rural schools in Belize.

World Challenge Expeditions Black Arrow House, 2 Chandros Rd, London NW10 6NE Ⓣ020/8728 7200, Ⓦwww.world-challenge.co.uk. A youth development organization that takes 18- to 24-year-olds to Belize for three- or six-month placements. Tasks can include teaching in a primary school, joining a conservation project or working in a children's home in Belize City. Around £2000 (which includes a return flight) plus £135/month for food and accommodation.

Mail

Belize has a reliable internal postal system, but its **international service** is patchy at best; many packages sent overseas, particularly between Belize and Europe, can spend months in transit, or may disappear altogether. An "express" service, considerably pricier than the cheap standard rates, has a better track record and is worthwhile when it comes to important parcels. Fedex and Global Express services are available in main towns and tourist centres, too, and there's a Mailboxes Etc. in Belize City.

From Belize, a **normal airmail letter** should take around four to five days to reach the US (Bz$0.60), a couple of days longer to Canada (Bz$0.60), eight to ten days to Europe (Bz$0.75) and two weeks to Australia and New Zealand (Bz$1). **Parcels** must be wrapped in brown paper and tied with string, and may be inspected by customs. Registration for mail isn't necessary, but it doesn't cost much extra and you'll get a certificate to give you some peace of mind.

Post offices are generally open Monday through Friday 8am–4.30pm; post offices in small villages – sometimes operated by a local out of their home – are often short on stamps and packing materials, so do any major mailing from a large town. Incoming mail (have it sent to **General Delivery**) is kept at the main post office in Belize City (or any town post office) for a couple of months; you'll need some kind of ID, preferably a **passport**, to pick it up. American Express cardholders can have mail sent to them c/o AMEX at Belize Global Travel, 41 Albert St, Belize City.

Maps

The best map of Belize is the **International Travel Map of Belize** (1:350,000), produced by International Travel Maps of Vancouver (Ⓦwww.itmb.com). It's available online from their website and from Ⓦwww.amazon.com; any good travel bookshop or map outlet should stock it. It's also available from several bookshops and gift shops in Belize and from *Belize First* magazine (see p.56). **Topographic maps** produced by Ordnance Survey in the UK are available for Belize: two sheets at 1:250,000 cover the whole country, with 44 sheets at 1:50,000 scale providing greater detail, though many are out of date and not all are readily available; try Stanfords or Elstead in the UK, or, in Belize, the Land Tax Office in Belmopan (see p.167).

Money

Prices and exchange rates are fairly stable, with the national currency, the **Belize dollar**, very conveniently fixed at the rate of two to the US dollar (**Bz$2=US$1**). US dollars (cash and traveller's cheques) are also accepted everywhere – and in some places even preferred – as currency. This apparently simple dual currency system can be problematic, however, as you'll constantly need to ask which dollar is being referred to; it's all too easy to assume the price of your hotel room or trip is in Belize dollars, only to discover on payment that the price referred to was in US dollars – a common cause of misunderstanding and aggravation. In San Pedro and other high-end destinations around the country, many businesses quote prices in US$. Prices in the Guide are usually quoted in Belize dollars – always preceded by the symbol Bz$.

The Belize dollar is divided into 100 cents. Banknotes come in denominations of 2, 5, 10, 20, 50 and 100 dollars; coins come in denominations of 1, 5, 10, 25, 50 cents and 1 dollar, although 10 and 50 cent pieces are less commonly seen. All notes and coins carry the British imperial legacy in the form of a portrait of Queen Elizabeth – and quarters are sometimes called "shillings".

For **currency exchange** on arrival, there's a branch of the Belize Bank at the international airport with an ATM that accepts foreign cards. Note that banks generally offer a lower exchange rate for US cash than if you simply spent the cash and got your change in Belize dollars. You'll find there's at least one bank, sometimes two or three (generally Mon–Fri 8am–2.30pm, some also Sat 8am–12pm) in every town. It's a good idea to keep some US cash, as it's in high demand and you may be asked to pay your **exit taxes** with it; try to get rid of all your Belize dollars before you go, since they're useless outside the country.

You can use most credit and debit cards at **ATMs** of the Belize Bank, Atlantic Bank and First Caribbean Bank (formerly Barclays) to get cash in Belize dollars at good rates. Other banks will process cash advances on cards at the counter, though at less favourable rates than an ATM. Always check what the charge will be for using your credit or debit card – many establishments add the extra five percent that the bank charges them. Visa is the most useful card in Belize (and throughout Central America), but MasterCard is also accepted fairly widely.

Officially, the only businesses in Belize other than banks allowed to exchange currency are the licensed **casas de cambio**, often offering better rates for US cash than banks, though they're hard to find. They're dotted around main towns, often inside shops or other businesses, and they change location regularly so you may have to ask around. Branches of Western Union are also licensed *casas de cambio*, with several offices in Belize City and other towns, sometimes inside a bank. There are no ATMs at Belize's land border crossings, but licensed **moneychangers** may exchange US cash at slightly higher rates than the standard Bz$2 for US$1, especially for larger sums and depending on demand; anywhere else, beware of rip-offs.

Opening hours and public holidays

It's difficult to be specific about **opening hours** in Belize, but in general most shops are open from 8am to noon and from 1 or 2pm to 8pm. The lunch hour (noon to 1pm) is almost universally observed and it's hopeless to expect to get much done then, though banks are open. However, a recent edict means government offices are supposed to remain open during the lunch hour, though you'll often find the person you really need is unavailable until after lunch anyway. Some shops and businesses work a half-day on Saturday, and everything is liable to close early on Friday. **Archeological sites**, however, are open 8am to 4pm daily. Public holidays, when virtually everything will be closed – though some public transport operates normally – are listed in the box below. Note that if the actual date of a particular holiday falls mid-week, the holiday will usually be observed the following Monday.

Phones

Belize's modern phone system is almost always easy to use, and payphones are plentiful. **Belize Telecommunications Limited (BTL)**, formerly a monopoly but still the country's dominant telephone service, has its main office (for international calls, fax, email and Internet access) at 1 Church St, Belize City (Mon–Fri 8am–5pm).

Payphones (good for both local and international calls) are a common sight throughout the country, and you'll find them all over Belize City. To use them you'll need a **phonecard**, which you can also use on any touchtone phone, pay or private. You can buy phonecards from BTL offices and from many hotels, shops and petrol stations; they come in units of Bz$5, $10, $20, $30 and $50. To use, first scratch off the patch to reveal the PIN and dial the (free) access code; then, at the voice prompt, dial the PIN, followed by the number you want to call.

There are no area codes in Belize, so wherever you're calling within the country you'll need to dial just the seven-digit number. Domestic call **charges** inside the local area are cheap at Bz$0.20/min; prices increase dramatically the further afield you dial, to between Bz$0.50 and Bz$1.50 per minute. **Cell phones** cover most of the country and visitors can easily rent one for about Bz$10–12/day, plus an activation fee – though you'll still need to buy a phonecard to use the phone.

It's simple enough (though expensive) to **dial home direct** using a phonecard: a call to a landline at peak time in North America costs Bz$1.26/min, to Europe Bz$1.05 and to Australasia Bz$1.07. Taking a telephone charge card with you is a good idea if you'll need to call home to the US, Canada or the UK; call your phone company to obtain one and have your calls billed to your home number. Calling home collect to these countries is also easy using **Home Country Direct**, available at BTL offices, most payphones and larger hotels. Simply dial the access code (posted on some payphones and in the phone book) to connect with an operator in your home country. You can also call toll-free numbers in North America; simply dial ⓣ001 before the number.

Public holidays

January 1 New Year's Day
March 9 Baron Bliss Day
Good Friday varies
Holy Saturday varies
Easter Monday varies
May 1 Labour Day
May 24 Commonwealth Day
September 10 National Day (St George's Caye Day)
September 21 Independence Day
October 12 Columbus Day (Pan America Day)
November 19 Garífuna Settlement Day
December 25 Christmas Day
December 26 Boxing Day

Photography

Everyone is different, but overall Belizeans are happy to pose for **photographs**, and on

Useful phone numbers

Calling Belize from abroad

The international direct dialing (IDD) code (also known as the country code) for Belize is ⓣ501. To call a number in Belize from abroad, simply dial the international access code (listed in your phone book), followed by the country code (501) and the full seven-digit number within Belize.

Calling home from Belize

Note that the initial zero is omitted from the area code when dialing the UK, Ireland, Australia and New Zealand from abroad.

US and Canada 00 + 1 + area code.

Australia 00 + 61 + city code.

New Zealand 00 + 64 + city code.

UK 00 + 44 + city code.

Republic of Ireland 00 + 353 + city code.

South Africa 00 + 27 + city code.

Useful numbers within Belize

Directory assistance ⓣ113
Operator assistance ⓣ115
International operator ⓣ114

seeing a camera many local children may pester you take their picture. Some adults are suspicious and will ask you what the photos are for, and a few may insist on a small payment. If someone refuses to let you take their photo, you should respect their wishes.

Daylight in Belize is very harsh, and for keen photographers, a UV or **polarizing filter** is a necessity. Taking photos in broad sunlight may also require a flash to ensure your subjects don't look washed out. The best time for photographs is during the **golden hour** – the hour before sunset when there is a warm glow to the light rather than a blue tone. This also applies to dawn light. Standard films are readily available, but look out for those kept in the sun and for expiry dates. Cards for **digital cameras** are expensive and not so easily found, so you should consider carrying at least one spare in case of loss or damage.

Time

Belize is on Central Standard Time, 6 hours behind GMT and the same as Guatemala and Honduras. Belize does not observe Daylight Savings Time, though Mexico does. This means that when DST is in operation (during the summer) the time in Belize is an hour earlier than in Mexico – something to bear in mind when you're crossing the border.

Tourist information

There's no shortage of **information about Belize** available from a variety of different sources, much of it online. Several excellent websites are dedicated to Belize, and these are the best places to start and refine your search for facts and practical details. See p.56 for a list of recommended sites.

Current political analysis and an interesting and informative overview of the society, economy and environment of Belize and all other Central American countries is provided by two specialist, independent publishers: the Resource Center (ⓦwww.irc-online.org) in the US, and the Latin America Bureau (ⓦwww.latinamericabureau.org) in the UK. Also in the UK are two very useful resources, open to the public: Canning House Library, 2 Belgrave Square, London SW1X 8PJ (ⓣ020/7235 2303, ⓦwww.canninghouse.com), which has the UK's largest publicly accessible collection of books and periodicals on Latin America, including a comprehensive section on Belize; and Maya – The Guatemalan Indian Centre, 94 Wandsworth

Bridge Rd, London SW6 2TF (Ⓣ & Ⓕ020/7371 5291, Ⓦwww.maya.org.uk), good for anyone planning to visit the Maya areas of Guatemala and Mexico as well as Belize. The Centre also hosts monthly cultural events.

Useful websites

Ⓦ**www.belize.gov.bz** The government's own website is worth checking – and you can sign up for news reports and press releases.
Ⓦ**www.belize.net** The best place to search for links to Belize websites.
Ⓦ**www.belizeaudubon.org** Website of the Belize Audubon Society (BAS), useful for the latest info on the growing number of reserves and national parks and their associated visitor centres. See Contexts, p.350 for more on the BAS.
Ⓦ**www.belizefirst.com** The best online magazine dedicated to Belize, featuring accurate reviews and articles about hotels, restaurants and destinations. The travel advice is definitely worth checking out before you go; subscribe to the print version by contacting the editor of *Belize First*, Lan Sluder – his email is Ⓔbzefirst@aol.com.
Ⓦ**www.belizemagazine.com** Online magazine produced in Belize with some worthwhile articles and listings; also available in German.
Ⓦ**www.belizenet.com** The best single tourism-related site in the country, with a huge range of accurate listings and links; also see Ⓦ**www.belize.com**, run by the same company.
Ⓦ**www.belizenet.de** If you're in Germany or you're a German-speaker, International Belize Tourism Marketing, a travel company specializing in visits to Belize, has plenty of worthwhile general information and some good links.
Ⓦ**www.channel5belize.com** Daily TV news broadcasts from Belize on an award-winning website.
Ⓦ**www.lanic.utexas.edu** The homepage of the Latin American Information Center (LANIC) leads to a seemingly never-ending series of great links; you can find information here on almost anywhere and anything in Belize.
Ⓦ**www.mesoweb.com** Fascinating articles and links, often written by archeologists, on the latest findings in Maya research.
Ⓦ**www.planeta.com** A valuable resource for information on ecotourism and travel in Latin America. You can peruse a database of articles by writers and concerned travellers, and you're welcome to contribute your own views and experiences.
Ⓦ**www.spear.org.bz** In-depth information on social, cultural, political and economic matters concerning Belize from the Society for the Promotion of Education and Research (SPEAR). Serious researchers can access the Spear resource centre, with an excellent collection of books, journals, newspapers and videos, at the Turton Library on North Front St in Belize City.

Travellers with disabilities

Travelling with a disability in Belize is possible, but certainly **not easy**. The very nature of Belize's abundant natural attractions often makes much of the country inaccessible to anyone with a disability, but there is increasing awareness of the differing needs of travellers. If you **plan ahead** and stay in higher-end resorts, you can still enjoy a visit to Belize but will need to rely on a certain level of help from staff and strangers, and your travel companion.

Travelling by **public bus** is virtually impossible, as they have no accessibility features and tend to get crowded. However, minibus **taxis** are plentiful and drivers will assist you when asked. Bicycle carts, though not the most dignified of transport options, can be a good solution in remoter areas. When

The Belize Tourism Board and the BTIA

The **Belize Tourism Board** website, Ⓦwww.travelbelize.org, is one of the best in the country, and from the main office in Belize City (see p.69) you can pick up city and regional maps, a transportation schedule and a list of hotels. The number of official tourist information offices in the country is increasing; local ones are covered in their respective chapters. The **Belize Tourism Industry Association** (BTIA; Ⓦwww.btia.org) represents most of the tourism businesses in the country and produces the annual *Destination Belize* magazine (free from tourist offices and many hotels), packed with helpful information, lots of ads and a telephone listing of every hotel in the country. The BTIA has local representatives in all resort areas.

travelling by **boat**, you'll be expected to tip staff to help you on and off. Streets in most areas can be difficult to negotiate, as they are mostly unpaved and **sidewalks** are rare.

Most **hotels** in Belize don't have rooms on the ground floor, and even those that do often have a few steps somewhere on the floor. There are a few hotels with some provision for disabled visitors, however: the *Radisson Fort George* in Belize City and the *Hok'ol K'in* in Corozal are the best, while *Clarissa Falls* near San Ignacio has **wheelchair-accessible cabins**, and the *Corona del Mar* in San Pedro has ramps, an elevator and helpful staff.

Resources for disabled travellers

The Disabled Traveller by Alison Walsh (BBC Books; order from Disabled Traveller, PO Box 7, London W12 8UD), full of information and contacts, is an excellent resource for anyone who wants to plan a trip independently.

In North America

The website ⓦwww.makoa.org/travel.htm, built and maintained by Jim Lubin, who is tetraplegic, outshines all others in providing masses of information and links for disabled travellers.

Access-Able Travel Service ⓣ303/232-2979, ⓦwww.access-able.com. A very useful organization for disabled travel generally, with travellers' reports on facilities in destinations.

Society for Accessible Travel and Hospitality (SATH) ⓣ212/447-7284, ⓦwww.sath.org. Nonprofit disability information service with a very organized website.

In the UK and Ireland

Irish Wheelchair Association Aras Chuchulainn, Blackheath Drive, Clontarf, Dublin 3 ⓣ01/8186 400, ⓦwww.iwa.ie. Useful information about travelling abroad for wheelchair-users.

RADAR (Royal Association for Disability and Rehabilitation) 12 City Forum, 250 City Rd, London EC1V 8AF ⓣ020/7250 3222, ⓦwww.radar.org.uk. A good source of advice on disability organizations, holidays and travel abroad.

In Australia and New Zealand

Both the following organizations provide lists of travel agencies and tour operators for people with disabilities.

ACROD (Australian Council for Rehabilitation of the Disabled) National Industry Association for Disability Services, Locked Bag 3002, 33 Thesinger Court, Deakin, ACT 2600 ⓣ02/6283 3200, ⓦwww.acrod.org.au.

Disabled Persons Assembly PO Box 27-524 Wellington 6035, New Zealand ⓣ04/801 9100 (also TTY), ⓦwww.dpa.org.nz.

Guide

Guide

1 Belize City 61–90

2 The north 91–122

3 The northern cayes and atolls 123–158

4 Cayo and the west 159–208

5 Tikal and Flores 209–232

6 The south 233–302

1

Belize City

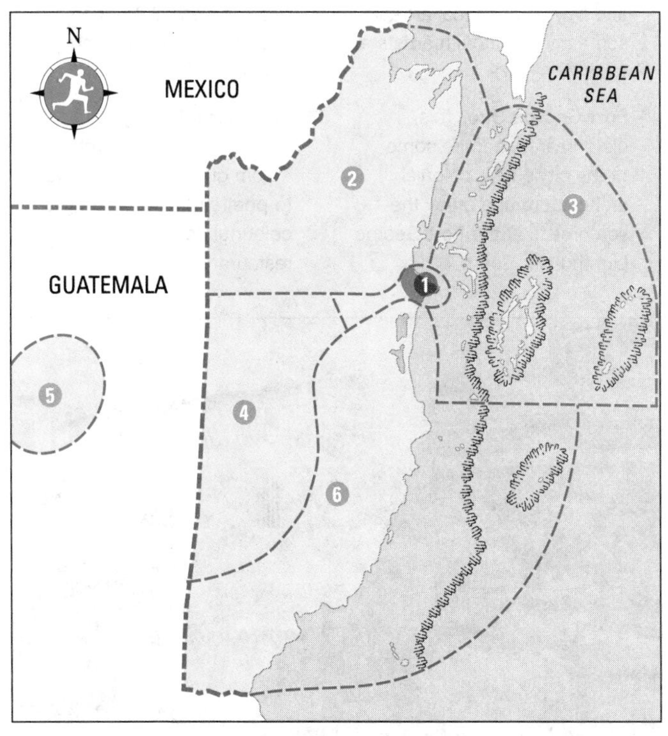

CHAPTER 1 Highlights

* **Swing Bridge** Watch the last manually operated swing bridge in the Americas open at dawn or dusk against a backdrop of brightly painted wooden fishing boats. See p.67

* **The Image Factory** Visit Belize's most provocative art gallery, where you can browse and buy unique local art and sometimes chat with artists at work. See p.72

* **Fort George** Stroll this historic area, admire some of the city's best colonial architecture and enjoy the sea breeze at the Fort George Lighthouse. See p.74

* **Museum of Belize** Marvel at the astonishing quality of Maya treasures on display in this world-class museum, housed in a beautifully restored Victorian prison. See p.75

* **The Belize Zoo** Take a day-trip from the city for close-up sightings of the animals and birds of Central America, notably Panamá the harpy eagle. See p.79

* **Faiyah Haat** Enjoy the best in Belizean eats and arts – from guava jelly pork chops to poetry readings – on the colourful deck of this lively restaurant. See p.82

△ Shoppers and vendors in Belize City

1

Belize City

The narrow, congested streets of **BELIZE CITY** can initially seem daunting and unprepossessing, even to travellers familiar with blighted urban centres. Dilapidated wooden structures stand right on road edges, offering pedestrians little refuge from the ever-increasing number of cars and trucks. Constricted bridges force traffic to cross in single file over almost stagnant canals, still used for some of the city's drainage. The overall impression is that the place is recovering from some great calamity – an explanation at least partly true. Belize City has suffered several devastating hurricanes, the latest in October 1961, when Hurricane Hattie tore it apart with winds of 240kmph and left behind a layer of thick black mud. Such hazards, however, are often overstated by people who have never set foot within the city limits. For those who spend some time here – that is, longer than it takes just to catch a bus or boat to the cayes – Belize City will reveal a distinguished history, several superb sights and fascinating cultural spectacles.

The city's astonishing energy comes from its 75,000 inhabitants, who represent every ethnic group in the country, with the **Creole** descendants of former slaves and British Baymen forming the dominant element and generating an easy-going Caribbean atmosphere. As you push your way through the throng, you'll see this relaxed attitude blending with an entrepreneurial flair, for this is the country's business capital. Banks, offices and shops line the main streets, while fruit and fast-food vendors jostle for pavement space with others selling plastic bowls or cheap jewellery. This apparent chaos finds some sort of order during the jubilant **September Celebrations**, which pack the already full streets with music, dancing and parades. **Carnival**, the culmination of the celebrations, ratchets up the excitement even further with gorgeously costumed dancers, who shimmer and gyrate through the city to electrifying Caribbean rhythms.

Some history

By the late sixteenth century, the Spanish treasure fleets in the Caribbean were attracting British and other European pirates, or **buccaneers**, who took advantage of the refuge offered by the reefs and shallows of Belize, using the cayes as bases for plundering raids. Ever the opportunists, they made money between raids by cutting the valuable logwood (a source of textile dye) that grew abundantly in the tropical swamps, and built a number of work camps from Campeche to Honduras. Their settlement at the mouth of the Belize River, constructed by consolidating the mangrove swamp with wood chips, rum bottles and coral, gradually became more permanent. By the 1700s, **Belize Town** was a well-established centre for **Baymen** (as the settlers called themselves), their families and their slaves, though the capital of the Bay settlement was off the

BELIZE CITY

ACCOMMODATION	
Bakadeer Inn	E
Barrack Road Guest House	I
Belcove Hotel	K
Belize Biltmore Plaza	D
Bellevue Hotel	R
Caribbean Palms Inn	P
Chateau Caribbean	M
Coningsby Inn	S
D'Nest Inn	B
Freddie's Guest House	F
The Great House	O
Isabel Guest House	L
Ma Ma Chen	G
Hotel Mopan	T
North Front Street Guest House	H
Radisson Fort George Hotel	N
Red Hut Inn	C
Seaside Guest House	Q
Three Sisters Guest House	J
Villa Boscardi	A

EATING & DRINKING	
The Big Apple	15
Big Daddy's Diner	16
Bird's Isle Restaurant	24
Caesar's Palace	1
Celebrity	11
Chateau Caribbean	M
Faiyah Haat	4
Gyros and Crepes	8
Harbour View	23
Iguana Rana	21
Jambel's Jerk Pit	22
Judith's Pastries	13
La Tavernetta	5
Le Petit Café	20
Club Level	3
Macy's	18
Ma Ma Chen	G
Marlins	14
Nerie's Restaurant I	9
Nerie's Restaurant II	12
Club Next	6
Pepper's Pizza	7
Riverside Patio	16
Riverside Tavern	10
Smoky Mermaid	O
Stonegrill	N
Sumathi	2
T-Quilea's	19
Wet Lizard	17

Municipal Airport
University of Belize
Marion Jones Sports Complex
BTL tower
KING'S PARK
Karl Heusner Memorial Hospital
National Library
Bus Stop
Flag Monument
San Cas Shopping Centre
Fire Station
Atlantic Bank
University of Belize
Lindbergh's Landing
BTL Park
Princess Hotel & Casino
Princess Marina
Mexico Belize Cultural Institute
Cinderella Plaza
Clock Tower
Belize Civic Center
CARIBBEAN SEA
Haulover Creek
Haulover Creek
NORTHERN HIGHWAY
HAULOVER ROAD
PRINCESS MARGARET DRIVE
PRINCESS MARGARET DRIVE
ST MATTHEW ST
ST MARK ST
ST LUKE ST
ST JOHN ST
EDWARD ST
ST CHARLES ST
LIZARRAGA DRIVE
GENTLE AVENUE
MOGUEL ST
SMITH ST
MEIGHAN AVE
L WAIGHT ST
LESLIE AVE
ST THOMAS STREET
19TH ST
18TH ST
17TH ST
16TH ST
15TH ST
14TH ST
13TH ST
10TH ST
9TH ST
8TH ST
7TH ST
6TH ST
4TH ST
3RD ST
2ND ST
1ST ST
5TH ST
H ST
F ST
I ST
K ST
G ST
D ST
B ST
A ST
C ST
F ST
BAYMEN AVENUE
NEWTOWN BARRACKS ROAD
BARRACK ROAD
ST PETER STREET
HOPKINS STREET
LANDIVER STREET
ST JAMES ST
DUNN STREET
GUADALUPE ST
HUESNER CRES
SIMON LAMB ST
NURSE SEAY ST
MATRON ROBERTS ST
CALLE AL MAR
WILSON STREET
FULLERS LAND
KELLY STREET
HUNTERS LANE
BARRACK ROAD
FREETOWN ROAD
FREETOWN ROAD
YORK STREET
CASTLE ST
JONES ST
SLAUGHTER-HOUSE RD
CRAN STREET
CLEGHORN STREET
MAPP ST
BELCAN BRIDGE
MOPAN ST

 (3.5km), ,  (3km),  (4km),  (4km), D (6km), Orange Walk & Corozal

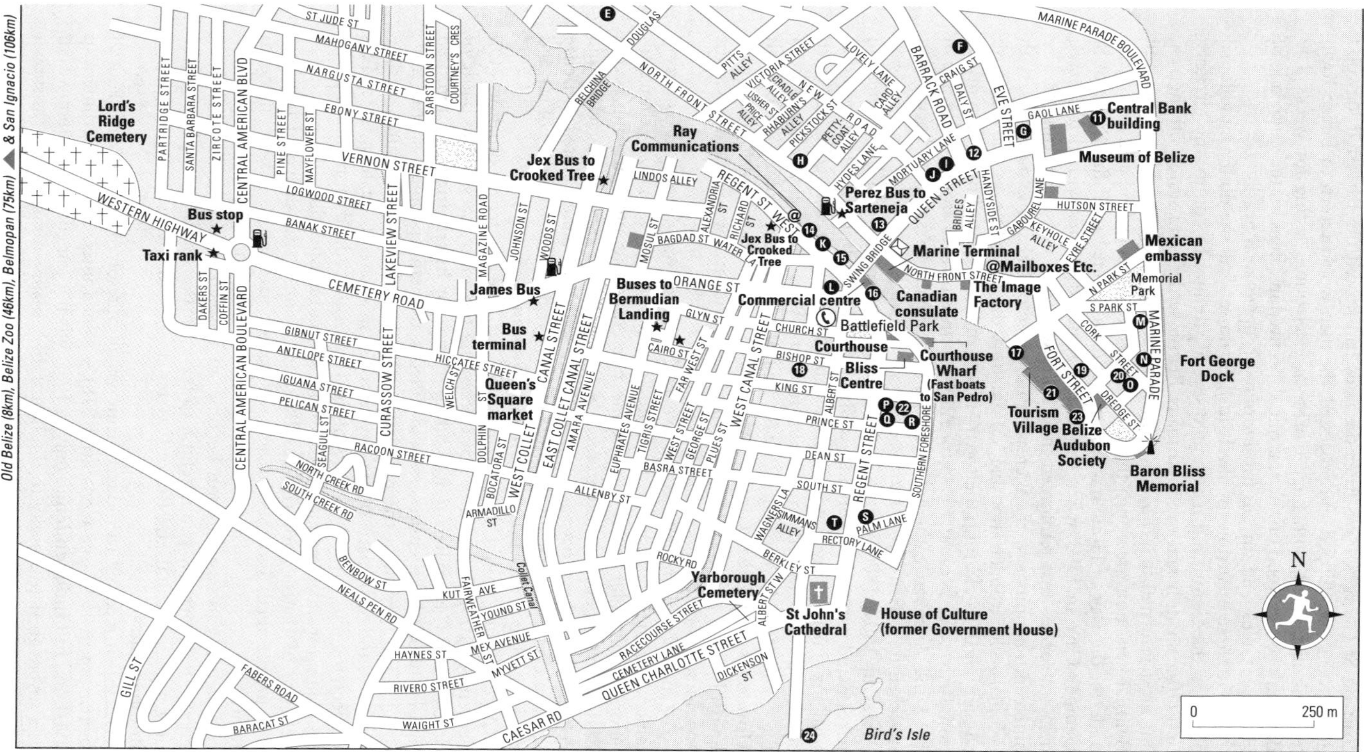
Old Belize (8km), Belize Zoo (46km), Belmopan (75km) & San Ignacio (106km)
Lord's Ridge Cemetery
Bus stop
Taxi rank
Jex Bus to Crooked Tree
Ray Communications
Perez Bus to Sarteneja
Jex Bus to Crooked Tree
Marine Terminal
@Mailboxes Etc.
Central Bank building
Museum of Belize
Mexican embassy
Memorial Park
Fort George Dock
The Image Factory
Canadian consulate
Commercial centre
Battlefield Park
Courthouse
Courthouse Wharf (Fast boats to San Pedro)
Bliss Centre
Buses to Bermudian Landing
James Bus
Bus terminal
Queen's Square market
Tourism Village Belize
Audubon Society
Baron Bliss Memorial
Yarborough Cemetery
St John's Cathedral
House of Culture (former Government House)
Bird's Isle
Collet Canal
N
0
250 m
ST JUDE ST
MAHOGANY STREET
NARGUSTA STREET
EBONY STREET
SARSTOON STREET
COURTNEY'S CRES
PARTRIDGE STREET
SANTA BARBARA STREET
ZIRCOTE STREET
CENTRAL AMERICAN BLVD
PINE STREET
MAYFLOWER ST
VERNON STREET
LOGWOOD STREET
BANAK STREET
WESTERN HIGHWAY
LAKEVIEW STREET
MAGAZINE ROAD
JOHNSON ST
WOODS ST
CEMETERY ROAD
DAKERS ST
COFFIN ST
CENTRAL AMERICAN BOULEVARD
GIBNUT STREET
ANTELOPE STREET
IGUANA STREET
PELICAN STREET
SEAGULL ST
RACOON STREET
CURASSOW STREET
HICCATEE STREET
WELCH ST
DOLPHIN ST
BOCATORA ST
WEST COLLET
CANAL STREET
EAST COLLET CANAL STREET
AMARA AVENUE
NORTH CREEK RD
SOUTH CREEK RD
ARMADILLO ST
BENBOW ST
NEALS PEN RD
KUT AVE
FAIRWEATHER ST
YOUND ST
MEX AVENUE
MYVETT ST
HAYNES ST
RIVERO STREET
WAIGHT ST
GILL ST
FABERS ROAD
BARACAT ST
CAESAR RD
DOUGLAS
BELCHINA BRIDGE
NORTH FRONT STREET
PITTS ALLEY
VICTORIA STREET
CRADLE ALLEY
USHER ST
PRICE ALLEY
RHABURN'S ALLEY
NEW ROAD
PICKSTOCK ST
PETTY-COAT ALLEY
HYDES LANE
LOVELY LANE
CARD ALLEY
BARRACK ROAD
CRAIG ST
DALY ST
EVE STREET
MORTUARY LANE
GAOL LANE
MARINE PARADE BOULEVARD
QUEEN STREET
HANDYSIDE ST
BRIDES ALLEY
GABOUREL LANE
HUTSON STREET
KEYHOLE ALLEY
EYRE STREET
N PARK ST
S PARK ST
CORK STREET
MARINE PARADE
FORT STREET
DREDGE ST
LINDOS ALLEY
REGENT ST WEST
ALEXANDRIA ST
RICHARD ST
MOSUL ST
BAGDAD ST
WATER LA
SWING BRIDGE
NORTH FRONT STREET
ORANGE ST
GLYN ST
CAIRO ST
FAR WEST ST
CHURCH ST
BISHOP ST
KING ST
ALBERT ST
PRINCE ST
WEST CANAL STREET
EUPHRATES AVENUE
TIGRIS STREET
WEST STREET
GEORGE ST
PLUES ST
BASRA STREET
DEAN ST
SOUTH ST
REGENT STREET
SOUTHERN FORESHORE
ALLENBY ST
WAGNERS LA
SIMMANS ALLEY
PALM LANE
RECTORY LANE
ROCKY RD
BERKLEY ST
ALBERT ST W
RACECOURSE STREET
CEMETERY LANE
QUEEN CHARLOTTE STREET
DICKENSON ST

coast on St George's Caye. After the rains had floated the harvested logwood downriver to be shipped and processed, the men would return to Belize Town to drink and brawl, with huge Christmas celebrations lasting for weeks. The Baymen's houses stood on the seafront, slaves lived in cabins on the south side of Haulover Creek, and various tribal groups occupied areas nearby.

Despite these incursions by the British, Spain was still the dominant colonial power in the region, and it mounted several attempts to control the territory. In 1779 a Spanish raid captured many British settlers and scared off the rest, but most returned in 1783, when Spain agreed to recognize their rights, and Belize Town soon grew into the main centre of the logwood and mahogany trade on the Bay of Honduras. Spanish raids continued until the Battle of St George's Caye in 1798, when the settlers achieved victory with British naval help – a success that reinforced their bond with the British government. The nineteenth century saw the increasing influence of **British expatriates**, with colonial-style wooden housing dominating the shoreline as the "Scottish clique" began to clean up the town's image and take control of its administration. Belize also became a base for Anglican missionaries around this time: in 1812 the Anglican cathedral of St John was built to serve a diocese that stretched from Belize to Panama.

Fires in 1804, 1806 and 1856 destroyed large swaths of Belize Town and necessitated extensive rebuilding, while epidemics of cholera, yellow fever and smallpox wreaked havoc on the population. Despite these obstacles, the town continued to grow with immigrants from the West Indies and refugees from the Caste Wars in Yucatán. In 1862 Belize became the colony of **British Honduras**, with Belize City (as it was now known) as its administrative centre; in 1871 it was upgraded to a Crown Colony, with its own resident governor appointed by Britain.

For the colony's inhabitants, the twentieth century was dominated by uncertainty over their relationship with the "mother country". In 1914 thousands among them volunteered to assist the war effort, but upon arriving in the Middle East they were confronted by a wall of prejudice and racism and consigned to labour battalions. In 1919 the returned soldiers rioted in Belize City, an event that marked the onset of black consciousness in the colony and the beginning of the **independence movement**.

More events would soon compound an already tense situation. On September 10, 1931, the city was celebrating the anniversary of the Battle of St George's Caye when it was hit by a massive **hurricane** that uprooted houses, flooded the entire city and killed a thousand people – at the time, roughly ten percent of the population. Disaster relief from Britain was slow to arrive, and many parts of the city were left in a state of squalid poverty. This neglect, together with the effects of the Depression, added momentum to the campaign for independence, and the city saw numerous rallies and marches in defiance of British authority. In 1961 Hurricane Hattie delivered her fury: 262 people died, and the damage was so serious that plans were made to relocate the capital inland to Belmopan. The instigators of the move assumed that Belize City would soon become an obsolete backwater as Belmopan grew, but in fact few people chose to leave for the sterile atmosphere of the new, nominal capital, and Belize City remains by far the most populous place in the country.

Belize – it received its modern name via an unresolved Guatemalan claim of ownership in 1945 (see Contexts, p.318) – gained internal self-government in 1964, and **full independence** only in 1981, when it joined the Commonwealth as a sovereign state. Loyalty to the monarchy remains strong, though, as shown by the tumultuous welcome given to Queen Elizabeth on her visits in 1985 and 1994. Since independence, the rise of foreign investment and tourism have contributed to ongoing development, and Belize City continues in its major construction boom.

Orientation

Although Belize City is by far the largest urban area in the country (the capital, Belmopan, is one tenth its size), its central area is compact enough to make **walking** the easiest way to get around. The city is divided neatly into north and south halves by **Haulover Creek**, a delta branch of the Belize River. The pivotal point of the city centre is the **Swing Bridge**, always busy with traffic and opened up sometimes twice a day, but usually several times a week, to allow larger vessels up and down the creek. **North** of the Swing Bridge, things tend to be slightly more upmarket; here you'll find the most expensive hotels, the majority of the embassies and consulates and – in the King's Park area – some very luxurious homes. **South** of the Swing Bridge is the market and commercial zone, with banks, offices and supermarkets; the foreshore is the prestige area, site of the former colonial governor's residence, now a museum and arts venue. The area south and west of the main thoroughfares of Regent and Albert streets is unsafe after dark.

△ The Swing Bridge

Arrival and city transport

Belize City has two airports. **International flights** land at **Philip Goldson International Airport**, 17km northwest of the city at Ladyville, just off the Northern Highway. Arriving here can be chaotic, with a crush of people waiting anxiously for their luggage to be unloaded from the planes. A recent expansion alleviated some of the overcrowding, but even this is sometimes insufficient for the huge increase in visitor numbers. Belize's **domestic airlines** also make stops at the international airport, so you could pick up an onward flight right away (though prices to all destinations are around Bz$40 more than from the **Municipal Airport**, on the seafront a few kilometres north of the city centre).

From the international airport, a taxi into town costs Bz$50. One option for cutting the cost is to share the ride with other travellers. It's best to arrange this within the airport and walk out as a group, as taxi drivers will sometimes charge more if they spot you making these plans outside. The only other way into town is by walking to the Northern Highway (25min) and flagging down one of the frequent passing buses (Bz$1.50 to the centre). From the Municipal Airport, a taxi to town costs around Bz$10; walking takes at least 25 minutes.

The main **bus terminal** is on the western side of the city centre along West Collet Canal, in a fairly derelict part of town known as Mesopotamia. It's only 1km from the Swing Bridge and you can easily walk – or, especially at night, take a taxi – to any of the hotels listed on pp.69–71. Most scheduled **boats** returning from the cayes pull in at the **Marine Terminal**, on the north side of the Swing Bridge, or at the **Courthouse Wharf**, on the south side of the creek; from either it's a fairly short walk or taxi ride to the bus terminal or any of the hotels.

Once you arrive downtown, you'll find that almost everything you need is within a kilometre of the Swing Bridge. **Taxis**, identified by green licence plates, cost Bz$7 for one or more passengers within the city; for other journeys,

Hassle

Walking in Belize City **during the day** is perfectly safe if you observe commonsense rules. The introduction of **tourism police** in 1995 made an immediate impact on the level of hassle and this, coupled with the legal requirement for all tour guides to be licensed, has reduced street crime. You'll soon learn to spot dangerous situations and in the city centre you can always ask the tourism police (☎227-2222; they sport green "Tourist Unit" badges on their sleeves) for advice or directions; they'll even walk you back to your hotel if it's near their patrol route. That said, it's still sensible to proceed with caution: most people are friendly and chatty, but quite a few may want to sell you drugs or bum a dollar or two. The best advice is to stay cool. Be civil, don't provoke trouble by arguing too forcefully and never show large sums of money on the street, especially American dollars. Women wearing short shorts or skirts will attract verbal abuse from local studs.

The chances of being mugged do increase **after dark**, though if you're with others, you can generally walk around some parts of the centre in relative safety. The tourism police keep watch on this area at night, especially during the high season and holidays. If you're venturing further afield, or if you've just arrived by bus or water taxi at night, you should travel by taxi. For more on security and avoiding trouble, see p.48.

be sure to agree on the fare in advance. Cars wait for passengers at the main bus station and Marine Terminal, or you can call one on ⓣ227-2888 or 224-4465; you should definitely take a **taxi** if you arrive anywhere at night. **City buses** operate to outlying residential areas but are of little use unless you know exactly where you're going.

Information and tours

The Belize Tourism Board (BTB) office is on Regent Street (Mon–Thurs 8am–5pm, Fri 8am–4pm; ⓣ223-1913, ⓦwww.travelbelize.org). Although it's not an essential visit, you can pick up free bus timetables, a hotel guide and city map, nature reserve brochures and copies of the (sometimes free) **tourist newspapers**.

Should you want to escape the city for a day or two, you can take one of the **day tours** inland. Most visit at least two of the following: the Belize Zoo, Bermudian Landing Baboon Sanctuary, Crooked Tree Wildlife Sanctuary, Altun Ha ruins and Lamanai ruins. However, all but the last two are very easy to visit independently – though with the exception of the zoo, you'll need to stay overnight if you don't have your own vehicle. Still, even with the extra cost of accommodation, it's likely to be less expensive than a tour. See Listings on p.88 for more information about tour operators and packages.

Accommodation

There are over fifty **hotels** in Belize City, around a third of which charge Bz$30–50 for a double room, with at least another half-dozen in the range of Bz$50–75; the selection here covers all price ranges, most with good rates for singles. For the comprehensive list, pick up a copy of *Destination Belize* from the tourism board or most hotels. There's usually no need to book ahead (unless you're eager to stay in a particular hotel), as you'll almost always find something in the price range you're looking for – though a phone call can save time and effort. The ones listed have been selected first on the basis of security and then of price; anything cheaper is likely to be unsafe. The more **upmarket hotels** (most take credit cards) are generally located north of the Swing Bridge, in and around the historic **Fort George area** or along the **seafront** south of the creek mouth, where the air is cooler thanks to sea breezes. If you want a comfortable hotel in a quiet location near the international airport and within easy reach of the city, take a look at the *Belize River Lodge* or *Black Orchid* (see p.95).

North of Haulover Creek

Inexpensive

Barrack Road Guest House 8 Barrack Rd ⓣ604-3615. A couple of blocks from the Marine Terminal and set back from the main road, this quiet, basic guest house has somewhat worn but clean rooms (with fans) arranged around a courtyard; some have private bath. The rate includes a simple breakfast of coffee and fruit. Discounts on extended stays. ❸

Freddie's Guest House 86 Eve St ⓣ223-3851. This long-time spot near the waterfront is the best value in its price range. The three well-maintained, secure and peaceful fan-cooled rooms have comfortable beds and bedside lamps; two rooms share a gleaming bathroom, and one has an immaculate private bath. ❸

Ma Ma Chen 7 Eve St ⓣ223-4568. A Taiwanese family runs this simple rooms-and-restaurant setup. The rooms (some with private bath and a/c, others with shared bath and fan) are sparsely furnished, and the beds a bit hard, but prices are low and it's relatively central. Being fairly new on the budget scene, they'll sometimes have rooms if other similarly priced places are full. The adjoining restaurant is the only fully vegetarian eatery in town (see p.82). ❶–❷

North Front Street Guest House 124 N Front St ⓣ227-7595. Friendly, simple guest house several blocks from the Marine Terminal, with a wide balcony overlooking the street. Although the rooms (including a triple) in this 120-year-old building are fairly small and none has a private bath (and there's only cold water in the shared bathrooms), it's cheap and clean. ❶

Three Sisters Guest House 36 Queen St ⓣ203-5729. Three large rooms in an airy, wooden building run by an amiable, mainly Spanish-speaking family. Each room, including a spacious triple, has a fan and refrigerator. It's hard to get more central – you can see the Swing Bridge from the sunny balcony overlooking Queen St. ❸

Mid-range to expensive

Bakadeer Inn 74 Cleghorn St ⓣ223-0659, ⓦwww.bakadeerinn.com. Twelve clean rooms with a/c, ceiling fan, TV and private bath with tub, though there's little natural light. The inn itself is secure, but you should take the usual precautions when walking this area after dark. They serve up a decent, reasonably priced Belizean breakfast. Rates are very good for three or four sharing. ❻

Belize Biltmore Plaza Mile 3, Northern Hwy ⓣ223-2302, ⓦwww.belizebiltmore.com. This hotel has a sun-flooded lobby with white wicker furnishings and spacious a/c rooms around a palm-filled courtyard. Although it's just off the highway, there's no traffic noise in the rooms or among the tranquil grounds featuring tropical plants and a lovely pool. The *Victoria Room* restaurant serves seafood, quality steaks and a lunch menu offering a changing daily cuisine. On Fridays, enjoy a lively happy hour (5–7pm) at the poolside *Palm Court Bar*, a steel band occasionally plays. Try the fine selection of Caribbean rums at the comfortable *Biltmore Bar*, where you can kick back on plush chairs. There's also a business centre for email (Bz$8/hr), a well-equipped fitness room and a massage room. Wheelchair-accessible and nonsmoking rooms available. ❾

Chateau Caribbean 6 Marine Parade ⓣ223-3888, ⓦwww.chateaucaribbean.com. Colonial-style hotel overlooking the seafront and Memorial Park. The well-appointed rooms all have spacious tiled bathrooms, a/c and cable TV, and some have sea views; the best views are from the two very large rooms with glass-fronted balconies on the top floor. There's also a good restaurant (see p.82), where you can start off the day with a hearty breakfast, like the Maya spread (Bz$11) of corn tortillas, fried beans and poached eggs. The *Chateau*, a former hospital, has featured in several movies. ❼

D'Nest Inn 475 Cedar St, Belama, 5km north of Belize City ⓣ223-5416, ⓦwww.dnestinn.com. The accommodating Gaby and Oty run this cheery, two-storey bed and breakfast in the quiet residential district of Belama. The four comfortable rooms, several with plush, four-poster beds and all with a/c and sparkling bathrooms, are named after birds that have nested in the garden, which flourishes with hibiscus, orchids and white lilies, amid antique planters and a splashing bird bath. Enjoy a tasty breakfast (included) in the bright dining room fronted by French doors. As is the case with most accommodation on the Northern Hwy, it's best if you have your own wheels to get to and from town. Alternatively, plan on staying here if you have a plane to catch the next day – the airport is just 11km away. ❺–❻

The Great House 13 Cork St ⓣ223-3400, ⓦwww.greathousebelize.com. This gorgeous, four-storey wooden building, originally built in 1927, has been modernized and expanded – in 1997, Mennonite contractors raised the entire ground floor by more than 1.5m – to become one of the most impressive hotels in the city. Located in the prestigious Fort George area, the sixteen spacious, well-equipped a/c rooms have private bath, coffeemaker, complimentary biscuits, TV, phone and dedicated fax lines and lustrous hardwood floors; some have a balcony. The *Smoky Mermaid* restaurant (see p.83), with a Friday evening happy hour, is in the courtyard with a gallery of shops and boutiques below. ❽

Radisson Fort George Hotel 2 Marine Parade ⓣ223-3333, ⓦwww.radisson.com/belizecitybz. The luxurious and extremely well-managed flagship of the city's hotels, on the north side of the harbour mouth. Even though it's by far the most expensive at around Bz$300–350 a night, you can expect substantial discounts on the "rack rates" when it's not full. All rooms have a huge cable TV, fridge and minibar. The Colonial Wing has carpeted rooms with views of the sea and the ground-floor rooms have balconies; rooms in the Club Wing, reached by the only glass elevator in Belize, feature marble floors and unbeatable sea views; and, across the road, all rooms in the Villa Wing have tiled balconies and some have wheelchair-accessible bathrooms. The business centre has Internet access, and there are two good restaurants and a cosy café (see p.82). The grounds are an oasis of calm on the edge of the sea, with two pools and a dockside marina, used by the larger live-aboard dive boats. 9

Red Hut Inn 90 Bella Vista, near Mile 3, Northern Hwy ⓣ663-8986, ⓦred-hut-inn-belize.50megs.com. The basic but well-maintained *Red Hut Inn* sits in the quiet, residential Bella Vista neighbourhood, on the northern outskirts of the city. Rooms feature firm beds along with wooden closets, a small sitting area, clean en-suite bathrooms, a/c, cable TV and free wireless service. Guests have access to a simple kitchen. The inn's owners offer airport pickup (and rides into town) for Bz$10. Note that the distance from town can be inconvenient, especially if you're relying primarily on public transport. 5

Villa Boscardi 6043 Manatee Drive ⓣ & ⓕ223-1691 or ⓣ602-8954, ⓦwww.villaboscardi.com. Spacious and immaculately clean guest rooms, each uniquely decorated, with a/c, private bath, TV and telephone in a house 4km from the city centre, just off the Northern Hwy. Gracious owner Françoise Boscardi is knowledgeable about local tours and activities, and can help plan itineraries catered to every budget. A filling breakfast, including eggs, fresh fruit and home-brewed coffee served in the sunny dining room, is included in the room rate. You can use email and send/receive faxes. No smoking in the house. 6

South of Haulover Creek

Belcove Hotel 9 Regent St W ⓣ227-3054, ⓦwww.belcove.com. Simple, tidy rooms, some with a/c and private bath, right next to the creek. Enjoy a view of the Swing Bridge from the yellow and red balcony. After dark, this part of town can be less than salubrious, though the attentive staff ensures that the hotel itself is secure. They can arrange a variety of tours including trips to the hotel's private island at Gallows Point, on the reef 15km from the city. 3–4

Bellevue Hotel 5 Southern Foreshore ⓣ227-7051, ⓔbellevue@btl.net. Fairly large hotel on the seafront, south of the Swing Bridge. Some of the rooms in this former colonial house have been renovated, while others are older and shabbier, so it's best to check what you're offered first. All have private bath, a/c and TV, and outside there's a relaxing, palm-shaded courtyard with a thatched bar and a pool (which is a bit murky at times). Upstairs, the *Harbour View* bar opens for a Friday evening happy hour (though usually only when the cruise ships are in), and the basement *Maya Tavern* disco features live music some Fridays. The *Bellevue* owners recently built a lovely restaurant and bar perched right on the water nearby, featuring a top-notch international menu and live music; call ahead to confirm open times. 4–5

Caribbean Palms Inn 26 Regent St, at King St ⓣ227-0472, ⓦwww.thecaribbean-palmsbelizeinn.com. Not a first choice, as it's overpriced for what you get, but they sometimes have rooms when everywhere else is full. Fairly central, with a/c, though a number of the rooms are shabby, so ask for a look around before deciding. There's also a basic patio, and a payphone. All rooms have private bath, but two have the bathroom outside – those are the cheapest ones (4). The cleaning lady will do a load of laundry for Bz$10. 6

Coningsby Inn 76 Regent St ⓣ227-1566, ⓕ227-3276. Ten clean, decent a/c rooms with TV and private bath in a quiet part of the city centre. There's a balcony over the street and the upstairs restaurant serves a simple Belizean breakfast, lunch and dinner daily; there's also a small bar for guests. Luggage storage available, and Internet (Bz$5/hr). 6

Isabel Guest House 3 Albert St, above and behind the Central Drug Store ⓣ207-3139. Small, welcoming, primarily Spanish-speaking guest house with four large rooms with private showers and small refrigerators. The room with four beds (5) is a good deal for groups. 4

Hotel Mopan 55 Regent St ⓣ227-7351, ⓦwww.hotelmopan.com. Wood-fronted building at the quiet end of Regent St near the colonial House of Culture. Welcoming and safe, it's run by Tomy and Jeannie, son and daughter of the late Jean Shaw, an avid conservationist. The original building is over 200 years old but all rooms have private bath and cable TV, some have a/c and there's Internet access for guests. Great views from the sun roof, and also a bar and several comfortable verandas for relaxing with an evening beer. The restaurant serves good-value breakfasts. 4–6

Seaside Guest House 3 Prince St ⓣ227-8339, ⓔseasidebelize@btl.net. A clean, well-run and secure hotel, popular with budget travellers, in a wooden building half a block from the southern foreshore. Two rooms come with four hostel-style dorm beds (Bz$29), and there are several private rooms (two with private bath). There's a payphone and Internet access for guests (Bz$10/hr). Lounge on the veranda – where you really can see the sea – or in the garden blooming with black orchids. Breakfast can be ordered (7–9am) and they sell beer and soda. 4

The City

Richard Davies, a British traveller in the mid-nineteenth century, wrote of the city: "There is much to be said for Belize, for in its way it was one of the prettiest ports at which we touched, and its cleanliness and order ... were in great contrast to the ports we visited later as to make them most remarkable." Many of the features that elicited this praise have now gone, though some of the distinctive **wooden colonial buildings** have been preserved as heritage showpieces, or converted into hotels, restaurants and museums. Yet even in cases where the decay is too advanced for the paintwork, balconies, carved railings and fretwork to be restored, the old wooden structures remain more pleasing than the concrete blocks that have replaced so many of them. Fires, too, have altered the architecture of the city, with the worst in recent years claiming the historic Paslow Building, which stood opposite the Marine Terminal.

The fate of the city's historic buildings is not all bad news, however. Two of the very best colonial structures have been carefully restored and are open to visitors; the former city jail, built in Victorian times, is now the **Museum of Belize**, and the even earlier **Government House** is a museum and cultural centre. There's a great deal of ongoing construction, too, with an enormous **cruise ship terminal** dominating the north side of the creek mouth, and beyond here, on the northern foreshore, a massive development is reclaiming land from the sea for real estate and improved vehicle and pedestrian movement.

Belize City's most recognizable landmark has changed through the years as well. The first wooden bridge was built in the early 1800s, replacing a system in which cattle and other commodities were winched over the waterway that divides the city – hence the name **Haulover Creek**. Its next incarnation, the Liverpool-made **Swing Bridge**, opened in 1923 and is the only manually operated swing bridge left in the Americas. Sometimes twice a day (around 5.30am and 5.30pm), but usually several times a week, the endless parade of vehicles and people is halted by policemen and the process of turning begins. Using long poles inserted into a capstan, four men gradually lever the bridge around until it's pointing in the direction of the harbour mouth. During the few minutes that the bridge is open, the creek traffic is busier than that on the roads, and cars are snarled up across the whole city.

The north side

Immediately on the **north side** of the Swing Bridge is the **Marine Terminal**, where you can catch boats for the northern cayes (see p.130 & p.145 for schedule). The Mundo Maya Deli (ⓣ223-1235), in the terminal, is a good place to find **information** on transport from Belize City; helpful owner Petty Cervantes keeps up-to-date bus schedules for Belize and sells tickets to Flores and Chetumal on the Flores-based buses and for the *Gulf Cruza* to Puerto Cortés. Amazingly, there's no restaurant inside the terminal, but the toilets are reasonably clean and there are also some rather expensive **luggage lockers**.

A block east of the Marine Terminal, at 91 N Front St, **The Image Factory** (Mon–Fri 9am–5pm; free but donations welcome; ⓣ610-5072, ⓦwww.imagefactory.bz) is home to Belize's leading contemporary artists. The gallery holds outstanding, sometimes provocative exhibitions and you often get a chance to discuss the works with the artists themselves. If you're looking for unique gifts, browse The Image Factory Shop, in front of the gallery, which sells Belizean art, books (including a wide range of contemporary local fiction),

Emory King

Any sailor shipwrecked on a foreign shore would doubtless be grateful to the land that saved him, but only one who'd been unfathomably moved by the experience would want to spend the rest of his life there. That's exactly what happened to **Emory King**, American-born wit, raconteur, realtor, historian, broadcaster, writer, businessman and film extra, when his schooner *Vagabond* crashed onto the coral off English Caye, British Honduras in 1953. Realizing almost immediately that the colony presented unrivalled opportunities to a young man of limited means but boundless entrepreneurial spirit, he stayed on, convinced he could play a major role in the development of this colonial backwater.

Finding the **Belize City** of the early 1950s much like a nineteenth-century village, with only a handful of cars (which, to his astonishment, drove on the left), a sickly electric power system and a few telephones to represent the modern age, he set about trying to change it. Within a year he managed to get appointed as the Secretary of the Chamber of Commerce, and then Secretary of the Tourist Committee – at a time when tourists were counted in dozens rather than hundreds of thousands. Believing that what the moribund colony needed to prosper was investment, and that the best way to attract investors was with minimal taxation, he waged a (so far still unsuccessful) campaign to abolish income tax. But although he advised investors and found land for American farmers in search of the next frontier, Emory King's most enduring gift to his adopted country was persuading the **Mennonites** (see box, p.105) to settle here in 1958; their back-breaking pioneer work is probably Belize's greatest agricultural success story.

Emory King's involvement in Belize has led to cameo roles in all the Hollywood movies filmed here. In perhaps the best-known, *The Mosquito Coast* (1985), based on the novel by Paul Theroux, he played a down-at-heel, drunken landowner offering to sell Harrison Ford a piece of land – a part he claims is not typecasting. In 1998 the government appointed him **film commissioner**, with a brief to attract more cinematic productions to Belize; he soon secured a production of *After the Storm*, based on the Hemingway short story and filmed in Placencia and Ambergris Caye. His success in this role has led to "reality television" productions such as *Temptation Island* being filmed here and the establishment of the **Belize Film Festival** (Ⓦwww.belizefilmfestival.com).

King's **books** on or about Belize and Belizean life are sold all over the country; a good one to start with is *Hey Dad, This is Belize*, a whimsical account of family life, followed by his second book, *I Spent it All in Belize* (see pp.366–375 for further titles). Most days he can be found in his office, in the forecourt of the *Radisson*, and will usually have time to sign a book or two – and if you're lucky, regale you with tales of Belize. King also writes a column ("Once Upon a Time") on historical anecdotes of Belize in the weekly *Belize Times*. His **website**, Ⓦwww.emoryking.com, provides everything you'll need to know about the man, or at least everything that he is prepared to tell.

music and videos, along with selected souvenirs, from wooden coasters to hand-woven baskets.

Continue east along North Front Street and you'll come to Fort Street. Here you'll see the **Maya Jade Museum**, at 8 Fort St, a gift shop-cum-mini-museum (April–Sept Mon & Fri 8am–3pm, Tues–Thurs 8am–5pm; Oct–March Mon–Fri 8am–5pm; Ⓣ203-1222) with a varied selection of jade jewellery – pendants, earrings, rings – for sale at decent prices, and fine replicas of jade artifacts culled from sites around Belize. In this area, you'll encounter the advance guard of trinket sellers, street musicians, hustlers and hair-braiders, announcing you're near the **Tourism Village**, Belize's **cruise**

ship terminal. This place often handles thousands of visitors in a single day; there will almost always be a cruise ship (or five) in view as you look out to sea. The city authorities, in an attempt to improve the area's image, try to keep the streets clear of vendors, but the lure of US cash tempts locals to set up improvised stalls. The Village itself is essentially a long dock used by cruise ship tenders to unload their passengers, with outdoor restaurants and bars and an attached shopping mall that houses the mega-store Diamonds International and the usual bevy of T-shirts-and-magnets souvenir shops; most are overpriced, so if you're stocking up on souvenirs, buy in town. The Village has expanded recently to an adjoining lot across Fort Street, called the Fort Street Plaza, with over a dozen gift and souvenir shops, a small pharmacy, a liquor store, a casual restaurant and the lively bar *T-Quilea's* (see p.85). Anyone can enter the Tourism Village, but note that the shops are only open when ships are in, usually Tuesday through Thursday. Cruise ship tourism is still a relatively new and often controversial phenomenon in Belize, with some stakeholders in the "traditional", low-impact overnight tourism stating that the sheer number of cruise ship tourists (expected to reach one million per year) exceeds the carrying capacity of the sites they visit, leading to irreversible environmental damage.

Beyond the Tourism Village, the road follows the north shore of the creek mouth – an area that was once Fort George Island until the narrow strait was filled in 1924 – eventually reaching the **Fort George Lighthouse**, which sits atop the tomb of and memorial to **Baron Bliss**, Belize's greatest benefactor (see p.77). Rounding the point and walking north along the shoreline, you pass the *Radisson Fort George Hotel*, in whose forecourt is the office of Emory King, one of Belize's most famous characters (see box, p.73). Natural history enthusiasts will benefit from a visit to two of Belize's foremost conservation organizations in the Fort George area: the **Belize Audubon Society**, 12 Fort St (Ⓣ223-5004, Ⓦwww.belizeaudubon.org), has information, books, maps and posters relating to the country's wildlife reserves and is very prominent in conservation education; nearby, at 1 Eyre St (Ⓣ227-5616, Ⓦwww.pfbelize.org), the **Programme for Belize** manages the Rio Bravo Conservation and Management Area (see p.111). The enthusiastic staff here will answer questions about Area access and progress. For more on these and other conservation organizations in Belize, see p.350 in Contexts.

Just north of the *Radisson*, the seafront **Memorial Park** honours the Belizean dead of World War I. In the streets around the park you'll find several colonial mansions, many of the best-preserved now taken over by upmarket hotels and embassies: the *Chateau Caribbean* and the Mexican embassy are a few fine examples. On the south side of the park, the **National Handicraft Center** (Mon–Fri 8am–5pm, Sat 8am–4pm; Ⓣ223-3636) sells high-quality Belizean crafts and art at fair prices. A little beyond here, at the corner of Hutson Street and Gabourel Lane, sits a superb "colonial" building – formerly the home of the US embassy, which moved to Belmopan in 2006 – that was actually constructed in nineteenth-century New England from American timber, before being dismantled and shipped to Belize.

Marine Parade, the seaward edge of Memorial Park, marks the beginning of the biggest civil engineering project in the city's history. A massive **seawall**, stretching for hundreds of metres along the shore to Barrack Road, encloses over fourteen acres of shallow sea, now in the process of being pumped dry. Soon this will become a boulevard for traffic and a pedestrian promenade, leading north for over a kilometre to the enormous *Princess Hotel*. Part of the reason for this seaward expansion of the city is to accommodate the ever-growing fleet of tour buses for the cruise ship industry, though it also creates lots of valuable new real estate for development. Beyond the northern end of this development, the attractive, seafront **BTL Park** was built on reclaimed land and it was in this area that Charles Lindbergh landed the *Spirit of St Louis*, the first aeroplane to touch down in Belize, in 1927. The park, with a children's playground, is popular with families and often hosts open-air concerts, with the biggest party taking place during the Independence Day celebrations in September.

The Museum of Belize

Near the Central Bank building at the north end of Queen Street, the former colonial prison has undergone a remarkable and very beautiful transformation to become the **Museum of Belize** (Mon–Fri 9am–5pm; Bz$10; ⓣ223-4524). Built in 1857 and used to house prisoners until 1993, it was reopened as the museum in 2002, the 21st anniversary of Belize's independence. While in use as a jail, the building almost certainly wasn't as impressive as it is today: the elegantly proportioned, two-storey structure of sand-coloured brickwork, set in lawns and gardens, looks more like a country mansion.

The lower floor, with plenty of exposed, original brick and bars on the windows, displays photographs and artifacts celebrating the history and the people of the city as it grew over the last 370 years, from a tiny settlement in the mangrove swamps to the bustling conurbation of today. Here you can also peruse a complete collection of the country's stamps; the earliest one, depicting Queen Victoria, dates to 1837. The building's original role is not glossed over, either; there's an old jail door, soon to be joined by a small exhibit of before-and-after photos chronicling the structure's evolution from prison to museum.

Fascinating though this is, the star attractions are upstairs, in the **Maya Masterpieces** gallery, a permanent, world-class collection of some of the best artifacts recovered from Belize's Maya sites. Well-lit glass cases display fine painted ceramics, representing all periods of Maya history. One of the most striking is the Buenavista Vase, which depicts the mythical Hero Twins dancing in the costume of the young Maize Gods after having defeated the Lords of Death – the central theme of the Maya creation story, the Popol Vuh (see Books, p.369). If you want to visit the site of Buenavista del Cayo, where the vase was found, see p.199. Other treasures include painstakingly formed **eccentric flints**, carved from a single piece of stone, and an exceptionally well-preserved wooden figurine, probably of a ruler, from a cave in Toledo District. Upstairs you'll also find the splendid **Jades of Belize** exhibit, which showcases the country's trove of jade discoveries, including a replica of the famous jade head from Altun Ha, stunning mosaic masks, pendants, ear flares and gorgeous necklaces.

On a different theme entirely, the museum also features one of the largest – and best-displayed – collections of insects in Belize, with each specimen pinned and clearly labelled. Bug-lovers won't want to miss it, but even those with merely a passing interest in insects will enjoy the close-ups of what they'll probably hear buzzing around them on their jungle treks.

The museum is overseen by the National Institute of Culture and History (NICH), an organization created by the Belize government in 2003 to preserve and promote Belizean culture. The House of Culture (see p.77) and the ICA (Institute of Creative Arts; see p.77), among other cultural and archeological entities, also fall under the NICH umbrella. Check out ⓦwww.nichbelize.org for more information.

The south side

The **south side** is generally the older section of Belize City; in the early days, the elite lived in the seafront houses while the backstreets were home to their slaves and labourers. These days it's the city's commercial centre, containing the main shopping streets, banks and travel agencies. Right by the Swing Bridge is the three-storey **commercial centre** (also called the new market), which opened in 1993 on the site of a rather decrepit old market dating from 1820. Though the new one is much cleaner, it's not very popular with either traders or shoppers, many of whom prefer the goods on display on the streets outside or the bustling Queen's Square market, next to the bus terminal.

Albert Street, running south from the Swing Bridge, is the main commercial thoroughfare, with banks, supermarkets and T-shirt and souvenir shops, including Sing's (see p.85). On the parallel **Regent Street**, a block closer to the sea, are the former colonial administration and court buildings, known together as the **Courthouse**. These well-preserved examples of colonial architecture, with their columns and finely wrought iron, were completed in 1926 after an earlier building on the same site was destroyed by fire. The Courthouse overlooks a square of grass and trees with an ornamental fountain in the centre, known as Central Park until it was renamed **Battlefield Park** in the early 1990s, commemorating the heated political meetings that took place here before independence; nowadays most of the noise in the park is the raucous chatter of grackles, which roost in their thousands every night.

Bliss Centre for the Performing Arts

On the waterfront a block south of the Courthouse is the extensively refurbished **Bliss Centre for the Performing Arts** (Mon–Fri 8am–5pm; ⓣ227-2110,

△ The Courthouse

Ⓦwww.nichbelize.org). A sleek, marble-lined entrance hall opens onto a 600-seat theatre behind, with space for drama workshops and the studios of the **Belize National Dance Company** upstairs. Benefiting from a generous grant from the Mexican government, which provides regular aid to Central American countries, this is the centre of Belizean cultural life, hosting concerts, plays and exhibitions as well as accommodating the country's **National Art Collection**. It's certainly worth a visit to the front desk to see what's on – here and elsewhere in the city – or to enjoy a drink at the café/bar. Concerts and events usually take place from 6 to 9pm.

The cultural programme is spearheaded by the **Institute of Creative Arts** (ICA), also housed here, with a remit to keep alive traditional culture and promote new talent. The organization was originally known as the Bliss Institute, funded by the legacy of Baron Henry Ernest Edward Victor Bliss, an eccentric Englishman with a Portuguese title and considerable wealth, the origins of which remain a mystery. A keen fisherman, Bliss arrived off the coast of Belize in his yacht *Sea King* in 1926 after hearing about the tremendous amount of game fish in local waters. Unfortunately, he became ill and died without ever having been ashore, but he must have been impressed by whatever fish he did catch, as he left most of his estate to the people of the colony – meticulously stipulating how the money was to be spent. This became the Bliss Trust, which has been used for various projects, helping to build markets and libraries, improve roads and water supplies and create the Bliss School of Nursing. In gratitude, the authorities declared March 9 (the date of his death) an official public holiday – **Baron Bliss Day** – commemorated by boat races and the La Ruta Maya canoe race (see p.190) from San Ignacio to Belize City. See p.74 for his tomb and memorial.

St John's Cathedral

At the southern end of Albert Street is **St John's Cathedral** (daily 6am–6pm; free), the oldest Anglican cathedral in Central America and one of the oldest buildings in Belize. Its construction lasted from 1812 to 1820 and used red bricks brought over as ballast in British ships. With its square, battlemented tower, it looks more like a large, English parish church than anything you might expect to find here. The main structure has survived almost 200 years of tropical heat and hurricanes, though a fire in 2002 destroyed most of the roof, now fully restored. In the first half of the nineteenth century, several indigenous kings of the Mosquito Coast held their coronation ceremonies here.

Just west of the cathedral, **Yarborough Cemetery** was named after the magistrate who owned the land and permitted the burial of prominent people here from 1781; commoners were admitted only after 1870. Although the graves have fallen into disrepair, a browse among the stones will turn up fascinating snippets of history. Nearby, connected to the mainland by a wooden causeway, **Bird's Isle** is a popular venue for parties and concerts, and there's a pleasant outdoor restaurant (see p.83).

The House of Culture

East of the cathedral, in a beautiful, breezy, seafront setting, shaded by royal palms and complete with an immaculate lawn, is the colonial Government House, now restored and renamed the **House of Culture** (daily 9am–4pm; Bz$10; Ⓣ227-3050, Ⓦwww.nichbelize.com). Built in 1814, it was the governor's residence when Belize was a British colony; at midnight on September 20, 1981, the Belize flag was hoisted here for the first time as the country celebrated independence.

The house has always been used for official receptions, particularly on Independence Day. But the present governor-general, Sir Colville Young, wanted to make this superb example of Belize's colonial heritage open to everyone, so in 1996 it was designated a **museum**, later becoming the House of Culture. A flight of steps under a columned portico leads to the front door; inside, a plush, red carpet stretches down the hall to a great mahogany staircase, and beyond here doors open onto the back porch, overlooking the sea. On the grounds, the carefully restored *Sea King*, the tender of Baron Bliss's yacht of the same name, stands as testimony to the skill of Belizean boatbuilders. The plant-filled gardens are a haven for birds and it's worth bringing a pair of binoculars.

A wide range of Belizean arts are presented here, among them painting, dance, **Garifuna** drumming, musical performances and, in a room off the front porch, contemporary visual art exhibitions. It's also a popular venue for weddings and banquets. In the main room, a panoramic painting of Belize City in the early 1900s overlooks the collection of colonial silverware, glass and furniture, and another wall is lined with prints of sombre past governors. A different room displays the **Eric King collection**, a fascinating compilation of vintage photographs and postcards of Belize.

Around Belize City

A number of sights near the city include the interesting Old Belize Cultural and Historical Center and the superb Belize Zoo, both making memorable day-trips and easily reached via the Western Highway.

Old Belize Cultural and Historical Center

The informative, well-run **Old Belize Cultural and Historical Center** (daily 10am–4.30pm; Bz$10; ⓣ222-4129, ⓦwww.oldbelize.com), on Mile 5 of the Western Highway, was created as an "appetizer to Belize" – a colourful, interactive overview of the country all under one roof, targeted towards time-pressed visitors like cruise ship passengers with their nine hours or less in port. The centre successfully draws the cruise crowd, but thanks to its adjoining open-air **restaurant** and man-made beach, it's also a hit with the locals. You enter the experiential museum through a mahogany tree, wander past ongoing videos on the country's varied ethnic groups and natural riches, and then explore a series of rooms, each of which highlights different eras in the country's history. Start off in the humid rainforest room, complete with a waterfall and a cage of fluttering Blue Morpho butterflies. Next is a dimly lit Maya village, with life-sized stone carvings and a replica wood-and-thatch home of Maya farmers. Belize's early industries are also featured, including sugar production, with a steam-powered sugar mill, the chicle (the base ingredient of chewing gum) trade and logging. You'll see a Garifuna dwelling – with piped-in beats of the ethnic group's traditional drumming – and walk along a re-created, early-twentieth-century Belize City street lined with wooden homes. Old Belize is also a great place for one-stop **souvenir shopping**, with reasonably priced wooden products, including cutting boards and coasters, local hot sauces and books on Belize.

After the museum, head for the *Sibun Bite Bar and Grill* (daily 11am–9pm), featuring high ceilings made of native hardwoods, where you can tuck into nicely priced Belizean specialities on the outdoor terrace overlooking Cucumber Beach. Dishes include pineapple curry shrimp, seafood burritos and stewed chicken with rice and beans, washed down with frothy fruit shakes. From Tuesday to Thursday, when the cruise passengers are scheduled to visit, you might catch Belizean dancing and singing, usually during the late morning and lunch. The **beach** (daily 10am–6pm; included in museum entrance fee, or Bz$5 for a beach-only pass), fashioned out of reclaimed land, is fairly small but well-groomed, with plenty of water activities for youngsters. Near the beach lies the marina, where both recreational and commercial boats can dock and refuel.

The Belize Zoo

Forty-six kilometres outside Belize City, at Mile 29 of the Western Highway, the **Belize Zoo** (daily 8.30am–5pm; Bz$16 adult, $8 for children, Peace Corps, VSO and military personnel; ⓣ220-8004, ⓦwww.belizezoo.org) is, for most people, the first point of interest outside the city and easily visited on a half-day trip or as a stop on the way to or from the west (see map, pp.162–163). And, unless you're a seasoned wildlife photographer, this is likely to be the best place to get excellent **photographs** of the animals of Belize. To **get to the zoo**, take any bus between Belize City and Belmopan and ask the driver to drop you off; there's a sign on the highway and zoo staff know the times of onward buses. A 200-metre walk brings you to the entrance and the Gerald Durrell Visitor Centre, with displays of children's art and exhibits on Belize's ecosystems.

Probably the finest zoo in the Americas south of the US, and long recognized as a phenomenal conservation achievement, the zoo originally opened in 1983 after an ambitious wildlife film (*Path of the Rain God*) left Sharon Matola, the film's production assistant, with a collection of semi-tame animals no longer able to fend for themselves in the wild. For locals and visitors alike, this now means the chance to see the native animals of Belize at close quarters, housed in spacious enclosures that closely resemble their natural habitats. Since the zoo opened, its menagerie has never been supplemented by animals taken from the wild – all are either donated or confiscated pets, injured wild animals brought in for healing and rehabilitation, sent from other zoos (often to take part in captive breeding programmes) or residents since birth. The zoo is actively involved in conservation education – all schoolchildren in Belize benefit from a free, official trip here – and it has achieved international recognition for its **captive breeding** programmes.

The zoo is arranged as "a walk through Belize", with a trail that takes you to the pine ridge, the forest edge, the rainforest, lagoons and the river forest; witty, hand-painted signs identify what you're seeing. Along the river forest trail you'll find the zoo's most famous resident: April, a venerable **Baird's tapir** (known locally as a "mountain cow") well known to the schoolchildren of Belize, who visit in their hundreds on her birthday (in April) to feed her a huge, vegetable birthday cake. Although April has been presented with potential mates, she hasn't produced any offspring; the prospect for progeny now rests between newcomer female Princess Navidad and male Ceibo, a pair of younger adult tapirs.

All the Belizean cats are represented and some, including the **jaguars**, have bred successfully; there's even a rarer melanistic (black) jaguar. One of the first aviaries you see houses a flock of vividly coloured **scarlet macaws**, and other birds include toucans, various parrot species, jabiru storks, a spectacled owl and several vultures and hawks. The real avian star of the show, however, is Panamá, a magnificent male **harpy eagle** (named for his home country) whose role in an ambitious captive breeding programme is crucial to the planned reintroduction of the largest eagle in the Americas to Belize. When you're on the viewing

△ Coatimundi at the Belize Zoo

platform outside his spacious enclosure, he'll look at you with seemingly all-knowing eyes – and you can be grateful you're out of reach of his enormous, steely talons.

Other zoo inhabitants include deer, spider and howler monkeys, peccaries, agoutis and numerous snakes. Both species of **crocodile** found in Belize thrive here, and you can get great close-ups of open jaws filled with powerful teeth.

To take part of your visit home with you, visit the **gift shop**: Sharon, the zoo's founder and a dedicated campaigner for conservation in Belize, has written several excellent and extremely popular children's books with a strong conservation message. These and other souvenirs are on sale, and if you're really keen on supporting the zoo, you can become a Friend and receive a regular newsletter. The zoo's website is also a good information source, with current information on conservation issues in Belize.

The Tropical Education Center

Across the highway from the zoo, and a few hundred metres back towards Belize City, the **Tropical Education Center** (Ⓣ220-8003 or 602-4980, Ⓔtec@belizezoo.org) focuses on school, college and tour guide training groups, though it's open to all and has research opportunities for overseas students. Study facilities include a classroom with Internet access and a well-equipped library, while outside there are self-guided **nature trails** and observation decks around two small lagoons.

Anyone can stay in the wonderful **accommodation** here, seated in the pine savannah and equipped with bug screens, electric lights, hot showers, flush toilets and a communal kitchen, open to all guests when large groups are absent. The three wooden **dorms** with tiled floors (Bz$60 per person) have either double or single beds and shared showers, though for a fraction more money, a couple can stay in the comfortable "Forest Cabana" (❻), on stilts and with shared showers. A third option is the secluded Guest House (❺–❻; lower long-term rates for researchers) with private bath, stove, fridge and peaceful views of the lagoon. **Internet** access is available and guests can take a special nocturnal tour of the zoo for Bz$20. If you're visiting the zoo by day and wish to stay the night here, ask at the office and TEC manager Celso Poot will come to pick you up.

Eating

The multitude of **restaurants** in Belize City offers a good deal of variety, though the tasty but humble **Creole** fare of rice and beans still predominates the lower end of the price scale. There's plenty of seafood and steaks, and a preponderance of **Chinese** restaurants – usually the best bet for **vegetarians** – as well as very good **Lebanese** and **Indian** establishments. The big **hotels** have their own restaurants, naturally quite expensive but with varied menus and good service. Generally, vegetables other than cabbage, carrots, onions and peppers are rarely served in the average Belizean restaurant, and these are likely to be the main components of any salad. Amazingly, the only US-based chain to make inroads into Belize is *Subway*, with a single branch. Until others inevitably arrive, *HL's Burger*, the self-proclaimed "Burger King of Belize", is the principal purveyor of fast food, with a growing number of outlets serving standard fare. A more grassroots version of takeaway food is greasy fried chicken – known as "dollar chicken", whatever the price –available from small stands all over the city.

If you're shopping for food, the main **supermarkets** – Romac's and Brodie's, the latter with a pharmacy (see p.89) – are worth a look; they're on Albert Street, just past Battlefield Park, and their selection is good, if expensive and largely imported. Milk and dairy products, produced locally by Mennonite farmers (see box, p.105), are delicious and of good quality. Naturally enough, local **fruit**, while highly seasonal, is cheap and plentiful – Belizean citrus is among the best in the world.

Note that some restaurants close fairly early in the evening (by 8.30 or 9pm and, if there are no customers, sometimes earlier). You can also expect that many smaller places will be closed on Sunday.

North of Haulover Creek

Celebrity Marine Parade, near the Volta Building and the Central Bank ☎223-7272. Enjoy international cuisine – thick T-Bone steaks, grilled butterfly snapper, shrimp kebabs, *köfte* meatballs, chicken fajitas – at this bright, airy restaurant. On breezy days, the pale blue curtains billow to reveal snatches of the Caribbean Sea in the distance.

Chateau Caribbean 6 Marine Parade, above the hotel ☎223-3888, ⓦwww.chateaucaribbean.com. For undisturbed views of blue sea and offshore islands, head up the steps to this cool, first-floor restaurant, where prices for Chinese (noodles with chicken, beef, shrimp or lobster) and international dishes are more reasonable than you might guess from the gleaming white linen and cutlery. In low season, the restaurant is often quite empty, but if you want post-meal drinks and conversation, you can always head to the outdoor bars at the *Radisson* and *Great House* nearby.

Faiyah Haat 164 Newtown Barracks ☎223-2865. At the lively new *Faiyah Haat* (Creole for "fire hearth"), local chef and entrepreneur Mark Usher aims to serve up "the best in Belizean food – and in Belizean arts and entertainment". He's successful on both counts, so, as they say on the menu, "Com een, siddown and loose dat deh pants button". Enjoy the daily happy hour (5–8pm) on the outdoor deck strung with coloured lights, then dig into superb local specialities, including guava jelly pork chops, blackened fish fillet with Cajun spices and coconut curry lobster with typical sides of fry jacks (fluffy, fried dough) and white coconut rice. Afterwards, stay on for the entertainment, which ranges from poetry nights (in association with the Belizean Poets Society), karaoke (Thurs, Fri & Sun) and, on Sat, "Laaf til yo cry wid backyaad theata".

Gyros and Crêpes 164 Freetown Rd ☎224-5841. Good Lebanese food, including tahini, falafel, hummus and kebabs – try the "Lebanese plate", which brings together everything above.

Harbour View 14 Fort St, just past the Tourism Village ☎223-6420. Fine dining and cocktails on the waterfront, featuring East Asian and Belizean specialities with lots of fresh seafood, including lobster tail with a Creole sauce and grilled snapper and grouper. Eat indoors in the a/c dining room or at tables on the deck.

Judith's Pastries 1 Queen St ☎223-3789. This family-owned cakeshop caters birthday parties across the city, and also serves up sugary slices from its simple storefront. The offerings change daily and might include banana cake, lemon meringue pie and rice pudding, made here with condensed and evaporated milk and whole eggs. Open Mon–Fri 8am–5pm, Sat 8am–3pm.

La Tavernetta 2 Dolphin Drive, Buttonwood Bay, 3.5km north of the city, off the Northern Hwy ☎223-7998. The city's only Italian restaurant serves up a respectable menu, thanks to the efforts of the Italian owner, who imports many of the ingredients. Try bruschetta heaped with tomatoes, pasta with shrimp and chicken and risotto enveloped in a creamy mushroom sauce. The sedate dining room has rose walls and white tablecloths, while the kitchen sports a brick oven. Top off the meal with gelato – try the tiramisu or caramel. If you're staying in Belize City proper, where there are plenty of dining options, it's probably not worth making the taxi trip out here, but if you're at any of the nearby accommodations (*Villa Boscardi*, *D'Nest Inn*, or the *Red Hut Inn*), then it makes for a convenient fine-dining option. Closed Mon & Tues.

Le Petit Café Cork St, in the Villa Wing of the *Radisson*. Enjoy fine coffee, baked treats, including croissants, and a pleasant café atmosphere at the outdoor tables. Ideal for a continental breakfast.

Ma Ma Chen 7 Eve St ☎223-4568. The only vegetarian restaurant in town, with a tasty Taiwanese menu of spring rolls stuffed with carrots, cabbage, mushrooms and tofu, sushi (on Fri) and a vegetarian lunchbox of tofu, soy meat and in-season vegetables. It's a no-frills but comfortable spot – the owners have a large extended family, and everyone from the kids to Grandma seems to walk through. Mon–Sat 10am–6pm. The adjoining guest house (see p.69) has basic, budget rooms.

Nerie's Restaurant II Queen St at Daly St ☎223-4028. Excellent Belizean fare served in clean, well-run and brightly lit surroundings. Just walk in, find a table and select from the chalkboard menu featuring local specialities, including a flavourful conch soup made with potatoes, okra and cocoa. Wash it down with a fresh-squeezed lime, watermelon or grapefruit juice. Very busy at lunchtimes, when there's always a daily special. Open daily 7.30am–10pm. On some weekend nights the *Bodega Lounge* upstairs features live music. *Nerie's I*, on 12 Douglas Jones St (Mon–Sat 7am–5.30pm), is just as good.

Pepper's Pizza 4 St Thomas St ☎223-5000. Popular pizza restaurant with reliable deliveries. Mon–Thurs 10am–10pm, Fri & Sat 10am–11pm, Sun 10am–9pm. There's also a small branch (until 5pm; closed Sun) on Albert St next to Romac's where you can buy by the slice.

Riverside Tavern 2 Mapp St ☎223-5640. A gleaming, four-sided bar, with bottles lining back-lit shelves, stands in the centre of this upscale tavern on the banks of Haulover Creek. Settle in at one of the ample wooden tables or on the breezy outdoor deck and fill up on "Coco Loco" shrimp, pan-seared grouper, seafood ceviche with corn tortilla chips and juicy burgers – among the best in the city. Come nightfall, the tavern swells with a lively crowd of Belizeans and travellers: see nightlife listings, p.85.

Smoky Mermaid 13 Cork St ☎223-4759. For al fresco dining, head here to sit amid the gnarled roots and heavy branches of native trees – breadfruit, soursap, mango – and a mermaid fountain, with the colonial *Great House* (see p.70) looming in the background. Try the grilled fish and seafood dishes, including ceviche, the catch of the day crusted with shredded yucca and "Naked Lobster", lightly steamed lobster tail served with a garlic or butter sauce. This is also a pleasant spot for an evening cocktail, either at the bar (with tree stumps for stools) or in the upstairs *Budda Bar*, where you can recline on low couches to the sounds of the wind rustling through the fan palms.

Stonegrill Cork St, in the Colonial Wing of the *Radisson* ☎223-3333. Poolside restaurant where you select your dish – seafood, chicken or beef, often on a skewer with vegetables – and cook it yourself on a slab of volcanic rock, delivered to your table, that's heated to 350°C. You get a range of mild or spicy sauces to accompany your creation. Sizzling fun and surprisingly healthful, as there are no added fats or oils.

Sumathi 190 Newtown Barracks Rd ☎223-1172. Excellent north Indian and tandoori food in a quiet, clean restaurant. Top-notch array of vegetarian dishes, including *kabuli channa* (chickpea curry) and *aloo gobi* (a curry of cauliflower, potatoes, sweet pepper and ginger). Tues–Sun 10am–11.30pm. There's also a *Sumathi* in the Tourism Village, serving an Indian buffet (Bz$20), and open 10am–5pm when the cruise ships are in.

Wet Lizard 1 Fort St, next to the Tourism Village ☎203-0400. Capture the feeling of the cayes at one of the brightly painted tables on a deck overlooking the creek mouth. The menu offers an eclectic range of well-prepared and very tasty dishes, including delicately flavoured seafood and tangy spring rolls stuffed with fish, shrimp, conch and lobster, along with Thai and Mexican specialities. Great desserts and cocktails, including a potent rum punch made with fresh juices. Mon–Fri 9am–4pm.

South of Haulover Creek

Big Daddy's Diner Upstairs in the commercial centre, just south of the Swing Bridge ☎227-0932. Great breakfasts – eggs, fry jacks, longanissa sausage – and Belizean dishes, with a daily lunch special, served cafeteria-style in clean surroundings. Try the fresh juices – watermelon, cantaloupe, orange and lime. Take your meal upstairs and enjoy the best harbour and bridge views in the city; a pity the windows don't open. Open Mon–Sat 7am–4pm.

Bird's Isle Restaurant Bird's Isle, at the south end of Albert St ☎207-6500. Relax under a thatched roof by the sea and enjoy nicely priced Belizean fare, like grilled conch, stewed chicken, plantains and, on Saturdays, a boil-up, the perennially popular, one-pot stew of root vegetables and chicken or beef (and a pig tail for flavour). This is a friendly, community-oriented place, and the neighbourhood kids are encouraged to stop in and use the adjoining basketball court. See if you can catch one of the spirited evening games between local teams. There's karaoke on Thurs and happy hour on Fri (6–8pm).

Jambel's Jerk Pit 2B King St ☎227-6080. Chef Garnet Brown and his crew cook up delicious, Jamaican-influenced dishes at reasonable prices in this amiable, wood-walled sister restaurant to the long-established *Jambel's* in San Pedro, Ambergris Caye (see p.143). Specialities include jerk chicken (obviously), but also try the delicious spicy fish and other seafood dishes, such as jerk lobster and soups and salads. Eat indoors or on the palm-shaded patio. Closed Sun.

Macy's 18 Bishop St ☎207-3419. Long-established Creole restaurant with plaid tablecloths, popular with locals and very busy at lunchtime. The menu includes whole snapper – pan-fried, steamed or broiled – and deep-fried chicken with tomato sauce, and also traditional game: armadillo, deer and gibnut (a type of large rodent).

Marlins 11 Regent St W, next to the *Belcove* ☎227-6995. Tasty, inexpensive Belizean and Mexican-influenced dishes – *escabeche*, stewed chicken, grilled catch of the day – in large portions, which you can eat on the veranda overlooking the creek. Local workers come by for the filling breakfasts, including eggs made every which way, ham with fry jacks or flour tortillas and refried beans.

Drinking, nightlife and entertainment

Belize City's more sophisticated **bars** and **clubs** are generally found in the upscale hotels, while at the other end of the scale are low-lit dives, effectively men-only. Though you might be offered drugs or feel uneasy in these places, you'll more likely end up spending a casual evening in the company of easy-going, hard-drinking regulars. Between these two extremes is a smattering of amiable, local spots – many with comfortable outdoor decks – perfect for enjoying a Belikin beer or two with a mix of residents and visitors.

A number of the top-end places tempt the after-work crowd with Friday evening **happy hours** (usually 5–7pm). Try the poolside bar of the *Biltmore*, occasionally visited by a steel band, or the *Radisson*, where you can sip frothy cocktails on an outdoor patio while tapping your toes to Caribbean tunes spun by a DJ. The *Smoky Mermaid* (see p.83), in the patio beneath *The Great House*, is another pleasant spot for an outdoor drink amid tropical foliage.

Karaoke is popular across the country, and you'll find a number of Belize City bars where you can belt out tunes on the weekends, including the poolside bar at the *Bellevue* (see p.71); call ahead, as the karaoke schedule changes often. *Bodega Lounge*, upstairs at *Nerie's Restaurant II*, also features karaoke some weekend nights, as well as live Caribbean music and dancing. *Nu Fenders Bar*, just opposite, does a brisk trade on the weekends with a local crowd knocking back local drinks.

One of the livelier strips in the city is the relatively safe stretch of Barracks Road facing BTL Park. On the weekends, the sidewalks fill with revellers traipsing from one nightspot to the next, like the semi-outdoor *Club Caribbean*, where a youngish, local crowd kicks back on the **outdoor deck** overlooking the park. The *Princess Hotel* looms over this part of town, and while it has a rather dismal reputation for its sub-par rooms and service, its nightlife offerings, including *Club Next* (see opposite), are generally top-of-the-heap by Belize City standards.

The *Princess* also features a flashy **casino**, where you don't have to be a high roller to try your luck, though you will need a passport or photo ID to gain temporary membership (free), and you must keep to the dress code: no shorts or sandals. The cash desk changes your Belize or US dollars into tokens for feeding the four hundred slot machines or playing blackjack, Caribbean poker and roulette. Officially there's a Bz$50 minimum to keep out the riff-raff (not always enforced); any tokens you don't use are changed back. Even if you don't win anything, a night's entertainment need only set you back around Bz$20–30. Local (as opposed to imported) drinks are free while you're playing. For the viceless or underage, there's an eight-lane bowling alley and Belize City's only **cinema**, showing the latest releases in air-conditioned comfort.

The Big Apple Regent St W, just southwest of the Swing Bridge. Red-lit club with live music (from merengue and reggaetón to salsa and pop), a local crowd and murals of toucans and apples. This part of town can get dodgy after dark, so take a taxi or go walking with others. It's one of the very few nightspots in the city open until the wee hours on Sun. Open Fri–Sun from 10pm to 3am (5am on Sat).

Caesar's Palace Newtown Barracks Rd, across from BTL Park. The nights get going here after

10pm on Fri and Sat, when a lively, packed house grooves to techno, Latin, soca and reggae on the small dancefloor.

Iguana Rana In the Tourism Village. By day, this large, breezy restaurant/bar, perched on the pier, is crammed with the cruise crowd, who sip tropical drinks with paper umbrellas while enjoying the rays and live Caribbean steel drums. On Fri nights (from 5pm), however, this festive spot becomes largely the territory of locals. A cheery mood pervades, as groups of friends and couples enjoy cocktails under the night sky, surrounded by the lapping Caribbean Sea.

Club Level Newtown Barracks Rd, near BTL Park. A smart venue attracting a more affluent crowd of young people and enforcing a fairly strict dress code. As with any other club around here, don't arrive before midnight or you'll find it next to empty. Open Fri & Sat from 10pm.

Club Next In the *Princess*. Hip DJs spin blaring tunes, from reggaetón to contemporary rock, for a dance-savvy crowd fuelled on potent cocktails. Fri & Sat 10pm–4am. Bz$15 cover.

Riverside Patio On the creekside behind the commercial centre. Depending on the crowd – usually lots of hard-drinking, local fishermen – this place can get loud and rowdy. If that's your scene, grab a beer with the guys and watch the bridge swing.

Riverside Tavern 2 Mapp St ⓣ223-5640. The classiest nightspot in this part of town, with a dark-wood-and-brass interior and an ample outdoor deck. The extensive cocktail menu includes the "Rainwater", watermelon and cranberry juice spiked with vodka. Secure parking lot.

T-Quilea's 6 Fort St. Sidle up to the inviting wooden bar at this jovial outdoor spot, where the speciality is – you guessed it – tequila, mixed in a variety of ways. Try it with a dash of coconut water, or opt for a shot chased by V-8 or Red Bull. On Fri nights, the Tequila Boys get the place going with tunes from reggae to jazz.

Shopping

Albert and Regent streets, south of the Swing Bridge, hum with commerce, from discount shoe stores to the city's largest supermarket and department store, **Brodie's** (see Listings, p.89). **Sing's**, at 35 Albert St, features a wide range of souvenirs, from mahogany carvings to Maya crafts and jewellery; there's also a Sing's in the Tourism Village.

On the north side of town lies the well-stocked department store **Mirab**, on Fort Street, with everything from postcards and batteries to appliances and furniture. For souvenirs, stop in at the **National Handicraft Center** (see p.74), with Belizean hardwood crafts, including bowls, picture frames and cutting boards, Maya basketry and hot sauces and spices. **The Image Factory** (see p.72) also carries quality souvenirs, as well as books and local art, and **Old Belize** (see p.78) has its own excellent array. Some of the larger hotels, including the *Biltmore* and the *Radisson* (see p.70), have small but thorough selections, slightly pricier than elsewhere.

Moving on from Belize City

Moving on from Belize City is easy, with regular departures by **bus** to all parts of the country, across the border to Chetumal in Mexico and to Benque Viejo in Cayo, for the Guatemalan border. Most transport tends to peter out at dusk and there are no overnight buses. Domestic **flights** to all main towns leave from the Municipal Airport; **boats** to the northern cayes leave from the Marine Terminal or Courthouse Wharf.

By air

Domestic flights: Domestic flights originate from Belize City's Municipal Airport, with dozens of scheduled flights to many destinations. Maya Island Air

Leaving Belize City by bus

Most buses from Belize City depart from and around a large terminal at 19 West Collet Canal (☎227-2255) on the western side of the city centre, in a fairly rundown section of town. It's safest to take a taxi to and from the terminal. The main bus company used to be called Novelo's until it dissolved in 2006; it now operates as **National Transport Services Limited (NTSL)**. Note, however, that you'll still see and hear the Novelo's name throughout town, including on bus brochures and bus signs. In addition to NTSL, there are numerous other private bus companies that service particular destinations.

You may be able to track down the latest schedules by either calling or stopping by the tourist office (see p.69) or asking locals such as Petty Cervantes (see below). You can also call the general bus terminal number; if someone answers, they can usually confirm the departures for that day. Very few of the bus companies have a contact number, however, and even when they do, you'll be lucky to get a response. If you're unable to confirm departure times for your destination, your best bet may be to arrive at the terminal in the morning (earlier rather than later) and inquire.

Bus contact information

Petty Cervantes at Mundo Maya Deli (see p.72) may have additional information and schedules.

NTSL ☎227-6372 or 227-2255; leaves from terminal.

James Bus ☎702-2049; leaves from the Shell station on Cemetery Rd, near the bus terminal.

Jex & Sons Bus ☎225-7017; leaves for Crooked Tree from Regent St W (Mon–Sat 10.50am) and from Pound Yard, Collet Canal (Mon–Fri at 5.15pm).

McFadzean's Bus Leaves from Euphrates Ave, off Orange St, near the bus terminal.

Perez Bus Leaves from Courthouse Wharf, N Front St, at 10.30, noon & 4pm.

Russell's Bus Leaves from Cairo St, near the corner of Cemetery Rd and Euphrates Ave.

Southern Transport ☎502-2160; leaves from terminal.

Western Transport ☎227-1160; leaves from terminal.

Bus schedule overview

The following chart is a rough schedule of buses departing from Belize City. It should not be used as a substitute for actual, up-to-date bus schedules acquired from the tourist office or bus companies.

and Tropic Air operate flights to: San Pedro (25min), stopping on request at Caye Caulker (15–20min), at least hourly from 7.30am to 5pm daily; and Punta Gorda (roughly 1hr), stopping on request at Dangriga (25min) and Placencia (45min), with 8–10 flights daily. See p.27 in Basics for further destinations.

International flights: Belize International Airport to: San Salvador (1 daily; 1hr 30min); Flores, for Guatemala City (2–4 daily; 45min); Roatán (1 daily; 1hr 45min); and San Pedro Sula (1 daily; 1hr). See p.27 in Basics for further destinations.

See Listings, p.88, for details of international and domestic airlines.

By boat

Scheduled **boats to Caye Caulker** leave from the Marine Terminal on N Front St by the Swing Bridge (roughly every 90min 8am–5.30pm; 45min; Bz$20 one way, Bz$30 same-day return; ☎223-5752); many of these services

	Duration (from Belize City)	Bus line	Frequency
Points north			
Chetumal, Mexico	up to 3hr 30min	NTSL, Linea Dorada and others	10 daily 5.30am– 7pm
Corozal	2hr 30min	NTSL, BBOC (to Mexican border), Gilharry, T-Line	hourly 5.30am– 7pm
Crooked Tree	1hr 30min	Jex	2 daily Mon–Fri, 1 Sat
Maskall (for Altun Ha)	1hr 30min	Maskall bus	Mon–Sat 3.30, 5.30 & 7pm
Orange Walk	1hr 30min	NTSL, Gilharry, T-Line	hourly 5am–7pm
Sarteneja (via Orange Walk)	3hr 30min	Perez	Mon–Sat 10.30am, noon & 4pm
Points west			
Belmopan	1hr 15min	NTSL, BBOC, James, Middleton's Transport, Shaw	at least hourly 5am–9pm
Benque Viejo (for the Guatemalan border)	up to 3hr	NTSL, BBOC, Middleton's Transport, Shaw	at least hourly 5am–9pm; the first usually runs to the border
Bermudian Landing	1hr 15min	McFadzean's, Russell's	3 daily Mon–Sat
San Ignacio (via Belmopan)	up to 2hr 30min	NTSL, BBOC, Middleton's Transport, Shaw	at least hourly 5am–9pm
Points south			
Dangriga	2hr via Coastal Rd; 3hr 30min via Belmopan	NTSL, BBOC, James, Usher	at least hourly 6am–5pm
Gales Point	1hr 40min	NTSL	5pm Mon & Fri only
Hopkins	4hr via Dangriga	NTSL, James, KC	6 daily 7am–2pm
Placencia	4–6hr via Dangriga	NTSL, James	4 daily 7am–2pm
Punta Gorda (via Belmopan & Dangriga)	5–7hr	NTSL, BBOC, James, Usher	12–15 daily 5.30am–3.30pm

also continue to **San Pedro, Ambergris Caye** and will call at St George's Caye on request. Other boats to these cayes leave from Courthouse Wharf. For more detail on boat schedules, see the boxes on p.130 & p.145.

Take the James bus at 5am to Mango Creek to connect with the *Gulf Cruza*, a fast boat to **Puerto Cortés**, Honduras (3hr; US$50); to book, call ⓣ202-4506 or 601-5289, or check with Petty Cervantes in the Mundo Maya Deli in the Marine Terminal (ⓣ223-1235).

From Mango Creek, you can also hop aboard the *Hokey Pokey* water taxi to Placencia, a ten-minute ride (see box, p.273). It's much faster than travelling to Placencia by bus, and it runs eight times daily.

For water transport to Guatemala, take a bus to Punta Gorda, and Requena's Charter Service (ⓣ722-2070) will bring you to Puerto Barrios (daily 9am & 2pm; 4hr; US$35). Memo's Water Taxi runs Mondays, Wednesdays and Fridays to Livingston, Guatemala.

Listings

Airlines American, New Rd at Queen St ⓣ223-2522; Continental, 80 Regent St ⓣ227-8309; Maya Island Air, Municipal Airport ⓣ223-1140 or 226-2435; Taca, in Belize Global Travel, 41 Albert St ⓣ227-7363; Tropic Air, Municipal Airport ⓣ224-5671 or 226-2012; US Airways toll-free to US office ⓣ0800/872-4700.

American Express In Belize Global Travel, 41 Albert St ⓣ227-7363.

Banks and exchange The main branches of Atlantic, First Caribbean, Belize and Scotia banks are on Albert St (usually Mon–Thurs 8am–2pm, Fri 8am–4.30pm). The Belize and First Caribbean banks have ATMs that accept foreign-issued cards; others will process cash advances over the counter. Cash in US$ is usually only available if you can show a ticket to leave the country. *Casas de cambio*, shops, hotels and restaurants change traveller's cheques and accept US$. Guatemalan and Mexican currency is often difficult to obtain except at the borders, but some shops in the Marine Terminal usually have quetzales and pesos. For more information, see p.53 in Basics.

Books In addition to the shops listed here, many of the larger hotels also sell books, magazines and newspapers; some budget hotels operate book exchanges. Both The Book Center, 4 Church St, opposite the BTL office (Mon–Thurs 8.30am–noon & 1.15–5.30pm, Fri 8.30am–noon & 1.15–9pm, Sat 8.30am–noon & 1.15–6pm; ⓣ227-7457), and Angelus Press, 10 Queen St (Mon–Fri 7.30am–5.30pm, Sat 8am–noon; ⓣ223-5777), have a wide range of books on Belize, maps and guides, including *Rough Guides*.

Car rental The following companies will arrange vehicle pickup and drop-off anywhere in the city, or at the Municipal or International airports (where most have offices), at no extra charge: Avis ⓣ225-2385 or 225-2629 (24hr), ⓦwww.avis.com.bz; Budget, Mile 2, Northern Hwy ⓣ223-2435, ⓦwww.budget-belize.com; Crystal, Mile 5, Northern Hwy ⓣ223-1600 or toll-free in Belize ⓣ0800/777-7777, ⓦwww.crystal-belize.com; Hertz, 11A Cork St ⓣ223-5935. Crystal has by far the largest rental fleet in the country, and is the only outfit that allows you to take vehicles over the Guatemalan border. Owner Jay Crofton, based in his antique-filled courtyard on the Northern Hwy, always gives a good deal on rentals and prides himself on service. For more information on renting and driving in Belize, see Getting around, p.26.

Embassies and consulates Though the official capital is Belmopan, some embassies remain in Belize City. These are normally open mornings Mon–Fri. Several EU countries have (mainly honorary) consulates in Belize City; current addresses and phone numbers for all embassies are in the Diplomatic Listings, at the back of the green pages in the telephone directory. Canada (cannot issue passports), 83 N Front St ⓣ223-1060; Guatemala, 8 A St, Kings Park ⓣ223-3150; Mexico, 18 North Park St ⓣ223-0194. The US Embassy is in Belmopan (see p.167).

Film developing For prints, slides and fast passport photos, try Spooner's, 89 N Front St (ⓣ223-1043), or Tito's Photo Studio, 7 Barrack Rd (ⓣ224-5340).

Immigration The Belize Immigration Office is in the Government Complex on Mahogany St, near the junction of Central American Blvd and the Western Hwy (Mon–Thurs 8.30am–4pm, Fri 8.30am–3.30pm; ⓣ222-4620). Thirty-day extensions of stay (the maximum allowed) cost Bz$25.

Internet and email Most accommodation offers Internet access; this is usually the most convenient way to check your email, particularly in the evenings, as few of the city's Internet centres are open outside of regular business hours (Mon–Fri 8 or 9am to 5 or 6pm). The high-end hotels, such as the *Radisson* and the *Biltmore*, have business centres with several computers and other services, while the smaller and/or budget places will generally have one or two computers available to guests (sometimes free, but more often Bz$5–10/hr). Increasingly, hotels also offer wireless service, so that you can access the Internet via your laptop. You'll find several Internet centres dotted about the city, with an average cost of Bz$5–10/hr. Angelus Press is one of the more affordable spots, with hourly Internet for just over Bz$3, as is the Internet centre inside Romac's supermarket (see p.81). M-Business Solutions, 2-A S Park St, offers Internet access, as does the National Handicraft Center (see p.74) next door. Both charge Bz$8/hr. You can also find Internet at Mailboxes Etc., 166 N Front St (near the Marine Terminal), in the Turton Library on North Front St and at the BTL office (see Phones, p.54).

Laundry Central America Coin Laundry, 114 Barrack Rd (Mon–Sat 8.30am–9pm; reduced hours Sun), and in many hotels.

Massage Oltsil Day Spa, 148A Barrack Rd ⓣ223-7722, ⓔoltsil@yahoo.com. Holistic massage, body scrubs, herbal wraps, facials, waxing, pedicures and spa treatments using local natural products and ingredients, including mud – properly sterilized

– from cave systems in northern Belize. Closed Sun.

Medical care Dr Gamero, Myo-On Clinic, 40 Eve St ⓣ224-5616; Karl Heusner Memorial Hospital, Princess Margaret Drive, near the junction with the Northern Hwy ⓣ223-1548.

Pharmacy In Brodie's, 2 Albert St, ⓣ227–7070. Open Mon–Thurs 8:30am–7pm, Fri 8:30am–8pm, Sat 8:30am–5pm, Sun 8:30am–1pm.

Police The main police station is on Queen St, a block north of the Swing Bridge (ⓣ227-2210). For emergencies, dial ⓣ90 or 911 nationwide. Alternatively, contact the tourism police; see the box on p.68.

Post office The main post office (including parcel office) is on N Front St, immediately north of the Swing Bridge (Mon–Fri 8am–4.30pm).

Telephones There are payphones (which need a phonecard) dotted around the city and at the main BTL office, 1 Church St (Mon–Sat 8am–6pm), which also has fax facilities and reasonably priced email service. Some hotels have a dedicated phone for guests to use with a phonecard.

Travel and tour agents The following travel agents are the best for information and bookings on transportation throughout the region; all can arrange tours within Belize: Belize Global Travel, 41 Albert St (ⓣ227-7363, ⓦwww.belizeglobal.bz), is an agent for most of the international airlines operating in Belize; Belize Travel Adventures, 168 N Front St (ⓣ223-3064, ⓦwww.belize-travel.net), is a rep for the Mundo Maya organization, linking tours in surrounding countries; Belize Trips (ⓣ223-0376 or 610-1923, or in the US, 561/210-7015, ⓦwww.belize-trips.com) is run by Katie Valk, a very experienced Belize travel specialist; Maya Travel Services, 42 Cleghorn St (ⓣ223-1623, ⓦwww.mayatravelservices.com), are inbound travel experts, very knowledgeable about tours and hotels within Belize; Travel and Tour Belize, 100 Albert Hoy Ave (ⓣ223-7604, ⓦwww.traveltourbelize.com), is a branch of the San Pedro-based agency, with the same excellent service; S & L Travel, 91 N Front St (ⓣ227-5145), offers birding and natural history tours, among others.

Western Union Belize Chamber of Commerce, 63 Regent St ⓣ227-0014.

2

The north

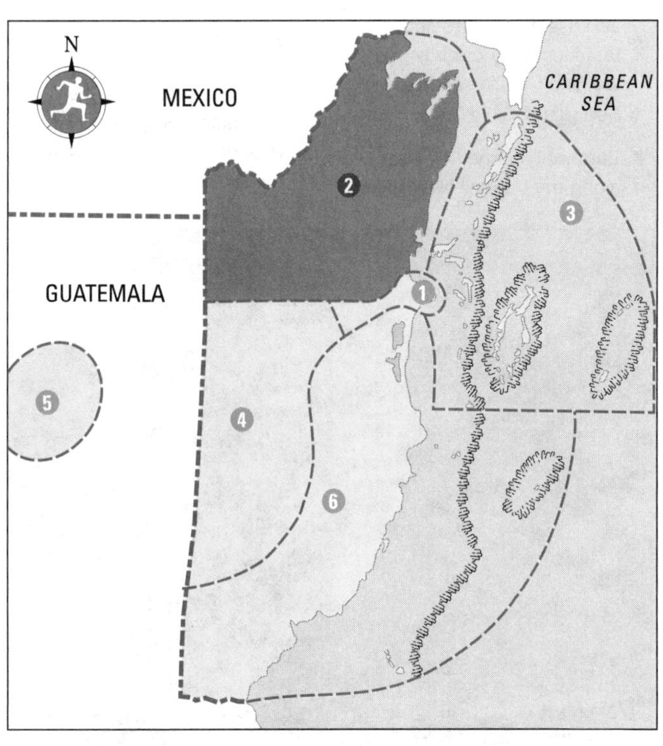

CHAPTER 2 Highlights

✱ **Bermudian Landing** Guaranteed close-ups of the black howler monkey – the largest primate in the New World – in this welcoming village on the banks of the Belize River. See p.97

✱ **Birding in Crooked Tree Wildlife Sanctuary** Spend the night in Crooked Tree village and rise at dawn to spot a fabulous array of birds in a wetland wildlife sanctuary. See p.100

✱ **Lamanai** Journey by boat along the tranquil New River to reach this astonishing Maya city, with some wonderfully restored temples. See p.108

✱ **Rio Bravo Conservation and Management Area** A massive swath of the best-protected forest in Belize, and the most likely place to catch a glimpse of a wild jaguar. See p.111

✱ **Sarteneja** Relax in this Mexican-flavoured village, within easy reach of the remarkable Shipstern Nature Reserve and a pair of Maya ruins. See p.114

△ *Chan Chich Lodge*, Gallon Jug

2

The north

Northern Belize is an expanse of relatively level land where swamps, savannahs and lagoons mix with rainforest and farmland. For many years this part of the country was largely inaccessible and had closer ties with Mexico than Belize City; most of the original settlers were refugees from the Caste Wars in Yucatán, who brought with them the sugarcane that formed the basis of the Belizean economy for much of the twentieth century. Indian and mestizo farming communities were connected by a skeletal network of dirt tracks, while boats plied the route between Belize City and Corozal. In 1930, however, the Northern Highway brought the region into contact with the rest of the country, opening up the area to further waves of settlers.

The largest town in the north is **Orange Walk**, the main centre for sugar production. Further north, **Corozal** is a small and peaceful Caribbean settlement with a strong Mexican element – not surprising, as it lies just 14km from the border. Throughout the north, Spanish is as common as Creole, and there's a distinctive Latin flavour to life.

Most visitors to northern Belize come to see the **Maya ruins** and wildlife reserves. The largest archeological site, **Lamanai**, features some of the most impressive pyramids in the country; it's served by regular boat tours along the New River and a good road to the nearby village of Indian Church, often used as a base for visiting the ruins. East of Lamanai, **Altun Ha**, reached by the Old Northern Highway, is usually visited as part of a day-trip from Belize City or San Pedro. Other sites in the region include Cuello and Nohmul, respectively southwest and north of Orange Walk, and Santa Rita and Cerros, both near Corozal.

The north is also a haven for wildlife, and each of the four main **reserves** in the region offers insight into a specific habitat or conservation strategy. At the **Community Baboon Sanctuary** in the Belize River valley, a group of farmers has combined agriculture with conservation, much to the benefit of the black howler monkey, while at **Crooked Tree Wildlife Sanctuary**, a network of lagoons and creeks gives protection to a range of migratory birds, including the endangered jabiru stork. By far the largest and most ambitious conservation project is the **Rio Bravo Conservation and Management Area**, comprising 970 square kilometres of tropical forest and river systems in the west of Orange Walk District. This vast, practically untouched area, containing several Maya sites, adjoins the borders of Guatemala and Mexico. The most northerly protected area is **Shipstern Nature Reserve**, where a large tract of tropical hardwood forest, mangroves and wetland is preserved with the help of a Swiss conservation organization.

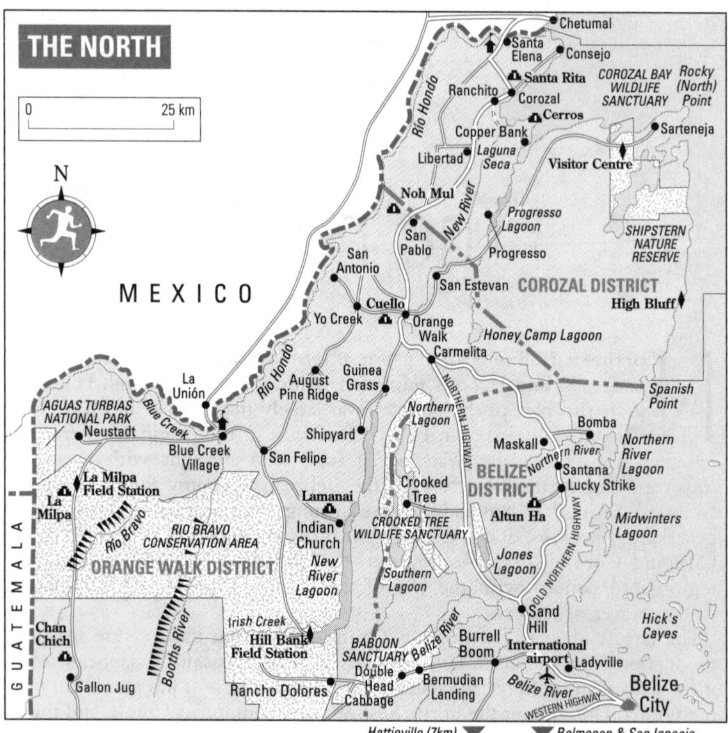

Getting around the north

Travelling around the north is fairly straightforward if you stick to the main roads. National Transport has bus services (5 daily 5am–7pm) along the Northern Highway between Belize City and Chetumal, Mexico, calling at Orange Walk, Corozal and the border town of Santa Elena along the way. Smaller roads and centres are served by a fairly regular flow of buses and trucks. Several companies operate tours to the Maya sites and nature reserves, though these can be expensive.

Belize City to Orange Walk

The start of the 88-kilometre Northern Highway in Belize City is marked by a roundabout adorned with the flags of the Caribbean Community (CARICOM) countries. Leaving the city, you pass spreading suburbs, where expensive houses sit upon reclaimed mangrove swamps; look to the east for a glimpse of the sea. Seven kilometres beyond the city limits, a metal-framed bridge carries the road over the mouth of the Belize River at the point where Haulover Creek branches away to the south. For the next few kilometres the road runs alongside the broad river, making it susceptible to flooding after heavy rains. If you look to your right, you may notice the large, brightly painted concrete building called Raul's Rose Garden; it's actually a brothel, so don't drop in expecting horticulture. At **Ladyville**, 15km from Belize City, you pass the turn-off to the international airport; another kilometre brings you to the road to Airport Camp, run by the Belize Defence Force and the main base of the British forces in Belize.

Heading a few hundred metres down either the first or second left turns along the road to the international airport, you arrive at the riverbank, just downstream from the peaceful *Belize River Lodge* (ⓣ225-2002, ⓦwww.belizeriverlodge.com; packages only, around US$3500/week for fishing, room and meals). Originally built as a fishing lodge in the 1960s, it still specializes in superb fishing packages, but is also renowned for its quality guides and meals and as a great base for visiting inland Belize. The spacious cabins have comfortable furniture, mahogany-panelled walls, private bathroom, air-conditioning and fan and a huge, screened porch with river views. Owners Mike Heusner and Marguerite Miles know Belize well and do all they can to ensure guests get the most out of a stay here. They also offer combination packages, including tours of Maya sites. In addition to its several skiffs, the *Lodge* has two **live-aboard boats**: the 52-foot *Blue Yonder* and the 58-foot *Cristina*.

Burrell Boom

Six kilometres down the Northern Highway turn-off to Bermudian Landing, you'll pass **BURRELL BOOM**, on the Belize River. In logging days, a huge, heavy, metal chain called a "boom" was stretched across the river to catch the logs floating down; you can still see the chain and the anchors that held it by the roadside, on the right as you pass through the village. Burrell Boom is a pleasant base for exploring the area, particularly with the advent of the restful *Black Orchid Resort* (ⓣ225-9028, ⓦwww.blackorchidresort.com; ⑧). Perched on the banks of the river, the **hotel** offers spacious, freshly scrubbed rooms with all the amenities – air-conditioning, TV, hot water – and large beds with plump comforters. Stroll the leafy grounds and pick your pastime: take a dip in the swimming pool, swing and snooze in a hammock or saunter down to the river's edge and float gently off in a canoe. The accommodating owners can fill you in on exploring the area further, from cave tubing to visiting the nearby Community Baboon Sanctuary (see p.96). The cosy **restaurant**, with a tree trunk rising up as a central pillar, features homemade Belizean specialities, and draws folks from Belize City and around, who come as much for the cuisine as for the peaceful riverside setting. Another option is the nearby *El Chiclero* (ⓣ225-9005, ⓦwww.elchicleroinn.com; ⑤–⑥), with large, tiled, air-conditioned rooms and a pool. It's run by a gregarious American expat and his wife, who dishes out American favourites – BBQ chicken, pork chops, lasagne, porterhouse steaks – in the simple restaurant.

In Burrell Boom, the river is never far from view, and to fully understand its role in the surrounding area, it's well worth taking a boat journey. **Old River Adventures** (ⓣ225-9008, ⓦwww.oldriveradventures.com), run by the knowledgeable Niall Gillett, is one of the more informative tours in the area. Board the small yet comfortable riverboat *Lorraine* for an entertaining trip that includes wildlife-watching – you may spot crocs, iguanas and howler monkeys – and cultural commentary as you peer through the bullet trees at Creole settlements and plantations. Tours last anywhere from one hour (Bz$50, minimum 3 people) to a full day (Bz$250 for 4–6 people).

If you have your own vehicle and are heading west to Cayo District after your visit, you can avoid the trouble of returning to Belize City by cutting south down from Burrell Boom to Hattieville, on the Western Highway, along a paved side road.

△ Black howler monkey

The Community Baboon Sanctuary

The **Community Baboon Sanctuary** (Ⓦwww.howlermonkeys.org), established in 1985 by primate biologist Rob Horwich and a group of local farmers (with help from the Worldwide Fund for Nature), is one of the most interesting conservation projects in Belize. A mixture of farmland and broadleaf forest, the sanctuary stretches along 30km of the Belize River valley – from Flowers Bank to Big Falls – and comprises a total of eight villages and over 250 landowners. Farmers here voluntarily harmonize their own needs with those of the wildlife in a project combining conservation, education and tourism; visitors are welcome and you'll find plenty of places to rent canoes or horses.

The main focus of attention here is the **black howler monkey** (locally known as a "baboon"), the largest monkey in the New World and an endangered subspecies of howler that exists only in Belize, Guatemala and southern Mexico. They generally live in troops of between four and eight, and spend the day clambering through the leafy canopy, feasting on leaves, flowers and fruits. You're pretty much guaranteed to see them up close, feeding and resting in the trees along the riverbank, and they're often as interested in you as you are in them. At dawn and dusk they let rip with their famous howl, a deep and rasping roar that carries for miles.

The sanctuary has proven so successful that some troops have been relocated to reserves elsewhere in Belize, with the aim of replacing populations wiped out by hunting or disease. In 1992, eighteen black howler monkeys were transferred to the Cockscomb Basin Wildlife Sanctuary in Stann Creek District, and in 1996 eight more were moved to the Macal River valley. Both relocations have resulted in breeding in these former parts of the monkeys' range, and Belize is considered to be at the forefront of successful primate relocation techniques. Howler numbers in the sanctuary now stand at around four thousand – almost double the number of people in the villages here.

The sanctuary is also home to around two hundred **bird** species, plus anteaters, deer, peccaries, coatis, iguanas and the endangered Central American river turtle. Special trails are cut through the forest so that visitors can see it at its best; you can wander these alone or with a guide, and canoe or horseback tours in the sanctuary are also possibilities.

Bermudian Landing

At the heart of the sanctuary, 43km northwest of Belize City, lies the Creole village of **BERMUDIAN LANDING**, a former logging centre dating to the seventeenth century. Buses make the 23-kilometre trip along the Northern Highway from Belize City to the turn-off for the village; see the box on p.86 for more information. Bear in mind that buses returning to Belize City leave Bermudian Landing between 5.30 and 6.30am, and occasionally in the afternoon as well.

On arrival at Bermudian Landing, you'll need to register at the sanctuary's **visitor centre** (daily 8am–5pm; Bz$10; ⓣ220-2181) at the western end of the village. The fee includes a short, guided trail walk and entry to Belize's first natural history museum, inside the centre, with excellent exhibits and information on the riverside habitats and animals you're likely to see. The education centre, at the rear of the visitor centre, has a library, satellite Internet access and a payphone. Sanctuary director Jessie Young, who lives nearby, can advise you on how to get the most out of your visit; her husband Fallet is the sanctuary tour director, and he can arrange longer guided walks, including night hikes (Bz$24), and canoe or horse rental for around Bz$50–55 a day. The visitor centre can also arrange for pickup and drop-off at the international airport for Bz$80, and Belize City for Bz$120.

You can **camp** at the visitor centre (Bz$10 per person), and a number of local families offer **bed-and-breakfast** rooms (❸), a wonderful way to experience village life. Booking ahead can be tricky, as few people have phones (try the community phone on ⓣ209-2001), though you'll always find somewhere to stay if you just turn up, as the visitor centre staff can direct you to rooms. *Nature Resort*, in a wooded field beside the visitor centre (ⓣ610-1378, ⓔnaturer@btl.net; ❹–❻), has several **cabins** (some thatched), most with private hot-water shower, fridge, fan, coffeemaker and hammocks on the porch. It's a great place to relax or follow the trails through the woods and along the river. Nearby lies the *Howler Monkey Lodge* (ⓣ220-2158, ⓦwww.howlermonkeylodge.com; ❸–❺) – spend the night here and chances are you'll be treated to a chorus of guttural howls from the monkeys scampering freely through the trees. That's the main draw, as the grounds sloping down to the river are a bit unkempt, and service can be lacking. The basic cabañas, most with private bath, have wood furnishings and air-conditioning or fan. One of the cabañas has a loft, making it a good fit for families or groups. The lodge also rents canoes and organizes nature treks and other tours.

Run by the village's women's group, the **community restaurant** at the visitor centre serves Creole meals, and there are a couple of other restaurants and **bars** in the village. *Russell's Restaurant*, right in the centre (where one of the buses parks for the night), has tables overlooking the river. *D's Cool Spot*, also in the village centre, serves up basic, local fare, including *panades* (cornmeal stuffed with fish and then fried) and fried chicken.

Rancho Dolores

About 12km west of Bermudian Landing, the village of **Rancho Dolores** is nestled within the nearly six thousand protected acres of the **Spanish Creek Wildlife Sanctuary**. Following the lead of their neighbours in Bermudian Landing, the Rancho Dolores villagers led an effort to protect their creek and surrounding tropical forest, and can offer guided tours and **homestays**. Visitor support, in turn, helps locals maintain the natural environment and support their families. The sanctuary has yet to see many visitors – facilities are minimal and it's far less established than Bermudian Landing – but the future holds promise. Before making the trip out here, it's best to either check in at the Bermudian Landing visitor centre (see p.97) for an update or contact the Spanish Creek Wildlife Sanctuary office (Mon–Fri 8am–5pm; ⓣ220-2191, ⓔspanishcreek@hotmail.com), which sits at the entrance to the sanctuary. Here you'll also find a small museum on the birds and other wildlife of the area.

There are a number of ways to explore the sanctuary: you can journey by dory or canoe along Spanish Creek, looking out for spider monkeys, iguanas, crocodiles and deer along the way, or trek the paths and trails that snake through the forest, where plenty of birds flit through the trees, including the **bare-throated tiger heron**. You can also visit various farms in the area, including a gibnut farm, where the nocturnal rodents (also called agouti) are raised for human consumption. Gibnut, which tastes like pork, is a favourite Belizean dish.

Technically, **buses** do travel to Rancho Dolores from Belize City, though the schedule is erratic and the last portion of road to the sanctuary is unpaved. If you'd like to stay overnight, several families rent out rooms (Bz$10 per person) and there is a basic **campsite** near the river.

Altun Ha

Fifty-five kilometres north of Belize City, and just 9km from the sea, is the impressive Maya site of **Altun Ha** (daily 8am–5pm; Bz$10). With a peak population of about ten thousand, it was occupied for around twelve hundred years until the Classic Maya collapse between 900 and 950 AD. The site was also inhabited at various times during the Postclassic (see p.308), though no new monumental building took place during this period. Its position close to the Caribbean coast suggests that it was sustained as much by trade as by agriculture – a theory upheld by the discovery of trade objects such as jade and obsidian, neither of which occurs naturally in Belize and both very important in Maya ceremony. The jade would have come from the Motagua valley in Guatemala, and much of it would probably have been shipped onwards to the north.

Around five hundred buildings have been recorded at Altun Ha, but the core of the site is clustered around two Classic-period plazas, with the main structures extensively restored, exposing fine stonework with rounded corners. Entering from the road, you come first to **Plaza A**. Large temples enclose it on all four sides, and a magnificent tomb has been discovered beneath Temple A-1, **The Temple of the Green Tomb**. Dating from 550 AD, this yielded a total of three hundred pieces, including jade, jewellery, stingray spines, jaguar skins, flints and the remains of a Maya book. Temple A-6, which has been particularly badly damaged, contains two parallel rooms, each about 48m long and with thirteen doorways along an exterior wall.

The adjacent **Plaza B** is dominated by the site's largest temple, B-4, **The Temple of the Masonry Altars**, the last in a sequence of buildings occupying this spot over the centuries. If its exterior seems familiar, it's because you might already have seen it on the Belikin beer label. The temple was probably the main focus of religious ceremonies, with a single stairway running up the front to an altar at the top; visitors must climb the modern wooden stairway at the side. Several priestly tombs have been uncovered within the main structure, but most of them had already been desecrated, possibly during the political turmoil that preceded the abandonment of the site. Only two of the tombs were found intact; in 1968 archeologists discovered a carved jade head of **Kinich Ahau**, the Maya sun god, in one of them. Standing just under 15cm high, it is the largest carved jade found anywhere in the Maya world. At the moment it's hidden away in the vaults of the Belize Bank, though there is a splendid replica in the Museum of Belize in Belize City (see p.75).

Outside these two main plazas are several other areas of interest that a good guide will point out, though little else has been restored. A short trail through the B Group leads south to **Rockstone Pond**, a literal translation of the Maya name of the site and also the present-day name of a nearby village. The pond was dammed in Maya times to form a reservoir (today it's home to a large crocodile); at the eastern edge stands Structure F-8 (Reservoir Temple), the oldest building at Altun Ha. Built in the second century AD, it housed a cache that contained green obsidian blades and other offerings imported from the great city of Teotihuacán in the Valley of Mexico. These artifacts have been dated to around 150 AD, evidence of early contact between the lowland Maya and Teotihuacán.

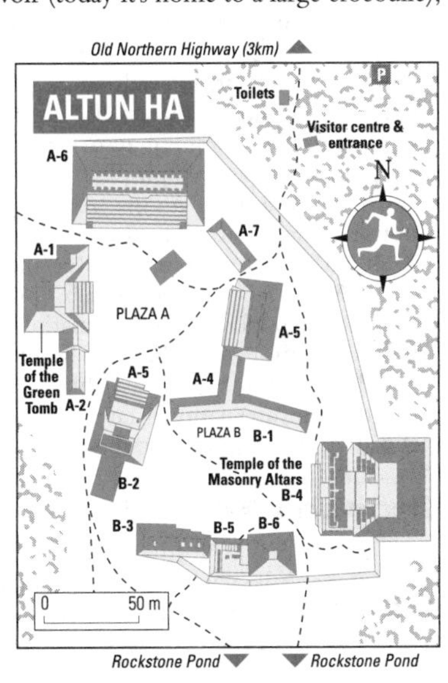

Practicalities

Altun Ha is fairly difficult to reach independently, as the track to the site is located along the Old Northern Highway and is not well served by buses. Any travel agent in Belize City will arrange a tour (see Listings, p.89), and increasing numbers of visitors come on day-trips from San Pedro. In theory there are buses from the terminal in Belize City (see box, p.86) to the village of **MASKALL**, passing the three-kilometre side road to the site from **Lucky Strike**, but the service is erratic and unreliable. You could try to confirm bus times by calling the Maskall community phone (Ⓣ209-1058), though it's usually hard to get through.

The best plan is to **stay nearby** and get to the site before the noise from the tour buses spoils the tranquillity. Despite being a little overpriced, *Pueblo Escondido* at Mile 30.5 of the Old Northern Highway, 3km from the turn-off to the site (Ⓣ614-1458, Ⓦwww.pueblo-escondido.net; ❹, camping Bz$20 per person), is a decent, secure option, with thatched, screen-sided huts and rooms in a main cabin – the owners will sometimes give a discount on a package with meals. They also offer bike rental and **horseback riding** on jungle trails. The name *Pueblo Escondido* is Spanish for "hidden village" (or "hidden people"), and indeed the place feels like a secluded wildlife haven, complete with lagoons where tapirs bathe. You'll have a good chance of seeing otters and foxes – maybe even ocelot or jaguar tracks – and there are always lots of birds.

The best budget accommodation in the area is the simple but welcoming *Silver Fox*, at Mile 38 in Maskall Village (Ⓣ205-5541 or 205-5522, Ⓦwww.silverfoxinbelize.com; ❶–❷), named after a little fox that lives in the grounds. The rooms, which come with a small basket of amenities (toothpaste, baby oil), have clean, shared bathrooms. The ground-floor **restaurant**, open when there are guests, features a local menu built around what the friendly owner decides to cook up that day, perhaps fried fish with rice and beans or lasagne. A continental breakfast is included in the price.

If money's no object, you can submit to the hedonistic (and undoubtedly therapeutic) pleasures at the primitive-meets-posh *Maruba Resort and Jungle Spa*, at Mile 40 near Maskall (Ⓣ225-5555, Ⓦwww.maruba-spa.com; ❾). Each room and suite is luxurious, verging on opulent: think gleaming mahogany ceilings, billowing silks, feather beds and wafting incense, along with hibiscus-strewn, mosaic-tiled bathrooms. What sets the *Maruba* apart from the usual high-end resort – and makes for a memorable and sexy stay – are the quirky, jungle-chic touches: a carved penis for a toilet paper holder in the lobby bathroom, rough-hewn walls studded with glass bottles of Belikin beer and Fanta, palm fronds as placemats. The message is clear: little goes to waste at this largely self-sustaining resort, where the lush, natural surroundings are incorporated whenever possible. With two gorgeous **pools**, piped-in jungle beats filling hideaways on the tropical grounds and a maximum of thirty-plus guests, it's a fabulous place for a romantic getaway. On the purely therapeutic side, you'd need to stay a week to take advantage of all the **spa treatments**; if the "African honey-bee scrub" or "mood mud body wrap" sound too decadent, then perhaps an aromatherapy massage or a "jungle sand scrub" would be more to your liking. The thatched **restaurant**, open to non-guests as well, is surrounded by palms and bougainvillea and serves excellent Belizean and international fare. The resort offers shuttle service to and from Belize City for US$75 round-trip.

Crooked Tree Wildlife Sanctuary

Back on the (new) Northern Highway, roughly midway between Belize City and Orange Walk, you pass the well-signposted branch road heading 5km west to **Crooked Tree Wildlife Sanctuary**, a twelve-square-kilometre reserve encompassing inland waterways, logwood swamps and four separate lagoons. Founded in 1984 by the Belize Audubon Society, it was designated Belize's first Ramsar site (after the Ramsar conference on wetlands in Iran) in 1998, as a "wetland habitat of international importance for waterfowl". It's an ideal nesting and resting place for the sanctuary's greatest treasure: tens of thousands of migrating and resident **birds**, including snail kites, tiger herons, snowy egrets, ospreys and black-collared hawks. Representatives of over three hundred bird species (two-thirds of Belize's total) have been recorded here.

The reserve's most famous visitor is the **jabiru stork**, the largest flying bird in the New World, with a wingspan of 2.5m. Belize has the biggest nesting population of jabiru storks at one site; they arrive in November, the young hatch in April or May, and they leave just before the summer rainy season gets under way. The **best time to visit** is from late February to early June, when the lagoons shrink to a string of pools, forcing wildlife to congregate for food and water. In a good day's birding, you can expect to see up to a hundred species. Visitors are welcome to participate in the May jabiru census; contact the Belize Audubon Society (see p.74) for details. If you set off to explore the lagoons you might also catch a glimpse of howler monkeys, crocodiles, coatis, turtles or iguanas.

Crooked Tree village

In the middle of the reserve, connected to the mainland by a causeway, the village of **CROOKED TREE** straggles over a low island in the wetlands. Over 300 years old, it's the oldest inland community in Belize, with an economy based on fishing, farming and, more recently, tourism. The Bz$8 visitor fee is payable in the **Sanctuary Visitor Centre** (Mon–Sat 8am–5pm, usually closes at noon on Sun), at the far end of the causeway. Inside, an amazing diorama displays fantastically lifelike models of the birds, mammals and insects found at Crooked Tree; there's also a good wildlife reference library with some books for sale. The reserve wardens, Steve and Donald Tillett and Rennie Jones, are excellent guides, hugely knowledgeable about the area's flora, fauna and rural culture. They also have trail maps and give information on accommodation and camping and canoe trips.

Although the main attraction at Crooked Tree – taking guided boat trips on the lagoons and along sluggish, forest-lined creeks – can work out to be quite expensive (upwards of Bz$75 per person, even in a group), it's still worth coming just to enjoy the unbelievably tranquil pace of life in the village. Strolling down the sandy, tree-lined lanes and along the lakeshore trails, you'll see plenty of birds and turtles, and hear frogs croaking languidly from the shallows. Villagers are courteous to strangers, and always have time to chat. **Guides** in the village are supremely knowledgeable, particularly about the many birds you'll encounter in the sanctuary, and impart their expertise with enthusiasm; even the children vie with each other to show off their bird-spotting skills. If you need a guide, ask at the visitor centre or at either of the hotels listed on p.102. Glen Crawford, who started out as a local birding guide, now helps leads tours in the area for Wildside Tours (in the US ⓣ610/564-0941, ⓦwww.adventurecamera.com), a US-based company.

Some of the mango and cashew trees here are over 100 years old, and in January and February the air is heavy with the scent of cashew blossoms. Since 1993 villagers and visitors have celebrated a **Cashew Festival** during the first week of May; though hardly a tradition in itself (it was started by a US tour company), it does highlight the economic importance of the famous nut, and the music, dance, storytelling and crafts offer a glimpse of village traditions and culture.

Practicalities

There are two daily **buses to Crooked Tree** from Belize City; see p.86 in Basics for details. Buses returning to Belize City leave early (Mon–Sat 6.30 & 7am). Phone service in the village is fairly good, with a **payphone** at the visitor centre and several others here and there, including one at *Bird's Eye View Lodge* (see below). A few stores sell basic supplies, including the Jex store, just past the visitor centre, and you'll find a number of quiet, friendly **restaurants** and **bars** in the village – *3 J's* in the centre serves good Creole meals. *Carrie's Kitchen* (Ⓣ205-7076; closed Sun), south of the village on the road (sometimes called Staine Road) behind the community centre, dishes up tasty Creole and Spanish fare, like fried fish, black beans and rice, chicken burritos, *panades* and bread pudding. The amiable restaurant at *Bird's Eye View Lodge* is another good option for local fare.

Accommodation

Crooked Tree offers several comfortable, family-run **bed-and-breakfasts** and simple but clean rooms rented out by locals, including *Rhaburn's Rooms* (Ⓣ225-7035; ❶), which has four simple rooms with fan and shared bath. When entering the village, turn left at the Crooked Tree sign to the Church of the Nazarene, from where *Rhaburn's* is clearly signposted. You can also check at the visitor centre for further accommodation information.

Bird's Eye View Lodge Ⓣ225-7027, Ⓦwww.birdseyeviewbelize.com. After a day of birding, relax at this lakeshore lodge, where you can catch the evening breeze on the upstairs deck and then get a good night's sleep in the comfortable, well-maintained rooms, all of which have a/c and private, hot-water bathroom. Some have lake views; rates are higher for upstairs rooms. The Belizean food is excellent, including a fresh catch of the day and fish balls with onions and black pepper. Finish it off with a glass or two of sweet cashew wine. ❻–❼

Sam Tillett's Hotel Near the village centre on the bus route Ⓣ220-7026 or 663-7497, Ⓔsamhotel@btl.net. Though it's not on the lagoon, it's the best-value hotel in the village, and the garden attracts an amazing variety of birds. Rooms are in a large, thatched cabaña, and have private bath; most have a balcony. More spacious accommodation is available in two comfortable, thatched suites, the wooden "Jacana" and the A-frame "Jabiru", each with a private deck. Sam, known locally as the "king of birds", is a great host. The restaurant serves superb Belizean food. ❹–❻

Around Crooked Tree: Chau Hiix

Visitors to Crooked Tree can benefit from a project promoting birding around the lagoons, carried out nearby by volunteers from two British-based conservation development organizations. An amazing 700-metre **boardwalk**, 3km north of the village, is supported 1.5m above the swamp on strong logwood posts. You'll need to get here by boat most of the year, but in the dry season it's possible to drive. Built in 1997, the walkway allows access through the otherwise impenetrable low forest at the edge of a lagoon, and a seven-metre-high observation tower affords panoramic **views** – a great place to enjoy the sunset.

Chau Hiix ("small cat"), a Maya site on the western shore of the lagoon, has escaped looting and therefore offers potentially enlightening discoveries to the teams currently excavating burials and other relics here. Climbing the nearby **observation tower** (also with a boardwalk), built in 1998 by volunteers from Trekforce Expeditions, will give you a clearer idea of the site, though admittedly much of what you'll see are just great, forested mounds. You'll experience a real thrill of discovery as you wander around the site, particularly if you're with one of the village guides, many of whom have worked on the excavations and can point out recent finds.

Orange Walk

With a population over 20,000, **ORANGE WALK** is the largest town in the north of Belize and the centre of a busy agricultural region. The tranquil, slow-moving **New River**, a few blocks east of the centre, was a heavily used commercial waterway during the logging days, and today provides a lovely starting point for a visit to the ruins of Lamanai, to which several local operators offer tours (see p.108).

Like Corozal to the north, Orange Walk was founded by mestizo refugees fleeing from the Caste Wars in Yucatán in 1849, who chose as their site an area that had long been used for logging camps and was already occupied by the local Icaiché (Chichanha) Maya. From the 1850s to the 1870s, the Icaiché Maya were in conflict with both the Cruzob Maya, who were themselves rebelling against mestizo rule in Yucatán (and supplied with arms by British traders in Belize), and with the British settlers and colonial authorities in Belize. The leader of the Icaiché, **Marcos Canul**, organized successful raids

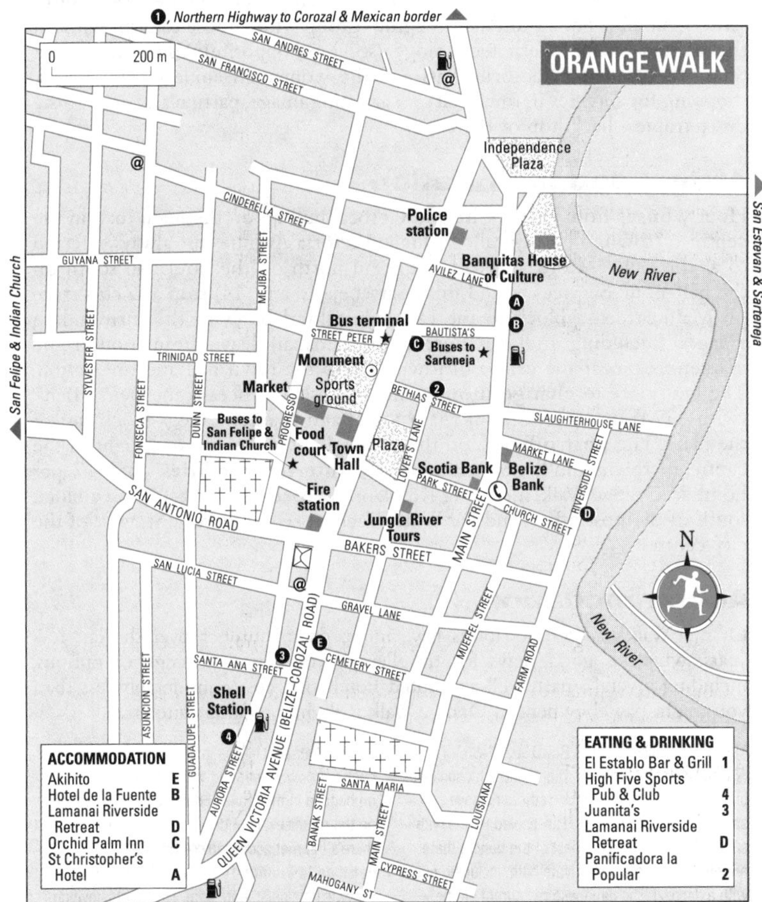

against British mahogany camps, forcing the logging firms to pay "rent" for lands they used, and Canul even briefly occupied Corozal in 1870. In 1872 Canul launched an attack on the barracks in Orange Walk. The West India Regiment, which had earlier retreated in disarray after a skirmish with Canul's troops, this time forced the Icaiché to flee across the Río Hondo, taking the fatally wounded Canul with them. This defeat didn't end the raids, but the Maya ceased to be a threat to British rule in northern Belize; a small monument opposite the park in Orange Walk commemorates the last (officially the only) battle fought on Belizean soil. Nowadays, the few remaining Icaiché Maya live in the village of Botes, on the Mexican border near the Río Hondo.

Orange Walk has traditionally thrived on its crops, first with the growth of the sugar (and the consequent rum distillation) and citrus industries, and after the fall in sugar prices, with profits made from marijuana. In the 1990s, however, pressure from the US government forced Belizean authorities to destroy many of the marijuana fields, and today the town has less of a Wild West atmosphere than it did several years ago. The land around the satellite villages of Blue Creek and Shipyard has been developed by **Mennonite** settlers, members of a Protestant religious group who choose to farm without the assistance of modern technology (see box, opposite). You'll often spot them, the men in wide-brim hats and the women in ankle-length dresses, shopping for supplies in town – it's an arresting image, particularly against the dusty, tropical backdrop of Belize.

Arrival and information

Hourly **buses** from Belize City and Corozal pull up on the main road in the centre of town, officially called Queen Victoria Avenue but always referred to as the Belize–Corozal Road, and head north on the hour and south on the half-hour. Services to and from Sarteneja (see p.114) stop at Zeta's store on Main Street, a block to the east, while local buses to the surrounding villages (including Indian Church, for Lamanai) leave from around the market area, near the centre of town behind the town hall and fire station. The best place to **change money** and get cash advances is the Belize Bank (with ATM) on the corner of Main Street and Market Lane, a block east of the plaza. The **post office** is on the west side of the main road, right in the centre of town. You'll find a number of **Internet facilities** (Bz$4–7 per hour) in Orange Walk, including K&N, on the Belize–Corozal Road a block south of the post office, and Far World Tech, at 65 Cinderella St, west of the city centre.

Accommodation

Orange Walk's accommodations have increased in number over the last few years, which is good news for travellers – you'll find a range of options, including several smart, well-appointed hotels that cost considerably less than you might pay elsewhere, as Orange Walk is slightly off the visitor trail.

Akihito 22 Belize-Corozal Rd ⓣ302-0185, ⓦwww.akihitobelize.com. Bland and a bit soulless, but rooms are clean and the bathrooms have strong hot-water showers. Fan-cooled rooms with shared bath are the cheapest of the bunch; there are others with a/c and private bath, including one with a Jacuzzi. The Japanese restaurant on the ground floor specializes in *shabu shabu*, where you cook your own meat and vegetables on burners embedded in the tables. Fresh noodles are made on the premises. Laundry costs Bz$10 per load and there's Internet access (Bz$4/hr). ❶–❸

Hotel de la Fuente 14 Main St ⓣ322-2290, ⓦwww.hoteldelafuente.com. This bright, inviting hotel has tidy rooms with a/c, cable TV, refrigerator and private hot-water bath, along with thoughtful extras like a coffeemaker with complimentary coffee and a computer desk and chair (though no computer). You'll find a range of rooms, from basic doubles (❸) to larger suites (❺). The wraparound balcony invites kicking back over a cool drink. Friendly owners Orlando and Cyndi de la Fuente can offer lots of tips on exploring the area, including tours to Lamanai. Take their recommendation for breakfast and head to the small *Luigi's* just down the street (20 Main St) for a substantial Belizean spread. Internet access available for guests. ❸–❺

Lamanai Riverside Retreat Lamanai Alley ⓣ302-3955, ⓔlamanairiverside@hotmail.com. This relaxing retreat is one of the few spots that takes full advantage of Orange Walk's prime perch on the New River. The three wooden cabañas, with a/c and hot-water bath, are simple, but it's the lush outdoors that you're here for: wake up to birds chirping and the gentle rush of the river, followed by a tasty breakfast served on the open-air deck of the restaurant (see p.106). Owner Raul Pelayo, a long-time wildlife advocate, is a consummate croc-spotter – follow his lead and keep your eyes peeled for telltale splashes on the river. He can arrange trips down the New River to Lamanai with Jungle River Tours (see p.110). Internet available for guests. ❹

Orchid Palm Inn Belize-Corozal Rd ⓣ322-0719, ⓦwww.orchidpalminn.com. This aptly named inn pays homage to its elegant namesake throughout, from the carefully tended garden to the glossy colour photos – taken by the owners' daughter – that hang in the spic-and-span rooms, all of which are outfitted with teak furnishings from Stann Creek. You'll find all the amenities, and then some: a/c, cable TV, coffeemaker, refrigerator and microwave. One room is wheelchair-accessible. ❹–❺

St Christopher's Hotel 10 Main St ⓣ322-2420, ⓦwww.stchristophershotelbze.com. Plain but clean rooms with sturdy, wooden furnishings, all with private bath and most with access to a balcony; some have a/c and fridge. The colourfully painted hotel, set on grounds sweeping down to the river, is run by the friendly Urbina family, who can arrange for tours to Lamanai departing from the hotel dock. Plenty of secure parking for guests with vehicles. Internet is Bz$4/hour. ❸–❹

Mennonites in Belize

The **Mennonites** arose from the radical Anabaptist movement of the sixteenth century and are named after the Dutch priest Menno Simons, leader of the community in its formative years. Recurring government restrictions on their lifestyle, especially regarding their pacifist objection to military service, forced them to move repeatedly. Having removed to Switzerland, they travelled on to Prussia, then in 1663 to Russia, until the government revoked their exemption from military service, whereupon some groups emigrated to North America, settling in the prairies of Saskatchewan. World War I brought more government restrictions, this time on the teaching of German (the Mennonites' language). This, together with the prospect of conscription and more widespread anti-German sentiments in the Dominion of Canada, drove them from Canada to Mexico, where they settled in the arid, northern state of Chihuahua. When the Mexican government required them to be included in its social security programme, it was time to move on again. An investigation into the possibility of settling on their own land in British Honduras brought them to the British colony of **Belize** in 1958.

They were welcomed enthusiastically by the colonial authorities, who were eager to have willing workers to clear the jungle for agriculture. Perseverance and hard work made them successful farmers, and in recent years prosperity has caused drastic changes in their lives. The Mennonite Church in Belize is increasingly split between the *Kleine Gemeinde* – a modernist section that uses electricity and power tools, and drives trucks, tractors and even cars – and the *Altkolonier* – traditionalists who prefer a stricter expression of their beliefs. Members of the community, easily recognizable in their denim dungarees and straw hats, can be seen trading their produce and buying supplies every day in Orange Walk and Belize City.

△ Mennonite boys near Lamanai

The Town

Orange Walk centres around a distinctly Mexican-style, formal plaza, shaded by large trees, and the town hall across the main road is called the Palacio Municipal, reinforcing the strong historic links to Mexico. The town isn't heavy on sights, but, on the riverbank just north of the centre, it does feature the **Banquitas House of Culture** (Mon–Fri 8.30am–5.30pm; free), a well-run museum and cultural centre overseen by the National Institute of Culture and History. The *banquitas* in the name refer to the little benches in a riverbank park, used for generations by courting couples and for simply relaxing on warm evenings. There's still a leafy park here, now with an amphitheatre for outdoor performances, but the highlights are in the main building, a renovated former market. The one-room permanent exhibition charts the history of Orange Walk District from Maya times to the present. Glass cases contain artifacts from local Maya sites, along with maps and drawings of the sites themselves. Other panels display archival materials documenting the stories of logwood, mahogany and chicle, which tell of the boom-and-bust cycles of extracting natural resources. Banquitas also hosts musical events and art exhibitions that include paintings, wood carvings and photo essays of daily life in Orange Walk.

Eating and drinking

Many of the **restaurants** in and around Orange Walk serve Mexican-influenced Creole fare. *Juanita's*, on Santa Ana Street by the Shell station towards the south end of town, serves up delicious Mexican dishes. Try *pan dulces* (sweet bread and pastries) and fresh bread at *Panificadora la Popular*, on Bethias Street, off the northeast side of the plaza. Behind the town hall, near the market, is the bustling **food court** (usually open daily until mid-afternoon), where you can graze cheaply on Mexican treats, from tacos to enchiladas. For outdoor dining, stroll over to the *Lamanai Riverside Retreat* (see p.105), where you can sip Belikin beer and savour local dishes – pork *salpicón*, conch salad – on an airy wooden deck overlooking the New River. In Indian Hill, three kilometres north of Orange Walk on the Northern Highway, the thatched-roofed ★ *El Establo Bar & Grill*

(☎322-0094; closed Mon) is run by a welcoming couple serving delicious Mexican-Belizean cuisine. The cosy dining room houses a collection of antiques – old steam irons, two-man logwood cutters – and the menu features spicy beef and chicken fajitas, *salpicón*, excellent *escabeche* and *relleno*, a black, annatto-based soup with chicken and ground pork. On the weekends, the owners fire up the brick grill.

As for **nightlife**, you'll find a sprinkling of bars dotted around town, though several serve as brothels and are packed to the rafters with hard-drinking local guys. A better bet is the *High Five Sports Pub & Club*, at 8 Aurora, just south of the Shell Station (☎322-0552). The pub has pool tables, TVs blaring sports events and pub grub – buffalo wings and burgers – to go with it. The adjoining club, with a lounge and dancefloor and occasional live music, sometimes revs up on the weekends until 3am. It's also worth checking if there's an event or performance at the House of Culture.

Maya sites around Orange Walk

Although the Maya sites in northern Belize (with the notable exception of Lamanai) are not as monumentally spectacular as those in Yucatán, they have been the source of some of the most important archeological finds anywhere in the Maya world. The area around Orange Walk has some of the most productive farmland in Belize, and this was also the case in Maya times; aerial surveys in the late 1970s revealed evidence of raised fields and a network of **irrigation canals**, showing that the Maya practised skilful, intensive agriculture. In the Postclassic era, this region became part of the powerful Maya state of Chactemal (or Chetumal), controlling the trade in cacao beans, which were used as currency and grown in the valleys of the Hondo and New rivers. For a while the Maya here were even able to resist the conquistadores, and long after nominal Spanish rule had been established in 1544, there were frequent Maya rebellions: in 1638, for example, they drove the Spanish out and burned the church at Lamanai.

Cuello and Nohmul

Cuello is a small Maya site 5km west of Orange Walk. It was excavated in 1973 by Norman Hammond, who found structures dating back to 1000 BC, making it one of the earliest sites from the Middle Preclassic Maya lowlands. That said, the site is more interesting to archeologists than the casual visitor; there's not much to look at except for a single small, stepped pyramid (Structure 350), rising in nine tiers – a common feature of Maya temples – and several earth-covered mounds.

The ruins are behind a factory where **Cuello rum** is made, and the site is on the Cuello family's land, so you should ask permission to visit by phoning ☎322-2141. Tours of the distillery are given on request. You can reach Cuello from Orange Walk by simply walking west from the town plaza for a little under an hour; a taxi to the site costs around Bz$15 each way.

A rather more arresting Maya site is **Nohmul** ("great mound"), situated on the boundary with Corozal District, 17km north of Orange Walk. It was a major ceremonial centre with origins in the Middle Preclassic period, but was abandoned before the end of the Classic and subsequently reoccupied by newcomers from Yucatán during the Early Postclassic (known here as the Tecep phase, around 800–1000 AD). The ruins cover a large area, comprising the East and West groups connected by a *sacbe* (causeway), with several plazas around them. The main feature is an acropolis platform (Structure 2) surmounted by a later pyramid, which, owing to the site's position on a limestone ridge, is the highest point for miles around. As at so many of Belize's Maya sites, looters have plundered the ruins and, tragically, at least one structure has been demolished for road fill – though as it's one of the sites earmarked for tourism, some structural restoration has taken place.

Nohmul lies amid sugarcane fields 2km west of **San Pablo**, on the Northern Highway. Any bus between Corozal and Orange Walk passes through the village. To visit the site, ask around the village for Estevan Itzab, who owns the land it's on and lives in the house on the west side of the highway, across from the water tower at the north end of the village; his son Guillermo will probably be your guide.

Lamanai

Extensive restoration of the ancient structures and a spacious museum make **Lamanai** (Mon–Fri 8am–5pm, Sat, Sun & holidays 8am–4pm; Bz$10) undoubtedly the most impressive Maya site in northern Belize. It's one of only a few sites whose original Maya name – *Lama'an ayin* – is known; it translates to "submerged crocodile", which explains the numerous representations of crocodiles among the ruins. "Lamanai", however, is a seventeenth-century mistransliteration that actually means "drowned insect". The site was continuously occupied from around 1500 BC until the sixteenth century, when Spanish missionaries built a church next door to lure the Indians from their "heathen" ways.

More than seven hundred structures have been mapped by members of the Lamanai Archeological Project, the majority of them still buried beneath mounds of earth, and the site extends far north and south of the restored area. Research is undertaken every year here, and you can join in the excavations, supervised by the nonprofit **Lamanai Field Research Center** (LFRC; Ⓦwww.lamanai.org). Since students stay at *Lamanai Outpost Lodge* (see p.111), these courses work out to around US$2200 for four weeks. The LFRC also arranges courses at the Las Cuevas Research Station in the Chiquibul Forest (see p.186).

The site

Lamanai's setting on the shore of the New River Lagoon, in an isolated swath of jungle protected as an archeological reserve, gives it a special serenity that is long gone from sites served by the torrent of tourist buses – though increasing numbers of speedboats now carry cruise ship visitors here. Over a dozen troops of black howler monkeys make Lamanai their home, and you'll certainly see them peering down through the branches as you wander the trails; mosquitoes too, are ever-present, so you'll need to be armed with a good **repellent**. Many trees and other plants bear name labels in English, Creole and Maya, and your guide will explain what the ancient Maya used them for.

The most impressive feature at Lamanai, prosaically named N10-43 (informally called the "High Temple", or "El Castillo", the castle), is a massive, Late Preclassic **temple**, towering 35m above the forest floor. When it was first built around 100 BC, it was the largest structure in the entire Maya world, though one which was extensively modified later. The view over the surrounding forest and along the lagoon from the top of the temple is magnificent and well worth the daunting climb. On the way to the High Temple you pass N10-27, a much smaller pyramid, at the base of which

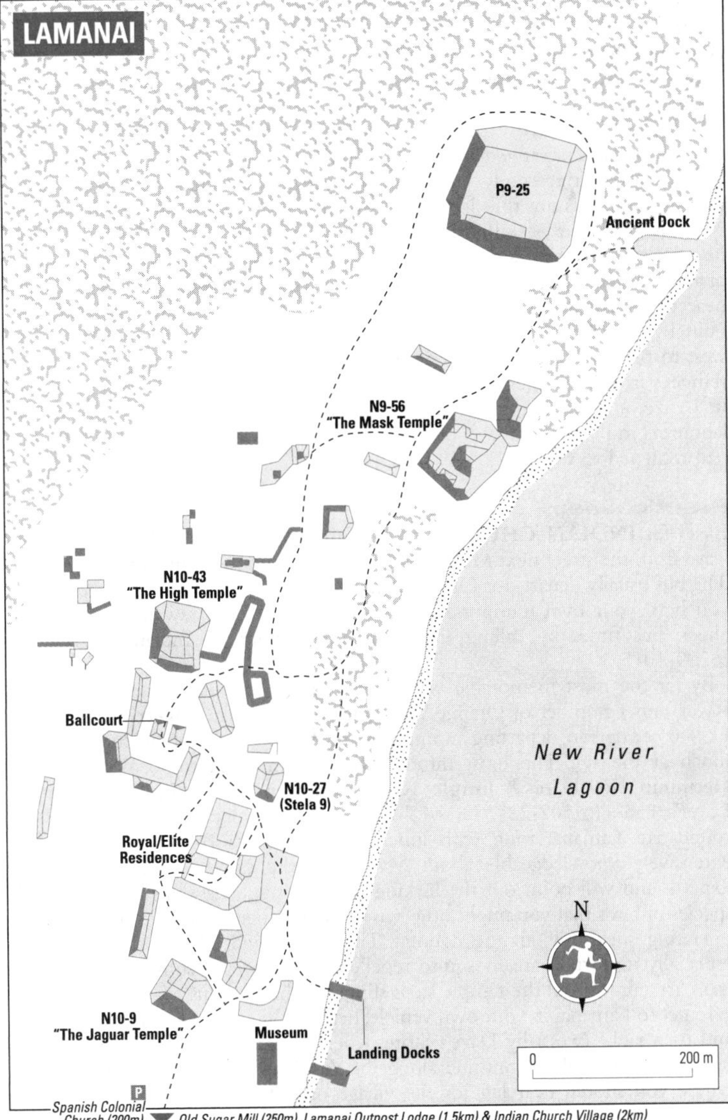

stands a fibreglass replica of **Stela 9**, which bears some of the best-preserved carvings at Lamanai. Dated to 625 AD, it shows the magnificently attired Lord Smoking Shell participating in a ceremony – probably his accession. This glyph has become emblematic of Lamanai and features on many of the T-shirts on sale here. North of the High Temple, structure N9-56 is a sixth-century pyramid with two stucco masks of a glorified ruler, represented as a deity (probably Kinich Ahau, the sun god), carved on different levels. The lower mask, 4m high, has survived especially well, and shows a clearly humanized face wearing a crocodile headdress and bordered by decorative columns. The temple overlies several smaller buildings, the oldest of which is a superbly preserved temple from around 100 BC, and there are a number of other clearly defined glyphs throughout.

The spacious **archeological museum** at the site houses an amazing collection of artifacts, arranged in chronological order; the majority of these are figurines depicting gods and animals, particularly crocodiles. The most beautiful exhibits are the delicate eccentric flints – star- and sceptre-shaped symbols of office – skilfully chipped from a single piece of stone. More unusual items include a drum the size and shape of a pair of binoculars and a phallus carved from a manatee bone. Traces of later settlers can also be seen near the museum: immediately to the south are the ruins of two churches built by Spanish missionaries, while a short trail behind the building leads west to the remains of a nineteenth-century sugar mill, built by Confederate refugees from the American Civil War. These refugees settled in several places in Belize, in an attempt to recreate the antebellum South using indentured labourers in place of slaves – but their effort failed, and within a decade most had returned to the States.

Practicalities

Buses for **INDIAN CHURCH**, 2km from the site (Mon & Fri 4pm; Bz$5), leave from the street next to the market, behind the town hall, in Orange Walk. The bus usually departs for Orange Walk at 5.30am on the same days, so, unless you have your own transportation, you'll have to stay a few nights. You can check bus times by calling the community phone in Indian Church on ⓣ309-1015.

By far the most memorable way to journey to Lamanai is along the New River, and a number of Orange Walk operators organize **day-trips** for about US$40 per person, departing around 9am; the price will usually include a picnic lunch at the site. The most informative are run by Antonio, Wilfrido and Herminio Novelo of **Jungle River Tours**, in the centre of town at 20 Lover's Lane (ⓣ302-2293 or 615-1712, ⓔlamanaimayatour@btl.net). Their round-trip Lamanai tour, with lunch included, costs Bz$80. Besides being extensively knowledgeable about Maya sites, the Novelos are also wildlife experts, and will point out the lurking crocodiles, iguanas, bats and dozens of species of birds that you might otherwise miss. The boat also floats past the only operating sugar mill in the country. The guides will advise what to bring; especially important are mosquito repellent and a pair of sturdy shoes, as the trails are muddy and the temple steps slippery when it rains.

To get to Lamanai in your own vehicle, head to the south end of Orange Walk and turn right (west) by Dave's Store, where a signpost gives the distance to Lamanai as 35 miles. Continue along the Yo Creek road as far as San Felipe, where you should bear left for the village of Indian Church, 2km from the ruins. If, for some reason, you decide to fly to Lamanai, *Lamanai Outpost Lodge* has a private **airstrip** (see opposite), and Tropic Air (ⓣ224-5671) offers flights if there's sufficient demand.

Staying in Indian Church on a budget is not especially convenient, but it enables you to visit Lamanai in the quieter times, as soon as it opens and after the crowds have left. If you're travelling here by bus, you won't have a choice anyway. The couple of places offering **rooms** (❸) are rather overpriced for what you get; you could also try asking in the Artisan Center, where you can see villagers making attractive jewellery and other craft items, if someone can rent you a room or let you **camp**. In either case you'll be invited to eat with the family.

Excellent **upmarket accommodation** is available nearby in the well-run and very comfortable thatched cabañas at *Lamanai Outpost Lodge* (Ⓣ672-2000, Ⓦwww.lamanai.com; ⑨), set in extensive gardens sweeping down to the lagoon just south of the site. Each cabaña has 24-hour electricity, hot water and a private deck; guests enjoy free **Internet** access in the dining room lobby, where there's also a small library. The restaurant, *Bushey's Place*, serves fantastic meals and has a wooden deck overlooking the lagoon. Guests can use the free canoes, take a "spotlight safari" (US$49) to spot nocturnal wildlife or go sunrise canoeing ($29); guides here are some of the best in Belize and the lagoon offers superb birding.

The Rio Bravo Conservation and Management Area

In the far northwest of Orange Walk District is the **Rio Bravo Conservation and Management Area**, an enormous tract of land designated for tropical forest conservation, research and sustainable-yield forest harvests. This astonishing conservation success story actually began with a disastrous plan in the mid-1980s to clear the forest, initially to fuel a wood-fired power station and later to provide Coca-Cola with frost-free land to grow citrus crops. Environmentalists were alarmed, and their strenuous objections forced Coca-Cola to drop the plan, though the forest remained threatened by agriculture.

Following this, a project to save the forest by purchasing it – known as the **Programme for Belize (PFB)** – was initiated by the Massachusetts Audubon Society and launched in 1988. Funds were raised from corporate donors and conservation organizations, but the most widespread support was generated through an ambitious "adopt-an-acre" scheme, enthusiastically taken up by schools and individuals in the UK and North America. Coca-Cola itself, anxious to distance the company from charges of rainforest destruction, donated more than 360 square kilometres of land it owned on the perimeter of the conservation area.

Today, rangers with powers of arrest patrol the area to prevent illegal logging and to stop farmers from encroaching onto the reserve with their *milpas* (slash-and-burn maize fields). The guarded boundaries also protect dozens of Maya sites, most of them unexcavated and unrestored, though many have been looted.

The **landscape** ranges from forest-covered, limestone escarpments in the northwest, near the Guatemalan border, to palmetto savannah, pine ridge and swamp in the southeast, around the New River Lagoon. Crossing through the middle of the region are several river valleys. The Rio Bravo area has 240 endemic tree species, and the forest teems with **wildlife**: no fewer than seventy mammal species, including tapirs, monkeys and all five of Belize's large cats, as well as four hundred bird species – almost ninety percent of the country's total. The strict ban on hunting, enforced for nearly twenty years now, makes this the best place in Belize to see these beasts; even pumas and jaguars, extremely reclusive creatures, are spotted fairly frequently. Wildlife-viewing is also excellent in the protected territory around **Gallon Jug**, a private estate to the south of the Rio Bravo area that's home to the fabulous *Chan Chich Lodge* (see opposite), regarded as one of the finest eco-lodges in the world and an incredibly beautiful place to stay.

There's no public transport to the Rio Bravo Conservation and Management Area, but if you want to visit or stay at either of the **field stations**, see below; for more information, see the PFB entry in Contexts on p.350. Getting here from Orange Walk means you have to pass through the modern Mennonite settlement of **Blue Creek**, high up on the Río Bravo escarpment, where you'll find one of the most astonishing artifacts in Belize: the fuselage (and more) of a **Super Constellation**, the world's first real airliner. On the Constellation's last flight from Mexico to Guatemala City, in the mid-1970s, it first lost a propeller before its two other engines cut out. The pilot attempted an emergency landing in Belize City, but on the final approach the port undercarriage failed to operate and the aircraft skidded off the runway. Luckily, no passengers were on board, and all three crew members survived. If you're an aviation buff, call in at Abe Dyck's house, next to the remains of the airliner, and he'll show you around and fill you in on the rest of the details, such as how the pieces reached their current resting spot.

In the valley below Blue Creek, the Río Hondo forms the boundary with Mexico. The border crossing here is usually only for use by Belizeans, who pole canoes over to the Mexican village of **La Unión**, where a brisk trade in cigarettes and beer fuels the local economy. The customs post won't stop you from strolling down to the riverbank and joining in the negotiations, though without pesos you won't find much available.

La Milpa and Hill Bank field stations

One of the aims of the PFB is environmental education; as such, **field stations** have been built at **La Milpa** and **Hill Bank** to accommodate both visitors and students. Both are quite difficult to get to, but you could visit either on a day-trip with your own vehicle, or you might be able to get a ride in with a ranger or other staff; see below for contact details.

Each field station has comfortable (though expensive) **dorms** (US$44 per person), facilities that utilize the latest green technology, including solar power and composting toilets, and a natural history library. Both sites also have lovely, thatched **cabañas** with private bath and a loft bedroom (sleep 4–6 people; US$55 per person, excluding meals and guided tours; discounts for student groups). With three meals and two excursions or lectures a day, it's roughly US$140 per person. To visit or stay at either station, contact the appropriate station manager (Ramon Pacheco at La Milpa, Efrain Cocom at Hill Bank) through the PFB office, 1 Eyre St, Belize City (Ⓣ227-5616, Ⓕ227-5635, Ⓔpfbel@btl.net, Ⓦwww.pfbelize.org), who will arrange transport.

La Milpa: the field station and Maya site

Set in a former *milpa* clearing in the higher, northwestern forest, **La Milpa Field Station** has a tranquil, studious atmosphere; deer and ocellated turkeys feed contentedly around the cabins, grey foxes slip silently through the long grass and vultures circle lazily overhead. There are binoculars and telescopes for spotting birds and you'll see turtles from the boardwalk bridge over the pond. Guests are mainly students on tropical ecology courses, though anyone is welcome to stay. A day-visit to the field station, which includes a guided tour of La Milpa ruins or one of the trails, costs US$20, but getting here on public transport is not easy: you'll have to catch a bus from Orange Walk to San Felipe,

Belize's reef and cayes

One of the most amazing and colourful ecosystems on earth, the Belize Barrier Reef is the longest in the Americas – a complex, living wall stretching nearly three hundred kilometres from just south of Cancún, Mexico down the entire coastline of Belize. The ocean here provides a firm floor, warm, shallow, unpolluted water and strong sunlight, all essential ingredients for coral growth, which happens gradually over thousands of years. Small sections of the reef are protected as World Heritage Sites, and many local reserves help to nurture this fragile and important environment, which in turn supports an array of land and sea habitats. Belize's cayes (pronounced "keys"), integral parts of the reef system, provide dry land for human settlements and bases for responsible, water-based recreation.

▲ Queen angelfish

Denizens of the sea

The reef is an underwater wilderness populated by creatures ranging in size from the practically microscopic to just plain enormous. Some of the tiniest organisms are the individual units of the reef itself: billions of **coral polyps**, most in the family of "hard" or "stony" corals, that come in an array of electric colours. "Soft" corals, such as gracefully wafting **sea fans** and stinging **fire corals**, are also integrated into the reef's structure.

Swarming around the coral are over four hundred species of **fish**, several playing important roles in the health of the ecosystem. **Cleaner wrasse** feed on the parasites of

Exploring the atolls

An **atoll** is a ring of coral reef enclosing a sheltered lagoon and often providing the foundation for a cluster of islands. There are four such formations in the Caribbean Sea, and Belizean waters contain **three** of them:

Lighthouse Reef: Belize's easternmost atoll, it surrounds the famous Blue Hole, best appreciated from the air but also a popular dive site. On the atoll's southeast edge is Half Moon Caye Natural Monument, the country's first marine conservation area and the site of a shipwreck and a protected colony of red-footed boobies. See p.156.

Turneffe Islands: Considered by some to be the most biologically diverse region in the Caribbean, these largely unsettled isles support many fish and crocodile nurseries as well as opportunities for snorkelling, diving and some of Belize's best fly-fishing. See p.155.

Glover's Reef: South of Lighthouse and Turneffe, the smallest and least accessible of Belize's atolls is a World Heritage Site with incredible diving and snorkelling and hundreds of marine species to admire. Sea kayaking between the atoll's islands, either solo or as part of a biologist-led expedition, is a popular pastime here. See p.258.

Caye carnivores

Belize is home to two dolphin species: the **spotted dolphin**, which lives beyond the reef and often frolics alongside boats to the outer atolls, and the more restrained **bottlenose**, larger in size but usually seen in smaller pods between the reef and land. Several species of large **shark** – including tiger, bull, lemon and hammerhead – patrol the outer Belizean waters, although the harmless **nurse shark** is usually the only one found within the reef. On full-moon nights between April and June, majestic and docile **whale sharks** congregate to feast on snapper eggs at Gladden Spit, offshore from Placencia; trips here can be arranged (see p.275).

larger species, and **butterfly fish** regulate algae build-up on the reef. Most reef fish also spend time among the mangrove roots on the edges of the cayes, where they lay their eggs and seek shelter from storms and predators.

Sometimes spotted within the reef, but more often in calm lagoons or just offshore, the **West Indian manatee** is a compelling aquatic creature distantly related to the elephant. Manatees are **endangered** around the world, but activists here are working hard to save them; in fact, Belize's manatee population is the largest in the region. The protected reserve of **Swallow Caye** and the Southern Lagoon at **Gales Point** offer the best chances to see them year-round, though entering the water is prohibited.

Protect and preserve

Despite Belize's herculean efforts to safeguard its natural treasures, the country's growing attraction as a tourist destination is forever altering the reef and cayes. Countless **conservationists** are working to ensure that tourism does not destroy the very environment it is dependent on, but, as the demand for infrastructure grows and developers cut down the mangroves to make room for resorts, a vital part of a vast ecosystem is being levelled.

Large swaths of reef have fallen victim to **coral bleaching**, caused by rising ocean temperatures linked to **global warming**. This bleaching is occurring around the world, leading some scientists to predict that reefs may disappear entirely within the next few decades. You can **do your part** by not causing immediate damage to the reef by touching or accidentally kicking it while you dive or snorkel; see p.128 for tips on proper reef etiquette.

▲ Sea kayakers at Tobacco Caye

Get wet

The best way to appreciate the amazing variety of marine life in Belize is in a bathing suit. **Diving** and **snorkelling trips** abound in the coastal communities, although the best tours can be found on the cayes, notably Ambergris Caye and Caye Caulker. Some of the southern cayes are so close to the reef that you can swim right out to it, though to do this you'll often have to stay at an exclusive – and expensive – **resort**.

You'll find plenty of above-water activities to enjoy, too. Belize's shallow seas and pleasant climate make for excellent **sailing** in either the shelter of the reef or the deeper water beyond. Since the reef rises to just below the surface in many places and charts can be sketchy, even veteran sailors should seek local expertise. **Skippered sailing tours** are available from several cayes and coastal towns.

Experienced (or would-be) **windsurfers** will have no problem finding rentals and lessons in either San Pedro or Caye Caulker. **Sea kayaking** is popular wherever there's water in Belize – in fact, the fishermen who ply the country's coastal and inland waterways have always used agile, kayak-like boats. All coastal resorts offer kayak rental, and many have organized tours.

For visitors who like to have something to show for their efforts (either in a photo or on a plate), all types of saltwater **fishing** trips are possible. Dedicated fishing lodges on the cayes attract anglers with all-inclusive packages, and local day-trips can be arranged virtually anywhere. Sand flats are the perfect, year-round locale for catch-and-release fly-fishing, and there's excellent deep-water fishing further offshore.

▼ Windsurfing off Caye Caulker

37km away, and arrange to be picked up there – the PFB office will give details. To get here in your own vehicle, take the road west from Orange Walk via San Felipe to the Mennonite village of Blue Creek. Beyond there the road is paved and in good condition, climbing steeply up the Río Bravo escarpment, then turning south to the field station and Gallon Jug. Charter flights use the airstrips at Blue Creek and Gallon Jug.

Five kilometres west of the field station is the huge, Classic-period **Maya city of La Milpa**, the third largest archeological site in Belize. After centuries of expansion, La Milpa was abandoned in the ninth century, though Postclassic groups subsequently occupied the site and the Maya here resisted both the Spanish conquest in the sixteenth century and British mahogany cutters in the nineteenth. Recent finds include major elite burials with many jade grave goods. The **ceremonial centre**, built on top of a limestone ridge, is one of the most impressive anywhere, with at least 24 courtyards and two ball-courts. The site also contains one of the largest public spaces in the Maya world: the **Great Plaza**, flanked by four temple-pyramids. The tallest structure in the group, the **Great Temple**, rises 24m above the plaza floor, and you can climb its steep, rocky face using roots for handholds and a rope for support. Beyond here are some of the site's *chultunes* – cave-like, underground chambers carved out of stone. For a unique perspective on a *chultun*, you can enter one through a collapsed side, view the tightly fitting capstone (similar to a manhole cover) from beneath and ponder what the ancient Maya used these spaces for.

Hill Bank Field Station

At the southern end of the New River Lagoon and 70km west of Belize City, **Hill Bank Field Station** is a former logging camp that has been adapted to undertake scientific forestry research and development. The emphasis here is more on extractive forest use, with the aim of revenue generation on a sustainable basis. Selective logging is allowed on carefully monitored plots, chicle is harvested from sapodilla trees and there's a tree nursery. These and other projects are at the cutting edge of tropical forest management, and there are often students and scientists working here. There's plenty of wildlife too, particularly birds and crocodiles, and butterflies abound. The **dorms** here (identical to those at La Milpa, opposite) have a screened veranda with table and chairs overlooking the lagoon, and there are also **cabañas**. For an even better view, climb the twelve-metre fire tower nearby.

There's **no public transport** to Hill Bank, but with your own vehicle you can get here by following the road west and north from Bermudian Landing (see p.97). It's also possible to approach Hill Bank from Lamanai, by boat along the New River Lagoon.

Gallon Jug and Chan Chich Lodge

Forty kilometres south of La Milpa Field Station, the former logging town of **GALLON JUG**, set in neat, fenced pastures, is today the private property of Barry Bowen, reportedly the richest Belizean. In the 1980s, his speculative land deals led to international outcry against threatened rainforest clearance. The experience apparently had a powerful effect upon Bowen, who is now an ardent conservationist, and most of the 500 square kilometres on his estate are strictly protected. Around twenty square kilometres of Gallon Jug are still under cultivation and produce the excellent coffee served at the luxurious, world-class **Chan Chich Lodge** (Ⓣ223-4419, in US Ⓣ1-800/343-8009, Ⓦwww.chanchich.com; ⑨), the focal point of the estate. The lodge, which regularly wins awards in the travel press, consists of twelve large, thatched cabañas (US$250) and suites (US$280), each with lovely verandas and hammocks, set in the grassy plaza of the Classic Maya site of Chan Chich ("little bird"). It's surrounded by superb forest and there's a refreshing, fully screened pool, complete with waterfall. Activities abound, from horseback riding through the jungle, canoeing on Laguna Verde and some of the best birding in Belize.

The construction of the lodge on this spot was controversial at the time (all Maya sites are technically under government control), but it received Archeology Department approval once its intent to cause minimal disturbance became clear. Certainly the year-round presence of visitors and staff does prevent looting, which has been a real problem in the past. It is a truly awe-inspiring setting: grass-covered temple walls, crowned with jungle, tower up from the lodge and the forest explodes with a cacophony of birdcalls at dawn. The 14km of **guided trails** are incomparable and the guides excellent; day and night wildlife sightings are consistently high, with around seventy jaguar sightings per year, half of them during daylight. You can drive here from Orange Walk (through Blue Creek and La Milpa), but most guests fly in to the airstrip at Gallon Jug; Javier's Flying Service (☎224-5332) has three scheduled flights a week from Belize's international or municipal airports.

Sarteneja and Shipstern Nature Reserve

The **Sarteneja peninsula**, jutting out towards the Yucatán in the northeast of Belize, is covered with dense forests, swamps and lagoons that support an amazing array of wildlife. Though the area is largely unpopulated and could once be reached only by boat, the lobster-fishing village of **Sarteneja**, the peninsula's main settlement, is beginning to attract tourism. Sarteneja and the shoreline are pretty enough, but the region's main attraction is **Shipstern Nature Reserve**, on the road 5km before the village.

Sarteneja

SARTENEJA, from Tzaten-a-ha (meaning "water among the rocks"), was largely settled in 1854 by refugees from the Caste Wars of Yucatán. Due to its historic isolation from the rest of Belize, it still retains close ties to **Mexico** – its inhabitants are primarily Spanish-speaking mestizos – which locals can easily reach by boat, though such services are currently not offered to tourists.

It's relatively easy to get here **by bus from Belize City** (see p.86). Buses pass through Orange Walk ninety minutes after departure, stopping at Zeta's store on Main Street, where the bus crew takes a break, and it's a further ninety minutes to Sarteneja. Buses returning to Belize City leave Sarteneja at 4.30, 5.30 and 6.30am, and a service from Chetumal passes through shortly after 6am. The *Thunderbolt*, a **skiff** running between Corozal and San Pedro on Ambergris Caye, stops at Sarteneja if there's sufficient demand (call ☎226-2904 to check); the dock is near the village centre. There's also a small airstrip, where Tropic Air **flights** between Corozal and San Pedro will stop on request (☎226-2012). If arriving by plane, arrange a pickup by your guest house in advance, as there are no taxis from the airstrip and the road into the village is long and rough.

Despite its remote location, the village is gearing up for an influx of visitors. There are several guest houses, and a number of bars and **restaurants** provide decent sustenance, among them Richie's, in the village centre (Ⓣ423-2031; 7am–9pm or later), offering fast food and homemade ice cream, and Lily's, at the eastern end of the village (no phone), serving Belizean staples. A group of enterprising residents has formed the Sarteneja Wildlife, Environmental and Ecotourism Team (SWEET), which works to promote sustainable tourism in the area through educational programs. As fish stocks decline, they're training local fishermen to be tour guides, and supporting the protection of sea creatures in the **Corozal Bay Wildlife Sanctuary**. SWEET's office, at the eastern end of North Front Street (daily 9am–12pm & 1pm–5pm; Ⓣ670-1793/6625), can fill you in on regional history and tours, and has an **Internet** café.

Accommodation

Sarteneja has a small but adequate choice of accommodation, given its size, and most places will serve meals if asked in advance.

Candelie's Sunset Cabañas and Bahia Verde Dinette Next to Krisami's Ⓣ423-2005, Ⓔcandeliescabanas@yahoo.com. Run by the same family that owns Krisami's, these two large cabañas, each with two double beds, cable TV and a/c, also have netted porches. The dinette serves meals on advance request, and on one wall displays a large mural, painted by local artist Eluterio Carillo, showing the village's history. The owners can arrange fishing and birding trips, as well as tours around the village and Bacalar Chico National Park and Marine Reserve (see p.141). ❹–❻

Fernando's Guesthouse Toward the western end of North Front Street Ⓣ423-2085, Ⓔsartenejabelize@hotmail.com. Sarteneja's original guest house offers comfortable rooms with private bath. With two hours' advance notice, meals are available to guests and non-guests alike, and you can also exchange money and arrange local tours (including to Bacalar Chico) here. ❹

Krisami's Bayview Lodge At the western end of the village Ⓣ670-3487, Ⓦwww.krisamis.com. Roomy quarters with private bath, cable TV, and wireless Internet. ❻

Oasis Guesthouse One block back from North Front Street, west of Fernando's Ⓣ403-2121 or 660-9621. Four large, breezy rooms with private shower and two double beds. ❸–❹

Shipstern Nature Reserve

Established in 1981, the unique **Shipstern Nature Reserve** (daily 8am–4pm; Bz$15; Ⓣ223-3271, Ⓦwww.shipstern.org) – named for an unexcavated Maya centre in its forested depths – crosses two biogeographical regions and is home to countless species, some found only in Belize. Its approximately 27,000 acres, dotted with small mangrove islands, saline swamps and wetlands, contain much of Shipstern Lagoon. Roughly a third of the reserve is tropical moist forest, which includes over a hundred plant species, though the effects of **Hurricane Janet**, which whipped through in 1955, still show in the absence of mature growth. Elsewhere are wide belts of savannah, covered in coarse grasses, palms and broadleaf trees. Several guided trails invite exploration, occasionally in one of the reserve's safari-type vehicles, and it's possible to arrange after-dark tours, as well as overnights in the guest house or further afield. Simply by spending an hour on the superb botanical trail from the **visitor centre** (where guides are available), you'll encounter more recorded plant species than on any other trail in Belize.

Indeed, Shipstern is a nature-lover's paradise. The lagoon system supports blue-winged teal, American coot, thirteen species of egret and huge flocks of American wood stork, while the forest is home to flycatchers, warblers, keel-billed toucans, collared aracari and at least five species of parrot. In addition to birds, there are crocodiles, manatees, coatis, jaguars, peccaries, deer,

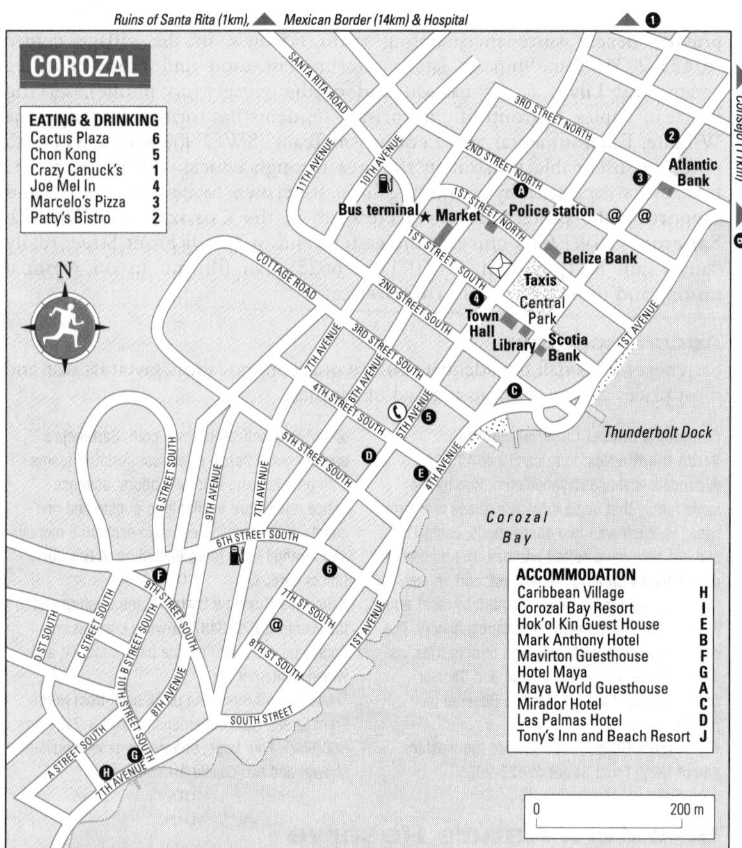

raccoons, pumas (though the tracks of larger animals are more commonly seen than the animals themselves) and an abundance of insects, particularly butterflies. The **butterfly farm** is being re-populated, and there's plenty of information about all the resident species in the excellent visitor's centre (just 100m from the main road, served by all Sarteneja buses). Camouflaged **treehouses** throughout the reserve enable you to get good views of wildlife without disturbing the animals, though you'll need a guide to find them, and the **Xo-Pol Ponds** offer an unparalleled chance to see Morelet's crocodiles and waterfowl through much of the year. Before trekking into the bush, make sure to cover exposed skin with clothing and a slathering of repellent – the bugs can be nasty.

The Shipstern management also runs the **Mahogany Tree Park and Museum**, with an informative visitor's centre (opened on request; included in reserve fee) detailing the life cycle of Belize's national tree and historic export. Further towards the village, the **Belize Crocodile Creche** (by appointment only; ⓣ423-2136, ⓔcroccreche@btl.net) raises American saltwater crocodiles for the first two or three years of their lives, giving this threatened species a safe environment before releasing them into the wild.

Corozal and around

COROZAL, 48km north of Orange Walk along the Northern Highway, is Belize's most northerly town, just twenty minutes from the Mexican border. Its location near the mouth of the New River enabled the ancient Maya to prosper here by controlling river and sea trade, and two archeological sites – Santa Rita and Cerros – are within easy reach. The town was founded in 1849 by refugees hounded south by the Caste Wars of Yucatán, and underwent substantial reconstruction after Hurricane Janet in 1955; today it's an intriguing mix of Mexican and Caribbean culture, with mestizos in the majority. This is a fertile area – the town's name derives from the cohune palm, which the Maya recognized as an indicator of fecundity – and much of the surrounding land is planted with sugarcane.

Until recently, there's been little to do in the area except transit through on the way to or from the Mexican border, but improved roads and local efforts to attract tourism are gaining Corozal more attention. It's an agreeable, hassle-free and relaxed town to spend a few days in and perhaps use as a base for day-trips throughout northern Belize, though the atmosphere is much more lively on Pan American Day (October 12; also known as Columbus Day), an occasion that merges the Mexican fiesta with Caribbean carnival. Palm trees shade Corozal's breezy, shoreline park, and the **town hall** is worth a look inside for a mural's vivid depiction of local history. The block northwest of Central Park, now containing the post office and police station, was previously the site of **Fort Barlee**, built in the 1870s to ward off Indian attacks; the brick remains of the fort's corners are preserved as historic landmarks.

Arrival and information

In addition to **buses** from Belize City to Corozal, those to Chetumal, Mexico pass through town roughly hourly from 7am to 9pm, and from 3.30am to 6.30pm in the opposite direction. A couple of local companies also operate shuttles to the border, which can be caught at the terminal on 7th Avenue near the market. Buses to the surrounding villages sometimes leave from behind the post office, but ask about these before planning an excursion, as their schedules change constantly. The *Thunderbolt* skiff provides a **fast boat service** to San Pedro, Ambergris Caye, leaving from the dock daily at 7am and 3pm (1hr 30min; Bz$45 one way, $90 return; ⓣ226-2904). Both Tropic Air and Maya Island Air operate daily **flights** between Corozal and San Pedro; the airstrip is a few kilometres south of town, and taxis meet all flights (Bz$8 into town). If you're in a rush to get to Tikal in Guatemala, check at *Hotel Maya* (see p.119) for information on the Linea Dorada **express bus from Chetumal to Flores**, which will stop at the hotel if you book ahead.

The tourist office in the historic customs building on the seafront has closed with no sign of reopening, so your best bet for **information** is *Caribbean Village*, an RV park and campsite at the southern edge of town. The library sells a helpful map detailing local birds, trees and history for Bz$2, and Corozal's well-designed **website** (ⓦwww.corozal.com), produced with help from the town's high school students, is another reliable source of information. The **post office** is northwest of Central Park (Mon–Fri 8.30am–4.30pm), and the nearby Belize and Scotia banks, as well as Atlantic Bank (three blocks north on 4th Avenue), all have ATMs. **Internet cafés** are plentiful, and several hotels have wireless access for guests – the Mirador has public wireless in its lobby. For organized **tours** to local nature reserves and

△ Corozal

archeological sites, contact Francisco Puck (☎423-0054) or Henry Menzies (☎422-2725), who is also an expert on travel to Mexico and able to arrange tours to the Maya sites of Quintana Roo, the state immediately over the border. The three Salvidar brothers (☎602-7722 or 625-0563) offer a variety of tours in the area and elsewhere in Belize.

Accommodation

Corozal has plenty of hotel rooms in all price ranges, and you'll always be able to find something suitable, though it's worth booking ahead for somewhere specific during the high season and holidays.

Carribean Village 2.5km south of the centre ☎422-2725. This RV park and campsite offers full hook-ups for Bz$20 and tent space for Bz$5 per person (bring your own equipment). Secure parking is available for Bz$5. The office is staffed daily 8am–6pm.

Corozal Bay Resort 3km south of the centre ☎422-2691, Ⓦwww.corozalbayinn.com. Large, thatched cabañas on a private beach, each with two double beds, a/c, TV with cable and nice bathroom. There's wireless Internet and a beach-front pool, and the *Rainforest Restaurant & Bar* serves snacks, steaks and a selection of nearly 300 cocktails. 8

Hok'ol K'in Guest House At the sea end of 4th St South ☎442-3329, Ⓔcorozal@btl.net. Modern hotel near the seafront with large, tiled private baths, balconies (with hammocks) and cable TV in most rooms. The ground floor is completely wheel-chair-accessible. Other features include a tour boat, a restaurant, a 24-hour bar and a TV lounge with Belize videos, and the small but pleasant gardens invite evening reflection. Prices vary according to room size and a/c or fan. 3–5

Mark Anthony Hotel On 3rd St North, close to the seafront ⓣ422-3141, ⓔmark@localgringos.com. Large, clean rooms, with a/c, cable TV and private bathrooms, above a local bar and restaurant serving Belizean food. Locals know it as "Butch's Place". 4

Mavirton Guest House On 6th St South. ⓣ422-0361, ⓔmavirton@btl.net. Quiet, family-run hotel with basic rooms, most with private bath. 2–3

Hotel Maya 2km south of the centre ⓣ422-2082, ⓔhotelmaya@btl.net. Clean, well-priced rooms with private bath, some with a/c and cable TV. There are several long-stay apartments starting at US$425/month, including utilities and Internet. The upstairs balcony gives refreshing sea views, and tasty breakfasts are served at the downstairs restaurant. The owner has extensive local knowledge and is an agent for domestic airlines and the Linea Dorada bus from Chetumal to Flores, which stops right outside. 5–6

Maya World Guesthouse 16 2nd St North, between 5th & 6th ⓣ624-4790. Clean, budget rooms with shared bath, and a good place to meet other travellers. Soon to offer rooms with a/c and TV. 2–3

Mirador Hotel 4th Ave at 2nd St South, on the seafront ⓣ422-0189, ⓦwww.mirador.bz. Large hotel with excellent rooftop views both across the bay and over Corozal, best enjoyed from the hammocks or chairs or with the telescope. Rooms (of varying sizes) come equipped with wireless Internet and cable TV, and some have a/c and beautiful bay views. 4–6

Las Palmas 123 5th Ave South, between 4th & 5th ⓣ422-0196, ⓦwww.laspalmashotelbelize.com. A variety of room styles, all with a/c, wireless Internet and cable TV. Secure parking is available, there's a restaurant for special events and groups and guests can rent bikes. 4–6

Tony's Inn and Beach Resort 3km south of the centre ⓣ422-2055 or 422-3555, ⓦwww.tonysinn.com. A touch of well-run luxury in a superb location with guarded parking. The spacious rooms with a/c and king-sized (or two double) beds overlook landscaped gardens and a gem of a beach bar, and the hotel's *Vista del Sol* and *Y-Not Grill* restaurants are excellent. There's Internet access for guests and tours can be arranged. 6–8

Eating

In addition to several small restaurants around town, some hotels serve good food. On Sundays, when many small businesses are closed, these may be your best bet. *Tony's Inn* has excellent fine dining, *Corozal Bay Resort* offers a decent menu, and the breakfasts at *Hotel Maya* are top-notch. Local restaurants are generally open either during the day for breakfast and lunch, or in the evening for dinner, but rarely both.

Cacus Plaza 6 6th St South ⓣ422-0394. This great cactus-shaped restaurant serves Mexican-style snacks and steaks, and a bar and weekend disco provide additional entertainment. A hotel is also in the works. Wed–Sun 5pm–2am.

Chon Kong 42 5th Ave ⓣ422-0169. The best – and most expensive – Chinese joint in town. Daily 10.30am–11pm.

Crazy Canuck's North of town ⓣ661-5902. Linked to the successful business of the same name in San Pedro, this restaurant/bar serves tasty burgers and complete meals. Tues–Sat all day, Sun until 2pm.

Joe Mel In 5th Ave near Town Hall ⓣ422-2526. Popular restaurant open for breakfast and lunch, serving different Belizean specials each day. Closed Sun.

Marcelo's Pizza 4th Ave, two blocks from Central Park ⓣ422-3275 or 422-2310. A reliable choice for late nights and Sundays, also delivering cheap fast food all over town. Daily 8am–12am.

Patty's Bistro 13 4th Ave, three blocks from Central Park ⓣ402-0174, ⓔmark@localgringos.com. Serving excellent Belizean, Mexican and American dishes. The walls are covered with graffiti from previous satisfied customers, locals and expats alike. Closed Sun.

Santa Rita

Of the two small Maya sites within reach of Corozal, the closer is **Santa Rita** (no opening hours, no charge), about a fifteen-minute walk northwest of town. Follow the main road toward the Mexican border and bear left at the fork, bringing you to the hospital, the power plant and the raised archeological site.

Founded as a small settlement around 1800 BC, Santa Rita appears to have been continuously occupied until the arrival of the Spanish, by which time it was in all probability the powerful Maya city known as Chactemal (Chetumal), which dominated regional trade. It was certainly still thriving in 1531 AD, when the conquistador **Alonso Dávila** entered the town, which had been tactically abandoned by its inhabitants; he was driven out almost immediately by Na Chan Kan, the Maya chief, and his Spanish adviser Gonzalo Guerrero (see Contexts, p.310).

Being so close to modern-day Mexico, it's not surprising that the site shares many attributes with ruins found to the north. **Pottery** found here connects the site with others in Yucatán, and, before it was bulldozed in the late 1970s, Structure 1 contained superb, Mixtec-style Postclassic murals similar to those found at Tulum in Quintana Roo. Due to this destruction, and the strong possibility that much of the ancient city lies beneath present-day Corozal, the only visible remains of Santa Rita are a few mounds and Structure 7, a fairly small but attractive **pyramid**. Burials excavated here include that of an elaborately jewelled elderly woman, dated to the Early Classic period, and the tomb of a Classic-period warlord, interred with the symbols of his elite status. Unfortunately the site is no longer maintained and bears some marks of abuse, namely litter and graffiti, the latter highly unusual for Belize.

Consejo

The tiny village of **CONSEJO**, on the tip of a peninsula eleven kilometres northeast of Corozal, is best known for its retirement community. That said, it's an idyllic, relaxed spot on palm-lined Corozal Bay, linked by intermittent bus service from Corozal (Bz$40 one-way by taxi), and has a couple nice places to stay. *The Smuggler's Den* (ⓣ614-8146 or 600-9723, ⓦsmugglersdenbelize.tripod.com) has three levels of accommodation, from a basic room (④) up to a two-bedroom beachfront bungalow (⑧); there are also camping facilities for Bz$3 per person. The restaurant, open to non-guests only on weekends, serves very tasty Belizean and American dishes and a **Sunday roast lunch** (book ahead). At the opposite end of the village, *Casablanca By the Sea* (ⓣ423-1018, ⓦwww.casablancabelize.com) offers great views across the bay to Mexico and a variety of comfortable rooms whose beautiful doors are carved with Maya reliefs (⑦–⑧). The **restaurant** is open seven days a week for breakfast and lunch (non-guests welcome). In the village centre, *Derek's Cozy Corner Bar* provides local colour in a quiet setting, but opening hours vary.

Cerros

On another peninsula jutting from the southern shore of Corozal Bay, the Preclassic Maya centre of **Cerros** (daily 8am–4.30pm; Bz$10) benefited from its position at the mouth of the New River, which enabled it to dominate regional water-borne trade. Beginning around 50 BC, it grew in only two generations from a small fishing village to a major city, one of the first to be ruled by a king. A kilometre-long canal bordered the central area, providing drainage for the town and the raised field system that sustained it. Despite initial success, however, Cerros was abandoned by the Classic period, made obsolete by shifting trade routes. The site today contains three large acropolis structures, ball-courts and plazas flanked by pyramids. The largest structure is a 22-metre-high temple with superb views of Corozal from its summit. The temple's intricate **stucco masks**, representing the rising and setting sun and Venus as morning star and evening star, are periodically covered to prevent erosion; if so, the informative **visitor centre** may compensate with its schematics of the site's buildings.

Practicalities

Cerros is easily reached from Corozal via a road starting at *Tony's Inn* (see p.119); you'll have to cross the New River on a free cable-winched ferry at Pueblo Nuevo. A water taxi from the centre of Corozal may start running soon, and there are also plans to open an airstrip to the north of Cerros. Hotels in Corozal can arrange transportation and tours for you as well. Daily buses also connect Corozal to the village of **Copper Bank**, whose accommodation is perfect for staying near the ruins, but departure points and times vary. Once you're in Copper Bank, it's easy enough to rent a bike for the twenty-minute ride to the site along a smooth, forested road.

Copper Bank has a few worthwhile **places to stay**, though you should call ahead to make sure they're operating. *The Last Resort* (Ⓣ665-6665, Ⓔjoe@lastresort.bz), set in shady gardens 200m along a signposted path from the centre of the village, has several cabins and a pleasant beach on the lagoon. Another option is *Copper Bank Inn* (Ⓣ608-0838, Ⓦwww.copperbankinn.com), whose large rooms (④) have a/c; there's also a pool and a pet spider monkey. Just off the road to Cerros, the eco-friendly *Cerros Beach Resort* (Ⓣ623-9766, Ⓦwww.cerrosbeachresort.com) is completely solar-powered, with several thatched cabañas offering single and double accommodation (④–⑥). The **restaurant/bar**, very popular with locals, is open all day (closed Mon). The grounds show evidence of ancient Maya occupation, and it's possible to walk along a wildlife-rich track to Cerros from here.

The Mexican border crossing

Corozal is only 14km from the Mexican border and one of the two land border crossings in Belize open to tourists. Many northbound buses heading into Mexico will take you to either the **bus terminal** in Chetumal (with plenty of onward express services up the coast to Cancún, or inland to Mexico City) or the nearby market. The whole journey from Corozal takes under an hour, including the **Santa Elena border crossing** on the south side of the Río Hondo. After you've cleared Belize immigration (paying the Bz$30 exit and Bz$7.50 PACT conservation taxes), the bus carries you to the Mexican immigration and customs posts on the northern bank.

Border formalities for entering Mexico are very straightforward, and few Western nationalities need a visa; simply pick up and fill out a **Mexican tourist card**. If you want visa advice, check with the Mexican embassy in Belize City (see Listings, p.88). There's no fee for entering Mexico, though you can conveniently convert your US or Belize dollars to pesos with the help of **money-changers** on the Belize side of the border. There's no such service on the Mexican side until you reach the banks in Chetumal (or the ATM in the bus terminal). **Entering Belize** from Mexico is also simple: there's no fee, and you'll get a maximum of thirty days by filling out the Belize immigration form. Note that you cannot import any fresh food into Belize.

In between the two border posts you'll pass through the **Corozal Free Zone**, a seemingly ever-growing and fairly chaotic area of shopping malls and petrol stations designed to encourage customers returning to Mexico to part with their US dollars – officially Belizeans aren't allowed in. Once you've left

Belize (the guard will check your passport stamp) you can enter this low-cost temple of Mammon, if only to wonder how so many shops all selling pretty much the same range of cut-rate electronic and household goods, clothes and canned food can survive – definitely worth a look if you've got an hour or two to spare. The buses do not allow time to stop here, though, so you'll need your own transport.

Travel details

Buses

Bus company information and details of services from Belize City to destinations in the north are given in the box on p.86.

Bermudian Landing to: Belize City (2–3 daily Mon–Sat; 1hr 15min), via Burrell Boom.

Chetumal to: Belize City (hourly 4am–3pm; 3hr 30min, express services 3hr), via Corozal and Orange Walk; Sarteneja (1 daily Mon–Sat at 6am; 3hr 30min).

Corozal to: Belize City (hourly; 2hr 30min), via Orange Walk (1hr); Chetumal (hourly; under 1hr).

Crooked Tree to: Belize City (several daily Mon–Sat; 1hr 30min).

Orange Walk to: Belize City (at least hourly from 5am–7pm; 1hr 30min); Corozal (hourly; 1hr); Indian Church, for Lamanai (3 weekly Mon, Wed & Fri in the afternoon; 2hr).

Sarteneja to: Belize City (3 daily Mon–Sat; 3hr 30min); Chetumal (1 daily Mon–Sat; 3hr 30min).

Flights

Tropic Air (Ⓣ226-2012) operates at least four daily flights between Corozal and San Pedro, calling at Sarteneja on request; Maya Island (Ⓣ223-1140) has flights between San Pedro and Corozal, but none to Sarteneja. There are no domestic services to Orange Walk.

3

The northern cayes and atolls

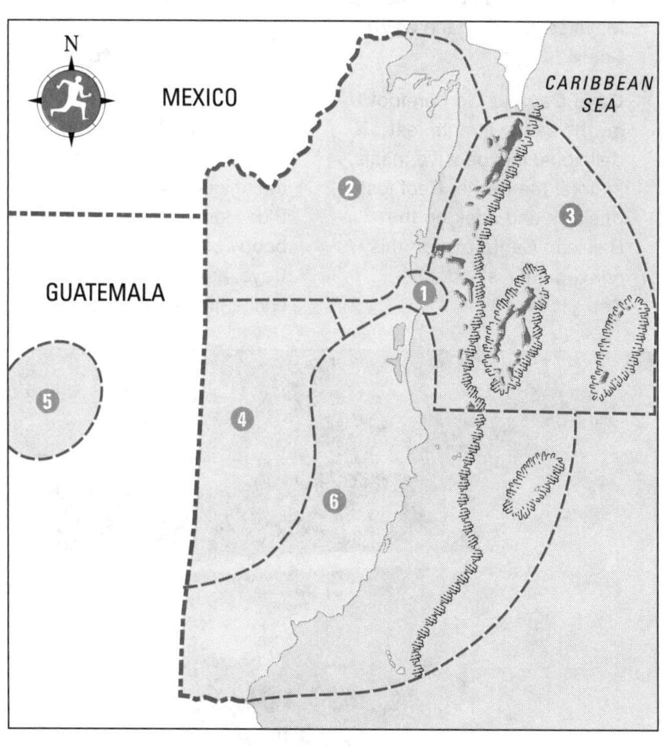

CHAPTER 3

Highlights

* **San Pedro** Sample some of the best food and nightlife in the country in this laid-back resort village, made famous by Madonna in her song *La Isla Bonita*. See p.129
* **Bacalar Chico National Park** Venture to this remote park on the northern tip of Ambergris Caye, stopping at ancient Maya seaports on the way. See p.141
* **Caye Caulker** Go barefoot on the sandy streets, eat delicious, inexpensive meals, snorkel the Barrier Reef just offshore and soak up the Belizean Caribbean on this relaxed little island. See p.144
* **Sail the Caribbean** Watch the glorious sunset from a handsome wooden sailing boat on an excursion from Caye Caulker, best enjoyed as an overnight trip. See p.151
* **Turneffe Islands** Spend the day snorkelling or diving, or stay overnight on Belize's largest atoll and marvel at the marine life in this virtually pristine, biologically diverse environment. See p.155
* **Lighthouse Reef** View it from the air, dive or snorkel the unique splendour of the Blue Hole, and then visit the booby birds on Half Moon Caye, arguably Belize's most enchanting island. See p.156

△ Snorkelling off Half Moon Caye

3

The northern cayes and atolls

Belize's spectacular **Barrier Reef**, with its dazzling variety of underwater life and string of exquisite islands – known as cayes (pronounced "keys") – is the main attraction for most first-time visitors to the country. The longest barrier reef in the western hemisphere, it begins just south of Cancún and runs the entire length of the Belize coastline at a distance of fifteen to forty kilometres from the mainland. One of the planet's richest marine ecosystems, it's a paradise for scuba divers and snorkellers, who come for the incredible coral formations teeming with hundreds of species of brilliantly coloured fish. Such is the importance of this astonishing marine ecosystem that virtually the entire reef, including the portions surrounding the outlying atolls, and all of Belize's marine reserves – known jointly as the **Belize Barrier Reef Reserve System** – were declared a **World Heritage Site** in December 1996. The announcement was greeted with tremendous enthusiasm by the country's dedicated and influential environmental organizations.

Most of the cayes lie in shallow water behind the shelter of the reef, with a limestone ridge forming larger, low-lying islands to the north and smaller, less frequently visited outcrops – often merely a stand of palms and a strip of sand – clustered toward the southern end of the chain. Though the four hundred cayes themselves form only a tiny portion of the country's total land area, and only around ten percent have any kind of tourism development, Belize has more territorial water than land, and the islands' lobster-fishing and tourism earnings account for a substantial proportion of the country's income.

In recent years the town of **San Pedro**, on **Ambergris Caye**, has experienced a transition from a predominantly fishing-based economy to one dominated by tourism. There are still some beautiful spots on Ambergris, however, notably the protected areas of the island, including **Bacalar Chico National Park** in the north and **Hol Chan Marine Reserve** in the south. **Caye Caulker**, south of Ambergris Caye and home to another marine reserve, is much smaller and more Belizean in feel. Still popular with budget travellers, it is also expanding into a more upscale market. Further south still, the original Belizean capital of **St George's Caye** holds a celebrated place in the nation's history and has some fine colonial houses along with an exclusive diving resort. **Swallow Caye**, near the tip of Belize City, is now protected as a manatee sanctuary; visitors can observe these gentle sea mammals on carefully monitored boat trips. Many of the other cayes are inhabited only by tiny fishing communities whose populations fluctuate with the season; a few have just a single upmarket lodge offering diving and sport-fishing to big-spending visitors.

Beyond the chain of islands and the coral reef are two of Belize's three **atolls**: the **Turneffe Islands** and **Lighthouse Reef**. In these breathtakingly beautiful formations, a ring of coral just below the surface encloses a shallow lagoon, often with a caye sitting right on its edge; here you'll find some of the most spectacular diving and snorkelling sites in the country, if not the world. The Turneffe Islands have a few resorts, and **Calabash Caye**, on the islands' eastern rim, contains a marine research station. To the east, Lighthouse Reef is the site of beautiful **Half Moon Caye**, where you can view nesting red-footed boobies, and the unique **Blue Hole Natural Monument** – an enormous, collapsed cave that attracts divers from all over the world. All of

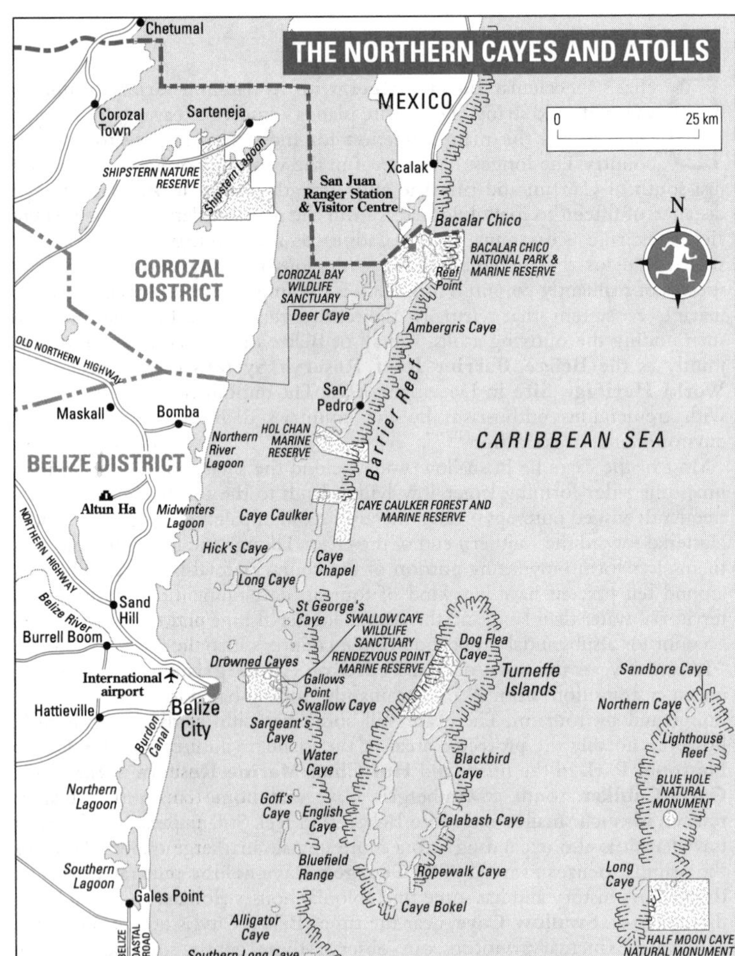

these destinations are regularly visited by day-trips or live-aboard dive boats from San Pedro and Caye Caulker.

A brief history of the cayes

The earliest inhabitants of the cayes were **Maya** peoples or their ancestors. By the Classic period (300–900 AD), the Maya had developed an extensive trade network stretching from the Yucatán to Honduras, with settlements and shipment centres on several of the islands. At least some cities in Belize survived the Maya "collapse", and the trade network lasted throughout the Postclassic era until the arrival of the conquistadores. **Christopher Columbus** may have sighted the coast of Belize on his last voyage to the "Indies" in 1502; his journal mentions an encounter with a Maya trading party in an immense dugout canoe off Guanaja, one of the Bay Islands of Honduras. Traces of Maya civilization remain on some of the cayes today, especially Ambergris Caye, which boasts the site of **Marco Gonzalez** near its southern tip, and the remains of a number of ports and trading centres on its northwestern shores. Evidence of coastal trade, such as shell mounds, has also been found on other islands, including Moho Caye off Belize City.

Probably the most infamous residents of the cayes were the **buccaneers**, usually British, who lived here in the sixteenth and seventeenth centuries, taking refuge in the shallow waters after plundering Spanish treasure ships. In time the pirates settled more or less permanently on some of the northern and central cayes. But life under the Jolly Roger grew too risky for them in the late 1600s, after Britain agreed to stamp out privateering under the terms of the Madrid Treaties, and a number of pirates turned instead to logwood cutting. The woodcutters, known as **Baymen**, kept their dwellings on the cayes – specifically **St George's Caye** – whose cool breezes and fresh water offered a welcome break from the steaming swamps where the logwood grew. The population of the cayes remained low during the seventeenth and eighteenth centuries, but the St George's Caye settlement remained the Baymen's capital until 1779, when a Spanish force destroyed it and imprisoned 140 Baymen and 250 of their slaves. The Baymen returned to their capital in 1783, but waited until 1798 to take revenge on the Spanish fleet in the celebrated **Battle of St George's Caye** (see p.315). After, although the elite of the Baymen still kept homes on St George's Caye, the population of the islands began to decline as Belize Town (later Belize City) grew.

During this period, fishermen and turtle hunters continued to use the cayes as a base for their operations, and refugees fleeing the Caste Wars in Yucatán towards the end of the nineteenth century also settled on the islands in small numbers. Descendants of these groups have steadily increased the islands' population since the mid-twentieth century, assisted by the establishment of **fishing cooperatives** in the 1960s, which brought improved traps, ice manufacturing (for shipping seafood) and access to the export market.

At around the same time the cayes of Belize, particularly Caye Caulker, became a hangout on the **hippie trail**, and then began to attract more lucrative custom. The islanders generally welcomed these new visitors: rooms were rented and hotels built, and a new prosperity began to transform island life. Luxuries not usually associated with small fishing communities in the developing world – colour televisions, telephones, skiffs with large outboard motors – are all evidence of the effects of tourism over the years. So profound are these changes that fishing has now become a secondary activity; many of the inhabitants of the two largest northern cayes, Ambergris Caye and Caye Caulker, now depend almost solely on tourism.

Visiting the cayes

The increasing popularity of Belize as a holiday destination has led to an escalation in land prices, and real estate offices proliferate on San Pedro's, and even little Caye Caulker's, main streets. Luckily, most of the islands are too small and remote to entice large-scale developers. Indeed, getting to many of the cayes and atolls can be difficult, especially if you're limited by time and finances, though access is much easier than it once was. Several organizations have **conservation projects** on the cayes, requiring self-funded volunteers (see p.350), or you could see if a visiting yacht owner needs a crew. Alternatively, **charter catamarans** are available in San Pedro and, if you can get together a group, you might **rent a sailing boat** for a few days – easily done on Caye Caulker – and let a local boatman show you the lesser-known parts of the reef.

Life on the cayes is supremely relaxing, tempting you to take it easy in a hammock, feast on seafood and sip rum punch as the sun sets. If you adopt the "no shirt, no shoes, no problem" philosophy of locals and expats alike, you'll fit right in. The most accessible and least expensive of the islands is Caye Caulker, and **snorkelling** or **diving** trips to the reef are easily arranged from here and

Safeguarding the coral reef

Coral reefs are among the most complex and **fragile** ecosystems in the world. Colonies have been growing at a rate of less than 5cm per year for thousands of years and, once damaged, the coral is far more susceptible to bacterial infection, which can quickly lead to large-scale, irreversible decline. Unfortunately, a great deal of damage has already been caused on Belize's Barrier Reef by snorkellers and divers standing on the coral or holding onto outcrops for a better look. On all the easily accessible areas of the reef you will clearly see dead white patches, especially on the large brain coral heads. All tour guides in Belize are trained in reef ecology before earning a licence (which must be displayed as they guide), and if you go on an organized trip, as most people do, the guide should brief you on the following **precautions** to avoid damage to the reef.

- Never anchor boats on the reef – use the permanently secured buoys.
- Never touch or stand on coral – protective cells are easily stripped away from the living polyps on their surface, destroying them and thereby allowing algae to enter. Coral also stings and can cause agonizing **burns**, and even brushing against it causes cuts that are slow to heal.
- Don't remove shells, sponges or other creatures from the reef or buy reef products from souvenir shops.
- Avoid disturbing the seabed around coral – aside from spoiling visibility, clouds of sand settle over corals and smother them.
- If you're a beginner or an out-of-practice diver, practise away from the reef first.
- Be aware of your position – particularly your feet – when diving and snorkelling, but don't panic if you find yourself very near the coral, as you may end up kicking it.
- If using a **camera**, ask someone to "spot" you so you don't drift into the coral.
- Don't use suntan lotion in reef areas – the oils remain on the water's surface. Wear a T-shirt instead to protect your skin from **sunburn**.
- Don't feed or interfere with fish or marine life; this can harm not only sea creatures and the food chain, but snorkellers too – large fish may attack, trying to get their share.
- **Report** guides that harass, touch or endanger the animals, or encourage you to do so. Touching fish damages the protective coating on their skin, making them vulnerable to infection.

from Ambergris Caye; dive instruction is also readily available. You can visit areas of almost unbelievable beauty and isolation by joining a group day-trip, visiting three or four different reef sites in a day, or by staying at a lodge on one of the atolls. For a spectacular aerial view of the **Blue Hole Natural Monument**, ask a local travel agent to book you onto a flight (Tropic Air runs one) over this amazing landmark and other sections of the reef; you can also choose from a variety of helicopter tours with Belize City-based Astrum Helicopters (Ⓣ222-9462, Ⓦwww.astrumhelicopters.com), whose flyover of San Pedro and the reef costs US$250 per person.

Birding in the cayes is fascinating, as it is almost everywhere in Belize. Over 250 species live in or visit the region, from ospreys and sandpipers to flamingoes and finches. Many otherwise rare birds are relatively common here; a sanctuary near San Pedro protects nesting roseate spoonbills, and red-footed boobies on Half Moon Caye have been protected since 1982. If you're keen on learning how, when and where to spot birds on the cayes, pick up a copy of *Bird Watching with Bubba*, self-published by expat Divemaster Elbert Greer and available on Ambergris Caye.

Catch-and-release **fly-fishing** for bonefish is popular, particularly on the Turneffe Island flats, where a couple of luxury fishing lodges can fulfil any angler's dream. Fishing trips for species such as snapper, barracuda and grouper are easily arranged from Caye Caulker or San Pedro, and a local guide can take you to the best spots.

Finally, some words of **warning**: occasionally the northern cayes (and other coastal areas of Belize) suffer direct hits by devastating hurricanes. The official **hurricane season** lasts from June to the end of November, though the worst storms usually occur during September and October – tourist low season. There are excellent warning systems in place, and if you are on the cayes during the hurricane season you should keep yourself informed about developing storms by checking Ⓦwww.belizenet.com/weatherix.shtml or The Weather Channel's "Tropical Update" (at ten minutes to the hour). If there is a hurricane developing *anywhere* in the Caribbean, prepare to leave as quickly as possible or postpone plans for a visit to the cayes. Hurricanes can and do change intensity and direction rapidly, so don't believe anyone who says it won't affect Belize – you can always return once the danger is over.

Ambergris Caye and San Pedro

Geographically part of Mexico's Xcalak Peninsula, **Ambergris Caye** is separated from Mexico by the narrow **Boca Bacalar Chico** channel, created partly by the ancient Maya. It's the most northerly and, at 40km long, by far the largest of the cayes, though the vast majority of its population is concentrated near the southern end. The island's main attraction and point of arrival is the former fishing village of **SAN PEDRO**, facing the reef just a few kilometres from the caye's southern tip. Development is spreading north from the town, with a number of beach resorts already established and plans for ever-larger hotels constantly in the making.

If you fly into San Pedro, as most visitors do, the views are breathtaking: the water appears so clear and shallow as to barely cover the sandy seabed, and the mainland and other islands stand out clearly. The most memorable sight is the white line of the reef crest, dramatically separating the vivid blue of the open sea from the turquoise water on its leeward side. The aircraft fly at such a low

Getting to and from Ambergris Caye

Flying to San Pedro is the easiest and most popular approach. Maya Island Air (ⓣ226-2435) and Tropic Air (ⓣ226-2012) both operate flights from Belize International Airport (Bz$114; see p.68) and Belize Municipal Airport (Bz$63; see p.68) to San Pedro (25min; at least hourly, 7.30am–5pm), calling at Caye Caulker on request (same price). Tropic Air also operates at least four daily flights from **San Pedro to Corozal**.

From Belize City, most **boats to Ambergris Caye** are operated by the Caye Caulker Water Taxi Association (1hr 20min; Bz$20 one way, $40 return; ⓣ226-0992, ⓦwww.cayecaulkerwatertaxi.com) and leave from the Marine Terminal at 8am, 9am, 10.30am, noon, 1.30pm, 3pm and 4.30pm, all calling at Caye Caulker on the way (except the 4.30pm express service). The least expensive boat on the run, the *Triple J* (Bz$20 one way, $35 return; ⓣ207-7777, ⓦwww.triplejbelize.com), leaves from Courthouse Wharf, on the south side of the Swing Bridge, every ninety minutes between 8am and 4.30pm. The *Thunderbolt* runs between **San Pedro and Corozal**, stopping at Sarteneja on request (1hr 30min; daily 7am & 3pm; Bz$45 one way, $90 return).

Caye Caulker Water Taxis **leave San Pedro** for Caye Caulker and Belize City at least every ninety minutes from 7am until 3.30pm (until 4.30pm on weekends and holidays). From San Pedro to other cayes, any of the boats above also stop at Caye Caulker, and will also call at **St George's Caye** or **Caye Chapel** on request, though you should check with them first for availability.

altitude (around 100m – there's no need to go higher on these short hops) that photographs taken from inside the cabin generally turn out well.

As you land at the tiny airport, with the sea on one side and the lagoon on the other, a glimpse of San Pedro shows it occupying the whole width of the island. Though not a large town – you're never more than a shell's throw from the sea – its population of over five thousand is the highest in all the cayes. San Pedro is the main destination for over half of all visitors to Belize, catering mainly to North American package tourists. Almost all prices in town are quoted in US dollars, which are accepted island-wide. Some of the country's most exclusive and luxurious **hotels**, **restaurants** and **bars** are here; the few budget places are in the "original" (pre-tourism expansion) village of San Pedro, which is also where most of the action takes place, particularly in the evenings.

During the daytime, for those not shopping, relaxing or enjoying some other land-based activity, the **water** is the focus of entertainment on Ambergris Caye, from sunbathing on the docks to **windsurfing**, **sailing**, **kayaking**, diving and snorkelling, fishing and even peering through the floor of a glass-bottomed boat. All of the trips described on pp.137–142 can be booked from local companies or through your hotel.

Arrival, information and getting around

Arriving at San Pedro's **airport**, you're at the north end of Coconut Drive and only 450m south of the centre. It's within easy walking distance of any of the hotels in town, though golf buggies and **taxis** will be waiting if you don't want to hoof it. A ride to the centre (or anywhere else in town) should cost Bz$6, but always verify this before agreeing to a ride, and never let a driver take you to a hotel of his choosing. Even if you arrive with a booking, call to confirm first if you can, as a common taxi-driver **scam** is to tell you your hotel is actually full or even closed, then take you to one where he earns (or extorts) a fat commission.

Boats usually pull in at the water taxi dock, on the front (reef) side of the island at the east end of Black Coral Street, or the Texaco Dock, at the east end

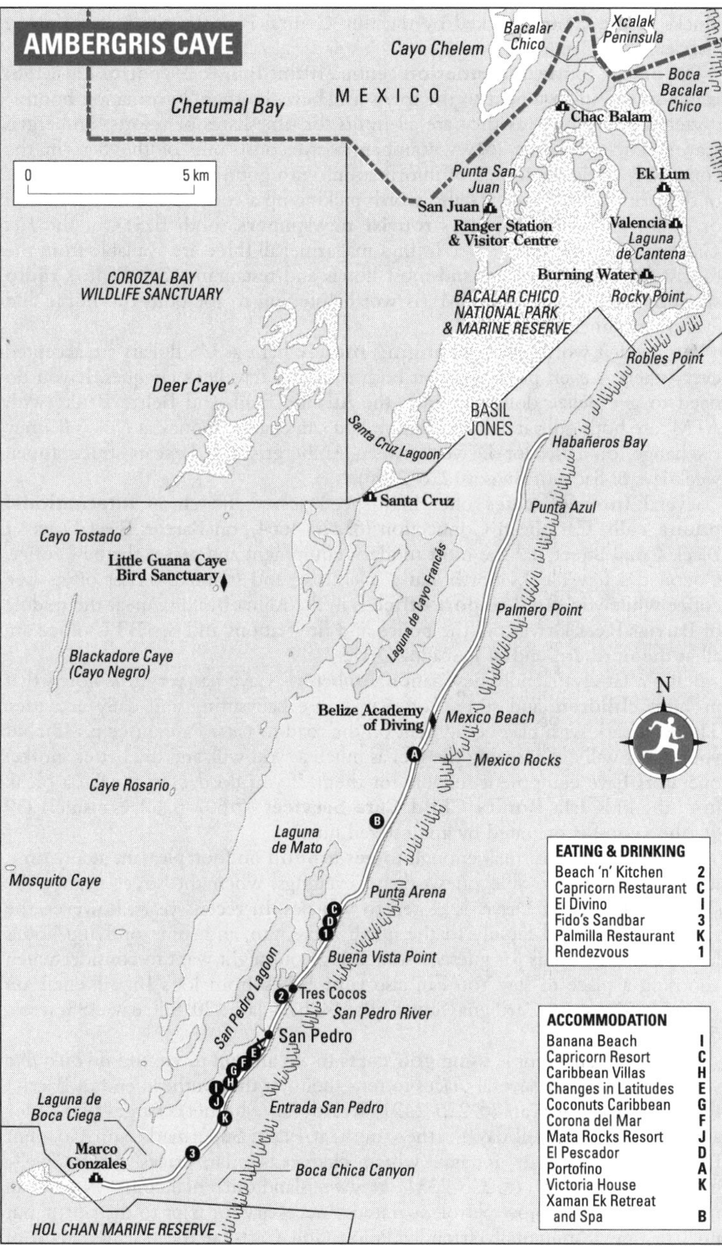

AMBERGRIS CAYE
Cayo Chelem
Bacalar Chico
Xcalak Peninsula
Boca Bacalar Chico
MEXICO
Chetumal Bay
Chac Balam
0
5 km
Punta San Juan
San Juan
Ek Lum
Ranger Station & Visitor Centre
Valencia
Laguna de Cantena
Burning Water
COROZAL BAY WILDLIFE SANCTUARY
BACALAR CHICO NATIONAL PARK & MARINE RESERVE
Rocky Point
Robles Point
Deer Caye
BASIL JONES
Santa Cruz Lagoon
Habañeros Bay
Santa Cruz
Punta Azul
Cayo Tostado
Little Guana Caye Bird Sanctuary
Laguna de Cayo Francés
Palmero Point
Blackadore Caye (Cayo Negro)
N
Belize Academy of Diving
Mexico Beach
Mexico Rocks
Caye Rosario
Laguna de Mato
EATING & DRINKING
Beach 'n' Kitchen 2
Capricorn Restaurant C
El Divino I
Fido's Sandbar 3
Palmilla Restaurant K
Rendezvous 1
Mosquito Caye
Punta Arena
Buena Vista Point
Tres Cocos
San Pedro River
San Pedro Lagoon
San Pedro
ACCOMMODATION
Banana Beach I
Capricorn Resort C
Caribbean Villas H
Changes in Latitudes E
Coconuts Caribbean G
Corona del Mar F
Mata Rocks Resort J
El Pescador D
Portofino A
Victoria House K
Xaman Ek Retreat and Spa B
Laguna de Boca Ciega
Entrada San Pedro
Marco Gonzales
Boca Chica Canyon
HOL CHAN MARINE RESERVE
Shark-Ray Alley (2km)

of Caribeña Street. The *Thunderbolt*, however, pulls in at Back Dock, at the back of the island at the west end of Black Coral Street. All docks are within a few blocks of the centre, marked by the tiny Central Park, on the seafront along Barrier Reef Drive.

The official tourist **information** centre (10am–1pm & 2–7pm; ⓣ226-2198) is in a small building next to the town hall; beware other "information booths" dotted around town, as they are all fronts for timeshares or resorts. Ambergris Caye's official website (ⓦwww.ambergriscaye.com), one of the best in the country, is a reliable source of information, with good maps and links to most of the island's businesses. It's also worth picking up a copy of *The San Pedro Sun* or *Ambergris Today*, the island's **tourist newspapers** (both Bz$1), or the *Hot Guide to Ambergris Caye*, a free listings magazine; all three are available from the tourist information centre and most hotels and restaurants. San Pedro's **radio station**, Reef Radio (92.3FM), is worth listening to for both the music and events announcements.

You needn't worry about **changing money** here, as US dollars are accepted everywhere – even preferred – in both cash and traveller's cheques. If you do need to get Belize dollars in cash, the Atlantic Bank and Belize Bank (with ATM) are both on Barrier Reef Drive. You can change money at Milo's Money Exchange, on Pescador Drive between Ambergris and Pelican streets (open weekdays & Sat mornings; ⓣ226-2196).

Several **Internet cafés** offer high-speed access and cheap **international phone calls**: Caribbean Connection (ⓣ226-4664), on Barrier Reef Drive at Black Coral Street, has the most modern equipment and serves the best coffee; Coconet, a few blocks north, has a lively bar, and Island Internet offers free coffee while you surf. The **post office** is in the Alijua Building near the middle of Barrier Reef Drive, and the police and fire stations and the **BTL** office are all at the northern end of Pescador Drive.

Being a family-friendly destination, Ambergris Caye has very few hotels that prohibit **children**, and several offer in-house babysitting and daily activities. There's a park with play equipment on the road to *Casa Picasso* (see p.143), but youngsters will enjoy seeing the reef as much as you will, and the better snorkel operators have equipment suitable for them. If you do decide to take a break from the kids, **Isla Bonita Child Care Services** (ⓣ607-8362, ⓔmsmel1939@yahoo.com) is operated by a registered nurse.

The town centre is small enough to **get around** on foot; pleasant at any time, it's particularly enjoyable on weekend evenings, when the street nearest the shore, Barrier Reef Drive, is closed to vehicles. In recent years, however, the town has expanded rapidly to the north and south, and some outlying hotels have **courtesy bikes** for guests – something you might want to consider when choosing a place to stay. You can also **rent bikes** from Joe's Bike Rental, on Pescador Drive at Caribeña Street (Bz$14/half-day, $20/full day, $85/week; ⓣ226-4371).

You'll see many people using **golf carts** to zip around town, and if you'd like your own, there are several places to rent them. At the southern end of Barrier Reef Drive, Castle Cars (ⓣ226-2421, ⓔcastlecars@btl.net) charges US$12 for an hour, $60 for a full day. Further south, at Island Supermarket on Coconut Drive, is Island Tour Rental, which charges similar prices for its well-maintained vehicles (ⓣ226-2351, ⓦwww.islandtourrental.com). Nearly all rental golf carts are now petrol-operated – necessary for trips to the north, but not very environmentally friendly. Polo's Golf Carts, at the northern end of Barrier Reef Drive (ⓣ226-3542), is the only place that still offers battery-powered ones. If you do rent a cart, observe the one-way system and look out

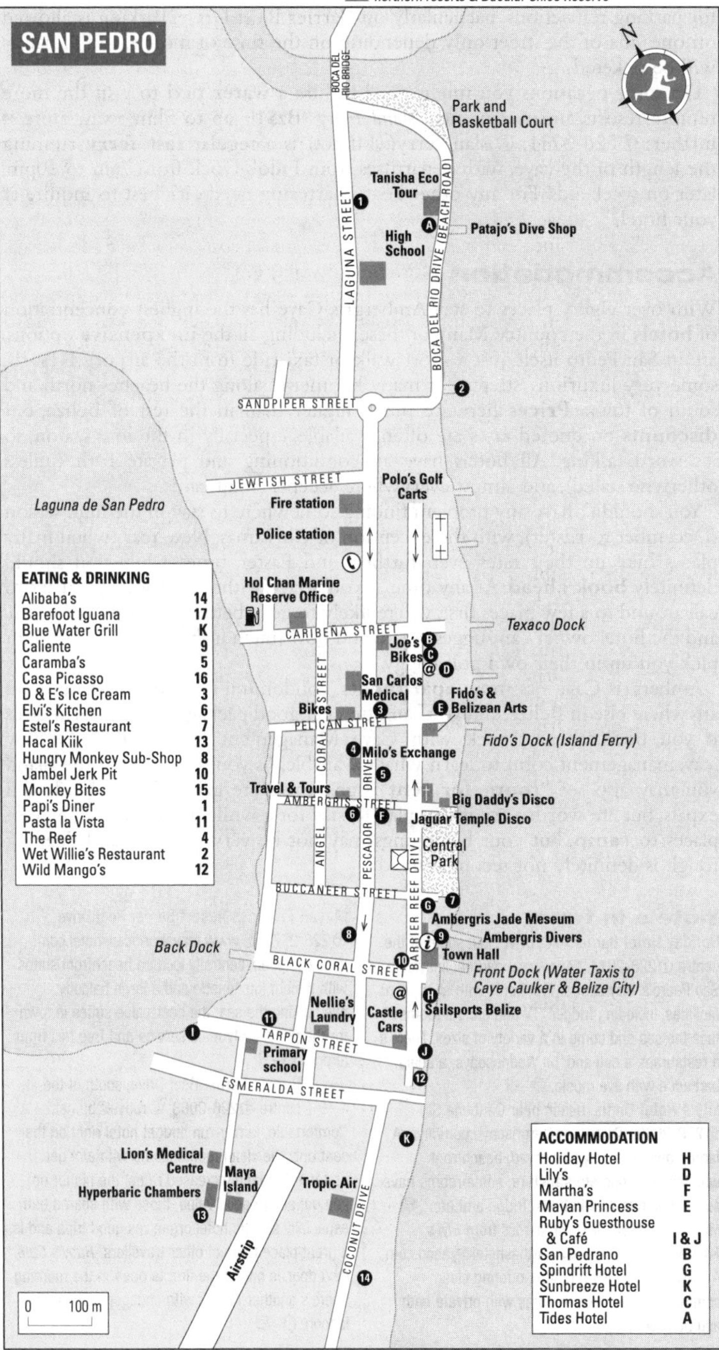

northern resorts & Bacalar Chico Reserve
SAN PEDRO
N
BOCA DEL RIO BRIDGE
Park and Basketball Court
Tanisha Eco Tour
LAGUNA STREET
BOCA DEL RIO DRIVE (BEACH ROAD)
Patajo's Dive Shop
High School
SANDPIPER STREET
JEWFISH STREET
Polo's Golf Carts
Laguna de San Pedro
Fire station
Police station
Hol Chan Marine Reserve Office
CARIBEÑA STREET
Texaco Dock
Joe's Bikes
CORAL STREET
San Carlos Medical
Fido's & Belizean Arts
Bikes
PELICAN STREET
Fido's Dock (Island Ferry)
Milo's Exchange
Travel & Tours
DRIVE
AMBERGRIS STREET
Big Daddy's Disco
Jaguar Temple Disco
ANGEL
PESCADOR
Central Park
BARRIER REEF DRIVE
BUCCANEER STREET
Ambergris Jade Meseum
Ambergris Divers
Back Dock
Town Hall
BLACK CORAL STREET
Front Dock (Water Taxis to Caye Caulker & Belize City)
Nellie's Laundry
Castle Cars
Sailsports Belize
TARPON STREET
Primary school
ESMERALDA STREET
Lion's Medical Centre
Maya Island
Hyperbaric Chambers
Tropic Air
Airstrip
COCONUT DRIVE
0 100 m
15 (1km), 16 (1km), 17 (1.5km) & Island Supermarket
EATING & DRINKING
Alibaba's 14
Barefoot Iguana 17
Blue Water Grill K
Caliente 9
Caramba's 5
Casa Picasso 16
D & E's Ice Cream 3
Elvi's Kitchen 6
Estel's Restaurant 7
Hacal Kiik 13
Hungry Monkey Sub-Shop 8
Jambel Jerk Pit 10
Monkey Bites 15
Papi's Diner 1
Pasta la Vista 11
The Reef 4
Wet Willie's Restaurant 2
Wild Mango's 12
ACCOMMODATION
Holiday Hotel H
Lily's D
Martha's F
Mayan Princess E
Ruby's Guesthouse & Café I & J
San Pedrano B
Spindrift Hotel G
Sunbreeze Hotel K
Thomas Hotel C
Tides Hotel A

for parking restrictions, particularly on Barrier Reef Drive. Parking is allowed on one side of the street only, depending on the time of month, and violators will be ticketed.

On some occasions you might need to hire a **water taxi** to visit the more remote resorts and restaurants. *Island Ferry* (Bz$10 up to 5km away, more if further; ⓣ226-3231, ⓔislandferry@btl.net) is a regular **fast ferry** running the length of the caye, with departures from Fido's Dock from 7am to 10pm, later on weekends. For any other boat-chartering needs, it's best to inquire at your hotel.

Accommodation

With over eighty places to stay, Ambergris Caye has the highest concentration of **hotels** in the country. Many of these, including all the **inexpensive** options, are in San Pedro itself, just a short walk or taxi ride from the airport. Resorts, some very luxurious, stretch for many kilometres along the beaches north and south of town. **Prices** here are much higher than in the rest of Belize, but **discounts** on quoted rates are often available, especially in the low season, so it's worth asking. All hotels have air-conditioning and private bath (unless otherwise stated), and almost everywhere accepts credit cards.

You shouldn't have any problem finding somewhere to stay in the high season (December to Easter), with the exception of Christmas, New Year (when many places hike up their rates even further) and Easter, times when you should definitely **book ahead**. At any time, if you arrive without a booking it pays to call around to a few places first; you're likely to get a better price on your room, and the hotel owner can suggest a taxi and how much it should cost – or might pick you up in their own golf buggy.

Ambergris Caye has more **apartments**, condominiums and timeshares than anywhere else in Belize, and you can often get good package or long-term deals if you book ahead; check with Caye Management (ⓣ226-3077, ⓦwww.cayemanagement.com) to learn what's available. As you walk around the island you may also see "**room for rent**" signs; these are generally for locals and expats, but are worth a try if you plan to stay for a while. There are a couple of places to camp, but your belongings may not be very secure – and sleeping rough is definitely not recommended.

Hotels in town

Holiday Hotel Barrier Reef Drive, just south of the centre ⓣ226-2014, ⓦwww.sanpedroholiday.com. San Pedro's very central first hotel, with all modern facilities, including fridges, TV and a/c. All rooms face the sea and come in a variety of sizes. There's a restaurant, a deli and, on Wednesdays, a beach barbecue with live music. ❽–❾

Lily's Hotel On the beach near Caribeña St ⓣ206-2059, ⓦwww.ambergriscaye.com/lilys. A family-owned, nicely preserved, beachfront wooden and concrete structure; some rooms have sea views, two double beds, fridge and a/c. ❼

Martha's Pescador Drive, across from *Elvi's Kitchen* ⓣ206-2053, ⓔmarthashotel@yahoo.com. A bargain in the town centre, offering clean, comfortable, fan-cooled rooms with private bath and bedside lamps. ❸–❹

Mayan Princess Resort Barrier Reef Drive ⓣ226-2778, ⓦwww.mayanprincesshotel.com. Well-equipped, centrally located beachfront suites with decent kitchenette and a large balcony overlooking the sea; the best-value suites in town for the price. Daily maid service and free taxi from airport. ❽–❾

Ruby's Barrier Reef Drive, south of the centre ⓣ226-2063, ⓔrubys@btl.net. Comfortable, family-run budget hotel right on the seafront. The clean rooms (some with a/c) get better views (and increased rates) the higher up you go; all are good value, those with shared bath especially so. The hotel organizes good trips and is a great place to meet other travellers. *Ruby's Café*, next door, is one of the first to open in the morning. There's another *Ruby's* with cheaper rates on the lagoon. ❸–❺

San Pedrano Barrier Reef Drive at Caribeña St ⓣ226-2054, ⓔsanpedrano@btl.net. Popular hotel in a wooden building with nice rooms, some with a/c. Set back slightly from the sea, but with fine views and breezy verandas. No single rates. ④–⑤

Spindrift Hotel On Barrier Reef Drive at Buccaneer St ⓣ226-2174, ⓦwww.ambergriscaye.com/spindrift. Centrally located and on the beach, this concrete hotel offers some rooms with great views across the sea and others around a patio. Four levels of rooms are available, the top three with a/c. ⑤–⑧

Sunbreeze Hotel South end of Barrier Reef Drive ⓣ226-2191, ⓦwww.sunbreezehotel.com. Curving around a sandy courtyard and a pool, this superbly run beachfront hotel has big rooms in three levels of comfort; all have large bathrooms and some have a Jacuzzi bath. The manager provides welcoming little touches to the rooms. Excellent restaurant and very good gift shop. ⑧–⑨

Thomas Hotel North end of Barrier Reef Drive ⓣ226-2061. A good budget option with clean and simple rooms. ④

The Tides On the beach, about 1km north of the centre ⓣ226-2283, ⓦwww.ambergriscaye.com/tides. Small, family-run hotel, with all rooms facing the pool and bar with the ocean beyond. Full breakfast included, and dive packages with Patojo's Dive shop are available. ⑨

Hotels south of town

The hotels below are listed in order of their distance from town.

Changes in Latitudes Coconut Drive, almost 1km south of town, near the Belize Yacht Club ⓣ & ⓕ226-2986, ⓔlatitudesbelize@yahoo.com. Very friendly B&B set in relaxing gardens half a block from the sea – guests can use the yacht club facilities, including the pool, next door. Smallish but immaculately clean rooms, with use of common area, including full kitchen, at all times. The owners are well informed about all tours and facilities on the island, and can make most arrangements for you. Rates include a wonderful cooked breakfast, different every day. ⑥

Corona del Mar On the beach, just over 1km south of town ⓣ226-2025, ⓦwww.ambergriscaye.com/coronadelmar. Lots of local flavour and very friendly, with beautiful, spacious rooms and suites – full kitchens, TV, phone and lots of extras. All are very good value; rates include a full breakfast, free rum punch all day and use of the *Coconuts* pool next door. Has the only elevator in San Pedro and good disabled access throughout, including wide steps to a swimming area from the pier. ⑥–⑨

Coconuts Caribbean Hotel On the beach, just over 1km south of town ⓣ226-3500, ⓦwww.coconutshotel.com. This popular hotel boasts beautifully decorated tiled rooms and suites, sited around a pool and hot tub with bar and beachfront restaurant. Excellent service, with free Internet access for guests and a free taxi from the airstrip. The Marauder Suite (US$283) has a private Jacuzzi. ⑦–⑨

Caribbean Villas Hotel Coconut Drive, about 1.5km south of town ⓣ226-2715, ⓦwww.caribbeanvillashotel.com. Large grounds given over to indigenous species, with a 4-storey wildlife-viewing platform and excellent birding. The best place for nature lovers close to town. A variety of large rooms and well-equipped suites, all with ocean views, on the beachfront. Plenty of peace and quiet and opportunities to relax; snooze in a hammock or immerse yourself in the hot tub. ⑥–⑨

Banana Beach Resort On Mar de Tumbo Beach, 1.5km south of town ⓣ226-3890, ⓦwww.bananabeach.com. Variety of spacious suites with one to four beds, cable TV, rattan furniture and colourful Mexican weavings; some with kitchens. All have balconies, some overlooking the grounds, pools and courtyard, others facing the ocean. Good weekly rates, and possible off-season discounts; a buffet breakfast at the excellent *El Divino* restaurant is included. Tours can be arranged by the friendly and efficient in-house Monkey Business Travel Shop (ⓦwww.ambergristours.com). Free taxi from the airstrip. Veranda rooms and courtyard suites ⑧–⑨; three-bedroom, three-bath ocean-view suite US$550/night.

Mata Rocks Resort Around 3km south of town ⓣ226-2336, ⓦwww.matarocks.com. Small family resort with rooms around the pool and bar, complimentary breakfast, transfers and free bikes for exploring. ⑦–⑨

Victoria House On the beach, 3km south of town ⓣ226-2067, ⓦwww.victoria-house.com. Award-winning hotel with a wide range of fabulous accommodation in a great location. The luxurious, colonial-style hotel rooms, thatched cabañas, suites and multi-room villas (the latter two options have varnished hardwood furniture and superbly equipped kitchens) are set in spacious grounds resembling a botanic garden. Service is excellent, and there's a beachfront pool and a fine restaurant. Prices start at US$320 for a double ("state") room in high season, and go up to US$980 for a two-bed villa in peak season. ⑨

Hotels north of town

The hotels below are listed in order of their distance from town. From February to June these are reachable by road, but the rest of the year the trip is better made by boat, as the road is deeply rutted.

El Pescador On the beach, about 5km north of town ⓣ226-2398, ⓦwww.elpescador.com. With a choice of several rooms (US$235) in a colonial-style house rich with hardwood furnishings, or one-, two- or three-bed villas (up to US$725), there's plenty of choice at this family-run establishment, where fishing and diving are the most popular activities. Complimentary bikes, kayaks and wireless Internet are available, and the family sits with guests at the hotel restaurant. ⑨

Capricorn Resort On the beach, just north of *El Pescador* ⓣ226-2809, ⓔcapricorn@btl.net. Most people come here for the incredibly good food (see p.144), but there are also some delightful, secluded wooden cabins (US$245 double) with porches overlooking a pristine beach; all make perfect hideaways. Breakfast is included, as is a water taxi from town on arrival and departure. ⑨

Xaman Ek Retreat and Spa 8km north of town ⓣ226-4455, ⓦwww.xamanekbelize.com. Sublime location for this resort, with a choice of thatched cabañas or two-bed suites, with pool, excellent beach and all spa facilities on site. Maya healing is a speciality here, and regular retreats are held. No restaurant, but three within walking distance, and rooms have microwave and fridge or full kitchen. Beachfront suites are US$325. ⑨

Portofino Resort On the beach, 9km north of town ⓣ220-5096, ⓦwww.portofinobelize.com. A mix of beautiful wooden and concrete cabañas arranged to one side of a large pool and all with ocean views, colourful, Mexican-tiled bathrooms and hardwood floors. All amenities, including free boat transfer to town. Service is friendly and helpful and the restaurant is excellent (see p.144). ⑧–⑨

The Town

San Pedro's main streets are only half a dozen blocks long, and the town does not boast any standout sights, but in a place so devoted to tourist pleasure you're never far from a bar, restaurant or gift shop (see opposite). Despite all the development, the town manages to retain some elements of its **Caribbean charm** with a few two-storey, clapboard buildings in the centre. However, lofty, concrete structures are an increasingly common feature, and in the built-up area

△ Ambergris Caye

most of the palms have either been cut down, destroyed by Hurricane Keith in 2000 or exposed to a "lethal yellowing" disease originating in the north. Traffic has increased considerably in recent years, and the busiest of the sand streets have recently been paved to alleviate some of the problems.

One of the most interesting (and hectic) times to visit San Pedro is during August's **Costa Maya Festival**, a week-long celebration featuring cultural and musical presentations from the five Mundo Maya countries (Belize, Mexico, Guatemala, Honduras and El Salvador). The festival began as a way to drum up visitors during the low season; it's now so popular you may need to book rooms. Another increasingly popular event is the **Annual Eco-challenge Lagoon Kayak Race and Reef Festival**, held at the end of April to raise awareness of the coral reef. Kayakers race 68km over two days, then celebrate at a blow-out beach party.

Shops and galleries

San Pedro's **gift shops** and **art galleries** offer some of the best shopping in the country. Highlights include Belizean Arts on Barrier Reef Drive (Ⓣ226-3019, Ⓦwww.belizeanarts.com), probably the best gallery in the country with an unparalleled range of **arts**, **crafts** and **jewellery** from all over Central America. Orange and Isla Bonita, galleries south of the centre along Coconut Drive, both display stunning works by Belizean artists, whom you can frequently meet. Look out for crafters of traditional **zericote wood carvings**, many of whom cluster on the beach at the south end of Barrier Reef Drive – you'll surely see their works around town. Also on the beach are numerous Maya women selling traditional cloth and baskets.

In the middle of Barrier Reef Drive, Ambergris Jade displays superb **carved jade** replicas of Maya artifacts. Owned by archeologist Pamela Killen, it's also a fascinating museum; you're free to browse and watch videos of Maya culture and sights. Some of the best classic and modern **sterling silver jewellery** in the country is on display at the Caribbean Connection Internet Café, and Isla Bonita Designs, near the north end of Barrier Reef Drive, sells creative and colourful **handmade clothing**.

Exploring the caye and reef

Fifteen hundred metres north of the town centre, the **Boca del Rio** (usually referred to simply as "the river" or "the cut") is a narrow but widening erosion channel now crossed by a substantial bridge (free on foot and after 10pm, Bz$2 for bikes and Bz$10 for golf carts during the day). The largest vehicle permitted across is a golf cart, although most rental companies don't allow clients to head much further north; check with your company, or call a taxi at Ⓣ602-1073 or 603-1073). On the northern side of the river, a rudimentary road (navigable for some distance in the dry season, much less during wet weather, though bikes can usually pass) leads to the village of **Tres Cocos** and the northern resorts along miles of gorgeous, mostly deserted beaches. The northernmost region of the caye, now accessible on organized day-trips or overnights, boasts the spectacular **Bacalar Chico National Park and Marine Reserve**, as well as several **Maya sites** (see p.142).

Following Coconut Drive **south** from the city, San Pedro becomes **San Pablo**, the semi-official name for this area of beach resorts and houses for the often Spanish-speaking workforce. Set back from the sea, the road runs for several kilometres to the Maya site of **Marco Gonzalez**, though the further you go, the swampier and more mosquito-infested the terrain gets. The site is hard to find and there's not much to see, but studies have shown that it was once an important trade centre with close links to Lamanai (see p.108); archeological teams still conduct excavations here. The southernmost tip of the caye is the terrestrial section of **Hol Chan Marine Reserve**.

Before **snorkelling** or **diving** here, whet your appetite for the wonders of the reef with a visit to the excellent Hol Chan Marine Reserve office and **visitor centre**, on Caribeña Street in San Pedro (Mon–Fri 8am–noon & 1–5pm; ⓣ226-2247). Photographs, maps and excellent models explain the marine reserve, and the staff will be pleased to answer any questions; you may even be able to get a ride with the ranger up to Bacalar Chico. For additional information on Hol Chan, contact Green Reef (ⓣ226-2833, ⓦwww.greenreefbelize.org), a nonprofit organization working to protect the marine reserves and ecology of Ambergris Caye. Founded in 1996, it promotes education and opportunities for self-funded volunteers interested in biological monitoring.

Diving

The reef in front of San Pedro is a heavily used area that's been subject to intensive fishing and souvenir hunting. You'll find it in much better condition to the north, toward **Mexico Rocks**, or south, toward **Hol Chan**, both

Dive tour operators on Ambergris Caye

In addition to the dive shops at several hotels and resorts, there are plenty of independent **dive operators**. The best are not necessarily the most well known, as these often cater to large groups and leave some divers unsatisfied. Smaller, locally owned outfits usually take smaller groups and provide more personal service. Beware any guides that encourage clients to touch the reef or animals or feed the fish.

Equipment sales and repairs and underwater camera rentals are available at **Island Diver Supplies** on Black Coral Street, near the Front Dock (ⓣ226-4023). San Pedro also has the only **hyperbaric chamber** in Belize, located behind the airstrip; your dive operator should have all the details in case of emergency.

Belize Academy of Diving 11km north of San Pedro ⓣ226-2873, ⓦwww.belize-academy-of-diving.com. Well run dive trips from the northern resorts, and training up to Advanced Open Water level.

Belize Diving Adventures ⓣ226-3082, ⓦwww.belizedivingadventures.net. Local, family-run business organizing dive trips to the Turneffe Islands, Blue Hole and other local dive sites, as well as fishing and inland tours.

Ecologic Divers North of the centre ⓣ226-4118, ⓦwww.ecologicdivers.com. Offers dive trips day and (even) night, with various local and atoll dives; few extras, but claims to be the most eco-aware.

Patojo's Next to *The Tides* ⓣ226-2283, ⓦwww.ambergriscaye.com/tides. A wide variety of local dives, and qualified to teach to Divemaster level. Offers good packages for keen divers (particularly for hotel guests).

Protech Belize In front of *Spindrift Hotel* ⓣ226-4690, ⓦwww.protechbelize.com. All the standard dive trips, with small groups. They're the only technical dive centre in Belize, offering IANTD rebreather and other courses (including cave diving), with oxygen and helium always in stock (all nitrox produced on the island).

White Sands Cove Dive Centre About 3km north of town ⓣ226-2405, ⓦwww.whitesandscovediveshop.com. Run by the well-known Elbert Greer, who is also a respected birder. Offering full PADI certification up to Instructor level, and packages for guests of *White Sands Cove*.

locations exhibiting fascinating "spur and groove" formations. Large marine life found here can include **sharks** (hammerhead, bull and tiger, as well as the common and harmless nurse shark), turtles, spotted eagle rays and, if you're really lucky, manta rays and whale sharks. For the best diving in Belize and high-voltage excitement in a relatively pristine environment, you really need to take a trip to one of the **atolls** (see box, opposite). **Night diving** and snorkelling, truly amazing experiences, are also available.

Open Water Certification, which turns novices into PADI-qualified sport divers, costs around US$420; **Advanced Open Water Certification** costs an additional US$325. A more basic, single-dive **resort course** (which doesn't lead to PADI certification) is around US$150. All options should include equipment. Qualified divers can purchase a two-tank local dive for around US$75. For diving trips to the Blue Hole, expect to pay around US$250; for the Turneffe Islands, around US$185.

Snorkelling

Almost every dive shop in San Pedro also offers **snorkelling** trips, although specialized snorkelling outfits will provide more personal attention; going with a dive boat may mean you're left on your own while the staff concentrates on the divers. Several trips are offered from San Pedro, the most popular being to Hol Chan Marine Reserve, focusing on a decent section of reef that is sometimes overcrowded. Local tours cost US$25–50 for two to four hours, depending on where you go and whether a beach barbecue is included.

Snorkelling **guides** (who must also be licensed tour guides) have a great deal of experience with visitors, and they'll show you how to use your equipment before setting off; if they don't seem willing to help novices, go with someone else. You might also prefer to snorkel in a lifejacket – this will give you greater buoyancy, and keep you from bumping into the coral (see p.128). Generally, trips either head north to the spectacular **Mexico Rocks** or **Rocky Point** or, more commonly, south to **Hol Chan Marine Reserve** and **Shark-Ray Alley** (see p.140). Trips to Caye Caulker are also popular,

Snorkel tour operators on Ambergris Caye

Adventure Belize On the Front Dock ⓣ226-2636. Offers a variety of tours, including Bacalar Chico.

Grumpy and Happy ⓣ226-3420, ⓦwww.grumpyandhappy.com. Private groups (up to eight people) from US$250. Good for special needs, also offering scuba tours and instruction.

Island Roots ⓣ226-3773, ⓔislandroots@btl.net. A small operation specializing in highly recommended tours to Bacalar Chico.

Reef Runner ⓣ226-2180, ⓦwww.ambergriscaye.com/reefrunner. The only glass-bottomed boat in San Pedro allows non-snorkellers to enjoy the reef. However, guides are known to pick up the animals, which should not be encouraged (see box, p.128).

Seaduced by Belize In the town centre ⓣ226-3221, ⓦwww.seaducedbybelize.com. Their sailing boats visit all the local snorkelling areas, and they also run sunset, sunrise and inland tours. Owner Elito Arceo is a great guide and does a lot of work in eco-education.

Searious Adventures In the town centre ⓣ226-4202, ⓦwww.seariousadventures.com. Snorkel tours by sailing boat; sunset and inland tours as well.

Tanisha Ecological Tours ⓣ226-2314, ⓦwww.tanishatours.com. Both snorkel and inland tours. Guide Daniel Nuñez, who runs the Lamanai trips, is a fantastic naturalist.

but travelling there on your own by water taxi and taking a local tour (see p.150) is cheaper. There are also several independent sailing boat owners who will charter their craft for the day; ask at your hotel or at the information centre next to the town hall.

Windsurfing, sailing and swimming

The best **windsurfing** and **sailing** rental and instruction on the caye is offered by SailSports Belize (☎226-4488, Ⓦwww.sailsportsbelize.com), on the beach in front of the *Holiday Hotel*. The English owners are both qualified Royal Yachting Association instructors, and provide a great learning environment; a beginner sailing course costs US$265 for a five-hour session. Boat rental is US$22–49 per hour or US$110–195/day, depending on the boat, and windsurfers are also available for rent at US$22–27 per hour or US$72–82/day; rates for both grow cheaper as rental hours increase.

Very comfortably equipped **charter catamarans** are a new, expensive and increasingly popular addition to Ambergris Caye's activities. If you can afford it, there are several companies to book with. TMM Bareboat Vacations, on Coconut Drive just past the Tropic Air Office (☎226-3026, in the US ☎1-800/633-0155, Ⓦwww.sailtmm.com), has a fleet with one 35-foot monohull and catamarans ranging from 38ft (sleeping up to eight) to over 46ft (sleeping up to twelve). All have VHF radio, dinghy, lifejackets, first-aid kit, cruising guide and snorkel equipment; a skipper and cook are also available for an extra daily fee.

If you plan on **swimming**, you should know that **beaches** on Ambergris Caye are narrow and the sea immediately offshore is shallow, with a lot of seagrass – meaning you'll usually need to jump off the end of a dock or take a boat trip to the reef if you want a proper paddle. A word of **warning**: there have been a number of swimming accidents in San Pedro caused by boats speeding past the piers. A line of buoys, not always clearly visible, indicates the "**safe area**", but speedboat drivers are sometimes recklessly macho; be careful when choosing where to swim.

The south: Hol Chan Marine Reserve and Shark-Ray Alley

Hol Chan Marine Reserve, 8km south of San Pedro at the southern tip of the caye, takes its name from the Maya word for "little channel", and it is indeed a break in the reef that forms the focus of the reserve. Established in 1987 and the first of Belize's marine reserves, its three zones – covering a total of around thirteen square kilometres – preserve a comprehensive cross-section of the marine environment, including **coral reef**, **seagrass beds** and **mangroves**. All three habitats are closely linked: many reef fish feed on the seagrass beds, and the mangroves are a nursery area for the juveniles. Approaching with a boat tour, you'll be met by a warden who explains the rules and collects the entry fee (Bz$20), which is sometimes included in the cost of your tour. If arriving in your own boat, purchase tickets beforehand at the Hol Chan office in town (see p.138). Feeding the fish is prohibited, but they're no longer hunted either, so you'll see plenty of **marine life**, including some very large snappers, groupers and barracuda. Much damage has already been caused to the **coral** here; see the box on p.128 for tips on avoiding further damage.

Included in most of the tours is another part of the reserve, **Shark-Ray Alley**, where you can swim in shallow water with three-metre **nurse sharks** and enormous **stingrays** – an extremely popular (though controversial) attraction. Watching these creatures glide effortlessly beneath you is an exhilarating experience and swimming here poses almost no danger to snorkellers, as humans are not part of the fishes' normal diet. Biologists, however, claim that the practice of feeding the fish to attract them alters their natural behaviour, exposing both the animals and humans to potential danger. In fact, the area is so crowded at times that any hope of communing with nature is completely lost amid the flailing limbs of the snorkellers, and there's also the possibility that a shark could accidentally bite a hand – as has occasionally happened. If you do want to experience a close encounter with sharks, never offer them food yourself, despite what your guide and other snorkellers do; just look at them and the rays from the boat, or jump in the water to simply swim among them. Touching them is also detrimental to their health and against regulations – though it often seems as though some guides aren't aware of this.

The north: Bacalar Chico National Park and the Maya sites

A visit to the remote and virtually pristine northern section of Ambergris Caye is a not-to-be-missed highlight, both for the obvious attractions of the **Bacalar Chico National Park and Marine Reserve** (ⓣ226-2833 for park manager) and for the chance to see a number of previously inaccessible **Maya sites** along the coast. Several companies offer trips up here, but only the most environmentally conscious outfits are allowed into the protected marine areas. On a day-trip from San Pedro you can visit several areas of the reserve and take in a few of more than ten Maya sites; the best trips are run by Island Roots and Adventure Belize (see p.139), both of which have permission to enter conservation areas.

On standard trips with local companies, you'll travel by boat through the Boca del Rio and up the west coast, stopping briefly to observe colonies of wading birds roosting on small, uninhabited cayes, such as the bird sanctuary of **Little Guana Caye**. Several species of heron and egret live in the area, and you might even spot the beautiful and much rarer **roseate spoonbill**, though landing on the islands or disturbing the birds is prohibited. To return to town you'll pass through **Bacalar Chico**, the channel partly dug by the Maya about 1500 years ago to create a shorter trading route between their cities in Chetumal Bay and the coast of Yucatán. It's so narrow you can practically touch the mangroves on either side as you sit in the boat. At the mouth of the channel the reef comes close to shore, so the boat has to cross into open sea and re-enter the leeward side of the reef on the approach to San Pedro – thus completing a circumnavigation of the island.

The national park and marine reserve

Covering the entire northern tip of Ambergris Caye, **Bacalar Chico National Park and Marine Reserve** is the largest protected area in the northern cayes. Its 110 square kilometres extend from the reef, across the seagrass beds to the coastal mangroves and the endangered **caye littoral forest**, and over to the salt marsh and lagoon behind. The sea area within the park is designated a Marine Reserve and is protected by Belize's Fisheries Department, while the terrestrial area is a National Park under the protection of Belize's Forest Department; both are patrolled by rangers based at the headquarters and **visitor centre** at **San Juan**, on the island's northwest coast, where you register and pay the park fee. Near the ranger station, a seven-metre-high **observation tower** allows views over undisturbed lagoon and forest – it's also used by rangers to control boat traffic.

Despite all the development to the south, there's a surprising amount of **wildlife** here, including crocodiles, deer, peccaries and, prowling around the thick forests, several of the wild cats of Belize, including jaguars. Birdlife is abundant and turtles nest on some beaches; contact the Belize Audubon Society (see p.74) or the Hol Chan Reserve office (see p.138) if you want to help patrol the beaches during the nesting season. The Peace Corps has been working with park management to provide a camping area and cabañas for rent; contact the park manager for details (Ⓔbacalarchicomr@gmail.com).

Maya sites

Some of the **Maya sites** in the north of the caye are undergoing archeological investigation, meaning there's a real air of adventure and discovery as you explore these ancient ruins buried in thick bush and jungle. About two thirds of the way up the west coast of the caye, **Santa Cruz** is a very large site, once used for the shipment of trade goods in the Postclassic era, though the precise function of most of its stone mounds remains uncertain. Further north, the beach at **San Juan** was another shipment centre for the ancient Maya; here you'll crunch over literally thousands of pieces of Maya pottery. But perhaps the most interesting site – at least, if archeologists are working there when you visit – is **Chac Balam**, an ancient ceremonial and administrative centre; getting here entails a walk through mangroves to view deep burial chambers, scattered with thousands more pottery shards.

Trips inland

Increasingly popular inland **day-trips** leave San Pedro for the Maya sites of **Altun Ha** (around US$85; see p.98) and even **Lamanai** (US$150; see p.108). Tour prices usually include lunch, soft drinks and beer, entrance fee and rum punch on the way back. Rounding the southern tip of the island in a fast skiff, you head for the mainland at the mouth of the Northern River, cross the lagoon and travel upriver to the tiny village of Bomba. With a good guide this is an excellent way to spot **wildlife**, including crocodiles and manatees, and the riverbank trees are often adorned with orchids. If you've enjoyed the wood carvings for sale in the gift shops on Ambergris Caye, stop and examine what's available in Bomba; prices here are lower, and the money goes directly to the carvers' families. The best naturalist **guides** for these trips are Daniel Nuñez of Tanisha Ecological Tours and Elito Arceo of Seaduced by Belize (see box, p.139).

Eating, drinking and entertainment

There are plenty of places to eat in San Pedro, including some of the best **restaurants** in the country, and the very top of the range compares favourably with resorts anywhere in the world. **Prices** are generally higher than elsewhere in Belize, though you can find a few local places offering excellent value. **Seafood** and **steaks** are on the menu at most restaurants, reflecting the tastes of the town's predominantly North American guests; thus you can also rely on plenty of shrimp, chicken, pizza and salads. Many hotels have their own dining room, and in some cases also hold **beach barbecues**. A few **Chinese** restaurants appear around town, but none especially stand out, unlike elsewhere in the country.

Buying your own food isn't particularly cheap: there's no local market and the supermarkets are stocked primarily with canned imports. The range and quality of groceries improves all the time, though, and one of your best bets is Island Supermarket, on Coconut Drive at the southern end of town. La Popular bakery, on Buccaneer Street, has a wide selection of bread and buns, including Mexican-style *pan dulces*, and there are some fruit and vegetable stalls dotted around the centre. *D & E's Ice Cream*, on Pescador Street at Pelican Street, is the best place in town for an **ice cream**.

Restaurants in town

Alibaba's Coconut Drive ⓣ226-4042, ⓔjazomarjaz@yahoo.com. Serving the only Mediterranean and Middle Eastern food on the island: Lebanese chicken from Bz$18, and kebabs and falafel also on the menu. Open 9.30am–9.30pm.

Blue Water Grill At the *Sunbreeze Hotel* ⓣ226-3347. On a deck overlooking the beach, this family-oriented restaurant, one of the best in town, serves imaginative seafood, wood-fired pizza and other treats from the extensive international and wine menus. Tuesday and Thursday are sushi nights.

Caliente On the beach at *Spindrift Hotel* ⓣ226-2170. A popular place for locals and tourists alike, with a Latin-flavoured menu. Ladies' night on Wednesday for the famous "chicken drop" (check out the *Spindrift*'s website). Closed Mon.

Caramba's Pescador Drive, between Pelican and Ambergris streets ⓣ226-4321. Extremely popular with expats and tourists, with a mixed menu and lively atmosphere.

Elvi's Kitchen Pescador Drive, across the street from *Martha's* ⓣ226-2176. A San Pedro institution known for great burgers and fries, *Elvi's* has now zoomed upmarket with an expanded menu of soups, Caesar salads, steaks, chicken and, of course, lobster and other seafood. The quality is high and the service slick, with prices to match; Friday is Maya Buffet night. Gentle live music in the evenings. Closed Sun.

Estel's Restaurant On the beach, at the end of Buccaneer St ⓣ226-2019. All-day breakfast and good local food at fair prices. One of the few locally owned businesses left on the beach.

Hacal Kiik On the street behind the airstrip ⓣ226-3115. Excellent snacks, Belizean food and baked goods – a hideaway treasure for those in the know.

Hungry Monkey Sub-Shop Pescador Drive ⓣ206-2221. Serving all variety of subs from Bz$14. Open 11am–6pm.

Jambel Jerk Pit Barrier Reef Drive ⓣ226-3515. A blend of Jamaican and Belizean specialities, including jerk chicken, pork, fish and always a vegetarian option. Good prices, decent food but unreliable service.

Papi's Diner Laguna Street, about 1km north of the centre ⓣ226-2047. Delicious, varied local fare at great prices. Some of the best seafood on the island and well worth the walk from town. Open for breakfast, lunch and dinner.

Pasta la Vista Tarpon Street ⓣ226-2651. Relaxed atmosphere, good pasta, calzones, pizza dishes and frozen lasagnes to take away. Open 3–10pm.

The Reef Pescador Drive between Pelican and Ambergris streets ⓣ226-4145. Very good Belizean food, including excellent seafood, at great prices in an atmospheric local restaurant cooled by a battery of fans. Commendable service.

Wild Mango's On the beach between Tarpon and Esmeralda streets ⓣ226-2859. Owned by locally renowned chef Amy Knox, featuring an innovative menu and good desserts. Tasty food at high prices.

Restaurants south of town

The restaurants below are listed in order of their distance from town.

Monkey Bites Café At *Exotic Caye Resort*, 1km south of town ⓣ206-2021. Excellent-value, hearty food with tables in front, inside and on the beach.

Casa Picasso Sting Ray Street, 1km south of the airstrip ⓣ226-4507, ⓔcasapicassobelize@yahoo.com. A popular place for evenings, with movie screen and happy hour. Good for pastas, tapas and vegetarian dishes, with a full wine list. Reservations are advised in peak season.

Palmilla Restaurant At *Victoria House* ⓣ226-2067, ⓦwww.victoria-house.com. Excellent fine-dining menu in a romantic, candlelit setting overlooking the hotel's pool. Also serves breakfast and lunch.

Fido's Sandbar On the beach, about 4km south of town ⓣ226-4210, ⓔchefadambelize@hotmail. A relaxing daytime hangout serving a variety of local and international dishes. Live music some evenings. Open 11am–9pm.

Restaurants north of town

The restaurants below are listed in order of their distance from town. They're best accessed by boat year-round, or by road from February to June.

Beach n' Kitchen About 1km north of the bridge ☎226-4456. Open for full breakfast and lunch, serving salads, sandwiches, Belizean food and daily specials at very reasonable prices.

Rendezvous On the beach, 5.5km north of town ☎226-3426. A delicious and unique fusion of Thai and French cuisines, accompanied by wines from the restaurant's own winery. Try the seafood sour curry, with shrimp, snapper and mussels. Expensive by Belize standards, at around US$21–29 for an entrée, but well worth it. Heavenly desserts, too.

Capricorn Restaurant At *Capricorn Resort* ☎226-2809. Unbeatable gourmet food in a beautiful location; try the French crêpes, stone-crab cakes or filet mignon/seafood combo. Great daily brunch from 10am to 2pm; you'll need to book in advance for dinner (til 9pm) in high season. Closed Wed in low season.

Portofino At *Portofino Resort* ☎220-5096. Excellent restaurant with great views, wines and cocktails and a wide range of seafood, poultry and meats. Call ahead for dinner reservations, which include free pickup from town. Open 7am–4pm & 6–9pm.

Bars and nightlife

San Pedro is the tourist **entertainment** capital of Belize, and its nightlife grows more sophisticated each year. At the very least you'll find **live music** somewhere every night of the week, and unless the band's a top-notch act, cover charges are rare. Many hotels have bars, several of which offer **happy hours** – usually two drinks for the price of one from 5 to 7pm – while small **cantinas** set back from the main street get the crowds warmed up. The best way to find out what's hot is to ask at your hotel or the information centre, or check the listings in the local press.

A block north of the park, *Fido's* showcases a reggae or rock band most nights, with resident Category X playing Saturdays. *Wet Willie's* (☎226-4136) is known for live music late on Wednesday evenings, attracting many mingle-minded tourists and expats. South of town, the seaside *Palapa Bar* next to *Beach n' Kitchen* (see above) is a good spot for an afternoon or evening drink, and *Fido's Sandbar* (see p.143), 4km south of town, occasionally hosts large bands.

For DJ beats and **dancing**, *Big Daddy's Disco*, near Central Park, is a popular weekend spot for young locals. The dance floor at *Jaguar Temple*, opposite the park, is usually packed, while the air-conditioned *Barefoot Iguana*, about 1.5km south of town on Coconut Drive, is the biggest club in town.

Caye Caulker

South of Ambergris Caye and 35km northeast of Belize City, **CAYE CAULKER** – whose name derives from a local wild fruit, the hicaco, or coco plum – has long had a reputation as a sleepy, laid-back fishing village, an image now rather outdated. Long an important stop on the backpacker trail in Belize, it now attracts families as well as upmarket travellers. The beautiful, palm-clad island is still a relaxing, traffic-free escape, but with many more opportunities for comfort and entertainment, and its wide spectrum of hotels runs from basic backpacker dormitories to luxury, poolside lodging.

Until about twenty years ago, tourism existed almost as a sideline to the island's main source of income, **lobster fishing**. Although the lobster catch increased for many years after fishing cooperatives were set up in the 1960s, the deployment of more traps over an ever-wider area led to the rapid depletion of the **spiny lobster**, once so common that it could be scooped onto the beaches

Getting to and from Caye Caulker

Most visitors to Caye Caulker arrive by **boat**: the Caye Caulker Water Taxi Association (ⓣ226-0992, ⓦwww.cayecaulkerwatertaxi.com) has departures at least every ninety minutes from 8am to 5.30pm from the Marine Terminal in Belize City (45min; Bz$15 one way). Most scheduled boats to San Pedro (see box, p.130) also call at Caye Caulker. Boats from **Caye Caulker to San Pedro** (Bz$20) depart and return at least every ninety minutes from 7am to 3.50pm (4.30pm on weekends and holidays).

Leaving for Belize City, boats (Bz$20) depart roughly every ninety minutes from 6.30am to 4pm (5pm on weekends and holidays). You can buy your ticket in advance but they don't take reservations. Standby boats are available at busy times.

Flights (Bz$63) on the San Pedro run stop on request at the Caye Caulker airstrip, 1.5km south of the village centre. The offices of Maya Island Air and Tropic Air are at the airstrip, and there are agents around the village.

with palm fronds. Their numbers remain low today, and in some years the creatures are so scarce that the fishermen call it quits by mid-January, a month before the end of the legal season. Despite this, there are always plenty of lobsters around for the annual **Lobster-Fest**, held on the first weekend of July to celebrate the opening of the season.

Caye Caulker's eight-kilometre length is split into two unequal sections by the "Split", originally a small passage cut by local fishermen that's since grown into a swiftly-moving boat channel, widened by successive tropical storms. The main village, and most hotels, are on the northern end of the south island. The north island was, until recently, mostly uninhabited and remains without electricity, but the caye as a whole is experiencing an unprecedented building boom on both sides of the Split. Still, most visitors have little reason to venture to the north island, except perhaps for an occasional trip to the land section of the **Caye Caulker Forest and Marine Reserve** (see p.149), whose littoral forest takes up roughly half a square kilometre on the northern tip of the caye. The smaller **Caye Caulker Mini Reserve**, on Back Street just north of the airstrip, makes for an easier trip, and has an informative visitor's centre and some interesting examples of indigenous vegetation, along with common foreign imports such as coconut palms.

Arrival and information

Arriving **by boat**, you'll be dropped off at one of two piers on the eastern edge of the caye, both in the main village. **Tricycle taxis** will be waiting to carry your luggage (and possibly you), but if you haven't pre-booked accommodation, the water taxi office will hold your belongings while you look for a place to stay. If you arrive by **plane**, golf cart taxis can take you 1.5km to the centre, or you can cover the distance on foot in ten to fifteen minutes.

Once in the centre, you'll find three sandy main streets running roughly parallel to the eastern shore; though their names have changed from "Front", "Middle" and "Back" streets to Avenida Hicaco, Avenida Langosta and Avenida Mangle, the original terms are used more often. Despite the impression given by some signs, a public path follows the shoreline, giving access to hotels right on the water. Outside the village, the main streets end and only a single road leads north and south, turning into a winding path beyond the airstrip.

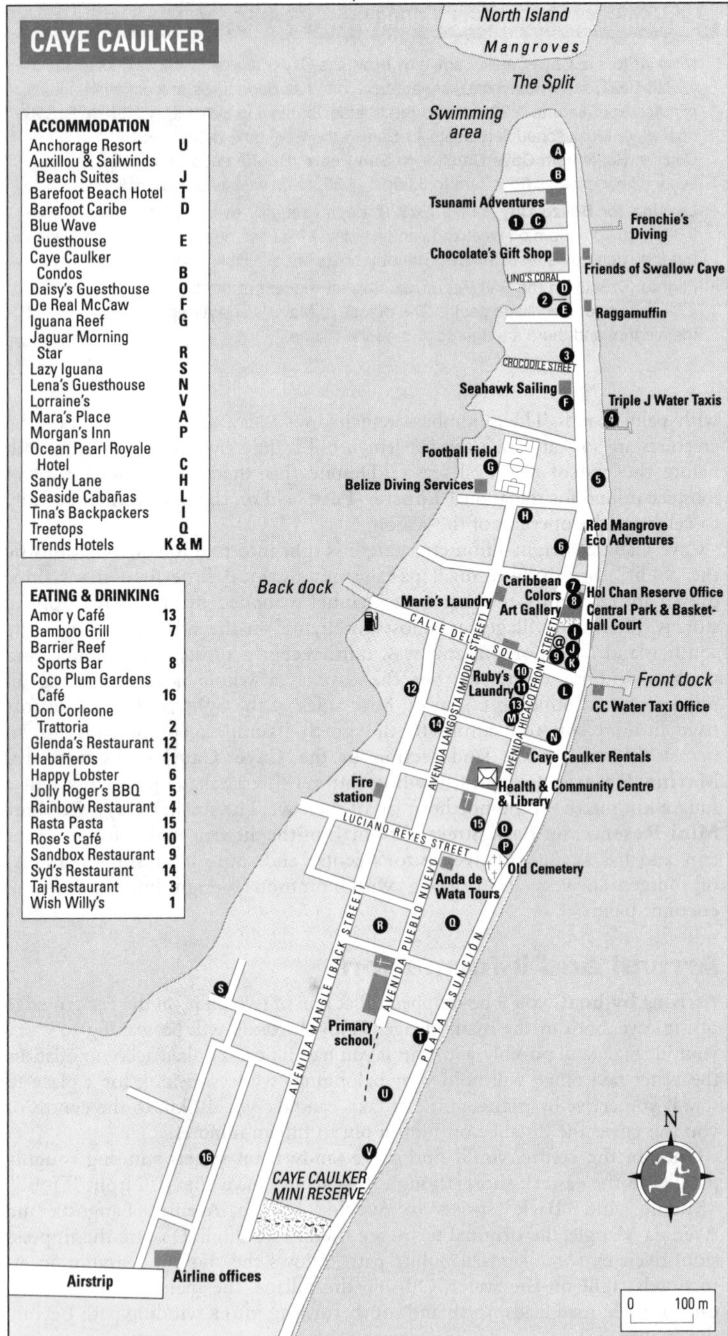
Caye Caulker Forest & Marine Reserve
CAYE CAULKER
North Island
Mangroves
The Split
Swimming area
ACCOMMODATION
Anchorage Resort U
Auxillou & Sailwinds Beach Suites J
Barefoot Beach Hotel T
Barefoot Caribe D
Blue Wave Guesthouse E
Caye Caulker Condos B
Daisy's Guesthouse O
De Real McCaw F
Iguana Reef G
Jaguar Morning Star R
Lazy Iguana S
Lena's Guesthouse N
Lorraine's V
Mara's Place A
Morgan's Inn P
Ocean Pearl Royale Hotel C
Sandy Lane H
Seaside Cabañas L
Tina's Backpackers I
Treetops Q
Trends Hotels K & M
EATING & DRINKING
Amor y Café 13
Bamboo Grill 7
Barrier Reef Sports Bar 8
Coco Plum Gardens Café 16
Don Corleone Trattoria 2
Glenda's Restaurant 12
Habañeros 11
Happy Lobster 6
Jolly Roger's BBQ 5
Rainbow Restaurant 4
Rasta Pasta 15
Rose's Café 10
Sandbox Restaurant 9
Syd's Restaurant 14
Taj Restaurant 3
Wish Willy's 1
Tsunami Adventures
Frenchie's Diving
Chocolate's Gift Shop
Friends of Swallow Caye
LINO'S CORAL
Raggamuffin
CROCODILE STREET
Seahawk Sailing
Triple J Water Taxis
Football field
Belize Diving Services
Red Mangrove Eco Adventures
Caribbean Colors Art Gallery
Hol Chan Reserve Office
Central Park & Basket-ball Court
Back dock
Marie's Laundry
CALLE DEL SOL
AVENIDA LANGOSTA (MIDDLE STREET)
AVENIDA HICACO (FRONT STREET)
Ruby's Laundry
Front dock
CC Water Taxi Office
Caye Caulker Rentals
Fire station
Health & Community Centre & Library
LUCIANO REYES STREET
Old Cemetery
Anda de Wata Tours
AVENIDA PUEBLO NUEVO
AVENIDA MANGLE (BACK STREET)
PLAYA ASUNCIÓN
Primary school
CAYE CAULKER MINI RESERVE
Airstrip
Airline offices
N
0
100 m

There's currently no official tourist office in Caye Caulker, but the village council (ⓦwww.cayecaulkerbelize.net) and the Belize Tourism Industry Association (BTIA; ⓦwww.gocayecaulker.com) both have excellent **websites**. The **post office** is just south of the centre on Front Street, and the **BTL** office is on Back Street, near the Back Dock, though there are plenty of payphones around. Excellent **Internet** access is available at Caye Caulker Cyber Café, just north of *Sandbox Restaurant*, and Cayeboard Connection is a bit further along Front Street. The Atlantic Bank, on Middle Street, has an ATM that takes foreign and local cards, and most businesses accept credit cards and US traveller's cheques; all take US dollars.

One thing to be aware of in Caye Caulker is the **tap water**, which smells sulphurous at times. This may be the result of natural chemicals in the groundwater, but since most businesses and residences use septic tanks for waste disposal, it could be the result of effluent seeping into the water table. A clean water system has been in the planning stages for quite some time, but until it actually materializes, tap water on the caye should be regarded as **unfit to drink**. Some hotels provide drinking water, or you can buy readily available bottled water.

Though there is a near-constant sea breeze, when this drops the air gets very sticky, and **sandflies and mosquitoes** can be unbearably irritating, making a good insect repellent essential.

Accommodation

Caye Caulker has an abundance of simply furnished, inexpensive shared-bath rooms in attractive **clapboard hotels**, plus plenty of more comfortable options with private bathrooms (and many with air-conditioning) – but to arrive at Christmas or New Year without a **reservation** could leave you stranded. Even the furthest **hotels** are no more than ten minutes' walk from the Front Dock. Almost everywhere has hot water and many accept credit cards. For excellent **house rentals**, check with Amanda Badger at Caye Caulker Rentals, south of the Front Dock (ⓣ226-0029, ⓦwww.cayecaulkerrentals.com). M&N Apartments (ⓣ226-0229) has some smaller apartments, and several of the hotels below have an

△ Palms on Caye Caulker

apartment or two for longer stays. You can also rent houses and cabañas from their owners; ask around town or look for signs.

The hotels below are listed in order of their appearance as you head north or south from the Front Dock.

North of the Front Dock

Trends Beachfront Hotel On the beach, immediately north of the Front Dock ⓣ226-0094, ⓦwww.trendsbze.com. Large rooms in a pastel-painted wooden building with comfortable beds, private baths and tiled floors. There's a deck with hammocks outside. Round the corner on Front St (left at *Habañeros Restaurant*) there's another *Trends* with slightly less expensive rooms. ❸–❺

Auxillou Beach Suites 50m along the beach from the Front Dock ⓣ226-0370, ⓦwww.auxiloubeachsuites.com. Four well-furnished, a/c suites with kitchenette in a glorious location overlooking the beach. The most spacious and comfortable apartments on the island, with living rooms opening onto a wide balcony. Good service, lots of extras and owner Wendy Auxillou can arrange tours throughout the country. ❼–❾

Tina's Backpackers 75m along the beach from the Front Dock ⓣ206-0019, ⓔtinasbackpackershostel@yahoo.com. A relaxing beach house with dorm beds (Bz$20 per person; shared bathroom) and private rooms from Bz$40. You can cook in the communal kitchen, and there's a book exchange. Outside is a pretty garden with hammocks and a dock for sunbathing. ❶–❷

Sandy Lane Hotel On Middle St, one block north of Atlantic Bank ⓣ226-0117. Small, quiet, clean and inexpensive, with shared-bath rooms in the original building and newer, slightly more expensive cabins on the grounds, with private bath; some have TV. ❶–❸

Iguana Reef Inn At the back (west side) of the caye, across the football field ⓣ226-0213, ⓦwww.iguanareefinn.com. The most luxurious hotel on the island, with thirteen well-furnished, beautifully decorated a/c suites with queen-sized beds, CD player, fridge and great sunset views. No TV. Free kayaks for guests, a pool and continental breakfasts. ❾

De Real Macaw Guest House Front St, next to Seahawk Sailing ⓣ226-0459, ⓦwww.derealmacaw.biz. Very comfortable, good-value rooms and thatched cabañas facing the sea. Variety of accommodation, from double rooms (some with a/c) through to two-bed condo with all amenities. Doubles ❸–❻, condo ❾

Blue Wave Guesthouse Toward the north end of Front St ⓣ206-0114, ⓔbluewave@btl.net. Very pleasant family-run place with basic rooms with shared bath. There are spacious a/c rooms with large showers and cable TV in a separate, newer building. ❷–❻

Barefoot Caribe Just past *Blue Wave* ⓣ226-0161, ⓦwww.barefootcariberesort.com. Large hotel (by island standards) with three levels of rooms, starting small with fan and TV (Bz$80) and going up to large with a/c (Bz$170). Run by a friendly family that also owns *Sobre las Olas* across the street, serving good breakfast and seafood. ❹–❼

Ocean Pearl Royale Hotel Toward the back of the island, two blocks from the Split ⓣ226-0074, ⓔoceanpearl@btl.net. Variety of rooms, some double, some twins and some with a/c, and two-bedroom cabins on the grounds for longer stays. Lots of local information available. ❹–❻

Caye Caulker Condos On the last block before the Split ⓣ226-0072. Excellent-quality apartments with full kitchens, wireless Internet, a safe for valuables, free bikes, a/c and large showers decorated with river stones. Large rooftop palapa with excellent views in all directions. The manager provides many extra touches to make you feel welcome. ❽–❾

Mara's Place One of the last buildings before the Split ⓣ206-0056. Six simple, comfortable and good-value wooden cabins facing the sea, with private bath, TV and porch. ❹

South of the Front Dock

Seaside Cabañas Just steps south of the Front Dock ⓣ226-0498, ⓦwww.seasidecabanas.com. Well-designed and furnished rooms and thatched cabañas, all with a/c, fridge, cable TV, DVD player and veranda with hammocks. Beautifully decorated both inside and out in rich colours with a Moroccan/Mexican feel, these are the best beach cabañas on Caye Caulker, arranged around a pool. There's also a thatched rooftop bar. No children under 11. Also available are five apartments in a development further south along the beach. Cabañas ❽, apartments ❾

Lena's Guest House On the beachfront ⓣ226-0106, ⓔlenas@btl.net. Budget rooms in a wooden building by the water, some with private bath. Great sea views from the shady porch at the front. ❹

Daisy's Guesthouse On Front St ⓣ206-0150. Set just back from the sea, these simple and delightful budget rooms, all with shared showers, are run by a friendly family. ❸

Morgan's Inn Opposite Galería Hicaco, where you enquire ☎226-0178, ©sbf@btl.net or siwaban@yahoo.com. Three quiet, roomy cabins, set just back from the beach; each sleeps at least three. Perfect for long stays and fine for just a night or two. Stoves available on request. The Galería has some artwork for sale, and the owner can take you on birding tours. Kayaks for rent (proceeds go to conservation efforts). ❹–❺

Treetops Guesthouse On the beachfront, past the cemetery ☎226-0240, ⓦwww.treetopsbelize.com. One of the best hotels on the island, just 50m from the water. Immaculately clean and very comfortable ground-floor rooms with fridge, cable TV and powerful ceiling fans, and luxury, rooftop a/c suites with fantastic views, all set in a small, peaceful garden. Deservedly popular, so booking ahead is advised. Rooms ❺, suites ❼

Jaguar Morning Star Guest House Across from the school ☎226-0347, ©joanne@btl.net. Two tiled rooms on the third floor with deck, and great views and an a/c cabin with a shady porch on the grounds; all rooms have private shower and fridge, and the cabin has a coffeemaker. A quiet, secure, relaxing place to stay. ❸–❹

Barefoot Beach Hotel On the beach, just south of the school ☎226-0205, ⓦwww.barefootbeachbelize.com. Four very comfortable, fan-cooled rooms with private bath and fridge in a concrete house right on the beach. There are also two roomy, wooden cottages. ❼–❾

Lazy Iguana Bed & Breakfast Follow the signs south from the dock to the back of the island ☎226-0350, ⓦwww.lazyiguana.net. The best B&B on the island, with just four beautifully decorated and very comfortable a/c rooms, each with a luxurious private bathroom. The shady gardens are filled with orchids and the top floor has a thatched deck with hammocks to enjoy all-round views over the sea and the lagoon. Friendly owners Mo and Irene Miller prepare a fantastic breakfast and also produce a unique range of perfumes in their own workshop. A massage can also be arranged on site. ❼

Anchorage Resort On the shore at the end the path past the school ☎226-0304, ⓦwww.anchorageresort.com. Lovely, clean, tiled rooms with comfortable beds, private bath, fridge, cable TV and balconies overlooking the sea in a three-storey concrete building in palm-shaded grounds. Rates for top-floor rooms are higher, but include great views. ❼

Lorraine's Guest House On the beach beyond *Anchorage Resort* ☎206-0162. A great bargain on the beach. Simple but comfortable wooden cabins with private hot-water showers run by the amiable Alamilla family; Orlando makes great wooden souvenirs. ❸

Exploring the caye and reef

The **Barrier Reef** lies only 1.5km from the shore, and the white foam of the reef crest is always visible to the east. The entire length of the reef off Caye Caulker was declared a **marine reserve** in 1998, and visiting it (Bz$10) is an experience not to be missed. You'll swim along **coral canyons**, surrounded by an astonishing range of fish, with perhaps a harmless nurse shark or two. Here, as everywhere, snorkellers should be aware of the reef's fragility and be careful not to touch any coral – even sand stirred up by fins can cause damage (see box, p.128).

At the island's northern tip is the **Caye Caulker Forest and Marine Reserve**, jointly managed by a local organization and the government and home to such trees as red, white and black mangroves, gumbo limbo and poisonwood. This area was a coconut plantation before Hurricane Hattie hit in 1961, but has not been in active use since, so the native littoral forest has had nearly fifty years to regenerate. The mangrove shallows support fish nurseries and small species called "sardines" by fishermen, who use them as bait to catch snapper. Sponges, anemones and other colourful sea creatures grow on the mangrove roots. As the trees' leaves fall and mud accumulates, some coastal areas rise just above sea level, at least in the dry season. Several lagoons, conversely, remain year-round and serve as excellent habitats for crocodiles, turtles and water birds. **American saltwater crocodiles** are sometimes seen here, but you're more likely to find them in the wild on the Turneffe Islands (see p.155) or in the more remote coastal areas – though if you're really keen to view these magnificent reptiles, head to the garbage dump by the airstrip. Other native inhabitants of the littoral forest include **boa constrictors**, scaly-tailed iguanas (locally called "wish willies"), geckoes and five species of land crab.

A small section of the original littoral forest has been preserved closer to town in the **Caye Caulker Mini Reserve**, just north of the airstrip and approached from the beach or Back Street (always open; free, but donations appreciated). The visitor's centre (8am–12pm) provides good information about the species you can see here. Walking the cleared paths will give you some idea of the variety and density of jungle that can grow on bare sand and coral rubble; stray off the path leading down to the southern tip of the island, and you'll realize just how spiky and impenetrable this forest really is.

Swimming and snorkelling

Caye Caulker has only a small beach, as the proximity of the reef stops sand building up on the foreshore, and the water's too shallow for true **swimming**, which is best done from the end of piers or at the Split at the north end of the village. Swimming out to the reef is discouraged, since it requires crossing a busy boat lane where fatal accidents have occurred in the past, as captains do not expect swimmers.

Recommended snorkelling tours

There are many snorkel shops on Caye Caulker, and their quality varies enormously. Cheaper tours may limit your time in the water, use inexperienced guides or overload boats. Many guides also touch the animals and allow clients to do so, which should be discouraged. The companies listed here are reputable, use motorboats to give you more time with the marine life, and are all on Front Street, unless otherwise noted.

Anda De Wata Tours On Luciano Reyes St ⓣ601-6757, ⓔandadewatatours@yahoo.com. Offers a variety of snorkelling and inland tours. Co-owner Vanessa was one of the first female guides on the island.

Anwar Snorkel Tours Two blocks north of the Front Dock ⓣ226-0327. One of the oldest tour companies, offering snorkelling tours and inland trips to Altun Ha and Lamanai.

Carlos Eco Tours Near the *Sandbox Restaurant* ⓣ600-1654, ⓔcarlosayala10@hotmail.com. Tours, led by conscientious guide Carlos Ayala, place an emphasis on conservation and education.

Chocolate's Manatee Tours At Chocolate's Gift Shop ⓣ226-0151, ⓔchocolate@btl.net. Lionel "Chocolate" Heredia is Caye Caulker's longest-serving tour guide, and was instrumental in securing Sanctuary status for Swallow Caye.

Ras Creek By the Front Dock and the Split. Ras runs laid-back trips in his little boat *Heritage* (Bz$25), taking you to the reef right in front of the caye. Plenty of rum punch is provided, and guests help prepare lunch, arriving back as the sun is setting.

Red Mangrove Eco Adventures Near the village centre ⓣ226-0069, ⓦwww.mangrovebelize.com. Highly recommended outfit offering educational and very eco-aware small-group tours by owner Carlos A. Miller, specializing in local sites and Turneffe. Also books flights and buses for onward transport, gives travel- and environment-related information, and runs a book exchange and gift shop.

Tsunami Adventures Near the Split ⓣ226-0462, ⓦwww.tsunamiadventures.com. Professional agency able to arrange all snorkelling and diving trips and book flights and tours throughout Belize. Also operates *Costa Maya Cabañas* next door.

Your most rewarding **snorkelling** experiences will likely be on an organized tour, which can educate you on what you're seeing. Tours are easily arranged and cost around Bz$50–150 per person, depending on duration and location – generally a half- or full day and stopping at a number of sites. Some trips visit Hol Chan Marine Reserve and Shark-Ray Alley (see p.140), but these tend to be busier and more expensive, and you'll be just as happy in either Caye Caulker's own marine reserve or the outer atolls, Turneffe in particular (p.155) – keep an eye out for the **dolphins** that often accompany boats on the way. Rental of decent equipment is usually included in the cost of your tour (though you'll get a reduction of around Bz$5 for using your own), but always make sure it fits well and try to practise breathing if you haven't snorkelled before.

Other popular snorkelling destinations include Goff's Caye, English Caye and Sergeant's Caye, tiny specks of sand and coral with a few palm trees. A trip to any of these may be combined with a stop at Swallow Caye Wildlife Sanctuary (see p.157), a mangrove caye with seagrass beds near Belize City, where you can view (but not swim with) **manatees**. You're almost certainly guaranteed a sighting, often of entire family groups; contact Chocolate for the best tours (around Bz$90; see box, opposite).

Diving trips and instruction

All dive shops on the caye offer great reef diving and visits to coral gardens (two tanks US$60, usually including equipment), as well as **night dives** (US$50). A day-trip to **Lighthouse Reef** and the **Blue Hole**, leaving at 6.30am (three dives, US$150), is an unforgettable experience, although some people are disappointed by the lack of marine life in the depths. After the unique, slightly spooky splendour of diving over 35m into the hole, many groups visit the fantastic eighty-metre wall off Half Moon Caye. A brief stop on the island itself lets you observe red-footed boobies and huge hermit crabs before climbing back in the boat for the Long Caye wall. The **Turneffe Islands** have world-class dive sites, too – some believe the best diving in Belize. North Turneffe (three dives, US$120) and Turneffe Elbow are the most popular trips from Caye Caulker.

Dive training is slightly cheaper here than on Ambergris Caye, and several dive shops offer PADI **instruction** (around US$250) for an Open Water or Advanced Open Water course. The best two outfits are Frenchie's, toward the northern end of the village (Ⓣ226-0234, Ⓦwww.frenchiesdivingbelize.com), and Belize Diving Services, at the far side of the football field (Ⓣ226-0143, Ⓦwww.belizedivingservices.com). Many shops sell disposable underwater cameras, but higher-quality photographic equipment is generally unavailable for rent. If you'd like to learn **underwater photography**, contact Red Mangrove Eco Adventures (see box, opposite), which occasionally runs specialized tours.

Sailing and other day-trips

A relaxing way to enjoy the sea and the reef is to spend the better part of a day on one of the caye's **sailing trips**, costing around Bz$60–75 and usually including two or three snorkelling stops and lunch before returning in the evening. Slightly cheaper **sunset cruises** (about Bz$50) are also on offer. The most tranquil, run by very experienced skipper Juni Zaldivar, is aboard *Trinity* (maximum eight people; Ⓣ226-0414); check at the house across from the basketball court. Other day-trips are offered by Seahawk Sailing (Ⓣ607-0323, Ⓔseahawksailingbelize@yahoo.com) and Raggamuffin Tours, near the north end of Front Street (Ⓣ226-0348, Ⓦwww.sailingadventuresbelize.com), with several beautiful wooden sailing boats. They also operate popular three-day **camping trips** (Bz$550) starting in Caye Caulker on Tuesdays and Fridays and ending in Placencia (see p.267).

Keen **sea kayakers** can join guide Allie Ifield's excellent mangrove, sunset or "expedition" tours (starting at Bz$30 for 1.5 hours; Ⓣ604-3553, Ⓔtoucancanoe @yahoo.com). Some trips are suitable for beginners. Experienced paddlers can **rent a kayak** for around Bz$25–40, or ask at Galería Hicaco (Ⓣ226-0178), where all rental fees go to conservation efforts. **Windsurfing lessons** are also on offer here.

A **fishing trip** is a common outing from the caye, and Anglers Abroad, near the Split (Ⓣ226-0303), has information on local guides and fly-fishing and dive equipment for sale. You can also simply ask around the village and you'll be pointed in the direction of a guide.

Informative **birding tours**, led by local naturalists, can be arranged through either Dorothy Beveridge (Ⓣ220-4079, Ⓔbzvisuals@btl.net) or Ellen Macrae at Galería Hicaco (Ⓣ226-0178, Ⓔsbf@btl.net or siwaban@yahoo.com). *A Guide to the birds of Caye Caulker*, available for purchase throughout the island, gives descriptions of the 130 species seen here, from waders, herons and sandpipers to spoonbills, hummingbirds and the ever-present pelicans and frigates.

Relaxing on land

After a day or two of water-based activity you might feel a need to slow down a little, perhaps get a massage or do some selective **shopping**. Eva McFarlane, next to *Don Corleone Trattoria* on Front Street (Ⓣ601-9731, Ⓔedenbelize@hotmail.com), offers several kinds of **massage** (Bz$100/hr), aromatherapy and many other treatments. CoCoPlum Gardens (Ⓣ226-0226, Ⓦwww.cocoplum.typepad.com) has a range of **massage and spa therapies**, as well as "aura soma colour" and Tarot readings. If it's art you're after, Caribbean Colors Art Gallery on Front Street (Ⓦwww.caribbean-colors.com) displays owner Lee Vanderwalker-Kroll's distinctive and very colourful paintings and photographs alongside the work of several talented **local artists**; you can also buy Belizean CDs and books. Many of the same artists also display their work on the beach, along Front Street or in their homes on the island. The Toucan gift shop, on Front Street near the Front Dock, is part of a large souvenir chain in Belize, and there are several smaller gift shops along Front Street as well.

Eating, drinking and entertainment

Good home-cooking, large portions and very reasonable prices are features of the island's many **restaurants**, half of which you'll pass while looking for a room. Aim to eat in the early-to-mid-evening, as many places close by 9.30pm. **Lobster** (in season) is served in every dish imaginable, from curry to chow mein; other **seafood** is generally well priced and accompanied by rice or potatoes and sometimes salad. Along Front Street are a couple of **fast-food** stands, serving tacos and burritos, and there's a good **bakery** on the street to the football field, which makes great cinnamon buns; local "cake-man" Lloyd, who walks around town in the late afternoon with a basket, sells some of Caye Caulker's best cakes. Many children also sell bread, pastries and other treats from baskets, and it's always worth seeing what's on offer. If you fancy an ice cream for dessert, try the *Ice Cream Parlour* on Front Street, near the basketball court. You can buy food at several well-stocked **shops and**

supermarkets around the village, the largest of which is Chan's, at the centre of the island. Unless noted otherwise, all restaurants below are on Front Street, and most will prepare food to take away. All are listed in order of their proximity to the Front Dock.

Restaurants north of the Front Dock

Sandbox Restaurant Immediately north of the dock ☎226-0200. Offering a variety of good meals and excellent breakfasts. A favourite evening hangout among expats.

Barrier Reef Sports Bar ☎226-0077. Serving decent food on the beach, with big-screen entertainment for sports fans.

Bamboo Grill Beachfront place serving quality lunch and dinners, including tasty appetizers. Late bar. Closed Fri.

Happy Lobster North of the centre. Inexpensive restaurant ladling out rice and beans, seafood and local dishes; one of the best values on the caye. Also has lodging in clean and pleasant rooms upstairs.

Jolly Roger's Barbecue On the beach, opposite *Oceanside* (see below). The very jolly Roger Martinez grills up the island's best lobster and fish at great prices. The healthy portions are served on picnic tables.

Rainbow Restaurant ☎226-0281. Very popular restaurant over the water, with respectable food and service. Closed Mon.

Taj Restaurant ☎621-6415. Serves fish, vegetarian and meat curries, and has rooms for rent behind the restaurant.

Don Corleone Trattoria ☎226-0025. Excellent pastas and salads in an upmarket dining atmosphere.

Wish Willy's At the north end of the island. Friendly, relaxed restaurant in a ramshackle building at the back of the island, where Belizean chef Maurice Moore creates some of the most delicious seafood dishes in the country.

Restaurants south of the Front Dock

Rose's Café On Calle del Sol ☎206-0085. Good for breakfasts, Belizean food and takeout pizza.

Habañeros Just south of the Front Dock ☎226-0487. The island's top restaurant, serving fantastic and creative gourmet international meals, with fine wine and slick bar service; it's often packed, so call for reservations. Closed Thurs.

Amor y Café Just south of the centre. An excellent place for full or continental breakfasts, using mostly organic ingredients.

Glenda's Restaurant At the back of the island, south of the Back Dock ☎226-0148. Justly famous for its delicious cinnamon rolls and fresh orange juice, this is a favourite breakfast meeting place. Closed Sun.

Syd's Restaurant On Middle St, just south of Alliance Bank ☎206-0294. Popular with locals and tourists alike, and often busy. A small place offering great-value Belizean dishes to eat inside, outside or wherever you like. Closed Sun.

Rasta Pasta Southern end of Front St. An extremely popular place, serving creative seafood and pasta dishes flavoured with owner Maralyn's unique blend of herbs and spices.

Coco Plum Gardens Café South of the centre, just north of the airstrip ☎226-0226. "Whole-food" café serving great breakfasts – think crêpes and homemade granola – as well as gourmet deli sandwiches, pizza and desserts in a lush garden setting with an art gallery; it's well worth the walk. Also has delicious Belizean fruit jams and wines and sells books, artwork and herbal remedies. Open 8am–5.30pm; closed Wed.

Bars and nightlife

Caye Caulker's social scene revolves around its various bars and restaurants, and **live music** and **happy hours** frequently add atmosphere to the evening, especially in the busier places along Front Street. Few establishments are strictly bars, though the three-storey *I & I's*, with its famous swing chairs, is one – just make sure to take care negotiating the stairs on the way down. Other popular bars are *Oceanside* and *Herbal Tribe* (where you can sometimes hear afternoon drumming demonstrations), on Front Street, and *Lazy Lizard*, with a great location at the Split. All can descend into late-evening, drunken rowdiness, so many visitors prefer quieter activities, such as relaxing in a restaurant over dinner and a drink, or gazing at the tropical night sky from the end of a dock.

Other northern cayes and atolls

Although Caye Caulker and San Pedro are the only villages anywhere on the reef, there are several **other islands** that you can visit and even stay on. Some of these are within day-trip distance of the main northern cayes or Belize City, and often contain a few superbly isolated, package-deal hotels, usually called **lodges**. Buildings are generally simple and either wooden or thatched, and in some cases your lodge will be the only one on the island, with just a few guests. Phones are scarce (though most lodges are in radio contact with Belize City), electricity comes from a generator and views of palm trees curving over turquoise water reinforce the sense of isolation.

Caye Chapel

Immediately south of Caye Caulker, privately owned **Caye Chapel** stands as a terrible example of a tropical island totally ruined by tourism development. There's an airstrip, hotel and marina, but it's the **golf course** – and the runoff from heavy applications of fertilizer and pesticides required to keep the grass green – that causes the worst environmental problems. Most of the mangroves have been cut down and the daily raking of the shore by tractors to create a beach has caused tremendous erosion. Virtually the whole island is now encased in an ugly, concrete sea wall – which you'll see if you're in a boat heading to Caye Caulker. On a historical note, it was on Caye Chapel that the defeated Spanish fleet paused for a few days after the **Battle of St George's Caye** in 1798. According to legend, some of their dead are buried here.

St George's Caye

Tiny **St George's Caye**, around 15km from Belize City, was the capital of the Baymen in the seventeenth and eighteenth centuries, and still manages to exude an air of colonial grandeur; its beautifully restored houses face east to catch the breeze and their lush, green lawns are enclosed by white picket fences. Eighteenth-century cannons are still mounted in front of some of the finer houses, and for another glimpse into the past you could head to the small graveyard of the early settlers on the southern tip of the island. Today St George's Caye is home to the villas of Belize's elite, a training centre for British forces in Belize and a few fishermen, who live toward the northern end in an area known, appropriately enough, as "Fisherman Town".

Though there's not much for the casual visitor, some fishing and snorkelling trips from other islands call here for lunch. Should you choose to stay, **accommodation** is available at *Pleasure Island Resort* (Ⓣ209-4020, Ⓦwww.stgeorgescayepleasure.bz; ❽), with double rooms for US$99, beach cottages for US$234 and a restaurant and bar. A more luxurious option is *St George's Lodge* (Ⓣ220-4444, Ⓦwww.gooddiving.com; ❾), an all-inclusive **dive resort** comprised of a ten-room main lodge, six luxury, wood-and-thatch cottages with private verandas and a beautiful dining room. The lodge was Belize's first dedicated diving resort and has long enjoyed a reputation as one of the very best in the country, consistently receiving rave reviews in the diving press. Rates depend on whether you're diving, but range from US$197 to US$328 per person. You'll get a better deal by paying in advance for a package, which includes airport transfer, diving and meals.

The Bluefield Range

In the **Bluefield Range**, a group of mangrove cayes 35km southeast of Belize City, visitors can stay at the remote **fishing camp** of *Ricardo's Beach*

△ Fly-fishing on the Turneffe Islands

Huts (Ⓣ614-4298), with simple, comfortable accommodation (minimum two nights) in huts built on stilts, right on the water. It's not cheap, at US$175 per person for three days and two nights, but the price includes transport to and from Belize City, all meals – including, as you might imagine, fresh fish and lobster – and a fishing or snorkelling trip to Rendezvous Caye, right on the reef. Owner Ricardo Castillo is a reliable, expert fishing guide and scrupulous conservationist, and has been known to extend discounts to *Rough Guides* readers.

The Turneffe Islands

Though shown on some maps as one large island, the virtually uninhabited and numerous **Turneffe Islands** are part of Belize's largest atoll, an oval archipelago rising over 300m from the seabed and enclosed by a beautiful coral reef. Situated 40km from Belize City, they are primarily low-lying mangrove islands – some quite large – and sandbanks around a shallow lagoon. Thanks to relatively minimal human development, the islands make up one of the most biologically diverse areas of the Caribbean. Conservation organizations are attempting to expand the several small protected areas on the islands, but may be thwarted by developers who have recently purchased tracts from the government.

Fishing the shallow flats here, typically for bonefish and permit, is world-class, and dedicated anglers can expect to fish at least six hours every day, with most of the sport-fishing on a catch-and-release basis. With over eighty logged sites, **diving** is sublime and **snorkelling** is just as wonderful. A few places offer all-inclusive **accommodation**, but the construction of resorts on this remote, fragile island has involved cutting down mangroves – a cause of controversy among conservationists.

Booking ahead for lodging is essential – and, though resorts here are very expensive (with one exception), most will offer discounts if you book through their websites. Prices include transport from Belize City (and usually from the international airport), all meals and whatever diving and/or fishing package is arranged; all the resorts have electricity and most have air-conditioning. Most guests will be fishing or diving much of the time, but there are always hammocks to relax in, there will usually be kayaks and windsurfers available to use, and the snorkelling right offshore is superb. Although staying out here has a heavenly, even dreamlike quality, **sandflies** and **mosquitoes** can bring you back to earth with a vengeance – so pack repellent.

The most northerly of the Turneffe resorts is *Turneffe Flats* (in US ⓣ1-888/512-8812, ⓦwww.tflats.com), offering diving and fishing packages at around US$2240 for a week. On **Blackbird Caye**, halfway down the eastern side of the archipelago, *Blackbird Caye Resort* (in US ⓣ1-800/326-1724, ⓦwww.blackbirdresort.com) has luxury wood-and-thatch cabañas and rooms (some with air-conditioning) and a beautiful thatched dining room. A week's high-season package, including transfers, all meals, diving/snorkelling and perhaps fishing, costs US$1915–2815; three- to four-night packages are available for US$950–1350.

Ropewalk Caye (also known as Pelican Caye), on the atoll's southeastern side, has *Amigos Dive Camp* (ⓣ622-0283, ⓦwww.amigosbelize.com), with simple accommodation aimed at budget travellers. The main thatched building is set in a palm grove on the beach, with the kitchen and dining room downstairs and rooms upstairs, and with separate, shared bathroom facilities. It's a bit rustic, but excellent value for what you get: a five-day package including ocean fishing, some diving and snorkelling is US$800, and three days without diving is US$450.

Finally, at the southern tip of the archipelago, **Caye Bokel** boasts *Turneffe Island Lodge* (in the US ⓣ1-800/874-0118, ⓦwww.turneffelodge.com), with luxurious, air-conditioned cabins on a twelve-acre private island. Catering to upmarket fishing and diving groups, packages cost US$1575–3500 per person for a week, depending on the activity. Half-weeks are also available.

If you'd prefer to visit the Turneffe Islands on a **day-trip**, you can do so easily from San Pedro or Caye Caulker; see the boxes on p.138 & p.150, respectively.

Lighthouse Reef, the Blue Hole and Half Moon Caye

About 80km east of Belize City is Belize's outermost atoll, **Lighthouse Reef**, made famous by Jacques Cousteau, who visited in the 1970s. The two main attractions here are the Blue Hole, which drew Cousteau's attention (he cleared the passage through the reef), and Half Moon Caye Natural Monument (Bz$80 entrance for both). The **Blue Hole**, now also protected as a Natural Monument, is technically a "karst-eroded sinkhole", a shaft about 300m in diameter and 135m deep that drops through the bottom of the lagoon and opens out into a complex network of **caves and crevices**, complete with stalactites and stalagmites. It was formed over a million years ago when Lighthouse Reef was a sizeable island – or even part of the mainland. Investigations have shown that caves underlie the entire reef, and that the sea has simply punctured the cavern roof at the site of the Blue Hole. Its great depth gives it a peculiar deep-blue colour, and even swimming across is disorienting as there's no sense of anything beneath you. Unsurprisingly, the Blue Hole and Lighthouse Reef are major magnets for **divers**, offering incredible walls and drop-offs, although seeing it from the air is arguably the best way to appreciate it (see p.129).

The **Half Moon Caye Natural Monument**, the first marine conservation area in Belize, was declared a national park in 1982. Its lighthouse was built in 1820 and has not always been effective: several wrecks, including the *Ermlund*, which ran aground in 1971, testify to the dangers of the reef. The medium-sized caye is divided into two distinct ecosystems: in the west, guano from thousands of seabirds fertilizes the soil, allowing the growth of dense vegetation, while the eastern half has mostly coconut palms growing in the sand. A total of 98 bird species have been recorded here, including frigate birds, ospreys, mangrove warblers, white-crowned pigeons and – most important of all – a resident population of four thousand **red-footed boobies**, one of only two nesting colonies in the Caribbean. The boobies came by their name because they displayed no fear of humans, enabling sailors to kill them in their thousands, and they still move only reluctantly when visitors stroll through their waddling crowds. Their nesting area is accessible from a platform and the birds are not in the least bothered by your presence. Apart from the birds, the island supports iguanas, lizards and both loggerhead and hawksbill turtles, which nest on the beaches; they in turn attract the biggest hermit and land crabs in Belize.

There's no accommodation on the caye, but **camping** is allowed with the permission of the Belize Audubon Society (Ⓣ223-5004; Bz$25), which manages the reserve; many of the overnight diving or snorkelling expeditions camp here, and are often your best bet, since independent campers are discouraged. Visitors must register with the rangers prior to arrival and pay the Bz$10 **entrance fee**; the **visitor centre** will help you understand the caye's ecology.

Swallow Caye Wildlife Sanctuary

Just a ten-minute boat ride from Belize City (forty from Caye Caulker), the Drowned Cayes (which include Swallow Caye) form the **Swallow Caye Wildlife Sanctuary** (Bz$10 entry fee), a secure refuge for the area's healthy population of **West Indian manatees**. Belize has the largest surviving population of these gentle giants, which congregate here to feed on the abundant turtle-grass beds, their primary food source, and use the deeper areas near Swallow Caye as resting places. The sanctuary, created in 2002 and covering over 36 square kilometres, sustains an array of other marine life including bottlenose dolphins, American crocodiles and the upside-down jellyfish. It's co-managed by the Friends of Swallow Caye and the Ministry of Natural Resources, and **day-trips** are available, mainly departing from Caye Caulker (see box, p.150). On one of these ventures, the skipper will turn off the motor as you near, quietly pushing the boat towards the manatees in order not to disturb them. Although you're not allowed in the water, you can generally get good photographs – of their heads and faces, at least. The Friends of Swallow Caye have built a visitor's centre for the sanctuary on Caye Caulker.

Travel details

For a rundown of **flights** and **boats** to the cayes from Belize City and between the cayes themselves, see the boxes on p.138 & p.150.

Cayo and the west

N
MEXICO
CARIBBEAN SEA
GUATEMALA
1
2
3
4
5
6

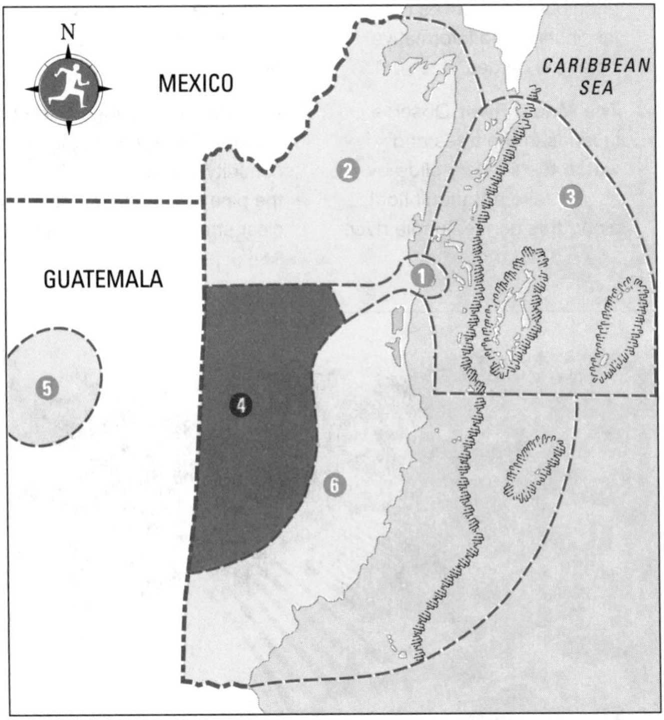

CHAPTER 4

Highlights

✱ **Actun Tunichil Muknal** Hike across rivers and through jungle before descending into an astonishing cave that was, for the Maya, the underworld and abode of the Lords of Death. See p.173

✱ **Green Hills Butterfly Ranch and Botanical Collections** Relax surrounded by clouds of colourful butterflies in this fascinating and informative botanical garden. See p.175

✱ **The Macal River** Observe iguanas in the trees and watch the scenery slide by as you take a tranquil float along this gentle, jungle river. See p.179

✱ **Caracol** The greatest Maya city in Belize, where you can ascend Caana, a 1200-year-old palace and temple complex that's still one of the tallest buildings in the country. See p.183

✱ **San Ignacio** Stay in a comfortable, affordable hotel and choose from dozens of adventure trips in this charming town, still full of colonial buildings. See p.186

✱ **Mountain Pine Ridge Forest Reserve** Escape the jungle's humidity to the cooler air of the pine forest and its many clear streams and waterfalls. See p.199

△ Maya ruins at Caracol

Cayo and the west

Heading along the **Western Highway** from Belize City to the Guatemalan border, 130km away, you trade the heat and humidity of the low-lying city for a range of varied landscapes, from pine savannah and river valleys to rolling hills and tropical forest. It's a fast, paved route that first traverses mangrove swamps, then heads further inland across open, sometimes swampy savannah, scattered with palmetto scrub and low pines. Before reaching Belmopan, the road passes several points of interest, including **Monkey Bay Wildlife Sanctuary and National Park** and **Guanacaste National Park**. Belmopan lies a short distance south of Guanacaste National Park; established in 1970, it is still the smallest national capital city in the world.

West of Belmopan, following the Belize River valley, the road skirts the lush foothills of the Maya Mountains, a beautiful area with clear air and astonishingly fertile land. You're now nearing the heart of **Cayo District**, the largest of Belize's six districts and arguably the most beautiful – a sentiment enthusiastically endorsed by the inhabitants when they declare "The west is the best." It's certainly one of the greenest: most of southern and western Cayo, including the entire mountain range, is under official protection as part of a vast network of national parks, wildlife sanctuaries and forest and archeological reserves stretching from the Caribbean coast to the Guatemalan border. The **Mountain Pine Ridge Forest Reserve**, to the south of the highway, is a pleasantly cool region of hills, pine woods and waterfalls, boasting some of the finest lodge accommodation in the country.

The ideal base for exploring the forests, rivers and ruins of western Belize is the busy main town of **San Ignacio**, on the Macal River just 15km from the Guatemalan border. A canoe or kayak trip through the **Macal River valley**, as the river tumbles from the Maya Mountains into the calmer waters of the tree-lined Macal gorge, is a highlight of any visit to Cayo, and cabins to suit all budgets line the riverbanks. South of San Ignacio, deep in the jungle of the Vaca Plateau, lies **Caracol**, the largest Maya site in Belize and a current focus of archeological research and restoration; many of its **caves** hold more astonishing Maya treasures for adventurous visitors.

Between San Ignacio and the Guatemalan border, the road climbs past the hilltop ruin of **Cahal Pech**, then descends along the valley of the **Mopan River**, passing several delightful riverside lodges. Belize's westernmost Maya site, **El Pilar**, 18km northwest of San Ignacio, actually extends into Guatemala, and is the first international archaeological reserve anywhere in the Maya region. A few kilometres before the border itself, at the village of **San José Succotz**, an ancient ferry crosses the Mopan River to bring visitors to **Xunantunich**, a hilltop Maya site whose highest structures offer stunning views into Guatemala's department of Petén.

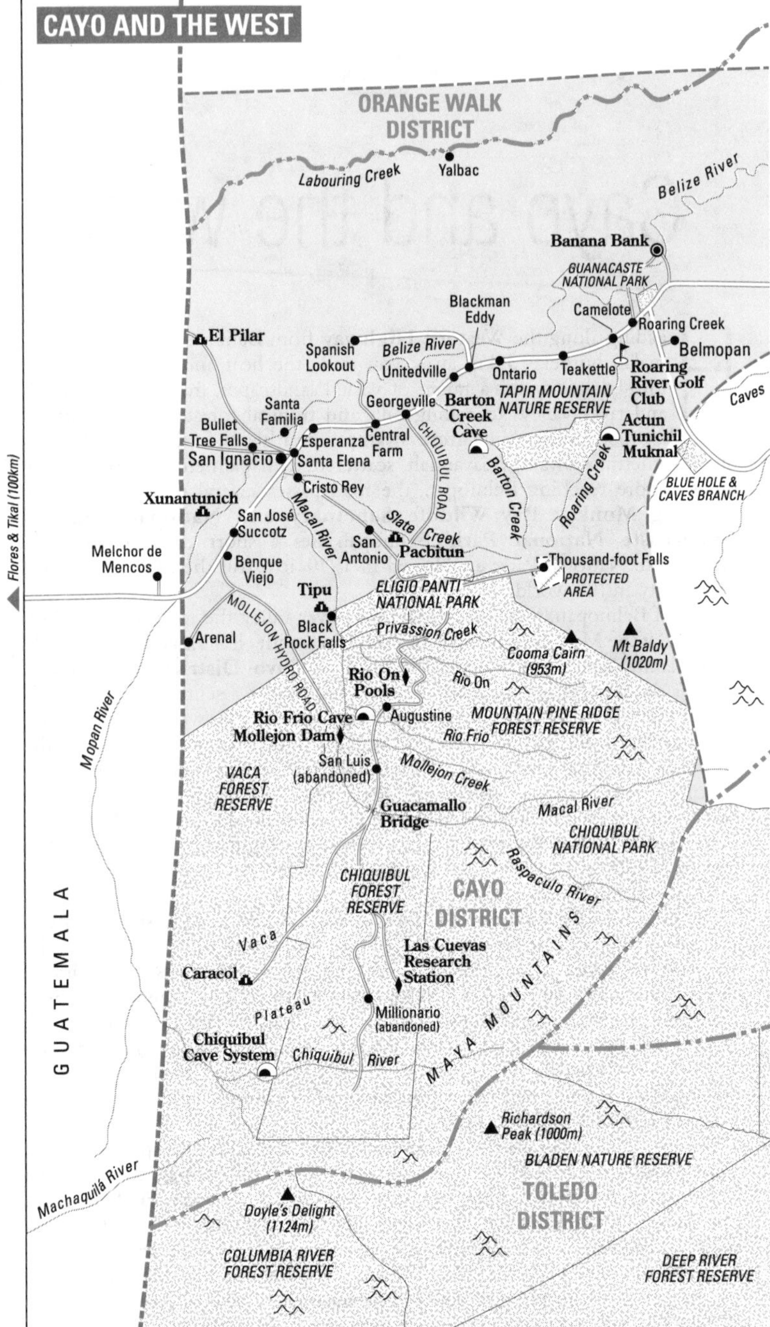
CAYO AND THE WEST
ORANGE WALK DISTRICT
Labouring Creek
Yalbac
Belize River
Banana Bank
GUANACASTE NATIONAL PARK
Blackman Eddy
Camelote
Roaring Creek
Belmopan
El Pilar
Spanish Lookout
Belize River
Unitedville
Ontario
Teakettle
Roaring River Golf Club
Caves
Georgeville
Barton Creek Cave
TAPIR MOUNTAIN NATURE RESERVE
Actun Tunichil Muknal
Santa Familia
Bullet Tree Falls
Esperanza
Central Farm
CHIQUIBUL ROAD
San Ignacio
Santa Elena
Cristo Rey
Barton Creek
Roaring Creek
BLUE HOLE & CAVES BRANCH
Flores & Tikal (100km)
Xunantunich
San José Succotz
Macal River
Slate Creek
San Antonio
Pacbitun
Melchor de Mencos
Benque Viejo
Thousand-foot Falls
PROTECTED AREA
ELIGIO PANTI NATIONAL PARK
Tipu
MOLLEJON HYDRO ROAD
Black Rock Falls
Privassion Creek
Arenal
Cooma Cairn (953m)
Mt Baldy (1020m)
Rio On Pools
Rio On
Rio Frio Cave
Augustine
MOUNTAIN PINE RIDGE FOREST RESERVE
Mollejon Dam
Rio Frio
Mopan River
San Luis (abandoned)
Mollejon Creek
VACA FOREST RESERVE
Guacamallo Bridge
Macal River
CHIQUIBUL NATIONAL PARK
Raspaculo River
CHIQUIBUL FOREST RESERVE
CAYO DISTRICT
GUATEMALA
Vaca
Las Cuevas Research Station
Caracol
MAYA MOUNTAINS
Plateau
Millionario (abandoned)
Chiquibul Cave System
Chiquibul
River
Richardson Peak (1000m)
BLADEN NATURE RESERVE
Machaquilá River
TOLEDO DISTRICT
Doyle's Delight (1124m)
COLUMBIA RIVER FOREST RESERVE
DEEP RIVER FOREST RESERVE

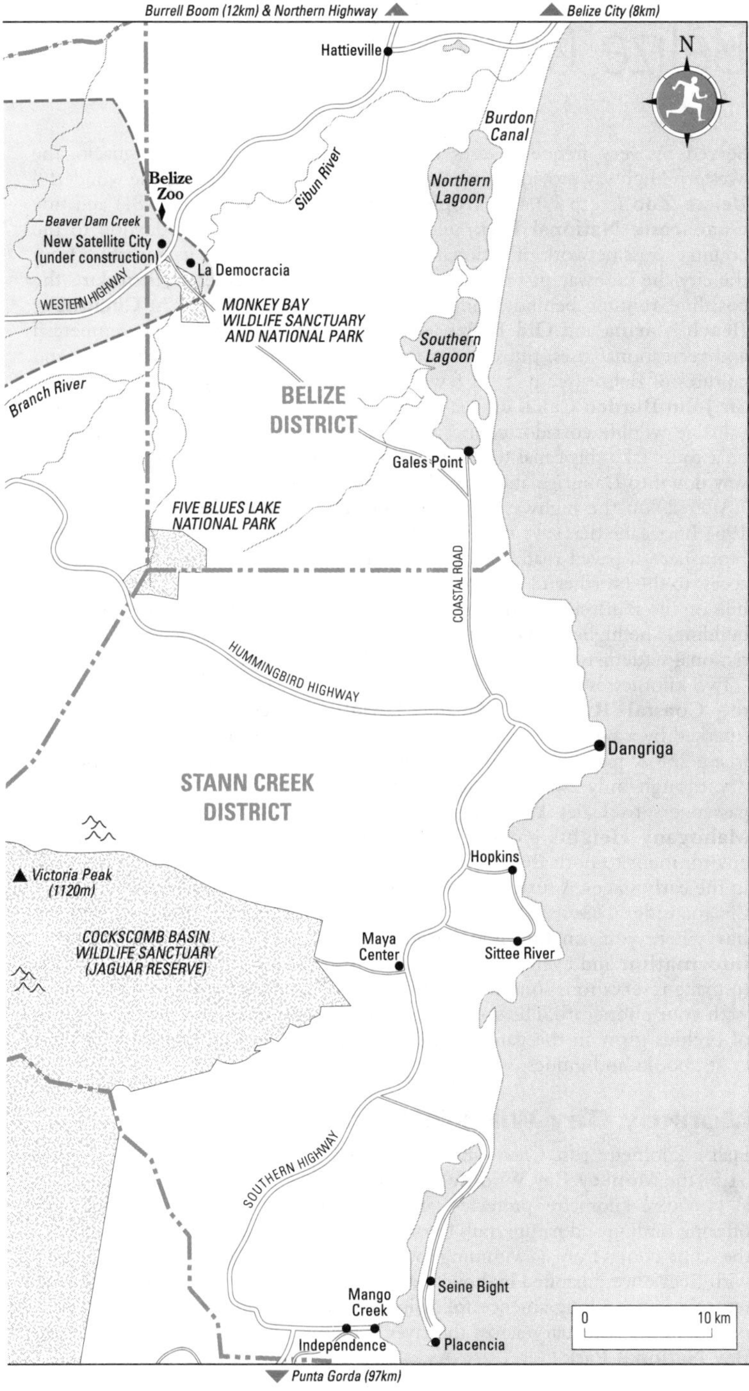

4 CAYO AND THE WEST

Belize City to Belmopan

Served by very frequent buses between Belize City and San Ignacio, the Western Highway provides easy access to nearby sights, including the wonderful **Belize Zoo** (see p.79), the **Tropical Education Center** (see p.81) and tiny **Guanacaste National Park**, which offers a fascinating introduction to the country's vast network of national parks and reserves. Upon its departure from the city, the highway passes through the Lord's Ridge cemetery, then skirts the coastline, running behind a tangle of mangrove swamps and past **Cucumber Beach Marina** and **Old Belize** – one an active marina for both commercial and recreational uses, the other a fine museum showcasing the history and cultures of Belize (see p.78). A few kilometres further, the highway crosses the **Sir John Burden Canal**, an inland waterway that serves as a nature reserve and valuable wildlife corridor connecting the Belize and Sibun rivers. Some small boat tours take this canal to the **Northern and Southern lagoons** on their way down to Dangriga and Gales Point; see p.238.

After 23km the highway passes through **HATTIEVILLE**, named after the 1961 hurricane that gave the village its first inhabitants in the form of refugees. From here, a paved road leads north to **Burrell Boom** (see p.95), providing access to the Northern Highway. Slightly west of Hattieville, the curiously steep hills on the south side of the highway are limestone outcrops, quarried for road-building. The highest is **Gracie Rock**, near the Sibun River, the location of the fictional settlement of Geronimo in the film *The Mosquito Coast.*

Two kilometres beyond the Belize Zoo and the Tropical Education Center, the **Coastal Road** (or Manatee Road) provides an unpaved shortcut (marked by a sign, a petrol station and a bar) to **Gales Point** and **Dangriga** (see p.238 & p.243, respectively). This rough road is served by several buses a day, though only two in either direction on Mondays and Fridays deliver passengers to Gales Point. Just past the junction, the residential area of **Mahogany Heights** provides inhabitants of the region with an alternative environment to both Belize City and Belmopan, though development is still in the early stages. A further 2km along the highway and set back 100m from the roadside, *Cheers* (Ⓣ822-8014) is a friendly, Canadian-run **restaurant/bar** where you can find good food at reasonable prices, as well as tourist **information** and even **accommodation** in cabañas (❻). Should you need to make reservations somewhere ahead, they'll likely let you use their phone with your phonecard. The staff offers guided **bird walks**, and several varieties of orchids grow in the garden. The **gift shop** has a good selection of local crafts, books and guides.

Monkey Bay Wildlife Sanctuary

Half a kilometre past *Cheers* and 400m south of the road (signposted at Mile 31.5), the **Monkey Bay Wildlife Sanctuary** (Ⓦwww.monkeybaybelize.org) is a 44-square-kilometre protected area extending to the **Sibun River** and offering birding and nature trails through five distinct habitats. The "bay" part of the name comes from a swimming spot by a sandy beach on the river, overhung with trees once inhabited by howler and spider monkeys; the monkeys are now returning after a long absence following hurricane disturbance to their habitat. Adjoining the sanctuary across the river is the nine-square-kilometre **Monkey Bay National Park**.

The Sibun River watershed supports abundant birdlife, jaguars, tapirs, howler monkeys, Morelet's crocodiles and the endangered **hawksbill turtle**, which lays its eggs in nests scraped out of beaches at the river mouth. Though the two protected areas covered above already serve as a wildlife corridor spanning the Sibun valley and extending south through karst limestone hills to the Manatee Forest Reserve, Belize government agencies and NGOs are currently joined in an ambitious conservation effort, the Mesoamerican Biological Corridor Project, which would turn these protected areas into a conservation "bridge" connecting similar areas in the north and the south.

From Monkey Bay you can arrange one- or multi-day guided **canoe, camping and birding trips** on the Sibun River and explore little-visited **caves** in the Sibun Hills to the south, all showing evidence of use by the ancient Maya. You'll need a guide (see p.169) for the three-day trek along the **Indian Creek Trail** to Five Blues Lake (see p.242) and, since Monkey Bay is primarily a research centre catering to student groups, this and other trips should be arranged in advance. Anyone can stay in the accommodation here, however, and there's a beautiful swimming spot on the Sibun, a twenty-minute walk from the field station. Monkey Bay is also the contact point for visits to **Cox Lagoon Crocodile Sanctuary**, a 120-square-kilometre private nature reserve north of the highway. This wetland area in the Mussel Creek watershed, home to over one hundred Morelet's crocodiles, also hosts at least a dozen other reptile species, jabiru storks, howler monkeys and jaguars, and visitors can camp, canoe, hike and fish. It's not as frequently visited as other wildlife destinations, so you should try to arrange trips well in advance.

Practicalities

The well-marked Monkey Bay is easily reached by any bus along the highway. The sanctuary headquarters comprises a handsome, wooden **field research station**, serving as library, museum and classroom, as well as a screened, three-tiered dining room and bunkhouses. An **Internet** café and free wireless access is available to guests. Although the field station specializes in hosting academic programmes in natural history and watershed ecology for students and teachers (it's also the Belize base for Conservation Corridors), it is a wonderfully relaxing **place to stay**, either in a single room (Bz$35) or the bunkhouse (Bz$25), or else camping on raised platforms under thatched roofs (Bz$12). If there's space available, you can also stay in the double rooms or the cabin used by teachers (both ❸–❹), or the new "Savanna Cabaña" – a private home next door to the sanctuary, with its own entrance, bath, veranda and kitchen (❼). None of these options, save the last, has a private bathroom, but the shared, tiled showers offer ample rainwater and all rooms sport mosquito-netted beds.

Monkey Bay attempts to be a viable exponent of "off-the-grid", **sustainable living**, utilizing solar and wind power, rainwater catchment and biogas fuel for cooking; the food, some of it grown in the station's organic gardens, is delicious, plentiful and inexpensive. It should fill you with plenty of energy to hike the Indian Creek Trail; if you're game, ask at Monkey Bay or contact Marcos Cucul (see p.169). To make a **booking** for the field research station, contact the directors, Matt and Marga Miller (ⓣ820-3032 or 600-3191, ⓔmbay@btl.net), or just turn up and ask the manager if there's space available. Next to Monkey Bay, *Amigos Bar* (ⓣ802-8000; daily 6am–10pm) has great **meals** and desserts, a daily happy hour and **Internet** access.

Banana Bank Lodge

Monkey Bay marks the boundary between Cayo and Belize districts, and here the open expanse of pine savannah begins to give way to rich pastures and citrus groves. Opposite the airstrip at Mile 46, 25km beyond Monkey Bay and 2km before the turn-off for Belmopan, a track heads north to **Banana Bank Lodge** (Ⓣ820-2020, Ⓦwww.bananabank.com; ⑧–⑨, includes a good breakfast). This 4000-acre working cattle ranch, half of which is still primary forest, is owned by Americans John and Carolyn Carr and managed by their daughter Leisa. They offer great horseback riding, canoeing and swimming, and there are also dozens of Maya mounds to explore. The **accommodation**, with views sweeping down to the Belize River, comprises five spacious, fan-cooled cabañas with two bedrooms, each with two beds and private bath, four air-conditioned rooms in the original lodge and air-conditioned suites with private balconies and Internet access. Tasty, home-cooked meals are served family-style in the thatched dining room.

The *Lodge* is on the north bank of the Belize River; the track from the highway ends at the south bank and you cross in a small boat. Vehicles can be left safely at the caretaker's house on the riverbank. An alternative route from Mile 49, signposted at the turn-off to the right just beyond **Roaring Creek** village, allows you to drive all the way, crossing the river over the new Agripino Cawich Bridge. If you're without your own vehicle, call the lodge to arrange a pickup in Belmopan.

Long before tourists began arriving in Belize, *Banana Bank* was renowned for **horseback riding** – the old racetrack here was popular with the elite from Belize City in the 1920s until the 1970s – and the lodge has expanded its equestrian capacity since then. It now has sixty well-trained horses for both English and Western riding styles, a stable block and a training arena. Complete beginners can learn to ride and experts can take some challenging trails, always with guides who are very friendly, knowledgeable and ready to help (non-guests welcome). If there's a full moon during your stay, a moonlight ride is an especially memorable experience.

The natural history of the *Lodge's* surroundings is astonishing: over two hundred bird species have been recorded here, and there's an observation tower for birding over a beautiful **lagoon** with resident Morelet's crocodiles. The ranch has its own small collection of animals, including a spider monkey and an aviary of over 25 birds. Carolyn is an accomplished artist and her work is exhibited all over the country; if time permits, you can visit her studio on-site. She recently designed the new **swimming pool**, drawing inspiration from the Inland Blue Hole, a peaceful lagoon in harmony with its environment (see p.240). She's also very proud of her "**mini observatory**" on the riverbank. The fourteen-inch, computer-controlled Meade telescope here (which guests can use under supervision) is the best in the country and the absence of light pollution enables you to view galaxies millions of light years away.

Immediately adjacent to *Banana Bank*, the *Belize Jungle Dome* (Ⓣ822-2124, Ⓦwww.belizejungledome.com; ⑧–⑨), is a good alternative if *Banana Bank* is full. It offers package accommodation, a variety of tours to surrounding regions, wireless **Internet access**, a café, a bookstore and a swimming pool.

Guanacaste National Park

Right by the highway, 73km from Belize City at the junction for Belmopan and the Hummingbird Highway, **Guanacaste National Park** (daily 8am–4.30pm;

Bz$5, includes a short, ranger-led tour) provides an opportunity to wander through a superb area of lush tropical forest at the confluence of Roaring Creek and the Belize River. At 52 acres, this is Belize's smallest national park, but it's also the easiest to visit – **buses** stop right outside the entrance. Sign in at the **visitor centre**, which has maps and information on park ecology – including a superb exhibit on the life cycle of leaf-cutter ants, which you'll see all over Belize – and have a look at the orchid display in the courtyard. Outside, three short **trails** take you through the park and along the banks of the Belize River, with the chance to plunge into a lovely swimming hole at the end of your visit; there's also a large wooden deck for picnicking and sunbathing.

The main attraction here are the many **guanacaste** (or tubroos) trees, tall spreading hardwoods that support some 35 other species of plants: hanging from their limbs are a huge range of bromeliads, orchids, ferns, cacti and strangler figs, which blossom spectacularly at the end of the rainy season. The partially water-resistant wood is traditionally favoured for feeding troughs, dugout canoes (a good-sized tree can make two or three) and mortars for hulling rice. In season, the tree produces ear-shaped fruit, used as cattle feed. Sadly, the park's "signature" tree – the largest and oldest – was cut in 2006 due to safety concerns, but another mature specimen can be found along the River Path.

Other botanical attractions include young mahogany trees, cohune palms, a ceiba (the sacred tree of the Maya, also known as a silk-cotton tree) and quamwood, while the forest floor is a mass of ferns and mosses. As the park is so close to the road, your chances of seeing any four-footed **wildlife** are fairly slim, though armadillos, white-tailed deer, jaguarundis, opossums and agoutis have nevertheless been spotted, and howler and spider monkeys use the park as a feeding ground. Birds abound, with around one hundred species present, among them blue-crowned motmots, black-faced ant-thrushes, black-headed trogons, red-lored parrots and squirrel cuckoos. Unfortunately, mosquitoes are common too, so bring repellent.

Belmopan

From Guanacaste National Park the Western Highway pushes on towards San Ignacio and the Guatemalan border, while a paved branch road leads 2km south towards Belize's capital, **BELMOPAN**. Beyond here, the road becomes the Hummingbird Highway, continuing all the way to the coast at Dangriga. For most people, the capital is no more than a pause in the bus ride to or from San Ignacio, though if you're heading to Dangriga or Placencia you may have to change buses here.

Belmopan was founded in 1970, nearly a decade after Hurricane Hattie swept much of Belize City into the sea. The government had decided to move to higher ground and, in a Brasília-style bid to focus development on the interior, chose a site in the geographical heart of the country. The name of the city combines the words "Belize" and "Mopan", the language spoken by the Maya of Cayo. The layout of the main government buildings is loosely modelled on a Maya city, with structures grouped around a central plaza; the National Assembly building even incorporates a version of the traditional roof comb, a decorative stonework and stucco crest. Although these long, grey, concrete buildings, set away from the road and surrounded by grass, won their British architect an award, they now present a rather dismal facade, out of line with their importance.

Though some of its elements have not aged well, Belmopan was originally meant to symbolize the dawn of a new era, with tree-lined avenues, banks, a couple of embassies and communications worthy of the capital of a freshly

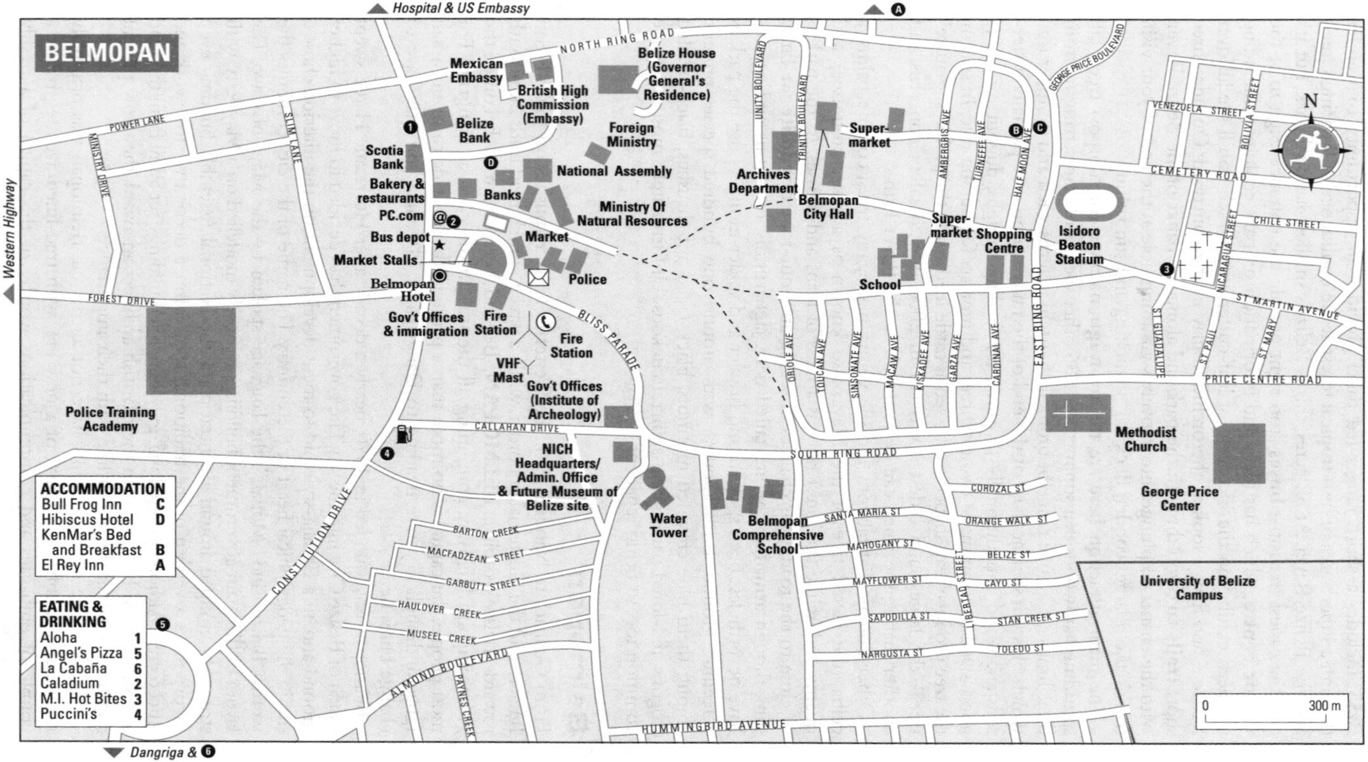

BELMOPAN

ACCOMMODATION

Bull Frog Inn	C
Hibiscus Hotel	D
KenMar's Bed and Breakfast	B
El Rey Inn	A

EATING & DRINKING

Aloha	1
Angel's Pizza	5
La Cabaña	6
Caladium	2
M.I. Hot Bites	3
Puccini's	4

Hospital & US Embassy
A
Western Highway
Dangriga & 6
North Ring Road
Belize House (Governor General's Residence)
Mexican Embassy
British High Commission (Embassy)
Foreign Ministry
Belize Bank
Scotia Bank
National Assembly
Bakery & restaurants
Banks
Ministry Of Natural Resources
PC.com
Bus depot
Market
Market Stalls
Police
Belmopan Hotel
Gov't Offices & immigration
Fire Station
Fire Station
VHF Mast
Gov't Offices (Institute of Archeology)
Bliss Parade
Callahan Drive
NICH Headquarters/ Admin. Office & Future Museum of Belize site
Water Tower
Belmopan Comprehensive School
Police Training Academy
Power Lane
Ministry Drive
Slim Lane
Forest Drive
Constitution Drive
Barton Creek
Macfadzean Street
Garbutt Street
Haulover Creek
Museel Creek
Almond Boulevard
Paynes Creek
Hummingbird Avenue
Unity Boulevard
Trinity Boulevard
Archives Department
Belmopan City Hall
Super-market
Ambergris Ave
Turneffe Ave
Half Moon Ave
George Price Boulevard
Super-market
Shopping Centre
School
Isidoro Beaton Stadium
Oriole Ave
Toucan Ave
Sinsonate Ave
Macaw Ave
Kiskadee Ave
Garza Ave
Cardinal Ave
East Ring Road
South Ring Road
Corozal St
Santa Maria St
Orange Walk St
Mahogany St
Belize St
Mayflower St
Cayo St
Sapodilla St
Stan Creek St
Nargusta St
Toledo St
Liberdad Street
Venezuela Street
Bolivia Street
Cemetery Road
Chile Street
Nicaragua Street
St Martin Avenue
St Guadalupe
St Paul
St Mary
Price Centre Road
Methodist Church
George Price Center
University of Belize Campus
N
0 300 m

independent country. The population was planned at 5000 for the first few years, with an expected increase to 30,000, but few Belizeans other than government officials (who had no option) have moved here. Although the population has doubled from 7000 to over 14,000 (and still growing) in the past few years, Belmopan is still the smallest capital city in the world.

Unless you've come here to visit a government department, there's no particular reason to stay any longer than it takes your bus to move on. If you find some time on your hands, however, visit the **George Price Centre** (Mon–Fri 9am–6pm; free; Ⓣ822-1054, Ⓦwww.gpcbelize.com), on the east side of the city. Here you will find the first flag that flew over the country, as well as an excellent display of documents, pictures and memorabilia in tribute to the first Prime Minister of Belize and the architect of the country's independence. Rotating exhibits of local artists, as well as movies and other activities, are scheduled regularly. Curator Elsie Alpuche is well informed and can provide information about new developments in Belmopan.

On the south side of town, next to the water tower, a newly constructed building currently serves as the administrative headquarters for the National Institute of Culture and History (NICH), but will soon become an extension of the Museum of Belize, with Maya artifacts on display; contact the NICH's Institute of Archeology (Ⓣ822-3302; office on second floor) for information. The **Archives Department**, 26–28 Unity Blvd (Mon–Fri 8am–5pm; free; Ⓣ822-2248, Ⓦwww.belizearchives.gov.bz), also welcomes visitors to its air-conditioned reading room, where photographs, documents, newspapers and sound archives provide fascinating glimpses of old Belize. The department regularly holds formal exhibitions of these materials.

Practicalities

Buses from Belize City to San Ignacio, Benque Viejo, Dangriga and Punta Gorda all pass through Belmopan, so there's at least one service every thirty minutes in either direction – the last bus from Belmopan to Belize City leaves at 7pm, to San Ignacio at 10pm. All buses currently stop in the main bus terminal. Heading south along the Hummingbird Highway, the first bus to leave is at 6.30am, with other buses leaving roughly hourly until 7pm. Not all buses heading south stop at every town along the way, so be sure to check if your destination is on the itinerary.

If you're in need of information, Dora at *DMD's Fast Food* (Ⓣ621-4229) can straighten you out; she's in the northwest corner of the wooden market stalls near the terminal. Here (or at the fire station) you might also find Marcos Cucul of the top-class **Maya Guide Adventures** (Ⓣ600-3116, Ⓦwww.mayaguide.bz); seek him out for one-of-a-kind jungle treks and cave tours.

Hotels in Belmopan tend to cater to the needs and expense accounts of diplomats and aid officials; San Ignacio, less than an hour away, has much more interesting and affordable accommodation. If you do have to stay here, the *El Rey Inn*, 23 Moho St (Ⓣ822-3438, Ⓔhibiscus@btl.net; ❸), is a pleasant and reasonably inexpensive option, with clean rooms, bedside lights and private bath. The best place in town is *Bull Frog Inn*, 25 Half Moon Ave (Ⓣ822-2111, Ⓔbullfrog@btl.net; ❼); its comfortable, air-conditioned rooms have cable TV, wireless Internet, telephone and balcony, and there's a very good restaurant and bar frequented by the political elite of Belize. Just behind, *KenMar's Bed and Breakfast*, 22–24 Half Moon Ave (Ⓣ822-0118, Ⓦwww.kenmar.bz; ❺–❻), offers homely rooms with air-conditioning, private bath, wireless Internet and a tropical breakfast in the morning. *Hibiscus Hotel*, off Constitution Drive near the banks on the other side of town (Ⓣ822-1418, Ⓔhibiscus@btl.net; ❺), has spacious rooms with private bath and air-conditioning, some with cable TV. There's a gift shop and restaurant serving Belizean mains here, too.

As for **restaurants**, the city's culinary diversity has benefited from the recent surge in new residents. The **market**, near the bus terminal, has several good fast-food and fruit stalls, and vendors will sometimes board the buses with snacks and drinks. The nearest restaurant to the terminal is *Caladium*, whose air-conditioning, nonsmoking policy and clean toilets make it one of the more pleasant eateries in the centre. It serves tasty, inexpensive Belizean dishes, including a daily special, and has a takeaway window. *Aloha*, immediately north of Scotia Bank, is a small diner dishing up Belizean and Taiwanese food, as well as burgers, coffee and ice cream. You can easily have your order to go in time to catch your next bus. If you're willing to walk a couple blocks from the terminal, *Puccini's* is a new, very popular Italian restaurant next to the petrol station, serving great pasta dishes. *M.I. Hot Bites* on St Martin Avenue serves a good selection of Indian and continental cuisine, but beware its high prices and dress code (no sandals or shorts). Near the roundabout on the southwest edge of the city are *Angel's Pizza* and *La Cabaña*, the latter a lively evening entertainment spot.

On to the Mountain Pine Ridge Forest Reserve

West of Belmopan the scenery becomes more rugged, with thickly forested ridges always in view to the south. Although the strictly protected **Tapir Mountain Nature Reserve** here is not open to casual visitors, you can get a taste of what it holds by visiting **Actun Tunichil Muknal**, one of the most extraordinary **caves** in the country. The Western Highway stays close to the valley of the Belize River, crossing numerous tributary creeks and passing through a series of villages: Roaring Creek, Camelote, Teakettle, Ontario, Unitedville, Esperanza and finally **Santa Elena**, San Ignacio's sister town on the eastern bank of the Macal River. There's been something of an accommodation boom along this route, with a couple of long-established, cottage-style **lodges** now joined by several newer enterprises. With your own vehicle, you might choose to abandon this route by turning south at Georgeville, 26km from the Belmopan junction, and taking the **Chiquibul Road** to the **Mountain Pine Ridge Forest Reserve** and the ruins of **Caracol**. Along this unpaved road are several places to stay, as well as Belize's best **butterfly exhibit** and **horseback riding**.

Roaring River Golf Club

CAMELOTE village, 8km west of Belmopan, holds the first attraction beyond the capital. **Roaring River Golf Club**, at Mile 50.25 of the Western Highway (☎614-6525), is the Belizean mainland's only public golf course. Its immaculately maintained fairways and greens, screened by mature and newly planted trees on the bank of the crystal-clear Roaring River, are the pride of South

African owner Paul Martin. Paul designed and built the nine-hole course himself, and it has gained a fine reputation from both locals and visitors. There's none of the snobbery here that can permeate other golf clubs, and prices are generous: weekend greens fees are only Bz$30, and it's Bz$10 to rent a set of clubs. During the weekdays, you can golf all day for Bz$15. The course is regularly patronised by diplomats and other members of the expatriate community, but you'll just as often encounter off-duty clerks or Mennonite families swinging their clubs. The abundance of wildlife on the course – a testament to Paul's policy of minimal pesticide use – means that it's now an official location on Audubon's annual Christmas Bird Count, and the water hazard on the eighth hole is home to thousands of fish and two crocodiles.

If you're arriving by bus along the highway, get off at *One Barrel Bar* at the junction of the three-kilometre track to the course; call from the bar and Paul will come pick you up.

Tapir Mountain Nature Reserve and Pook's Hill Jungle Lodge

Ten kilometres south of the highway, between Roaring and Barton creeks, **Tapir Mountain Nature Reserve** protects 28 square kilometres of the northern foothills of the Maya Mountains. The reserve, managed by the Belize Audubon Society, is a rich, well-watered habitat covered in high canopy and moist tropical forest, and home to all of Belize's **national symbols**: Baird's tapir, the keel-billed toucan, the black orchid and the mahogany tree. Nature reserves are Belize's highest category of protected land and, as one requirement of the designation is to "maintain natural processes in an undisturbed state", Tapir Mountain can only be visited by accredited researchers. Unfortunately, the category does not guarantee protection from hunters, or even from farmers encroaching on the reserve.

Although you aren't allowed to enter, you can enjoy the reserve's spectacular scenery from a distance by staying at **Pook's Hill Jungle Lodge** (Ⓣ820-2017, Ⓦwww.pookshilllodge.com; ⑨), run by the extremely hospitable Ray and Vicky Snaddon. The turn-off from the highway clearly signposted at Mile 52, at the village of **Teakettle**, and the nine-kilometre track up to the lodge is bumpy but in good condition. If you're travelling by bus, call ahead – someone will pick you up from the junction, where there's a payphone.

The lodge is set in a clearing on a terraced hillside within a 300-acre private holding. Eleven comfortable, thatched cabañas overlook the thickly forested Roaring River valley, with breathtaking views across Tapir Mountain Nature Reserve to the Mountain Pine Ridge beyond. Just below here are two additional cabañas, reached by a bridge high over a small creek and offering even more comfort and seclusion; all have electricity and hot water. This spectacular location clearly held attractions for its previous inhabitants, too: the lodge sits atop a Maya platform, and the cabañas are arranged around the remains of ancient habitation, plans of which you can view in the lodge. The site was recently excavated and consolidated; the most interesting find is the only purpose-built "sweatbath" found so far in Belize. Excellent **meals** (not included in rates) are served in a dining room at the edge of the forest; above, a thatched, open-sided deck with easy chairs and hammocks serves as a bar in the evenings. There's also a small **library** here, with a focus on archeology and natural history.

To see **wildlife**, you don't have to stray far. Birding here is in a league of its own and there is almost always a raptor of some kind, perhaps a **bat falcon**, hunting or feeding in view of the lodge. Every year a pair of spectacled owls raises a brood near the cabañas, and *Pook's Hill* is also a centre of Belize's green iguana breeding programme. There are wonderful, self-guided **nature trails** and superb **horseback riding trails** along farm and forest tracks, and you can hike or ride to more substantial ruins, including **Actun Tunichil Muknal**, further up the valley (see box, opposite). To cool off you can swim or go **tubing** in the river.

△ Hiking to Actun Tunichil Muknal

Actun Tunichil Muknal

A few kilometres up Roaring Creek valley, south of the *Pook's Hill Lodge*, lies **Actun Tunichil Muknal** ("cave of the stone sepulchre"), one of the most spectacular caves in the country. Often referred to as "ATM", the cave was discovered in 1986 by archeologist Thomas Miller, who named it for the astonishingly well-preserved skeletons of Maya human sacrifices he found within. A total of fourteen individual skeletons have been identified, including six infants under 3 years old and a child of about 7; the ages of the adults range from the twenties to forties. None was actually buried: they were simply laid in or near shallow pools in natural travertine terraces. Alongside the skeletons are over 150 ceramic vessels, probably originally containing food offerings, most of which have been ceremonially "killed" by piercing the base to release the powerful energy or spirit of the vessel.

Although looting has occurred in one chamber, the main chamber, much higher up the cave wall, has not been touched and the **megalithic artifacts** here are absolutely spellbinding: carved slate representations of a huge obsidian blade and an enormous stingray spine – a symbol of human sacrifice – lean upright against each other, encircled by stones. These models of bloodletting implements are an indisputable indication of the sacred ceremonies performed here over 1200 years ago. Perhaps the most dramatic sight, however, is the skeleton of a young woman lying below a rock wall – and, nearby, the stone axe that may have killed her. To the ancient Maya, caves were entrances to Xibalba – "the place of fright" and the abode of the Lords of Death – yet the worshippers made the difficult descent over one kilometre underground with only pine torches to light their way. Such rituals must indeed have been terrifying journeys to an utterly frightful place.

As the cave is a registered archeological site (entry fee Bz$30), only specially trained guides are allowed to lead groups inside. Currently, there are a number of qualified and experienced guides based in San Ignacio (see p.186), who run excellent, adventurous trips (around US$80 with transportation, entrance fee and lunch included). You'll need to be pretty fit and able to swim to make the trip: you'll be wading waist- or even chest-deep in water much of the time. Good **hiking shoes** or closed-toe footwear are mandatory for navigating the underground river's slippery and sharp rocks, and don't wear anything you don't want to get muddy.

While ATM is certainly well worth exploring, its growing popularity places great stress on its carrying capacity and begins to compromise the experience and **safety** for visitors. The best tack is to find a reputable guide to take you when fewer people are visiting, and to go with the smallest group possible.

Spanish Lookout and Caesar's Place

Heading west from Teakettle, you'll pass the roadside eatery *McWolf's*, a great spot for fresh, delicious burgers and fries (Mon-Sat 11am-7pm, Sun 11am-5pm). No matter which direction you're headed, you can get off the bus here and catch the next one in half an hour. Once you've filled up and arrived at the village of **Blackman Eddy** (Mile 57), a well-paved and signposted road turning right from the highway leads to **Spanish Lookout**, one of Belize's most successful **Mennonite** farming settlements. Its neat farmhouses, white-fenced fields, paved roads, car and tractor showrooms and the *Golden Coral* diner (closed Sun) successfully evoke the American Midwest. The Mennonites here have enthusiastically embraced modern technology, and have the best-stocked auto parts shops in the country.

Crude oil was discovered here recently, bringing this already burgeoning settlement further into the spotlight and provoking (or rekindling) several national debates. While the oil strike suggests a windfall for this debt-strapped country, Belize's modest infrastructure cannot keep up with the sheer volume of product – of an available 50,000 barrels per day, only 3000 are moved – and there are rising concerns that government mismanagement and greed will allow international industry to spoil the country's protected natural resources. The oil is currently trucked along narrow, unpaved roads to Big Creek, where a 45,000-barrel barge transports it to Texas – creating the possibility (or probability, as many experts warn) of oil spills and other disasters. The issues don't stop here, either: Guatemala has never relinquished its long-standing claim to much of Belize's border region, including Spanish Lookout, so the countries' smouldering territorial dispute could quickly erupt into a political crisis if Guatemala decides it wants a piece of the pie (see Contexts, p.318).

Further along, on the north side of the highway at Mile 60, **Caesar's Place** (ⓣ824-2341, ⓔinfo@belizegifts.com; ❺–❻) is Caesar and Antonieta Sherrard's café and **guest house**, right on the bank of Barton Creek. Guests stay in comfortable, attractive and secure rooms with private bath, though trailer hook-ups and camping spots are available as well (both Bz$10). The open-air dining area is a great place for lunch, serving delicious, pan-Central American **home cooking**, and there's always a vegetarian option. It's also a renowned **music** venue, featuring local band Mango Jam on the first Saturday of the month. A short trail leads down to a beautiful **swimming** hole on the creek, and Caesar's son Julian can organize canoe or caving trips along the Macal River – on the bank of which sits *Black Rock River Lodge*, another of Caesar's ventures (see p.201). The *Caesar's Place* **gift shop** is one of the largest and best in Belize, featuring wood carvings (properly dried in a solar kiln), slate reproductions of Maya artwork, a wide selection of Belizean contemporary art, Guatemalan textiles and silver jewellery from Taxco in Mexico. The book section is a good place to pick up information about the Maya, and it carries several maps and guides to Guatemala and Mexico.

Beyond *Caesar's*, just over the Barton Creek bridge, two prominent grass-covered **pyramids** mark the unexcavated Maya site of **Floral Park**; simply looking out the bus window as you pass by will give you a good sense of what's there. Six kilometres further lies the **Georgeville** junction, from where (with your own transport) you can head south along the **Chiquibul Road** into the Mountain Pine Ridge Forest Reserve (see p.179). A few kilometres past the junction is Central Farm, the University of Belize's Agricultural Research station. On the right of the highway, another road leads to **Spanish Lookout** via a ferry crossing. The Western Highway continues for another 7km to Santa Elena and San Ignacio (see p.176 & p.186, respectively).

The Chiquibul Road

Well used by villagers, foresters and tourists, the Chiquibul Road reaches deep into the Mountain Pine Ridge Forest Reserve and heads for Caracol (see p.183), with some entertaining diversions along the way. From Georgeville, where the road begins on the Western Highway, you could hitch to the reserve headquarters at **Augustine/Douglas Silva**, but a mountain bike or four-wheel-drive vehicle is ideal for exploring this fascinating area of hills, waterfalls, caves and jungle. The road, usually in reasonable condition, may be experiencing upgrades to enable easier and faster access to Caracol.

Barton Creek Cave

Of the many **cave trips** in Cayo, one of the most fascinating is to **Barton Creek Cave**, accessible only by river, and only on a tour with a licensed guide (around 4hr; Bz$60 plus $20 entry fee). Like all caves in Belize, Barton Creek Cave is a registered archeological site and nothing must be touched or removed. Although almost everyone now offers trips here, the original and **best guide** to the cave is David Simpson, a multilingual Belizean who runs David's Adventure Tours from San Ignacio (see p.189). He'll carefully and responsibly show you the astonishing Maya artifacts in the cave, and will usually include a visit to Green Hills Butterfly Ranch (see below).

Though the official, signposted turnoff to the cave is 7km along the Chiquibul Road from Georgeville, this route has become impassable even for many four-wheel-drive vehicles. Luckily, the traditional Mennonite settlement of **Upper Barton Creek** has been kind enough to temporarily allow tour groups access to a private track, turning east off the Chiquibul Road after 3km, that fords Barton Creek and eventually reaches a jade-green pool. On the far side, the water disappears into the jungle-framed cave entrance, and you follow the river underground in a canoe, crouching down in places where the cave roof dips low. After 1600m you emerge into a gallery blocked by a huge rockfall. If it's been raining, a subterranean waterfall cascades over the rocks – a truly unforgettable sight. Beyond lie many more miles of passageways, accessible only on a fully equipped expedition. The clear, slow-moving river fills most of the cave's width, though the roof soars 100m above your head in places, and you must illuminate the way ahead with powerful lamps. Several **Maya burials** surrounded by pottery vessels line the banks, the most awe-inspiring indicated by a skull set in a natural rock bridge used by the Maya to reach the sacred site.

After a tour of Barton Creek Cave, you can also stop by the **Barton Creek Outpost** (Ⓣ662-4797, Ⓦwww.bartoncreekoutpost.com), complete with restaurant and bar, showers, rope swings and canoe rental (Bz$20). If you're inclined to stay overnight, camping is free – mattress and sleeping bag rental is Bz$10 and you can catch a ride back to San Ignacio with a tour the next day. Check at *Café Cayo* (see p.192) in San Ignacio for more information.

Mountain Equestrian Trails

Eleven kilometres along the road from Georgeville, **Mountain Equestrian Trails** (Ⓣ820-4884, in the US Ⓣ1-800/838-3918, Ⓦwww.metbelize.com; ❾) is unquestionably Belize's premier **horseback riding** vacation centre, with nearly 100km of superb forest trails encompassing various ecosystems. It offers very comfortable **accommodation** – ten rooms in thatched, oil lamp-lit cabañas, set in tropical forest on the edge of the Pine Ridge – and the *Cantina* restaurant dishes out tasty Belizean and Mexican **meals** in large portions. Managers Allison and Arran Bevis can also arrange hiking, birding, kayaking and caving trips into little-visited regions of the interior, and the centre is a base for low-impact wildlife safaris deep into the Chiquibul Forest.

Owner Jim Bevis and his wife, Marguerite, are founding members of the Slate Creek Preserve, a privately owned, sixteen-square-kilometre tract of limestone karst forest bordering the Mountain Pine Ridge Forest Reserve. Landowners, recognizing the importance of conservation and sustainable development, helped to establish the preserve in 1992 by following the guidelines in UNESCO's Man and the Biosphere Programme – one example of how concern for the environment in Belize has been translated into practical projects benefiting local people.

Green Hills Butterfly Ranch and Botanical Collections

On the opposite side of the road from *Mountain Equestrian Trails*, the **Green Hills Butterfly Ranch and Botanical Collections** (daily 8am–4pm; Bz$10 with guided tour, last tour at 3.30pm; ⓣ820-4017, ⓦwww.green-hills.net) is Belize's biggest and best butterfly exhibit. It's run by Dutch biologists Jan Meerman and Tineke Boomsma, both experts in the field who have published many scientific and popular articles and books – including a *Checklist of the Butterflies of Belize* – on insects, reptiles, amphibians and flowers (see the excellent website for the full list, where most of the articles can be downloaded free of charge). They've also discovered several new species in Belize, including a **tarantula** – *Citharacanthus meermani* – at Green Hills itself.

The main attraction is the enclosed, beautifully landscaped **flight area**, where flocks of gorgeous tropical butterflies flutter around, settling occasionally on flowers to sip nectar. Over eighty different species have been bred here, though you'll usually see around twenty-five to thirty at any one time, depending on the time of year and the breeding cycle. As this is a breeding centre, you can watch one of nature's wonders (particularly in the early morning) as the butterflies emerge from jewelled chrysalises; many of the chrysalises are shipped to approved butterfly exhibits in the US. Fascinating as this is, there's lots more to see, and enthusiastic, well-trained local guides give fantastic briefings and welcome all questions. To raise butterflies you also need to know about their food plants, so there's an amazing botanical garden, home to **Belize's National Passionflower Collection**, as well as countless **epiphytes** (air plants), cycads, heliconias and orchids and a tropical fruit orchard.

Santa Elena and the Cristo Rey Road

Immediately to the east of San Ignacio, **SANTA ELENA** sits on the eastern bank of the Macal River. Though quite a large town, Santa Elena has few of the attractions of its larger neighbour, serving primarily as the starting point of the Cristo Rey Road – another route, like the Chiquibul Road, into the Mountain Pine Ridge Forest Reserve. Though San Ignacio is a nicer place to stay, there is a very reasonable **hotel** here: the *Aguada* (ⓣ804-3609, ⓦwww.aguadahotel.com; ❹), signposted on the right of the highway near the town entrance. Run by a very welcoming family, the hotel has clean, comfortable rooms, all with air-conditioning and private bath. There's an inexpensive restaurant, a pool and patio in the landscaped grounds and **Internet** access for guests. Another of the town's few notable sights is Dr Rosita Arvigo's **Ix Chel Wellness Center**, where you can learn about tradition Maya healing methods and the medicinal plants of the rainforest (see p.202).

Nearly half a kilometre east of Santa Elena's **Hawkesworth Bridge**, built in 1949 over the Macal River and still the only road suspension bridge in Belize, the **Cristo Rey Road** sets out toward the Mountain Pine Ridge. It holds a few points of interest along its length, starting with the excellent *Maya Mountain Lodge* (ⓣ824-2164, ⓦwww.mayamountain.com; ❻–❾), set in rich tropical forest two kilometres south of Santa Elena and providing a fascinating overview of Belize's wildlife. **Accommodation** is in colourfully decorated, individual cabañas, each with private bath and electricity; the "Parrot's Perch" is a larger wooden building housing seven rooms with private bath, air-conditioning and a huge, shared deck with hammocks. Delicious **meals** are served in an open-sided dining room that's also a great spot for birding: motmots, aracaris and trogons fly just metres from your table. The lodge sometimes hosts student groups and has a lecture area and well-stocked library; after dinner most evenings there's an informed cultural or educational presentation. Families are especially welcome and kids will have plenty of entertainment, including a pool and the best illustrated trail guide in Belize. Great tour packages are available, as are discounts for *Rough Guides* users.

After another few kilometres you come to **CRISTO REY**, a pretty village of scattered wooden and cement houses and gardens on a high bank above the Macal River. Near the entrance to the village, Orlando and Martha Madrid run *Sandals Restaurant* and a few simple, inexpensive **cabins** (Ⓣ614-7446; ❷–❸); you can also **rent canoes** at good rates. At the other end of the village, *Crystal Paradise Resort* (Ⓣ824-2772 or 824-4014, Ⓦwww.crystalparadise.com; ❼–❾) offers a wide range of accommodation and tours. Built and owned by the Belizean Tut family, it's a welcoming, relaxed place with accommodation in wooden rooms and thatched cabañas; all have private baths with hot water. The deck outside the dining room overlooks the valley (though you can't see the river) and is tremendous for spotting hummingbirds. Teresa's in charge of the cooking, Victor built many of the thatched roofs at the resorts in Cayo and sons Jeronie and Everald arrange tours throughout the district and over to Tikal; see the box on p.188. Free pickup in San Ignacio and **Internet** service is provided. Rates include delicious and filling home-cooked breakfast and dinner each day. As icing on the cake, they offer a discount to *Rough Guides* readers.

San Antonio and Pacbitún

Nestled in the Macal River valley, 10km further along the Cristo Rey Road, is **SAN ANTONIO**, a village surrounded by scattered *milpa* farms with the forested Maya Mountains in the background. Its inhabitants are descendants of Yucatec Maya (or *Masawal*) refugees who fled the Caste Wars in Yucatán in 1847. Most people here, whose oral history is transcribed in Alfonso Antonio Tzul's fascinating *After 100 Years*, still speak Yucatec and Spanish as well as English. San Antonio was the home of the famous Maya *curandero* (healer) **Don Eligio Panti** (see p.201), and his house has become a small, informal museum dedicated to his life and work and the simple tools he used; opening times are by request. Don Eligio's memory has been further honoured by naming a new national park after him (see below).

The village is a fine place to learn about traditional **Maya healing** methods. Go see Don Eligio's nieces, the **Garcia sisters**, who grew up in the village determined not to let their Maya culture be swamped by outside influence. The sisters run the newly renovated *Chichan Ka Guest House* (Ⓣ820-4023, Ⓔartistmai1981@btl.net; ❷) at the approach to the village; the **Mesh bus** from San Ignacio (4 daily Mon–Sat; 1hr) stops right outside. **Meals** are catered upon request and are prepared in traditional ways, often using organic produce from the garden. Maria Garcia is president of the Itzamna Society, a local organization formed to protect the Maya's environment and culture, and she also offers courses in the gathering and use of medicinal plants. The sisters are renowned for their **slate carvings**, and the **gift shop** here has become a favourite tour-group stop. Next door is the small **Tanah Museum** (Bz$6), with displays of village life and history and slate carvings; the Sa'k Tunich Gift Shop (Ⓣ670-8166) in the village has more carvings for sale.

Maria Garcia has played a prominent role in the establishment of the new **Eligio Panti National Park**, part of a project to allow the Maya of San Antonio to manage a protected area for conservation and tourism. The park covers over fifty square kilometres of rugged forest, hugging the northernmost perimeter of the Mountain Pine Ridge Forest Reserve. Park wardens and guides are well trained, and there's a visitor centre, trails among medicinal plants, and campsites (Bz$10). The park receives few visitors at present, but the

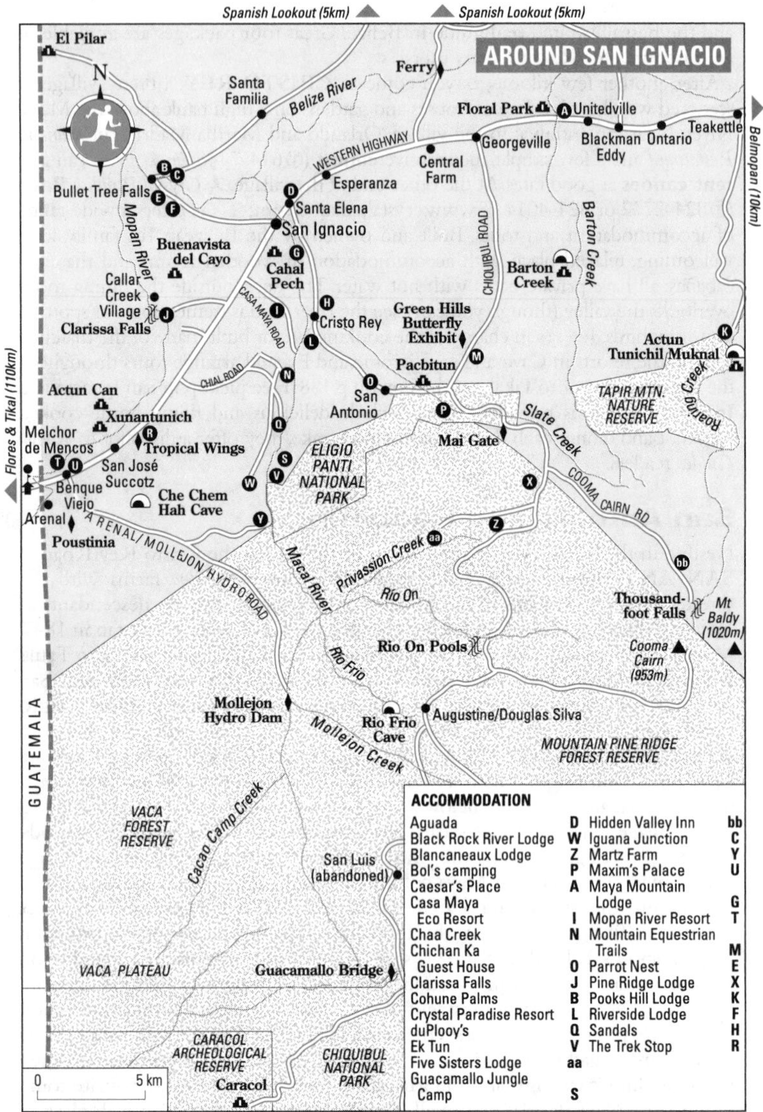

landscape is breathtaking and guides from the village can take you on horseback to see caves and waterfalls.

Three kilometres east of San Antonio, towards the entrance to the Mountain Pine Ridge Forest Reserve, lie the **ruins of Pacbitún**, a major Maya ceremonial centre. One of the oldest known Preclassic sites in Belize (it's been dated to 1000 BC), it continued to flourish throughout the Classic period, and farming terraces and mounds are still evident in the surrounding hills. Pacbitún, meaning "stones set in the earth", has at least 24 temple pyramids, a ball-court and several raised causeways, though only Plaza A and its adjacent structures have been cleared; this is the highest point in Pacbitún, created when the Maya reshaped an entire hilltop. Here, the tombs of two elite women yielded the largest haul of Maya musical instruments ever found in one place: drums, flutes, ocarinas and the first discovery of Maya maracas. Though the site is not always open to casual visitors, José Tzul, who lives just to the right of the entrance to the ruins, runs Blue Ridge Mountain Rider and can arrange wonderful **horseback tours** of the area (US$50/day); he can even guide you along little-known trails to the lodges in the Mountain Pine Ridge. If he's not home, Maria at the Tanah Museum in San Antonio can help you find him.

The Mountain Pine Ridge Forest Reserve and beyond

Southeast of San Ignacio and accessed by both the Chiquibul and Cristo Rey roads, the **Mountain Pine Ridge Forest Reserve** is a spectacular range of rolling hills, peaks and gorges. Its heights are formed from some of the oldest rocks in Central America, granite intrusions that have thrust upwards from the bedrock that underlies the entire isthmus. Amongst this are also some sections of limestone, riddled with superb caves, the most accessible of which is **Rio Frio Cave** in the village of Augustine/Douglas Silva. For the most part, the landscape here is a mixture of grassland and pine forest growing in the nutrient-poor, sandy soil, although in the warmth of the river valleys the vegetation is denser. The pines give way to rainforest south of the Guacamallo Bridge, which crosses the upper Macal River on the road to **Caracol**.

Plentiful rainfall renders the smooth roads in the Pine Ridge difficult to use in the wet season, but these rains feed a number of small streams, most of which run off into the Macal and Belize rivers. One of the most scenic is the **Río On**, rushing over cataracts and forming a gorge – a sight of tremendous natural beauty within view of a picnic shelter. On the northern side of the

The Pine Ridge lives on

Belizeans regard their beautiful pine forest as a national treasure, so news of a very severe infestation of the **southern pine bark beetle** in the Mountain Pine Ridge in early 2000 caused anguish throughout the country. As they feed, the beetle larvae kill the trees, and a new generation of larvae appears every four or five weeks. The deadly pests swept through the forest, their progress helped by the government's policy of fire suppression, which had allowed the trees to grow more densely than they would naturally. Initially, it was thought that the entire forest might be destroyed, but a rapidly implemented **reforestation programme** and abundant natural regeneration have made it clear that the forest will eventually recover. As you drive around the sandy roads in the Pine Ridge, you will see large areas of bare, lifeless pines, stretching to the horizon in places, but already the vigorous saplings are up to 2.5 metres tall and growing rapidly. Even the dead trees make important contributions to the habitat, providing hunting grounds for woodpeckers and other insect-eaters and thinning the forest as they fall, which makes recurrences of the infestation less likely and reveals new vistas for visitors to enjoy. Though the forest's appearance has been altered, it's still a beautiful place, and, by good fortune, the trees around Thousand-foot Falls were untouched – you can still see this magnificent sight in all its glory (see p.180).

ridge is **Thousand-foot Falls**, actually over 1600ft (490m) and the highest in Central America.

The Pine Ridge is virtually uninhabited but for a handful of **tourist lodges** and one small forestry settlement, **Augustine/Douglas Silva**, site of the reserve headquarters. The whole area is perfect for **hiking** and **mountain biking**, but **camping** in the reserve is allowed only at Augustine/Douglas Silva and at Bol's Nature Tours, by the Mai Gate at the entrance to the reserve (see below). Officially you need permission from the Forest Department in Belmopan to camp in these spots, but in practice you'll almost certainly be allowed if you ask the checkpoint officers politely when you arrive. It's fairly hard – though rewarding – to explore this part of the country on your own, and unless you have a car or a mountain bike or come on an organized tour, you may have to rely on hitching, making sure you're near somewhere to stay when it gets dark. To explore the many forestry roads branching off the Chiquibul Road, you really need to study one of the 1:50,000 topographic maps of the area, on display at many area resorts and attractions but, unfortunately, available for purchase only at the Forest Department in Belmopan. See p.178 for a map showing the Macal River valley and the Mountain Pine Ridge.

Arrival and getting around

There are **two entrance roads** to the reserve: the **Chiquibul Road**, from the village of Georgeville on the Western Highway (see p.174), and the **Cristo Rey Road**, from Santa Elena, served by the Mesh bus from San Ignacio and passing through the village of **San Antonio** (see p.176). If you're up to it, a good way to explore these routes is to rent a **mountain bike** in San Ignacio; buses on the Cristo Rey Road transport bikes, though you could also put it in the back of a passing pick-up truck. Any travel agent or resort in the area can arrange **organized tours**: if you're staying at a Cayo resort, a full-day tour of the Pine Ridge costs around US$35–55 per person for a group of four, more if you want to go to Caracol (see p.183). Ongoing road improvements, particularly on the road to Caracol (the last part now has an all-weather surface), make a trip in a **rental jeep** perfectly feasible most of the year, but always check road conditions first and heed the advice of the forestry officials.

Exploring the reserve

Not far beyond Pacbitún (see p.178), the Cristo Rey and Chiquibul roads converge and begin a steady climb toward the official **entrance to the reserve**. One kilometre south of this junction is a **campsite** (Bz$10 per person) run by Fidencio and Petronila Bol, owners of Bol's Nature Tours. On a ridge with views over to Pacbitún and Xunantunich, it's a good base for exploring the park. Fidencio can guide you to several nearby **caves**, including the aptly named Museum Cave, which holds dozens of intact bowls and other ceramics. Across from the campsite is *Misty Mountain* restaurant and bar, where Mick serves tasty food (burgers, pizzas and Belizean fare) at a bargain. About 5km uphill is the **Mai Gate**, a forestry checkpoint offering information about the reserve as well as toilets and drinking water. Though there are plans to levy an **entrance fee**, for the moment all the guard will do is write your name, or that of the tour group, in the visitors' book (this is done to ensure there's no illegal camping).

Once you've entered the reserve, pine trees quickly replace the dense, leafy forest that lined the approach roads. After 3km, the often-rough Cooma Cairn Road heads off to the left, running for 16km (through an area of dead pines) to a point overlooking **Thousand-foot Falls**. The setting is spectacular, with rugged, thickly forested slopes visible across the gorge. The long, slender plume of water disappears into the valley below, giving rise to the falls' other, more poetic name: Hidden Valley Falls. The waterfall itself is about one kilometre from the viewpoint, but try to resist the temptation to climb around for a closer look: the slope is a lot steeper than it first appears, and even if you manage to make the descent, the scramble back up is more difficult. Dawn and dusk are perhaps the best times to view the falls, as you'll very likely be the only visitors. However, you'd almost certainly need your own vehicle to do this, or a room at the nearby *Hidden Valley Inn*; see Accommodation, below. You can't see the river below, but this is the headwaters of Roaring River (or Creek), whose confluence with the Belize River you can appreciate in Guanacaste National Park (see p.166). There's a shelter with toilets at the viewpoint, and since the site is also a **National Monument**, you'll be approached by caretaker Pedro Mai for the entrance fee (Bz$2).

One of the reserve's main attractions has to be the **Rio On Pools**, a gorgeous spot for a swim, back on the Chiquibul Road and 11km further on. Here the river forms pools between huge, granite boulders before plunging into a gorge right beside the main road. Another 8km from here you reach the reserve headquarters at **Augustine/Douglas Silva**. Now housing only a few forestry workers, this small settlement was known as Augustine until it was renamed **Douglas Silva** after a local politician; however, only some of the signs have been changed and a complete transition to the new name never occurred. If you're heading to **Caracol**, Forest Department staff in the headquarters will give advice on road conditions. You can also **camp** here, and be sure to make the short hike to Big Rock Falls, one of the area's waterfall treasures.

A twenty-minute walk from Augustine/Douglas Silva, along the signposted track from the parking area and through the forest, is **Rio Frio Cave**. It burrows under a small hill, and the Río Frio flows right through it and out the other side. If you enter the foliage-framed cave mouth, you can clamber over limestone terraces the entire way until you're back out in the open. Sandy beaches and rocky cliffs line the river on both sides.

Accommodation

The **resorts** in the Mountain Pine Ridge Forest Reserve include some of the most exclusive accommodation in the interior of Belize. These lodges, mostly cabins set amongst pines, are surrounded by undisturbed natural beauty and have quiet paths to secluded waterfalls; they're also ideal places to stay if you're visiting **Caracol** (see p.183). The listings below are in order of their location along the entrance road (see map on p.178).

Hidden Valley Inn 8km along the Cooma Cairn Rd to Thousand-foot Falls ⓣ822-3320, in the US ⓣ866/443-3364, ⓦwww.hiddenvalleyinn.com. Twelve roomy, well-designed cottages at the highest elevation of any accommodation in Belize, and set in a thirty-square-kilometre private reserve bordering on Thousand-foot Falls. You may forget you're in the tropics here: each cottage has a fireplace stacked with logs to ward off the winter chill, and the vegetation – pines and tree ferns – appears distinctly temperate. Hiking and 4WD trails take you to mountain overlooks and secret waterfalls, and mountain bikes are free of charge. However you choose to roam, you'll have a detailed map and a two-way radio with you in case you get lost. There are so many waterfalls in the area that guests can arrange to have one entirely to themselves – a popular option with honey-mooners. Meals (not included in room rates) are served in the spacious main lodge, with its wood-panelled walls, crackling log fire and well-stocked

△ Waterfall in Mountain Pine Ridge

library. Days are hot enough for swimming in the pool, but if you get chilly you can jump in the hot tub. The *Inn* has an impressive list of bird sightings, and you can frequently see the rare orange-breasted falcon. ⑨

Pine Ridge Lodge On the Chiquibul Rd to Augustine/Douglas Silva, just past the Cooma Cairn junction ⓣ606-4557, in the US ⓣ1-800/316-0706, ⓦwww.pineridgelodge.com. A small resort on the banks of Little Vaqueros Creek, with a choice of simple, Maya-style thatched cabins or more modern ones with red-tiled roofs. The grounds and trees are full of orchids, and trails lead to pristine waterfalls. The restaurant is a favourite refreshment stop on tours of the Pine Ridge. Continental breakfast included. ⑦–⑧

Blancaneaux Lodge 1km beyond *Pine Ridge Lodge*, then 2km down a signposted track to the right, by the airstrip ⓣ824-3878, in the US ⓣ1-800/746-3743, ⓦwww.blancaneauxlodge.com. Owned by Francis Ford Coppola, *Blancaneaux* is the most sumptuous lodge in the Pine Ridge and features a few Hollywood luxuries – not least the prices, though these are considerably lower during the off-season. Guests stay in comfortable and very spacious hardwood and thatched cabañas, and even more spacious villas overlooking Privassion Creek. The grounds are beautifully landscaped, from the palm-lined driveway to the croquet lawn and organic garden. Villas (up to US$525, sleeping 4) have two enormous rooms with varnished hardwood floors, are decorated with Guatemalan and Mexican textiles, and boast huge, screened porches with gorgeous views over the creek. Cabañas (US$215 for garden view, $250 for river view, US$325 for the honeymoon version) are perhaps a better value and equally luxurious. The restaurant enlists a wood-fired pizza oven and an espresso machine, and meals feature Italian specialities served with home-grown organic vegetables and Coppola's wines. The latest additions to the attractions here are a delightful hot pool and a massage house built entirely with materials from Indonesia. The staff and service is exceptional, and thanks to the new conch "shell phones", you have a direct line to the front desk for your every need. Coppola also owns the equally luxurious *Turtle Inn* in Placencia (see p.267) and *La Lancha* near El Remate, Guatemala (see p.217). 9

Five Sisters Lodge 4km past *Blancaneaux*, at the end of the main reserve road ⓣ820-4005, ⓦwww.fivesisterslodge.com. Set on a hillside among granite and pines, this lodge has the best location in the Pine Ridge. It's also the only Belizean-owned resort here and is the pride and joy of owner Carlos Popper. There are nineteen very comfortable palmetto-and-thatch cabañas and suites, each with hot showers and a deck with hammocks. Electricity is provided by a small, unobtrusive hydro, but the oil lamps are wonderfully romantic and the resort is very popular with honeymooners. The grounds are a profusion of flowers, and there's a nature trail through broadleaf forest to Little Vaqueros Falls. The Five Sisters Falls, of which the dining-room deck offers tremendous views, can also be explored, though you can opt to ride up and down in the tiny funicular rather than climb. Below the main lodge, on a rocky island in Privassion Creek, there's a thatched beach bar and a small beach. The meals here are a good value even if you're just passing by on a day-trip. 8–9

Caracol

The main ridges of the Maya Mountains rise up to the south of Augustine/Douglas Silva, while to the west is the Vaca Plateau, a fantastically isolated wilderness. Sixteen kilometres past the reserve headquarters, the Chiquibul Road crosses the Macal River (and a fault line) over the low **Guacamallo Bridge**. South of this point, the vegetation changes dramatically: the pines of the northern riverbank change to the broadleaf jungle of the **Chiquibul Forest**. The turn-off for Caracol is 2.5km past the bridge, and 18km along this road brings you to the **visitor centre**, where you sign in before exploring the ruins. Many tour operators in San Ignacio run trips to Caracol: Everald Tut has a daily **shuttle** (US$50 per person; ⓣ820-4014). All groups depart for the site by 9am and, due to robberies in the area, travel with a military escort. For a directory of tour operators, see the box on p.188.

Caracol (daily 8am–4pm; Bz$15), the most extensive and magnificent Maya site in Belize (and one of the largest in the Maya world), was lost in the rainforest for over a thousand years until its rediscovery by chiclero Rosa Mai in 1937. Research has revealed that the name the ancient Maya gave to the city was **Oxwitzá**, or "three hill water", making this one of the few sites whose true name is known. The locale was first systematically explored by A.H. Anderson in 1938; he renamed the site Caracol – Spanish for "snail" – because of the large number of snail shells he found there. Anderson was accompanied by Linton Satterthwaite of the University of Pennsylvania in the 1950s, but many of their early records were destroyed by Hurricane Hattie in 1961, and several altars and stelae were deliberately broken by logging tractors in the 1930s.

In 1985 the first detailed, full-scale excavation of the site, the "Caracol Project", began under the auspices of Drs Arlen and Diane Chase of the University of Central Florida. Research continues to unearth a tremendous amount of artifacts relating to all levels of Maya society. Over a hundred **tombs** have been found, one of the best-preserved being B-19, under the largest temple on the summit of Caana (see opposite). This is almost certainly the tomb of **Lady Batz Ek**, or "black monkey", who married into the ruling K'an dynasty in 584 AD and who may even have been a ruler in her own right. Other ceremonially buried caches contain items as diverse as mercury and amputated human fingers. There are also many hieroglyphic inscriptions, enabling epigraphers to piece together a virtually complete dynastic record of Caracol's Classic-period rulers from 599 to 859 AD.

Apparently there was a large and wealthy middle class among the Maya of Caracol, and dates on stelae and tombs suggest an extremely long occupation, beginning around 600 BC. The last recorded date, carved on Stela 10, is 859 AD, during the Terminal Classic; evidence points to a great fire around 895 AD. At the height of its dominion, roughly 700 AD during the Late Classic period, Caracol covered 88 square kilometres and had a population estimated at around 150,000, with over 30,000 structures – a far greater density than at Tikal, another important centre of the Maya world. So far, only around ten percent of greater Caracol's full extent has been mapped, and research continues each field season. What continues to puzzle archeologists is why the Maya built such a large city on a plateau with no permanent water source – and how they managed to maintain it for so long.

The site

If you've driven here on your own, you may be asked to comply with certain safety regulations; at the very least, you'll be accompanied on your visit by one of the site rangers (who know a great deal about recent excavations) or, if excavation is in progress, by an archeology student. This is not so much to inform you – though you will undoubtedly gain from their expertise – as to ensure you're not about to damage any recently exposed surfaces or artifacts.

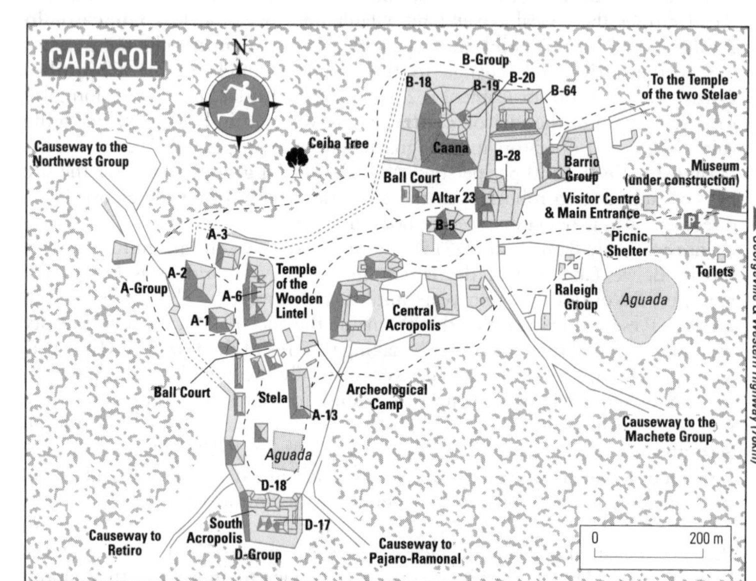

Recent work over the last few years has resulted in the discovery of many new monuments and stucco carvings, and several have been left under simple, thatched shelters until they can be removed to proper storage and laboratory facilities. A **stela house** is under (seemingly interminable) construction to display these findings, but until it's complete you'll learn much more about the latest discoveries from your guide. Despite the presence of the archeology teams and rangers, Caracol's isolated, remote location near the Guatemalan border makes it vulnerable to looting; the British Army and Belize Defence Force frequently patrol the area.

The **visitor centre**, the best at any Maya site in Belize, is an essential first stop. There's a scale model and a map of the ruins, some excellent, very informative display panels (follow them from right to left) and several unearthed artifacts. There's also a large, thatched picnic shelter and clean toilets. Only the city's core, covering 38 square kilometres and containing at least 32 large structures and twelve smaller ones around five main plazas, is currently open to visitors – though this is far more than you can effectively see in a day. It's an amazing experience to be virtually alone in this great, abandoned city, the horizon bounded by jungle-covered hills, only three hours by foot from the Guatemalan border.

Towering above the forest, Caracol's largest structure – **Caana**, or "sky place" – is, at 43m in height, the tallest Maya building in Belize (and still one of the tallest buildings in the country); several others are over 20m tall. Caana is the central structure of the **B Group**, the most massive architectural complex at Caracol. At the top of this immense, restored edifice is another plaza, with yet three more sizeable pyramids above this. When you finally climb B-19, the tallest of the three pyramids, you'll be rewarded with views of seemingly endless ridges and mountains – a perfect environment to contemplate the Maya concept of time's enormity while you regain your breath.

Beneath Caana, a series of looted tombs still show traces of original, painted glyphs on their walls; some have lintels of iron-hard sapodilla wood supporting their entrances and are decorated with painted text. Excavation on **Temple B5**, facing Caana across Plaza B, has uncovered fantastically detailed, stucco **monumental masks** on either side of the central staircase. They portray jaguars and the Witz ("sacred mountain") monster, wearing a headdress of water-lily pads being nibbled by small fish. In Maya cosmology, this design symbolizes the evening sun transforming into the jaguar god of the underworld and descending into the watery underworld of Xibalba to fight the Lords of Death. Legend dictates that if he's successful, he will rise again as the sun god.

To the side of Plaza B lies **Altar 23** – the largest altar at Caracol – clearly depicting two bound, captive lords from Ucanal and Bital, once-subdued cities located in present-day Petén; the glyphs above and between them date the structure to 810 AD. Other glyphs and altars tell of war between Caracol and **Tikal** (see p.308), with control over a huge area alternating between the two great cities. One altar dates Caracol's victory over Tikal at 562 AD – one that set the seal on the city's rise to power.

Not only a haven for archeologists, Caracol is also a **Natural Monument Reserve** and home to abundant wildlife. Bird sightings include the **orange-breasted falcon** and the very rare **harpy eagle**. You may catch sight of ocellated turkeys feeding in the plazas, and tapirs dine at night on the succulent shoots growing on cleared areas. One of the most awe-inspiring sights in this fantastic city is an immense, centuries-old **ceiba tree** – sacred to the Maya – with enormous buttress roots twice as tall as a human being.

The Chiquibul Cave System

Fifteen kilometres beyond the Caracol turn-off, the Chiquibul Road arrives at the vast **Chiquibul Cave System**, the longest cave system in Central America, containing what is probably the largest chamber in the western hemisphere. The entire aboveground area is dotted with caves and sinkholes, which were certainly known to the ancient Maya and probably used for ceremonies; as yet there has been no cave found in Belize that does not contain Maya artifacts. At present, the area is impossible to reach on your own – you'll need to come on a properly organized expedition, with permission from the Forest Department in Belmopan – but some tour operators are planning to run trips in the future, so it's worth checking with those recommended on p.188.

Slightly northeast of the cave system is the **Las Cuevas Research Station**. Although it's generally closed to the public, visitors on organized tour groups sometimes stay in the wooden cabins here; if you're lucky, you might get a lift to the station with the researchers or a group. South of the cave system, **Puente Natural** is an enormous, natural limestone arch.

San Ignacio and around

On the west bank of the Macal River, 35km from Belmopan, **SAN IGNACIO** is a friendly, relaxed town that draws together much of the best of inland Belize. The beating heart of Cayo District and the focus of tourism in western Belize, it offers good food, inexpensive hotels and restaurants and frequent bus connections. The town's best feature, however, is its location on the Macal River, amidst beautiful countryside and near several reserves. It's an excellent base for day-trips and overnights to the surrounding hills, streams, archeological sites, caves and forests. Several local tour operators run excursions south into the **Mountain Pine Ridge Forest Reserve** and beyond to the ruins of **Caracol**.

Just downstream from San Ignacio, the Macal and Mopan rivers, after tumbling down the northern and western slopes of the Maya Mountains, join to form the Belize River; the forested hills that begin at this confluence roll all the way south to Toledo District and west across Guatemala. The evenings are relatively cool here, and the days fresh – a welcome break from the sweltering heat of the coast – and there's a virtual absence of mosquitoes and other biting insects. The **population** is typically varied, mostly made up of Spanish-speaking mestizos, but with significant populations of Creoles, Mopan and Yucatec Maya, Mennonites, Lebanese, Chinese and even Sri Lankans.

Although you can easily use San Ignacio as a base for day-trips, numerous guest houses and ranches in the surrounding countryside offer **cottage- and lodge-style accommodation** and organized trips. On the whole, standards are very high, and most lodgings cater mainly to upmarket, package tourists who come here after a spell on the cayes – a phenomenon known as a "surf and turf" holiday. However, there are plenty of admirable places in every price bracket, a wide selection covered under Accommodation on p.191. Many are booked up in the peak season (Christmas to Easter), but, if open, can offer reduced prices in the low season. Most provide a very comfortable night's sleep

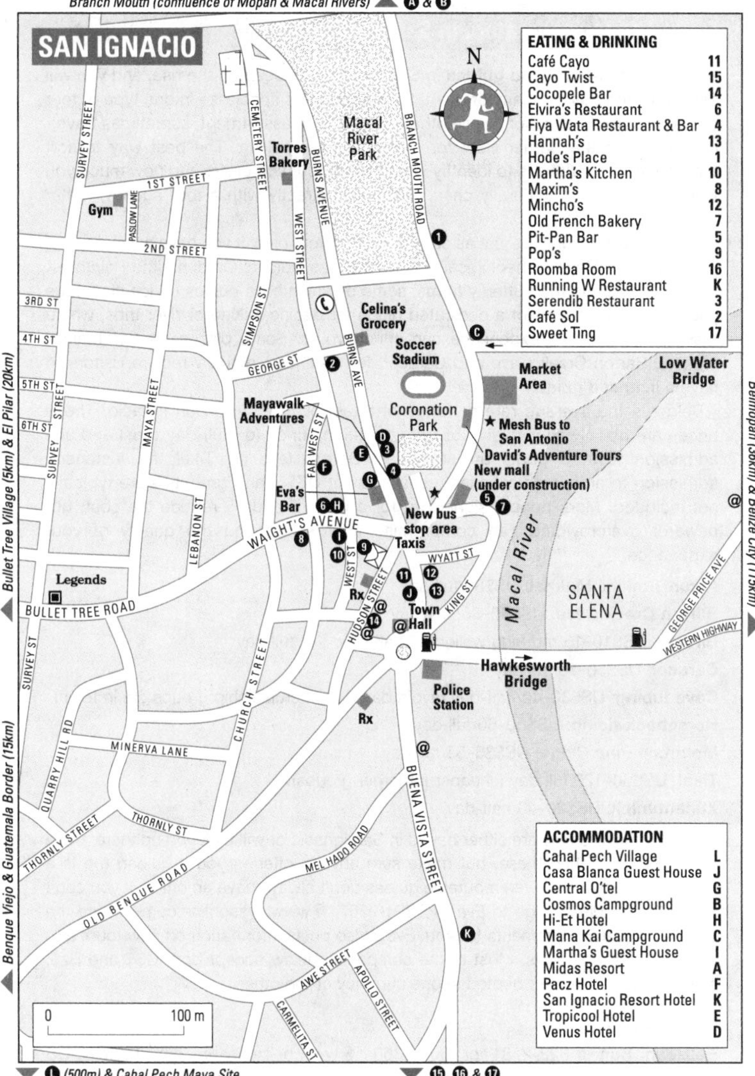

and good home-cooking – even gourmet dining – as well as horseback riding, birding, canoeing and other trips into the surrounding area. All can be reached by road and are well signposted from San Ignacio, though to get to a couple of them you'll have to cross the Macal River in a canoe or small boat.

Some history

The name the Spanish gave to the area around modern-day San Ignacio was **El Cayo**, the same word they used to describe the offshore islands. (The town is usually referred to as **Cayo** by locals, and this is the name you'll often see indicated

Tours and tour operators in San Ignacio

The number of **tours and guides** in San Ignacio has been on the rise, and you will see signs and ads for many of them. Some operators specialize in one type of tour or one specific destination, while others offer a wide assortment, sometimes travelling as far as the Barrier Reef for diving and snorkelling. The best way to sort through all the options is to identify what kind of tour you prefer and how much you want to spend. It's generally cheaper to book directly with a tour agency, rather than through a hotel.

Several destinations are just as easy to visit on your own: if you have a vehicle, you can reach the Maya archeological sites, the Belize Botanic Gardens, the Rainforest Medicine Trail and the butterfly farms, some of which have guides on location once you arrive. You may want a dedicated guide for birding, hiking or river trips, where their knowledge and experience can enrich yours. Some places – Actun Tunichil Muknal, Barton Creek Cave and Caracol, for instance – actually require visitors to have a **licensed guide**.

Below is the average rate or range of rates for trips from San Ignacio. These prices are usually all-inclusive of transportation, lunch (on full-day trips) and any admission fees to parks and reserves. Border fees (to Tikal, for instance), admission to archeological sites (usually about US$5) and gratuities are typically not included. More people signed up for a trip will usually reduce the cost, but beware: overcrowding can compromise your safety and the quality of your experience.

Actun Tunichil Muknal: US$80/full day

Barton Creek Cave: US$30–65/half-day

Birding: US$10–15/morning walk, $50/half-day, $75/full day

Caracol: US$50–75/full day

Cave tubing: US$30–40/half-day (avoid days when cruise ship groups are in town)

Horseback riding: US$30–60/full day

Mountain Pine Ridge: US$35–55/full day

Tikal: US$60–120/full day (cheaper for larger groups)

Xunantunich: US$20–40/half-day

All the guides below are either based in San Ignacio or will pick you up there; there are many more than these, but make sure anyone offering you a guided trip is a **licensed tour guide**. Even reputable guides don't always have an office; if you can't contact them directly, go to *Eva's* (Ⓣ824-2267, Ⓦwww.evasonline.com), where the staff will make arrangements for you. *Eva's* also posts information on new tours and alternate tour operators. Most of the companies below accept both US$ and Bz$, whether their prices are quoted in one currency or the other.

Operators and guides

Belizean Sun Ⓣ823-2781 or 601-2360, Ⓦwww.belizeansun.com. Former US forester Ken Dart organizes individual trips to the interior of Cayo, and can take you to amazing caves that nobody else visits. He also customizes family trips as well as adventure tours to most of the attractions in the region.

on buses headed here.) It's an apt description of the location, on a peninsula between two converging rivers, and also a measure of how isolated the early European settlers felt, being surrounded by forest. It wasn't just the jungle they had to fear; the forest was also home to the indigenous inhabitants of a province that valued its independence. **Tipú**, a Maya city that once stood at Negroman on the Macal River, about 9km south of San Ignacio, was the capital of Dzuluinicob,

Cayo Adventure Tours ⓣ824-3246, ⓦwww.cayoadventure.com. Customized group tours, in reliable off-road vehicles, to all Cayo attractions. Run by Elbert Flowers and Ces Neal – based in Santa Elena.

David's Adventure Tours In a blue booth around the corner from the bus stop, across from the market ⓣ804-3674, ⓦwww.davidsadventuretours.com. Multi-lingual Belizean David Simpson is the original (and best) guide to Barton Creek Cave (around Bz$65). David's African and Maya heritage lends added perspective to his tours. He also leads overnight jungle trips and tours to Caracol. See *Guacamallo Jungle Camp*, p.200.

Easy Rider On Burns Ave under Central O'tel ⓣ824-3734, ⓔeasyrider@btl.net. Charlie Collins organizes the best day of horseback riding in San Ignacio, and she carefully matches riders to the right mount (US$30 half-day, US$40 full day).

Everald's Caracol Shuttle At *Crystal Paradise Resort* (see p.177) during the day, Snooty Fox Tours (see below) evenings ⓣ820-4014 or 804-0050. Everald Tut runs affordable van tours to Caracol almost daily (US$50); he also operates King Tut Tours, for other excursions around Cayo and to Tikal.

Hun Chi'ik Tours at *Martha's* ⓣ670-0746, ⓔhunchiik@belizemail.net. A group of six guides from the nearby village of San José Succotz organizes a range of archeological and naturalist tours in the Cayo district. Each guide draws from his Maya heritage, family knowledge, or experiences working at key tourist attractions in Belize to add perspective to your excursion.

Mayawalk Adventures 19 Burns Ave ⓣ824-3070, ⓦwww.mayawalk.com. Aaron Juan leads a unique overnight trip to Actun Tunichil Muknal (around US$80), as well as other overnight caving and rock climbing expeditions.

Pacz Tours At *Pacz Hotel* ⓣ824-2477, ⓔpacztours@btl.net. Specialist archeology guide Jamal Crawford arranges expert trips to Actun Tunichil Muknal and other Maya sites in Cayo.

Paradise Expeditions At *Crystal Paradise Resort* ⓣ824-4014 or 610-5993, ⓦwww.birdinginbelize.com. Jeronie Tut runs superb, personalized bird and nature tours throughout Cayo and Belize. Multi-day trips and packages to some of the best birding sites are also available. Spotting scopes and up-to-date equipment provided.

River Rat ⓣ625-4636, ⓦwww.riverratbelize.com. Gonzo Pleitez, who lives up the Macal River, arranges customized cave and jungle trips, as well as archeological tours. For river tours, Gonzo can put you in touch with Henry Link of Phoenix Tours.

Snooty Fox Tours West St at Waight's Ave, opposite *Martha's* ⓣ824-2720 or 600-0683. Michael Waight has the best canoe rental in Cayo (Bz$40/full day, including a cooler for your lunch) and offers drop-off and shuttle service to points along the Macal River (Bz$100/half-day, $125/full day, canoe included).

Toni's River Adventures Ask at *Eva's* ⓣ824-3292, ⓔevas@btl.net. Toni Santiago runs what is by far the oldest and best guided canoe trip on the Macal River; it's under US$25 for an expert paddle upriver to the Rainforest Medicine Trail (see p.201). He also organizes fantastic overnight camping trips along the river.

where for years the Maya resisted attempts to Christianize them. The early wave of European conquest, in 1544, made little impact here, and the area remained a centre of rebellion through the following decades. Two **Spanish friars** arrived in 1618, but a year later the entire population was still practising "idolatry". Outraged, the friars smashed the idols and ordered the native priests flogged, but by the end of the year the Maya had once again driven out the Spaniards. In 1641 the friars returned to Tipú, determined once again to Christianize the inhabitants. To express their defiance to the Spanish clerics, the Maya priests conducted a mock Mass, using tortillas as communion wafers, and ejected the friars. From then on, Tipú remained an outpost of Maya culture, providing refuge to other Maya fleeing Spanish rule, and apparently retaining a good measure of independence until 1707, when the population was forcibly removed to Flores.

Like many places in Belize, San Ignacio probably started its present life as a logging camp. A map drawn up in 1787 simply states that the Indians of this general area were "in friendship with the Baymen" – an intriguing situation, considering the strained relations of less than a century earlier. Later it was a centre for the shipment of chicle, and the self-reliant chicleros, as the collectors of chicle were called, came to know the forest – and most of the Maya ruins – intimately. When the demand for Maya artifacts sent black market prices rocketing, many chicleros turned to looting.

Until the Western Highway was built in the 1930s (though the section beyond San Ignacio wouldn't be paved until the 1980s), local transport was by mule or water. It could take ten days of paddling to reach San Ignacio from Belize City, though later small steamers shortened the trip. Nowadays river traffic, which had at one point almost died out, is enjoying a revival, as increasing numbers of tourists opt for this peaceful mode of transport. Indeed, a good time to visit San Ignacio is at the start of Belize's premier **canoe race**, La Ruta Maya, held annually in early March to celebrate Baron Bliss Day (see p.77), when teams of paddlers race all the way to Belize City. Anyone can enter the race, but local guides always win.

Arrival and information

Several **buses** run regular services from Belize City to San Ignacio, stopping at the south end of Coronation Park before continuing to Benque Viejo for the Guatemalan border; a shared **taxi** to the border from San Ignacio costs Bz$5 per person. While looking for a room, you can **leave luggage** at David's Adventure Tours, just around the corner from the bus stop and across from the market. If David is around, he can help guide you to a hotel appropriate to your budget.

Although there's no official tourist office in San Ignacio, you'll be bombarded with **information**: Bob Jones, owner of the long-established *Eva's Bar* on Burns Avenue, knows almost everything about Cayo, and the walls of his bar are festooned with framed brochures listing what the town has to offer. *Eva's* also has **Internet access**, as do several other places, but for Internet cafés with more computers try the Cayo Community Computer Center or *Tradewinds*, both on Hudson Street.

San Ignacio's main street is **Burns Avenue**; along it, or nearby, you'll find almost everything you need, including the best produce market in Belize. This is also where you'll find the **banks**; Belize, Scotia and Atlantic banks all have ATMs. If you need Guatemalan quetzales, you can avoid extra time at the border (but get slightly less favourable rates) by using the services of the **moneychangers** who will approach you. The **post office** is next to Courts furniture store in the centre of town, and the **BTL office** is on the north end of Burns Avenue near Macal River Park. **Car rental** is available at Western Auto Rental (☎824-3328 or 668-2819), right next to the Venus Hotel. For domestic and international **air tickets**, try Exodus Travel, 2 Burns Ave (☎824-4400). A number of good gift shops can be found on Burns Avenue near *Eva's*; past here, Caesar's Gift Shop sells the same jewellery and wood carvings as he does at his place on the Western Highway (see p.174). You can also ask him about his *Black Rock River Lodge* in the Macal River Valley (see p.201). **Laundry** can be dropped off at *Martha's Guest House* on West Street (see Accommodation, below).

Accommodation

Hotels in San Ignacio offer some of the best budget accommodation in the country, and lodging in all price ranges is constantly improving in quality and services. You'll almost always find space somewhere once you arrive, but you should book ahead if you want to stay at a particular place during busy periods. If pickings are slim, try the *Aguada*, just over the river in Santa Elena (see p.176), or the hotels in nearby Bullet Tree Falls (see p.195). All but the really inexpensive places take credit cards. *Mana Kai Campground*, at the start of Branch Mouth Road (Ⓣ824-2317), with showers and electricity, has **camping** spaces for Bz$10 for two people in their own tent, or you can rent one for Bz$5 per person; for other camping options near town, check out *Cosmos Campground* and *Midas Resort*.

Cahal Pech Village On Cahal Pech Hill, just across from the Maya site (see p.194), 2km from town Ⓣ824-3740, Ⓦwww.cahalpech.com. Offering a spectacular view of San Ignacio, this well-designed "village" has spacious, private rooms in its main building as well as comfortable, thatched cabañas. Each room and cabaña – named after a Belizean Maya site – has a private bath and TV, and the interiors are decorated with Guatemalan textiles; cabañas have wooden decks with hammocks. There's a good restaurant and complimentary Internet access for guests. ❼

Casa Blanca Guest House 10 Burns Ave Ⓣ824-2080, Ⓦwww.casblancaguest-house.com. Great value, with immaculate rooms – all with private bath, cable TV and a/c – and a comfortable sitting area with microwave, fridge, coffee and tea, though no stove. It's a bright, friendly place, and owner Betty Guerra is quietly proud that it won Belize's "Best Small Hotel" award soon after opening. Laundry services also available and booking is advised. ❸–❹

Central O'tel 24 Burns Ave Ⓣ824-3734, Ⓔeasyrider@btl.net. Simple, clean rooms, all sharing a couple of small bathrooms in an old wooden building, and one of the best-priced budget places in town. The front balcony (with hammocks) is a great place to watch the street below. ❷

Cosmos Campground On Branch Mouth Rd (just past *Midas Resort*), a fifteen-minute walk north from town Ⓣ824-2116. A campsite (Bz$10 per person) and a simple cabin with three beds (Bz$50), with flush toilets and shared, hot-water showers. The site extends right down to the river, and you can rent canoes, bicycles and horses at affordable prices – ask at the manager's house, signposted on the left just before the campsite.

Hi-Et Hotel West St, behind *Courts* Ⓣ824-2828. A phenomenally popular and very well-priced hotel, in an attractive, wooden colonial building with a wraparound balcony and a bench-swing. The original rooms, each with its own tiny balcony, share a hot-water bathroom, while the larger rooms in an adjacent, concrete building have private bathrooms. Guests can use the fridge in the comfortable sitting room. ❷–❸

Martha's Guest House West St, behind *Eva's* Ⓣ804-3647, Ⓦwww.marthasbelize.com. Recent renovations have made this popular hotel in San Ignacio even better, but owners Martha and John August have managed to keep the homey atmosphere that made the original hotel so popular, and booking is advised. The rooms are very comfortable and well furnished, and most have beautiful, tiled bathrooms and cable TV; there are also two guest lounges with TV. Each room has either a private balcony or access to a shared one, and the suite on the top floor has an enormous, full-width balcony, with views over the whole town. The restaurant below (see p.193) is a favourite meeting place. There's a range of good books on Belize to read, a gift shop, drop-off laundry, wireless Internet and a shuttle service to Belize City. ❹–❻

Midas Resort Branch Mouth Rd, a ten-minute walk from the bus terminal Ⓣ824-2322, Ⓔmidas@btl.net. Set in trees and pasture above the riverbank, *Midas* is the only resort actually in town – and it's one of the best cabaña places in Cayo, within walking distance of the town centre but with the peace and quiet of the countryside. Accommodation is in comfortable wooden or concrete cabañas, all with a porch and private bath. There's also a restaurant, wireless Internet, and laundry service. Camping (Bz$8 per person) and trailer hook-ups are available. ❺

Pacz Hotel 4 Far West St, two blocks behind *Eva's* ⓣ824-4538, ⓔpaczghouse@btl.net. Five clean, comfortable, tiled rooms (some with private hot showers) at bargain rates, especially for three people sharing, all opening onto a quiet, upstairs sitting area. A restaurant serving excellent Belizean meals is below. ❸

San Ignacio Resort Hotel 18 Buena Vista St ⓣ824-2034, from the US ⓣ1-800/822-3274, ⓦwww.sanignaciobelize.com. Just ten minutes' walk uphill from the town centre, in a superb location with views over the Macal River valley, San Ignacio's premier hotel is locally renowned for hosting Queen Elizabeth on her most recent visit. All rooms are comfortable, spacious and a/c, and some have balconies. The best values are the one remaining economy room (❽) or the newly constructed honeymoon suite (US$225), complete with a private Jacuzzi on the balcony. The *Running W* restaurant (see opposite) has a terrace overlooking the pool (Bz$10 for non-guests), and the *Stork Club* has a happy hour on Friday and karaoke on Thursday. There's also a tennis court, complete with racquets and balls (small fee for non-guests). A computer in the lobby is available for Internet access, and there's Wi-Fi for laptop-users. The tranquil Medicinal Jungle Trail, with lots of informative labels, leads down to the Macal River and up to a forested hilltop; it's ideal for early-morning birding. The hotel also hosts a highly interpretive and educational exhibit on the conservation of the threatened green iguana. Iguanas here are raised for one year before they're released into the wild. ❾

Tropicool Hotel Burns Ave, 75m north of *Eva's* ⓣ804-3052, ⓔtropicool@btl.net. Bright, well-priced and clean (nonsmoking) rooms with bedside lights and shared, hot-water bathrooms; also, wooden cabins in the garden, with private hot showers and cable TV. Ground-floor rooms are wheelchair-accessible from the street, but upstairs rooms are bigger. There's a sitting room with TV and a laundry area. ❸–❹

Venus Hotel 29 Burns Ave ⓣ824-3203, ⓦwww.venushotelbelize.com. A two-storey hotel, one of the biggest in town, with good rates and San Ignacio's only 24-hour front desk; the best deal around if you want to stay a few days. The modern rooms have clean, tiled bathrooms, a/c and TV, while the rear balcony has views over the market down to the river. *Rough Guides* readers can receive a discount here. ❹

Eating

Like its budget hotels, San Ignacio's **restaurants** are plentiful and of high quality. If you have somewhere to cook, then the Saturday **market** is worth a visit; it's one of the best in Belize, with local farmers bringing in fresh-picked produce. It's also a good place to stock up on provisions for trips; see Chris Lowe at the market for his Fruit-A-Plenty trail mix, granola bars and homemade peanut butter, also available from local shops. There are several reliable **fast-food stalls** here, including a taco stand (in front of the post office) that's very popular with locals, who gather for the incredibly spicy food until 2–3am, sometimes later. For general **groceries**, Celina's Store, two blocks down from the *Venus Hotel* on Burns Avenue, has the widest selection. In the centre of town there are plenty of **fruit stands** laden with bananas, oranges and papayas, and you can pick up fresh **bread** and other baked goods from *Torres Bakery*, at the end of Far West Street. On most afternoons, small boys sell tasty, freshly cooked *empanadas* and *tamales* on the street.

Cafe Cayo 12 Burns Ave. A simple, friendly place offering good international food, draft beer and Internet access. Large pizzas are Bz$30–38, pastas Bz$16–26, and there are good vegetarian options as well. There's a TV lounge and a spacious patio area to check out the local scene over a drink. Ask here about *Barton Creek Outpost* campsite (see p.175). Open 7am–9pm.

Elvira's 6 Far West St. One of the best deals in town, Elvira and her family serve delicious meals all day – mains are typically less than Bz$10. Some of their tastiest treats aren't even on the menu, so make sure to ask if the *escabeche* or any other house specials are available. The homemade chocolate cake is delectable. The great food and personal service might convince you to make their small guest house your base when in town. Open 7am–8pm, occasionally later.

Fiya Wata Burns Ave, next to Mayawalk Adventures. One of the town's newer restaurants, serving mouth-watering barbecue for Bz$12–15. The grill is out front, its tempting aroma drawing customers toward the shady, outdoor seating area. At night, it turns into a bar with pool table, darts and live music. Open from 2pm until late.

Hannah's 5 Burns Ave. A small restaurant with some of the most delicious food in the country at great prices (Bz$12–20), much of it grown on the owner's farm. Serves everything from Belizean specialities to Burmese curry, all accompanied by freshly prepared salads; get here early or you'll have to wait. Open 6am–9pm.

Martha's Kitchen and Pizza Parlour West St, behind *Eva's*. Located below the guest house of the same name and just as well run. Great breakfasts with strong, locally grown coffee, and main dishes of traditional Creole food and pizza (Bz$20–35). There's always a vegetarian choice and delicious cakes for dessert. Good service, too. The patio tables, romantically candlelit in the evenings, are a popular place to plan an excursion. Open from 7am–10pm.

Maxim's Far West St, behind *Martha's*. The best of San Ignacio's many Chinese restaurants, rapidly serving large portions of the standards. Chow mein dishes are Bz$6–8; fried chicken is Bz$5. Open 10am–3pm & 5–10.30pm.

Mincho's Burns St, next to *Hannah's*. Identified by a blue awning, this takeaway food stand serves incredible *salbutes* and burritos at even more incredible prices (Bz$2–4). Arguably the best bargain if you're on a tight budget. There are great breakfast burritos here as well.

Old French Bakery On the main square. Delicious croissants, baguettes, cinnamon rolls, and more – all at very affordable prices. The popular ham and cheese croissants are just under Bz$2. Open 7am–6pm.

Pop's West St, across from *Martha's*. A tiny and popular local restaurant, serving very tasty Belizean dishes, including a daily lunch special and all-day breakfast (Bz$6). Open 6.30am–2pm.

The Running W Restaurant At the *San Ignacio Resort Hotel*, 18 Buena Vista St. Excellent food in tranquil surroundings, and not too expensive. Good steaks and seafood (including fish and chips) with a distinctive Lebanese influence, accompanied by real Mediterranean olives. Breakfasts are an especially good value.

Serendib Restaurant 27 Burns Ave. Excellent Sri Lankan curries and seafood at very reasonable prices (Bz$9–12) and with good service. Open 10am–3pm & 6–10.30pm, closed Sun.

Café Sol 25 West St. Fresh and attractive vegetarian meals, soups, salads, sandwiches and great desserts, served in an atmosphere inspired by similar cafés in Antigua, Guatemala. There's always a daily special (Bz$10–15), and you can eat indoors or in the patio garden. Also has computers and Internet access. Open 7am–10pm, closed Mon.

Drinking and nightlife

Nightlife in San Ignacio is evolving as growth in tourism and population inspires new developments. The range of evening festivities makes the town a weekend destination for many Belizeans, and there's plenty of **live music and dancing** on offer. *Roomba Room*, at the intersection of Old Benque Road and Buena Vista Street, blasts reggae and punta rock until the early morning on weekends, and *Legends*, on Bullet Tree Road, is an after-hours spot featuring a number of local artists, often lively until 5am. Frequented by a youngish crowd, *Cocopele*, on Hudson Street, opens nightly for both tourists and locals; its full bar, several foosball and pool tables, dart boards, TV projector and free popcorn do their best to keep you entertained. Should you tire of these, you can place bets on how soon your waitress will arrive after you switch on your table's red "service" light bulb. San Ignacio mainstay *Eva's*, also on Burns Avenue, is renowned as the town's prime hangout, and is a great place to meet other travellers and tour guides. *Hode's Place Bar and Grill* on Branch Mouth Road has a large, open-air patio with pool tables, TV and a playground for children, and *Pit-Pan*, a local bar near the *Old French Bakery*, is open most nights.

For a relaxed drink in more sophisticated surroundings, the *Stork Club* at the *San Ignacio Resort Hotel* is the place to be; it's quite popular during the Friday evening **happy hour**, after which things liven up with a DJ or band. You can also join the **Latin dance classes** here on Wednesday evenings (Bz$10) or belt out your favourite karaoke tunes on Thursdays.

Around San Ignacio

The people of San Ignacio are justifiably proud of their surrounding countryside and beautiful river valleys, and there are several specific attractions to visit near town, including the Green Iguana Exhibit at the *San Ignacio Resort Hotel* and the Maya site of **Cahal Pech**. Slightly further afield, the **Rainforest Medicine Trail** and the **Belize Botanic Gardens** can be seen on relaxing **canoe trips** along the mostly gentle **Macal River**; resorts along the faster **Mopan River** offer tubing or **kayaking**. The nearby farmland and forest are ideal for exploring on **horseback** or **mountain bike** (you can take a bike on the Mesh bus to San Antonio and the Mountain Pine Ridge; see p.177). For bike rental, check at *Eva's* or the *Crystal Paradise Resort* office on Branch Mouth Road (Ⓣ824-2823); for canoes, see Snooty Fox Tours in the box on p.188.

Most of the bigger hotels and lodges have their own tour desks, but there are several small-scale, local operators who offer trips to the many attractions around San Ignacio. Some of these are difficult, even impossible, to visit on your own; the increasingly popular activity of **caving**, for instance, is practically verboten without a licensed guide who's qualified in cave rescue. In addition to the operators recommended in the box on p.188, you could check with Iain Anderson at Caves Branch and Marcos Cucul of Maya Guide Adventures, both on the Hummingbird Highway; see p.239.

Branch Mouth

Perhaps the easiest introduction to the area around San Ignacio is to take the twenty-minute walk north of the town centre to **Branch Mouth**, where the Macal and Mopan rivers merge to form the Belize River. The track leads from the football field past clapboard houses on the edge of rich farmland, with thick vegetation, tropical flowers, iguanas and butterflies on either side. At the confluence of the rivers is a huge tree, with branches arching over the jade water. A rusted mooring ring in the trunk is a reminder of the past importance of river transport, though the swallows skimming the water's surface, parrots flying overhead and scores of tiny fish in the water indicate that nature has reclaimed this particular spot. The scar of raw earth on the opposite bank is evidence of severe flooding in recent years, which has risen within metres of the Hawkesworth Bridge and even inundated the streets of San Ignacio. Local boys leap off the pedestrian **suspension bridge** across the final stretch of the Mopan River here, but for most visitors just walking along the swaying structure is enough of an adventure.

Cahal Pech

A twenty-minute, uphill walk out of town to the southwest, clearly signposted along the highway to Benque Viejo, the hilltop Maya site of **Cahal Pech** (daily 6am–6pm; Bz$10) has undergone extensive restoration and is well worth a visit. The **visitor centre and museum** has a model of the site, excellent display panels showing paintings of Cahal Pech in its heyday and the history of the Maya in Belize, plus lots of artifacts, such as ocarinas, chocolate pots, projectile points and carved flints, including one that looks remarkably like a modern wrench; watch the 47-minute **video** (also for sale on DVD) for a deeper understanding of the site and its treasures.

Cahal Pech means "place of ticks" in Mopan and Yucatec Maya, but that's certainly not how the elite who lived here would have known it; this was the royal acropolis-palace of a Maya ruling family during the Classic period. There's evidence of construction from the Early Preclassic, around 1200 BC, after which the city probably dominated the central Belize River valley. Studies of the buildings and ceramics show that the site was continuously occupied until around 800 AD; most of what you see dates from the eighth century AD.

Entering the site through the forest, you arrive at **Plaza B**, surrounded by temple platforms and the remains of dwellings, and your gaze is drawn to Structure 1, the **Audiencia**, the site's largest building. If you're used to finely executed, exposed stonework at reconstructed Maya sites, then the thick overcoat of lime-mortar on the buildings here may come as a shock. The Classic Maya viewed bare, stone facings as ugly and unfinished, and covered all surfaces with a heavy layer of plaster or stucco, which was then brightly painted. You can climb the steps at the front of the structure, but the best way to enjoy your surroundings is to walk around the side and through **Plaza D** and a maze of ancient corridors and stairways, which gradually reveal an enchanting view of **Plaza A** – a sacred space entirely enclosed by walls and tall buildings. You're now across the plaza from Structure 1; make your way to the front of the site, and you can then descend to your starting point.

Sunset is a particularly pleasant and peaceful time to visit Cahal Pech. After your visit, you can poke around the **gift shop** for local crafts, then head downhill to *Cayo Twist* (ⓣ605-2527; Thurs–Sun 4–11pm), at the intersection of Old Benque Road and Buena Vista Street, for the only soft-serve ice cream in town and other ice cream-related treats. Just around the corner on Old Benque Road, *Sweet Ting* (ⓣ610-4174; daily 2–9pm) has delicious pastries served in restaurants around the country; if you can't make up your mind, try the cheesecake.

Bullet Tree Falls and El Pilar

Five kilometres northwest of San Ignacio, along Bullet Tree Road, is **BULLET TREE FALLS**, a predominately Spanish-speaking, mestizo farming village spread out along the forested banks of the Mopan River. A bridge crosses the river at the falls – really just a set of rapids – and several nearby cabañas offer some very pleasant **places to stay** on the riverbank. Many of these will arrange transport from San Ignacio for guests; all make a good base for visiting El Pilar (see p.196). Several restaurants and bars in Bullet Tree Falls create quite a busy scene here on weekends; of these, the restaurant at the *Riverside Lodge*, right by the bridge, is an agreeable place to enjoy a meal or a drink.

In the middle of the village, immediately before the bridge, is the **El Pilar Cultural Centre**, or *Be Pukte*, which means "road to Bullet Tree" in Maya (opening hours vary; call Don Beto at ⓣ662-2079 to check). Inside there's a good model of the Maya site of El Pilar, as well as trail guides and other informational booklets relating to the site; if you'd like a **local guide**, ask in the village for Teddy Waight. **Tony Chuc** (ⓣ667-6060, ⓔcherica@hotmail.com) specializes in river sports (rafting, kayaking) and can lead you on an excellent combo tour that includes a visit to El Pilar and then rafting five sets of rapids back to Bullet Tree Falls. His wife Erica worked on the archeological team at El Pilar (see Contexts, p.336), and, when available, can share her perspective on the site. Closer to town, the **Three Sister Rock Medicinal Trail** has been established along the river, and you can join a guided tour (Bz$10).

A shared taxi from San Ignacio to Bullet Tree Falls costs Bz$2.50 per person; catch one at the bus stop where the road to the village leaves the Western Highway. Bullet Tree Road passes through Bullet Tree Falls and eventually leads to Spanish Lookout, a route along which many well-known artists live, including George Landero and Marcos Manzanero (ⓣ600-6225). Visit their studios to say hello and view their work. Before Spanish Lookout is the village of **Santa Familia**, where Beatrice Waight (ⓣ602-2655, ⓔmarlin_waight@hotmail.com; donations accepted) – a **traditional Maya healer** – works next to the village community centre. Beatrice is not only a seventh-generation shaman, but was also trained by the legendary Don Eligio (see p.201). A visit to her Healer's Hut can help cure you of your spiritual illnesses; she currently offers a variety of Maya treatments such as prayers, herbal baths, massages, teas and other services.

Accommodation

Just a ten-minute drive from San Ignacio, Bullet Tree Falls offers even better-value accommodation. Its location along the river is ideal for exploring, relaxing after a tour or simply appreciating the beautiful landscape. Most places either have or can easily procure kayaks, tubes or mountain bikes.

Cohune Palms ⓣ824-0166 or 669-2738, ⓦwww.cohunepalms.com. Four unique, thatched, wooden cabins in a beautiful riverbank setting, each with private bathroom and strong ceiling fan. Cabins are screened but you don't have to worry too much about mosquitoes here anyway. The restaurant serves delicious Belizean and vegetarian meals on a veranda with a view of the Mopan River. Guests can lounge on the outdoor decks with hammocks or else try the rope swing. There's also a good gift shop, and Internet service is available. Owners Mike and Bevin Waight provide free pickup in San Ignacio, but you'll need to call ahead. Mike is a drummer for the Bullet Tree Boys, whom you can sometimes catch at *Legends* in San Ignacio. ❻

Iguana Junction ⓣ820-4021, ⓦwww.iguanajunction.com. Four elevated, simple, wooden cabins on the riverside, all with private half-bath and shared showers. A good location for extended stays. ❹

Parrot Nest Lodge ⓣ820-4058 or 602-6817, ⓦwww.parrot-nest.com. Right on the riverbank, six simple, clean, thatched cabins of varying size, two sitting very securely in a grand guanacaste tree. All are among beautiful gardens, some have verandas and two have private toilets and washbasin. The shared bathrooms have hot showers. Owner Theo Stevens serves filling meals and guests are welcome to hitch a ride to and from San Ignacio with her. ❹–❺

Riverside Lodge ⓣ824-3580, ⓦwww.riversidelodgebelize.com. Uninspired cabins with balconies overlooking the Mopan River. Rooms have hot showers and a/c, and the restaurant serves good meals all day. ❺

El Pilar

The Maya site of **El Pilar** (daily 8am–4pm; Bz$10), the largest in the Belize River valley, is a rough, uphill but enjoyable 14-kilometre drive northwest of Bullet Tree Falls. Taxis from the village charge Bz$55 for a carload, and drivers will wait for two hours while you explore the site with caretaker Marcos Garcia or other staff. When the **archeological team** from the University of California is working (usually March–June), you may be able to get a lift either to or from the site with them. They also welcome volunteer participation (see Contexts, p.336). Should you wish to make the journey to El Pilar by horse or mountain bike, check at *Eva's* in San Ignacio (see p.190) or the hotels in Bullet Tree Falls. **Trail guides** and other information on El Pilar are on sale at the *Be Pukte* cultural centre in Bullet Tree Falls, and are downloadable from El Pilar's very informative and well-organized website (ⓦwww.marc.ucsb.edu/elpilar), which also has information on the annual **El Pilar Fiesta**, a cultural event well worth planning your visit around. The *Trail of El Pilar* guide details the story of the ruins according to the archeologists who have worked here.

The Belize River Archaeological Settlement Survey ("BRASS"; see Contexts, p.336) has conducted investigation and restoration at El Pilar since 1993. One theory they are studying is that the forest was originally a garden cultivated by the Maya, who used the tree cover to support a variety of food crops – a method known as "forest garden" agriculture. Much more than "slash and burn", this "select and grow" technique relied on maintaining the forest through strategic cutting and controlled burning. Researchers have been simulating this method in an experimental, educational exhibit that also includes a re-creation of a traditional Maya house discovered on the Lakin trail on the east side of the road from Bullet Tree Falls. The "Tzunu'un" (meaning

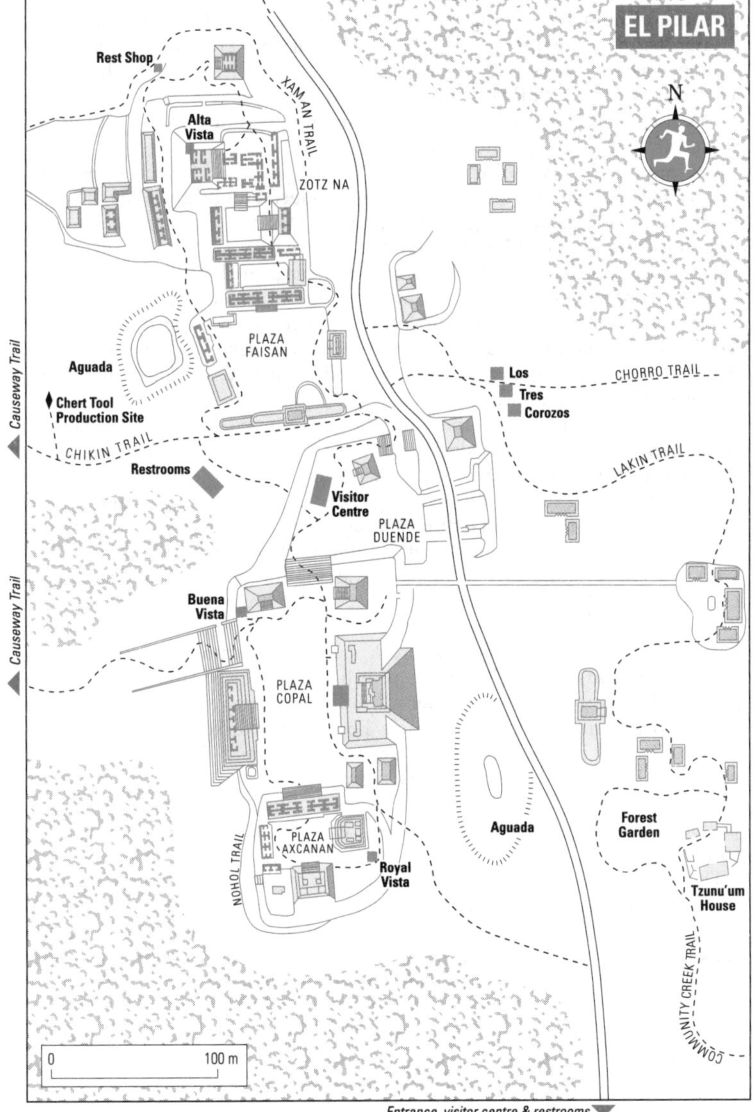

"hummingbird", the guardian of the forest and flowers) residential area of El Pilar was excavated and consolidated in the late 1990s to provide the first, and so far only, view into the suburban communities that surrounded all ancient Maya cities.

The site

Construction on El Pilar began in the Preclassic period, around 800 BC, and continued right through to the Terminal Classic, around 1000 AD, when some of the largest existing structures were completely rebuilt. One reason for such a long period of continuous occupation was almost certainly the presence of numerous springs and creeks in the area – El Pilar is Spanish for "water basin". The prosperity of the civilization here still shows in the seventy major structures grouped around 25 plazas, all of which can be appreciated along six **hiking trails** that criss-cross the 5000-acre reserve. The site is also considered one of the finest **birding** areas in Cayo, so enthusiasts should definitely bring binoculars.

The most impressive structures – four large pyramids between fifteen and twenty metres high and a ball-court – are grouped around the **Plaza Copal**, from whose west side a flight of steps leads down to a thirty-metre-wide causeway running to **Pilar Poniente** in Guatemala. Because of the strong conservation policy dictated by the management plan at El Pilar, most of the structures are still largely mantled by the forest in order to avoid the severe erosion that can result from removal of this protective covering; some portions of caved-in stonework, however, have been uncovered and are on display. Among these is an underground, corbelled tunnel, a standing temple and examples of architecture for the elite.

Very few of the ruins have been significantly altered since their discovery; indeed, visitors see El Pilar almost exactly as it was when archeologists first explored it. Scattered all around are shards of pottery of different styles and colours, indicating the various periods of the site's occupation. **Chert flakes** – by-products of the manufacture of household and agricultural implements – are visible in huge quantities at a stone tool production site along the Chikin Trail. It's quite easy to imagine walking this path without shoes, and construe that the ancient Maya had a concern for properly disposing of "hazardous wastes" (sharp stones, in this case) by setting aside a place for the flakes. The El Pilar Community Creek Trail is a strenuous path with some steep slopes, and structural remains, as well as evidence of land use and water access, allow you to piece together a historical narrative of the people who inhabited the area in the last century. For a longer hike, the 2.3-kilometre Chorro Trail brings you to a delicate waterfall where there's also a minor centre with prehistoric monuments and pyramids, currently inaccessible to the public. The Chorro settlement was inhabited from the Classic period nearly to the present, continually attracting residents by its proximity to fresh water.

The site's location on the Guatemalan border might have led to difficulties of access, or even curtailed further study, but the countries' governments, urged on by concerned local leaders and the international archeological community, have set aside generations of mutual suspicion to create the **El Pilar Archaeological Reserve for Maya Flora and Fauna**, covering an area of nine square kilometres on both sides of the border. Plans are afoot to open the Guatemalan side to visitors, so that there will soon be a single archeological destination spanning two countries.

Buenavista del Cayo

On the east bank of the Mopan River, halfway between San Ignacio and the border, the small Maya site of **Buenavista del Cayo** was once the centre of a political region that included Cahal Pech as a satellite. The ruins are on private land, and to visit you need permission from the owner, Pablo Guerra, a shopkeeper in Benque Viejo. The best way to get here is on horseback – Easy Rider (see box, p.188) runs tours. The site was excavated between 1984 and 1989 by Jennifer Taschek and Joseph Ball, who discovered a palace, ball-courts, carved stelae, plazas and courtyards. A number of important burial items were also found here, including the famous Jauncy vase, now in the Museum of Belize in Belize City (see p.75). There's also evidence that the Maya established workshops on the site to mass-produce pottery. Since excavation, most of the structures have been overgrown by vegetation, but you can still visit a small but charming palace structure and arched courtyard in a glade.

Along the Mopan and Macal rivers

The main tributary creeks of the **Mopan River**, which runs north between San Ignacio and the Guatemalan border before curving east and joining the Macal at Branch Mouth, begin in the Maya Mountains. From here, the river they create first flows into Guatemala before it re-enters Belize at the village of **Arenal**, 5km south of the Benque Viejo border post. The **international boundary** runs right through the middle of this Maya-mestizo village of stick-and-thatch houses, bisecting a football pitch with a goal in each country. The river then leaves Belize briefly again, rushing under a bridge just over the border, before the final (and perhaps most picturesque) 25-kilometre stretch to its confluence with the Macal River, just north of San Ignacio (see p.186). There are some attractive and not too serious **white-water rapids** along this stretch, and it's easy enough to arrange kayak or rafting trips here; check at *Clarissa Falls* or *Trek Stop* (see p.200 & p.205, respectively). Take care when swimming, though, as rapids that appear minor from the bank can present a real danger when you're swept over them; for your own safety, you should always wear a **lifejacket** in the river.

The Mopan's counterpart, the Macal River, arises from tributaries in the Mountain Pine Ridge and the Chiquibul Forest, and in its upper reaches is sometimes fast and deep enough for **white-water kayaking**, though you'll need an expert guide for this (see box, p.188). If instead the idea of a gentle day (or more) on the river appeals, then any of the resorts south of the Western Highway will rent canoes (as will Snooty Fox Tours; see p.189), though you'll see far more wildlife with a guide than you ever will alone. A very popular choice is to take a **guided canoe trip** up the Macal to *The Lodge at Chaa Creek* to visit the famous **Rainforest Medicine Trail** and **Chaa Creek Natural History Centre**, two of Cayo's premier attractions and both on the lodge grounds; a combined ticket costs Bz$18, though lodge guests visit for free. Even further upstream, there's the impressive and rapidly growing **Belize Botanic Gardens** at *duPlooy's*. Heading in the opposite direction, you can also make the trip downriver all the way to Belize City: up to a week of hard paddling, camping on the riverbank each night.

Steep limestone cliffs and forested hills edge the lower Macal valley, and there's plenty of **accommodation** in all price ranges along the river. On any branch over the river or amidst the bank-side vegetation you can see **green iguanas**, the males resplendent in spring with their orange and brown mating colours. Higher up, you might hear the deep-throated roar of **howler monkeys**, which have been successfully reintroduced to the Macal valley from Bermudian Landing, north of Belize City, and the Monkey River, in Toledo District.

Accommodation

Most accommodation is along the Macal River rather than the Mopan, and tends toward upmarket **cabaña-style resorts**, beautifully located in the forest above the riverbank. There are some cheaper options, though, and these often give discounts to *Rough Guides* readers. A taxi from San Ignacio to most Macal River lodgings costs around Bz$30–40, more for the furthest places. Any of them can organize superb **horseback tours** to nearby Maya ruins, and some also have **mountain bikes** and **canoes** for rent. If you'd like a relatively easy but picturesque **canoe float** down the Macal River to San Ignacio after your stay, your host can take your luggage ahead while you drift along and enjoy the scenery.

The listings here are in order of their appearance as you travel away from San Ignacio. All except *Clarissa Falls* and *Martz Farm* can be reached by taking the well-signposted Chial Road/Negroman Road turn-off from the Western Highway, 10km from San Ignacio towards Benque Viejo. A couple of places require that you cross the river by boat. See the map on p.178 for accommodation locations.

Clarissa Falls 2km along a signposted track on the right of the Western Hwy, just past Mile 70 ⓣ824-3916, ⓦwww.clarissafalls.com. Although it's part of a working cattle ranch (ask to help with the round-up), this is a very restful place right by a set of rapids on the Mopan River. The simple, clean, thatched cottages are all wheelchair-accessible and have private bath; suites have a full kitchen. There's also a "bunkhouse" cabin with shared, hot-water showers (Bz$30 per person), space for camping (Bz$15 per person) and hook-ups for RVs. Chena serves great home-cooking and there's a quiet bar overlooking the falls. The resort offers an overwhelming variety of activities, including horseback riding, canoeing, rafting and tubing. Guided jungle walks are available, and birding here is stellar. 4–6, discounts for students.

Casa Maya Eco-Resort 2.5km southwest of San Ignacio on the Casa Maya Road ⓣ820-4020, from the US ⓣ877/833-0679, ⓦwww.casamayaresort.com. A jungle lodge close to town but with a good measure of tranquillity. Private cabañas sleep two and a family room in a guest house with shared bath is US$35. Cabañas are well screened and baths spacious, with plenty of hot water. The grounds are filled with tropical vegetation and are perfect for relaxing after a day's excursion. The friendly staff can help you set up a tour, point out the new swimming pool or make you a nice meal in their open-air restaurant. 4–8

The Lodge at Chaa Creek On the west bank of the Macal, at the end of the Chial Rd ⓣ824-2037, ⓦwww.chaacreek.com. Beautiful, whitewashed, wood-and-stucco cabañas (US$230–300) and wooden "treetop" Jacuzzi suites (US$450; sleep four) in gorgeous grounds high above the Macal River, with a justly deserved reputation for luxury and ambiance. The cottages have very comfortable beds, tiled floors, large bathrooms, screened windows and spacious, wooden decks. The stunning hilltop spa is the most modern in Belize, with separate rooms for each treatment and a private, outdoor palapa. Naturally, there's a fine restaurant and a great bar, with a large, outdoor deck. A cheaper option on the grounds is *Macal River Camp*, eminently comfortable camping in wooden cabins with tarp roofs (US$55 per person, including meals). *Camp* guests can avail themselves of all the *Chaa Creek* luxuries: free, guided tours to the *Lodge's* attractions, an early-morning bird walk, use of canoes, and Internet access in the conference centre. 5–9

duPlooy's Along a signposted road beyond the *Chaa Creek* turn-off ⓣ824-3101, ⓦwww.duplooys.com. First-rate accommodation, beautifully located in farmland and forest on the west bank of the Macal River, and home to the Belize Botanic Gardens (see p.202). There are spacious, private bungalows with deck, king-sized and sofa beds, fridge and coffeemaker (US$185); "Jungle Lodge" rooms, each with queen-sized bed and private porch (US$145); and the budget-rate Belize River House (which can be rented by groups), with seven rooms, each with a double and single bed, a kitchen and a large, screened porch (US$450, up to 14 people). A very eco-friendly business that turns off its generators at midnight and is researching alternative sources of energy to power the lodge. 5–9

Guacamallo Jungle Camp On the east bank of the river; contact David's Adventure Tours in San Ignacio for transport ⓣ804-3674, ⓔdavidtours@belizemail.net. Simple cabins high above the river (which you cross in a canoe), located on the edge of a huge and mysterious Maya site; you'll have the pleasure of exploring this on your own. Lots of tasty food, much of it organically grown on location, and a wonderful sense of timelessness at night as you sit on a Maya mound outside your cabin, watching the stars. Bz$60 per person, including transport, dinner and breakfast.

Ek Tun Near the end of the road to *Black Rock* (see below), and across the river ⓣ820-3002, ⓦwww.ektunbelize.com. The most luxurious stick-and-thatch cabañas in the country; there are only two units, the better to preserve the sublime isolation. Gourmet dinner is served overlooking the river, which by day is an idyllic setting for swimming and tubing. The turquoise, spring-fed pool is the most beautiful of any resort in the country – and the overflow disappears mysteriously into a cave. Trails lead through the forest and along river cliffs dotted with more cave entrances; you can hear howler monkeys in the trees, and the rare orange-breasted falcon nests on the limestone bluffs opposite. The owner makes sure that everything here is as environmentally friendly as possible. No smoking, no singles and no children. US$190 double, US$55 for each extra person; meals are extra and there's usually a three-night minimum stay. ⑨

Black Rock River Lodge At the very end of the "Black Rock road" ⓣ824-2341, ⓦwww.blackrocklodge.com. Drive here on your own, or call at *Caesar's Place* on the Western Highway (see p.174) or his gift shop in San Ignacio (see p.190) to make transport arrangements. Set high above the west bank of the Macal River, with stunning views of the jungle-clad limestone cliffs of the upper Macal valley, these solidly built deluxe cabañas have private hot showers and floors made of smooth river stones. All have river views and are powered by hydro and solar power. It's a fairly easy hike from here up to Vaca Falls, from where you can tube back, or to Vaca or Flour Camp caves, containing some amazing Maya pottery; there are also fine horses and mountain bikes to ride. You can canoe down to San Ignacio with Caesar's son, Julian Sherrard, who's a leader in the Belize Canoe Association and can advise on long-distance paddles in Belize. ⑧–⑨

Martz Farm 13km along the Arenal/Mollejon Hydro Road from Benque Viejo ⓣ662-2849 or 614-6462, ⓦwww.martzfarm.com. Run by the grown-up children of the Martínez family, this is far upriver from the other places on the Macal, and difficult to reach on your own – but someone from the *Farm* usually visits San Ignacio daily, or you could check with Bob Jones at *Eva's*, where guests are met for free transport to the *Farm*. It's well worth the effort to get here, with comfortable thatched cabins perched in trees above a rushing, crystal-clear creek, inexpensive rooms and plenty of home-cooked food. Reaching the river involves a climb down a gorgeous, 30-metre waterfall (by which you can also camp for Bz$10 per person) to a remote beach; across the river, the forest beckons and there's great riding on the Martz mules. ④

The Rainforest Medicine Trail

A canoe trip along the Macal is one of the best ways to get to *Chaa Creek*'s **Rainforest Medicine Trail** (daily 8am–5pm; free for lodge guests, Bz$11 for non-guests, $18 combined ticket with Natural History Centre, $31 with guided tour at 9am and 2pm). When first built, the trail was dedicated to Don Eligio Panti, a Maya bush doctor from San Antonio village who died in 1996 at the age of 103; the naming of a national park near San Antonio after him was a fitting tribute (see p.177). At the entrance to the trail, there's a large, thatched shelter with hammocks to rest in, and visitors can enjoy a refreshing drink during the explanatory talk before the hike, which winds through the forest above the riverbank.

The medical knowledge of the Maya was extensive, and signs along the trail identify about a hundred species of healing plants, many still used in modern medicine. It's a fascinating journey: there are vines that provide fresh water like a tap; poisonwood, with oozing black sap; its antidote, the peeling bark of the gumbo limbo tree, always growing nearby; and the bark of the negrito tree, once sold in Europe for its weight in gold as a cure for dysentery. You'll also see specimens of tropical hardwoods that have been exploited for economic reasons. The more mundane, but still interesting, products of the forest range from herbal teas to blood tonic, and there's quite a selection available in the **gift shop**. Traveller's Tonic, a preventative for diarrhoea, really works, as does Jungle Salve, for insect bites.

Before his death, Don Eligio passed on his skills to Dr Rosita Arvigo, who founded the Medicine Trail and still lives nearby. She now operates the **Ix Chel Wellness Center** in Santa Elena (1458 Eve Street, just off the highway on Loma Luz Boulevard; open year-round, but Rosita is there only in winter), and visitors can benefit from her skills in natural and traditional Maya healing methods and massage. Call ⓣ804-0264 for an appointment and visit ⓦwww.arvigomassage.com for details of the classes she teaches in medicine and cooking; she also gives herb walks around San Ignacio. Several plants from the Belize rainforest are being investigated as potential treatments for AIDS, and Rosita and the staff at Ix Chel, in collaboration with the New York Botanical Garden, have been at the forefront of this research. Rosita has written about her apprenticeship to Don Eligio (see Books, p.372) and is a founding member of the Belize Association of Traditional Healers; you can purchase their excellent newsletter, *Tree of Life*, and any of Rosita's books in the Ix Chel gift shop.

Chaa Creek Natural History Centre and Butterfly Farm

A visit to the marvellous **Chaa Creek Natural History Centre** (daily 8am–4pm; Bz$11, includes guided tour, every hour on the hour), on the grounds of *The Lodge at Chaa Creek* next to the Rainforest Medicine Trail, is a great sampler of Cayo's history, geography and wildlife. If you're spending more than a couple of days in the area, try to see this first: call ⓣ824-2037 to check on the current events programme. The centre has fascinating and accurate displays of the region's flora and fauna, vivid archeological and geological maps, a scale model of the Macal valley and a library with relevant books and journals – all of which make for an engaging visit.

Nearby, at the **Blue Morpho Butterfly Breeding Centre** (included in Natural History Centre entry fee), you can walk among enormous, magnificent Blue Morpho butterflies, and even watch them emerge from chrysalises most mornings. There's also a **Maya Farm**, where *Chaa Creek* staff use traditional methods to grow corn, beans, tomatoes, squash and other crops; the produce is incorporated into the meals served at the lodge (see p.200).

The Belize Botanic Gardens

South of *Chaa Creek*, and reached either by road or river (see p.199), the ★ **Belize Botanic Gardens** at *duPlooy's* (daily 8am–5pm; Bz$10, $20 with guided tour; ⓣ824-3101, ⓦwww.belizebotanic.org) are an ambitious and remarkable project established in 1997 on fifty acres of former farmland and forest. The garden is the brainchild of *duPlooy's* owners and avid plant-lovers Ken and Judy duPlooy. Ken, who died in 2001, was held in such high esteem that a new species of orchid was named after him – *Pleurothallis duplooyii*, a tiny, purple variety. Daughter Heather duPlooy now manages the gardens, where there are over four hundred tree species, a nursery with over a thousand seedlings and several kilometres of interpretive **trails**. The gardens have become a first-class educational and study resource and conserve many of Belize's native plant species within small-scale reproductions of their natural habitats. You approach the gardens through an avenue of fruit-bearing trees, intended to attract wild **birds**, and you can either explore on your own or follow the guidance of **expert naturalists** Lloyd and Martin. A firetower on the grounds, dedicated to Ken DuPlooy, offers breathtaking views of the gardens and surrounding hills, and bird hides on the two ponds allow you to spy on least grebes, black-bellied whistling-ducks and northern jacanas. The magnificent, specially designed **orchid house**, with over one hundred species, is the largest in Belize and the best in Central America.

San José Succotz and Xunantunich

Back on the Western Highway, the village of **SAN JOSÉ SUCCOTZ** lies beside the Mopan River about 12km southwest of San Ignacio, just before **Benque Viejo**. It's a very traditional village in many ways, inhabited largely by Mopan Maya, who throw a fiesta here on the weekend after Holy Saturday (Easter).

△ Sculpture at Xunantunich

administration, the Maya of Succotz cooperated with the British, gered other groups, such as the Icaiché (see p.320), who burnt the ground in 1867. The people here still identify strongly with their and many of the men work as caretakers at Maya sites throughout

sta times, the village is fairly sleepy, and the main reason most people ;e the Classic-period site of **Xunantunich**, up the hill across the river. Ju Succotz, *Trek Stop*'s wooden cabins (see opposite) offer some great budget **accommodation**, well positioned for visiting the ruins. *Trek Stop* has great meals, but for more variety you can head into the village, about three blocks uphill from the bus stop on the highway, to *Benny's Kitchen* (Ⓣ823-2541). This open-air **restaurant** serves Belizean dishes at very reasonable prices, and the milkshakes are excellent. *On 'D'Way* restaurant, on the highway between *Trek Stop* and Xunantunich, sells delicious, fried tacos and *salbutes* – quick, delicious snacks. For souvenirs, the Magaña family's art gallery and **gift shop** (Ⓣ823-2285), just south of Hua Young Supermarket, deals in superb wood and slate carvings.

Xunantunich

El Castillo, the tallest building in the impressive Maya city of **Xunantunich** (daily 7.30am–4.30pm; Bz$10) dominates the countryside for miles around – you'll see it clearly as you approach from San Ignacio. Pronounced "Shun-an-tun-ich", the site's name means "the stone maiden" in Mopan Maya – though this is not what the ancient Maya would have called it, as is the case with many sites. In fact, one of the most significant finds at Xunantunich is a chunk of stone frieze bearing the site's original name: **Kat Witz**, or "clay mountain".

Xunantunich was first explored in the 1890s by Dr Thomas Gann, a British medical officer; in 1904, Teobalt Maler of the Peabody Museum took photographs and drew up a plan of El Castillo. Gann returned in 1924 and unearthed (looted, in modern terminology) large numbers of burial artifacts, removing as well the carved glyphs of Altar 1, whose whereabouts are unknown. In 1938, British archeologist J. Eric S. Thompson excavated a residential area and found pottery, obsidian, jade, a spindle, seashells, stingray spines and hammers. Recent excavations have found evidence of Xunantunich's role in the power politics of the Classic period: it was probably allied as a subordinate partner, like Caracol, with the regional superpower Calakmul against Tikal. By the Terminal Classic, Xunantunich was already in decline, though still apparently populated until around 1000 AD, shortly after the Classic Maya collapse.

To **get here**, take any bus or shared taxi running between San Ignacio and the border, but try to visit in the afternoon or, better yet, on days when cruise ship groups aren't in town; the site can get unpleasantly crowded. You'll be dropped off by the hand-winched **cable ferry** (daily 7.30am–4.30pm; free), which carries foot passengers and vehicles across the Mopan River. From the opposite bank, you'll have to walk or drive up a steep, two-kilometre road to the site entrance. Your first stop should be the marvellous **visitor centre**, one of the best in Belize. There's a superb scale model of the city here, and the labelled exhibits will answer most questions. One of the centre's highlights is a fibreglass replica of the famous hieroglyphic frieze around El Castillo (see opposite), from which you get a much better idea of the real thing's significance. Nearby, the smaller original **museum** has several well-preserved stelae from the site.

The site

Built on top of an artificially flattened hill, Xunantunich incorporates five plazas, although the remaining structures are grouped around just three of

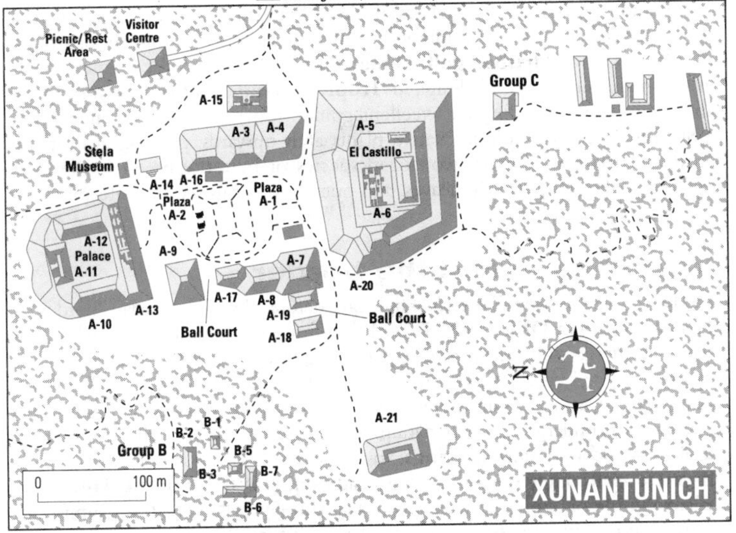

them. The entrance road brings you to Plaza A–2, with large buildings on three sides.

To the left, Plaza A–1 is dominated by structure A–6, commonly known as **El Castillo**, the city's tallest building at 40m high and a prominent symbol of Belize's national identity. As is so often the case, the building is layered, with later versions built on top of earlier ones. It's ringed by an extensively restored **stucco frieze** decorated with abstract carvings, human faces, jaguar heads and a king performing rituals associated with assuming authority. The climb up El Castillo is a challenge, but the views from the top are superb, with the forest stretching out all around and the rest of the ancient city clearly laid out beneath you.

To your right as you enter the site, Plaza A–3 is almost completely enclosed by a low, acropolis-like collection of buildings, known as the **Palace**. Artifacts found here in 2003 suggest that this was the place where the ruler met important officials. The remains of a human sacrifice found in a lower room of the palace may be connected with ceremonies conducted while the structure was being deliberately filled in and abandoned in the Late Classic – but well before the entire site was abandoned in the Terminal Classic.

Trek Stop and Tropical Wings Nature Center

Five hundred metres before the village of Succotz and the ferry over the Mopan River is the wonderful *Trek Stop* (Ⓣ823-2265, Ⓦwww.thetrekstop.com; ❸–❹). Set in a quiet forest clearing near the highway (signposted on the left), these ten nonsmoking **cabins** with comfortable beds, mosquito nets and a porch cost just Bz$20 per person. Run by Succotz resident and a pair of American biologists, it's an environmentally friendly place, with composting toilets and shared, solar-heated showers. Plants here include Maya medicinal varieties, and the excellent library focuses on the Maya and natural history. The **restaurant** serves some of the largest portions in Cayo, always with good vegetarian choices, and there's a self-catering kitchen. Bikes (Bz$20/day), kayaks (Bz$50/day for one or two people) and tubes (Bz$20/day) are available for rent, and guided river and nature trips can be arranged. A rather unique activity, popular with visiting school groups, is to play a round of **frisbee golf** on the only such course in the country.

Also on the site, the well-designed **Tropical Wings Nature Center** (daily 8am–5pm; Bz$6, including an excellent guided tour) is a delicate, enchanting world full of tropical colour. Native plants arch upwards, pressing against the netting on the roof. About two dozen species of butterfly breed successfully here, laying their eggs on the leaves, and outside you can see the caterpillars in all stages of development.

Benque Viejo and the border

The last town on the Western Highway before the Guatemalan border is **BENQUE VIEJO DEL CARMEN**, 13km from San Ignacio. Here Belize and Guatemala merge with almost equal potency, and Spanish is certainly the dominant language, despite English street names such as Elizabeth and Victoria. Benque, as it's usually known, is a pleasant, quiet town, home to many artists, musicians and writers, and is undergoing a fascinating cultural revival. Several villagers produce excellent **wood and slate carvings**; you'll see them for sale at Xunantunich.

If you're really interested in mestizo tradition, visit the **Benque House of Culture** in the old police station (Mon–Fri 8am–5pm; ⓣ823-2697), supported by the Community of Artists for Cultural and Historical Endeavours (CACHE). Inside are displays of old photographs and documents, logging and chicle-gathering equipment, paintings and musical instruments. The collection's keepers are behind another manifestation of the area's artistic spirit: **Poustinia**,

Poustinia Land-Sculpture Park

It's hard to imagine a more impressive and atmospheric venue for an art exhibition than this thirty-acre rainforest setting. The brainchild of Benque Viejo-born architect Luis Ruiz (with assistance from his brother David and some British artists), the **Poustinia Land-Sculpture Park** holds a collection of around thirty sculptures from both Belizean and foreign artists, both provoking and portraying contemporary Belize. Poustinia seeks to create an awareness of the **natural environment**, reforestation and land beautification following human industrial abuse. Some of the sculptures themselves are organic, and in time will disappear to be replaced by new works. *Returned Parquet*, by Welsh artist Tim Davies, is a fine example of this philosophy. In Davies' piece, reclaimed mahogany parquet flooring has been laid as a path through a forest glade; the material will eventually biodegrade and return to the forest whence it came. Other works include installations from David and Luis Ruiz and the schoolchildren of Benque Viejo.

Given their engaging, thought-provoking mission, it's difficult to see why Poustinia is not better known – but its location 5km south of Benque Viejo on the Arenal Road ensures that it's not on the tourist trail and that it remains the property of the environment around it. On any given day you are likely to have the park to yourself, giving you an opportunity for peaceful reflection a million miles from the usual city gallery environment. The walk around the park is best enjoyed in sunny weather and at leisure – allow three hours of daylight to complete the route, and bring plenty of water. The **entry fee** is Bz$20 and visitors are provided with maps for a self-guided tour. Guided tours are available for Bz$50, but you need to call ahead. Bookings and further information can be obtained from the Benque House of Culture (see above), by visiting the Poustinia Foundation's website (ⓦwww.poustiniaonline.org) or by contacting Luis Ruiz at ⓣ822-1574. Taxis ply the route from Benque Viejo to Arenal, so transport shouldn't be a problem unless you're returning late in the day – even then, the one-hour walk back to town is an enjoyable one.

a surreal **earth art** sculpture park, 5km south of town on the Arenal/Mollejon Hydro Road (see box, opposite).

Further along the same road, about 8km from Poustinia, is **Che Chem Ha Cave** (daily tours at 9.30am and 1.30pm; 90min; ⓣ820-4065). Maya for "running water," Che Chem Ha boasts one of the largest collections of Maya pottery discovered anywhere in Belize. Scattered throughout the cave and its chambers are several ceremonial pots, largely intact, some two thousand years old. The cave was primarily used for food storage and ceremonies, and remains just as it was found in 1989, when William Morales stumbled upon its mouth during a hunt with his father. William leads tours into the cave, and can pick you up from Benque if your group is large enough. Be sure to bring sturdy shoes, insect repellent and water, and the will to get muddy – you'll be able to rinse off in a waterfall at the site, and Vaca Falls is an easy, thirty-minute hike away.

Crossing the border, 2km beyond Benque, is straightforward, and there's a constant stream of taxis to and from the border post (Bz$2–3 per person); full details are given in the box on p.212.

Accommodation

Maxim's Palace 41 Church Hill St, Benque Viejo ⓣ823-2360, ⓔcayobenque@yahoo.com. A clean, safe, well-run hotel popular with Belizeans. Twelve rooms with private bath and hot showers; some rooms have king-sized beds, others two double beds. ③–④

Mopan River Resort On the west bank of the river, opposite the park in Benque Viejo ⓣ823-2047, ⓦwww.mopanriverresort.com. Belize's first all-inclusive inland resort, this is the place to enjoy luxurious pampering while you stay in some of the most spacious thatched cabañas in the country. All have comfortable beds and rattan furniture, private bathrooms with tubs, a fridge, a/c, cable TV and a large porch. There are also three cabaña suites with fitted kitchens for longer stays. It's ideal for those seeking a social vacation experience: meals are served family-style, and each evening after dinner you're briefed on the next day's group excursion. Prices start with a 3-night package ($597 per person), which includes accommodation, sumptuous gourmet meals, all drinks, an excellent tour every day (including Tikal and Caracol), use of kayaks and transfers from the international airport. With all the extras on offer, it's actually a very good value, quite possibly the best deal of this calibre in the country. No smoking allowed in the cabañas. Closed during the low season, from July to October inclusive. ⑨

Travel details

The following schedules are for the main bus lines; several smaller companies also frequently run along the same western and southern routes. A shared taxi to the border costs Bz$2–3 per person from Benque, though it's often easier and quicker to take a shared taxi (Bz$4–5 per person) from the market area in San Ignacio.

Belize City to: Destinations along the Western Highway, terminating in Benque Viejo (for the Guatemalan border; 3hr 30min), are served by at-least-hourly NTSL buses (5am–9pm). There is an express service, stopping only in Belmopan, every 3–4hr, saving an hour on the journey time above.

Belmopan to: Dangriga (roughly hourly 5am–7pm; 1hr 40min); Placencia (3–4 daily 8.30am–2.30pm; 3hr 15min); Punta Gorda (3–4 daily 6.30am–4.30pm; 4hr); San Ignacio and Benque Viejo (hourly Mon–Fri 6.30am–10pm, fewer on weekends; first bus of the morning usually continues to Melchor, Guatemala)

Benque Viejo to: Belize City, calling at San Ignacio and Belmopan (half-hourly daily 4am–5pm, express service every 3–4hr).

San Antonio to: San Ignacio (Mon–Sat 6am, 7am, 1pm & 4pm; 1hr).

San Ignacio to: Belmopan and Belize City (half-hourly & some express 3.30am–6pm); Benque Viejo (half-hourly until 11.30pm; 20min); Guatemalan border (usually once daily at 7.30am); San Antonio (4 daily Mon–Sat 10.30am–5.15pm; 1hr)

Tikal and Flores

N
MEXICO
CARIBBEAN SEA
GUATEMALA
1
2
3
4
5
6

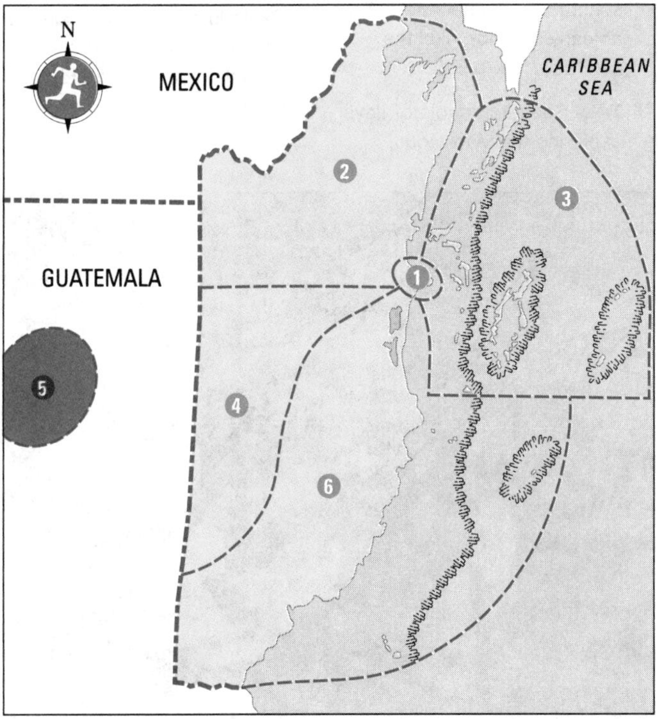

CHAPTER 5

Highlights

* **Laguna Yaxhá** This sublime lake, with the impressive, restored ruins of Yaxhá towering above its shore, is one of the best-kept secrets in Petén. See p.214

* **El Remate** Stay overnight in this relaxed little village on the eastern edge of Lago Petén Itzá, watch a spectacular sunset and get an early start for Tikal the next day. See p.216

* **Tikal** Spend a couple of days exploring this enormous, ancient Maya metropolis, amid protected rainforest teeming with wildlife. See p.218

* **Flores** Stroll around the cobbled streets of this tiny colonial capital set on an island, then enjoy cocktails at a lakeside bar. See p.226

* **Jungle trekking** Extend your Tikal trip by hiking through pristine rainforest to more-distant Maya sites like El Zotz or Río Azul. See p.230

△ Locals Flores

5

Tikal and Flores

No visitor to Belize should pass up the chance to make a side-trip into **Guatemala** to see the famous **Maya sites** and spectacular **nature reserves**, and it's relatively easily done, either independently or on an organized tour. Here, in the vast northern department of **Petén**, are literally hundreds of ruins – many completely buried in the jungle – but few combine intrigue and accessibility as well as **Tikal**, arguably the most magnificent of all Maya sites and situated less than two hours from the border. Its monumental temple-pyramids tower above the rainforest, testament to the fact that Petén was the heartland of ancient Maya civilization during the Preclassic and Classic periods (around 300 BC–900 AD), and that here Maya culture reached the height of its architectural achievement.

En route to Tikal, there are other Maya sites worth stopping for, and you'll see signs for several as you head west along the road from the bustling yet nondescript border town of **Melchor de Mencos**. The first major sites are **Yaxhá**, the third largest in Petén, and the much smaller **Topoxté**. Both occupy beautiful settings on opposite shores of Laguna Yaxhá, about 30km from the border, and there's camping and cabaña accommodation nearby. At **Macanché**, another 30km beyond the Yaxhá junction on the lake of the same name, the private nature reserve of **El Retiro** boasts several fine examples of *chultunes* – underground chambers carved out of limestone whose real function is still a mystery – as well as a serpentarium and a **crocodile sanctuary**.

If you're travelling directly to Tikal by bus from the Belizean border, you'll need to change buses at the village of **Ixlú**, from where it's only a couple of

Guatemala basics

Getting there

From Belize City, **buses** leave hourly for Benque Viejo (all calling at San Ignacio; see p.86), just 2km from the Guatemalan border. After you disembark at Benque Viejo, you'll need to take a *colectivo* taxi (around US$1 per person) the rest of the way to the border (though the first bus of the day from Belize City usually continues to the border). Alternatively, the Linea Dorada bus line (Ⓦwww.tikalmayanworld.com) will take you directly from the Belize City bus terminal to Flores or Tikal, with a stop at the border for formalities. Finally, and much more expensively, you could **fly**: Tropic Air and Maya Island Air each have two daily flights from Belize International to Flores/Santa Elena in Guatemala (up to US$103 one-way, plus departure taxes totalling US$35). These flights generally depart Belize at 8.30am and 3pm, returning at 9.30am & 4pm.

Border practicalities

Both the Belizean and Guatemalan border posts are on the eastern bank of the Mopan River, 15km west of San Ignacio. Even if you're leaving Belize for just one day, you'll have to pay the **exit tax** of Bz$30 and the PACT conservation fee of Bz$7.50; keep your receipt, as it could reduce your next exit tax. Although **visas** are not needed by most nationalities, and most visitors aren't required to pay an entry fee, everyone must fill in the immigration form – and you may still be asked to pay, anything from Q10 to US$10. If you're driving a vehicle from Belize, there will a Q50 (about US$6.50) fee, plus smaller, often variable fees for spraying with insecticide and a bridge toll. At immigration, make sure you request enough time to cover your visit, and ask for the maximum if you're travelling onwards – though the most you're likely to get is thirty days.

Although there is a **bank** just beyond immigration, which gives reasonable rates (Mon–Fri 8.30am–6pm; no ATM or cash advances), it's mainly used by truck drivers for paying import charges and doesn't always deal in dollars. It's quicker and easier to use the moneychangers who'll pester you on either side of the border; bargain with a couple and you'll get a fair rate. There's a LADATEL (long distance) **telephone** just past immigration, though the cards it takes are not easy to find nearby. There's no official tourist information office at the border – the closest locations of the Guatemalan Tourist Commission, aka INGUAT, are in Flores and at the airport.

If you need **accommodation** at the border (thereby allowing you to get a really early start the next day), the best option is the *Río Mopan Lodge* (Ⓣ7926-5196, Ⓦwww.tikaltravel.com; 3), on the riverbank just past Guatemalan immigration and before the bridge. Swiss owner Marco Gross knows Petén and its archeology extremely well, and he organizes trips to remote Maya sites. You can also safely change money here. The cheap, sleazy hotels in the centre of Melchor are best avoided.

Phones

The international calling code for Guatemala is **502**.

Language

Guatemala is a **Spanish**-speaking country and you'd be wise to acquire at least some knowledge of the language; overcharging foreigners is routine, and the better you are at getting by, the less likely you are to be ripped off. See p.381 for a brief Spanish-language guide.

kilometres to the peaceful community of **El Remate** – a good base if you plan to spend more than a day exploring the area. Those with the time for a more extended trip could make for the village and ruins of **Uaxactún**, to the north of Tikal, which also serves as a jumping-off point for expeditions to El Zotz and the remote northern sites of Río Azul and El Mirador.

Money and costs

The Guatemalan unit of **currency** is the quetzal (Q), currently trading at Q7.70–8.00 to the US dollar. At the border, you can easily exchange money (US or Belize) or cash travellers' cheques. If you're not going directly to Flores/Santa Elena (where there are ATMs), make sure you have enough cash (quetzales or dollars) to last at least the first day of your trip. Only the more expensive hotels will take credit cards.

Costs are generally far cheaper than in Belize; for transport, accommodation and food they can be as much as forty or fifty percent less. El Remate (roughly on the way to Tikal) and Flores have some of the best budget accommodation in the country; in either town you can get a decent double for around US$20, much less for a room with shared bath.

Crime and safety

In Guatemala you'll need to take even greater **safety precautions** than in Belize. The border crossing (and indeed travel to Tikal) is best undertaken in daylight – which is not difficult, as the journey is short enough to allow for an early breakfast in San Ignacio and arrival by early afternoon at the latest. In the past, violent robberies and assaults on tourists have taken place in and around El Remate and within Tikal itself, though the introduction of **Tourism Police (POLITUR)** patrols in vehicles and on foot has successfully driven most violent criminals elsewhere. You should check with fellow visitors and owners of the recommended hotels for information on the security situation where you are. If you see a robbery or are a victim yourself, contact the Tourism Police at ⓣ110 or the regular police at ⓣ120.

Beyond the border

The only way to go directly from the border to **Tikal** or **El Remate** is to take a **private minibus** (1hr 20min; around US$10–15 per person, depending on the number of people) or **taxi** (around US$15 per person, depending on the number of people); this is generally the quickest and most comfortable way to travel. It is, however, also quite easy to use public transport and change at the **Ixlú junction** (see p.216) to a bus (or more likely a minibus) that will take you the rest of the way.

All public buses to **Flores/Santa Elena** (under 2hr; every couple of hours from 5am to 7pm) can be picked up just over the bridge at the border. If there isn't one waiting when you arrive, you may find one in the market in Melchor – take a shared taxi from the border for a couple of quetzales, or walk fifteen minutes over the bridge and up the hill to the right. The official **bus fare** to Flores is Q15; even if you're only going as far as Ixlú, you'll still be asked for at least this by the Pinita bus employees, so get a Rosita or a Fuente del Norte bus if there's a choice. All public buses from Ixlú will eventually drop you off on Calle Principal in Santa Elena, on the mainland opposite Flores. Getting to Flores from here is an easy (if hot) fifteen-minute walk across the causeway. Alternatively, you can catch one of the frequent local buses (Q1) from the junction of Calle Principal and the road to the causeway.

Colectivo **minibuses** (known locally as microbuses) provide a faster and more frequent service than the public buses; they wait just over the bridge and charge around Q25–30 to Santa Elena.

But archeology isn't the only thing to tempt you over the border. Petén is a huge, rolling expanse of tropical forest, swamps, lakes and dry savannahs, stretching into the Lacandón forest of southern Mexico. Tikal itself lies at the centre of a large national park, which forms part of the **Maya Biosphere Reserve**, covering 16,000 square kilometres of northern Petén. As one of the

Guatemala accommodation price codes

Accommodation in this chapter has been given a **price code** according to the scale below, which represents the cost of **a double room in high season**. The scale is in US$, due to possible fluctuation in the exchange rate of the quetzal.

❶ under US$10	❹ US$25–40	❼ US$75–100
❷ US$10–15	❺ US$40–55	❽ US$100–125
❸ US$15–25	❻ US$55–75	❾ over US$125

largest tropical forest reserves in Central America, it's extraordinarily rich in **wildlife**, particularly birds, though you're also virtually guaranteed to see **howler** or **spider monkeys**. One of the best places to get an understanding of the forest (apart from Tikal itself) is to visit the **Biotopo Cerro Cahuí** reserve near El Remate.

Finally, the departmental capital, **Flores**, is a picturesque town set on an island in Lago Petén Itzá, while close by, on the mainland, the town of **Santa Elena** is its transport hub.

Melchor de Mencos to El Remate

The sixty kilometres from the **Belize border to the Ixlú junction** takes you through rolling countryside and farmland, past a series of small villages, populated mainly by fairly recent immigrants to Petén, and the Maya sites of **Yaxhá** and **Topoxté**. The road from Melchor de Mencos is in reasonable condition, with only the first few kilometres beyond the border still unpaved, and runs roughly parallel to a chain of lakes – the largest of which is **Lago Petén Itzá** – used in Maya times as the main route across the region. Other lakes along the way include **Macanché**, with more ruins and a nature reserve, and Sal Petén, where there's another major Maya site. Near the shore of Lago Petén Itzá, the Melchor road meets the Flores–Tikal road at the village of **Ixlú**, from where you can continue west to Flores, or north, through **El Remate**, to Tikal.

Yaxhá and Topoxté

Thirty kilometres from Melchor the road passes about 8km to the south of **lagunas Yaxhá and Sacnab**, beautiful bodies of water ringed by dense rainforest. Laguna Yaxhá is home to two Maya ruins well worth a visit: **Yaxhá**, on a hill overlooking the northern shore, and **Topoxté**, on an island near the southern shore. The turn-off is clearly signposted and the bus driver will stop if you ask. If you haven't arranged accommodation at *El Sombrero* (see opposite) in advance, you'll probably be faced with a sweltering two-hour walk to get there. However, there is occasionally traffic to and from the village of La Máquina, 2km before the lakes. Here you'll also find the restaurant-bar *El Portal de Yaxhá* (Ⓣ5477-4414), run by two sisters, where you can inquire about transport to the sites (one of the locals may offer to take you for a small fee). Just before you reach the lakes, you'll pass a **control post** where you pay the Q80 entry fee and may be asked to sign in. From here it's 3km to Yaxhá: head along the road between the lakes, then turn left (signed) for the site.

Yaxhá, a huge ruin covering several square kilometres of a ridge overlooking the lake, is primarily a Classic-period city. Although a great deal of restoration has been completed in recent years, don't expect the manicured splendour of Tikal. What you can count on here, though, is real atmosphere as you try to discover the many features still half-hidden by the forest. The site is open daily; if you're not on a guided trip, one of the knowledgeable guardians will show you around for a small fee. The scale model of the site near the entrance is another good source of information. The ruins are spread out over nine plazas and more than five hundred structures have been mapped so far, including several huge pyramids and large acropolis complexes. The tallest and most impressive pyramid, **Structure 216**, 250m northeast of the entrance, rises in tiers to a height of over 30m; the restoration enables you to climb to the top for spectacular views over the forest and lake.

Topoxté, a much smaller site on the easternmost of three small islands, is best reached by boat from *El Sombrero*. There is a four-kilometre trail to a spot opposite the islands, but you still have to get over to them – and large crocodiles inhabit the lake. The structures you see are not on the scale of those at Yaxhá, and date mainly from the Late Postclassic, though the site was occupied since Preclassic times. Work is in progress to restore some structures.

If you want to **stay** nearby, the wonderful, solar-powered *Campamento El Sombrero* (ⓣ7783-3923 or 7783-3924, ⓦwww.ecosombrero.com; ❸–❺), 200m from the road on the south side of the lake, has rooms in wooden jungle lodges, a less expensive shared room and space for **camping**. The thatched restaurant and lounge overlooking the lake, outfitted with low couches and hammocks, is a peaceful spot to stop for lunch even if you're not staying. The Italian-born owner is a great source of information about Yaxhá, and can arrange boat trips on the lake and horseback trips to other sites; she'll pick you up from the bus stop if you call in advance. On the far side of the lake, immediately below the Yaxhá ruins, locals run another excellent *campamento* (owned by INGUAT) where you can **pitch a tent** or sling a hammock beneath a thatched shelter for free.

Macanché and Ixlú

Beyond the Yaxhá junction the road continues for around another 30km to the village of **MACANCHÉ**, on the shore of **Laguna Mancanché**, where a signed track leads north for 1.8km to another wonderfully tranquil place to stay, the *Santuario Ecológico El Retiro* (ⓣ5751-1876, ⓦwww.retiro-guatemala.com; ❶–❹). Set in forested grounds on the north shore of the lake are private, two-person **bungalows** with hot shower and shady porch for US$50, as well as spacious, ready-to-use **tents** for Q50 per person; if you bring your own tent, you can **camp** for Q25 per person. There's a bar and a dock for swimming – and the crocodiles are not usually seen at this end of the lake. A **serpentarium** houses over twenty species of snakes native to Guatemala (including the deadly fer-de-lance) and a venomous beaded lizard (*escorpión* in Spanish), all in glass tanks in a very secure building and under licence by the Guatemalan government. A tour, which can include watching the snakes catch and devour rats, costs Q40; other tours are described below.

On top of the hill behind the grounds lie the stone remains of ancient **Maya residential complexes** – but far more intriguing are the numbers of *chultunes* found here. A *chultun* is a roughly spherical or gourd-shaped hole carved out of the rock, with a very narrow entrance on top capped by a circular stone. Their exact use is still unknown, though suggested functions include storage chambers, a refuge or a place to conduct ceremonial or religious rites. The best example

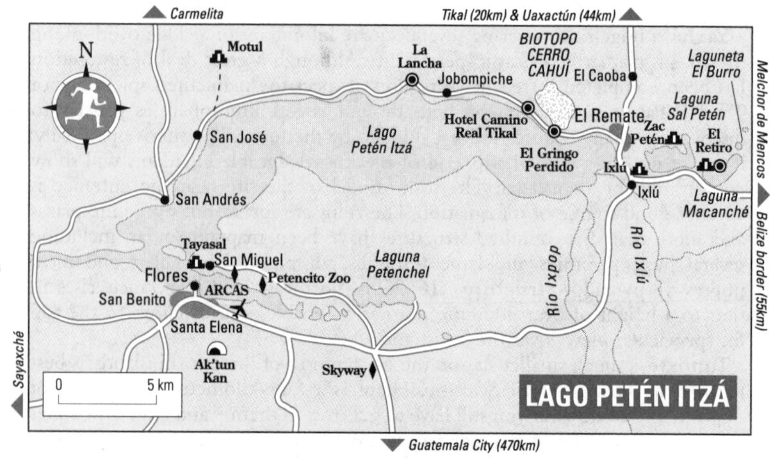

found so far is just behind the bungalows; it has a main chamber with two or possibly three side chambers accessed by a spiral ramp. Anyone brave enough is welcome to sleep inside.

El Retiro forms part of an extensive, private nature reserve and **crocodile sanctuary** that extends along the lake and into two other lakes beyond. The caretaker and guide at *El Retiro* can take you on a 45-minute hike through the forest or a ten-minute boat ride to reach the gorgeous **Laguneta** (meaning "small lagoon") **El Burro**, just beyond the north shore of Laguna Macanché and surrounded by thick rainforest dotted with Maya ruins; use of a canoe to paddle around the *laguneta* is included in the tour. Other trails (each about 45min) lead to another large lake, **Laguna Tintal**, and then onwards to a *cenote*, a limestone sinkhole 100m across and almost 100m deep. A day tour, which includes a visit to the serpentarium and all three lagoons, costs Q140; a night tour, with a hike and boat trip to spot the crocodiles, is Q200.

A few kilometres past Macanché, you reach the tiny village of **IXLÚ**, at the junction with the Flores–Tikal road; coming from the Belize border by public transport, you'll need to get off here if you want to continue to Tikal. Inside the **information** hut you'll find a large map of the area, showing the little-restored **ruins of Ixlú**, 200m down a signposted track from the road, on the shore of Laguna Sal Petén.

El Remate and around

EL REMATE, 2km north from Ixlú along the shore of Lago Petén Itzá, is a small, friendly village and, if you intend to spend more than a day at Tikal, a convenient place to base yourself. The accommodation here is cheaper and nicer than at the site itself, and all buses and minibuses to and from Tikal pass through the village. Transportes Hillary and a couple of other companies run regular **minibuses** between Santa Elena (for Flores) and El Remate, passing through Ixlú every couple of hours, and the daily Pinita **bus to Tikal** leaves from the marketplace in Santa Elena at 1pm and passes through Ixlú and El Remate about 45 minutes later, continuing to Tikal and Uaxactún. Many minibuses stop here to allow visitors to buy beautiful **wooden handicrafts**, often directly from the carvers and at better prices than in the gift shops in Flores.

Two kilometres further west along the lake, an unpaved road passes the **Biotopo Cerro Cahuí** (daily 7am–5pm; Q20), a 6.5-square-kilometre **nature reserve** with a lakeshore, ponds and trails leading through the forest to hilltop Maya ruins. Beyond here is the village of **Jobompiche**, served by buses from Santa Elena, and the road continues on to circle the entire lake – good for exploring by mountain bike. A few hotels have bikes for guests to borrow or rent. There are plenty of **guides** in El Remate who can lead you on multi-day trips to remote Maya sites; the best way to find a good one is to ask at the recommended hotels.

Accommodation

Accommodation in El Remate is dotted along the main road and the one that runs along the northern shore of the lake. Though few, if any, have exact addresses, most are clearly signposted from the road, and El Remate is small enough that you'll pass many of them on a stroll through the village. There's a fairly broad selection, from simple rooms with shared bath, where the going rate for a bed is around Q30 per person, to well-appointed cabañas with private bath.

La Casa de Don David At the junction with the road to Biotopo Cerro Cahuí ⓣ7928-8469 or 5306-2190, ⓦwww.lacasadedondavid.com. Comfortable and secure wooden bungalows and rooms with private hot-water bath set in extensive, lovely plant-filled grounds just back from the lakeshore. The popular restaurant serves *guatemalteca* home-cooking. The staff can arrange trips to Tikal and bus tickets for Belize and Guatemala City. There are usually a couple of bikes to borrow, and guests can use the Internet. Their website has lots of useful information on the area. 3–4

Casa Roja 500m past *Don David*, down the road to Biotopo Cerro Cahuí ⓣ5909-6999. Laid-back, no-frills cabañas, all with shared bath, scattered about leafy grounds right by the lake. Popular with European backpackers. The inexpensive restaurant serves only vegetarian food, including curried vegetables and fresh-squeezed juices. Kayaks for rent. 1

Las Gardenias On the main road ⓣ7928-8377 or 5992-3380, ⓔhotelasgardenias@yahoo.com. Central, well-run spot, with clean a/c and fan rooms with private bath. The simple restaurant, with thatch-and-stick-style walls and a stone floor, serves filling, local fare, including scrambled eggs with tomato, onion and refried beans for breakfast. 3–4

El Gringo Perdido On the north shore, 3km from *Don David's* ⓣ2334-2305, ⓔgringo_perdido@hotmail.com. Long-running, relaxed place on the tranquil shores of the lake. Simple rooms with wooden beds, with private and shared bath. You can also camp (Q25 per person). The open-air restaurant serves plenty of vegetarian options. 3–5

La Lancha In Aldea Jobompiche, about 15km west of El Remate along the north shore of the lake ⓣ7928-8331, ⓦwww.blancaneaux.com. For true lakeside comfort, head to Francis Ford Coppola's third and latest resort in Central America. Winding paths lead though verdant grounds to plush casitas featuring Balinese headboards, bright red-and-orange Guatemalan fabrics, marble bathrooms and ample wooden decks overlooking the placid lake. Other than a shell phone to call reception, the casitas are decidedly gadget-free – no TVs, real phones or a/c. In keeping with Coppola's belief in environmental sustainability, the casitas are designed from local materials and benefit from natural ventilation. The rustic-chic restaurant – think wooden canoes as planters – serves top-notch *guatemalteca* fare. Breakfast included in the price. 9

La Mansión del Pájaro Serpiente On the main road ⓣ5702-9434. Set in a gorgeous tropical garden with a pool, these stone-built, two-storey cabañas have immaculate baths and superb lake views. When available, the smaller cabañas, usually used by tour guides, are available at a discount. 5

El Mirador del Duende On the main road, high above the lake and reached by a stairway cut into the cliff ⓣ5301-5576, ⓔmicuchitril@hotmail.com. Whitewashed, stucco cabañas that look like igloos decorated with Maya glyphs. The restaurant serves vegetarian food. 1

El Muelle On the main road, across from Pájaro Serpiente ⓣ5514-9785 or 5529-1374. The El Muelle gift shop and restaurant has seven ample rooms upstairs with finished wooden floors and private or shared bath. Some have balconies with partial views of the lake. They also rent out pedal boats and kayaks. 4–5

Posada Filin Down a small alley off the main road ⓣ5908-7506. Very simple fan-cooled rooms with wood-and-bamboo doors and clean, shared bath with stone floors, run by friendly owners. 1

Sun Breeze Hotel On the main road ⓣ7928-8044 or 5898-2665. Clean, basic, fan-cooled rooms with lake views and comfortable beds equipped with mosquito nets. 2–3

△ Visitors at Tikal

Eating

El Remate is dotted with casual **restaurants**, many offering outdoor dining with lake views. A number of the hotels also have attached restaurants. The restaurant at *Don David* (see p.217), which features views of the leafy grounds and the lake in the distance, serves nightly dinner specials like *pollo al jocón* (chicken with green tomatillo-cilantro sauce). *Restaurant Cahuí* on the lake side of the road in the centre of the village is also worth trying for its range of vegetarian dishes served on the wooden deck. For casual, open-air dining, head to *El Muelle* ("the pier"; see p.217), on the main road, where you dine at sturdy wooden tables overlooking grounds that slope to the lake. At the thatched-roofed *Las Orchideas* (Ⓣ5701-9022), on the road to Biotopo Cerro Cahuí, the amiable Angelo serves up homemade dishes – aubergine parmesan, fresh breads and pastas – from his native Italy.

Tikal

Immediately north of El Remate, the road climbs a limestone escarpment, and though most people's minds are already fixed on the mighty ruins of **Tikal**, only 30km ahead, a quick glance behind will reward you with superb views of the lake. The landscape becomes more undulating and the settlements begin to thin out as you approach the entrance to **Tikal National Park**, a protected area of some 370 square kilometres that surrounds the archeological site. As you get closer, the sheer scale of Tikal as it rises above the forest canopy becomes overwhelming, and the atmosphere spellbinding. Dominating the ruins are five enormous **temples**: steep-sided pyramids that rise up 60m from the forest floor, and around which lie literally thousands of other structures, many still hidden beneath mounds of earth and covered with jungle.

Some history: the rise and fall of Tikal

According to archeological evidence, the first occupants of Tikal had arrived by 900 BC, during the **Middle Preclassic**, making this amongst the oldest of Maya sites, though at that time it was little more than a village. Its inhabitants called it **Mutul**, or "knot of hair", an image depicted in the city's emblem glyph – a rear view of a head with what appears to be a knotted headband around it. The earliest definite evidence of buildings dates from 500 BC, and by about 200 BC ceremonial structures had emerged, including the first version of the **North Acropolis**. Two hundred years later the **Great Plaza** had begun to take shape, and Tikal by this point was established as a major site with a large permanent population. For the next two centuries, art and architecture became increasingly ornate and sophisticated, though Tikal remained a secondary centre to **El Mirador**, a massive city about 65km to the north.

The closing years of the Preclassic (250–300 AD) saw trade routes disrupted and alliance patterns altered, culminating in the decline and abandonment of El Mirador. In the resulting power vacuum, the two sites of **Tikal** and **Uaxactún** emerged as substantial centres of trade, science and religion. Less than a day's walk apart, the expanding cities grappled for control of the region. A winner emerged in 378 AD, when, under the inspired leadership of **Great Jaguar Paw (Toh Chac Ich'ak)**, Tikal's warriors overran Uaxactún, securing its dominance over central Petén for much of the next five hundred years.

This extended period of prosperity saw the city's population grow to somewhere between 50,000 and 100,000, spreading to cover an area of around thirty square kilometres. Crucial to this success were Tikal's alliances with the powerful cities of Kaminaljuyú (in present-day Guatemala City) and Teotihuacán (to the north of modern Mexico City); stelae and paintings from the period show that Tikal's elite adopted Teotihuacán styles of clothing, pottery and weaponry. In the middle of the sixth century, however, Tikal suffered a huge setback. Already weakened by upheavals in central Mexico, where Teotihuacán was in decline, the city now faced major challenges from the east, where the city of **Caracol** (see p.183) was emerging as a significant regional power, and from the north, where **Calakmul** (see Contexts, p.308) was becoming a Maya "superstate". In an apparent pre-emptive strike against a potential rival, **Double Bird**, the ruler of Tikal, launched an "axe war" against Caracol and its ambitious leader, **Lord Water (Yahaw-te)**, in 556 AD. Despite capturing and sacrificing a noble from Caracol, Double Bird's strategy was only temporarily successful; in 562 AD Lord Water hit back in a devastating "star war", which crushed Tikal and almost certainly sacrificed Double Bird. The victors stamped their authority on the humiliated nobles of Tikal, smashing stelae, desecrating tombs and destroying written records, ushering in a 130-year "**hiatus**" during which no inscribed monuments were erected and Tikal was overshadowed by Caracol and its powerful ally, Calakmul. When research from more recent discoveries at Temple V (see p.224) is published, however, the "hiatus" may come to be viewed in a new light.

Towards the end of the seventh century, however, Caracol's stranglehold had begun to weaken and Tikal gradually started to recover its lost power. Under the formidable leadership of **Heavenly Standard-bearer (Hasaw Chan K'awil)**, who reigned from 682 to 723 AD, the main ceremonial areas were reclaimed from the desecration suffered at the hands of Caracol. By 695 AD, Tikal was powerful enough to launch an attack against Calakmul, capturing and executing its king, **Fiery Claw/Jaguar Paw (Ich'ak K'ak)**, and severely weakening the alliance against Tikal. The following year, Heavenly Standard-bearer repeated his astonishing coup by capturing **Split Earth**, the new king of Calakmul, and Tikal

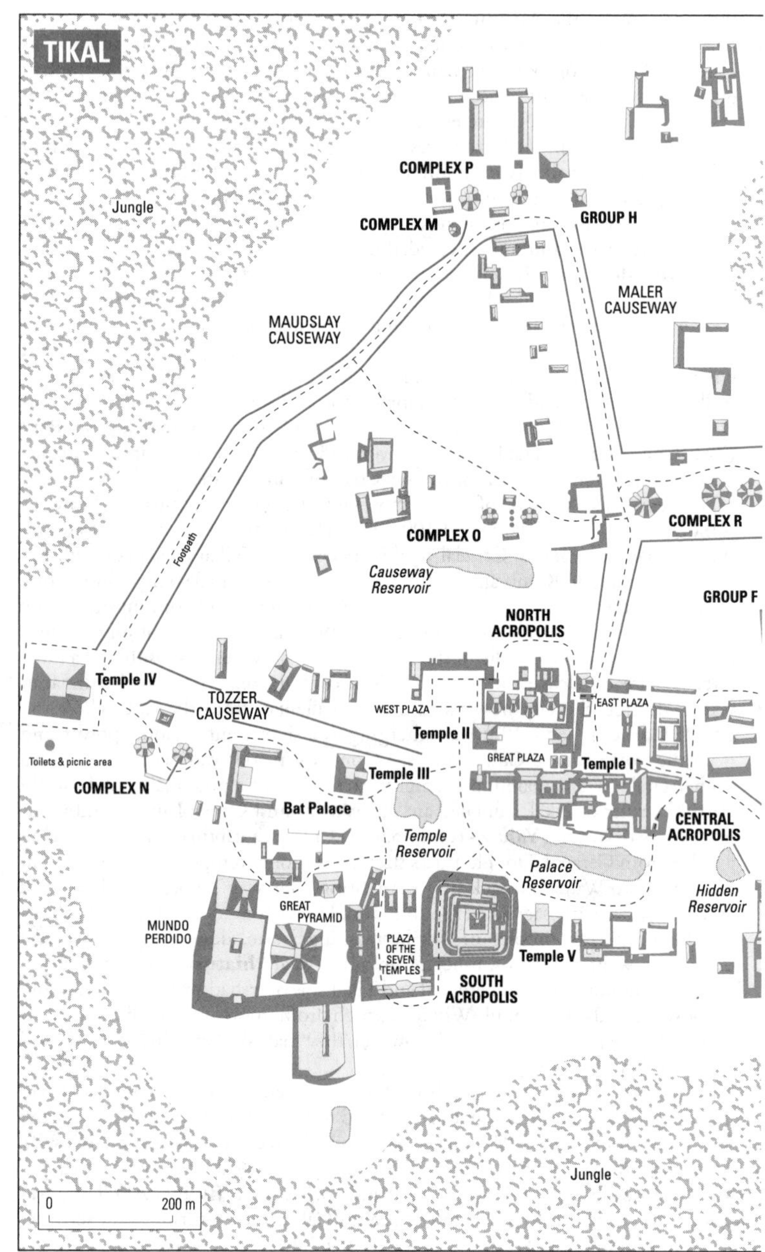

TIKAL
Jungle
COMPLEX P
COMPLEX M
GROUP H
MALER
CAUSEWAY
MAUDSLAY
CAUSEWAY
Footpath
COMPLEX O
COMPLEX R
Causeway
Reservoir
GROUP F
NORTH
ACROPOLIS
Temple IV
TOZZER
CAUSEWAY
WEST PLAZA
EAST PLAZA
Temple II
GREAT PLAZA
Temple I
Toilets & picnic area
COMPLEX N
Temple III
Bat Palace
CENTRAL
ACROPOLIS
Temple
Reservoir
Palace
Reservoir
Hidden
Reservoir
GREAT
PYRAMID
MUNDO
PERDIDO
PLAZA
OF THE
SEVEN
TEMPLES
Temple V
SOUTH
ACROPOLIS
Jungle
0
200 m

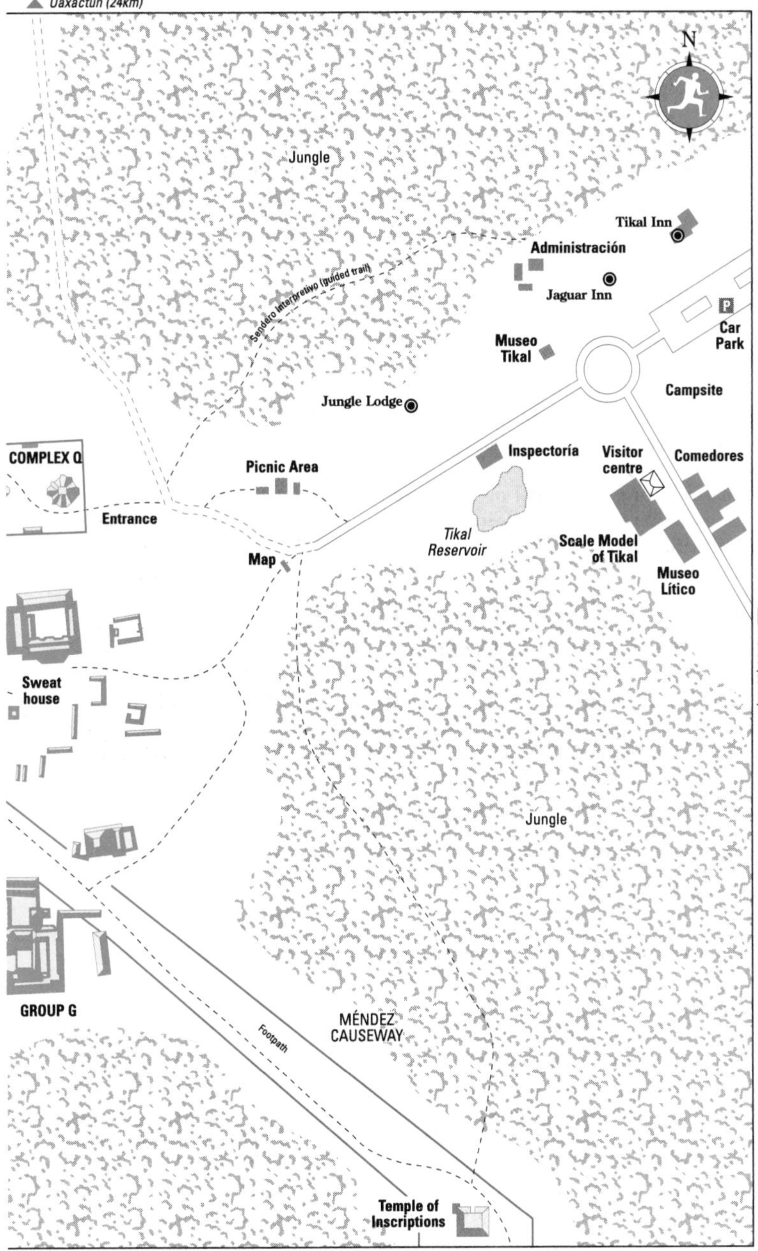
Uaxactún (24km)
N
Jungle
Tikal Inn
Administración
Jaguar Inn
Sendero Interpretivo (guided trail)
P
Car
Park
Museo
Tikal
Campsite
Jungle Lodge
COMPLEX Q
Picnic Area
Inspectoría
Visitor
centre
Comedores
Entrance
Tikal
Reservoir
Scale Model
of Tikal
Map
Museo
Lítico
Flores (63km)
Sweat
house
Jungle
GROUP G
Footpath
MÉNDEZ
CAUSEWAY
Temple of
Inscriptions

regained its position among the most important of Petén cities. Heavenly Standard-bearer's leadership gave birth to a revitalized and powerful ruling dynasty: in the hundred years following his death, Tikal's five main temples were built and his son, **Divine Sunset Lord (Yik'in Chan K'awil)**, who ascended the throne in 734 AD, had his father's body entombed in the magnificent **Temple I**. Temples and monuments were still under construction until at least 869 AD, the last recorded date in Tikal, inscribed on Stela 24.

What brought about Tikal's final **downfall** remains a mystery, but it's certain that around 900 AD, almost the entire lowland Maya civilization collapsed, and that by the end of the tenth century, Tikal had been abandoned. Afterwards, the site was used from time to time by other groups, who worshipped here and repositioned many of the stelae, but it was never formally occupied again.

Getting to Tikal

Coming by bus **from the Belize border**, you'll need to change buses at **Ixlú** (see p.216); look for the *Zac Petén* restaurant on the left. At the junction, local buses to Socotzal and Jobompiche can drop you in El Remate (Q3), where there's abundant, inexpensive accommodation. Alternatively, you can just hop on any passing *colectivo* minibus, which will take you directly to Tikal for around Q15–20 per person.

From Flores, any hotel or travel agent will arrange transport in one of the many minibuses leaving at least hourly from 4am to early afternoon; tickets cost Q40 with return. Mundo Maya generally has the best buses, with departures at 5am, 8.30am and 3.30pm. At the **airport**, minibuses to Tikal (via El Remate) connect with flights from Belize City.

From Santa Elena, the daily Pinita bus to Tikal leaves from the marketplace at 1pm, passing through El Remate about 45 minutes later and continuing to Tikal (Q10; 50min from El Remate) and **Uaxactún**, 24km north of Tikal.

Car rental is available from the airport or in Santa Elena (see Listings, p.231). If you're **driving to Tikal**, you'll be given a time-stamped ticket when you enter the national park to ensure you don't break the 30kmph speed limit on park roads; authorities will check this when you arrive at the site and report you to the police if you've taken less than twenty minutes.

Visiting the site: entrance fee, information and tours

At the national park entrance barrier, 15km before the site itself, you pay a Q50 **entrance fee** (due every day you stay at the site). If you arrive after 3pm you'll be given a ticket for the next day, which you can also use the day you buy it. The ruins are open from 6am to 6pm; extensions to 8pm can sometimes be obtained from the *administración* (Mon–Sat 7am–noon & 2–5pm), a complex of bungalows opposite the roundabout at the end of the paved road.

At the entrance to the ruins is a **visitor centre** with the standard overpriced café and gift shop, though the latter has a good selection of books. The best guide to the site is William R. Coe's *Tikal, A Handbook to the Ancient Maya Ruins*, while *The Birds of Tikal* is useful for identifying some of the hundreds of species you might come across as you wander round. The highlights here, though, are the **Museo Tikal** (see opposite), the **scale model of Tikal** and the **Lithic Museum** (Museo Lítico; daily 8am–4pm; entry included in site ticket), containing a selection of the finest stelae and carvings from the site. Also at the entrance are a **post office** and a few stalls selling *típica* – Guatemalan weavings and handicrafts.

A **licensed guide** (many speak English) can show you the site for around US$40 for four hours for groups of up to five. A number of tour companies and guides in El Remate and Flores also offer sunrise tours of Tikal, which involve a departure time of 3.30am and offer the chance to observe the jungle waking up around the mist-shrouded temples; most hotels and guesthouses in El Remate and Flores can set you up with the tour.

If you fancy aping Tarzan, try the **Canopy Tour Tikal** (daily 7am–5pm; US$30; ⓣ5819-7766 or 7926-4270, ⓦwww.canopytikal.com). After a 25-minute walk through lovely forest, you're strapped into a harness suspended at tree-height, clipped onto a cable and launched off toward the next platform, 100m away. Once you get used to flying through the forest canopy, you can begin to look around and enjoy the views, which can include birds and monkeys.

Accommodation

Although you can comfortably see the main Tikal temples and sights in one day, the park hotels can be especially convenient if you plan on spending several days exploring the site, and want a chance to wake up to the jungle coming to life around you. There are three **hotels** (all with restaurants) near the entrance. They're fairly expensive by local standards (better deals are available in Flores and El Remate), but you can often get discounts out of season. During the high season they're often booked up weeks in advance; **reservations** can be made through a recommended travel agent in Belize or Flores.

The least expensive is *Jaguar Inn* (ⓣ7926-0002, ⓦwww.jaguartikal.com), with comfortable, private bungalows (❺), hammocks (Q40 per person) and camping (Q25 per person if you have a tent, Q50 without). The cheery restaurant serves up simple fare of grilled chicken, pastas, burgers and omelettes. *Tikal Inn* (ⓣ7926-0065, ⓔhoteltikalinn@itelgua.com; ❺–❻) has attractive, thatched bungalows around an inviting pool; this place can be the best value if you book a package that includes meals. The largest and most luxurious option, *Jungle Lodge* (ⓣ7861-0446 or 7861-0447, ⓦwww.junglelodge.guate.com), has large, private bungalows on shady grounds (❼) and some more basic rooms with shared bath (❹), although the latter are often full. The well-appointed restaurant features fine international and local fare.

There are several **comedores** at the park entrance, offering a limited menu of traditional Guatemalan specialities – eggs, beans, grilled meat and a few "tourist" dishes; the best of these is *Comedor Tikal*, at the end of the row. For longer (and pricier) menus, try the hotel restaurants. Cold drinks (*refrescos*) are sold throughout the day from numerous spots around the ruins, though you should always carry a supply of water.

Museo Tikal

At the entrance, between *Jungle Lodge* and *Jaguar Inn*, the one-room Museo Tikal (Mon–Fri 9am–5pm, Sat & Sun 9am–4pm; Q10) houses some of the stelae found here, including the remains of **Stela 29**, Tikal's oldest carved monument (dating from 292 AD), as well as many artifacts: tools, jewellery, pottery, eccentric flints and obsidian and jade objects. There's a spectacular reconstruction of **Hasaw Chan K'awil's tomb**, one of the richest ever found in the Maya world, with beautiful polychrome ceramics, 180 jade ornaments, including bracelets, anklets, necklaces and earplugs, and delicately incised bones, among them a famous, carved human bone depicting deities paddling the dead to the underworld in canoes. A larger bone shows a poignant image of a bound captive with his head bowed – no doubt awaiting a sacrificial death.

The site

The sheer size of Tikal can at first be daunting, and the site is certain to exhaust you before you exhaust it. However, even if you only make it to the main plaza, and spend an hour relaxing atop a temple, you won't be disappointed. The **central area**, with its five main temples, forms by far the most impressive section and should be your priority. Outside the main area are countless smaller, **unrestored structures**, and though they pale beside the scale and magnificence of the main temples, these rarely visited sections can be exciting if you're armed with a good map (the best is in Coe's guide to the ruins, available from the gift shop; see Books on p.370).

You should take great care **climbing the temples**: the steps are narrow and can be slippery after rain, and getting down is always more difficult than getting up. Visitors have been injured (and one killed) by falling from great heights, so the authorities close the taller structures from time to time, especially in the rainy season. Temple I has been closed for many years, though you're almost certain to be allowed up Temple IV.

From the entrance to the Great Plaza

As you walk into the site, the first structures that you come to are the rather unevocatively named **Complex Q** and **Complex R**. Dating from the reign of Hasaw Chan K'awil, these are two of the seven sets of twin pyramids built to mark the passing of a *katun* (a period of twenty 360-day years). Only one of the pyramids (in Complex Q) is restored, with the stelae and altars re-erected in front of it. The carvings on the copy of **Stela 22** (the original is in the Museo Lítico), in the small enclosure set to one side, record the ascension to the throne in 768 AD of Tikal's last known ruler, **Chitam**, portrayed in full regalia, complete with enormous, sweeping headdress and staff of authority.

Following the path as it bears to the left, you approach the back of the restored **Temple I**, a steep pyramid topped by a three-room building and a hollow roof comb that was originally brightly painted. Unfortunately, the stairway is roped off and you're strictly forbidden to climb. The temple towers 44m above the **Great Plaza**, the heart of the ancient city; surrounded by four massive structures, this plaza was the focus of ceremonial activity at Tikal for around a thousand years. Now the celebrated symbol of the entire site, Temple I was built as a burial monument to contain the magnificent **tomb of Hasaw Chan K'awil**. Within the tomb at the temple's core, the ruler's skeleton was found facing north, surrounded by an assortment of jade, pearls, seashells and stingray spines – a traditional symbol of human sacrifice. Some magnificent pottery was also discovered here, depicting a journey to the underworld made in a canoe rowed by mythical animals.

Standing opposite, like a slightly shorter, wider version of Temple I, **Temple II** rises 38m, although when its roof comb was intact it would have been the same height as Temple I. When open, it's a fairly easy climb to the top, and the view, almost level with the forest canopy, is incredible, with the Great Plaza spread out below. As an added bonus, you'll almost certainly see toucans in the nearby branches.

The North Acropolis, the Central Acropolis and Temple V

The **North Acropolis**, which fills the whole north side of the plaza, is one of the most complex structures in the entire Maya world. In traditional Maya style, it was built and rebuilt on top of itself; beneath the twelve temples visible today are the remains of about a hundred other structures, some of which,

The Maya world

From 1500 BC to 1000 AD, the Maya dominated Central America, developing an advanced society that left behind some of the most magnificent and mysterious relics on the entire continent. Their cities were far larger and more elaborate than anything in Europe at the time, a feat made all the more remarkable without the aid of wheeled transport or metal tools. The Maya also showcased their brilliance by producing highly accurate calendars, sophisticated counting and writing systems and intricate jade jewellery.

▲ Mask in Plaza B, Caracol

The collapse

The ancient Maya still fascinate archeologists, not least because of the civilization's sudden and inexplicable decline in the tenth century, when its grand cities were emptied and abandoned in the jungle. The enigma of the Maya's "**collapse**" remains unsolved to this day, though lengthy droughts, overpopulation, exhaustion of arable land, social revolution, disease, extended warfare or a combination of such factors have all been proposed as possible explanations. As you explore the archeological sites and gaze at the impressive ruins, however, it's difficult to imagine how the civilization responsible for such eternal structures could simply have vanished.

The hard evidence

Whatever the reason for their fall, the Maya certainly left behind a treasure trove of **remains**, visible at most sites throughout the country. Closely observing the glyphs and **stelae**, fine jade artwork and stone and ceramic vessels, you'll find scenes depicting mythology, science, politics and warfare – as well as the events of everyday life. Some sites are littered with **pottery shards**, and by examining the colour and consistency of the clay, you can estimate the time of their origin. Murals on temple walls provide a wealth of information about community life, especially aspects of work and trade. Etchings chronicle the births, coronations, marriages, conquests and deaths of Maya kings.

Many Maya structures are incredibly tall – **Tikal**, especially – and after climbing their steep stairs you will arrive breathless, but you'll be greeted at the top by outstanding panoramas of ruins and the surrounding forest. In most cases you'll be in the midst of deep jungle, revealing just how hidden these sites were before excavation. The layout of many structures was carefully aligned with the stars to draw upon their perceived powers, and often designed to mirror other elements of the natural world. An interesting feature that most sites share is the "**ball-court**", the venue for a violent game that symbolized the epic battle between the Hero Twins and the Lords of Death as depicted in the Popol Vuh, the Maya creation story.

▲ Altun Ha

Tips for an enjoyable site visit

- Before settling on a tour guide, always check for an **official licence** from the Belize Tourism Board. Also, a guide who either is of Maya descent or has worked on the site with an archeology team will make your visit more rewarding.
- **Dress appropriately** for jungle terrain: sturdy shoes, long pants, high socks and insect repellent. Sunscreen, sunglasses and a hat are also essential.
- Many sites are havens for **wildlife**, so don't forget your binoculars. El Pilar (see p.196) and Lamanai (see p.108) have the best reputations for birding.
- Leave your valuables at the hotel. **Robberies** are not unknown at sites near the Guatemalan border, and though these are usually well protected by military personnel, you can never be too safe.
- Don't remove anything from a site, not even a tiny pottery shard – it's a **crime**, and visitors' bags are searched at the airport.

Exploring the Maya underworld

Though most evidence of the Maya is aboveground, the culture was fascinated by the subterranean, and **caves** held sacred status. They were considered entrances to the underworld, called **Xibalba**, the "place of fright", but despite their fearsome nature they also provided privileged access to the dwelling of gods, ancestors and spirits. Almost every cave in Belize – and, thanks to the country's porous karst limestone, there are plenty – has revealed unique findings, including wall paintings, pottery shards and the remains of fires. Because the Maya gods had to be appeased with **sacrifices**, you'll also see weapons, altars and skeletons, typically left just as archeologists first discovered them.

Perhaps the best cave to visit for its cache of Maya artifacts is **Actun Tunichil Muknal** (or ATM) in Cayo District, involving a short swim and, depending on the water level, a forty-minute hike through waist-deep water. **Che Chem Ha**, also in Cayo District, is another highlight, with some of the most intact artifacts in the country. In addition to their attraction as Maya sites, caves also invite a slew of adventure activities, heavily promoted by tour organizers. **Cave tubing**, **abseiling** (or rappelling) and **canoeing** are some of the most popular activities and run the gamut from relaxing to exhilarating.

▼ Artifacts in Actun Tunichil Muknal cave

▲ Maya women in San Miguel, Toledo District

The Maya today

Although their glorious past now lies in ruins, the Maya themselves did not disappear – nine million still live throughout Central America, and another million in the US – and most have retained their pre-Hispanic traditions and customs. Just as their ancestors did, contemporary Maya regard **corn** as the key to their existence; in fact, Maya belief holds that the first man was made from corn kernels. Modern Maya generally make their living from **subsistence farming**, producing corn, cacao and beans and raising cows, pigs and chickens, and some along the Caribbean coast rely on **fishing**. With the rapid rise of Belize's tourism industry, however, many Maya have turned to hospitality work, and you'll likely interact with them on a daily basis during your visit to the country.

Stay with the Maya

The best way to understand the Maya of today is to venture south to **Toledo District**, where most reside; incidentally, it's also home to some remarkably remote and unspoilt landscapes. Villages here are rich in tradition, and many inhabitants still speak **Maya dialects**, such as Mopan, Kekchí and some Yucatec. Several villages have a **homestay** or guest house program (see p.290), allowing you to interact with the Maya and gain insight into their past. You'll sample traditional food and drink, listen to music, stories and myths, and may even learn how to make chocolate the Maya way – especially if you visit during the **Toledo Cacao Festival** in May. What's more, major archeological sites and artifact-filled caves are usually just a short hike away.

along with two large **masks**, have been uncovered by archeologists. One of the masks, facing the plaza and protected by a thatched roof, remains quite distinct. In front of the North Acropolis are two lines of **stelae** carved with images of Tikal's ruling elite, with circular altars at their bases. These and other stelae throughout the site bear the marks of **ritual defacement**, carried out by newly enthroned rulers to erase any latent powers that the image of a predecessor may have retained.

On the other side of the plaza, the **Central Acropolis** is a maze of tiny, interconnecting rooms and stairways built around six smallish courtyards. The buildings here are usually referred to as palaces rather than temples, although their precise use remains a mystery. The large, two-storey building in Court 2 is known as **Maler's Palace**, named after the archeologist Teobert Maler, who made it his home during expeditions in 1895 and 1904.

Further behind the Central Acropolis, a wide path leads to **Temple V**, though the best approach is from the Plaza of the Seven Temples, where you'll catch a particularly good view of the creamy limestone of the restored monumental staircase. Unfortunately, you can't climb this, though an extremely steep wooden stairway to the left of the stone one is sometimes open to visitors, and the view from the top is superb. Temple V has been the focus of intensive research (funded by the Spanish government) for much of the past two decades. It was once thought to be among the last of the great temples to be built, but findings from the many burials here indicate that it was in fact the earliest, dating from around 600 AD and almost certainly constructed by **Kinich Wayna**, Tikal's governor at the time. This discovery alone overturns most previous views of this era of Tikal's history, as it was built early in the Mid-Classic "hiatus", which followed Tikal's defeat by Lord Water of Caracol in 562 AD; experts previously thought that no new monuments were erected at Tikal during this period. More intriguing discoveries are sure to be announced as the research data is analyzed and published.

From the West Plaza to Temple IV

The **West Plaza**, behind Temple II, is dominated by a large, Late Classic temple on its north side, and scattered with various altars and stelae. From here, the **Tozzer Causeway** – one of the raised routes that connected the main parts of the city – leads west to **Temple III**, covered in jungle vegetation. Around the back of the temple is a huge palace complex, of which only the **Bat Palace** has been restored, while further down the causeway, on the left-hand side, is **Complex N**, another set of twin pyramids. In the northern enclosure of the complex, the superbly carved **Stela 16** depicts Hasaw Chan K'awil.

Looming at the end of the Tozzer Causeway, the massive **Temple IV**, at 64m, is the tallest of all the Tikal structures. Built in 741 AD, it is thought by some archeologists to be the resting place of the ruler **Yik'in Chan K'awil**, whose image was depicted on wooden lintels built into the top of the temple. To reach the top you have to ascend secure wooden ladders (one to go up and another to come down). Slow and exhausting as this is, it's always worth it, offering one of the finest views of the whole site. All around you the green carpet of canopy stretches to the horizon, interrupted only by the great roof combs of other temples. At any time this view is enthralling – at sunrise or sunset, it's unbeatable.

The Plaza of the Seven Temples and Mundo Perdido

The other main buildings in the centre of Tikal lie to the south of the Central Acropolis. Here, reached by a trail from Temple III, you'll find the

△ Entrance to Flores

Plaza of the Seven Temples, which forms part of a complex dating back to before Christ. There's an unusual triple ball-court on the north side of the plaza, and to the east, the unexcavated South Acropolis. **Mundo Perdido**, or Lost World, lies immediately to the west, another magical and very distinct section of the site with its own atmosphere and architecture. The main feature of this area, the **Great Pyramid**, is a 32-metre-high structure whose surface conceals four earlier versions, the first dating from 700 BC. From the top of the pyramid you'll get incredible views toward Temple IV and the Great Plaza, and it's another excellent place to watch the dramatic sunrise or sunset.

Flores and Santa Elena

Although it's the capital of Petén, **FLORES** is an easy-going, sedate place with an old-fashioned atmosphere – quite different from the rough, bustling commercialism of other towns in the region. A cluster of cobbled streets and ageing houses built around the white, twin-domed church of Nuestra Señora de Los Remedios, it sits beautifully on an island in Lago Petén Itzá, connected to the mainland by a causeway; even if you're heading back to Belize after visiting Tikal, it's worth making a detour here on the way.

The **lake** is a natural choice for settlement and its shores were heavily populated in Maya times. **Noh Petén** ("great island"), which would become modern Flores, was the capital of the Itzá – the last independent Maya kingdom to succumb to Spain, which conquered and destroyed it in 1697. Cortés, the conqueror of Mexico, passed through here in 1525, and once in a while Spanish friars would visit, though they were rarely welcome. For the entire colonial period (and indeed up to the 1960s), the town languished in virtual isolation, having more contact with neighbouring Belize than the Guatemalan capital.

Eventually Flores acquired its modern elements, the ugly, sprawling twin towns of **Santa Elena** and **San Benito**, which lie across the water. Santa Elena, opposite Flores at the other end of the causeway and strung out between the airport and the market, has banks, hotels and buses; there's no need to venture into the chaotic mire of San Benito.

Today, despite the steady flow of tourists passing through for Tikal, Flores retains a genteel air, with residents greeting one another courteously as they meet in the streets, and offers pleasant surroundings in which to stay, eat and drink. If you're not going to the Guatemalan highlands but want to buy *típica* clothing and **gifts**, you'll find the shops here have better prices than at Tikal.

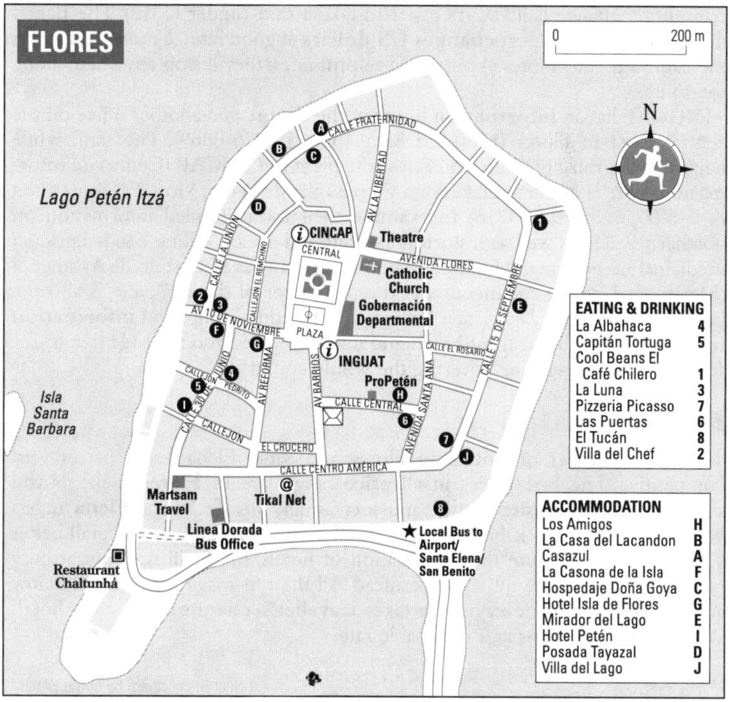

FLORES

EATING & DRINKING
La Albahaca 4
Capitán Tortuga 5
Cool Beans El Café Chilero 1
La Luna 3
Pizzeria Picasso 7
Las Puertas 6
El Tucán 8
Villa del Chef 2

ACCOMMODATION
Los Amigos H
La Casa del Lacandon B
Casazul A
La Casona de la Isla F
Hospedaje Doña Goya C
Hotel Isla de Flores G
Mirador del Lago E
Hotel Petén I
Posada Tayazal D
Villa del Lago J

Causeway to Santa Elena (approx 750m)

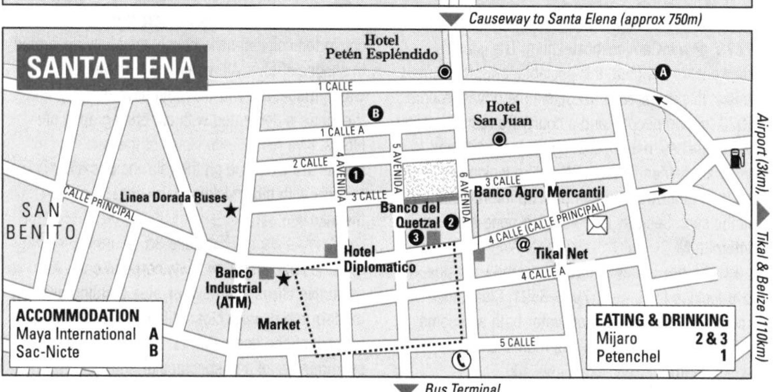

Bus Terminal

Flores holds its annual **fiesta** from January 12 to 15, celebrated by processions, a fair, beauty contests and fireworks. At midnight on the last day, a local wit reads *El Muerto* – a carefully compiled list of the peccadilloes of various townspeople during the previous year – and the drunkest person around (selected from a large cast) is placed in an open coffin and paraded through town.

Arrival and information

Arriving by bus from Belize or Tikal, you'll be dropped on or near Calle Principal (aka 4 Calle) in Santa Elena, just a few blocks from the paved causeway to Flores. The **airport** is on the road to Tikal, 3km east of the causeway; **local buses** (*urbanos*) make the trip into town for Q1, but as this entails a time-consuming change halfway, it's easier to take a **taxi** (under US$2). The Banco del Quetzal at the airport **changes US dollars** at good rates. *Urbanos* run across the causeway into Flores about every ten minutes; they'll stop anywhere along the route.

INGUAT has an **information** booth at the airport, and another office on the central plaza in Flores (Mon–Fri 8am–4pm; ⓣ7926-0669). The staff, while helpful, will probably direct you across the plaza to CINCAP (Centro de Información sobre la Naturaleza, Cultura y Artesanías de Petén; Mon–Fri 8am–noon & 2–5.30pm; ⓣ7926-0718) to examine their more detailed information on northern Petén, as well as historical exhibits and a shop selling handicrafts and medicinal herbs. The old building is known to many as El Castillo de Arismendi (Martín de Ursúa y Arismendi was the conqueror of the Itzá), and is also the production office of *Destination Petén*, a free monthly listings and **information magazine**, available at most hotels and travel agencies; also available free is *The Revue*, a bigger magazine covering the whole country.

Accommodation

The sheer number of **hotels** in Flores and Santa Elena keeps prices very competitive. The best places in all price ranges are in **Flores** itself, so you shouldn't stay in noisier, dirtier, and increasingly unsafe **Santa Elena** unless you're looking for rock-bottom rates – and even then, you'll find overall better value in Flores. Despite the proliferation of hotels, many fill up early at busy periods, so you may want to book ahead. All the top-range hotels listed below accept **credit cards**, everywhere takes **traveller's cheques**, and most hotels will change US dollars at a reasonable rate.

Flores

Los Amigos Calle Central ⓣ5584-8795 or 5521-2873, ⓦwww.amigoshostel.com. The island's backpacker hangout, this sociable, brightly painted hostel has dorm beds (Q25), simple private rooms (Q70 for two people) and a courtyard restaurant/bar with couches, hammocks, resident parrots and a vegetarian-friendly menu. If you're looking to meet up with other travellers or pick up information, this is the spot. Security lockers, ping-pong and Internet. ❷

La Casa del Lacandón At the island's far side, overlooking the lake ⓣ7926-3591. Clean, tiled rooms, all with private hot-water bath and some with a/c. Ask for the upstairs rooms, a couple of which feature lovely lake views. ❷

Casazul Near the northern tip of the island ⓣ7926-1138, ⓦww.corpetur.com. Stylishly converted colonial-style house, tastefully decorated in shades of blue. All rooms have private bath, hot water, fridge, a/c and TV, some have balcony, and the lobby is decorated with old photographs of Flores. Five rooms with views of the lake, and all guests are welcome on the relaxing upstairs terrace, with blue wicker chairs, that juts over the lake. ❺

La Casona de la Isla Calle 30 de Junio ⓣ & ⓕ7926-0593, ⓦwww.corpetur.com. An attractive citrus and powder-blue building offering modern rooms with clean, tiled hot-water bath, a/c, telephone and cable TV. There's also a swimming pool and spectacular sunset views from the terrace restaurant/bar. Internet access in lobby for guests. ❺

Hospedaje Doña Goya Calle la Unión ⓣ7926-3538. Friendly, family-run budget guest house offering well-lit rooms, some with private hot-water bath and balcony, others with clean, shared bath. They also have dorms. Breakfast available and there's a rooftop terrace with hammocks. ❶–❷

Hotel Isla de Flores Avenida de la Reforma ⓣ7926-0614, ⓦwww.junglelodge.guate.com. A lobby with white wicker furniture gives way to clean, a/c rooms with TV, private bath and bright bedspreads; about half the rooms feature lake views. A skylight and hanging plants liven up each floor. ❺

Mirador del Lago I and II Calle 15 de Septiembre ⓣ7926-3276. Basic, well-furnished rooms with private hot-water bath and fan. The fridge is stocked with beer and soft drinks, and the restaurant has tables on a lakeshore terrace. No. I is on the lakeshore and no. II is across the street. Great lake views from the roof of either hotel, and well-priced meals. ❷

Hotel Petén Calle 30 de Junio ⓣ7926-0692, ⓦwww.corpetur.com. Modern hotel with friendly staff. The rooms have private hot-water bath, fan, TV and a/c, and most have lake views. The lobby features a small pool and the restaurant, with a menu of grilled fish, pastas, burgers and burritos, sits on a terrace overlooking the lake for fabulous sunset views. Internet access for guests and kayaks for rent. ❺

Posada Tayazal Calle la Unión ⓣ & ⓕ7926-0568, ⓔhotelposadatayazal@hotmail.com. Decent budget rooms, some with private hot-water bath; shared baths have hot water. Prices and views increase as you head upstairs and some rooms have a balcony. Internet available on ground floor. ❷–❸

Villa del Lago Calle 15 de Septiembre ⓣ7926-0508, ⓦwww.hotelvilladelago.com. Modern, three-storey building with comfortable, pretty rooms with private hot-water bath, a/c and TV. The breakfast terraces at the rear are great places to enjoy the sunrise. Good restaurant and laundry service in this well-run hotel. ❹

Santa Elena

Hotel Maya International On the lakeshore ⓣ2334-1818, ⓦwww.villasdeguatemala.com. Set in gardens right over the lakeshore opposite Flores. Good-sized rooms with private bath, TV, phone and a balcony. There's a reasonable restaurant with a pool outside, and they'll also exchange dollars and euros. ❼

Sac-Nicte 1 Calle A 4–45 ⓣ & ⓕ7926-0092. Basic rooms with fans and private hot shower; those on the second floor have balconies and views of the lake. The well-stocked shop next door is handy if you don't want to venture too far into Santa Elena. They offer free pickup and drop-off at the airport. ❷

Eating and drinking

There are plenty of good, reasonably priced **restaurants** in Flores and a couple in Santa Elena. Many restaurants serve a tourist-oriented menu, with pasta, grilled chicken, fish or beef, pizzas, kebabs (*pinchos*) and other international fare. Several restaurants on the island also serve **wild game**, often listed on menus as **comida silvestre**. Virtually all this has been taken illegally from the reserve, and you should avoid ordering items such as *tepescuintle* (paca, a large relation of the guinea pig), *venado* (deer) or *coche de monte* (peccary, or wild pig).

Flores

La Albahaca Calle 30 de Junio ⓣ7926-0505. Dine on simple Mediterranean fare at this quiet corner restaurant with pastel-green walls and checked tablecloths. Chicken cutlets are grilled with a tamarind sauce, and shrimp tossed with garlic and olive oil and served over rice. You could fill up on the crusty homemade bread alone – and don't miss the delicious chocolate mousse. Closed Mon.

Capitán Tortuga Calle 30 de Junio ⓣ7926-0247. Large restaurant, often catering to groups, with a terrace on the lake at the back. Good grills and salads, chicken burritos and fine cocktails.

Cool Beans "El Café Chilero" Calle 15 de Septiembre ⓣ5571-9240. Pleasant restaurant with wicker lamps overlooking a coconut-strewn garden and the lake beyond. Come for the hearty, reasonably priced breakfasts, including green-pepper omelettes with beans and pancakes, plus sandwiches and salads, served with whole wheat bread. Daily happy hour. Closed Tues.

La Luna At the far end of Calle 30 de Junio ⓣ7926-3346. Pleasant, colourful, plant-filled restaurant, very popular with locals and visitors. The international menu includes grilled fish, garlic shrimp over rice, *spaghetti a la carbonara*, chicken, steak and vegetarian choices like falafel and squash stuffed with vegetables.

Pizzeria Picasso Calle 15 de Septiembre, near *El Tucán* ☎7926-0673. Wide range of good, filling pizzas and pastas. They also deliver.

Las Puertas Signposted off Calle Santa Ana ☎7926-1061. Cheery, high-ceilinged restaurant with six *puertas* (doors), hanging rattan lamps and healthful offerings like generous salads, grilled shrimp and vegetarian omelettes. Occasional live music, and they also run a small *cine*, or movie theatre, across the street.

El Tucán Reached from Calle Centro América ☎7926-0527. Tasty fish and shrimp ceviche and great Mexican fare, including enchiladas stuffed with beef loin strips, cheese and onions – but prices can be relatively steep and there's occasionally wild game on the menu.

Villa del Chef Calle La Unión. A quiet, even romantic, restaurant serving Guatemalan and Arab cuisine, like grilled meats and chicken shish kebab, along with a range of vegetarian choices, including ratatouille. The tables on the lakeshore terrace are candlelit in the evenings.

Santa Elena

Mijaro Two locations; one at the top of the road from the causeway, the other around the corner on Calle Principal ☎7926-1615. The best Guatemalan restaurant in Santa Elena, with good food at local prices and a daily special. You can usually leave luggage here while you look for a room.

Petenchel 2 Calle, beyond *Hotel San Juan*, past the park. No-frills eatery with tasty, local food.

Around Flores

On the peninsula opposite Flores, the **Petencito Zoo** (daily 7am–5pm; Q20) houses a surprisingly well-looked-after collection of local fauna, including jaguars and other cats, monkeys and macaws, all in generally spacious enclosures in an authentic, hilly, jungle setting on the lakeshore. A *lancha* to get there will cost around US$10, and for this price the boatman will wait for as long as it takes you to look around. Slightly nearer, the animal rescue centre of **ARCAS** is also open to the public (daily 8am–5pm; Q15).

At the **Skyway Ixpanpajul**, 10km from Santa Elena, just off the road to Guatemala City (daily 6am–6pm; Q100; ☎2336-0576, Ⓦwww.ixpanpajul.com), an amazing system of suspension bridges and stone paths connects 3km of forested hilltops in a nine-square-kilometre private reserve. From the middle of the bridges you enjoy a monkey's eye view of the canopy, and on top of the highest hill there's an enormous *mirador* with views of virtually the whole of the

Jungle tours and travel agents

Besides Tikal, there are many other Maya sites within the Maya Biosphere Reserve; the agents listed below are the best around for visiting these. They'll provide a guide (an English-speaking one can be arranged but may cost more), food and all equipment, including tents, hammocks and mosquito nets where necessary. In most cases being in a group will cut costs, and it's always worth asking for a discount on multi-day trips. Some trips are arduous expeditions, involving hiking through muddy jungle, but the rewards are often spectacular and you'll feel a real sense of achievement as you climb to the top of a temple and peer out over nothing but rainforest.

The best travel agent in Flores is the English-speaking **Martsam Travel**, at the western end of Calle Centro América (☎7926-3225, Ⓦwww.martsam.com), which runs a daily trip to Yaxhá (p.214) for US$30 per person (minimum two people) and also offers overnight jungle trips to El Zotz, El Perú and many other sites. **Explore**, on 2 Calle 3–55, Zona 1, Santa Elena (☎7926-2375, Ⓦwww.exploreguate.com), is expert in trips to Ceibal, on the Río Pasión (daily, US$40), as well as other sites southwest of Flores, such as Aguateca and Dos Pilas, on Laguna Petexbatún (overnight US$165, including Ceibal).

Moving on from Flores

Buses to **Melchor de Mencos** (for the Belize border; around 2hr; Q15–20) leave from the marketplace in Santa Elena; all pass through Ixlú (for El Remate and Tikal). Most are crowded "chicken buses", though all companies have some more comfortable "Pullman" services. Pinita (the worst service) leaves at 5am, 8am and 11am; Rosita leaves at 7am, 11am, 2pm, 4pm and 6pm; Fuente del Norte has a Pullman at 4.30pm, leaving from its office on Calle Principal. Mundo Maya in Flores runs daily luxury buses **to Belize City** (terminating at the Marine Terminal; see p.68) at 5am & 8am (4hr; around US$18), continuing on to Chetumal, Mexico (a further 4hr; around US$25 in all) where they connect with a Mexican bus service servicing **Cancún** (5hr 30min; first class US$9). *Colectivo* **minibuses** for Melchor (Q20–25) depart every half-hour or so from the terminal on Calle Principal in Santa Elena.

All the bus companies heading to **Guatemala City** also have offices on Calle Principal, and there are around thirty departures daily to the capital (8hr). ADN and Linea Dorada offer the best and fastest services, with departure four times daily from Flores itself, which saves the hassle of getting to the mainland and is much safer; buy tickets (US$20–25) from hotels and travel agencies. Fuente del Norte, usually much cheaper, is the best of the rest.

Tickets for **flights to Belize City** (2 morning & 2 afternoon daily; US$80) and **Guatemala City** (at least 8 daily; US$55–75) can be bought at the airport or at any travel agent in Santa Elena or Flores. There are also flights to **Cancún** with Aviateca (daily at 4.30pm) and Aerocaribe (Mon, Wed & Fri at 8am).

Petén Itzá basin. It's best to go in the early morning or after mid-afternoon; allow a few hours so you can take your time inspecting the trees and orchids. You can even sign up for a special "spotlighting" tour at night, when the wildlife really comes to life. There's a good self-guided trail leaflet (in Spanish only), and you can get there from Flores by bike (45min) or any Poptún-bound *microbus*, which will drop you at the entrance.

Listings

Banks and currency exchange Not all banks in Flores and Santa Elena change cash dollars, but the Banco Banrural (Mon–Fri 8.30–5pm) in Flores's main plaza usually does. You can also try the Banco Agro Mercantil in Santa Elena, at the intersection of Calle Principal and the road to the causeway (Mon–Sat 8.30am–5pm). Many travel agents, including Martsam Travel in Flores (see box, opposite), will change dollars and traveller's cheques.

Bike and motorbike rental Backabush Bike Tours on Avenida Barrios (☎5695-7481) has good mountain bikes; rent one for around Q15/hr or take one of their excellent tours. For motorbikes (Q120 for 2 hrs) see Martsam Travel, opposite.

Car rental Budget, Hertz, Koka and Tabarini (which has the widest choice; ☎7926-0253) operate from the airport, and there are some offices in Santa Elena. Rates (usually including insurance) start at around US$50/day for a small or mid-sized car and go up to over US$80/day for a double-cab pickup with 4WD. It's always worth checking with a recommended travel agent first, though – they will be able to point you in the direction of reliable small firms.

Communications and Internet You'll find a number of Internet centres in Flores, particularly on Calle Centro América, where you can also make phone calls, including Tikal Net, on Calle Centro América (also on Calle Principal, directly across the causeway in Santa Elena).

Doctor Centro Médico Maya, 4 Avenida near 3 Calle in Santa Elena, by the *Hotel Diplomático* (☎7926-0180), is helpful and professional, though no English is spoken.

Laundry Lavandería Amelia, behind CINCAP in Flores, or Petenchel on Calle Centro América (both Q25 to wash and dry).

Post office In Flores, on Avenida Barrios; in Santa Elena, on Calle Principal, two blocks east of the Banco Agro Mercantil (both Mon–Fri 8am–5pm).

6

The south

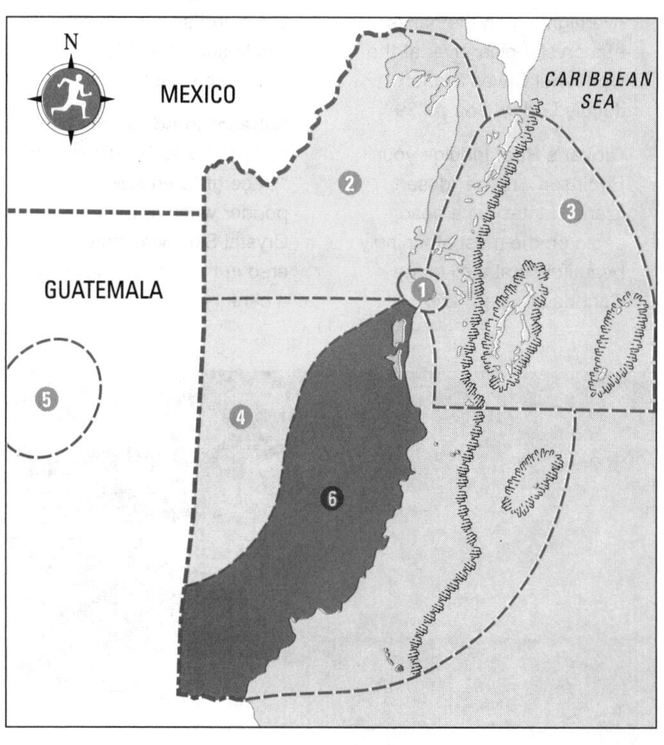

CHAPTER 6

Highlights

* **Gales Point** Stay in this tiny Creole village, where you can listen to drums in the evening, then rise early to spot manatees and wading birds at dawn. See p.238
* **The Hummingbird Highway** Take the most scenic drive in the country, stopping to visit Blue Hole National Park, or overnighting on the banks of a crystal-clear river at the wonderful Caves Branch Jungle Lodge. See p.239
* **Glover's Reef** Indulge your Robinson Crusoe "desert island" fantasy in a beach cabin on the most stunningly beautiful coral atoll in the Caribbean. See p.258
* **The Cockscomb Basin Wildlife Sanctuary** Spend a night or two in the world's first jaguar reserve, following the tracks of the largest cat in the Americas. See p.260
* **Placencia** Stroll along the best beaches in the country, or head out to sea for snorkelling off Laughing Bird Caye and swimming with whale sharks at Gladden Spit. See p.267
* **Lubaantun** Admire the beautifully restored buildings of the "place of fallen stones" – and ponder whether the famous Crystal Skull was truly discovered in this ancient city nearly a century ago. See p.295

△ Laughing Bird Caye

6

The south

Belize's southern half contains its wildest terrain. Stretching along the coast south of Belize City is an elongated band of swamp, lagoon and savannah, whose nutrient-poor soil supports large, incongruous stands of Caribbean pine. Beyond Dangriga, at the far end of this **coastal strip**, the shoreline becomes a combination of sandy bays, peninsulas and mangrove lagoons, gradually changing to river-hewn valleys and forested ridges on the way inland toward the impressive Maya Mountains. The climate grows more humid further south, promoting dense, wildlife-rich **rainforest** – which has also developed resilience in the face of periodic Caribbean hurricanes and selective mahogany logging. In the far south, the estuaries of the slow-moving Temash and Sarstoon rivers, lined by the tallest **mangrove forest** in Belize, form **Sarstoon-Temash National Park**, adjoining protected land in Guatemala.

Inland from the coast and the Southern Highway, the Maya Mountains remain unpenetrated by roads, forming a solid barrier to land travel except on foot or horseback. Successive Belize governments, showing supreme foresight, have placed practically the entire mountain massif under some form of legal protection, whether as national park, nature reserve, wildlife sanctuary or forest reserve. The most accessible area of this rainforest, though still little visited by tourists, is **Cockscomb Basin Wildlife Sanctuary**, designed to protect a sizeable jaguar population and a perfect base for exploring the forest. You'll come across plenty of jaguar tracks here, but don't count on seeing what left them. The sanctuary is also the starting point of the **Victoria Peak Trail**, an arduous but very rewarding trek to the summit of the second-highest mountain in Belize.

Population density in the south of Belize is low, with most of the towns and villages located on the coast. **Dangriga**, the largest settlement, is the headquarters of the **Garifuna** people – descended from Carib Indians and shipwrecked African slaves (see box, p.246) – and allows access to a number of idyllic cayes, sitting right on top of the barrier reef, and the **South Water Caye Marine Reserve**. The villages of **Gales Point**, north of Dangriga, and **Hopkins** and **Sittee River**, on the coast to the south, are worth visiting to experience the tranquil way of life practised there. Further south along the Southern Highway, the **Placencia peninsula** has become the focus of coastal tourism in southern Belize. From here you can visit **Laughing Bird Caye National Park** and the unique **Gladden Spit and Silk Cayes Marine Reserve**, established specifically to protect **whale sharks** – the largest fish in the world. The highway reaches its terminus in **Punta Gorda**, from where you can head south to Guatemala, visit **ancient Maya sites** and modern **Maya villages** in the southern foothills, or embark on the adventurous hike along the **Maya Mountain Divide Trail**.

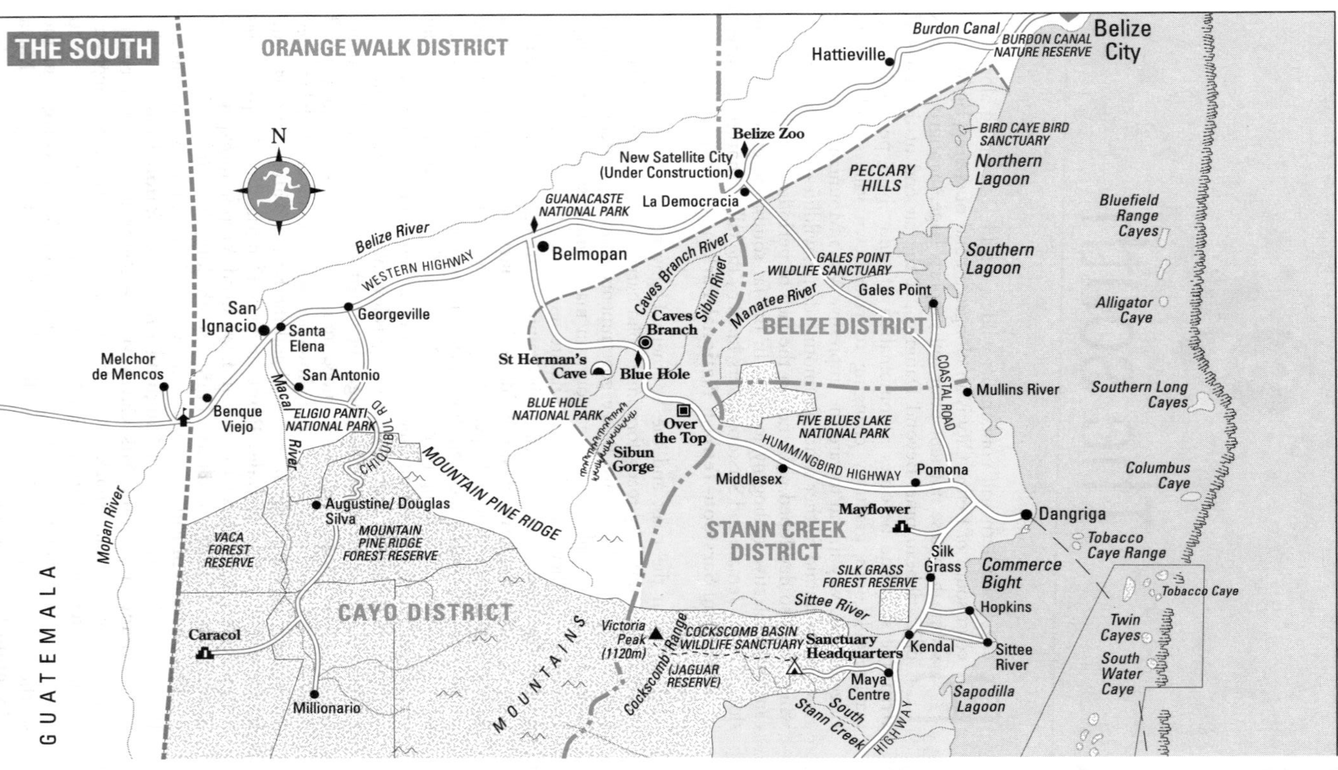
THE SOUTH
ORANGE WALK DISTRICT
Belize City
Burdon Canal
BURDON CANAL NATURE RESERVE
Hattieville
Belize Zoo
New Satellite City (Under Construction)
La Democracia
GUANACASTE NATIONAL PARK
Belmopan
Belize River
WESTERN HIGHWAY
San Ignacio
Santa Elena
Georgeville
Melchor de Mencos
Benque Viejo
San Antonio
Macal River
ELIGIO PANTI NATIONAL PARK
CHIQUIBUL RD
MOUNTAIN PINE RIDGE
Augustine/ Douglas Silva
MOUNTAIN PINE RIDGE FOREST RESERVE
VACA FOREST RESERVE
Mopan River
GUATEMALA
Caracol
CAYO DISTRICT
Millionario
MOUNTAINS
Flores & Tikal
N
St Herman's Cave
Caves Branch
Blue Hole
BLUE HOLE NATIONAL PARK
Over the Top
Sibun Gorge
Caves Branch River
Sibun River
Manatee River
GALES POINT WILDLIFE SANCTUARY
Gales Point
BELIZE DISTRICT
PECCARY HILLS
BIRD CAYE BIRD SANCTUARY
Northern Lagoon
Southern Lagoon
Bluefield Range Cayes
Alligator Caye
Southern Long Cayes
Mullins River
COASTAL ROAD
FIVE BLUES LAKE NATIONAL PARK
HUMMINGBIRD HIGHWAY
Middlesex
Pomona
Columbus Caye
Dangriga
Mayflower
STANN CREEK DISTRICT
Tobacco Caye Range
Tobacco Caye
Silk Grass
Commerce Bight
SILK GRASS FOREST RESERVE
Sittee River
Hopkins
Twin Cayes
South Water Caye
Victoria Peak (1120m)
COCKSCOMB BASIN WILDLIFE SANCTUARY
(JAGUAR RESERVE)
Cockscomb Range
Sanctuary Headquarters
Kendal
Sittee River
Maya Centre
South Stann Creek
HIGHWAY
Sapodilla Lagoon
Glover's Reef (see inset) via Dangriga (50km)

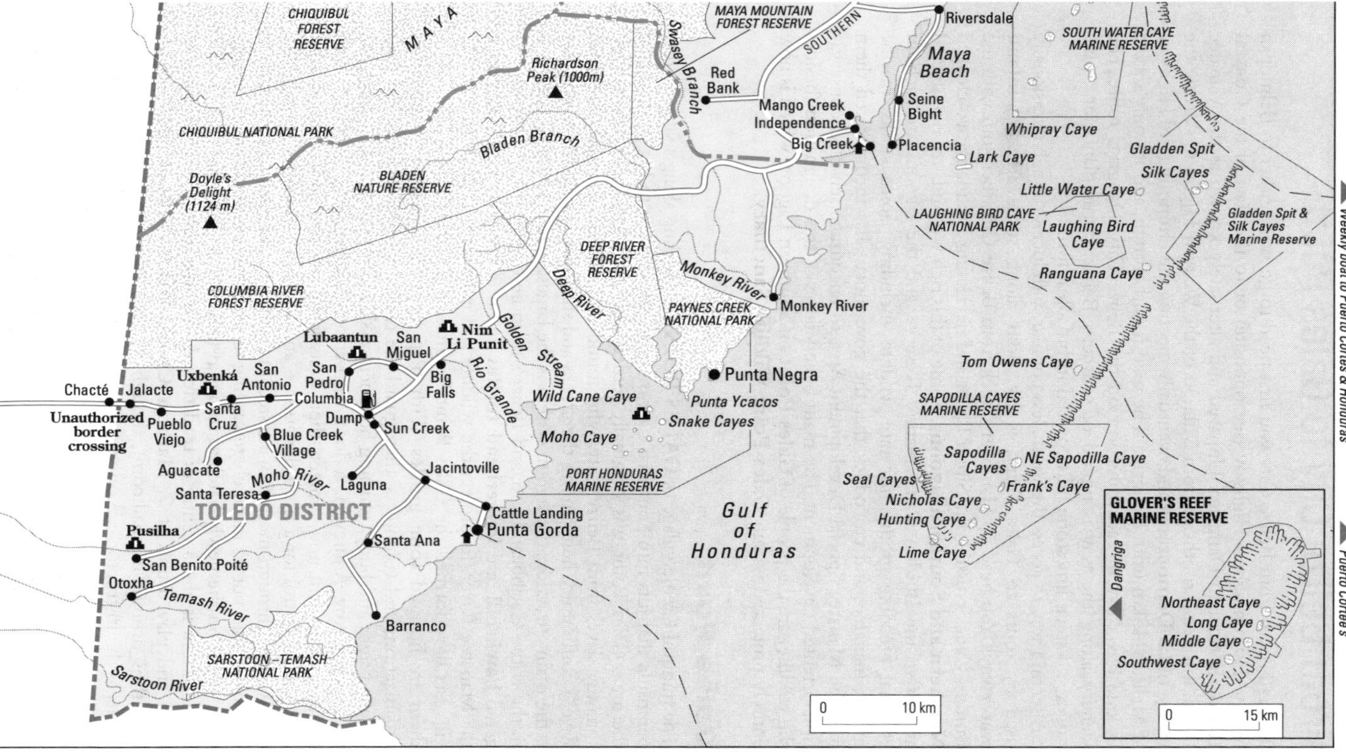

CHIQUIBUL FOREST RESERVE
MAYA
MAYA MOUNTAIN FOREST RESERVE
SOUTHERN
Riversdale
SOUTH WATER CAYE MARINE RESERVE
Richardson Peak (1000m)
Swasey Branch
Red Bank
Maya Beach
Seine Bight
Mango Creek
Independence
Big Creek
Placencia
Whipray Caye
CHIQUIBUL NATIONAL PARK
Bladen Branch
Lark Caye
Gladden Spit
Silk Cayes
Doyle's Delight (1124 m)
BLADEN NATURE RESERVE
Little Water Caye
LAUGHING BIRD CAYE NATIONAL PARK
Laughing Bird Caye
Gladden Spit & Silk Cayes Marine Reserve
Weekly boat to Puerto Cortés & Honduras
DEEP RIVER FOREST RESERVE
Deep River
Monkey River
Ranguana Caye
COLUMBIA RIVER FOREST RESERVE
PAYNES CREEK NATIONAL PARK
Monkey River
San Luis & Poptún
Lubaantun
San Miguel
Nim Li Punit
Golden Stream
Tom Owens Caye
Punta Negra
Chacté
Jalacte
Uxbenká
San Antonio
San Pedro Columbia
Big Falls
Rio Grande
Wild Cane Caye
Punta Ycacos
SAPODILLA CAYES MARINE RESERVE
Unauthorized border crossing
Pueblo Viejo
Santa Cruz
Dump
Sun Creek
Snake Cayes
Blue Creek Village
Moho Caye
Sapodilla Cayes
NE Sapodilla Caye
Aguacate
Moho River
Laguna
Jacintoville
PORT HONDURAS MARINE RESERVE
Seal Cayes
Frank's Caye
Santa Teresa
TOLEDO DISTRICT
Cattle Landing
Gulf of Honduras
Nicholas Caye
GLOVER'S REEF MARINE RESERVE
Pusilha
Punta Gorda
Hunting Caye
Santa Ana
Lime Caye
Puerto Cortee's
San Benito Poité
Dangriga
Otoxha
Temash River
Northeast Caye
Long Caye
Barranco
Middle Caye
Southwest Caye
SARSTOON–TEMASH NATIONAL PARK
Sarstoon River
0 10 km
0 15 km
Guatemala (Puerto Barrios & Livingston)

From Belize City to Gales Point

To head south from Belize City you first need to go west, either to Belmopan for the Hummingbird Highway (see opposite) or to the start of the **Coastal Road** shortcut to Dangriga. Unpaved and alternately known as the Manatee Road, this heads southeast from Mile 30 of the Western Highway, skirting the village of **La Democracia** and eventually meeting the Hummingbird Highway at Melinda, 15km from Dangriga. The road is fairly rough, and it's only served by one bus a day in each direction on the Belize City–Dangriga route. The scenery along the way is typical of southern Belize: citrus plantations, pine ridges and steep limestone hills covered in broadleaf forest.

A second way to access the south, less popular with locals though occasionally used by tours to Gales Point, is **by boat** along some amazing **inland waterways**. You head up Haulover Creek from Belize City, then join with the Burdon Canal, crossing the Sibun River and navigating the mangrove-cloaked **Northern and Southern lagoons**. Some of this rich wetland area is protected as part of the Burdon Canal Nature Reserve, and the lagoons are such an essential breeding ground for rare wildlife, including jabiru storks, marine turtles, manatees and crocodiles, that the government has incorporated them into the Manatee Special Development Area to encourage sensitive, conservation-oriented development. The main beneficiaries of this designation (besides the wildlife) are the people of **Gales Point** on Southern Lagoon, which is now entirely protected within **Gales Point Wildlife Sanctuary**.

Gales Point

The tranquil Creole village of **GALES POINT**, straggling along a very narrow peninsula that juts into Southern Lagoon, is the ideal place to begin exploring the area. Gales Point was originally settled over two hundred years ago by runaway slaves from Belize City, who founded a maroon (meaning "escaped slave") community here among the creeks and shallow lagoons. Today, **wildlife** is the main attraction: the lagoon system is the largest manatee breeding ground in the entire Caribbean basin, and Belize's main nesting beaches of the endangered **hawksbill** and **loggerhead turtles** lie on either side of the mouth of the Manatee River. To protect the wildlife and encourage tourists to visit, the villagers have formed the Gales Point Progressive Cooperative, and several of them are licensed **tour guides**. With help from international conservation organizations and volunteers, they guard the turtles' nesting beaches and have installed signs and buoys warning boatmen to slow down to avoid harming the manatees. Leroy Andrewin, a local conservation hero who grew up here hunting turtles but now protects their nests from predators, will take you out on his night patrol for a small donation – and you can **volunteer** for a longer stay. Wading through mosquito-infested mangroves in search of turtles can be uncomfortable, but it's infinitely rewarding to see adult females laying their eggs or to cheer on the newly hatched babies as they race for the sea.

Gales Point is also a centre of **traditional drum-making**. You can learn to make and play drums at **Maroon Creole Drum School** (Ⓣ603-6051, Ⓔmethos_drums@hotmail.com), though it's best to make advance arrangements as the instructors are often out performing. Making a drum costs around Bz$250, including materials and instruction, and it's Bz$16 per hour to learn to play (group rates available). You'll also absorb much about local history, culture and crafts, all while sipping home-produced cashew or berry wine in the evenings. With your newly acquired skills, you may be able to participate in a

sambai, a fertility dance ritual that's one of the most significant gatherings in Creole culture. The drummers here, playing in a circle around a fire, are supremely talented, and the dancers take turns interpreting their rhythms.

Practicalities

Gales Point is directly served by two NTSL (the ones going through Gales Point are still marked "Southern Transport") **buses** weekly in each direction on the Coastal Road, leaving Belize City at 5pm and Dangriga at 5am on Mondays and Fridays. Other traffic passes the junction, 4km from the village; it's a pleasant walk into town if you're not carrying much luggage, and hitching in is relatively easy.

Walking along the village's only street, you'll see several signs pointing to houses offering simple bed-and-breakfast **accommodation** (❷–❸). Ionie Samuels, who runs Martha's Store, has a room and can arrange other meals and tours; call the community telephone on Ⓣ209-8031 for more possibilities. *Gentle's Cool Spot*, a small bar and restaurant where the buses turn around, also has a few clean, basic rooms in a wooden house with fan, electric light and shared bath (❷), and a room with private bath (❸). You can **camp** at *Metho's Coconut Camping* (Bz$10 per person), in a sandy spot north of the village centre. The most luxurious accommodation is the *Manatee Lodge* (Ⓣ220-8040, in the US Ⓣ1-877/462-6283, Ⓦwww.manateelodge.com; ❼), a white-painted, colonial-style building with green trim set amidst lush lawns and coconut trees at the tip of the peninsula. The rooms (all nonsmoking) are spacious and comfortable, and the meals are superb. On the upper floor, a deck with hammocks is an ideal spot to take in a sunrise or sunset over the lagoon; indoors, the book and video library has a good collection of Belizean topics, and guests can use the **Internet** for free. Explore the lagoon on canoes and small sailing boats (free for guests; non-guests can rent by the day, Bz$20 for a canoe and Bz$40 for a sailing boat), or call ahead to arrange a boat trip along the inland waterways from Belize City (Bz$350, 1–4 people; Bz$35 per extra person) or Dangriga (Bz$200, 1–4 people; Bz$20 per extra person).

The best **restaurant** in the village is at *Manatee Lodge*, for which you'll need reservations if you're not a guest – well worth it for the delicious coconut crisps served here. Otherwise, there's Creole cuisine at *Gentle's Cool Spot*, which also makes its own wine, or pre-arranged meals with a local family. Amazingly, you can get a **cappuccino** or a latte at the *Sugar Snack Café and Gifts*, which also serves cakes and other sweets.

Gales Point is at the centre of a wildlife sanctuary, and renting a **dory** (a traditional dugout canoe) or taking a boat tour is a great way to experience the waterways; rent either from someone in the village (about Bz$25/day) or from *Manatee Lodge*. Raymond Gentle, owner of the *Cool Spot*, leads trips in his large, motorized dory to **Ben Lomond's Cave**, on the north shore of the lagoon, and several other guides in the village will take you fishing or hiking; Delroy Andrewin offers **yoga lessons** for Bz$30 per hour.

The Hummingbird Highway

Heading southeast from Belmopan through hills and lush forest, with the green, eastern slopes of the **Maya Mountains** rising to the right, the **Hummingbird Highway** offers the most scenic drive in Belize. For years much of this forest lay untouched, but here and there Salvadoran or Guatemalan refugees have hacked down a swath of jungle to plant maize and beans, and you're rarely out of sight of citrus plantations. About 19km out of Belmopan the road crosses the **Caves Branch River**, a tributary of the Sibun whose valley holds some of Belize's finest **caves**, as well as **Blue Hole National Park**, a wildlife-rich zone with an intriguing natural landmark. Further on, just past the highest point on the road, are **Five Blues Lake National Park** and the start of the **Indian Creek Trail**, beyond which the highway follows the Stann Creek valley all the way to Dangriga.

Blue Hole National Park

Blue Hole National Park (BHNP), established in 1986 and managed by the Belize Audubon Society (BAS), is named for its most famous feature: the **Blue Hole** (often referred to as the "Inland Blue Hole", to distinguish it from the one on Lighthouse Reef), a short, ten-metre-wide stretch of underground river revealed by a collapsed karst cavern, or *cenote* in Maya. The river continues to flow on the surface for about 50m beyond the "hole" before disappearing beneath another rock face. Its cool, fresh, turquoise waters, surrounded by dense forest and overhung with vines, mosses and ferns, are perfect for a refreshing dip. Despite the park's small size (only 2.5 square kilometres, though it's adjacent to other protected areas), it boasts an abundance of wildlife. Three of the five species of **cats** found in Belize – the jaguar, ocelot and jaguarundi – have been sighted within park boundaries. Black howler monkeys are occasionally heard, and mammals seen here include tapir, collared and white-lipped peccaries, tamandua (anteaters), gibnut, coatimundi, opossum, deer, kinkajou and many species of bats. It's also home to more than 175 species of birds, including the slaty-breasted tinamou, black hawk-eagle, crested guan, lovely cotinga, nightingale wren and red-legged honeycreeper. The **Hummingbird Loop**, a 1.5-kilometre, self-guided trail undulating through the forest, provides a worthwhile glimpse of the park – but to enjoy it comfortably you'll need insect repellent.

St Herman's Cave and Crystal Cave

Just beyond the Caves Branch River, by the roadside on the right, is **St Herman's Cave** (daily 8am–4pm; Bz$8, includes the Blue Hole), one of the most accessible caves in Belize. Any bus between Belmopan and Dangriga will drop you at the cave or the Blue Hole, making this an easy day-trip (the rangers know the times of onward buses), but to really experience the excitement of caving in Belize you need to stay nearby, preferably at *Caves Branch Jungle Lodge* (see opposite).

You pay the entrance fee at the National Park **visitor centre**, which has good displays on the plant, bird and animal life found here – particularly bats – then follow the marked trail for ten minutes to the cave entrance, beneath a dripping rock face. You'll need a torch to descend the steps from the opening, originally cut by the Maya. Inside, you scramble over rocks and splash through the river for about twenty minutes, admiring the strange formations, before the cave appears to end. To continue beyond, and emerge from another opening, you need to go on a **tour**; one of the best is organized by Marcos Cucul of Maya Guide Adventures (see p.169), great for any sort of caving, climbing or jungle survival trip, including a tour of the amazing **Crystal Cave**, also in the park (US$80 includes entrance fee, all equipment and lunch). Behind the cave – which sports some crystal formations and intriguing Maya artifacts – an **interpretive trail** leads past some unusually shaped rocks, yet more caves and a spectacular observation platform, arriving after 4km at a **campsite**. For more information on these caves and others nearby, contact the visitor centre (which also has information on nearby **accommodation**) or call BAS at ⓣ223-5004.

Caves Branch Jungle Lodge

The best place to stay near the Blue Hole (and indeed along the whole Hummingbird Highway) is **Caves Branch Jungle Lodge**, at Mile 41.5 (ⓣ822-2800, ⓦwww.cavesbranch.com; ❼–❾). It's located 1.5km beyond St Herman's Cave and a few hundred metres before the Blue Hole, 1km in from the highway along a level track, easily accessible and signposted; all passing buses will stop at the entrance.

The lodge is set in a huge area of superb, high canopy forest on the banks of the beautiful **Caves Branch River**, and offers a range of comfortable, rustic **accommodation** to suit all budgets. The highlights are the luxurious treehouse suites, elevated twenty feet off the ground with a spectacular view of the river (❾), spacious jungle suites with a sitting room and wicker furniture (❾), and the bungalows with tiled roofs and wraparound verandas (❽), all of which have private hot showers, though only the treehouses have electricity. The screened cabañas on stilts, with a ceiling fan (❼), are slightly less expensive, but the real bargains are the screened **bunkhouse** (Bz$30 per person) and the **campsite** with hammock space (Bz$10 per person), both with clean showers and flush toilets; there's no service charge and you can save money by booking a complete package. Delicious and filling buffet-style meals are served in a simple dining room above the river, and cold beer is always available. Try to plan at least two nights here; even if you don't take any of the trips on offer, one day just won't seem long enough, and the birding is superb.

Caves Branch is run by Canadian Ian Anderson, who has recruited and trained some of the most experienced guides in the country to lead amazing wildlife treks, ruin tours, overnights and survival courses through the area's most spectacular caves and along sparkling rivers (starting at about US$90 per person, including lunch and equipment). All the caves contain **Maya artifacts**, furnishing abundant evidence of the Classic-period ceremonies that were held in them. Some caves are dry, and you must take great care not to touch the glittering, crystal formations as you clamber over rocks and around stalagmites. You can float on inner tubes 10km down a subterranean river, your headlamp piercing the intense darkness, or head several kilometres upstream along another underground river and climb stupendous waterfalls that thunder into caverns. Other (perhaps more challenging) activities include **rappelling** – descending the sheer wall of a sinkhole through forest canopy to the enormous Actun Loch Tunich cave entrance, over 90m below – and **rock-climbing**, with walls graded according to your level of experience. All equipment is provided (climbing shoes can be rented), and participants on all expeditions need good hiking boots; the lodge has a good selection if you need to borrow a pair.

Caves Branch also runs the *Sibun Adventure Lodge* (ⓣ822-2800, ⓦwww.adventuresinbelize.com; groups only, US$95 per person per night), 6km further along the highway, in a lovely forest-and-garden location overlooking the Sibun River. The thatched, three-storey lodge is aimed mainly at student groups, with comfortable dorm accommodation and hot showers on the ground floor and classrooms with fantastic views above. It's an ideal place to study tropical ecology, and the private bungalows will provide even more comfortable accommodation for adult guests. **Kayak trips** on both the white-water of the upper Sibun and the calmer lower section are available.

Five Blues Lake National Park

Beyond the Blue Hole, the Hummingbird Highway undulates smoothly through the increasingly hilly landscape, eventually mounting a low pass. This is the highest point on the road, and the downhill slope is appropriately, if unimaginatively, called Over the Top. On the way down, the road cuts through St Margaret's Village, where a women's cooperative arranges **bed-and-breakfast** accommodation in private houses (❸); call the community phone (Ⓣ809-2005), which rings at the nearby *Over the Top Restaurant*, a good rest stop on the trip south.

Across from the restaurant, at Mile 32, is the turnoff to **Five Blues Lake National Park** (Ⓦwww.5blueslake.org), seventeen square kilometres of luxuriantly forested karst scenery, centred on what was until very recently a beautiful lake. Since the summer of 2006, the lake, named for its constantly changing colours, has lost approximately 75 percent of its water, and consequently much of its appeal for visitors. Scientists, however, are intrigued by the phenomenon and have so far determined that the same blockage that created the lake may have dissolved, allowing the water to exit through the limestone underground. There are no rangers at the park, and because of the changing landscape, it's advised to visit with a guide; some (see p.169) may be willing to lead you along the **Indian Creek Trail**, co-managed by the St Margaret's and La Democracia communities, which ends here after snaking its way over 25 kilometres from Monkey Bay Wildlife Sanctuary (see p.164). The trail winds through dense riparian forest, perfect for observing rare flora and fauna, jungle-draped cave systems and Maya artifacts dating back hundreds of years.

Continuing south on the Hummingbird Highway, 3km from Over the Top, there's more **accommodation** at *Palacio's Mountain Retreat*, Mile 31 (buses stop right outside; Ⓣ822-3683 or 600-2248, Ⓦwww.palaciosretreat.com; ❺, camping Bz$20 per person). The four simple cabañas with private hot shower and electricity overlook a beautiful river lined with sandy beaches and boulders; it's great for swimming, and you can hike upstream to a ten-metre jungle waterfall. The family that runs the place is very proud of its Garifuna heritage, and guests can enjoy the restaurant's Garifuna food and learn about other customs.

On towards Dangriga

Palacio's Mountain Retreat marks the start of the **Stann Creek valley**, the centre of the Belizean citrus fruit industry. Bananas were the first crop to be grown here, and by 1891 half a million stems were being exported through Stann Creek (now Dangriga) every year. However, this banana boom came to an abrupt end in 1906, when disease destroyed the crop, and afterwards the government set out to foster the growth of **citrus fruits**. Between 1908 and 1937 the valley was even served by a small railway – many of the highway bridges were originally rail bridges – and by 1945 the citrus industry was well established.

Today, citrus comprises a major part of the country's agricultural exports and, despite widely fluctuating prices, is heralded as one of the nation's great success stories – although for the largely Guatemalan labour force, housed in rows of scruffy huts, conditions are little better than on the oppressive coffee *fincas* at home. The presence of tropical parasites, such as the leaf-cutter ant, has forced the planters to use powerful insecticides, including DDT.

Further along, at Mile 25, signs appear for **Billy Barquedier National Park**, a 1500-acre expanse whose highlight is a 100-metre hike up to a refreshing waterfall. Though there are two entrances to the park, be sure to use the northern one, the first you'll pass on the way to Dangriga – otherwise your walk will be much longer. Currently the park is officially open only on weekends (Bz$8), but you may be able to arrange a guided tour on a weekday by calling the Stedfast village community phone (☎509-2011) and asking for a ranger.

The last stretch of the Hummingbird Highway is flat and relatively uninteresting. The petrol station ten kilometres before Dangriga is a useful place to refuel without heading into town; just beyond this is the junction with the now-paved **Southern Highway**, heading to Punta Gorda.

Dangriga and around

DANGRIGA, formerly called Stann Creek, is the capital of Stann Creek District and the largest town in southern Belize. It's also the cultural centre of the **Garifuna**, a people of mixed indigenous Caribbean and African descent, who make up about eleven percent of the country's population. Since the early 1980s Garifuna culture has undergone a tremendous revival; as a part of this movement the town was renamed Dangriga, a Garifuna word meaning "sweet (or standing) waters", in reference to the North Stann Creek flowing through the town centre.

Dangriga is home to some of the country's most popular **artists**, some of whom have small galleries here. Fine **crafts** – distinctive brown-and-white basketware, woven palm-leaf hats and dolls in Garifuna costume – are easy to find. The large, bronze **"Drums of Our Fathers" monument**, on the roundabout at the southern entrance to town, is local Nigerian artist Stephen Okeke's ode to the centrality of **drumming** in Garifuna culture.

This musical tradition plays an important role in local celebrations, the most important of which is **Garifuna Settlement Day**, on November 19, when the town erupts into wild celebration, packed solid with expatriate Dangrigans returning to their roots. The party begins the evening before, and the drumming and punta dancing (see p.362) go on all night long. In the morning there's a re-enactment of the Garifuna's original arrival from Honduras, with people landing on the beach in dugout canoes decorated with palm leaves. Similar exuberance goes into Christmas and New Year, when you might see the *wanaragu* or *Jonkunu* (John Canoe) dances, where **masked and costumed performers** represent a cast of historical archetypes, including eighteenth-century naval officers and Amerindian tribal chiefs.

During quieter times the atmosphere is enjoyably laid-back, though there's little to do during the day and not much nightlife outside weekends. As the south of the country becomes more accessible, however, Dangriga is increasingly useful as a base for visiting south-central Belize, the cayes offshore and the mountains, Maya ruins and Jaguar Reserve inland.

Arrival, orientation and information

In addition to **buses** heading just for Dangriga, all services between Belize City and Punta Gorda call here (see p.86 for details on transport from Belize City). In general, there should be either a James or NTSL bus passing by every hour or so from 7am to 6pm. Buses enter Dangriga at the southern end of town and stop at the monument by the petrol station; those continuing to Hopkins leave from the dock near the *Riverside Restaurant* in the town centre. Dangriga's **airstrip**, served by at least eight daily flights in each direction on the Belize City–Punta Gorda run, is by the shore, just north of the *Pelican Beach Resort*; you'll need a taxi (at least Bz$6) into town.

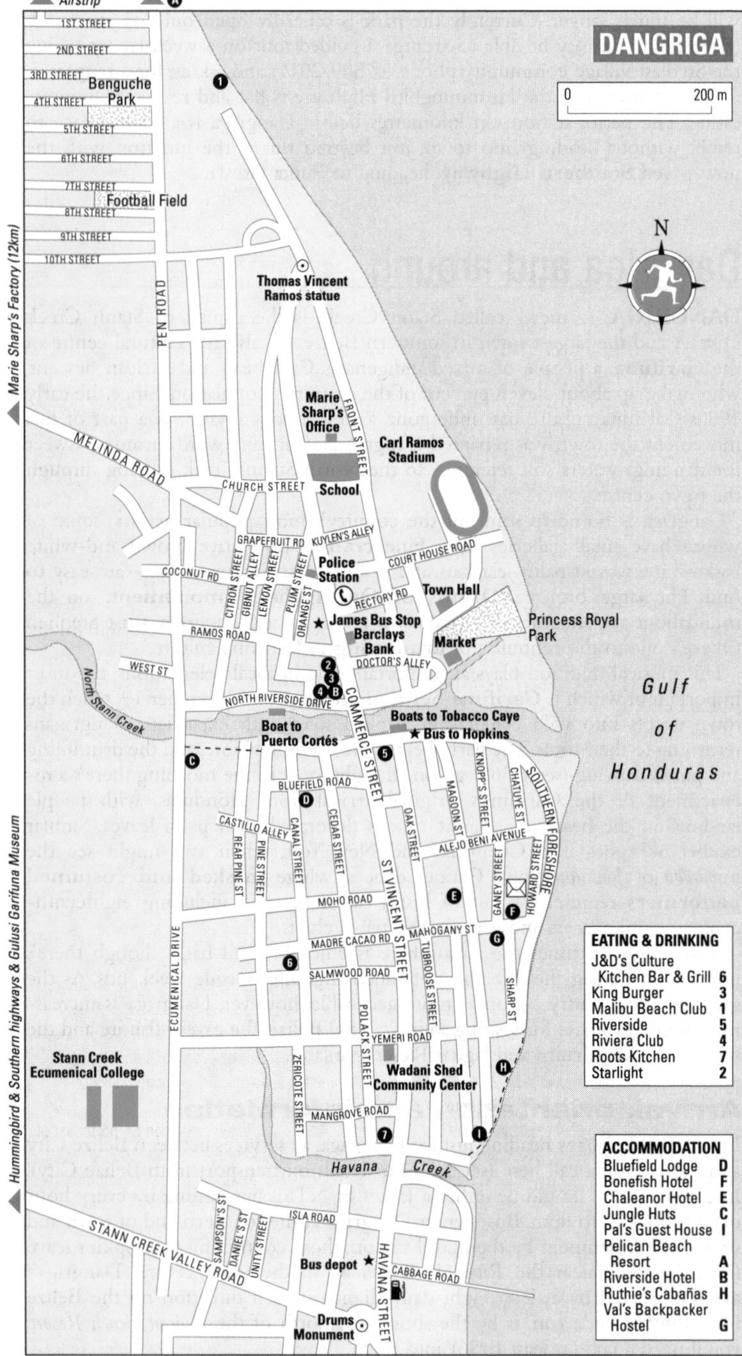

DANGRIGA
0
200 m
N
Airstrip
A
Marie Sharp's Factory (12km)
Hummingbird & Southern highways & Gulusi Garifuna Museum
1ST STREET
2ND STREET
3RD STREET
4TH STREET
5TH STREET
6TH STREET
7TH STREET
8TH STREET
9TH STREET
10TH STREET
Benguche Park
Football Field
PEN ROAD
Thomas Vincent Ramos statue
Marie Sharp's Office
FRONT STREET
Carl Ramos Stadium
MELINDA ROAD
CHURCH STREET
School
KUYLEN'S ALLEY
GRAPEFRUIT RD
COURT HOUSE ROAD
COCONUT RD
CITRON STREET
GIBNUT ALLEY
LEMON STREET
PLUM STREET
ORANGE ST
Police Station
RECTORY RD
Town Hall
James Bus Stop
Barclays Bank
Princess Royal Park
RAMOS ROAD
Market
DOCTOR'S ALLEY
WEST ST
North Stann Creek
NORTH RIVERSIDE DRIVE
COMMERCE STREET
Gulf of Honduras
Boats to Tobacco Caye
Bus to Hopkins
Boat to Puerto Cortés
BLUEFIELD ROAD
CASTILLO ALLEY
REAR PINE ST
PINE STREET
CANAL STREET
CEDAR STREET
OAK STREET
MAGOON ST
KNOPP'S STREET
CHATUYE ST
SOUTHERN FORESHORE
ALEJO BENI AVENUE
ST VINCENT STREET
GANEY STREET
HOWARD STREET
MOHO ROAD
MAHOGANY ST
MADRE CACAO RD
SALMWOOD ROAD
TUBROOSE STREET
SHARP ST
ECUMENICAL DRIVE
POLACK STREET
YEMERI ROAD
Stann Creek Ecumenical College
Wadani Shed Community Center
ZERICOTE STREET
MANGROVE ROAD
Havana Creek
SAMPSON'S ST
DANIEL'S ST
UNITY STREET
ISLA ROAD
STANN CREEK VALLEY ROAD
Bus depot
HAVANA STREET
CABBAGE ROAD
Drums Monument
EATING & DRINKING
J&D's Culture Kitchen Bar & Grill 6
King Burger 3
Malibu Beach Club 1
Riverside 5
Riviera Club 4
Roots Kitchen 7
Starlight 2
ACCOMMODATION
Bluefield Lodge D
Bonefish Hotel F
Chaleanor Hotel E
Jungle Huts C
Pal's Guest House I
Pelican Beach Resort A
Riverside Hotel B
Ruthie's Cabañas H
Val's Backpacker Hostel G

At Dangriga's centre is a **road bridge** over North Stann Creek, with the main thoroughfare leading north as Commerce Street and south as St Vincent Street. Almost everything you're likely to need, including **hotels**, **restaurants**, **banks** and **transport**, is on or very near this road. There's no official tourist office, but the town hall has a visitor's **map**, which you can also download (along with up-to-date tourist information) from the city's new website (Ⓦwww.dangrigalive.bz). Most hotels, along with *Riverside Restaurant*, just south of the bridge in the centre of town, may also provide some information – especially if you need a **boat to the cayes**. The Belize Bank, on St Vincent Street just before the bridge, and First Caribbean, near the BTL office a block north of the bridge, have ATMs that accept foreign cards. The **post office** is on the corner of Mahogany and Ganey streets in the southern half of town, a block back from the sea. High-speed **Internet** access is available at *Val's Hostel* on Mahogany Street, opposite the post office, where you can also have your **laundry** done.

For **bookings and tours**, contact C&G Tours (Ⓣ522-3641, Ⓔcgtours@btl.net), with a fleet of comfortable, air-conditioned vehicles providing transport to nearby sights. If you're an experienced paddler you can rent high-quality **sea kayaks** from Island Expeditions (on Southern Foreshore, next to *Ruthie's Cabañas*; Ⓦwww.belizekayaking.com). A double kayak costs US$55/day or US$350/week, and the expedition leaders can shuttle you out to the cayes along with camping equipment and everything else you'll need for an extended outing. Just beyond the downtown area, fans of Belize's ubiquitous hot sauce can take a tour of **Marie Sharp's Factory** (Mon–Fri; Ⓣ520-2087, Ⓦwww.mariesharps-bz.com), where Marie herself will likely give you a history-filled tour. You can sample and purchase all the sauce varieties here, or you can visit the downtown office on Pier Road (Ⓣ522-2370).

Accommodation

Dangriga experienced something of a hotel-building boom a few years ago, resulting in a wider choice of places to stay; with some real bargains on offer, there's no need to settle for a cheap dive.

Bluefield Lodge 6 Bluefield Rd Ⓣ522-2742, Ⓔbluefield@btl.net. This small hotel is very clean, secure and well run – everything a budget place should be but rarely is. Extremely welcoming, with comfortable beds and bedside lights, and some rooms have private bath and TV. There's a dedicated payphone for BTL phonecards, and a quite reliable information board. ③

Bonefish Hotel 15 Mahogany St Ⓣ522-2243, Ⓔbonefishhotelbelize@yahoo.com. Good hotel with cable TV, hot water, carpets and a/c, in a quiet, seafront location. Specializes in fishing trips and is the office for *Blue Marlin Lodge* on South Water Caye (see p.251). Quoted rates include hotel tax. ⑤–⑦

Chaleanor Hotel 35 Magoon St Ⓣ522-2587, Ⓔchaleanor@btl.net. Very hospitable place with clean, spacious rooms, all with private bath and some with a/c. Next to the main hotel are some equally clean budget rooms in a wooden building, some with private bath; all are very good value. Free coffee, fruit and purified water are available in the lobby. The owner's son Elihue is a skilled guide. ⑤–⑥

Jungle Huts Lodge 4 Ecumenical Drive Ⓣ522-0185. Sixteen pleasant rooms alongside North Stann Creek with private bath and some with a/c, set around a peaceful courtyard on the quiet side of town. The owner's amiable family serves good food in the restaurant. Cabañas and units with kitchenettes are available for longer stays or groups. ③–⑤

Pal's Guest House 868 Magoon St, northeast of the Havana Creek bridge Ⓣ522-2365, Ⓦwww.palsbelize.com. Reasonably priced accommodation in two buildings: budget rooms (some with private bath and TV) are in the older part; newer beachfront rooms have private baths and TV (some with a/c). ①–④

Pelican Beach Resort On the beach, 2km north of town Ⓣ522-2044, Ⓦwww.pelicanbeachbelize.com. Dangriga's largest and most expensive hotel, with the best beachfront location, is also extremely well managed. Six standard rooms, two honeymoon suites and two economy rooms (no balconies) are in a wooden, colonial-style structure, and eight spacious sea-view rooms with large baths are in a modern, two-storey concrete building. Most rooms have TV, a/c and balconies facing the beach. It's popular with tour groups, and frequently used by scientists and conservation organizations. The hotel also offers some wonderful accommodation on South Water Caye (see p.250); contact the office here for details. Room and package prices do come down out of season and it's worth asking for a discount. The restaurant is the best in Dangriga and features a large marine aquarium. 8–9

Riverside Hotel Commerce St, right beside the bridge ⓣ522-2168. Clean rooms with shared bath in a convenient location, with a view over the river. Prices are per person, so it's a good deal for singles. 2

Ruthie's Cabañas 31 Southern Foreshore ⓣ502-3184. Two bargain, thatched cabañas right on the sand, with private bath and porch

A Garifuna history

The **Garifuna** (or Garinagu) trace their history back to the island of **St Vincent**, one of the Windward Islands in the eastern Caribbean. At the time of Columbus's landing in the Americas, the islands of the Lesser Antilles had recently been settled by people from the South American mainland, who subdued the previous inhabitants, the Arawaks. These new arrivals called themselves Kalipuna or Kwaib, from which the names Garifuna, meaning cassava-eating people, and Carib probably evolved. When Europeans came ashore here, the people they encountered were descendants of Carib men and Arawak women; a few thousand people who trace their heritage to the original Caribs still live in Dominica and St Vincent.

In the early seventeenth century, Britain, France and the Netherlands vied for control of the islands, fighting each other and the Caribs. The admixture of African blood came in 1635 when two Spanish ships, carrying **slaves** from Nigeria to Spanish colonies in America, were wrecked off St Vincent and the survivors took refuge on the island. The Caribs and Africans initially clashed with each other, but the former had already been weakened by war and disease, and the foothold the Africans gained eventually led to the rise of the **Black Caribs** or Garifuna. Though the British nominally controlled St Vincent for most of the seventeenth and eighteenth centuries, for all practical purposes it belonged to the Garifuna.

In the mid-1700s, however, the British attempted to gain full control of St Vincent, but were driven off by the Caribs, with French assistance. Another attempt twenty years later was more successful, and in 1783 the British imposed a treaty on the Garifuna, granting themselves ownership of over half the island. The treaty was rejected, however, and the Garifuna continued to defy British rule through frequent uprisings, consistently supported by the French. The last serious attempt by the Garifuna to establish their independence was initiated in 1795, a drawn-out battle that inflicted horrendous casualties upon both sides. After a year of bitter fighting and the loss of their leader, Chief Joseph Chatoyer, the Garifuna (along with the French) surrendered on June 10, 1796.

Since the British colonial authorities could not countenance free blacks living amongst slave-owning European settlers, they decided to **deport** the Garifuna, whom they hunted down, destroying their homes, uprooting their culture and causing hundreds to die through starvation and disease. The survivors of this round-up – 4300 Black Caribs and 100 Yellow Caribs, as designated by the British – were transported to the nearby island of Balliceaux; within six months over half died, many of yellow fever. In March 1797, the remaining survivors were loaded aboard ships and sent to **Roatán**, one of the Bay Islands off the coast of Honduras. The Spanish commandeered one of the ships and redirected it to the mainland colony of Trujillo, in present-day Honduras. Barely two thousand Garifuna lived to see Roatán, where the British promptly abandoned them.

Perhaps in response to pleas for help from the Garifuna, who continued to die on Roatán, the Spanish *comandante* of Trujillo arrived and took possession of the island, with hammocks, and some even cheaper rooms, one with bunkbeds, in a concrete building. Ruthie cooks delicious meals by arrangement. ❸–❹

Val's Backpacker Hostel 1 Sharp St, corner of Mahogany St ⓣ502-3324, ⓔvalsbelize@yahoo.com. A one-stop shop for tourists, especially those on a budget. Bunkbeds (Bz$15) and private rooms available at bargain rates, and same-day laundry service 7.30am–7.30pm. The Internet café has several computers, and you can enjoy ice cream or Val's delicious banana bread while you browse. ❶–❸

Eating

Despite Dangriga's central position in Garifuna culture, there are few restaurants here specializing in Garifuna food; only a couple occasionally serve such dishes,

shipping the survivors to his jurisdiction to augment his labour force. The Spanish hadn't managed to succeed in agriculture, and the introduction of the very proficient Garifuna benefited the colony considerably. Boys and men were conscripted into the army and proved to be very effective soldiers and mercenaries. As their renown spread, they were brought to other areas along the coast, and in 1802, 150 arrived in Stann Creek and Punta Gorda to be woodcutters. The understanding they gained of the rivers and coastline made them expert **smugglers**, able to evade Spanish enforcement that forbade trade with the British in Belize.

In spite of this economic relationship with the British, the Garifuna's incursion into Belize did not please its colonizers, and in 1811 Superintendent Barrow ordered their expulsion – to little effect. The Garifuna were already established in Stann Creek when European settlers arrived there in 1823, and they continued to flow in, finding work in clearing land. Among the Europeans were many **Methodist missionaries**, who found the Garifuna's mix of Catholicism, ancestor worship and polygamy outrageous; their attempts to completely Christianize the Garifuna, however, were met with little success. The largest single Garifuna migration to Belize took place in 1832, when, under the leadership of Alejo Benji, several hundred fled Honduras (by then part of the Central American Republic) after supporting the losing side of a planned overthrow of the Republic's government. This arrival is still celebrated as **Garifuna Settlement Day**, though many Garifuna had come before and continued to do so after.

By the start of the **twentieth century**, Stann Creek (later to be called Dangriga) was a stable Garifuna community, with its women employed in bagging and stacking cohune nuts and men working in agriculture. As in the previous century, however, the Garifuna continued to travel widely in search of work. They initially confined themselves to Central America (where they can still be found all along the Caribbean coast from Belize to Nicaragua), but in World War II Garifuna men joined the crews of both British and US merchant ships. Since then, trips abroad have become an important part of the local economy, and there are small Garifuna communities in New York, New Orleans, Los Angeles and even London.

Today, Belize has a National Garifuna Council, whose scholars are refining a written language; the council has already published *The People's Garifuna Dictionary* as well as school textbooks. *The First Primer on a People Called Garifuna*, by Myrtle Palacio, is in English and available throughout the country. In Dangriga, make sure to visit the **Gulusi Garifuna Museum**, in Chuluhadiwa Park on Stann Creek Valley Road (Bz$10; ⓣ502-0639), for fascinating exhibits on Garifuna culture and history, including historical pictures and documents, clothing, food and music. There's also an exhibit on Thomas Vincent Ramos, the Garifuna leader who established the first Garifuna Settlement Day in 1941.

△ Fisherman in Dangriga

and you'll probably find the cuisine more available in Hopkins (see p.252). If you do happen upon them, **Garifuna dishes** frequently feature fish and vegetables such as yam, plantain, okra and cassava, often served in *sere*, a rich, thick, coconut-milk sauce similar in consistency to a chowder. This is typically accompanied by rice, but more reliably by the Garifuna staple of thin, crispy **cassava bread**, baked on a metal sheet over an open fire. Try your luck at the restaurant at *Pelican Beach* (see p.245), the best in town, where the staff is skilled at preparing all of Belize's cultural specialities. If Chinese food is more to your liking, head to *Starlight*, just north of *King Burger*.

For picnic supplies, you could try the **market** on the north bank of the creek, near the seashore, but it's very small; for other groceries, it's best to head for the supermarket just south of the bridge.

J&D's Culture Kitchen Canal St at Madre Cacao Rd. Off the beaten path, serving daily specials and hearty, home-style portions of traditional Creole and Garifuna dishes at good prices (around Bz$10). Mon–Sat 8am–9pm.

King Burger Commerce St, north of the creek. Serves good rice, chicken, burgers, fish, fruit juices and conch soup, a Belizean delicacy. Mon–Sat 7am–3pm & 6–10pm.

Riverside Restaurant South bank of the creek. Tasty Creole and Garifuna food for Bz$10–20, including great breakfasts and a daily special. Also a good place for information on sights and activities in the area. Open 7am–9pm.

Roots Kitchen Just north of Havana Creek. One of the few reliable and affordable (Bz$10–15) places to find traditional Garifuna dishes like *hudut* (mashed, half-ripe plantain with fish) and *bundiga* (savoury dish made from fish and banana). Open 6am–9pm.

Drinking and nightlife

There's no shortage of **bars** in Dangriga, though some, particularly those calling themselves clubs, like *Kennedy Club*, *Culture Club* and *Harlem Club*, are rather dubious. Slightly more reputable is *Riviera Club*, right in the centre of town, with a very local scene and popular karaoke nights. The best nightspots are *The*

Beach Place and *Malibu Beach Club*, just before *Pelican Beach Resort*, north of the centre. Both are good places to mix with locals and dance on the sand, though they're generally open only on weekends.

Offshore from Dangriga: Tobacco Range and Columbus Reef

The **Tobacco Range** is a group of mangrove cayes just before the beautiful **Columbus** and **Tobacco reefs**, about 16km east of Dangriga. The largest caye in the range, **Man-O'-War Caye**, is a **bird sanctuary** named after the frigate (or man-o'-war) birds you'll see hanging on the breeze with outstretched wings. In the breeding season the males develop an immense, bright red balloon on their throats and the island fills with nesting birds; watching them from a boat is permitted, but you can't land on the caye. Beyond Columbus Reef, with its scattering of small cayes, including tiny **Tobacco Caye**, lies Tobacco Reef with the slightly larger **South Water Caye** at its southern end. Each caye has a number of delightful places to stay, and sunsets out here can be breathtakingly beautiful, outlining the distant Maya Mountains with a purple and orange aura.

Tobacco Caye

Tobacco Caye, ideally situated right on the reef, is the easiest to reach in the area and has the most accommodation. **Boats** leave from near the bridge in Dangriga every day, but there are no regular departures; check at the *Riverside Restaurant* in Dangriga, where you can meet the skippers. Captain Buck runs the most prompt and reliable service, though any of the caye's hotel owners will take you if they're in town, and perhaps arrange a package deal. It's a thirty-minute trip and the one-way fare is Bz$35 per person.

The cayes of Columbus Reef were originally visited by turtle fishermen; Tobacco Caye was a trading post where passing ships could pick up supplies,

Moving on from Dangriga

Returning **to Belize City** (2–3hr), NTSL **buses** (some express services) leave every hour or so from 4.30am to 7.30pm; most go via **Belmopan** (1hr 45min), though the 5am departure on Mondays and Fridays travels the Coastal Road, calling at **Gales Point**. All buses board at the Drums monument at the southern end of town.

If you're **continuing south**, bear in mind that buses to **Punta Gorda** (3hr 15min; up to fifteen daily, including expresses) don't necessarily originate here and delays are possible. The first and last buses, the only express services, leave at 7.30am and 6pm. All stop at **Independence** (under 2hr) – also known as **Mango Creek** – where you can hop on a boat to Placencia (see p.267).

There are usually four daily buses from Dangriga to **Placencia** (2hr), but departure times are constantly changing; they currently leave at 10.30am, 11.30am, 4pm and 5.15pm. Most also call at **Hopkins** (30min) and **Sittee River**. Hopkins has its own bus as well, leaving from the dock near the *Riverside Restaurant* at 10.30am and 1pm, Monday through Saturday.

Tropic Air and Maya Island Air have **flights** every couple of hours between Dangriga and Belize City's Municipal Airport (15min; Bz$75), and south to Placencia (20min; Bz$83) and Punta Gorda (40min; Bz$137).

A **fast skiff** leaves for Puerto Cortés, Honduras each Saturday at 9am (3hr; US$50) from the north bank of the creek, two blocks west of the bridge; be there at 8am with your passport so that the skipper (☎522-3227) can take care of the formalities.

including the tobacco that gave the island its name. At just five acres, the island is tiny, and if you stand in the centre you're only a couple of minutes from the shore in any direction, with unbroken reef stretching north for miles. On the island's southern edge, a huge storm beach of coral rubble, thrown up by Hurricane Mitch in 1998, encloses a tiny lagoon – creating a lovely natural swimming pool – and the tons of sand dumped on the leeward side by the storm created new beaches. Since the reef is within wading distance of the shore, you don't even need a boat for some superb **snorkelling and diving**, saving precious time to eat, drink or relax in a hammock the rest of the day. Some of the resorts have dive shops, and Tobacco Caye Dive Center (ⓣ670-0558) offers trips to the atolls. A two-tank dive just off the island (including equipment) costs US$80, and there's plenty to see, since the caye is part of the **South Water Marine Reserve**, one of the best-protected areas for snorkelling and diving. The entrance fee is Bz$10/day or Bz$30/week, usually collected at the hotels by rangers.

Accommodation

Accommodation here is simple but comfortable, and generally of good value; you'll stay in either a wooden building on the sand or a cabin right over the shallows. Prices vary with demand (bargaining is possible at slack periods), but here more than anywhere it's essential to check what you're paying for – and whether the price is quoted in US or Belize dollars. Unless you've arranged a package in advance, the hotels charge per person per night, and typically include all meals in the rate. Any lodging can also arrange scuba, snorkelling and fishing trips.

Gaviota Coral Reef Resort ⓣ509-5032. Five cabins on the sand, and budget rooms in the main wooden building, all very clean and with shared bath; this place is well run and usually the best deal on the caye. Electricity comes from a solar panel, and there's a thatched shelter with hammocks and good snorkel equipment for rent. ❺–❻

Lana's on the Reef ⓣ520-5036. Four simple, neat rooms in a lovely wooden house; the upstairs quarters, with private shower and opening onto a balcony, are more expensive. Great food and good coffee in a romantic atmosphere. ❻–❼

Reef's End Lodge ⓣ522-2419, ⓦwww.reefsendlodge.com. Stay right on the shore in the large wooden building (upstairs rooms cost more) or one of the spacious, private cabañas, all with private hot showers and deck. The beachfront suite with a/c goes for US$195. The restaurant and bar hover over the sea at the tip of the reef, a fantastic place to enjoy the sunset. Delicious food, a good dive shop and discounts for *Rough Guides* readers. ❻–❾

Tobacco Caye Lodge ⓣ227-6247 or 520-5033, ⓦwww.tclodgebelize.com. The largest area of any hotel on the island, stretching from the reef at the front to the lagoon at the back. Accommodation comprises six spacious, comfortable, two-room houses with private bath, deck with hammocks, and solar-powered lights, and there's a good beach bar by the dock. ❾

Tobacco Caye Paradise ⓣ520-5101, ⓔbluefield@btl.net. Simple rooms in a wooden house, all with shared bathroom (Bz$50 per person), and thatched cabañas over the sea (Bz$70 per person), some with great views of the reef. ❸–❹

South Water Caye

Eight kilometres south of Tobacco Caye and about three times larger, **South Water Caye** is arguably one of the most beautiful and exclusive islands in Belize. The island takes its name from a well at its centre, still in existence, which provided fresh water for passing ships. Like Tobacco Caye, the island sits right on the reef and offers fantastic, very accessible snorkelling and scuba diving in crystal-clear water; it's also the centre of the **South Water Marine Reserve** – a World Heritage Site – and its southern end is part of a small nature preserve. Turtles nest in the sand here, and the reef curves around offshore, protecting the pristine beach. Most of the resorts have their own

very good **dive shops** and can arrange trips to **Glove**
The tiny island off the caye's south end is **Carrie Bow**
Smithsonian Institute has a research station; you can ask yo
a visit, but there's no overnight accommodation.

Accommodation

The island's **accommodation** is mainly upmarket and must
advance; rates are typically either for groups or all-inclusive packag
rates are possible, but probably won't include the US$125 (each dir
from Dangriga.

Blue Marlin Lodge ⓣ520-5104, in the US ⓣ1-800/798-1558, ⓦwww.bluemarlinlodge.com. The most luxurious accommodation on the island, set in a wide expanse of raked white sand under the coconut trees, and comprising three dome-shaped, carpeted a/c cabins with beautiful bathrooms, five comfortable a/c cabins with a deck over the sea, and wood-panelled rooms in a typical "caye house". The thatched dining room serves delicious meals. *Blue Marlin* specializes in diving and fishing: there's a fleet of boats with top guides. Prices (based on two sharing, and including all taxes) are around US$1360 for six nights, including transfers from/to the international airport and all meals, and around US$1660 for a diving package. ⑨

Leslie Cottages ⓣ670-5030, in the US ⓣ1-800/548-5843, ⓦwww.ize2belize.com. Very comfortable private-bath cabins and shared-bath dorm rooms, all cooled by fans, in a tropical field research station. The cabins have a lounge area and wraparound decks, and two are right over the reef. Although many guests come on study trips – the manager is a biologist whose courses focus on reef ecology – it's still a wonderful place for anyone to stay. A complete package for private guests, including transportation, accommodation, meals and daily boat tour, costs about US$1465/week per person. Internet access for guests. ⑨

Pelican Beach Resort ⓣ522-2024, ⓦwww.pelicanbeachbelize.com. A range of idyllic options in a stunning location on the south half of the island. Choose from seven private cabañas and five sea-view rooms, some in a former colonial convent; rates (starting at US$220 for a double) include meals and snorkel gear. Electricity is provided by solar cells, and most accommodation has composting toilets. *The Pelican's University*, on the west side of the island, has a bunk-and-shared-bath design ideal for groups of students or travellers. ⑦–⑨

The Southern Highway to the Jaguar Reserve

South of Dangriga the country becomes more mountainous, with settlements mainly restricted to the coastal lowlands. The only road heading in this direction is the **Southern Highway**, spanning 170km from Dangriga to Punta Gorda. For its entire length the highway is set back from the coast, running beneath the peaks of the Maya Mountains and often passing through pine forest and vast citrus and banana plantations. Several branch roads lead off to settlements such as **Hopkins**, a Garifuna village on the coast, and the nearby Creole village of **Sittee River**, where you can catch the *Glover's Atoll Resort* boat to Long Caye on **Glover's Reef** (see p.258). From the village of **Maya Centre**, 36km south of Dangriga, a road leads west into the Cockscomb Basin Wildlife Sanctuary (generally referred to as the **Jaguar Reserve**); your first reason to pull off the highway, however, might be to visit the Maya site of **Mayflower**.

Mayflower and Mama Noots Backabush

Ten kilometres south of the junction with the Stann Creek Valley Road, an unpaved, six-kilometre branch road twists through citrus groves and forest to s of the Maya Mountains and the Late Classic site of **Mayflower**. re really three Maya sites here: Mayflower, near the end of the branch d, and Maintzunun ("hummingbird") and T'au Witz ("dwelling-place of the mountain god"), both a short distance through the forest. Apart from a few medium-sized stone mounds and areas that are clearly plazas, the sites have not yet been fully cleared, so there's not much to see architecturally. The location, however – on a creek where the coastal plain meets the forested mountains – is sublime, rich in bird and animal life. The sites are currently being excavated by the Mayflower Archaeology Project – see Contexts, p.337, for details of how to participate in the dig – and the area around them is now protected in the 7000-acre **Mayflower Bocawina National Park** (Bz$10), whose hiking trails lead to waterfalls tumbling into Silk Grass Creek.

You can stay in the midst of this natural beauty at **Mama Noots Backabush** (Ⓣ670-8019, Ⓦwww.mamanoots.com; ❼), set in a large grassy clearing surrounded on three sides by forest-covered hills. Owner Nanette Beamer and her two daughters are very hospitable, creating a cheerful and creative experience for their guests. Most of their fifty acres of primary and secondary forest have been left intact (much of the land is steep hillside anyway), and they make the most of **alternative energy**, using solar and wind power. It's an utterly tranquil place, and even the occasional visits by a jaguar only add to the natural atmosphere. All buses heading south from Dangriga pass the side road to the resort; call ahead and they'll pick you up from the junction, 6km away. The accommodation consists of one family-sized cabaña, a two-room thatched house and six rooms in a wheelchair-accessible concrete lodge. All rooms are large, with private bath, fan, 24-hour electricity and balconies with hammocks, and guests can use the Internet. The **restaurant** serves delicious food and is open to non-guests; organic vegetables grown in the resort's garden show up in many dishes. A short trail near the lodge has descriptions highlighting various plants' medicinal properties, while other trails lead to nearby waterfalls: there's an easy, 35-minute hike to Three Sisters Falls, and a very steep trail to the ridge of the ninety-metre Antelope Falls, visible from the grounds and excellent for early-morning, guided birding trips.

Hopkins

Stretching for more than 3km along a shallow, gently curving bay, **HOPKINS** is home to around 1200 Garifuna, who, until recently, made their living from small-scale farming and fishing, often paddling dugout canoes to pull up fish traps, or using baited handlines. Their houses, traditionally small wood-and-thatch structures, have now mostly been replaced by less visually appealing but more secure concrete buildings. The village, named for a Roman Catholic bishop who drowned nearby in 1923, was first settled in 1942 after a hurricane levelled its predecessor, the community of Newtown, a few kilometres to the north. The population is proud of its customs (everyone speaks Garifuna as a first language), and **Garifuna Settlement Day** on November 19 is celebrated enthusiastically with singing, dancing and, above all, the beating of drums – an integral part of Garifuna culture. Only recently inducted into the tourist circuit, Hopkins still sees relatively few visitors, and as a stranger you'll be made to feel welcome by the exuberant friendliness of the villagers, particularly the children.

Delicious food and accommodation in all price ranges makes Hopkins a pleasant place to spend a few days relaxing, but it's also well equipped for outdoor activities. You can rent **kayaks** at *Tipple Tree Beya*, **windsurfers** at

Windschief (Ⓣ523-7249) and **bicycles** (Bz$20/day) from Tina's Bike Rental, on the road toward the south end of the village. Many hotels can arrange trips to the reef and cayes, and **diving** here is excellent and uncrowded; check at the resorts just south of the village, including *Hamanasi Adventure and Dive Resort* (Ⓣ520-7073). Second Nature Divers (Ⓣ523-7038, Ⓔdivers@starband.net), based at *Jaguar Reef Lodge*, offers PADI courses by two very experienced English instructors, as well as **dive excursions** and equipment rental. Call ahead and they'll arrange accommodation for you based on your budget. Day-trips are US$98 for a two-tank offshore reef dive and US$175 for a three-tank dive on Glover's Reef. Prices include tanks, boat and guide.

Just north of the village, a narrow creek gives way to a large, peaceful lagoon – a good place for kayaking – but construction of timeshares and condominiums nearby threaten its accessibility. Still, the view inland from here, with the village and the high ridges of the Maya Mountains in the background, is breathtaking. Unfortunately, the water immediately offshore has a silty appearance, and the coconut trees that once shaded the entire village have been wiped out by a "lethal yellowing" disease advancing inexorably down the coast from Mexico. The disease-resistant variety of trees planted to replace them is growing vigorously, but taking a while to mature.

The Drumming Center at *Lebeha* (Ⓦwww.lebeha.com) showcases **Garifuna drumming and dancing** every Friday night around 8pm, and you can sometimes catch the musicians at resorts in False Sittee Point (see p.255). Drumming lessons are available for Bz$25 per hour, and if you're interested in making a drum, visit Mr Coleman (Ⓣ523-7217) on the north side of the village.

Arrival and orientation

The **bus** service to Hopkins has improved recently, with KC's Bus leaving from the dock outside the *Riverside Restaurant* in Dangriga (Mon–Sat 10.30am & 1pm, returning from Hopkins at 7am; Bz$5). Most bus services to Placencia also pass through the village, continuing south via Sittee River; see p.86 for details. There are plenty of trucks between Dangriga and Hopkins, making **hitching** a fairly reliable option, best attempted from the bus shelter at the junction with the Southern Highway outside Dangriga. The best way to arrive, though, is by **boat** – ask around the bridge in Dangriga whether anyone from Hopkins is in town, as they may be willing to give you a lift.

If you do hitch a ride, it is customary to give a couple dollars for petrol, which comes at a high price in the country. As there are no street names in Hopkins, the best way to locate anything is to describe its position in relation to the point where the road from the Southern Highway enters the village centre. The main road from the highway, which heads south through the village, is paved (as are a couple other streets in the village), though the asphalt gives way to sand at the southern end; this road continues 5km to **Sittee River** (see p.256).

Accommodation

Hopkins has plenty of **accommodation** in all price ranges, and booking ahead is only really necessary for the days around November 19, Garifuna Settlement Day. That said, it's always a good idea if you want a particular place at Christmas or Easter. There are also several **houses for rent**, and a couple of places to **camp**. Almost all hotels in the main village have bicycles for guests to use, quite useful as Hopkins extends so far along the beach. Beyond the southern edge of the village, a growing number of luxury resorts line a beautiful beach called **False Sittee Point**; some of these are included in the list on p.255.

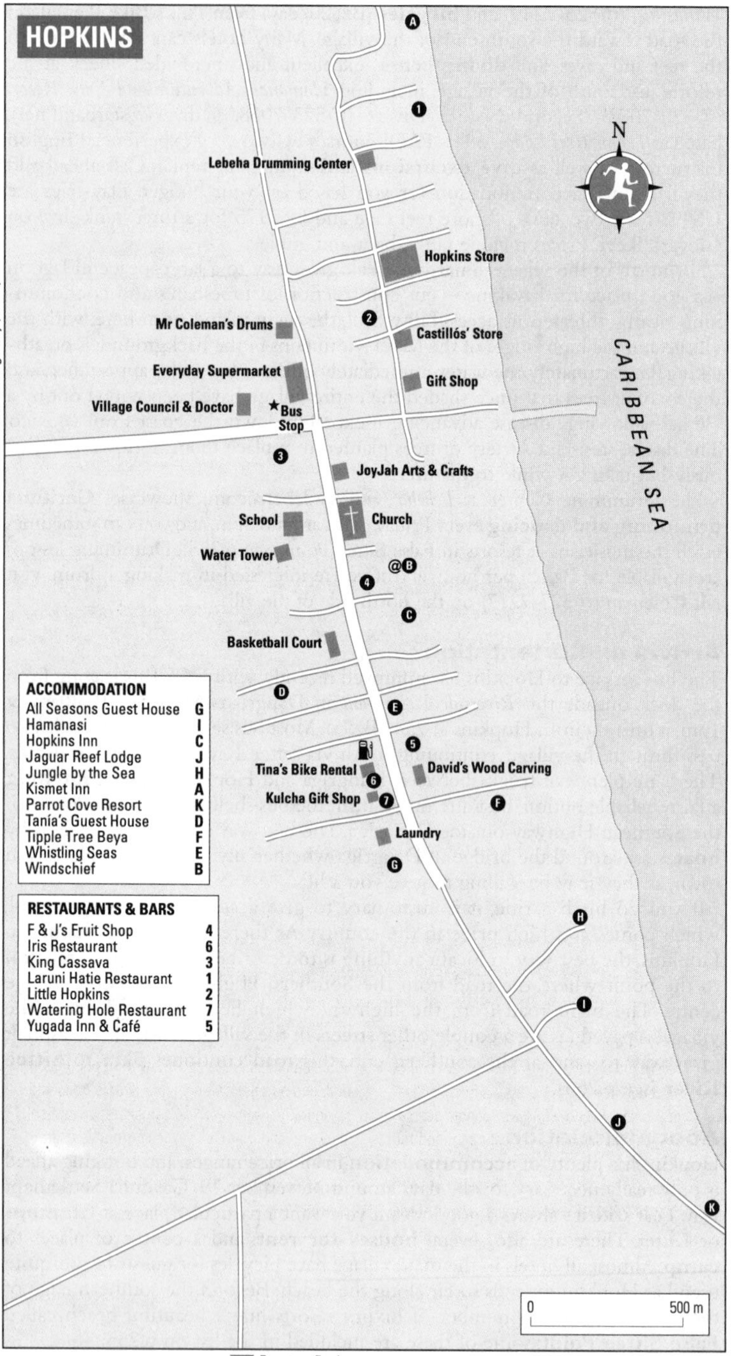

HOPKINS
Lebeha Drumming Center
Hopkins Store
Mr Coleman's Drums
Castillós' Store
Everyday Supermarket
Gift Shop
Village Council & Doctor
Bus Stop
JoyJah Arts & Crafts
School
Church
Water Tower
Basketball Court
Tina's Bike Rental
David's Wood Carving
Kulcha Gift Shop
Laundry
CARIBBEAN SEA
N
Southern Highway (6.5km)
Sittee River Hotels & Sittee River (3km)
Bocatura Bank
0
500 m
ACCOMMODATION
All Seasons Guest House G
Hamanasi I
Hopkins Inn C
Jaguar Reef Lodge J
Jungle by the Sea H
Kismet Inn A
Parrot Cove Resort K
Tanía's Guest House D
Tipple Tree Beya F
Whistling Seas E
Windschief B
RESTAURANTS & BARS
F & J's Fruit Shop 4
Iris Restaurant 6
King Cassava 3
Laruni Hatie Restaurant 1
Little Hopkins 2
Watering Hole Restaurant 7
Yugada Inn & Café 5

All Seasons Guest House At the south end of the village ⓣ523-7209. Three beautifully decorated rooms, all with a/c, private bath, coffeemaker and fridge, set in a lovely garden with a tranquil, Mediterranean-style patio. Dune buggy rental is available, and German and Dutch spoken. ❹

Hamanasi Adventure and Dive Resort False Sittee Point, 1.5km south of the village ⓣ520-7073, in the US ⓣ1-877/552-3483, ⓦwww.hamanasi.com. One of the top dive resorts in the country, with a range of luxuriously appointed suites (US$350), beachfront deluxe rooms (US$315), standard rooms (US$275) and six "treehouse" cabañas on three-metre stilts (US$350), located on a beautiful beach. All accommodation has a/c, ceiling fans, king or queen-size beds, gorgeous Belizean hardwood furniture, colourfully tiled bathrooms and private porches. Service here is excellent, and the resort has a number of fast, modern dive boats and superb equipment for diving or snorkelling on the reef or any of the atolls; inland tours to caves, ruins and Cockscomb are also available. ❾

Hopkins Inn On the beach, just south of the centre ⓣ523-7013, ⓦwww.hopkinsinn.com. Friendly place with four immaculate, white-washed cabins with showers, fridge and coffee-maker. The owners can help arrange snorkelling, fishing and boat activities with local guides. Ample continental breakfast included and free bikes for guests. German spoken. ❺

Jaguar Reef Lodge False Sittee Point, 2km south of the village ⓣ520-7040, in the US ⓣ1-800/289-5756, ⓦwww.jaguarreef.com. A luxury resort with large, thatched, two-room cabañas, all with a/c, in beautifully landscaped grounds and in a superb location, often used by top nature tour companies. The restaurant, under a huge, thatched roof overlooking the beach and pool, is excellent and so is the service. Kayaks and bikes are available free for guests, and there's a full-service dive shop with instruction. ❾

Jungle by the Sea Beyond the south end of the village ⓣ523-7047, ⓦwww.junglebythesea.com. Three hardwood cabañas with private bath and an economy lodge in a shady, relaxed setting with views of the sea. Friendly owners "Jungle Jeanie" and "Jungle John" also have a restaurant and rent kayaks. Camping is available. ❺

Kismet Inn On the beach at the north end of the village ⓣ523-7280, ⓦwww.kismetinn.com. Lovely, thatched, individually decorated stone cabañas with private bathrooms, budget rooms in a wooden house (some with shared bath) and a furnished house (Bz$500/month). The *Kismet* experience is quite unique; you're bound to meet characters of all ages and backgrounds and leave with plenty of stories. Breakfast of fresh homemade bread and local fruit is included, and you can use the small guest kitchen. RV hook-ups are Bz$20, camping is Bz$10 per person and use of bike is free for guests. ❶–❸

Parrot Cove Resort False Sittee Point, 2.5km south of the village ⓣ523-7225, in the US ⓣ1-877/207-7139. An intimate seaside resort with ten rooms and a separate beach villa for longer stays or larger groups. All rooms have a/c and coffee-makers. The restaurant and bar serves international fare, and for special events guests can request a private meal served at the thatched-roof dock. ❽

Tania's Guest House South of the centre, on the west side of the road ⓣ523-7058. Although not directly on the beach, this small, friendly hotel is a great bargain. All rooms have private shower (most with hot water) and some have bedside light, fridge and cable TV – and there's complimentary coffee. ❷–❸

Tipple Tree Beya On the beach near the south end of the village ⓣ520-7006, ⓦwww.tippletree.com. Good-value, clean rooms in a wooden building with deck and hammocks; one has cold-water shower, others have hot shower and coffee-maker. Run by the friendly Patricia Sturman, who provides great information and does all she can to ensure you have an enjoyable visit. There's also a furnished wooden house to rent, with fridge and microwave, for Bz$100/day, or you can camp for B$10 per person. ❹

Whistling Seas Inn On the beach towards the south end of the village ⓣ523-7203, ⓔmarcello@whistlingseas.com. Five brightly painted cement cabañas with private bathroom and a veranda. The friendly Belizean owners offer great value and run a restaurant too. ❹

Windschief On the beach, south of the centre ⓣ523-7249, ⓦwww.windschief.com. Two simple and clean cabins, a smaller one with one double bed, and a larger one with two double beds and refrigerator. Both have coffeemakers, private cold showers, and a great view facing the beachfront. There's a shared hot shower and Internet access. The owner offers windsurfing lessons and rental as well. ❸–❹

Eating

Though your choice may be limited outside of the tourist season, Hopkins has a good selection of inexpensive **restaurants**. You'll always find delicious Garifuna and Creole meals, and usually very good seafood. Bear in mind that service can be slow (they might have to send the kids out to buy ingredients), so be prepared to wait for your meal to arrive – at least you'll know it's fresh. For more upmarket dining you could sample the restaurants in the lodges at False Sittee Point, some way beyond the south end of the village. If you want to attempt your own shopping, a great selection of fresh **fruit and vegetables** can be found at *F&J's Fruit Shop*.

Iris Restaurant Near the southern edge of the village. Good Belizean mains and burgers at great prices, served from 8am to 9pm.

King Cassava In the centre at the junction. Full Belizean and international menu with complete bar service in an open-air dining space. Daily specials may include fresh, local game such as gibnut. Nightly entertainment. Open late, closed Mon.

Laruni Hatie Beyabu Restaurant On the beach, north of the centre. The only Belizean-owned eatery with a beachfront view, serving delicious Belizean food and Garifuna specialities like *hudut* (see p.248). A favourite among locals.

Little Hopkins North of the centre, across from Hopkins Store. A small stand serving simple meals in hearty portions. Popular for its late hours (until midnight or later).

Watering Hole South of the centre, near the edge of the village. One of the best restaurants in town, serving great seafood and daily specials.

Yugada Café On the main street, south of the centre. The Nuñez sisters serve tasty international fare, fresh seasonal juices and good desserts in a pleasant, warm and friendly dining room. Entertainment sometimes provided.

Drinking and nightlife

Most businesses in Hopkins close from 2 to 4pm, at which point they remain open late into the evening. Bars are often open until midnight, restaurants until 10pm. For a drink with the locals head to *King Cassava*, where **live music and drumming** on weekends add zest to the full **bar**. Some resorts, as well as *Lebeha* (see p.253), also feature live drumming, but it's best to check dates and times before you go. Since bars are constantly opening and closing in Hopkins, it's a good idea to ask your hotel's staff about evening activities – most locals are very aware of what's going on in the community.

Sittee River

A few kilometres south of the Hopkins turn-off from the Southern Highway, another side road leads to the pleasant village of **SITTEE RIVER**, most useful as a jumping-off point for Glover's Reef (see p.258). The eight-kilometre dirt track roughly follows the north bank of the community's namesake, and the village sits right on the river as well. On the way in, you'll see signs to the ruins of the nineteenth-century **Serpon Sugar Mill**, now preserved as a local park and a good spot for birding. Wildlife is abundant all around the village, and freshwater crocodiles and turtles bask along the riverbanks.

You can also reach Sittee River along a dirt road from Hopkins; raised and improved, it's still a little rough in places. The village is served by the same **buses** as Hopkins along the Dangriga–Placencia route, and it's about a 25-minute ride from Hopkins by **bike**. If you're stopping by on your way to *Glover's Atoll Resort* (see p.259), as most visitors are, the bus driver will drop you at the appropriate spot (see *Glover's Guest House*, p.258). Should you spend much time here before heading to sea, though, be warned that the sandflies can be atrocious; guest houses provide screens and mosquito nets for good reason.

The great-value *Toucan Sittee* (Ⓣ523-7039, Ⓦwww.toucansittee.info; ❸–❼), signposted at the entrance to the village from the Hopkins road, is the best **accommodation** option in Sittee River, set on the beautiful riverbank and graced by toucans most mornings. The extremely hospitable owners offer a wide range of rooms, including some of the best budget accommodation in the

△ Drummer in Hopkins

country, in five solidly built, well-furnished wooden cabins with electric lights and fans; most have a private hot-water bathroom and a fridge. **Rooms** start at Bz$40, and there are also a couple of apartments, each with a small kitchen and fridge (Bz$160, good discounts for longer stays), and very comfortable dorm beds in the "bunkhouse" (Bz$23). The food served here is excellent, with lots of fresh fruit (including nine varieties of mango) and organic vegetables. **Bike** and **canoe** rentals are free for guests, and excellent guide Udell Foreman (☎522-7027) can take you on an exciting night paddle.

Nearby, *Glover's Guest House* (ⓣ509-7099, ⓔinfo@glovers.com.bz; ❷–❹), where you check in for Glover's Reef trips, has dorm beds for Bz$36 and double rooms in elevated cabins for Bz$76. Two nights here earns you a free third one. The **restaurant** is right on the riverbank, and the boat to the reef ties up outside. If you need to stock up on **supplies** for your trip to Glover's Reef, Hill Top Farm stocks fresh vegetables and Reynold's Store covers the rest of the groceries. Check your **email** at Sittee River Internet (ⓣ603-8358) before heading out to sea.

Just downstream from Sittee River, reached by a kilometre-long, signposted track from the road to Hopkins, there's a range of comfortable accommodation at *Bocatura Bank* (ⓣ606-4590, ⓦwww.bocaturabank.com; ❸–❼). Its main attractions are spacious, whitewashed, wooden **cabins** on the riverbank, each with at least one bedroom with queen-sized bed, futon, kitchenette and large, screened porch with rattan furniture and hammocks. There's also a budget cabin overlooking the river and a "treehouse" cabin on stilts. The delicious meals are US$30/day. The owner, a biologist from the northeastern US, is a keen sailor and not only has a Sunfish sailing boat, kayaks and canoes for guests, but also a forty-foot catamaran for **sailing charters**. Guests can call ahead for a free lift from Hopkins or Sittee River.

Slightly further downriver, **Possum Point Biological Station** (ⓣ523-7071, ⓦwww.marineecology.com) is a tropical ecology field station with cabins, primarily for student groups, and courses that include a spell offshore at the marine ecology lab on **Wee Wee Caye**, a tiny mangrove island 15km off the coast. Phone to inquire about opportunities for independent travellers.

Glover's Reef

The southernmost of Belize's three coral atolls, **Glover's Reef** lies roughly 50km off Dangriga. Named after British pirate John Glover, the reef is oval in shape, about 35km from north to south, and its main cayes are in its southeastern section. Physically, it's the best-developed atoll in the Caribbean, rising from depths of 1000m, with the reef wall beginning less than ten metres offshore. It offers some of the most spectacular **wall diving** in the world – the fantastic Long Caye Wall is less than 100m offshore – with visibility of over 300m. Glover's Reef is home to rare seabirds such as the white-capped noddy, all its cayes have nesting ospreys, and Belize's **marine turtles** lay their eggs on the beaches. The vitally important snapper spawning grounds on the atoll attract dozens of immense **whale sharks**, which congregate during the late spring full moons to feast on snapper eggs. Within the beautiful, aquamarine lagoon are hundreds of smallish patches of coral, or **patch reefs** – a snorkelling wonderland. All of these unique features helped bring about the decision in 1993 to declare the entire atoll a protected area – **Glover's Reef Marine Reserve**, a status further enhanced by its designation as a World Heritage Site in 1996. The atoll is divided into management zones and, while no fishing is allowed from any of the cayes themselves, you can fish in the zones shown on the map you should receive when you pay the Bz$20 **entry fee**, collected most of the time.

Three of the four main cayes offer some **package accommodation**, mostly in purpose-built camps and cabins; these are often used by **sea kayaking** and diving groups. Apart from its biological attributes, there's another feature that makes Glover's Reef so unusual among the remote atolls: one of its cayes, Northeast Caye, has accommodation within the reach of budget travellers (see opposite). Staying on one caye doesn't mean you're confined there; you can easily hop between the four, by either boat or kayak. Most accommodation in the reserve runs weekly boat shuttles to and from the mainland, and the ride is usually included in week-long packages. Since a chartered boat from Dangriga or Hopkins/Sittee River will cost you US$350 each way, package transport is the best way to arrive and depart. If you must use a charter, ask at your hotel or try Michael Jackson (Ⓣ620-8913), who may be inclined to give discounts to *Rough Guides* readers.

The cayes

Northeast Caye, covered in thick coconut and broadleaf forest and with evidence of Maya fishing camps, is home to *Glover's Atoll Resort* (Ⓣ614-7177 or 520-2016, Ⓦwww.glovers.com.bz), owned by a French-American family that's lived here for several decades. All accommodation overlooks the sea and reef, and here more than anywhere else in Belize you can indulge your Robinson Crusoe fantasy to the utmost. The quoted prices apply year-round (though the resort sometimes closes in September and October, at the height of the rainy season) and are per person per week, including transport from Sittee River on the resort's boat – either a 55-foot motor sailing boat, a fast skiff or a diesel-powered catamaran – leaving on Sunday morning and returning the following Saturday. No meals are included, but if you stay for a month the fourth week is free. Twelve simple, wood-and-thatch, self-catering **beach cabins** perch on stilts on the sand (US$199) or over the water (US$269), and there's a dorm room in a wooden house (US$149) and space for **camping** (US$99, including the tent and bedding). Some cabins on the sand have loft bedrooms, making them ideal for families. Kitchens include a kerosene stove and there are barbecues outside; one evening each week features a potluck supper. You can either bring your own food for the week (fish, lobster, bread and basic supplies are available to buy, but bring your own booze) or eat at the thatched **restaurant**, where Chef Tony serves outstanding meals (place orders in the morning). Five gallons of drinking water per person are provided free – you pay to use more – but bear in mind that **coconuts** are free, too, and the green ones contain lots of delicious water. Showers are taken in water drawn from a shallow well. While here, you're pretty much left to your own devices and you can choose to enjoy a simple "desert island" experience, but your stay will be greatly enhanced if you partake in the fee-based **activities** on offer, including sea kayaking, fishing, snorkelling, scuba diving with PADI certification (less expensive than most other places) and visits to the other cayes. Resident dive instructor "Breeze" knows the atoll very well and can show you some of the best dive sites. Those into fishing will have an adventure with young Warren – born and raised on the atoll – who promises a record catch on his watch, or at least a tall tale from past triumphs.

Just across the channel from Northeast Caye, **Long Caye** is the base of Slickrock Adventures (Ⓦwww.slickrock.com; see p.23), which provides wonderful **sea kayaking expeditions** and lodging. Guests are picked up in Belize City and transported by fast launch to their **accommodation** in sturdy, comfortable cabins on stilts, with a deck and hammock overlooking the reef, or in tents on a wooden deck under a thatched roof. There's collected rainwater to drink, and varied, filling meals are served in the spacious dining room. Slickrock is a very experienced adventure outfitter (they also offer windsurfing, kayak surfing and fishing here, plus river and jungle trips inland) and its base camp is eco-friendly, with composting toilets and some electric lighting provided by wind and solar power. **Diving** on the caye is run by the well-managed *Off the Wall Dive Center and Resort* (Ⓣ614-6348, Ⓦwww.offthewallbelize.com), offering responsible and professional PADI courses, snorkelling and fishing packages for around US$1395–1995/week per person, depending on the activity, and including all meals and boat transfer from

Dangriga. Guests stay in charming wooden cabañas with separate showers, and the only **gift shop** on the atoll sells souvenirs.

Four kilometres to the southwest, **Middle Caye** is in the wilderness zone of the reserve, with a marine research and monitoring station and laboratory run by the Wildlife Conservation Society (see Contexts, p.351). This is also the base for the Fisheries Department's **conservation officers**, who rigorously patrol the reserve. Only staff and authorized scientists and students stay on the caye, but you can usually visit with permission. The ecology of the atoll is explained in some interesting displays, and you might even see some research in progress. Visitors can also contribute to the conservation efforts here by purchasing excellent T-shirts found only on the caye.

Southwest Caye, 5km beyond Middle Caye, is the headquarters of Vancouver-based Island Expeditions (Ⓦwww.islandexpeditions.com; see Basics, p.23), a very experienced **sea kayaking** outfitter with superb guides and an exemplary environmental record. Guests are typically flown to Dangriga and taken by fast skiff to the caye, where they sleep in spacious, comfortable white tents with proper beds and eat gourmet meals in the screened dining room. Beginners receive training in paddling a kayak, and veterans can visit the other cayes or even take part in overnight camping expeditions to uninhabited islands. Island Expeditions also offers excellent, biologist-led educational trips.

Southwest Caye was sliced into two distinct islands by Hurricane Hattie in 1961, and on the other part, across a narrow channel, is *Isla Marisol Resort* (Ⓣ520-2056 or 610-4204, Ⓦwww.islamarisolresort.com). Eleven attractive, spacious wooden cabañas stand on the beach, each with a queen-sized bed, ceiling fans, private hot-water shower and a shady veranda with hammocks. The food is excellent and the bar is built on a deck over the water. *Isla Marisol* is a PADI dive centre, offering courses from beginner to Advanced Open Water; a week's **package** in high season, including transport from Dangriga, all meals and seventeen dives (including two night dives) is US$1850. During your stay you can expect to dive on all three of Belize's atolls, depending on weather conditions; in April, May and June you can dive with the **whale sharks** at Gladden Spit. A week's fly-fishing is US$2450, or you can just relax and swim off the gorgeous beach for US$1300; three- or four-day packages are also available.

The Cockscomb Basin Wildlife Sanctuary and Maya Centre

Back on the mainland, the jagged peaks of the **Maya Mountains** rise to the west of the Southern Highway, their lower slopes covered in dense rainforest. The tallest summits are those of the Cockscomb range, which includes Victoria Peak, at 1120m the second-highest mountain in Belize and a dramatic sight on a clear day. In 1888 the Goldsworthy Expedition made the first recorded successful attempt on the summit of Victoria Peak, though it's reasonably certain that the ancient Maya were first to make it to the top. Beneath the sharp ridges is a sweeping bowl, part of which was declared a **jaguar reserve** in 1986. It has since been expanded to cover an area of over four hundred square kilometres – the **Cockscomb Basin Wildlife Sanctuary**.

This area was inhabited in Maya times, and the ruins of **Kuchil Balam**, a Classic-period ceremonial centre, still lie hidden in the forest. It was also exploited by mahogany loggers; the names of their abandoned camps, such as Leave If You Can and Go to Hell, illustrate how they felt about life in the forest. In more recent times the residents of Quam Bank, a logging camp and Maya village, moved out of the Cockscomb when the reserve was established,

The Victoria Peak Trail

Viewed from the sea, the jagged granite peaks of the Cockscomb range take on the appearance of a colossal, recumbent head, whose sloping forehead, eyebrows, nose, mouth and chin have earned the range the nickname of "The Sleeping Maya". **Victoria Peak** the highest point in the Cockscomb at 1120m (3675ft), and the second-highest mountain in Belize after Doyle's Delight (1124m), is no giant by world standards, but the trek to the summit should not be undertaken lightly. You'll need to find a guide in Maya Centre (or contact Maya Guide Adventures; see p.169), since the trip involves scaling some of the rock faces below the peak using climbing equipment, and to be able to carry supplies for three to five days. It's best to begin each day's walk at first light to make the most of the cool morning; **heat exhaustion** is a very real danger and you must carry plenty of water. Creeks cross the trail at least every couple of kilometres and the water is generally safe to drink, though you may prefer to purify it first. Simple **shelters** along the way mean it's not absolutely necessary to bring a tent, but bringing one will at least give you protection from biting insects. Currently there's no charge for use of the trail itself – you just pay the reserve entrance fee and backcountry campsite charges – although there are plans to introduce a **user fee**.

The trail begins at the reserve headquarters, first following a relatively level, abandoned logging road through secondary forest for 12km to the first rest point, where the **Sittee Branch River** beckons with the chance of a cooling swim. On the far bank is the first **campsite**, a sturdy, thatched shelter with a kitchen and pit toilets. Beyond here the trail begins to climb steeply – and then descend equally steeply – in a series of energy-sapping undulations until you reach kilometre 17, at which point you walk up and along a very steep ridge before descending to the second campsite, just before kilometre 19. A **helipad**, hacked out of the forest on a tiny patch of flat land at kilometre 18, provides the first real views of the peak. If you've set off early and are fit you can reach this campsite in one day, but be warned that the 7km from the first campsite are so rigorous that this section can take as much time as the first 12km. At the campsite you can hang hammocks in an open-sided wooden shelter, and your shower is a small waterfall cascading over smooth rocks.

The final stretch to the peak is almost four hours of relentless, uphill struggle, with much of the trail along a steep, rocky creek bed – too dangerous to attempt in heavy rain. As the ascent becomes ever more vertical and you rise above the forest canopy, the views increase in splendour; closer to the ground, wildflowers cling to rock crevices. Just below the peak, you have to haul yourself up through a narrow gully on a rope suspended from a tree. Above here the track along the final ridge passes first though an elfin **cloud forest**, with gnarled tree limbs draped in filmy moss and tiny ferns, before reaching the summit itself. Low, waxy-leaved bushes and grass offer only scraps of shade here, and the Belize flag flutters in the breeze. Tethered to the rock that marks the actual peak is an exercise book, stuffed inside a screw-topped plastic pipe, for recording the names of successful climbers. Spread beneath you are the rocky peaks of a series of deep green, thickly forested ridges and valleys – on a very clear day you can see to the Caribbean – and not a sign of humanity's impact on the environment. The trek down is almost as arduous as the ascent, but it takes about an hour less to reach the campsite. With an early start the next morning, you can walk all the way out to the sanctuary headquarters in a single day.

relocating to the village of **Maya Centre** on the Southern Highway (see p.262). The sanctuary is managed by the Belize Audubon Society, with some financial assistance from international conservation organizations. There's an opportunity for a limited amount of **volunteer work** in the reserve, maintaining trails, working on displays in the visitor centre or even tracking howler monkeys; contact BAS in Belize City for more information (see p.74).

Maya Centre: arrival and reserve information

All buses heading south from Dangriga pass **MAYA CENTRE** (35min), from where a somewhat rough 10-kilometre track leads to the sanctuary headquarters. You'll need to sign in and pay the reserve entrance fee at the Craft Centre (daily 7.30am–5pm; Bz$10; ⓣ603-9256) at the road junction. It's run by the village women's group, and there's information here about accommodation in the reserve as well as inexpensive slate carvings and embroidery. The Mopan Maya families living in Maya Centre are enthusiastic proponents of eco-tourism, and staying here (perhaps before entering the reserve) is a perfect way to learn about forest life and to experience Maya culture. You can also spot lots of **wildlife** along the adjacent Cabbage Haul Creek, a particularly good birding site.

Although many tour operators will tell you that you can't get into the Jaguar Reserve without going on a tour, you can easily walk in from Maya Centre – it takes a couple of hours or so along the gentle uphill slope, and you can leave any excess luggage at Julio's Store (see below). If you've come by bus and don't fancy walking, a taxi or truck to the headquarters will cost about Bz$35–40 for up to five people – you can ask at the Craft Centre to call you a car. For the best experience, though, don't go it alone – the people of Maya Centre know the reserve intimately, and are by far the best guides around. A guide for the **Victoria Peak Trail** (see box, p.261) will cost upwards of Bz$100/day, and the cost can be shared by groups; if you need help with carrying supplies you'll need to hire porters, too. Greg Sho is one of the most experienced guides in Maya Centre, and among the best bush and river kayaking guides in the country, but if he's booked up, ask for Gregorio Chun, Raul Balona or William Sho. William also has a **butterfly exhibit** (daily 6am–5pm; Bz$5; ⓣ660-0587) across the creek from the Craft Centre, featuring a dozen species. Just beyond the Craft Centre, **Julio's Store** sells basic supplies and cold drinks (there's no restaurant or shop in the reserve) and also has a **bar** and **Internet access**. Owner Julio Saqui runs Cockscomb Maya Tours (ⓣ520-3042, ⓔjulio_saqui@hotmail.com) and can arrange **guides and transport** into the reserve, as can most hotels.

Maya Centre: accommodation and eating

Maya Centre has several reasonable **places to stay**, generally simple rooms with electricity and sometimes a private bathroom; all serve good, inexpensive meals. You can **camp** at any of these for Bz$10 per person, though not all of the places have tents for rent. Contact *Nu'uk Che'il Cottages* (see opposite) to arrange a **homestay** with a village family for Bz$40 per person, including dinner and breakfast. The sanctuary headquarters (see opposite) can inform you of other accommodation options.

On the highway just before the junction, *Tutzil Nah Cottages* (ⓣ520-3044, ⓦwww.mayacenter.com; ❷–❸) has two neat, clean cabins – one with private bath. The concrete cabin also happens to be a hurricane shelter. They're run by the Chun family, and the brothers, Gregorio, Julian and Ouscal, are excellent guides and can arrange amazing **kayak trips** along South Stann Creek, which flows through the reserve. The family also manages a store and small gift shop, where you can stock up on supplies and souvenirs.

Set in lovely gardens behind the Craft Centre, *Mejen Tz'il Lodge* (ⓣ520-3032, ⓔlsaqui@btl.net; ❷–❸) has rooms in a thatched cabaña with private bathroom, as well as dorm rooms in a large wooden cabin with a large balcony (Bz$16 per person). Co-owner Yoli serves great **meals**, and you can rent **tents** here for use on the Victoria Peak Trail.

Some 500m up the track to the reserve, the *Nu'uk Che'il Cottages* (Ⓣ520-3033 or 615-2091, Ⓔnuukcheil@btl.net; ❸–❹) offer simple but delightful rooms with private hot-water bathroom (Bz$60), and rooms with shared showers and dorm beds (Bz$20). The **restaurant**, serving Maya and Belizean food, is great for a filling meal on your way to or from the reserve. Aurora is one of the Garcia sisters from San Antonio, Cayo District (see p.177), and has developed a medicinal trail (Bz$5) in the forest next to the cottages. She also makes **traditional herbal medicines** (for sale in the H'men Herbal Center and Gift Shop), arranges Maya cultural events – featuring marimba music and dancing – and gives talks on Maya history and healing methods.

The Jaguar Reserve

Heading through towering forest and fording a couple of fresh, clear streams, the road from Maya Centre crosses the Cabbage Haul Gap before reaching the sanctuary headquarters, in a grassy area surrounded by beautiful foliage. Technically, this is a **tropical moist forest**, with an annual rainfall of up to 300cm that feeds a complex network of wonderfully clear streams and rivers, most of which eventually run into Swasey River and South Stann Creek. A sizeable percentage of Belize's plant and animal species live in this verdant habitat; among the mammals are tapirs, otters, coatis, deer, anteaters, armadillos and, of course, jaguars, as well as other cat species. Over three hundred species of birds have also been recorded, including the endangered scarlet macaw, the great curassow, the keel-billed toucan and the king vulture. The sanctuary is particularly important as a refuge for the largest raptors, including the harpy eagle, the solitary eagle and the white hawk-eagle. Reptiles and amphibians abound, including the red-eyed tree frog, the boa constrictor and the deadly fer-de-lance snake, known in Belize as "yellow-jaw tommy-goff". The forest itself is made up of a fantastic range of plant species, including orchids, giant tree ferns, air plants (epiphytes) and trees such as banak, cohune, mahogany and ceiba.

At the headquarters, the excellent **visitor's centre** has a relief model of the Cockscomb Basin, displays on the area's ecology and maps and trail maps. You can also pick up a copy of *Cockscomb Basin Wildlife Sanctuary* (see Contexts, p.373), a superb and detailed guide to the history, flora and fauna of the reserve, and the shop sells drinks and snacks. **Accommodation** is available here, giving you the opportunity to fully experience Cockscomb by listening to its amazing night-time sounds. Most is aimed at student groups and researchers, but anyone can stay; choose from a private furnished cabin (❺), solar-powered wooden dorm rooms with shared showers and composting toilets (Bz$37 per person) or simple but comfortable dorm beds in "rustic" cabins (Bz$16 per person). There's also space for **camping** (Bz$10 per person), with tents available to rent. Meals aren't served here, but the cabins have a kitchen with a gas stove. Camping at designated sites along the trails is Bz$5 per person, and you'll need to get a permit from the ranger at the headquarters.

Although roughly sixty of Belize's seven hundred **jaguars** are believed to live in the sanctuary, your chances of seeing one are very slim. However, it's an ideal environment for plant-spotting, serious birding or seeking out other ever-evasive wildlife, and the trail system is the best-developed in any of Belize's protected areas. Several well-maintained short trails lead through the forest to the riverbank or to exquisite waterfalls framed by jungle, and **Ben's Bluff Trail** is a strenuous four-kilometre hike to the top of a forested ridge – where there's a great view of the entire Cockscomb Basin – with a chance to cool off in a delightful rocky pool on the way back. Similarly scenic is the two-kilometre trail to **Tiger Fern Falls**, a picturesque, two-tiered waterfall with a pool at the

△ Cockscomb Basin Wildlife Sanctuary

upper level. **Inner tubes** (Bz$5) are available from the ranger's office; follow the marked trail upstream and float down South Stann Creek for a soothing, tranquil view of the forest. For a longer (or overnight) trip using inflatable kayaks, check with the Chuns at *Tutzil Nah* in Maya Centre (see p.262). If you're suitably prepared, you can climb **Victoria Peak** (see box, p.261); 3km along the route, a side trail leads to the Outlier Overlook, perfect for either a challenging day-hike or an overnight camp.

Kanantik Reef and Jungle Resort

About six kilometres south of Maya Centre a side road heads east to the sea, ending at **Kanantik Reef and Jungle Resort** (Ⓣ520-8048, Ⓦwww.kanantik.com; US$365/day per person including meals and activities; ⑨), one of Belize's all-inclusive luxury resorts. The brainchild of Italian investors, the resort has 25 very spacious, elevated cabañas with tall, conical thatched roofs – the pinnacle of jungle and beach elegance. Composed of the finest local materials, Guatemalan textiles and four-poster beds, and surrounded by a wooden deck and tropical gardens, the resort fuses rustic simplicity with style and sophistication more successfully than anywhere else in the country. *Kanantik* means "to take care" in Mopan Maya, and you're certainly well cared for here; all the cabañas are air-conditioned and the meals and service are simply superb, but thankfully without the fussy formality of some other luxury places. It's set in three hundred acres of beach, jungle, pine forest and wetlands just south of Sapodilla Lagoon, and the area abounds with wildlife, including jaguars, crocodiles and birds, which can be spotted from two birding towers. The pool is just metres from the sea, and guests can choose from a variety of expertly guided activities, including scuba diving, snorkelling, sailing, canoeing, horseback riding and expeditions to Maya sites and the Jaguar Reserve; the only extra charge is for fly-fishing. Most guests arrive on scheduled Tropic Air flights (Fri–Mon), landing at the resort's own paved airstrip, but the staff will pick you up at the Dangriga airstrip as well.

The Placencia peninsula

Sixteen kilometres south of Maya Centre, a good dirt road cuts east from the Southern Highway, heading through pine forest and banana plantations and eventually reaching the sea at the tiny settlement of **Riversdale**. This marks the start of the **Placencia peninsula**, a narrow, sandy finger of land sheltering Placencia Lagoon from the sea. The road then curves down 26km to **Placencia**, a small, laid-back fishing village light years from the hassle of Belize City, and catering to an ever-increasing number of tourists. The road first passes through a beautiful stretch of coast called **Maya Beach**, halfway along the peninsula, where there are several restaurants and a range of accommodation.

Travelling south down the peninsula you'll pass around twenty resorts and hotels, most owned and operated by expatriate North Americans. Accommodation is usually in cabins with private bathrooms and electricity, and Internet access may be available; while pricey, most places will give *Rough Guides* readers worthwhile discounts. Meals, if not included in the rates, come to around US$40/day. In addition to the pleasures of a sandy Caribbean beach just a few steps away, most resorts also give access to Placencia Lagoon and can arrange fishing and diving trips offshore, as well as tours inland to the Jaguar Reserve and several Maya sites. Many have bikes and kayaks for guests, and it's a relatively easy paddle to False Caye. Below here, the Garifuna village of **Seine Bight** has several more upmarket places; the majority of the peninsula's budget accommodation is in Placencia village itself. The entire peninsula is served by four daily **buses** from Dangriga (see box, p.249), hitching is relatively easy and the sand road is ideal for cycling.

Maya Beach practicalities

Hungry Gecko, run by a friendly Honduran family (which also owns a store below the restaurant), serves tasty Belizean **breakfasts** and Central American snacks, plus soups, sandwiches, burgers and seafood at great prices (closed Wed). *Maya Beach Hotel and Bistro* (closed Mon; see p.266) has a sophisticated menu of delectable combinations from around the world. If you're putting together your own meal, the *Maya Point Market* is a local **grocery store** that also has cold beer.

Some hotels along Maya Beach have self-catering kitchens (grocery vans make regular trips down the peninsula and hotel owners know the times and days they call) and a selection of **restaurants** within walking distance, though most are at hotels. A **taxi** to or from Placencia costs around Bz$25–30. **Hotels** are listed in the order you approach them from the north, and all are right by the road; for more information on accommodation, visit Maya Beach's **website** (Ⓦ www.gotobelize.com).

Hotels and cabañas

Barnacle Bill's Beach Bungalows 400m south of *Maya Breeze* Ⓣ 523-8010, Ⓔ taylors@btl.net. Two large, very well-equipped wooden houses on stilts on a beautiful sandy beach. Each house has a double bedroom, bathroom with tub, living room with sofa bed and kitchen with microwave, stove, coffeemaker, fridge and even a spice and condiment package; call ahead with a list and they'll stock you up with groceries. Kayaks and bikes for guests. ⑧

Green Parrot Beach Houses 50m south of the *Maya Beach Hotel* Ⓣ 523-2488, Ⓦ www.greenparrot-belize.com. Six spacious wooden houses (sleeping up to five) raised on stilts, and two secluded, thatched, wooden "honeymoon" cabins on the beach. Each house has a living room, a loft bedroom with a queen-sized and single bed, a superb kitchen and a deck with hammocks. There's also an excellent restaurant, and the rates include transport from Placencia airstrip, continental breakfast and use of kayaks. ⑨

Maya Beach Hotel and Bistro 13km north of Placencia village ⓣ520-8040, in the US ⓣ1-800/503-5124, ⓦwww.mayabeachhotel.com. The six "beach-basic" rooms here are an excellent value with a/c, private bath and queen beds. Apartments are also available for longer stays. The popular restaurant, with fantastic food and service, consistently draws guests from other hotels. Online booking, particularly at the last minute, can yield a good discount. ❻–❽

Maya Breeze Inn Immediately south of *Green Parrot* ⓣ523-8012, in the US ⓣ1-888/458-8581, ⓦwww.mayabreezeinn.com. Beautifully furnished wooden cabins and suites on a gorgeous beach, plus four comfortable hotel rooms back from the road. All accommodation has a/c, private tiled bathrooms, fridge and balcony or deck; suites have a full kitchen. The *Monarch Café* serves breakfast only. ❼–❽

Maya Playa 250m south of *Singing Sands* ⓣ523-8020, ⓦwww.geocities.com/mayaplaya. Three palmetto-and-thatch, A-frame cabañas in a beautiful, beachfront location. Main bedrooms are upstairs, with a queen-sized bed and small balcony; the ground-floor living room has a couch and an extra bed, and the spacious semi-circular bathroom has jungle plants growing up the wall. Friendly owner Chuck Meares has built a very tall palapa on the beach for his kitchen and dining room, where guests are welcome to cook and eat their meals. There's a fridge in each cabaña, plus free bikes, kayaks, coffee and fruit for guests. ❻

Singing Sands Inn 200m south of *Barnacle Bill's* ⓣ523-8022, ⓦwww.singingsands.com. Six lovely, ground-level wood-and-thatch cabins, each with a porch, hammock, rocking chair and a tiny garden in front; there are less expensive rooms overlooking the shady, orchid-filled garden. There's a good restaurant, especially for vegetarians, the only pool in Maya Beach and a new swimming dock. Kayaks, canoes and bikes are complimentary for guests. Owner Marti Cottrell offers massage service and also has a furnished apartment for longer rentals. ❽

Seine Bight to Placencia

Three kilometres beyond Maya Beach the Garifuna village of **SEINE BIGHT** has several resorts and hotels, some looking out of place alongside the settlement's often dilapidated shacks. That said, the inhabitants' economic situation has been gradually improving, and many can now afford to build better homes. Reputed to have been founded by privateers in 1629, Seine Bight was possibly given its present name by French fishermen deported from Newfoundland after Britain gained control of Canada. The present inhabitants are descendants of the Garifuna settlers who arrived in Seine Bight around 1869.

The village is certainly worth a visit even if you're not staying: Seine Bight has its own **Garifuna band**, Lumalali Beidi ("voice of the Bight"), who sing and dance accompanied by powerful, evocative drumbeats; the band also gives drumming lessons. *White Sand Tiki Bar*, a distinctive, two-storey bamboo-and-thatch building on the beach near the centre of the village, plays Garifuna music and Western rock, and often has live music at weekends, when the management runs a shuttle service from Placencia. You could also check out Lola Delgado's superb (and affordable) oil and acrylic paintings of village life at *Lola's Art Gallery and Cat's Claw Bar and Café*, further south behind the soccer field. Lola is a great entertainer and a wonderful cook, serving superb Creole and Garifuna meals most days, and her dinners are often followed by **music and drumming** – call ⓣ601-1913 to check if she's cooking that evening. Lola can also arrange a taxi to pick you up in Placencia.

Resorts from Seine Bight to Placencia

Beyond Seine Bight, another series of resorts offers upscale **accommodation**, listed here from north to south. All have **restaurants** that are among the best in the country, so you'll usually need to book for dinner.

The Inn at Robert's Grove Just over 1km south of Seine Bight ⓣ523-3565, in the US ⓣ1-800/565-9757, ⓦwww.robertsgrove.com. A very well-managed luxury resort with spacious, elegant, a/c rooms and suites, all with cable TV and private balcony overlooking the sea; there are also three pools, several rooftop Jacuzzis and an oceanfront spa facility. *Seaside Restaurant*, with tables on a wooden deck on the beach, serves superb international and local dishes, and *Habañeros Mexican Café* offers Mexican-influenced fare under a thatched roof. Activities include diving, snorkelling, fishing, sailing, kayaking and canoeing, windsurfing and tennis. There are also three private cayes for guests to enjoy – all with overnight accommodation. Doubles US$215–235; suites US$285–485. 9

Mariposa Beach Suites 300m south of the airstrip ⓣ523-4069, ⓦwww.mariposabelize.com. Set on a beautiful beach, these gorgeous suites, with tiled floors and full kitchen, are the best value in their price range. Each has comfortable queen-size beds, a patio and a private beach palapa. There are also two brightly painted wooden cottages in the grounds, simpler and less expensive than the suites, but just as comfortable. *Mariposa* is Spanish for butterfly – an appropriate name, as you'll see lots as you wander the paths in the tranquil gardens. 9

Miller's Landing 300m south of *Robert's Grove* ⓣ523-3010, ⓦwww.millerslanding.net. Small, secluded resort set amid original vegetation just off a quiet beach. Very laid-back and a bit more rustic than many of the places here, with comfortable rooms in wooden cabins, all with private bathroom, ceiling fans and a porch; also two "economy" rooms with shared bathroom. There's a good bar and restaurant, locally famous for its pizza. Kayaks and bikes for guests. 6–8

Rum Point Inn Just north of the airstrip, 4km from Placencia ⓣ523-3239, ⓦwww.rumpoint.com. The giant, mushroom-shaped, whitewashed cabañas, with skylights and indoor plants, are spacious, cool and very comfortable; the enormous suites have the biggest bathrooms in the country. There's also a pool, to help with dive instruction, and the *Auriga II*, with its highly professional crew, is an excellent dive boat. Massage is available, and the library, with an emphasis on archeology, science and natural history, is the best of any resort in the country. Non-guests need to book for meals. Doubles US$179–209. 9

Turtle Inn 1km north of the village ⓣ523-3244 or 824-4912, ⓦwww.turtleinn.com. Francis Ford Coppola's resort in the Caribbean, set on a gorgeous, palm-lined beach and just as sumptuous as his *Blancaneaux Lodge* in Cayo (see p.182) and *La Lancha* near El Remate, Guatemala (see p.217). The thatched seafront "cottages" (US$385) have lots of varnished wood and Indonesian art and furnishings, plus fabulous tiled bathrooms and a big, screened deck. Other cottages in the garden are just as comfortable and a trifle less expensive, and a two-bedroom, two-bathroom beachfront villa with spacious sitting room is US$600. The atmosphere here is somehow more relaxed than *Blancaneaux*, and the spa will soothe you further. Pool, dive shop and free kayaks and bikes for guests. 9

Placencia

Perched on the tip of the peninsula, shaded by palm trees and cooled by the sea breeze, **PLACENCIA** is a welcome stop after the bus ride from Belize City or Dangriga. It also has some of the country's most beautiful **beaches**, and these, together with the abundant, inexpensive accommodation, make it a great place to relax. The villagers enjoy the easy life as much as visitors – as you'll find out during **Lobster-Fest**, celebrated over a fun-filled weekend in late June, shortly after the opening of the lobster season. You could also try to visit during the **Sidewalk Arts Festival**, held around Valentine's Day, when you can meet some of the artists and musicians of Belize's vibrant arts scene. If Placencia has one drawback, it might be that its remote location and distance from the reef put many of its tours out of the reach of budget travellers; more options are always becoming available, however.

Getting there and orientation

The easiest way to reach Placencia is on one of the regular Maya Island Air or Tropic Air **flights** from either of Belize City's two airports (about 45min). There will usually be a **taxi** (Bz$10) waiting to take you the 3km to the village. If not, ask someone at the airport to call one for you (Kingfisher ⓣ601-1903; Percy's ⓣ614-7831; or Noel's ⓣ600-6047). **Flights** from Placencia to Dangriga are Bz$83 (20min), and Bz$144 to Belize Municipal (45min).

Much cheaper are the direct **buses from Dangriga**, which currently leave at 10.30am, 11.30am, 4pm and 5.15pm and end up at the beachfront petrol

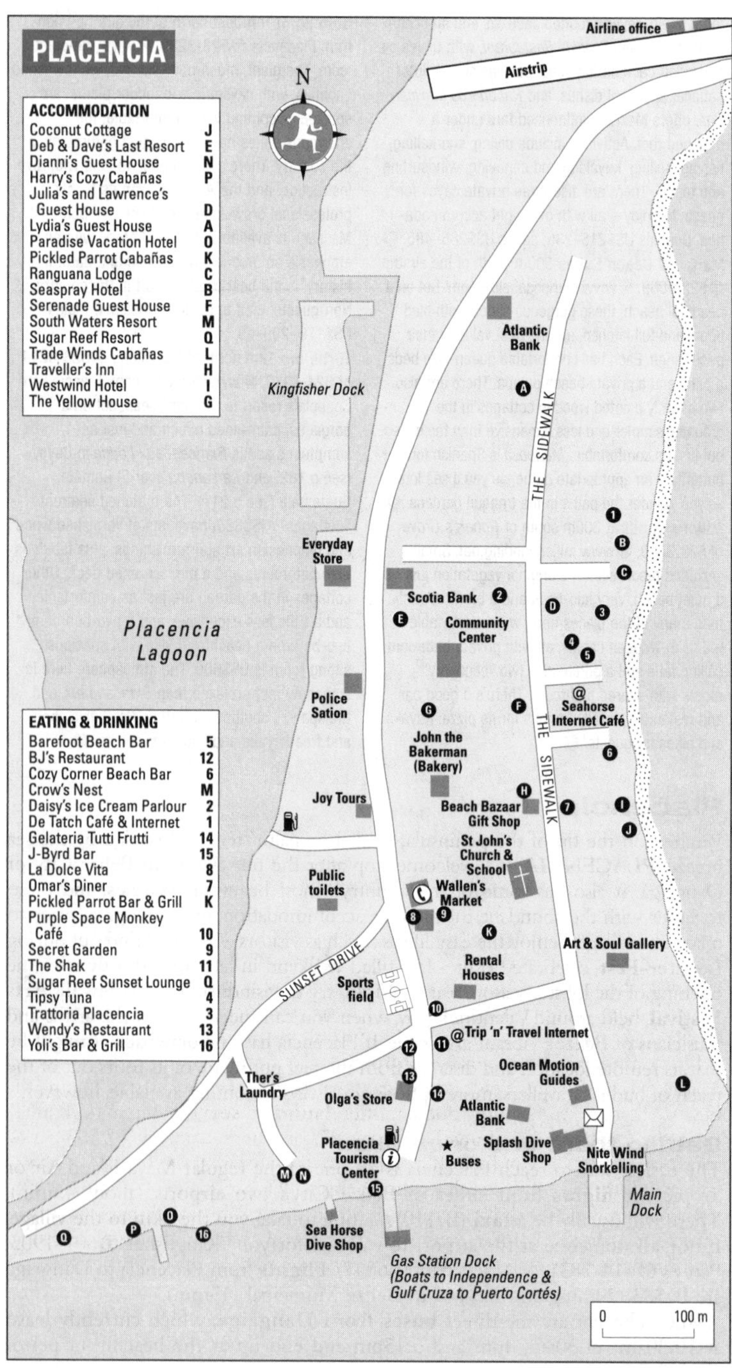

PLACENCIA
ACCOMMODATION
Coconut Cottage J
Deb & Dave's Last Resort E
Dianni's Guest House N
Harry's Cozy Cabañas P
Julia's and Lawrence's Guest House D
Lydia's Guest House A
Paradise Vacation Hotel O
Pickled Parrot Cabañas K
Ranguana Lodge C
Seaspray Hotel B
Serenade Guest House F
South Waters Resort M
Sugar Reef Resort Q
Trade Winds Cabañas L
Traveller's Inn H
Westwind Hotel I
The Yellow House G
EATING & DRINKING
Barefoot Beach Bar 5
BJ's Restaurant 12
Cozy Corner Beach Bar 6
Crow's Nest M
Daisy's Ice Cream Parlour 2
De Tatch Café & Internet 1
Gelateria Tutti Frutti 14
J-Byrd Bar 15
La Dolce Vita 8
Omar's Diner 7
Pickled Parrot Bar & Grill K
Purple Space Monkey Café 10
Secret Garden 9
The Shak 11
Sugar Reef Sunset Lounge Q
Tipsy Tuna 4
Trattoria Placencia 3
Wendy's Restaurant 13
Yoli's Bar & Grill 16
N
Airline office
Airstrip
Seine Bight (5km) & Dangriga (75km)
Atlantic Bank
Kingfisher Dock
THE SIDEWALK
Everyday Store
Scotia Bank
Community Center
Placencia Lagoon
Police Sation
Seahorse Internet Café
John the Bakerman (Bakery)
Joy Tours
Beach Bazaar Gift Shop
St John's Church & School
Public toilets
Wallen's Market
Art & Soul Gallery
SUNSET DRIVE
Sports field
Rental Houses
Trip 'n' Travel Internet
Ocean Motion Guides
Ther's Laundry
Olga's Store
Atlantic Bank
Placencia Tourism Center
Buses
Splash Dive Shop
Nite Wind Snorkelling
Main Dock
Sea Horse Dive Shop
Gas Station Dock (Boats to Independence & Gulf Cruza to Puerto Cortés)
0 100 m

station, right at the end of the peninsula; they generally return at 5.15am, 6am, 1.15pm and 2pm, but check locally for the times of the next day's departures (1hr 30min; Bz$10). If you're looking for budget rooms, you should get off the bus when you see the sign for the *Seaspray Hotel*, about halfway through the village on the left-hand side of the road. Head for "The Sidewalk", a concrete walkway that winds through the village and the palms like an elongated garden path, and you'll be at the centre of a cluster of inexpensive hotels and restaurants.

You can also hop over easily on the regular *Hokey Pokey* **boat service** from **Independence/Mango Creek** (20min; Bz$10), the small town just across the lagoon, where residents go to buy supplies and the older children go to school. It usually arrives at the main dock by the petrol station, though you can also get on or off at the Kingfisher Dock on the lagoon side. Independence is on the Dangriga–Punta Gorda bus route and the ferry meets most arriving buses; see box on p.273 for full details of transport to and from Indepdendence.

The *Gulf Cruza*, a large, fast, covered skiff, leaves Placencia for **Puerto Cortés**, Honduras, every Friday at 9.30am (4hr; US$50; ⓣ202-4506), going first across the lagoon to Big Creek, where passengers often face a lengthy delay to clear immigration; the onward journey from Big Creek to Puerto Cortés is only 2hr 30min. The *Cruza* returns to Placencia on Mondays, arriving around 2pm. Alternative water taxis are available, and you can find additional information at the Tourism Center. If you're **arriving by boat**, walk along the main dock to the end of the road through town; the Tourism Center is just ahead, and The Sidewalk will be to your right.

Information

The **Placencia Tourism Center** (Mon–Fri 9–11.30am & 1–5pm; ⓣ523-4045, ⓦwww.placencia.com) is the best tourist information office in the country, with a comprehensive website; call to find out what's going on locally, or stop by to call hotels on the payphone. The Center produces the excellent *Placencia Breeze* **newspaper** (Bz$1), with full local listings, transport schedules and a good map of the village and peninsula. The **post office** is upstairs in the wooden building at the end of The Sidewalk; the **BTL office** is at the roadside near the soccer field, and there are several payphones around town. **Internet connections** are everywhere: Placencia Office Supply has a fast connection with many terminals, and offers many additional services. Other options include *De Tatch Café* and Sea Horse Internet Café. The **Atlantic Bank** (24-hour ATM; Mon–Thur 8am–3pm, Fri 8am–4pm), across from the main dock by the petrol station, deals swiftly with cash advances; they have a second ATM on the main road, conveniently located next to *Gelateria Tutti Frutti* (see p.272). If you're heading to Honduras and want US dollars to exchange for lempiras, you'll need to present your ticket to the teller.

There are several self-service **shops** in the heart of the village: Wallen's Market, by the sports field, and Olga's, just before the petrol station, are the best-stocked. If your hotel doesn't offer **laundry service**, then find Julia's Laundry (ⓣ503-3478) along The Sidewalk, or Ther's Laundry (ⓣ503-3019) southwest of the sports field. If you're near the airstrip, Live Oak Plaza has a laundry with Internet as well as the Peckish Deli Store (ⓣ523-3636), selling gourmet groceries and a variety of deli items: smoked provolone, baked brie, prosciutto, smoked salmon and more for the perfect sandwich. There's no dedicated travel agent in the village, but many hotels and all tour operators can book **domestic flights**, and Maya Island Air and Tropic Air both have offices at the airstrip. Several **gift shops** sell souvenirs: The Beach Bazaar, on The Sidewalk south of the centre, has the best selection, and Art 'n' Soul Gallery, 30m south along The Sidewalk, showcases and sells a wide variety of arts and crafts made on consignment by local artisans. A number of enterprising Maya craftspeople from surrounding villages also set up shop, selling baskets and textiles along The Sidewalk, and approaching visitors on the beach from time to time.

Accommodation

There are plenty of **accommodation** options in Placencia, in all price ranges, and you should have no problem finding a room – provided you don't arrive at Christmas, New Year or Easter without a booking. Possibilities begin at The Sidewalk, once listed in the *Guinness Book of World Records* as the narrowest street in the world, and as you wend your way down it seems as though every family is offering **rooms**.

If you want to **rent a house**, bear in mind that many hotels here (and along the peninsula) also manage houses and self-catering apartments. One of the best-value places is offered by Ted Berlin (just before the *Purple Space Monkey Café*; ⓣ523-3172), who, in addition to being a qualified acupuncturist, has a couple of simple but charming places to rent for around Bz$250/week – and they do get booked up quickly. For something larger, ask Merlene at *Yoli's*, at the south end of the village (see p.272; ⓣ503-3153 or 625-2765, ⓔyolandaestephan@hotmail.com; Bz$550/week), who has two bedrooms (one with queen-sized bed), a full kitchen and bathroom, a comfortable living room with cable TV and DVD player and a patio. Also worth trying are *Be Back Cabañas* (ⓣ523-3143; Bz$350/week), just before the end of the road, with two houses on stilts with hot-water showers and basic kitchens with a fridge. The best-value **rental apartment** in the village is *Colibrí House* (ⓣ523-4046, ⓔcatalina@btl.net), a beautiful, fully furnished studio apartment in an octagonal wooden house on the beach, with a double bed and single sofa bed for US$55 per night. For other good rentals, visit the Tourism Center's website (ⓦwww.placencia.com) or contact Caribbean Tours (ⓣ523-3047), which represents a large variety of properties in the village.

Unless noted otherwise, all places listed here have **hot water**.

Inexpensive

Deb & Dave's Last Resort In the village centre (buses stop outside) ⓣ523-3207, ⓔdebanddave@btl.net. The nicest budget place in the village; very comfortable wooden rooms with clean, shared bathrooms and set in lovely gardens. You can rent kayaks here and Dave Vernon, who runs Toadal Adventure (see p.275), is a superb tour guide. ③

Julia's and Lawrence's Guest House In the centre of the village, south of the *Seaspray* ⓣ503-3478. Simple, comfortable rooms in a wooden building near The Sidewalk and cabins nearer the beach, all with private bath and porch; also a small furnished house for rent, Bz$130/night. ③–④

Lydia's Guest House Near the north end of The Sidewalk ⓣ523-3117, ⓔlydias@btl.net. Quiet, clean, secure and affordable rooms in a great location, all sharing immaculate bathrooms, in two wooden houses. There's a fridge for guests' use, and Lydia will cook breakfast on request. Also several good beach houses and kayaks for rent. ③

Paradise Vacation Hotel On the south beach, 250m west of the south dock (turn right at the petrol station) ⓣ523-3179, ⓔpvh@btl.net. Most rooms have private, hot-water shower, and some have a/c (though these have no windows), in this two-storey wooden building with a spacious upstairs deck overlooking the sea. There's a kitchenette with fridge, microwave and coffeemaker; no single rates. ③–④

Seaspray Hotel On the beach in the centre of the village ⓣ & ⓕ523-3148, ⓦwww.seasprayhotel.com. A popular, well-run hotel with a range of accommodation, from budget rooms to a private beach cabin, all with private bathroom and some with refrigerator, kitchenette, TV and balcony. The owners can arrange tours and give reliable information, and there's *De Tatch* restaurant on the beach for tasty meals and Internet access. ③–⑥

Traveller's Inn On The Sidewalk, just south of the centre ⓣ523-3190. Five basic rooms – the cheapest in the village – with shared bath and a communal porch for relaxing. Owner Lucille also has some comfortable rooms with private bath in a separate building. ③–④

The Yellow House In the centre of the village, east side of the road ⓣ523-3047, ⓔinfo@ctbze.com. Bargain rooms with comfortable beds and private bathrooms (two also have kitchenette) in a bright yellow wooden building with balcony and hammocks. French spoken. ③–④

Mid-range to expensive

Coconut Cottage On the beach south of the centre ⓣ523-3234, ⓔkwplacencia@yahoo.com. A comfortable, well-decorated and deservedly popular wooden cabin on the beach, with full kitchen; very popular, so you'll need to book in advance. ⑥

Dianni's Guest House On the south beach ⓣ523-3380, ⓔhotelserenade@btl.net. ⓦwww.diannisplacencia.com. A very comfortable two-storey hotel with clean, well-furnished rooms, all with private bathroom, a/c, fridge and coffeemaker. The wide, breezy verandas with hammocks are great for relaxing and you can borrow a cooler to take to the beach. Internet access, laundry service and kayaks and bikes for rent. ⑤

Harry's Cozy Cabañas 300m west from the south dock, turn right at the petrol station ⓣ523-3155, ⓔharbaks@yahoo.com. Spacious wooden cabins on stilts, with a screened porch, on a quiet little beach. Each cabin has a double and single bed, fridge and coffeemaker, and one has a small kitchen. The plant-filled gardens are an iguana sanctuary. According to Harry, kicking back with a Belikin under his "Tree of Knowledge" actually does impart wisdom. Usually a three-night minimum stay. ⑥

Pickled Parrot Cabañas Signposted just past Wallen's Market, towards the south end of the village ⓣ604-0278, ⓦwww.pickledparrotbelize.com. Two varnished wooden cabins with double beds, private bath, fridge and coffeemaker, and a deck with lounge chairs and a hammock, set in luxuriant tropical gardens. The bar and restaurant here (see p.272) is a great place to exchange information and arrange trips. *Rough Guides* readers may get a discount. ⑤–⑥

Ranguana Lodge On the beach in the centre of the village ⓣ523-3112, ⓦwww.ranguanabelize.com. Five beautiful white cabañas with porches, hammocks and optional a/c; three are on the beach, and the other two also have sea views. Inside are comfortable beds, bathrooms with tubs, hardwood floors and fittings, a big fridge and a coffeemaker, and there are palapas on the beach for relaxing. ⑥

Serenade Guest House On The Sidewalk just south of the centre ⓣ523-3380, ⓔhotelserenade@btl.net. Good-value rooms with private bath and a/c in a large, white-painted concrete building. There's also a good restaurant upstairs. This is where you book for Frank's Caye (see p.292). ⑥

South Waters Resort On the south beach, 100m west of the south dock ⓣ523-3308, ⓔsouthwatersresort@yahoo.com. Another spacious and comfortable hotel, with pastel-painted cement cabañas on the beach, each with fridge, microwave and coffeemaker, and a private patio in front. There are also a/c suites with full kitchen and living room in a two-storey building with wide verandas and great views. The open-air *Crow's Nest Café* serves excellent conch fritters. ⑧–⑨

Sugar Reef Resort On the south beach, near the end of Sunset Drive ⓣ523-3289, ⓦwww.thesugarreef.com. The British owners run a hospitable and wonderfully landscaped hotel, situated between beautiful views of both the lagoon and sea. Accommodations vary to suit singles, couples, and families with optional a/c, spacious bathrooms, and some kitchens. You can relax at the sunbathing pool, rooftop lounge, or docks on both the sea (with hammocks) and lagoon sides. The restaurant and bar here is particularly good, serving delicious Caribbean-inspired dishes. The bar hosts a number of festive events – Saturdays are especially lively, with horseshoes in the afternoon and the Saturday Night Fever party later on. Kayaks and canoes available for rent. ⑤–⑥

Trade Winds Cabañas On the south point ⓣ523-3122, ⓔtrdewndpla@btl.net. Eight brightly painted cabins (the biggest has a kitchenette and king-sized bed; ⑦) and three bargain rooms, all with private bath, fridge, coffeemaker and deck with hammocks, on the largest and sandiest beach in the village. Run by Janice Leslie, Placencia's former postmistress and owner of *J-Byrd Bar*, who's a mine of local knowledge. ④–⑥

Westwind Hotel Across from the Beach Bazaar gift shop ⓣ523-3255, ⓦwww.westwindhotel.com. An eccentric but functional wooden hotel offering rooms with private bath and decks with a beach-front view. You can "crack back" in one of many hammocks arranged around a large and spacious palapa out on the beach. ⑤–⑥

Eating and drinking

There are plenty of good **restaurants** in Placencia; however, even more so than elsewhere in Belize, places here change management fast, so it's always worth asking a resident's advice. There are also a number of good establishments at the resorts along the peninsula, and it may be worth taking a cab to try one of these. Most places close early; you'll certainly have more options if you aim to eat by 8pm. Fresh **bread** is available from John the Bakerman, just north of the Wallen's Market, and from a number of local women who bake johnny cakes, Creole bread and buns.

BJ's Restaurant By the road junction just past the sports field. Some of the best Belizean food in the village at genuine local prices, with friendly service in clean surroundings. Mon–Sat 7am–10pm, Sun 7am–3pm.

Cozy Corner Beach Bar & Grill On the beach just south of the centre. A heavily trafficked open-air restaurant and bar serving an array of blended drinks and large portions of international fare such as burgers, seafood and steaks. The daily specials are a deal here. Open 11am–11pm (later on weekends).

Daisy's Ice Cream Parlour On The Sidewalk in the centre. Long-established and deservedly popular place for ice cream, cakes and snacks, also serving complete Belizean meals. Daily until 10pm.

De Tatch Café On the beach, just north of the centre ⓣ503-3385. The best Belizean-owned restaurant in town, with a lovely, thatched open-air dining room and a scenic view of the ocean. Serves Caribbean cuisine at very affordable rates and delicious seafood mains at all hours; the fry-jacks are especially good at breakfast. There are also computers with high-speed Internet access. 7am–10pm.

Gelateria Tutti Frutti Near the end of the road. Genuine Italian ice cream, quite simply the best in Belize; it's available in literally dozens of flavours and you should try at least one every day you're in town. Daily until 9.30pm.

La Dolce Vita In the centre near Wallen's Market. A charming restaurant serving a good variety of Italian food and imported wines. The air-conditioned dining room is tastefully adorned with scenes from Fellini's movie, and dinner is served nightly. Open from 5.30pm until late.

Omar's Diner On The Sidewalk, across from Beach Bazaar. Very inexpensive joint for rice and beans, great, filling burritos, seafood and daily specials. Closed Sun.

Pickled Parrot Bar & Grill At *Pickled Parrot Cabañas* (see p.271). Friendly place under a big thatched roof. Consistently the best restaurant in the village and deservedly popular, serving fresh seafood, great pizza, pastas, salads with a daily special. The bar has wonderful blended tropical drinks and a 5–6pm happy hour. Open Mon–Sat 11am–9.30pm.

Purple Space Monkey Café Opposite the sports field. Serving good coffees and great American/Belizean-style breakfast, lunch and dinner under a huge thatched roof. Also has a paperback exchange and wireless Internet. Opens early, closes late.

Secret Garden Opposite the sports field near Wallen's Market. As the name implies, this café's location makes for a peaceful respite; it's tucked away right in the centre of town, serving not only as a coffeehouse but also a full-service restaurant, massage and spa centre and wireless Internet hotspot. Also a good place to find homemade baked goods and Sunday brunch. Closed Mon.

The Shak Opposite the south end of the sports field. Serves a variety of smoothie combinations using the freshest fruits and juices around. Healthy eats and vegetarian-friendly menu.

Trattoria Placencia On the beach near the centre. Authentic Italian meals – handmade pasta accompanied by good wines – in a very relaxed atmosphere. Open Mon–Sat from 5pm.

Wendy's Restaurant Near the south end of the main road. A comfortable, air-conditioned diner serving fresh juices and delicious Spanish and Creole dishes. Open daily 7am–10pm.

Yoli's Bar & Grill On the south beach, near *Paradise Vacation Hotel* ⓣ503-3153. Great for breakfast, serving good coffee and fantastic homemade bread and fry-jacks. Lunch and dinner are equally good, especially for fish, but the place is small so you may have to book. The exuberantly friendly owner is renowned for her cakes – if you have a birthday to celebrate, ask if she can make one for you. Open Mon–Sat 7am–9pm.

Nightlife

Evenings in Placencia are as relaxed as the days, but there are a few places with a lively **bar** atmosphere – ideal for drinking rum and watching the sun set – and an increasing number have **live music** to enhance the party mood. Some places in the village and many resorts along the peninsula have regular evening entertainment – happy hours, bar games, music and drumming, or a special dinner or barbecue; check the *Placencia Breeze* for what's on where. Both *Tipsy Tuna Sports Bar* and *Barefoot Beach Bar* on The Sidewalk are popular evening spots and open late. *J-Byrd Bar* (with adjacent gift shop), by the south dock and open all day, is a great place to meet local characters, and sometimes has live music at weekends. Turn right on Sunset Drive at the sign by the sports field for the *Sunset Lounge* at *Sugar Reef Resort* (see p.271), featuring a daily **happy hour**, bar games, karaoke, a regular DJ and occasional bands.

Around Placencia, offshore and inland

Trips from Placencia can be tailored to your preference and perhaps your pocket, covering everything from a day on the water to a week of camping, fishing, snorkelling or sailing on or around any number of idyllic islands. Diving or snorkelling at the cayes or along the reef is excellent, with shallow **fringing and patch reefs**, and some fantastic **wall diving**. You can visit several virtually pristine protected areas, including **Laughing Bird Caye National Park** and **Gladden Spit and Silk Cayes Marine Reserve**. **Placencia lagoon** is ideal for exploring in a **canoe or kayak**, available from several places in the village; you may even spot a manatee, though it's more likely to be a series of ripples as the shy giant swims powerfully for cover. The reefs and shallows off Placencia are rich **fishing** grounds too, and the village is home to a number of renowned fly-fishing guides.

It's also worth **heading inland** from Placencia – up the thickly forested banks of the **Monkey River** or to the **Jaguar Reserve** (see p.276 & p.263, respectively). Although many tour operators offer day-trips to the Jaguar Reserve (around Bz$135), it's quite feasible to do the trip independently by bus, leaving Placencia in the early morning and returning on the afternoon bus from Dangriga as it passes Maya Centre. **Car rental** is another option, especially useful if you're

Independence travel connections

Just across the lagoon from Placencia, **Independence**, though of little intrinsic interest, is a useful travel hub, served by all **buses** between Dangriga and Punta Gorda (see p.243 & p.284, respectively). Although some maps show **Mango Creek** and Independence as separate places, the creek just lends its name to one end of town; Independence begins at the road junction, a kilometre or so away. There's a regular fast **boat to Placencia** from here – the ironically named *Hokey Pokey* (20min; Bz$10 one way) – and the boatman usually meets arriving buses, often with a truck to carry your luggage. The *Hokey Pokey* leaves Independence/Mango Creek at 6.30am, 7.30am, 8am, 11am, 12.15pm, 2.30pm, 4.30pm and 5.30pm, returning from Placencia at 6.30am, 10am, 4pm and 5pm, sometimes with even more frequent departures. Alternatively, a charter costs at least Bz$45, and you may be able to get a lift on a local's boat.

NTSL and James **buses** have, between them, at least twelve departures daily in each direction along the Southern Highway (including some express services), heading **north to Dangriga** (under 2hr), Belmopan and Belize City between 6am and 4pm, and **south to Punta Gorda** (2hr) from 9am to 7pm. Catch the bus where the crews take their meal break: *Café Hello* for NTSL, and, across the road, *Sherl's Restaurant* for James; both serve inexpensive Belizean dishes and snacks.

With all these transport connections, you should be able to avoid getting stuck overnight in Independence. If you do, the *Hotel Hello* (☎523-2428; ④–⑤), mainly used by businesspeople, has air-conditioned rooms. You could also try the clean, simple *Ursula's Guest House* on Gran Main Street (☎608-7109; ③).

combining many inland sights. SUV Peninsula Car Rental (Ⓣ624-4903), conveniently located a short walk north of the airstrip, has a good selection of four-wheel-drive vehicles for roughly US$75/day. If the high petrol prices turn you off car rental, you may choose simply to explore the peninsula on a **bike**, which you can rent from *Dianni's Guest House* for around Bz$25/day.

After a long day of outdoor activity, you'll probably feel in need of some pampering: Z-Touch (Ⓣ523-3513) has a **massage**, spa and beauty parlour in the town centre, and Secret Garden Massage (Ⓣ523-3420) also offers massage services.

Diving and snorkelling

The Barrier Reef is wider here than in the north of Belize, and it's not as continuous, breaking into several smaller reefs and cayes and creating even more coral canyons and drop-offs. Because it lies about 30km offshore, though, snorkelling and diving trips are more expensive here than at many other places. The upside is that there are several smaller mangrove islands and coral heads closer to the coast, and you can still see a lot of fish and some coral by snorkelling just offshore. For detailed information on the reefs and all aspects of the ecology of the protected marine areas off Placencia, visit the **Friends of Nature** office (Ⓣ523-3377, Ⓦwww.friendsofnaturebelize.org). Friends of Nature co-manages the area's reserves, and you can support their efforts by becoming a "Friend" or buying a beautiful and eye-catching whale shark T-shirt.

Day-trips to the cayes (including visits to see **whale sharks** in season) are offered by several operators (the best are listed below), and the choice of dive sites is so wide that during a month-long stay you need never visit the same one twice. PADI Open Water Certification costs around Bz$700, and a two-tank dive trip roughly Bz$150–200. Snorkelling trips cost from Bz$65 to $85, depending on the location; they usually include lunch and sometimes snorkelling equipment. If not, you can rent snorkels, masks and fins for around Bz$10. Several resorts along the peninsula have their own **dive shops**; in the village, go to Splash Dive Shop at the end of the sidewalk (Ⓣ523-3345 or 661-8160, Ⓦwww.splashbelize.com) or Brian Young at Sea Horse Dive Shop, on the south dock (Ⓣ523-3166, Ⓦwww.belizescuba.com), for the best diving instruction, excursions and equipment rental. For **snorkelling** or **manatee-watching**, check with Nite Wind Guides (Ⓣ523-3847, Ⓔdoylegardiner@yahoo.com) or Ocean Motion Guides (Ⓣ523-3363, Ⓔoceanmotion@btl.net), both at the south end of The Sidewalk.

Sailing, kayaking and fishing

Sailing among the reefs and cayes off Placencia is, if anything, even more beautiful than from the northern cayes, and the village is a base for top-tier catamaran charter companies TMM and The Moorings. If you'd like (and can afford) a week's sailing, you'll usually need to book well in advance; see p.23 in Basics for contact details and prices. Some of the resorts along the peninsula have Hobie Cats (small catamarans) for rent, but other than these the only regular one-day **sailing trip** is aboard the *Next Wave*, a fifty-foot catamaran operated by British couple Rory and Michelle McDougall. A day-trip to the cayes, including buffet lunch and open bar, is US$88, while a sunset cruise with drinks and snacks is US$50; to book, call Ⓣ523-3391 or 610-5592, or visit Ⓦwww.nextwavesailing.com.

Let's Go Sailing has been around for thirty years and has a large fleet of sailing boats and catamarans, including the *Talisman*, a wonderful and very comfortable

52-foot ketch; it's sometimes available for a day's sailing, but often booked for overnight trips. At US$120 per person for a day-trip (9.30am–5.30pm) it's fairly expensive, but the price includes snorkelling, kayaking, snacks, a full lunch and an open bar; there are also three staterooms for overnight trips. In addition to the *Talisman*, Let's Go Sailing offers day and overnight packages on fully crewed or bareboat charters (ⓣ523-3138 or 523-3312, ⓦwww.belize-sailing-charters.com) from US$300 to over $1000 per night. You could also contact Raggamuffin Tours on Caye Caulker (see p.151), which arranges weekly overnight sailing trips from there to Placencia; they typically arrive in Placencia between Tuesday and Thursday, and may have space aboard for the return journey.

Several places rent **canoes** and sit-on-top kayaks for around Bz$35/day – try *Sugar Reef Resort* in the village (see p.271) – and some resorts have free ones for guests. For top-quality double **sea kayaks** (Bz$75/day) and tours (Bz$120 per person) contact Dave Vernon at Toadal Adventure (ⓣ523-3207, ⓦwww.toadaladventure.com). Dave is one of the best tour guides in Belize, and is a great natural historian as well as a superb river and kayaking guide.

World-class **fishing** draws anglers eager to test their skill by catching the permit, tarpon, snook and bonefish that abound in the seas around Placencia, and a day out with a boat and a guide will set you back around US$300; any of the dive or snorkel places can arrange this. You could also go with Trip 'n' Travel's Earl Godfrey, one of the best fly-fishing guides around (ⓣ523-3614, ⓔlgodfrey@direcway.com), or Bernard Leslie at Ocean Motion Guides (see opposite). Fishing rods, flies and tackle are available from Fred's Fishing Gear (next to *Dianni's*; ⓣ523-3304 or 601-1914, ⓔfredsea1@yahoo.com).

Laughing Bird Caye

The Bugle Cayes, with a good section of reef, are only a few kilometres from Placencia, though most operators prefer to take you to uninhabited **Laughing Bird Caye National Park** (Bz$20), about 18km away. The caye itself (named for the laughing gull) is tiny, under 1.5 acres, and the gulls themselves no longer nest here, but the national park protects over 10,000 acres of the surrounding sea as a "no take zone" (fishing prohibited), and it is a World Heritage Site. The caye sits on top of a "faro", a rhomboid-shaped limestone reef rising steeply from the sea bed, with an outer rim enclosing a lagoon, and thus similar to (though not the same as) an atoll. There's a ranger station on the caye, and many tours stop for lunch on the beach here, where there's a picnic shelter, tables and a barbecue pit. The northern tip of the caye protects the native vegetation and nesting birds and turtles, and is off-limits to visitors.

Gladden Spit and Silk Cayes Marine Reserve

Twenty kilometres beyond Laughing Bird Caye, the exquisitely beautiful Silk Cayes form part of the **Gladden Spit and Silk Cayes Marine Reserve** (Bz$10), a much larger protected area designated to safeguard the seasonal visitation of the enormous yet graceful **whale shark**. These migratory fish, found throughout tropical waters, are attracted to Gladden Spit during the full moons of April, May and June by huge numbers of spawning snappers. The sharks are filter-feeders, so it's the protein-rich spawn they're after, not the fish themselves. Research conducted by the University of York and the Nature Conservancy indicates that this is one of the largest and most predictable aggregations of whale sharks in the world. Radio-tracking the sharks has demonstrated that they travel at least as far as Cancún in Mexico and down to Honduras – and it's likely they go even further afield. Any guide taking you to see whale sharks will have undergone special training in how to approach them without harming or disturbing their feeding. Boats should stay fifteen metres away from the sharks, and snorkellers and divers must keep at least three metres away. *Isla Marisol*, on Glover's Reef, runs trips here (see p.260).

Ranguana Caye

Ranguana Caye, 35km southeast of Placencia and visited by some snorkel trips from town, is a jewel of an island just 120m long by 25m wide, surrounded by patch reefs perfect for snorkelling. For divers, the shelf and 800-metre drop-off begin 750m offshore. The sand on Ranguana is softer than in Placencia, the palm trees are taller and the sunsets are glorious, silhouetting mountain ranges in Honduras and the Maya Mountains in Belize. It's owned by *Robert's Grove* near Placencia (see p.266), and you can stay here in beautiful wooden cabins facing into the almost constant breeze. Each has an immaculate private bathroom, there's hot water and electricity, and meals are served in a large palapa-covered dining area. As you might expect, it's expensive, at US$325 per night per person, including transport, meals, drinks and use of kayaks and snorkel gear; a week's stay is US$1120 per person.

French Louie Caye

Kitty Fox and Ran Villanueva offer a great **sea kayaking** or overnight trip to beautiful **French Louie Caye** (Ⓦwww.frenchlouiecayebelize.com), a tiny island fringed with mangroves just 12km offshore. There's great snorkelling all around the caye, with numerous hard and soft corals, sea anemones and huge schools of tiny fish among the mangrove roots; you can also visit at least half a dozen uninhabited cayes nearby. French Louie has a resident pair of ospreys, who nest in a mature white mangrove and successfully rear chicks every year. If you want to stay you can have exclusive use of the caye, sleeping in a two-storey wooden house with delicious meals prepared and served by the resident cook, or you can cook for yourself. This simple paradise costs US$190 per night per person, including transport (you're taken out in a skiff, or you can paddle a kayak if you like), use of a double kayak, a dory and snorkelling gear; camping is half the price. Mosquitoes are not a problem as there's no open fresh water; drinking water (in a rainwater vat) is available, and there are composting toilets. You can inquire about the caye at the Peckish Deli in Placencia (see p.269).

Whipray Caye

Whipray Caye (shown on some maps as Wippari Caye), 13km northeast of Placencia, is another small, idyllic island, surrounded by reef corals and coral heads, and it also has some fine cabin accommodation, a little less expensive than on the previous two cayes. *Whipray Caye Lodge* (Ⓣ608-8130, Ⓔwhipraycaye@yahoo.com; ❼, meals US$40/day per person and transport US$40 per person each way) has two comfortable wooden cabins with private bathrooms, ceiling fans and windows on all sides so you can enjoy the views and the breeze. Run by expert fishing guide Julian Cabral and his wife Beverley, it's an ideal base for some serious angling, or just relaxing, and you'll be eating plenty of fresh fish.

The Monkey River

One of the best inland day-trips from Placencia takes you by boat 20km southwest to the practically untouched **Monkey River**, teeming with fish, birdlife and **howler monkeys**. Monkey River Magic, in Placencia, runs the best **tours** (US$40, minimum 4 people; contact Trip 'n' Travel, Ⓣ523-3614), led by Evaristo Muschamp, a very experienced local guide from Monkey River

△ Kayaks on the Monkey River

Town. You can also arrange some good packages with accommodation in the village. Tours from Placencia set off by 8am, leaving from the petrol station dock, and a thirty-minute dash through the waves is followed by a leisurely glide up the river and a walk along forest trails. Binoculars are essential if you want to make the most of the amazing **birding** here, as well as the chance to see turtles, crocodiles and, of course, howler monkeys along the river. The

Monkey River area was badly hit by Hurricane Iris in 2001 (which also caused tremendous damage in Placencia), and the forest will take several years to fully recover. Most of the monkeys survived the ordeal, however, and continue to breed successfully.

If you've brought a picnic, lunch is taken on a sandbank in the river, or you can get a meal in *Alice's Restaurant* in **MONKEY RIVER TOWN** (in reality a small village). There's also time to enjoy a stroll around the village and have a drink at one of the **bars**: *Ivan's Cool Spot*, where the river meets the sea, is one of the best. If you want **to stay**, *Enna's Guest House* (Ⓣ720-2033 or call community phone Ⓣ709-2069; ❶–❷) has a nice river view with shared bath, fans and electricity, and Enna's brothers are tour guides. You can also find the *Sunset Inn* (Ⓣ720-2028, Ⓔsunsetinn@btl.net; ❸) on a tiny bay at the back of the village. Rooms are in a two-storey wooden building with comfortable beds, private bath and fan. A wide, shady veranda overlooks the river, and you can get tasty Creole food in the restaurant; owner Clive Garbutt is an excellent guide (contact him on the village's community telephone, see above). Eloy Cuevas, also from the village, is one of the best **fly-fishing guides** in Belize; contact him at Ⓣ523-2014 or through the Placencia Tourism Center (see p.269).

If you'd rather **drive** to Monkey River, take the 22-kilometre dirt road that connects the village to the Southern Highway, south of Independence. The road ends on the opposite bank of the river from the village, but just call out and someone will give you a ride over in a boat.

The far south: Toledo District

South of the Placencia and Independence junctions, the newly paved **Southern Highway** leaves the banana plants and the grim settlements squashed beside the plantation roads, twisting at first through pine forests and crossing numerous creeks and rivers. Though it still sees little traffic, this is now the best highway in the country. People are scarce down here, with only a few villages along the way, but the neat ranks of new citrus plantations are frequently in view, with trees marching over the hills. The mountains to the west are all part of the country's system of forest and nature reserves and national parks, though conflicts over the status of some protected areas are emerging as **Toledo District** (whose residents often feel they live in Belize's "forgotten district") becomes more developed. Wildlife is abundant but the reserves are often inaccessible – though on the northern border of Toledo, at **Red Bank**, you can see one of the largest concentrations of **scarlet macaws** in Central America, and further south you can stay in a field station on the west bank of the **Bladen River**, surrounded by wild jungle and mountains. As you head south you'll still see scars on the mountainsides and trees with their top branches torn off – evidence of the havoc wreaked on the landscape as Hurricane Iris ripped a narrow but devastating swath through southern Belize in October 2001. A few more **lodges** have opened their doors in recent years, most of them expensive, upmarket places, but there are a few more affordable options as well.

Although the Maya of Belize are a fairly small minority within the country as a whole, in Toledo the two main groups – Mopan and Kekchí – make up about half of the population. For the most part they live in simple villages, very similar in appearance to their Guatemalan counterparts; in fact, the verdant, mountainous landscape of the far south resembles that of Guatemala's Alta Verapaz and southern Petén, where the ancestors of most of Toledo's Maya came from. The biggest of the Maya villages in Toledo are **San Antonio** and **San Pedro Columbia**, reached by a good side road heading west from the highway. These villages have hotels, though in many others you'll stay in simple guest houses.

There's plenty of evidence that the ancient Maya lived here too, with ruins scattered in the hills around the villages. The best-known site is **Lubaantun**, where the famous Crystal Skull was "discovered" (see box, p.294), and **Nim Li Punit**, with some impressive stelae, is an easy visit from the highway; near the Guatemalan border, **Pusilhá** is a little harder to reach, but contains the best example anywhere of a Maya bridge. The Southern Highway ends at **Punta Gorda**, the southernmost town in Belize and the only proper town in Toledo. It's the base for visits both to the inland villages and to the little-visited southernmost **cayes and marine reserves**. Several daily skiffs connect it to **Puerto Barrios** in Guatemala.

Red Bank

Fourteen kilometres south of the junction to Riversdale and Placencia, a side road heads 6km west to the small Maya village of **Red Bank**, the focus of a campaign to preserve the habitat of the largest-known concentration of **scarlet macaws** in Belize – if not Central America. These spectacular members of the parrot family, formerly considered uncommon in Belize, congregate during the winter months to feed on ripe fruit. Knowledge of the flock, which could number over two hundred birds, only came to light when word reached conservation organizations in Belize City that villagers (who had no idea of the macaws' protected and endangered status) were hunting them for food. The Programme for Belize and the Belize Audubon Society immediately devised proposals to establish a tourism project in the hope that income from visitors would save the macaws and bring economic benefits to the people of Red Bank.

Near the village, there's **accommodation** in a four-roomed cabin (Bz$50 per person) with a deck and a separate dining room, overlooking a pretty creek and in sight of the macaws feeding in the surrounding hills. Villagers have been trained to guide visitors to see the macaws and hike along forest **trails** to nearby waterfalls and caves. Keep in mind that the macaws aren't always here, however, so before you visit you should call to ask if the birds are around (see below for phone numbers). There's currently no regular transport to Red Bank, but trucks leave daily from and to Independence. For details on staying or visiting, contact the Programme for Belize or the Belize Audubon Society in Belize City (see p.74), or telephone Geronimo Sho or Julio Teul on the Red Bank **community telephone** (Ⓣ509-3110).

The Belize Foundation for Research and Environmental Education

Twenty-five kilometres past the Independence junction, and 7km beyond the bridge over the Bladen River, a track heads west for 10km to the **Belize Foundation for Research and Environmental Education** ("Bfree"; Ⓣ614-3896, Ⓦwww.bfreebelize.net). Here you can stay in a **field station** on the riverbank, surrounded by some of the most magnificent forest and mountain scenery in the country. Bfree is a research and educational facility, founded in 1994 by biologists Jacob and Kelly Marlin, and the field station is open to all. They particularly welcome **interns** (who pay only Bz$40/day, including food and accommodation) to help with tropical forest conservation and research and to undertake practical tasks such as maintaining the garden and buildings.

All buses on the Southern Highway pass the turn-off for Bfree (200m before the Gomez sawmill, the only building around), which is signposted as "**Bladen Nature Reserve**". Unless you're in your own vehicle (and don't attempt to drive this road without a high-clearance four-wheel-drive, preferably one equipped with a winch) you'll have to walk in (2hr), and even study group participants usually arrive on foot, learning about the local ecosystems on the way. It's a pleasant hike along level ground, passing first through pine and palmetto savannah, then through the shade and scent of the pines, reaching the broadleaf forest as you approach the riverbank; call out and someone will paddle a canoe over to carry you across. Alternatively, you can charter a ride on "Grizzly", Bfree's 4x4, which will pick you up at the Gomez sawmill.

Bfree's location is nothing short of stunning. The field station is set in over 1100 acres of private reserve, at the meeting point of four enormous protected areas: the Cockscomb Basin Wildlife Sanctuary, the Deep River and Maya Mountain Forest Reserves and the Bladen Nature Reserve – the last only accessible to accredited, authorized researchers. The jade-green Bladen River emerges from a steep-sided valley just upstream, and the jungle-clad triangle of **Richardson Peak** – the third-highest peak in Belize, at just over 1000m – is just the largest in an entire range of mountains rising on the western horizon. You can climb this with a guide from Bfree or, suitably prepared, take any route in the fifty-kilometre trail system. The beautiful "**blue pool**", among rocks in the river, is perfect for a swim, and canoes are available for river trips. Nearby is a tranquil lagoon, full of fish and overhung by trees laden with bromeliads, where crocodiles lurk, tapirs bathe and monkeys howl. Jaguars and other cats prowl the forest.

There's a range of comfortable, rustic **accommodation** here, though you'll most likely get a dorm bed in the comfortable wooden bunkhouse (Bz$60 per person, including meals), or you can **camp** (Bz$60 per person, including meals, and tents are available). The private wooden cabins are usually reserved for researchers. Substantial, delicious meals, often using produce from the organic garden, are served in the thatched dining room. Amazingly, despite the remote location, there's **Internet access** and phone service.

Biodiversity is rich here, with over 300 bird and 180 reptile and amphibian species, and many of the definitive books on Belizean and regional wildlife have been researched here. With 21 amphibian species in eight families, Bfree is an ideal site for long-term amphibian research, and work undertaken at the field station is vital to the goals of the Maya Forest Anuran Monitoring Project (supported in part by the Wildlife Conservation Society; see p.351 in Contexts). The data collected is particularly relevant in light of concern about the decline in amphibian populations in supposedly undisturbed environments – even if you're here just as a visitor or intern, you could easily share in a discovery.

Nim Li Punit to Big Falls

About 58km from the Independence junction, near the Maya village of **Indian Creek**, you pass the entrance to **NIM LI PUNIT**, a Late Classic-period Maya site that was probably allied to nearby Lubaantun (see p.295). This site, discovered only in 1976, is home to the largest and one of the best-preserved stelae in Belize, and recent restoration work has revealed many more features. It's only 1km west of the highway and the entrance track is well signposted – making

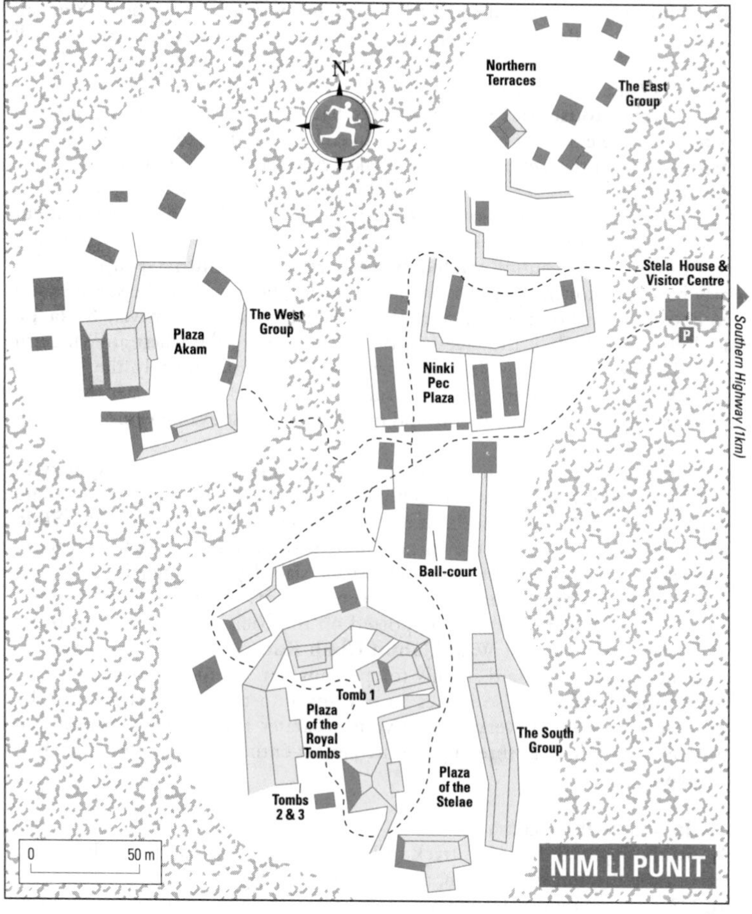

for an easy and very worthwhile visit. The site is often included on tour itineraries, and nearby, two of Toledo's luxury lodges, *Indian Creek Lodge* and *The Lodge at Big Falls*, provide upscale **accommodation** (see pp.282 & 283, respectively). The village of **Big Falls** also has some budget rooms.

Ten kilometres south of Indian Creek, the road to **Silver Creek** branches off to the right (west); with your own transport you can use this route to visit Maya villages and the site of Lubaantun (see p.295).

Nim Li Punit

Nim Li Punit (daily 9am–5pm; Bz$10) occupies a commanding position on a ridge above Indian Creek, with views over the maize fields to the southern coastal plain beyond – a scene largely unchanged since ancient times. It's believed to have been linked politically with all the other sites in southern Belize, as well as to Copán in Honduras. **Getting to the site** is relatively easy: all passing buses go by the entrance road, so you could head up here from Punta

Gorda in the morning and catch a bus back to town in the afternoon. You can leave luggage at the little shop by the roadside, and the family that runs it will know the times of onward buses; Pop's, the village bus service, leaves for Punta Gorda at 6am, 7am and 11.30am.

The **Stela House and Visitor Centre** has a good map of the site, and wall panels provide excellent explanations – in Kekchí and English – of some of the texts carved on the stelae. The site caretaker, Adriano Mas, may be able to show you around.

You enter the site through a plaza surrounded by walls and buildings of cut stones held together without mortar, a characteristic of sites in the region, and pass through the beautiful **walled ball-court** to the **South Group** – which may have functioned as an observatory to record the sunrise at the solstices and equinoxes. A total of 25 stelae were found here, eight of them carved. **Stela 14**, at almost 10m high, is the tallest in Belize, and one of the tallest anywhere in the Maya world – although it was never erected. Unfortunately, the site was badly looted soon after its discovery, and in 1997 several of the stelae were again badly damaged – this time by fire and machete. The best examples are now kept securely indoors.

Although Stela 14 lives in the Stela House, it's still an impressive sight, with panels of glyphs above and a richly attired ruler below: it's his elaborate headgear that gives Nim Li Punit its name, being Kekchí for "big hat". **Stela 15**, dated to 721 AD and the earliest here, is slightly smaller yet even more impressive. Carvings on this great sandstone slab depict a ruler in the act of dropping an offering – perhaps *copal* incense or corn kernels – into an elaborately carved, burning brazier supported on the back of a monster, in order to conjure up a vision of **Waxaklahun Ubah Kan**, or "Mosaic War Serpent", the ruler's battle standard. To his (or perhaps her – expert opinion differs) right, a smaller figure also makes an offering into the brazier, while on the left side a column of very clear glyphs separates the main figure from an attendant, or guard; all three figures are almost entirely surrounded by panels of glyphs.

Indian Creek Lodge

Across the highway from the track to Nim Li Punit, and set on a hilltop with views over the forest, savannah, and two artificial lagoons, *Indian Creek Lodge* (Ⓣ223-6324, Ⓦwww.belizelodge.com; ⑨) offers splendid **accommodation** in twelve spacious and very comfortable hardwood and stone cabins. Some are air-conditioned and the interiors of all are richly appointed: the four-poster beds are draped with mosquito nets, the bathrooms are luxurious and each has a large deck for enjoying the views. There's a private zoo in the grounds, providing native birds and animals (including a black jaguar from Mexico) almost as much luxury as the human guests. The lodge is set in the huge, privately owned **Boden Creek Ecological Reserve**, covering thirteen thousand acres from the highway to the coast.

Indian Creek manages three other lodges nearby. The closest, *Ballum Ha*, is just 3km south of *Indian Creek*, alongside Boden Creek. It's equally luxurious, with suite accommodation, and is home to two male jaguars. Eight kilometres south of *Indian Creek* and accessible only by water, *Jungle Camp* has safari-style bungalows and an elegant, spacious dining room overlooking Golden Stream. From here you can take **hiking** trips into the forest and **boat trips** along the river and into Payne's Creek National Park and Port Honduras Marine Reserve with superb naturalist guides. Seafaring boats will take you to the Sapodilla Cayes (see p.292) or the Snake Cayes, site of *Moho Cay Lodge*, just

1.5km off the coast. The lodging on this private island consists of elevated, thatched-roof "tents" with tiled bathrooms, hardwood floors, wicker furnishings and private verandas. You can snorkel, relax and enjoy the panorama of the Caribbean here, and feast on fresh seafood caught and prepared on-site. Guests are typically flown to the private airstrip, and most come on a package (starting around US$1015 per person for three nights, US$1950 for six nights), which typically includes stays at two or more of the properties, as well as a choice of numerous excursions in the ecological reserve, to sites throughout Toledo and to the cayes offshore.

Big Falls accommodation

Just beyond the Silver Creek junction is the village of **BIG FALLS**, with a petrol station, a store and a major bridge over the Río Grande, as well as a luxury resort. It's not a particularly pretty village (though the river is gorgeous) but it does boast Belize's only **hot spring**, a sumptuous spot for a warm bath. The spring feeds a creek that flows into the Río Grande, just upstream of the bridge in the village centre. Alongside the highway is *Coleman's Café*, an excellent and delicious local spot for a **meal** or snack.

Just north of the bridge, and signposted 800m off the highway, *The Lodge at Big Falls* (Ⓣ671-7172 or 671-6677, in the US Ⓣ1-888/865-3369, Ⓦwww.thelodgeatbigfalls.com; ⑨) provides decadent **accommodation** in very spacious thatched cabañas, set in 29 landscaped and flower-filled acres on a meandering bend of the Río Grande. The six fully screened cabañas, all with tiled floors, powerful ceiling fans, roomy bathrooms, hardwood furniture and a large deck with hammocks, offer plenty of comfort and privacy. You'll see lots of nature right here; two hundred species of birds have been recorded, and butterflies are everywhere. Trails lead though the lush growth on the riverbank and kayaks are available; you can be put in at San Miguel, 8km upstream, for a wonderful float back to the *Lodge*. The grounds were once a citrus orchard, with more than enough trees left to provide all the fresh juices served in the restaurant. Food is also served at an outdoor grill near the swimming pool.

Big Falls to Punta Gorda

Seven kilometres south of Big Falls, a road branches off west to **San Antonio** (see p.299), from where you can explore the forested southern foothills of the Maya Mountains, dotted with ruins and some delightful riverside Maya villages. Paving of this road has been delayed, but eventually it will lead to a **new border crossing** point into Guatemala; until this happens the existing unofficial crossing is not a legal exit point from Belize. The road's junction with the highway goes by the unfortunate name of **Dump**; there's a **petrol station** here, selling beer and cold drinks, and if you're driving it's a good place to pick up information. From the Dump junction the Southern Highway heads southeast, smooth and fast along the 22km to Punta Gorda. Along the way you'll pass a few small villages, mostly founded and inhabited by members of Belize's East Indian community, and a handful of places to stay. At **Jacintoville**, 11km from Punta Gorda, a branch road heads south to the Garifuna village of **Barranco**, Belize's southernmost coastal settlement.

At **Sun Creek**, 3km south of the Dump junction, *Sun Creek Lodge* (Ⓣ614-2080 or 662-0496, Ⓦwww.toucantrail.com/sun-creek-lodge.html; ④, including breakfast) has five beautiful thatched cabañas, all with electricity and one with a private bathroom. The lodge is a "naturalist's paradise", providing all the necessary modern conveniences through creative applications of rustic living.

The jungle showers (with "bucket" showerheads) are particularly innovative, making guests feel as though they're standing under a waterfall in the rainforest. German co-owner Bruno knows Toledo District and the entire country very well and runs International Belize Tourism Marketing, offering a range of often hard-to-find services for visitors to southern Belize, including tours, **jeep rental** (US$65/day) and high-speed and wireless **Internet** access.

At **Jacintoville**, 7km past Sun Creek, *Tranquility Lodge* (no phone, ⓦwww.tranquility-lodge.com; ➎, including breakfast), on the bank of beautiful Jacinto Creek, offers air-conditioned comfort at a bargain price in spacious, tiled, en-suite rooms set in orchid-laden gardens. Above the rooms, the fully screened thatched restaurant serves excellent meals, and gives great all-round views of the grounds. *Tranquility*'s location, just 300m from the paved highway at the entrance to the road to Barranco, makes it an ideal base for visiting the inland Maya villages and ruins or the southern coast. The place is very popular with birders, with over two hundred species seen along the forested trails here, and the natural, rock-lined pool in the creek is perfect for a refreshing dip. If you want to meet locals, stroll over to *Miss Flora's Beer Parlour*, in the village about a kilometre from the lodge. Flora also serves snacks and simple meals. If you're arriving at *Tranquility* by bus, get off on the south side of the bridge at the junction for Barranco, then follow the signs.

Six kilometres beyond Jacintoville, a signposted road leads left (north) to another of Toledo's upscale resorts, *Machaca Hill Lodge* (ⓣ722-0050; ➒), whose glorious hilltop setting on landscaped grounds high above the Río Grande offers wonderful views over the surrounding forest. Though the service can be a bit rusty, the location is superb. Guests stay in spacious, beautifully furnished wooden cabañas, each with a private deck shaded by trees, and **meals** are served in the main lodge building. From here you can embark on a number of adventures into Laughing Falcon Reserve, eleven thousand acres of privately protected land. **Fly-fishing** packages into Port Honduras Marine Reserve can also be arranged, starting at US$1170 per person for three nights and two days of fishing. A funicular tram takes you down the steep slope to the river and the waiting boats, and if you're not fishing you can relax in and around the **pool** atop the hill, enjoy a breathtaking panorama from the main lodge or walk the **nature trails** through the forest. Overnight rates are US$210 for a double, and packages of three to seven nights are available, including tours, local transfers and all meals.

The highway reaches the sea a few kilometres beyond the *Machaca Hill* junction at a place called **Cattle Landing**, where you can **rent a room** for a week or more in *Casa Bonita Apartments* (ⓣ722-2270, ⓔcba4cnn@btl.net). Here there's a range of private, good-value, furnished apartments with full kitchens in a concrete building facing the sea – ideal for long stays. They cost around Bz$75–150/week, though there are discounts for students, and meals can be arranged. Beyond Cattle Landing the road continues along the attractive shoreline for the last few kilometres to Punta Gorda.

Punta Gorda

The Southern Highway comes to an end in **PUNTA GORDA** (commonly known as "PG"), the heart of still-isolated **Toledo District** – until recently, a hard-to-reach area largely overlooked by planners and developers. Access is much easier now that the majority of the Southern Highway is paved, and visitors who make it out here can reward themselves by spending a few days at the inland **Maya villages** (see p.294), with a way of life far removed from

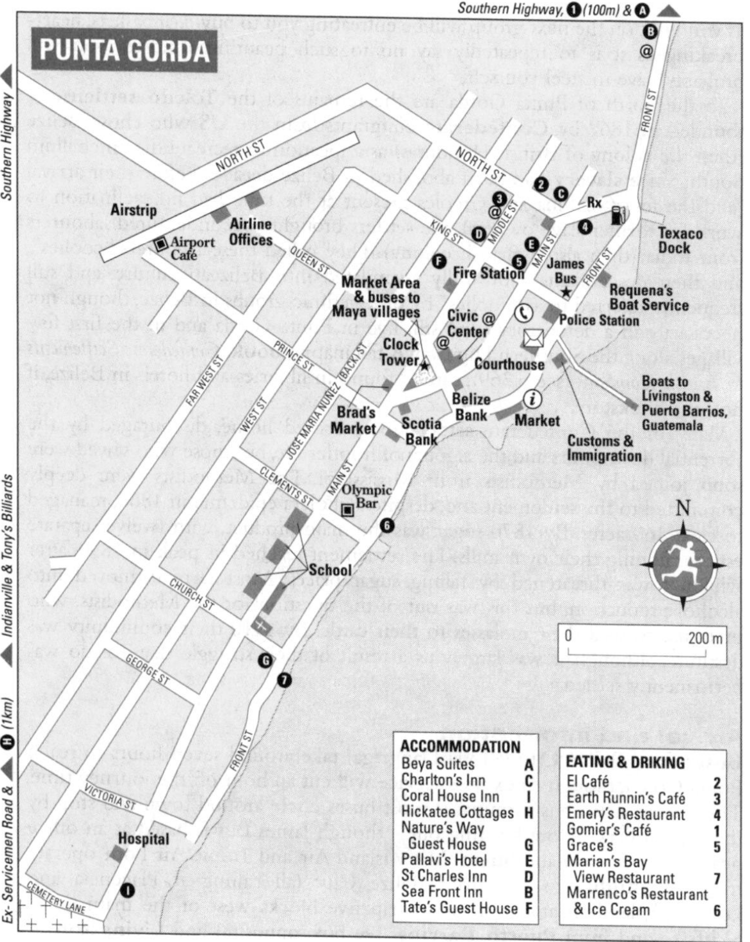

that of greater Belize. Offshore, the **Sapodilla Cayes** and **Port Honduras** form the focus of Belize's southernmost **marine reserves**. Punta Gorda's position on low cliffs means that cooling sea breezes reduce the worst of the heat and, though this is undeniably the **wettest** part of Belize, with trees heavy with mosses and bromeliads, most of the extra rain falls at night, leaving the daytime no wetter than, say, Cayo District.

The town has a population of around six thousand, including Garifuna, Maya, East Indians, Creoles and some Lebanese and Chinese, and is the business centre for a large number of nearby villages and farming settlements. The busiest day is Saturday, when people from the surrounding villages come into town to trade. Despite a recent minor building boom, Punta Gorda remains a small, unhurried and hassle-free town – though as a tourist (here and in the villages) you'll constantly be approached by Maya women and girls, imploring you to buy the small and undeniably attractive **decorative baskets** they make from a local vine. These salespeople are polite and utterly charming rather than forceful, but as you walk on the next group will be entreating you to buy *their* baskets; heart-breaking as it is to repeatedly say no to such beautiful children, you will probably have to steel yourself.

To the north of Punta Gorda are the remains of the **Toledo settlement**, founded in 1867 by **Confederate** emigrants from the US who chose Belize (then the colony of British Honduras) as a location to recreate the antebellum South. Since **slavery** had been abolished in Belize decades before their arrival (and the few Garifuna and Creoles present at the time had no inclination to work for former slave owners), the settlers brought over indentured labourers from India (then also a British colony). They called these labourers "coolies", and their descendants (now fully assimilated into Belizean culture, and still frequently referred to as "coolies" by other ethnic groups in Belize, though not necessarily in a derogatory way) still live in Punta Gorda and in the first few villages along the Southern Highway. A fascinating **book**, *Confederate Settlements in British Honduras* (see p.369), can be found in libraries and hotels in Belize, if not in a bookstore.

Many of the Confederate settlers soon drifted home, discouraged by the torrential downpours and the rigours of frontier life, but those who stayed were soon joined by Methodists from Mississippi. The Methodists were deeply committed to the settlement and, despite a cholera epidemic in 1868, managed to clear 160 acres. By 1870 sugar was the main product, with twelve separate estates running their own mills. The settlement reached its peak in 1890, after which it was threatened by falling sugar prices. Most farmers moved into alcohol production, but this was out of the question for the Methodists, who preferred to feed their molasses to their cattle. By 1910 their community was destitute, although it was largely as a result of their struggle that Toledo was permanently settled.

Arrival and information

Buses from Belize City (all via Dangriga) take around seven hours to reach Punta Gorda, though an express service will cut an hour off the journey time. There is no main bus terminal – most buses circle around town and stop by the central park before heading out – though James Bus is based at an office near the dock on King Street. Maya Island Air and Tropic Air both operate five daily **flights** to and from Belize City (all calling at Placencia and Dangriga), landing at the small airstrip five blocks west of the main dock. **Skiffs** to and from **Puerto Barrios** (see box, opposite) and **Lívingston** in Guatemala use the main dock, roughly in the centre of the seafront; the **immigration** office is nearby. See the box opposite for details of moving on from Punta Gorda.

Despite having relatively few visitors, Punta Gorda has an excellent **information** centre. The Belize Tourism Industry Association (BTIA) has a very informative office on Front Street, just south of the dock (Ⓣ722-2531), where Zoara Gutierrez can help with transportation schedules to the Maya villages and set up **tours** of Toledo District's interior and outlying cayes. Across the street is Tide Tours (see p.290; Ⓣ722-2129), which can give information regarding their many conservation programmes and help you arrange tours to the marine reserves. If you'd like to plan a tour prior to your arrival, a good place to start is with the Toledo Tour Guide Association (Ⓦwww.puntagordabelize.com/ttga/index.htm). For information on visiting other Toledo destinations, see p.289.

The main **bank** is the Belize Bank (with 24-hour ATM; Mon–Thurs 8am–3pm, Fri 8am–4.30pm), on the main square across from the Civic Center, though there's also a Scotia Bank just across the street from the clock tower.

There will usually be a **moneychanger** outside the immigration office when international boats are coming and going, and you can also change money in *Grace's Restaurant*, a block from the dock. If you're leaving the country from Punta Gorda, keep in mind that it's best to get rid of your Belize dollars before you cross the border.

The **post office** is in the government buildings a block back from the ferry dock, and the **BTL office** is across the parking lot. PG has abundant **Internet access**: some options include the long-established Cyber Café, just past the *Sea Front Inn* on Front Street (Mon–Sat 8am–2pm); V-Comp on Main Street (Mon–Sat 8am–8pm), which also has a DVD rental service; and the air-conditioned Carysha Internet Café, on Queen Street across from the park (Mon–Fri 8.30am–12pm & 2.30pm–6pm, Sat 8.30am–12pm), complete with business centre services, café and gift shop.

For **car rental**, check at *Charlton's Inn* (see p.288) or Galvez Taxi & Auto Rental (Ⓣ722-2402), or contact Bruno Kuppinger at *Sun Creek Lodge* (see p.283; Ⓣ614-2080, Ⓔsuncreek@hughes.net). For a reliable taxi service, call Allan Hines (Ⓣ607-5337), who will take you anywhere in the region and can also pick you up from the airstrip. For **bike rental** go to Aba Iseni, on North Street (Ⓣ722-2338), or Disha's Bike Rental at 23 Main Street (Ⓣ622-7809). **Laundry** can be dropped off at PG Laundry on Main Street, across from Belize Bank (Ⓣ722-2273).

Moving on from Punta Gorda

NTSL **buses** (see p.86) leave for **Belize City** (5–7hr) at 3pm and 4.30pm; James buses (see p.86) depart at 4am, 5am, 6am, 8am, 10am, noon, 2pm and 3pm. James bus sometimes runs an **express service** at 6am, though this isn't always reliable. Usher buses leave at 5am and 1.30pm, and the BBOC bus leaves at 9am.

Buses for the **Maya villages** and **Barranco** leave around noon on market days (Mon, Wed, Fri & Sat) from the streets next to the Civic Center; Zoara Gutierrez in the BTIA office (see p.56) has full details. Most village bus companies are literally one-man operations and Sunday is their day off. The only village bus departing in the afternoon is Pop's, which leaves for **Indian Creek** (near **Nim Li Punit**, see p.280) Monday through Saturday at 5pm.

Of the Maya villages, **San Antonio** is the biggest and has two daily buses, Chun's and Prim's – at least one will continue to **Jalacte** on the Guatemalan border (not yet a legal crossing for visitors). If you're heading for **Lubaantun** (see p.295) you'll need the bus for **San Pedro Columbia**, though you can also usually get there any day with rides in pickup trucks. If you're heading for **Uxbenka**, **Río Blanco** or **Pueblo Viejo Falls** (see p.301) you'll take the **Pueblo Viejo** or **Jalacte** bus; for **Pusilhá**, take the **San Benito Poité** bus. Returning from the villages, all buses leave early, around 3–6am.

There are three regular daily **skiffs** to **Puerto Barrios** in Guatemala (1hr in good weather; Bz$35–38). Julio Requena's *Mariestela* leaves at 9.30am (Ⓣ722-2070; Ⓔwatertaxi@btl.net), Carlos Carcamo's *Pichilingo* leaves at 2pm and Rigoberto James's ferry leaves at 4pm (Ⓣ722-2870). Rigoberto James also runs the daily ferry to **Lívingston**, departing at 10am (1hr; Bz$38). There's no need to buy your ticket in advance (though you can); just turn up at the dock half an hour or so before departure so the skipper can get the paperwork ready. You'll have to pay the PACT **exit tax** of Bz$7.50 at the immigration office.

Each domestic airline has five daily **flights** from 7am to 4pm to Belize City Municipal Airport (1hr; Bz$185), calling at Placencia and Dangriga on the way; check the Maya Island Air and Tropic Air offices at the airstrip.

Accommodation

There has been a spate of **hotel construction** in PG during the last few years and, although visitor numbers have increased, few people spend long here, so there are plenty of bargains. For **longer stays** see *Casa Bonita Apartments* (see p.295) and the entries for the *Sea Front Inn* and *Coral House Inn*. An alternative to staying in town is *Nature's Way Guest House* (see below), which, along with the Toledo Ecotourism Association, coordinates an award-winning programme of guest house accommodation in surrounding villages. The only **campsite** near town is *Irie Camping*, 3km away at Cattle Landing (all buses pass by), with tent sites for Bz$8 per person and some simple cabins (no phone; ❷). It's in a good location near the seafront but there's rarely anyone there, so you may still have to head back into town.

Beya Suites Front St, 1km north of the centre ⓣ722-2188 or 621-0140, ⓦwww.beyasuites.com. Named Belize's Small Hotel of the Year in 2006 by the Belize Tourism Board, this is the only Belizean-owned luxury accommodation around town. Located on the seafront just outside the centre, all rooms (most with balconies) offer a/c and TV, and you can watch the sun rise from the rooftop "sunbathing deck". Internet and laundry services are available and delicious meals are served all day in the restaurant and bar downstairs. ❼

Charlton's Inn 9 Main St ⓣ722-2197, ⓔcharlstin@btl.net. Rooms with hot-water showers and most with a/c in a two-storey concrete building with safe parking. Owner Duwane Wagner can arrange car rental and sells domestic air tickets. ❸–❺

Coral House Inn 151 Main St ⓣ722-2878, ⓦwww.coralhouseinn.net. At the southern end of town and next to the cemetery, this beautifully renovated guest house makes you feel truly at home. The four comfortable rooms feature décor from local artisans, and you can relax in the pool or a hammock on the veranda upstairs. The owners can pick you up from the airport in their red, vintage VW van. Breakfast and bicycles are complimentary, as is the wireless Internet access. ❻–❼

Hickatee Cottages Ex-Servicemen Rd, 2 km from town centre ⓣ662-4475, ⓦwww.hickatee.com. Best-value accommodation set in peaceful jungle just outside town. Three charming cottages tastefully decorated with local furniture, with private bath and veranda. The owners aspire to minimal impact on the environment while benefiting the community. Kate serves the best meals in the area using fresh ingredients grown on their farm; many people come just for dinner, so reservations are highly recommended. Bikes are complimentary for guests and pickup is available from the airport or town centre. ❺

Nature's Way Guest House 65 Front St ⓣ702-2119. The best budget place in PG and renowned as a meeting place and information point. Private rooms and clean, comfortable dorm accommodation (Bz$23–33), but no private baths and no hot water. The owner, a committed environmentalist, has been in PG for over thirty years and is a driving force behind the Toledo Ecotourism Association; he can arrange trips to the Maya villages. Good breakfasts and other meals served. ❶–❷

Pallavi's Hotel 19 Main St, next to *Grace's Restaurant* ⓣ722-2414. Clean rooms with private bath and TV in a two-storey concrete building in the centre of town. ❸

St Charles Inn 23 King St ⓣ722-2149. One of PG's smartest options, with clean, quiet rooms with TV and a/c in a charming wooden building with hammocks on the balcony. Located right in the centre of town and close to all the main activity. ❸

Sea Front Inn Front St, 600m north of the centre ⓣ722-2300, ⓦwww.seafrontinn.com. A four-storey, stone-and-wood-fronted building with steep Alpine-style eaves, this hotel is strikingly different from any other in the country. Rooms are spacious, with tiled floors, a/c, TV and balcony, and some with fridges; there are also furnished apartments from around Bz$450/week. The restaurant usually only serves breakfast unless it's booked for a function. Email available for guests. The *Sea Front* is the base for Wild Encounters, which arranges tours in Toledo and throughout Belize. ❼

Tate's Guest House 34 José María Nuñez St, two blocks west of the town centre ⓣ722-0147. A very quiet, friendly, family-run hotel close to the centre. Rooms have a/c and TV, and one has a private kitchen. ❸–❹

Eating, drinking and nightlife

It's easy to get a good, filling **meal** for a reasonable price in Punta Gorda, and **nightlife** heats up when a band is playing at the *PG Sports Bar* opposite the clock tower; there are also a few **bars** where you can meet locals and fellow travellers. Visitors wanting a quiet chat over a beer will get a warm welcome from Olympia Vernon in her tiny *Olympic Bar*, near the corner of Main and Clements streets. You'll find reggae vibes at *Earth Runnin's* (see below), popular with the expat NGO crowd (surprisingly large in PG) and occasionally featuring live music. Another good place to enjoy an early-evening drink (and possibly some nightlife) is *Waluco's*, though it's 2km from the centre; follow Front Street north across the metal bridge over Joe Taylor Creek. It, too, is popular with expats, and there's a deck to enjoy the sea breeze and beers at normal (not inflated) prices. In the back of town, toward Indianville, *Tony's Billiards* is the best spot around to play pool and is typically open from 3pm to midnight (closed Tues). A range of dishes is served here, from *panades* and tacos to burgers and fried chicken, and there's karaoke on weekends.

El Café North St, behind *Charlton's Inn*. Good, inexpensive Belizean dishes, often incorporating local organic produce; opens for breakfast at 6am and serves good coffee.

Earth Runnin's Café and Bukut Bar Corner of North and Middle streets. Punta Gorda's most sophisticated dining option, and a bit pricier than the others, with a changing menu that always features good breakfasts, fresh seafood, pasta and delicious vegetarian meals. It's also a popular bar, serving a range of creative cocktails, and an Internet café.

Emery's Restaurant Main St, near intersection with North St. One of the best restaurants in town, serving fresh fish and seafood caught daily, and the fried chicken here is an excellent option. The restaurant has a spacious, open-air dining room.

Gomier's Café Front St, 100m north of *Sea Front Inn*. A tiny place serving delicious, organic vegetarian, soy and seafood meals, with a daily special. Eat inside or at a table beneath a thatched roof and enjoy the sea breeze.

Grace's Restaurant 19 Main St, opposite the BTL office. Inexpensive, tasty Belizean dishes served in very clean surroundings. You can change money here, and all buses heading north stop across the road.

Marian's Bay View Restaurant Front St, across from *Nature's Way*. Daily menu serving fresh food for breakfast, lunch and dinner. Enjoy a delicious meal while gazing at the magnificent ocean from your table. Vegetarians welcome.

Marrenco's Restaurant & Ice Cream Parlour Front St, 1 block south of the clock tower. Serves good burgers and Belizean dishes, as well as some Chinese food. The highlight here is the variety of desserts, ice cream treats and milkshakes. Open late.

Around Punta Gorda: Toledo's eco-tourism projects

Eco-tourism is a buzzword throughout Belize, and several projects in Toledo District are reaping the benefits. Their aim is to achieve a balance between two needs: economic development and preserving the area's rich natural and cultural heritage. One such project, the **Punta Gorda Eco-Trail**, incorporates both public and private land in the immediate vicinity of the town, taking in **howler monkey** habitat on nearby forested hilltops, a **green iguana** breeding project and a **medicinal plant** trail; check at *Nature's Way* (see opposite) for details. It's hoped that small numbers of "low-impact" visitors to the area will provide additional income to villages without destroying the communities' traditional way of life.

Many Maya villages in Toledo are sited on **Indian Reservations**, designated as such in colonial times to protect the Maya's subsistence lands. Title, however, remained with the government (which leases logging concessions), not the Maya who actually occupied the reserves. Recent developments in forestry policy have alarmed community leaders, who fear that so-called "conversion forestry", where all trees over a certain size on the reservations are cut down for timber, will cause severe erosion and silt up previously clear streams used for drinking. In response, international conservation organizations have stepped up to support better policy initiatives.

The **Toledo Ecotourism Association (TEA)**, in the BTIA office on Front Street in Punta Gorda (722-2531, ttea@btl.net or vinsackul @hotmail.com), is countering the destruction of the forest by offering visitors a **Guest House and Eco-Trail Programme**. Ten villages in southern Toledo are involved in the project; each has an eight-bed guesthouse (Bz$20 per person) and meals are taken at different houses to allow distribution of income. Each village has its own attraction, be it a cave, waterfall, river or ruin, and there are guided walks or horseback rides (around Bz$8/hr; 4-hour minimum); there may also be canoes for rent. The villagers have extensive cultural knowledge of medicinal plants and ancient Maya myths, and a visit to the villages can be an excellent way to find out about their life and culture without feeling like an intruder. The programme has also raised awareness among villagers about both eco-tourism and the political process of protecting their forest. The guest houses covered on pp.294–297 are involved in the programme.

As an alternative to the guest house programme, Yvonne and Alfredo Villoria of Dem Dats Doin (722-2470, demdatsdoin@btl.net) coordinate the Maya Village Homestay Network (MVHN), which lets visitors stay in a village with a Mopan or Kekchí Maya family, participate in village work – grinding corn, chopping firewood, cooking tortillas and the like – and sleep in a hammock. In either programme you'll find few modern conveniences like electricity and flush toilets (though most villages have community telephones operating on a solar panel), but if you go with an open mind you'll have a fascinating and rewarding experience, and the villagers will be happy to teach you some Maya words. Dem Dats Doin also operates a self-sustaining organic farm and tropical botanical garden near San Pedro Columbia that's well worth a visit.

An especially interesting commercial and environmental project in the villages is the cultivation of organically grown cacao (cocoa) beans for the production of **chocolate**; almost all the crop around here is used to make the delicious Maya Gold chocolate sold abroad. The ancient Maya used cacao beans as money, and the beans were traded over great distances. Today you'll often see cacao beans drying on special concrete pads as you meander through the villages, and if you've never seen cacao growing, ask in the BTIA office how you can visit a farm. In 2007, the district inaugurated a Cacao Festival to be held during the month of May; check at the information centre or *Coral House Inn* (see p.288) for more information.

TIDE, the **Toledo Institute for Development and Environment** (722-2129, www.tidetours.org), is an excellent local NGO that manages **Payne's Creek National Park**, north of Punta Gorda, and **Port Honduras Marine Reserve** offshore, plus 16,000 acres of private land. These reserves form part of the continuous Maya Mountain Marine Corridor (MMMC), protecting a wide swath of southern Belize stretching from the cayes to the Guatemalan border. They're also linked with other marine protected areas in Guatemala and Honduras under the umbrella of the **Tri-national Alliance for the Conservation of the Gulf of Honduras** (*La Alianza Trinacional* in Spanish; www.trigoh.org), a group comprising prominent NGOs from the three countries promoting conservation and sustainable livelihoods for the people living in or near the reserves. If you're interested in **volunteering** for these conservation programmes, contact Celia Mahung, TIDE's executive director.

TIDE's subsidiary, Tide Tours, offers a range of **tours** (722-2129, www.tidetours.org, info@tidetours.org), including a full-day **kayak** trip along the lower Moho or Río Grande (Bz$80–95), **snorkelling** at Moho Caye or the

Snake Cayes (Bz$65–100) and **mountain bike** trips to all the local attractions. Overnight camping and fishing trips to Payne's Creek and Port Honduras use the basic **bed and breakfasts** available in the tiny, isolated seaside community of **Punta Negra**, 30km north of Punta Gorda. Contact Pablo Ack in the Tide Tours office on Front Street, across from the BTIA office.

Tours of the Toledo interior, the coast and the cayes are available from a few other local operators, including Green Iguana Adventures (Ⓣ608-0431 or 722-2475, Ⓔsouthernexplorars@hotmail.com), which offers superb birding, fishing, **camping** and **kayaking** trips in addition to the more usual Maya village and ruins tours. Dan Castellanos of Blue Belize Tours, on 139 Front Street (Ⓣ722-2678, Ⓦwww.bluebelize.com), is a traditional fisherman-turned-tour guide and a PADI Divemaster; he offers an array of marine tours, and his excellent knowledge of southern Belize is extremely helpful if you're fishing or snorkelling with him. TASTEE Tours, at 12 Front Street near the dock (Ⓣ722-2795, Ⓔtastetours@btl.net), offers inland tours to archeological sites and national parks.

Out to sea: the cayes and the coast

The cayes and reefs off Punta Gorda mark the southern tip of Belize's Barrier Reef. Though the area is becoming more accessible from Punta Gorda and is visited by specialist sea kayaking tours, it gets relatively little attention from visitors and is very interesting to explore. The roughly 130 low-lying mangrove cayes closest to PG cluster in the mouth of a large bay to the north of town, whose shoreline is a complex patchwork of islands and swamps. Six hundred square kilometres of the bay and its coast are protected in the **Port Honduras Marine Reserve**, partly to safeguard the many **manatees** living and breeding in this shallow water habitat. Sport-fishing, especially **fly-fishing**, is particularly good in this little-visited region; one of the best local guides is Bobby Polonio (Ⓣ722-2135). The Garbutt Brothers – Scully, Oliver or Dennis – are also good and reliable (Ⓣ702-2651 or 604-3548, Ⓔgarbuttsmarine@yahoo.com). For others, and for details of how to visit the reserve and the cayes, see TIDE (opposite) or TASTE on p.292.

Though the cayes and coastline north of Punta Gorda are virtually uninhabited today, they were once home to ancient **Maya sea traders** and salt works. Since 1981, archeological fieldwork by Heather McKillop's project through Louisiana State University has documented sea-level rise since the end of the Classic period (900 AD) that submerged ancient sites and created the modern mangrove landscape. The ancient Maya port of **Wild Cane Caye**, a mostly mangrove-covered caye 20km north of Punta Gorda, was once responsible for the inland trade of salt (produced in the salt works in nearby Punta Ycacos Lagoon) – a basic biological necessity for the inhabitants of the great inland cities. The salt works were abandoned with the Classic Maya collapse, but Wild Cane Caye continued to participate in long-distance sea trade with Postclassic cities as far away as Chichén Itzá in Yucatán. McKillop's project has also documented unique **coral architecture** at Wild Cane Caye and other islands, in which coral rock was mined from the sea to build platforms for structures of perishable material. The coastal area here is managed by TIDE (see opposite), and before visiting the site visitors must check in at the **ranger station** on nearby **Abalone Caye**. Boat trips in the reserve often visit the ranger station so that clients can climb to its top deck for spectacular views over the reserve and to the mountains inland.

The first real beaches north of Punta Gorda appear on the idyllic **Snake Cayes**, a group of four main islands surrounded by glorious white coral sand beaches. Roughly 27km northeast of PG, they're quite easy to visit from town. Beyond here the main reef is fragmented into several clusters of cayes, each surrounded by a small independent reef. The largest and most easterly of these are the stunningly beautiful **Sapodilla Cayes**, a chain of five main islands – each almost wholly encircled by coral and with gorgeous soft-sand beaches – and several rocky outcrops.

Some cayes have accommodation and new resorts are going up all the time; it's clear the area faces increasing visitor pressure, though a management plan for the Sapodilla Cayes, co-devised by the Fisheries Department and the **Toledo Association for Sustainable Tourism and Empowerment** (TASTE; ⓣ722-0191), aims to limit damage to the environment and ensure that local people benefit from the reserve. TASTE is very active in environmental education, taking boatloads of local schoolchildren to the Sapodillas to learn about marine ecosystems and participate in beach clean-ups; committed **volunteers** can ask at TASTE's office, at 53 Middle Street in PG, if there's any extra room in a boat.

The Sapodilla Cayes

These beautiful islands lie at the heart of the **Sapodilla Cayes Marine Reserve**, proving them some protection, though the presence of day-trippers from Guatemala and Honduras challenges the already thinly stretched conservation agencies. Of the five main islands, uninhabited **Northeast Caye**, thickly covered with coconut trees and under government ownership, is the **core zone** of the reserve, to be left undeveloped. You'll pay the Bz$20 reserve entrance fee at **Hunting Caye**, an immigration post handling foreign visitors and the site of some limited camping and picnicking possibilities. The sand at the incredibly beautiful Crescent Moon Beach, on the caye's east side, attracts hawksbill turtles to nest. **Nicolas Caye** has an abandoned resort, and you could **camp** here or ask the caretaker for permission to sleep in a half-finished cabin. The most southerly main island, **Lime Caye**, also has tourism development planned, but for the moment (if you can afford to get here; contact the TASTE office, above) you can savour its glorious isolation.

Frank's Caye, a small island flanked by two even tinier ones, is currently the only one in the group to have a functioning tourist resort, the idyllic *Serenade Island Resort* (ⓣ523-3380; ⓔhotelserenade@btl.net; US$210 double, including meals; transport is US$200 return), with comfortable, white-painted wooden cabins, each with a private bathroom and a deck with hammocks. Most guests arrive by skiff from Placencia (about an hour's trip in good weather), and for details you can contact the *Serenade Guest House* (see p.271) there. Meals are served in the spacious restaurant built over the water, also with a deck and hammocks. The fishing is excellent, you can snorkel right off the beach and the reef is only 200m offshore; rates include use of canoes.

Barranco and the southern coast

From Punta Gorda you can see range upon range of mountains in Guatemala and Honduras, but the Belizean coastline south of here is flat and sparsely populated. Tidal rivers meander across a coastal plain covered with thick tropical rainforest that receives over 3.5m of rain a year, forming a unique ecosystem in Belize with a very high diversity of plant species, particularly orchids and palms. The **Temash River** is lined with the tallest mangrove forest in the country, **black mangroves** towering more than 30m above the riverbanks, while in the far south the **Sarstoon River**, navigable by small boats, forms the border with Guatemala; the land between these rivers is

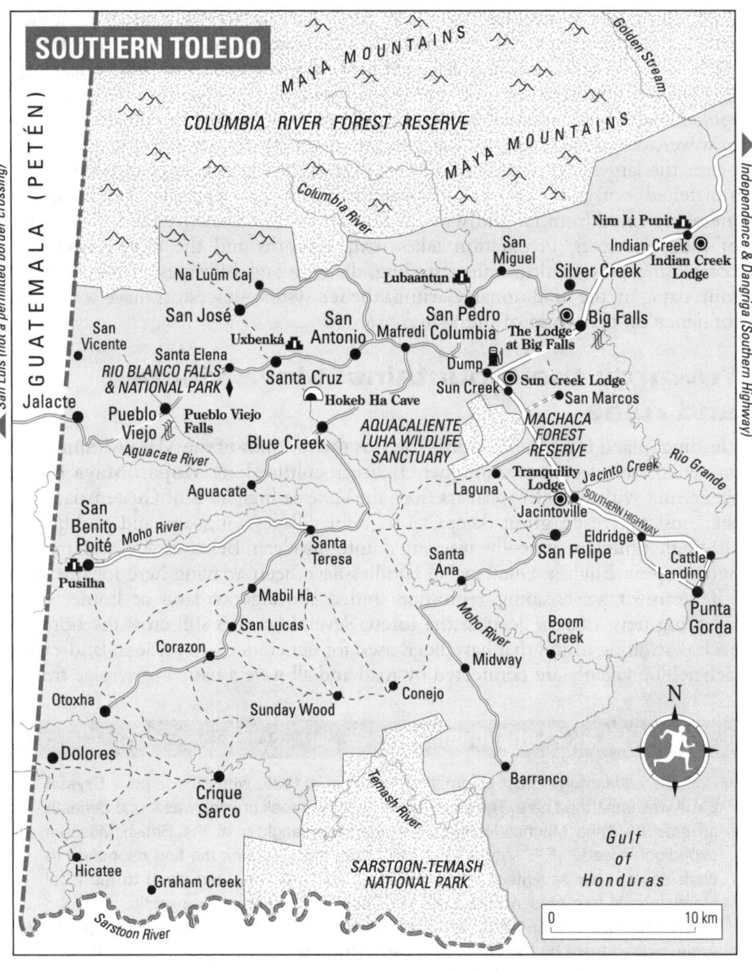

known as **Sarstoon-Temash National Park** (Ⓦwww.satiim.org.bz). You can arrange tours from operators in Punta Gorda and the rivers are sometimes paddled on trips run by sea kayaking companies, using inflatable river kayaks.

The only village on the coast down here is **BARRANCO** (community phone Ⓣ709-2010), a small, traditional Garifuna settlement of around 150 people, where you can stay through the TEA village guest house programme (see p.290). A rough road connects the village with the Southern Highway (buses run to Punta Gorda at 6am on Mon, Wed, Fri & Sat, returning to the village at noon on the same days), crossing the Moho River over a high-level bridge. Some people, though, rely on motorized dories to get to Punta Gorda.

Several jungle trails can be explored on foot or horseback, and Derek Zuniga, a local **guide**, can show you excellent birding spots; you could also check with village chairman Alvin Lindo.

The birthplace of celebrated musician Andy Palacio (see Contexts, p.359), the village is set amongst forest and savannah, with scattered houses shaded by trees. Many villagers of working age have left to seek opportunities elsewhere, leaving the village populated by children and the elderly, and Garifuna is regularly spoken here only by older people. Other aspects of Garifuna culture live on, however: despite virtually all the villagers being Roman Catholics, Barranco boasts the largest *dabuyaba* (a traditional **Garifuna temple**, built of poles with a thatched roof) in the country. It's occasionally used for *dugu* rites, when family members come from far and wide to honour deceased relatives and the spirits of their ancestors. Preparation takes many months and the **ceremonies** – comprising prayers, drumming, singing, dancing and offerings of food – last four days. In the traditional Garifuna belief system, ancestors have a direct influence on the world of the living.

Towards the mountains: Maya villages and ruins

Heading inland from Punta Gorda towards the foothills of the Maya Mountains, you encounter yet another uniquely Belizean culture: here **Mopan Maya** from Petén mix with **Kekchí** speakers from the Verapaz highlands of Guatemala. For the most part each group keeps to its own villages, language and traditions, although both are partially integrated into modern Belizean life and many people speak English. Guatemalan families have been arriving here for the last 130 years or so, escaping repression and a shortage of land at home, and founding new villages deep in the forest. Several families still cross the border each year, along routes that have been used for generations, to settle in land-rich Belize. The villages are connected by road and all have a basic bus service from

The Crystal Skull of Lubaantun

Perhaps Lubaantun's most enigmatic find came in 1926, when the famous **Crystal Skull** was unearthed here. The skull, made from pure rock crystal, was found beneath an altar by Anna Mitchell-Hedges, the adopted daughter of the British Museum expedition's leader, F.A. Mitchell-Hedges. By a stroke of luck the find happened to coincide with her seventeenth birthday, and the skull was then given to the local Maya, who in turn presented it to Anna's father as a token of their gratitude for the help he had given them. It is possible that the "discovery" was a birthday gift for Anna, placed there by her father after he'd acquired it on previous travels, although she strenuously denied such allegations.

While mystery and controversy still surround the original skull, London's British Museum has another crystal skull which – according to Dr G.M. Morant, an anthropologist who examined both skulls in 1936 – is a **copy** of the one found at Lubaantun. He also concluded that both life-size crystal skulls are modelled on the same original human head, but could give no answer as to their true age and origin. The skull was formerly on display in the Museum of Mankind in London, but when this closed the British Museum decided not to exhibit it, as its origin could not be proved. While on display in the Museum of Mankind, its label was suitably vague: "Possibly from Mexico, age uncertain...resembles in style the Mixtec carving of fifteenth-century Mexico, though some lines on the teeth appear to be cut with a jeweller's wheel. If so it may have been made after the Spanish Conquest." There is a similar, smaller crystal skull in the Musée de l'Homme in Paris, and others exist too; all attract great interest from **New Age** mystics, who believe that crystal has supernatural properties.

Punta Gorda (see box on p.287), although moving around isn't that easy and in many places you'll have to rely on hitching – despite the fact that there isn't much traffic. A good option is to **rent a bike** from Punta Gorda (ask at *Nature's Way*, TEA or TIDE) and put it on the bus, cycling between the villages in the **guest house** programme. The people here are of course used to walking, and the villages are also connected by an intricate network of footpaths. And, when the development plan for Toledo is implemented, the road from the Southern Highway at the Dump junction (see p.283) will be paved to Jalacte on the Guatemalan border, to serve as a feeder road in the **Plan Pueblo-Panamá** – a truly massive infrastructure project that includes upgrading highways throughout southern Mexico and the Caribbean coast of Central America, in part to facilitate the impending implementation of the Free Trade Area of the Americas. For years, this has been a controversial proposition, as some Maya communities argue that they will be further marginalized as international developers follow in the wake of the highway.

For now though, the existing unpaved roads provide access to small villages (almost always on a river) and numerous **Maya sites**, **caves** and **waterfalls** in the surrounding countryside. The area offers wonderful possibilities for hiking (see especially San José, p.300) and you can usually find a guide to lead you on foot or horseback through the lush valleys and over the hills.

Lubaantun and San Pedro Columbia

The Maya site of **Lubaantun**, near the mainly Kekchí village of **San Pedro Columbia**, is an easy visit from Punta Gorda, as the village has its own bus service on market days and many pickup trucks head here from the Dump junction. To **get to the site**, head through the village and cross the bridge over the Columbia River, just beyond which you'll see the track to the ruins, a few hundred metres ahead on the left. If you ask around in the village one of the older boys will gladly show you the way; the ruins are about a twenty-minute walk from where the bus drops you. San Pedro itself has limited possibilities for staying overnight (though you might find a room with a local family), but there are a couple of bars and simple restaurants and you should be able to get someone to paddle you to the **"source" of the Columbia River** – a gorgeous spot a couple of kilometres from the village where the river re-emerges from an underground section, gushing forth among the rocks in an enormous, crystal-clear spring overhung with jungle foliage.

Lubaantun

Lubaantun (daily 8am–5pm; Bz$10) is a major Late Classic city which at one time covered a much larger area than the remains – impressive though they are – that you see today. The name means "place of the fallen stones" in modern Maya, though the site's original name is unknown, and it's thought to have been occupied only briefly, from around 730 AD to sometime before 880 AD. The ruins sit on a high ridge, and from the top of the tallest building you could once (just) see the Caribbean, over 30km away, though climbing the high pyramids is now not allowed. However, with eleven major structures, five main plazas and three ball-courts, it's nonetheless a very interesting site – essentially a single **acropolis**.

Lubaantun was brought to the attention of the colonial authorities in 1903, and the governor sent Thomas Gann to investigate. A survey in 1915 revealed many structures, and three ball-court markers were removed and taken to the Peabody Museum at Harvard University. The British Museum expedition of 1926 was joined in 1927 by J. Eric S. Thompson, who was to become the most

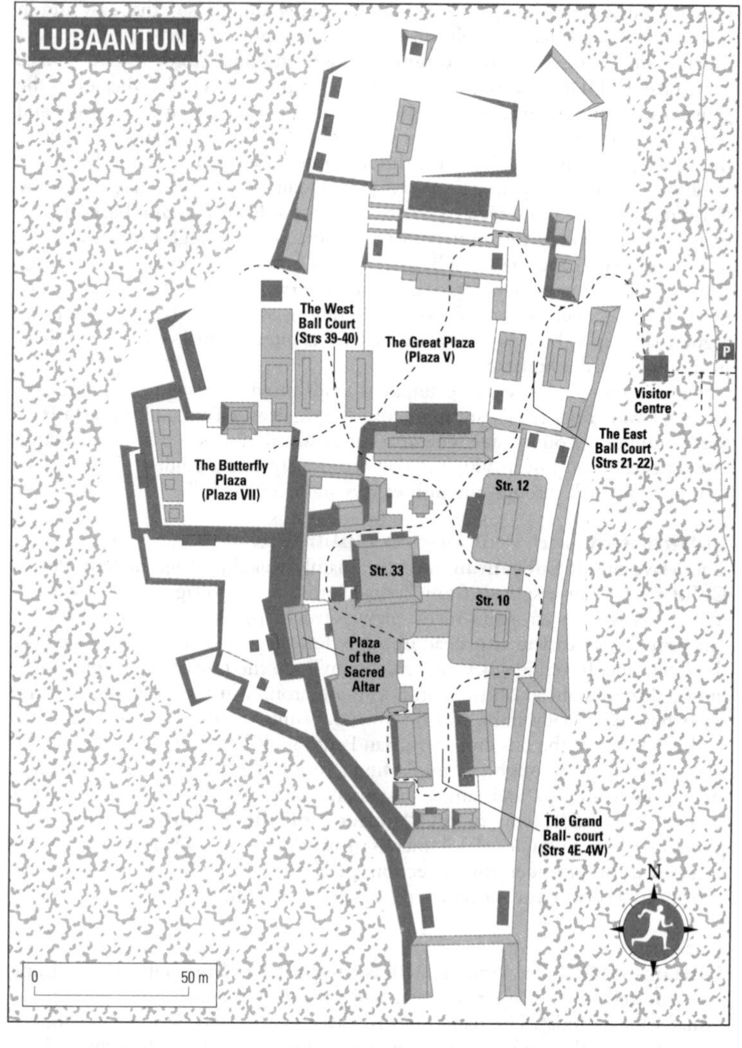

renowned Maya expert of his time. No further excavations took place for over forty years until Norman Hammond mapped the site in 1970, showing the inhabitants' links with communities on the coast and inland – trade relationships likely enhanced by Lubaantun's wealth of cacao beans.

To visit the site, sign in at the **visitor centre** (which, incidentally, has good toilets), where glass cases display some of the finds made at the site – astonishing eccentric flints (symbols of a ruler's power) and ceramics. Wall panels give accounts of the site's discovery and excavation and depict life in a modern Maya village. The very knowledgeable head caretaker Santiago Coc, who's assisted with excavations here for 35 years, or his son Kenan may be able to give you a superb guided tour of the site. Santiago also makes wonderful working replicas of the many ocarinas – clay whistles in the shape of animals – that have been found here; when you hear their evocative notes floating through the ruins, you can imagine the sounds that may have accompanied Maya ceremonies. There are also dozens of mass-produced ceramic figurines littered about the site, often depicting ball-players – items found nowhere else in such quantities.

Restoration has confirmed that the famous Maya **corbelled arch** was never used here. Instead, buildings were constructed by layering and fitting together precisely carved stone blocks, Inca-style, with nothing to bind them. This technique, and the fact that most of the main buildings have **rounded corners**, give Lubaantun an elegance sometimes missing from larger, more manicured sites. Another anomaly is that no stelae were found here, and it's conjectured that Lubaantun was the regional administrative centre while Nim Li Punit, only 17km away and with numerous stelae, had a more ceremonial or religious function for the same political unit. The relative plainness and monumentality of Lubaantun's architecture is also similar to the later buildings at Quiriguá in Guatemala (another site with numerous stelae), and there may have been some connection between these two sites.

San Pedro Columbia practicalities

The TEA guest house is really the only place to stay in San Pedro Columbia (community phone ⓣ702-2303), though you may also be able to find **accommodation** with a local family though the MVHN (see p.290).

You might also be able to stay as a volunteer or student intern at the **Belize Agroforestry Research Center** (BARC; ⓦwww.tcf-barc.org), in a beautiful riverside setting on the outskirts of the village. The centre is located on 150 acres of forest and farmland, and attempts to provide a model of sustainable agro-ecology, with a tree nursery, dozens of fruit and ornamental trees and organic gardens of raised beds. The study facilities include a classroom, a library and an herbarium, and there are several kilometres of trails (you can walk to Lubaantun from here). **Accommodation** is in private rooms, a dorm or the campsite (all US$15 per person), and all have shared bathrooms. Courses and volunteer projects usually need to be planned well in advance; if you're interested, contact director Mark Cohen in the US at ⓣ740/448-2044 or ⓔmarkdcohen@hotmail.com.

Blue Creek

At the tiny village of **Mafredi**, about 9km from San Pedro Columbia, a branch road (served by buses from Punta Gorda) heads south and west to **BLUE CREEK**, where the main attraction is the village's namesake – a beautiful stretch of water that runs through magnificent rainforest. The Mafredi junction is marked by *Roy's Cool Spot*, a well-stocked shop where you can get a snack, a drink and possibly a meal and a room to stay. Four kilometres along the road to Blue Creek is the home of Pablo Bouchub, who runs the tour company Roots and Herbs (ⓣ722-2834 or 603-1304). Pablo is a great **guide**: he can take you to nearby **Aguascalientes Lagoon** for some fantastic birding and knows fascinating routes to caves and ruins. He and his wife Sonia can also teach you about the medicinal plants of Toledo, and Sonia cooks delicious meals.

Another 3km brings you to Blue Creek itself, with the river flowing through the middle of the village. To get to the best **swimming** spot, walk upriver along the right-hand bank (facing upstream), and in about ten minutes you'll come to a lovely turquoise pool and the wooden cabins of *Blue Creek Rainforest Lodge* (ⓣ523-7076 or 722-2199, ⓦwww.ize2belize.com; US$45 per person, including meals), set among the trees. The lodge, used by both student and adventure tour groups, is under the same ownership as *Leslie Cottages* on South Water Caye (see p.251), where you should make reservations. It's set in the **Blue Creek Rainforest Preserve**, a 200-acre private park, and it's mainly used as a field study centre for students of rainforest ecology, though other visitors can arrange to stay. A student package, including four nights here and five nights on South Water Caye, starts at US$1250; for non-student prices check with *Leslie Cottages*. Since the lodge is privately owned, and you have to pass right by the cabins, the management here sometimes asks you to pay a fee to use the path – so you should know that all rivers and riverbanks in Belize are publicly accessible, and you can in fact walk freely along. The villagers, however, seeing a lucrative source of income, may also wish to charge a small fee for you to use their beautiful river, so you may have to pay up gracefully anyway.

The **source of Blue Creek**, where the water gushes from beneath a mossy rock face, is about another fifteen minutes' walk upriver. Alongside is the entrance to **Hokeb Ha Cave**, fairly easy to explore. The entire area is made of limestone bedrock honeycombed with caves, many of which were sacred to the Maya, and plenty of others are doubtless waiting to be rediscovered. If you want to experience the cave in solitude don't come on a Sunday – it can get crowded and you'll be besieged by village children trying to sell you souvenirs, though most other days you'll probably have it to yourself. Sylvano Sho, who lives by the bridge at the entrance to the trail, is the best **guide** in Blue Creek and can take you to Maya altars deep in Hokeb Ha Cave; he's also a great guide to Pusilhá (see below) – and you should not venture there without a local guide. Delphina, Sylvano's wife, serves simple, tasty **meals** in their house.

Pusilhá

About 7km southwest of Blue Creek is the Kekchí village of **Aguacate**, beyond which the road climbs a ridge leading to the valley of the Moho River, near the border with Guatemala. Further up the valley, almost on the Guatemalan border (and accessed by road via **Santa Teresa**, south of Blue Creek), lies **Pusilhá**, the largest Maya site in southern Belize, where you can view the finest example of an **ancient bridge** anywhere in the Maya world. The site is located in and around the present-day village of **San Benito Poité**, served by a bus on market days from Punta Gorda (up to 2hr, and returning on market days only). At the entrance to the village there's a new bridge over the clear, fast-flowing Pusilhá River, with a lovely **camping** spot nearby. Just downstream from here the Pusilhá and Poité rivers join to form the **Moho River**, the middle stretch of which has some of the best **white-water rapids** in Central America – occasionally paddled by rafting and kayaking expeditions from the US and Canada (see Basics, p.23).

It's really best to **visit the site** when the archeologists from the **Pusilhá Project** (undertaken by the State University of New York at Buffalo) are working, usually in spring and early summer, as none of the structures here have been fully excavated or restored. Even more importantly, bear in mind that the villagers are not used to seeing outsiders (most speak only Kekchí and a little Spanish), and may not be as immediately welcoming as you expect. You must **ask permission** from the alcalde (similar to a mayor) to visit the site as soon as you enter the village, and you're strongly recommended to go only with a Kekchí-speaking guide – see if you can get Sylvano Sho in Blue Creek (see p.297). If you haven't come with your own, the alcalde will supply a guide from the village (for whom you'll have to pay a small fee), and he can also arrange food and lodging with a local family. He, or Bruno Kuppinger at *Sun Creek*

Lodge (see p.283), might also have a copy of the excellent **information sheet** on the site written by Dr Geoffrey Braswell, the Pusilhá Project's director.

The site

The city, strategically built on high land between the confluence of the Poité and Pusilhá (Machaca) rivers, has yielded an astonishing number of carved monuments and stelae, including **zoomorphic altars** (great, rounded stone tablets carved with stylized animals) in a style similar to those at Quiriguá in Guatemala. This initially led archeologists to suggest that at some stage Pusilhá may have been under Quiriguá's control, but recent studies indicate a closer connection with Copán, in Honduras.

Although most of the monuments and stelae have been removed (mainly to the British Museum, where they were taken by colonial expeditions in the late 1920s), the **Stela Plaza** – the sacred centre of the ancient city, reached by a *sacbe* (ceremonial road) – still has a few badly eroded stelae and three zoomorphic altars resembling frogs. Nearby you can also see the remains of an enormous **walled ball-court**. The real highlight, however, is the **Maya bridge**, built at a narrow point over the Pusilhá River. Clearly visible are the remains of the main bridge abutments, solid vertical walls of cut stones several metres high and supported by ramps of rock, and if you look carefully you can see more large, cut stones lining the river bed. In ancient times the bridge supports would have been spanned by beams of sapodilla wood, carrying the road leading to the **Gateway Hill Acropolis** – the residential palace complex of Pusilhá's rulers and the administrative centre of the city. During construction the river would have been held back and diverted by a coffer dam upstream, and on either side of the main span are diversion channels, built to take the extra volume of water pouring down the valley during rains.

The mystery is, why build a bridge at all? The ancient Maya built very few bridges, and rivers were usually crossed by canoe. As such, it would appear this magnificent feat of engineering was constructed solely to provide a suitably impressive **processional route** to the **Acropolis**, the most imposing remains at Pusilhá. Here, a series of pyramidal platforms, terraces and facades, skilfully blended with natural features on the hill slope, have created an awe-inspiring edifice rising 80m above the river – almost twice the height of Belize's tallest free-standing Maya structure, Caana at Caracol, and even higher than Temple IV at Tikal.

San Antonio

The Mopan Maya village of **SAN ANTONIO**, perched on a small hilltop, is the easiest of the villages to reach, as it's served by daily buses from Punta Gorda, 34km away. In addition to the TEA village guest house here, you can also find *Bol's Hill Top Hotel* (community phone ⓣ702-2144; ❶), which has simple **rooms** with electric light and superb views. There are a couple of shops in the village and you can get **meals** at Theodora's or Clara's house, behind *Bol's*. The area is rich in wildlife, surrounded by jungle-clad hills and swiftly flowing rivers. Further south and west are the villages of the Kekchí Maya, including many fairly recent immigrants who still retain strong cultural links with Guatemala.

The founders of San Antonio came from the Guatemalan town of San Luis, just across the border, and they maintain many age-old traditions, including the worship of their patron saint; opposite *Bol's Hotel* is the beautiful **stone church** of San Luis Rey, currently looked after by an American Jesuit order. The church is the third to stand on the site (two previous versions were destroyed by fire), and its most remarkable feature is a set of superb **stained-glass windows**

△ Maya village near San Antonio

depicting the twelve apostles and other saints, donated by St Louis, Missouri. The villagers also observe their own pre-Columbian traditions and fiestas, the main one taking place on June 13 and featuring marimba music, masked dances and much heavy drinking.

San José

Nestled among the southern foothills of the Maya Mountains, **SAN JOSÉ** is one of the northernmost villages in the area. The village bus leaves Punta Gorda for San José at noon on market days (about 1hr) and if you're travelling in your own vehicle the turn-off is about 2km east of San Antonio. To stay at the **guest house** here, call the community phone on ⓣ702-2072. If you're fit, you can take some amazing hikes higher up into the mountains; ask in the village for Valentino Tzub, who can guide you as far as **Little Quartz Ridge**, a steep and isolated plateau with an ecosystem unique to Belize, or even to (at least) the lower slopes of **Doyle's Delight**, the highest peak in Belize. For either of these trips, you'll need camping gear and supplies for at least three days, plus a great deal of stamina. An even more adventurous hike is the extremely arduous five-day **Maya Mountain Divide Trail** (ⓦwww.mayadividetrail.com) from San José to **Las Cuevas**, at the end of the Chiquibul Road in Cayo (see p.186); if you're interested, contact Marcos Cucul at Maya Guide Adventures (see p.169).

Uxbenká

Seven kilometres west from San Antonio and 300m before the village of **Santa Cruz**, the ruins of relatively small **UXBENKÁ** ("ancient place") are superbly positioned on an exposed hilltop with great views towards the coast. Uxbenká's existence only became known to archeologists in 1984 after reports of looting in the area; though there's still no official site caretaker, the community of Santa Cruz is increasingly involved in excavation and developing the site as a tourist destination. You can inquire in the village about a guided tour – someone involved in the TEA guest house program will gladly show you around. During your visit you're likely to encounter research in progress: currently, Dr Keith Prufer from Wichita State University heads the **Uxbenká Archeological**

Project, which began in the summer of 2005 to catalogue and identify new monuments and sculptures.

The core area of Uxbenká consists of seven architectural plazas spread across three sets of ridges and hilltops that overlook the foothills and valleys of the Maya Mountains. The site appears to contain the civic, ceremonial and elite residential components of Maya society, and has been roughly grouped into three clusters: the **Stela Plaza** (Group A), an "**acropolis**" residential group (Group G), located atop the highest hill with dramatic views, and a set of five conjoined **plazas** (Groups B–F), the site's main ceremonial groups.

Uxbenká is the earliest known Maya political centre in southern Belize, having risen to prominence in at least the Early Classic period, and it may even have existed as a settlement in the Preclassic. It might also have had links to Tikal, a theory first proposed by Richard Leventhal after he surveyed the site in 1989 and 1990. Leventhal made other important discoveries as well, particularly of the **Stela Plaza**, containing at least 22 carved and uncarved monuments and stelae that clearly date the site to at least the Early Classic. His team also discovered an intact, but collapsed, tomb in the floor of the Stela Plaza, which so far has been left intact. In the fifteen years between Leventhal's survey and the current effort, Uxbenká was not studied – and, with its dispersed layout and no caretaker, it was an easy victim of vandals and looters. Probably as a result, no new carved monuments have been found in recent pit excavations.

Nevertheless, the research currently underway has led to several intriguing discoveries. One is the notion that Uxbenká was a major **agricultural center** and likely engaged in the commercial production of cacao, a theory supported by the numerous terraces on the surrounding hills, which hold the richest soil in the Maya lowlands. Excavations in the Stela Plaza and the discovery of an intact **ball-court marker** in Group D suggest that, despite Uxbenká's early origins, it was still operating in the Late Classic. The star finding, however, is an **ancient canoe** – likely the oldest discovered in Mesoamerica – dated to somewhere between 200 and 800 AD, though carbon testing will produce a more accurate estimate. Archeologists hypothesize that the canoe was part of a funerary offering which, prior to looting, contained a cut-stone crypt. The canoe was found in a cliff-top cave at the site, believed to have been used as a royal burial crypt and containing remains of an ancient tomb. The craft's placement was very symbolic of the Maya's spiritual journey through the underworld, as caves, many with navigable waterways running through them, were closely associated with the afterlife. The canoe is scheduled for eventual display in the Museum of Belize in Belize City.

If you'd like to stay nearby to explore the area around the ruins, there's a **guest house** at the entrance to Santa Cruz, and buses run on market days; some continue to the border village of **Jalacte** (see p.302). All around Santa Cruz are forest **trails** to rivers and waterfalls, and you can walk to **San José** in about three hours (see opposite).

On to Jalacte

Continuing west toward the Guatemalan border, you can enjoy some wonderful **waterfalls** within easy reach of the road. Twelve kilometres west of San Antonio, between Santa Cruz and Santa Elena, the **Rio Blanco Falls** tumble five metres over a wide, rocky ledge into a deep pool, perfect for a dip and a picnic. The falls form part of **Rio Blanco National Park**, and the bus passes right by the (generally deserted) visitor centre; walk down the short trail at the side of the building to reach the falls. At **Pueblo Viejo**, 7km further on, an impressive series of cascades on Pueblo Creek proves an even more spectacular sight. Above the falls, a steep trail leads through orchid-laden rainforest to a mountaintop overlook; ask in the village for a guide to lead you. Trucks and buses continue 13km further west to **Jalacte**, at the Guatemalan border, used regularly as a crossing point by nationals of both countries, though it's not currently a legal entry or exit point for tourists.

Travel details

The Southern Highway has almost as many buses running along it as the Northern and Western highways, with more frequent services and new express buses to cut journey times even further. The main routes are listed here; other buses to smaller villages are covered in the text. Bus company offices and departure frequencies from Belize City to Dangriga, Placencia and Punta Gorda are covered in the box on p.86.

Buses

Dangriga to: Belmopan (1hr 40min) and Belize City (12 daily; 2–3hr); Hopkins and Sittee River (6 daily; 30min); Placencia (4 daily; 2hr); Punta Gorda (12–15 daily; 3hr 30min). All buses between Dangriga and Punta Gorda stop at Independence/Mango Creek, where there's a regular ferry to Placencia (see p.273).
Hopkins and Sittee River to: Dangriga (6 daily, first one around 7am; 30min).
Placencia to: Dangriga (4 daily; 2hr); all connect with departures to Belmopan and Belize City.
Punta Gorda to: Dangriga (3hr 30min) and Belize City (5–7hr; 12–15 daily), all calling at Independence/Mango Creek.

Flights

In Belize City, Maya Island Air (☎223-1140) and Tropic Air (☎226-2012); each has five daily flights from Belize City to Dangriga (25min), continuing on to Placencia (a further 20min) and Punta Gorda (20min beyond Placencia).

International boats

Dangriga to: Puerto Cortés, Honduras (weekly skiff, on Sat; 4hr).
Placencia and Big Creek to: Puerto Cortés, Honduras (weekly skiff, on Fri; 4hr).
Punta Gorda to: Lívingston, Guatemala (daily; 1hr); Puerto Barrios, Guatemala (3 daily; 1hr).

Contexts

Contexts

History 305
Chronology of the Maya 325
Chronology of Belize 327
The Maya achievement 329
Archeology 335
Landscape and wildlife 338
Conservation 345
Human rights and democracy 354
Ethnic Belize 356
Music 358
Dance 365
Books 366

History

Belize is the youngest nation in Central America, only gaining full independence from Britain in 1981, and its history has been markedly different from the surrounding Latin American republics since at least the mid-seventeenth century. Although the whole region, including Belize, was (to a greater or lesser degree) colonized by Spain in the sixteenth century, it was the colonial entanglement with Britain that gave Belize its present cultural, social and political structures.

Prior to the arrival of Europeans, the area now called Belize was part of a vast region known to archeologists as **Mesoamerica**, stretching from north-central Mexico to El Salvador and Honduras. Within this imprecisely defined geographical area the individual cultures shared several common characteristics, including a complex, accurate calendar, hieroglyphic writing, a similar cosmology and religion and a highly organized, stratified society. They may also have shared a common origin in the **Olmec** civilization, which arose in southern Mexico around 3000 years ago. This definition is designed to exclude the native tribes of North America (whose culture remained largely nomadic) and to group together the pre-Columbian civilizations of their southern neighbours. By far the most important of these (as far as Belize is concerned) are the **Maya**, whose culture began to emerge here as early as 2500 BC and whose cities were at the height of their power between 250 and 900 AD.

Prehistory

Delving further into the past, archeologists are on uncertain ground, piecing together a general idea on the basis of scattered archeological remains and a handful of written texts. Prior to the advent of Maya civilization very little is known about the area, and the earliest Maya remain fairly mysterious. Set out here is a brief overview of many separate theories, none of which can claim to dominate the academic debate. Over the last few years the situation has, if anything, become even more confused, as excavations of important new sites (especially in Belize) throw up information that casts doubt on many accepted notions. At any moment our whole understanding could be overturned by new discoveries, and there is certainly still a great deal to learn.

Archeological opinions differ as to when the first people arrived in the Americas, but the most widely accepted theory is that **Stone Age hunter-gatherers** crossed the Bering land bridge from Asia in several waves, beginning probably around 25,000 BC and travelling via an ice-free corridor (and possibly in small boats along the coastline) at a time when sea levels were lowered by advancing glaciers. These early hunters rapidly spread southwards, developing the **Clovis** culture (named after characteristic stone projectile points first identified in Clovis, New Mexico) at least 11,000 years ago; worked stone flakes from this era have been found at Richmond Hill, a site in Orange Walk District. The Clovis people subsisted primarily on hunting the abundant large mammals, including mammoths, mastodons, deer and horses. By 9000 years ago, however, the northern ice sheets were in full retreat, and the big game disappeared during the long period of hot, dry weather that followed.

The scarcity of game, combined with climatic change and altered vegetation patterns, forced the hunter-gatherers to adopt a different way of life, turning to more intensive use of plant foods. During this period (known as the **Archaic** period) the food plants vital to the subsequent development of agriculture, such as peppers, squash, beans and, most important of all, maize, were domesticated. Analysis of pollen grains from that time, found in lake deposits in Petén, Guatemala, reveal that the region (and presumably adjacent Belize too) was an area of savannahs and broad-leaved woodland; the tropical forests did not appear until the Classic period, by which time the Maya could more easily control its profuse growth.

This transition into more settled, primarily agricultural societies enabled the development of an identifiable culture, which has become broadly known as **Proto-Maya**. There is archeological evidence of Archaic sequences in Belize dating from 7500 BC until later than 2000 BC, though few visible remains from that period can be seen today. An early language, Proto-Maya, was in use in the western highlands of Guatemala, and probably in other places too, including Chiapas in Mexico.

The early Maya in Belize

Somewhere between 2000 and 1500 BC we move into the **Preclassic** (also known as the Formative) period (2000 BC–250 AD). These periods are terms used by archeologists to describe the earliest developments in the history of the culture we recognize as distinctly Maya; each main period is itself usually subdivided into Early, Middle and Late. The boundaries of the different periods are not marked by exact dates, and should be understood as cultural and technological milestones, when particular architectural, artistic and administrative advances were in widespread use; current excavations appear to be pushing back the date when the earliest breakthroughs were made.

The **Early Preclassic** (roughly 2000 BC–1000 BC) marks the beginning of recognizable patterns of agriculture, notably the annual cutting and burning of forest by people living in settled villages in order to plant maize. Crops would have provided part (and increasingly the main part) of their food needs, supplemented by hunting, fishing and foraging for wild plants. There's currently no evidence of structures larger than dwellings for this period, but ceramics were produced; pottery found at **Cuello**, near Orange Walk, dates from around 1000 BC and is among the earliest ceramics in the Maya lowlands.

Elsewhere in Mesoamerica, big changes were taking place that were to have a far-reaching impact throughout the region. The first great culture to emerge was the Olmec civilization, originating in the coastal plain of Veracruz, in Mexico. The Olmecs, often regarded as the true ancestors of Maya culture, developed a complex polytheistic religion, an early writing system and a calendar known as the "long count", later adopted by the Maya (see p.325).

By the **Middle Preclassic** (1000 BC–300 BC) there was a substantial increase in population – evidence of numerous settlements can be found right across the Maya area, from southern Guatemala to northern Yucatán, including almost all of Belize, in particular the main river valleys. Similar styles of red and orange monochrome pottery of the Mamóm style, and stone metates for grinding corn, have been found in all the settlements. It is thought that a common Maya language was spoken throughout the area, and that a universal belief system, practised from a very early date, may have provided the stimulus and social cohesion to build bigger towns. At the same time, as in all early agricultural communities, food surpluses would have eventually freed some to become seers, priests and astronomers. By 750 BC Nakbé, in northern Petén, was a large city, perhaps the first one in the Maya world, evidence that the Maya had progressed far beyond a simple peasant society.

Further advances in architecture and what amounted to an explosion of Maya culture and population came in the **Late Preclassic** (300 BC–250 AD), when the **Chicanel culture** dominated the northern and central areas of the Maya world. The famous Maya corbelled arch (not a true arch with a keystone, but consisting of two sides, each with stones overlapping until they eventually met, thus able to span only a relatively narrow gap) was developed in this period, and the whole range of buildings became more ambitious. Large pyramids with elaborate temples were built at Tikal, El Mirador and Río Azul in Petén. In northern Belize, Cuello, Nohmul, Lamanai and Cerros were the great centres, all featuring major examples of public architecture, some of which can still be seen today. Lamanai and Cerros controlled Preclassic trade routes, and probably continued to do so right through the Classic and into the Postclassic period. The Belize River valley was fully settled, with local centres such as Cahal Pech, Pacbitún and El Pilar expanding and consolidating their power.

The question of what sparked this phase of rapid development is a subject of much debate, though most archeologists agree that the catalyst was the Olmec culture. The Maya adopted and adapted these outside influences, and developed complex administrative mechanisms to feed and control the growing population. As in any advancing society, a hierarchical ruling structure evolved. In the Maya world ultimate military and spiritual power was vested in kings, who established ruling dynasties and communicated with the gods by spilling their own blood at propitious festivals.

The Classic period

The development that separates the Late Preclassic from the **Early Classic** period (250 AD–600 AD) is the introduction of the long count calendar and a recognizable form of writing. This appears to have taken place before the fourth century AD and marks the beginning of the greatest phase of Maya achievement.

Developments in the Maya area were still powerfully influenced by events to the north. The cultural influence of the Olmecs was replaced by that of **Teotihuacán**, which dominated Central Mexico during the early Classic period. Armed merchants spread the power of Teotihuacán as far as Yucatán, Petén and Belize, bringing new styles of ceramics and alternative religious beliefs: complete military invasion and subjugation, however, were a fairly unlikely scenario. Whatever happened around 400 AD, the overwhelming power of Teotihuacán radically altered life in Maya lands. In Petén, **Tikal**'s rise to power must have been helped by close links with Teotihuacán, and both cities prospered greatly: Tikal has a stela (a freestanding carved monument), with inscribed text and dates, depicting a lord of Tikal on one side and a warrior from Teotihuacán on the other.

Most of the cities we now see as ruined or restored sites were built during the Classic period, almost always over earlier structures. Elaborately carved stelae, bearing dates and emblem-glyphs, tell of actual rulers and of historical events in their lives – battles, marriages, dynastic succession and so on. The deciphering of these dates has provided confirmation (or otherwise) of archeological evidence and offered a major insight into the Maya elite. Broadly speaking, the Maya region was made up of independent city-states, bound together by a coherent religion and culture and supporting a sophisticated trade network. The cities jostled for power and influence, a struggle that occasionally erupted into intense warfare. Exactly how the various centres related to one another is unclear, but it appears that three or four main centres dominated the Maya area through an uncertain process of alliances, though no city held sway throughout the entire region. **Calakmul**, in Campeche, Mexico, and Tikal were the nearest of these "superstates" to Belize, and in 562 AD an alliance of Calakmul and Caracol, in southern Cayo District, defeated Tikal, as shown by an inscription on Altar 21 at Caracol. Other detailed carvings on wooden lintels and stone monuments at the site depict elaborately costumed lords trampling on bound captives. It's unclear whether this victory of a previously subordinate city over the dominant regional power was the cause of the major upheaval that followed, but dramatic change was to come.

The collapse of Teotihuacán in the seventh century caused shock waves throughout the civilizations of Mesoamerica as advances were temporarily halted by what is known as the **Middle Classic Hiatus**. No stelae were erected in the Maya cities, and many existing monuments were damaged and defaced. In all likelihood the dominant Maya centres suffered revolts, and warfare raged as rival lords strove to win political power. However, as the new kings established dynasties, now free of Teotihuacán's military or political control, the Maya cities flourished as never before. Architecture, astronomy and art reached degrees of sophistication unequalled by any other pre-Columbian society. Many Maya centres were much larger than contemporary Western European cities, then in their "Dark Ages": Caracol had an estimated 150,000 people.

The prosperity and grandeur of the **Late Classic** (600–850 AD) reached all across the Maya lands: from Bonampak and Palenque in the west, to Calakmul and Uxmal in the north, Altun Ha and Cerros in the east, and Copán and Quiriguá in the south, as well as hundreds of smaller centres. Masterpieces of painted pottery and carved jade (the Maya's most precious material) were created, often to be used as funerary offerings. Shell, bone and, rarely, marble were also exquisitely carved; temples were painted in brilliant colours, inside and out. Most of the pigments have faded long ago, but vestiges remain, enabling experts to reconstruct vivid images of the appearance of the ancient cities.

The Terminal Classic and Postclassic periods

Though it was abrupt when the end came for each Classic Maya centre, it took a century or so (**Terminal Classic**; 800–c.1000 AD) for the Classic Maya civilization to be extinguished in Belize. By 750 AD political and social changes began to be felt; alliances and trade links broke down, wars increased and stelae were carved less frequently. The sacking of Dos Pilas, in the Petexbatún region of southwest Petén, by nearby Tamandarito in 761 AD is generally regarded as the first phase of the **Classic Maya collapse**. Warfare became more widespread and destructive, cities gradually became depopulated and new construction ceased over much of Belize after about 830 AD. Bonampak, in Chiapas, was abandoned before its famous murals could be completed, while many of the great sites along the River Usumacinta (now part of the border between Guatemala and Mexico) were occupied by militaristic outsiders. By the end of the Classic period there appears to have been strife and disorder throughout Mesoamerica.

The decline and subsequent collapse of the Classic Maya civilization was probably a result of several factors. There is strong evidence that a prolonged drought in central Yucatán caused competition for scarce resources, with the effects rippling outward. Additionally, the massive increase in population during the Classic period may have put intolerable pressure on food production, ultimately exhausting the fertility of the soil. Finally, the growth and demands of the unproductive elite may have led to a peasant revolt, leading to the abandonment of city life. By the tenth century, the Maya had largely abandoned their central cities and most of those that remained were reduced to a fairly primitive state.

But not all Maya cities were entirely deserted: those in northern Belize, in particular, survived and indeed prospered, with Lamanai and other cities in the area remaining occupied throughout the **Postclassic period** (c.900–1540 AD). The Yucatán peninsula, which appears to have escaped the worst of the depopulation, came under the influence (possibly by outright conquest) of the militaristic **Toltecs**, who came from central Mexico in 987 AD, creating a hybrid of Classic Maya culture.

From around 900 AD to the time of the Spanish Conquest the Yucatán peninsula and northern Belize consisted of over a dozen rival provinces, bound up in a cycle of competition and conflict. Northern Belize was part of the Maya province of **Chactemal** (later known as Chetumal), covering an area from around Maskall, near the site of Altun Ha, to Laguna Bacalar in southern Quintana Roo in Mexico, and with Santa Rita, near Corozal, as its possible capital. Chetumal was a wealthy province, producing cacao and honey; trade, alliances and wars kept it in contact with surrounding Maya states up to and beyond the Spanish conquest of Aztec Mexico. Further south, the forests were thicker and the ridges of the Maya Mountains intruded across the land. To the Maya of Chetumal this area was known as **Dzuluinicob** – "land of foreigners" – whose capital was Tipú, located at Negroman, on the Macal River south of San Ignacio. The Maya here controlled the upper Belize River valley and put up strenuous resistance to attempts by the Spanish to subdue and convert them.

The first Europeans

The general assumption that Belize was practically deserted by the time Europeans arrived is now widely discredited. In 1500 AD the native population in the area which was to become Belize is estimated to have been around 200,000 – almost as high as it is today – and the Maya towns and provinces were still vigorously independent, as the Spanish found to their cost on several occasions.

The first **Europeans** to set eyes on the mainland of Belize were the Spanish sailors Pinzón and de Solis in the early sixteenth century, though they didn't attempt a landing. The first, accidental, contact occurred in 1511, when a small group of shipwrecked Spanish sailors managed to reach land on the southern coast of Yucatán: five were immediately sacrificed and the others became slaves. At least one of the slaves must have escaped and regained contact with his fellow countrymen, because when **Cortés** reached Cozumel in 1519 he knew of the

△ Hernán Cortés

existence of two other enslaved survivors of the shipwreck, and sent gifts to their masters for their release. Geronimo de Aguilar immediately joined Cortés, but the other survivor, **Gonzalo Guerrero**, refused: Guerrero had married the daughter of Na Chan Kan, the chief of Chactemal, and preferred life among his former captors. Because of his knowledge of Spanish tactics he became a crucial military adviser to the Maya in their subsequent resistance to Spanish domination: the archeologist Eric Thompson calls him the first European to make Belize his home.

In the early years of the conquest few reports were made of contact with the Maya in Belize, probably because the Spanish heard no stories of gold or treasure – their overriding obsession. In 1525 Cortés himself almost certainly passed through southern Belize on his epic march from Veracruz in Mexico to punish a rebellious subordinate in San Gil de Buena Vista, near the mouth of the Río Dulce on the Bay of Honduras. The course of his march took Cortés and his retinue of 140 Spanish soldiers and 3000 Indians across the unknown territory of the Maya heartland, which still contained many thriving towns and cities. At Tayasal on Lake Petén Itzá, he was welcomed by Can Ek, chief of the Itzá, who had heard of Cortés' cruelty in conquering Mexico and decided not to oppose him. The expedition continued southwards, to the valley of the Sarstoon River, the present boundary with Guatemala. After reaching and pacifying the rebels, Cortés sailed north to Mexico, apparently without realizing that Yucatán was not an island.

Attempted conquest

For the Spanish it proved relatively simple to capture and eventually kill the "living god" leaders of such militaristic, unified and highly organized empires as the Aztecs and Incas. However, at the time of the conquest, the Maya of present-day Yucatán and Belize were not united into a single political entity, and the rulers of the Maya provinces were accustomed to dealing with enemies either by fighting or forming temporary alliances to retain their independence – one reason why the Spanish found this region so difficult to subdue.

In 1528 **Francisco de Montejo**, granted permission by the Spanish Crown to colonize the islands of Cozumel and Yucatán, established a settlement called Salamanca on the mainland coast south of Cozumel. At the same time his lieutenant, **Alonso Dávila**, led an overland expedition south. Neither was particularly successful: both groups encountered hostile Maya, and Dávila was forced to turn away from Chetumal (Chactemal) by Maya under the command of Gonzalo Guerrero. A second attempt by Dávila to found a town at Chetumal, in 1531, was marginally more successful but nevertheless short-lived. This time (on the advice of Guerrero, who realized they could not defeat the Spanish outright) the Maya had abandoned the town; it was then occupied by Dávila and renamed **Villa Real** – the first attempt by Spain to conquer and settle the area that later became Belize. Once established, however, Dávila and his troops were continually harassed by the Maya and were driven out eighteen months later, fleeing south along the coast of Belize, eventually reaching Omoa in Honduras. For some years after Montejo and Dávila's unsuccessful attempts to conquer Chetumal, the Maya in Belize remained largely free from Spanish interference. Chetumal regained its important trading links and was also a powerful military ally, sending fifty war canoes to Omoa in 1542 to assist the local chief fighting the Spanish.

Montejo's vision of ruling a vast province of the Spanish empire comprising the whole of Yucatán, Belize and Honduras was not to be fulfilled. His son, Montejo the Younger, completed the conquest of Yucatán, establishing his capital at Mérida in 1542: Montejo himself was occupied in settling Honduras. In theory, the area of the Montejos' colonial administration initially stretched from Honduras to Yucatán, and would have included Belize, but in practice the interior was never completely pacified nor were administrative boundaries clearly defined.

Late in 1543, however, **Gaspar Pacheco**, his son Melchor and his nephew Alonso began another chapter in the sickeningly familiar tale of Spanish atrocities, advancing on Chetumal, destroying crops and food stores and ruthlessly slaughtering the inhabitants. In a letter to Spain, cleric Fray Lorenz de Bienvenida wrote: "Nero was not more cruel [than Alonso Pacheco]. He passed through and reached a province called Chetumal, which was at peace.…This captain with his own hands committed outrages: he killed many with the garrotte, saying 'This is a good rod with which to punish these people'."

By 1544 the Pachecos had subdued Maya resistance sufficiently to found a town on Lake Bacalar, and claim *encomienda* (tribute) from villages around Chetumal. It is likely that the Pachecos also conquered parts of Dzuluinicob to the south, though for a time Tipú was the centre of an alliance between the two adjacent Maya provinces, showing that there was still armed resistance to Spanish domination.

During the second half of the sixteenth century missions were established, including one at Lamanai in 1570, and the Spanish, with difficulty, strengthened their hold over northern Belize. However, the Maya resentment that was always present beneath the surface boiled over into total rebellion in 1638, forcing Spain to abandon the area of Chetumal and Tipú completely and more or less permanently.

In the mid-seventeenth century the nearest permanent Spanish settlements to Belize were Salamanca de Bacalar in southern Yucatán and Lago de Izabal in Guatemala. Records are scarce, but it is likely that the Maya of Belize were under some form of Spanish influence even if they were not under Spanish rule. Perhaps the determination of Maya resistance deterred Spain from attempting to fully colonize the area; perhaps the Maya fled to inaccessible forests in an attempt to retain their independence. Repeated **expeditions** were mounted by Spanish friars and colonial leaders during the seventeenth century in an attempt to bring the heathen Maya of Tipú into the fold of the Catholic Church, though these were never more than partially successful.

In 1695 a Spanish mission met leaders of the Itzá to discuss the **surrender of the Itzá**. The negotiations were fruitless, and in 1697 Spanish troops attacked Tayasal, the Itzá capital on Lake Petén Itzá (near the site of modern Flores), bringing Maya independence in Petén to an end – at least in theory. At Tipú the struggle was to continue with simmering resentment until 1707, when the population was forcibly removed to Lake Petén Itzá. This cruel act effectively ended Spanish attempts to settle the west of Belize, as it would be impossible to establish a successful colony without people to work for the Spanish landowners.

In the late seventeenth century Bacalar was abandoned after years of **Maya and pirate attacks**. Spain's forces were simply too stretched to cope with securing the vast (and relatively gold-free) territory from Campeche on the Gulf of Mexico to Nicaragua. English, and later British, trade and territorial ambitions now focused on America and the Caribbean, resulting in almost continuous conflict with Spain. The capture of Jamaica in 1655, after 150 years of Spanish rule, gave England a base in the Caribbean from which it could harass Spanish shipping and support the growth of its own colonies.

The arrival of the British

The failure of the Spanish authorities to clearly delineate the southern boundary of Yucatán subsequently allowed **buccaneers** or pirates (primarily

British) preying on the Spanish treasure fleets to find refuge along the coast of Belize, and ultimately led to Guatemala's claim to British Honduras and refusal to recognize Belize's independence. Had Spain effectively occupied the area between Yucatán and Honduras it is unlikely that British influence – and a British colony – would have been allowed to become established. When Spain attempted to take action on various occasions to expel the British pirates and woodcutters there was confusion over which Spanish captain-general maintained jurisdiction in the area. Consequently the pirates were able to flee before the Spanish arrived and could return in the absence of any permanent Spanish outposts on the coast.

British incursions along the Bay of Honduras were first made by buccaneers, resting and seeking refuge after raids on Spanish ships and settlements. Some of the great Elizabethan sailors, such as Raleigh, Hawkins and Drake, may have landed on the coast of Belize, though there are no records to prove this. Indeed records of any kind concerning settlements or even temporary camps until the 1700s are scarce; while the dates of the establishment of other British colonies in the Caribbean are known, there was no attempt on the part of the British government to colonize Belize itself.

Other European powers, notably **France** and **the Netherlands**, were also keen to establish a foothold in the Caribbean. Companies were set up to equip privateers, who were really government-sanctioned pirate ships, to raid the Spanish treasure fleets. Treasure wasn't always easy to come by and sometimes they would plunder the piles of **logwood**, cut and awaiting shipment to Spain. The wood itself, hard and extremely heavy, was worth £90–110 a ton, and the trade was controlled by Spain. Back in Europe logwood was used in the expanding textile industry to dye woollens black, red and grey. Naturally such an abundance of convertible wealth attracted the attention of the buccaneers, once they learned of its importance. By the mid-seventeenth century (possibly as early as 1638) British buccaneers had settled on the coasts of Campeche and the Spanish Caribbean.

The various treaties signed between Britain and Spain from the late seventeenth to the mid-eighteenth century, initially designed to outlaw the buccaneers, eventually allowed the British to establish logwood camps along the rivers in northern Belize. However, this was never intended to legitimize permanent British settlement of a territory which Spain clearly regarded as its imperial domain. Thus, the British settlements in Belize periodically came under attack whenever Spain sought to defend its interests. But the attention of the European powers rarely rested long upon the humid and insect-ridden swamps where the logwood cutters, who were becoming known as **Baymen**, worked and lived. The British government, while wishing to profit from the trade in logwood, preferred to avoid the question of whether or not the Baymen were British subjects. For the most part they were left to their own devices.

Life in the logwood camps was uncomfortable, to say the least. Though the wood was mainly cut in the dry season, it was too heavy to float, and the men had to build rafts to float it down to the river mouth in the rainy season, where it was stored awaiting shipment. The Baymen lived in rough huts thatched with palm leaves (known as "Bay leaf", and still seen today, mainly in tourist cabañas), surviving on provisions brought by ships from Jamaica. These ships also brought rum, which the Baymen drank with relish whenever it was available. An English merchant (writing in 1726) reports: "Rum Punch is their Drink, which they'll sometimes sit for several Days at…for while the Liquor is moving they don't care to leave it."

Though many of the woodcutters had "voluntarily" given up buccaneering, raiding of Spanish ships still occurred in the later years of the seventeenth century, only to be punished by Spain whenever it had the will and opportunity. One such reprisal against British woodcutters in the Bay of Campeche left the survivors imprisoned in Mexico and led to Belize becoming the main centre for logwood cutting.

As the gangs of woodcutters advanced further into the forests in search of **mahogany** (which had overtaken logwood as the principal export by the 1760s and was increasingly valuable for furniture-making), they came into contact with the Maya of the interior. Although the Baymen had no wish to colonize or convert the Maya, they did capture some for slaves, and records show that the early buccaneers took Maya captives to trade in the slave markets of Jamaica. By the mid-eighteenth century the Maya had been so weakened by disease and depopulation that they could offer only limited resistance to British incursions into their territory.

Spanish attacks on the settlements in Belize occurred throughout the eighteenth century, with the Baymen being driven out on several occasions. Increasingly though, Britain – at war with Spain from 1739 to 1748 (the War of Jenkins' Ear) and France from 1743 to 1748 (the War of the Austrian Succession) – began to admit a measure of responsibility for the protection of the settlers. For the British there was little to lose.

In 1746, in response to requests from Belize, the governor of Jamaica sent troops to aid the Baymen, but this assistance didn't stop the Spanish laying waste to the settlement in 1747 and again in 1754. The **Paris Peace Treaty** of 1763 was the first (of many) to allow the British to cut logwood, but since it did not define boundaries the governor of Yucatán sent troops from Bacalar to ensure that the cutters confined themselves to the Belize River. In 1765 Admiral Burnaby, the British commander-in-chief at Jamaica, visited Belize to ensure that the provisions of the treaty, vague though they were, were upheld. As so often in the reports of naval officers concerning the condition of the settlers, he found them "in a state of Anarchy and Confusion". The admiral, recognizing that the Baymen would benefit from some form of British law and regulation, drew up a simple set of laws concerning the maintenance of justice in a remote and uncouth area where the British government did not care to become too closely involved. These rules, known as **Burnaby's Code**, gave authority to a bench of magistrates, supported by a jury, to hold quarterly courts with the power to impose fines. The Baymen attached an importance to the Code (though they apparently rarely obeyed it) beyond that which Burnaby had intended, and even voted to increase its scope a year later.

A century of antagonism, boundary disputes and mutual suspicion between the Spanish colonial authorities and the woodcutting (ex-buccaneering) Baymen meant that relations were never secure: the Spanish feared raids on their treasure ships, and the Baymen feared being driven out of what was ostensibly Spanish imperial territory. Spanish reprisals and animosity to Britain had fostered in the settlers a spirit of defiance and self-reliance, and led to the realization that British rule was preferable to Spanish, as long as they could choose which of its institutions to accept.

The Baymen's tenure in Belize was still very uncertain, however. In 1779 Spain (then allied with France on the side of the American colonies fighting for independence from Britain) sent a fleet from Bacalar to Belize and captured all the inhabitants of St George's Caye – the capital of the Baymen – imprisoning them in Mérida and Havana. The **Versailles Peace Treaty** (1783) did little to resolve the question of the Bay settlement, but a convention signed three years later allowed timber to be cut as far south as the Sibun River. The clause that rankled with the independent-minded settlers most was that no system of government could be established without approval from Madrid. True to their "turbulent and unsettled disposition", the Baymen ignored the strictures of the convention, cutting wood where they pleased and being generally unruly. After 1791 the settlement was without even the little-regarded authority of a superintendent appointed by the governor of Jamaica.

The Battle of St George's Caye

The final showdown between the waning Spanish empire and the Bay settlers (supported this time by a British warship and troops), the **Battle of St George's Caye**, came as a result of the outbreak of war between Britain and Spain in 1796. Field Marshal **Arthur (Don Arturo) O'Neil**, an Irishman and the captain general of Yucatán, assembled ships and troops, determined to drive out the British settlers and this time to occupy Belize. The Baymen appealed to Lord Balcarres, the governor of Jamaica, for help, and a **Lieutenant-Colonel Barrow** was despatched to Belize as superintendent to command the settlers in the event of hostilities. At a vital Public Meeting held on June 1, 1797, the Baymen decided by 65 votes to 51 to defend the settlement rather than evacuate. A few companies of troops were sent from Jamaica, and slaves were released from woodcutting to be armed and trained. The sloop **HMS Merlin**, under the command of Captain John Moss, was stationed in the Bay, local vessels were armed and gun rafts built and an attack was expected at any time. Throughout the next year the mood of the defenders vacillated between aggression and despair. Under the supervision of Colonel Barrow the men of Belize, now under martial law, prepared for war – albeit grudgingly in some cases. The Baymen (and their slaves) would have to defend themselves with the scant resources at their disposal.

The **Spanish fleet**, reported to consist of 32 vessels, including sixteen heavily armed men-of-war and 2000 troops, arrived just north of St George's Caye in early September 1798. On September 3 and 4 several of the Spanish warships attempted to force a passage over Montego Caye Shoals, between Long Caye and St George's Caye, but were repulsed by the Baymen's sloops. Stakes put down by the Spanish to mark the channels through the shoals were removed by the defenders, who knew these waters well. Colonel Barrow and Captain Moss correctly guessed that the Spanish would now try to seize St George's Caye. The *Merlin* and part of the Baymen's tiny fleet sailed there on the evening of September 5, securing it just as twelve of the heaviest Spanish warships were attempting to do the same.

The next few days must have passed anxiously for both sides: the Spanish with their massive firepower severely restricted by the shallow water; and the Baymen with their small but highly manoeuvrable fleet awaiting the impending attack – with the Baymen's slaves apparently at least as eager to fight the Spanish as were their masters. On the morning of **September 10, 1798**, fourteen of the largest Spanish ships sailed to within 2.5km of St George's Caye, keeping to the deep water to the east, and began firing. Captain Moss of the *Merlin* held his fire – the Spanish broadsides were falling short. At 1.30pm he gave the order to open fire. Guns blazing, the *Merlin* and the Baymen's fleet swept forward, wreaking havoc among the heavy and crowded Spanish ships. The Spanish fleet, already weakened by desertions and yellow fever, suffered heavy losses and fled in disorder to Caye Chapel. There they remained for five days, burying their dead on the island. On the morning of September 16 the defeated fleet sailed for Bacalar, still harassed by the Baymen.

Though a victory was won against overwhelming odds, the Battle of St George's Caye was not by itself decisive. No one in Belize could be sure that the Spanish would not once again attempt to remove the Baymen by force. The legal status was as before: a settlement where the inhabitants could cut timber but which did not constitute a territory of the British empire. Sovereign rights remained, nominally at least, with Spain.

However, in purely practical terms the power of the Spanish empire was waning while the British empire was consolidating and expanding. But in Belize the slaves were still slaves, though they had fought valiantly alongside the Baymen: their owners expected them to go back to cutting mahogany. Emancipation came no earlier than elsewhere in the British empire. Indeed controversy still exists within Belize over the fact that the battle was fought between two European powers to establish rule over a colony. It created the conditions for Belize to become an integral part of the British empire and enabled the slave owners to claim that the slaves were willing to fight on behalf of their masters. Whatever its legacy, the 1798 expedition was the last time that Spain attempted to gain control over Belize; Britain gradually assumed a greater role in the government of the settlement.

Settlers and slaves

A report by a Spanish missionary in 1724 mentions the ownership of **slaves** by English settlers, and it's possible that slaves were brought in (from Jamaica and Bermuda) before that time. The British population of the settlements in the Bay of Honduras during the century and a half following the arrival of the first buccaneers had never been more than a few hundred, their livelihoods dependent on the attitude of the authorities in the adjacent Spanish colonies. In order to gain concessions from Spain favourable to the Belize settlement, Britain had agreed to relinquish claims to the Mosquito Coast (a British protectorate along the coasts of Honduras and Nicaragua) in the **Convention of London** in 1786. Many of the aggrieved inhabitants displaced by the convention settled in Belize, and by 1790 the population had reached over 2900, of whom over 2100 were slaves.

Over the years the view that slavery in Belize was somehow less harsh than elsewhere in the Caribbean has emerged. It's a misconception that may have arisen because of the differences between plantation slavery as practised in the West Indies and the southern United States, and the mainly forest labour that slaves in Belize were required to perform. The misconception has evolved into a myth, skilfully manipulated by apologists for colonialism, who maintain that during the pivotal Battle of St George's Caye slaves voluntarily fought "shoulder to shoulder" with their white masters, and thus preferred slavery over the freedom offered by the Spanish authorities to any slave who escaped to Spanish territory. Although some slaves did fight alongside their masters in 1798, they also continued to escape: in 1813 fifteen slaves belonging to Thomas Paslow, one of the heroes of the battle, escaped "because of ill-treatment and starvation", their desperation evidence enough to refute the myth. Records of **slave revolts** from 1745 to 1820 are further indication that relations between master and slaves were not as amicable as some would like to believe.

The whites in the settlement, always vastly outnumbered by their slaves, feared rebellion at least as much as they feared attack by the Spanish. The biggest (and arguably most successful) revolt occurred in 1773 when six white men were murdered and at least eleven slaves escaped across the Hondo River, where they received asylum from the Spanish authorities. This was not a display of altruism on the part of the Spanish, since encouraging slaves to flee the British settlement was calculated to weaken its economy.

The nature of slavery in Belize was, however, very different from that on the sugar plantations in the West Indies. The cutting of mahogany involved small gangs working in the forest on their own or on a fairly harmonious level with an overseer. The slaves were armed, with firearms in some cases, to hunt for food and for protection against the Maya. Skills developed in searching for the trees, cutting them down and transporting them to the coast gave the slaves involved a position of trust that their masters depended on for the continuation of their own way of life. **Manumission**, whereby a slave might purchase freedom or be freed as a bequest in a will, or simply a gift, was much more frequent in Belize than in the Caribbean islands, perhaps as an indication of the greater informality of Belizean society. However, treatment could still be harsh and little protection was offered by the law. Owners could inflict up to 39 lashes or imprison their slaves, and if a slave was hanged for rebellion the owner could be compensated for the loss of property.

Ironically, it was the **Abolition Act of 1807** – which made it illegal for British subjects to continue with the African slave trade but not illegal to transport slaves from one British colony to another – that gave the settlers in Belize recognition as **British subjects**. If Belize was not a colony (which it clearly was not) then slaves could not be transported between Jamaica and the settlement. Superintendent Arthur, the British government's representative and upholder of the law in Belize, decided that the settlers in Belize were British subjects and therefore forbidden to engage in the slave trade. The **Abolition Act of 1833** ended slavery throughout the British empire, and contained a special clause to include Belize. The passing of the Act, however, did not end slavery immediately: "freed" slaves were to be called "apprentices", required to work for their masters for forty hours per week with no pay before being allowed to work for payment. This abuse continued until 1838, when the former slaves were fully and legally free. Despite the inherent immorality in the institution of slavery the Act provided for **compensation** to be paid to the owners for the loss of property, rather than to the former slaves for the suffering they had undergone for so long – and, at £53 per slave, the compensation paid was higher than in any British colony.

The settlement becomes a colony

The consolidation of British logging interests in the eighteenth century and the grudging, tentative steps towards recognition from Spain, led to a form of **British colonial government** gradually becoming established in the Belize settlement. The **Public Meeting**, with its origins in the early 1700s, was the settlers' initial response to the need for some rudimentary form of government. At first informal, the meetings slowly assumed greater importance, and by the 1730s were electing magistrates with powers to hold courts and impose fines, though in the democratic spirit of the time only property-owning white men could vote. Free black men were allowed to vote at the Public Meeting after 1808, though their franchise was limited by burdening them with higher property requirements than that of whites. **Burnaby's Code** in 1765 reinforced and enlarged the jurisdiction of the magistrates, and allowed the laws passed at the Meeting to be enforced by the captain of a British naval ship, though reports by visiting naval officers almost invariably commented on the lamentable inability of the settlers to keep their own laws.

These early examples of Britain's acceptance of some form of responsibility to the settlers led to the appointment in 1784 of the first **superintendent**, Captain Despard, who took up his post in 1786. The office of superintendent, always held by an army officer, appears to have been a difficult one. They often faced an unsupportive Public Meeting, which wanted to run the settlement without "interference" from London. Gradually though, the powers of the superintendent grew, while those of the magistrates lessened. The election of magistrates ceased altogether in 1832, after which they were appointed by the superintendent. The office of superintendent was moving towards the role (though not the title) of a lieutenant-governor of a colony, and in 1854 an elected **Legislative Assembly** was formed, establishing the beginnings of colonial-rule parliamentary democracy. The assembly began petitioning for recognition as a colony, arguing that the settlement was in fact, if not in law, already a British colony. Earl Grey, at the Colonial Office, supported the assembly and Palmerston, the British prime minister, agreed. On May 12, 1862, the Belize settlements, with the boundaries that still exist today, became the **Colony of British Honduras**.

Partly as a result of arguments about raising finance, the Legislative Assembly dissolved itself in 1870 and was replaced by a Legislative Council. This enabled the British government to establish a **Crown Colony** form of government in 1871, in line with colonial policy throughout the West Indies. Now under the control of a governor appointed by the Colonial Office, the self-determination of the settlers was effectively reduced.

Mexican and Guatemalan claims

After the Battle of St George's Caye in 1798 Spain continued to maintain its claim to Belize, and the **Treaty of Amiens** in 1802 required Britain to hand back to Spain the territory captured during the war. Spain took this to include Belize, though the Baymen had no intention of leaving. But in the face of gathering difficulties throughout the Spanish empire, and Britain's willingness to assist the settlers in the defence of Belize, Spain's claim became increasingly insupportable.

Although **Mexico's independence**, achieved in 1821 and followed two years later by the colonies in Central America, marked the end of the Spanish empire on the mainland of the Americas, it didn't signal the end of external claims to Belizean territory. The years between the collapse of the Spanish empire and the close of the nineteenth century were filled with claim and counter-claim and with treaties made and broken – a situation not entirely resolved today.

Mexico's claim to at least the northern part of British Honduras as an extension of Yucatán was unacceptable to the British government, and eventually, after numerous diplomatic exchanges, an **Anglo-Mexican Treaty** was ratified in 1897. However, Mexico stated at the time that should Guatemala successfully revive any of its claims to British Honduras then Mexico would press a claim to the area north of the Sibun River.

Guatemala's claim has been the source of more belligerent disagreement with Britain, and there's no doubt that the British government shares much of the blame for the confusion. In treaty after treaty Britain regarded Belize as a territory under Spanish sovereignty, and long after Spain's expulsion from the area, Britain maintained the fiction of Spanish sovereignty, which only complicated relations with the independent Guatemala. The Guatemalan claim to the territory of Belize rested upon the acceptance in international law of *uti possidetis* – the right of a colony that successfully gains independence from a colonial authority to inherit the rights and territory of that authority at the time of independence. For this to be valid, however (even if Britain accepted the premise of *uti possidetis* – which was doubtful), the entire territory of Belize would have had to have been under Spanish control in 1821. Since this was clearly not the case the British position was that Guatemala's claim was therefore invalid.

In a vain attempt to reach a settlement, Britain and Guatemala signed the **Anglo-Guatemalan Treaty** in 1859: the interpretation of this treaty and its various clauses has been the source of controversy and dispute ever since. The treaty, which in the British view settled the boundaries of Guatemala and Belize in their existing positions, was interpreted by Guatemala as a disguised treaty of cession of the territory outlined – if the crucial and controversial Article 7 of the treaty was not implemented – and not a confirmation of the boundaries. Under the provisions of Article 7, Britain agreed to fund and build a road from Guatemala City to the Atlantic coast and in return Guatemala would drop its claim to Belize. If the road was not built then the territory would revert to Guatemala. Although a route was surveyed in 1859, Britain considered the estimated cost of £100,000 to construct the road too high a price to pay to secure the territory of Belize, and for this and other reasons the road was never built. The disputes were no nearer resolution when the settlement became the colony of British Honduras in 1862. The provisions of this article continued to be a cause of rancour and disagreement between the two countries for decades, and despite conventions and negotiations no agreement was reached. Finally, in 1940, Guatemala repudiated the treaty on the grounds that the provisions of Article 7 were not fulfilled, and the new constitution of 1945 declared Belize – *Belice* in Spanish – to be the 23rd department of Guatemala. In 1948 Guatemala made the first of several **threats to invade** Belize to "recover" the territory; Britain responded by sending cruisers and troops, the first of many military deployments required to counter this threat over the next four decades. In hindsight, £100,000 in 1859 would have been a comparative bargain.

The Caste Wars of Yucatán

The terrible, bloody **Caste Wars** of Yucatán began with a riot by Maya troops at Valladolid in 1847. They sacked the town, killing whites and spreading terror throughout the peninsula, and came within a hair's breadth of capturing the capital, Mérida, and throwing off white rule completely. From 1848, as Mexico sent troops to put down the rebellion, thousands of Maya and mestizo **refugees** fled to Belize, increasing the population of Orange Walk and Corozal and clearing the land for agriculture. The superintendent in Belize encouraged them to stay as they brought sugar cane and much-needed farming skills.

The rebellious **Cruzob Maya** (taking their name from a sacred "talking cross") occupied a huge, virtually independent territory in the east of the Yucatán peninsula. They established their capital at Chan Santa Cruz ("little holy cross" in English), the modern town of Felipe Carillo Puerto, well to the north of Belize, giving them their alternative name – the **Santa Cruz Maya**. At this time, the border between Belize and Mexico was not clearly defined, and the Belize woodcutters came into conflict with the Santa Cruz Maya, who attacked the mahogany camps and took prisoners for ransom. The alarm spread throughout Belize and eventually a compromise was reached, whereby the settlers would pay a ransom to secure the prisoners' release, and would furthermore pay royalties to the Santa Cruz for the rights to cut wood in the Maya territory. In fact British merchants in Belize profited from the war by selling the Santa Cruz Maya arms, provoking strong protests from Mexico.

The story is further complicated by suspicion between the Santa Cruz and another Maya group, the **Icaiché**, who were not in rebellion and consequently were not trusted by the Santa Cruz. In 1851 the Icaiché were attacked by the Santa Cruz Maya, leading the Mexican government to propose an alliance between themselves and the Icaiché against the Santa Cruz. The Icaiché leaders requested British help in their negotiations, and since the woodcutters wanted to enter Icaiché lands to log mahogany, the Belize timber companies were also signatories to the treaty. In the **treaty of 1853** the Icaiché were granted virtual autonomy in the lands they occupied in return for recognizing the authority of Mexico, and the British were allowed to cut wood under licence in the Icaiché lands, in what was to become the northwest of Belize. The British woodcutters viewed the agreement as a means to expand their territory at the expense of both the Icaiché and a weakened Mexico.

It was now the turn of the Icaiché to demand rent from the British loggers; again this was only paid after **Maya attacks** on the camps. The continuing British arms trade with the Santa Cruz Maya incensed the Icaiché, and the flames were fanned further when they were attacked by the Santa Cruz. After years of broken agreements and betrayal the Icaiché, supported by Mexico and led by **Marcos Canul**, attacked mahogany camps on the Río Bravo and the New River in 1866, capturing dozens of prisoners and spreading panic throughout the colony. The lieutenant governor declared martial law and sent for reinforcements from Jamaica. Raids and counter-raids continued for years, as the Maya sacked villages in Belize and colonial troops destroyed Maya villages and crops in reprisal. Canul briefly occupied Corozal in 1870, and even his death following a battle at Orange Walk in 1872 did not put an end to the raids. Corozal became a fortified military base, and, although the violence diminished, the danger of Maya attacks wasn't over until 1882 when the Icaiché leader, Santiago Pech, met the governor in Belize City to recognize British jurisdiction in the northwest.

The twentieth century: towards independence

By 1900, free for the moment from worries about external threats, Belize was an integral, if minor, colony of the British empire. The population in the census of 1901 was 37,500, of whom 28,500 were born in the colony.

Comfortable complacency set in, and the predominantly white property owners could foresee no change to their rule. The workers in the forests and on the estates were mainly black, the descendants of former slaves, known as "Creoles". Wages were low and the colonial government and employers maintained strict controls over workers, with the power to imprison labourers for missing a day's work and stifling any labour organizations.

Belizeans rushed to defend the "mother country" in **World War I** but the black troops from Belize were not permitted to fight a white enemy and were instead placed in labour battalions in British-held Mesopotamia. On their return in 1919, humiliated and disillusioned, their bitterness exploded into violence, and the troops were joined by thousands of Belize City's population (including the police) in looting and rioting, an event which marked the onset of **black consciousness** and the beginnings of the independence movement. The ideas of **Marcus Garvey**, a phenomenally industrious and charismatic black Jamaican leader, and founder of the Universal Negro Improvement Association (UNIA), were already known in Belize – the colonial government's ban on *Negro World*, the UNIA's magazine, contributed to the severity of the 1919 riot – and in 1920 a branch of the UNIA opened in Belize City. Garvey believed that the "Negro needs a nation and a country of his own" – a sentiment which found increasing support among all sectors of black society in Belize. Garvey himself visited Belize in 1921.

The status of workers had improved little over the previous century, and the Depression years of the 1930s brought extreme hardship, the disastrous hurricane of 1931 compounding the misery. The disaster prompted workers to organize in 1934 after an unemployment relief programme initiated by the governor was a dismal failure. **Antonio Soberanis** emerged as a leader, founding the Labourers and Unemployed Association (LUA), and holding regular meetings in the "Battlefield" – a public square outside the colonial administration buildings in Belize City. Soberanis was arrested in October 1934 while arranging bail for pickets at a sawmill who had been arrested. He was released a month later, and the meetings resumed. The colonial government responded by passing restrictive laws, banning marches and increasing the powers of the governor to deal with disturbances.

World War II gave a boost to forestry and the opportunity for Belizeans to work abroad, though conditions for the returning soldiers and workers were no better than they had been following World War I. Even in 1946 political power lay with the tiny wealthy elite who controlled the Executive Council and with the governor, a Foreign Office appointee. The devaluation of the British Honduras dollar at the end of 1949 caused greater hardship. A cautious report on constitutional reform in 1951 led to a new constitution, and in 1954 a **general election** was held in which all literate adults over the age of 21 could vote. These elections were won with an overwhelming majority by the **People's United Party** (PUP), led by **George Price**, and ushered in a semblance of ministerial government, though control of financial measures was retained by the governor. Belize became an **internally self-governing** colony in 1964, a step intended to lead to full independence after a relatively short time, as was the policy throughout the Caribbean. Until then, however, the British government, through the governor, remained responsible for defence, foreign affairs and internal security. The National Assembly became a bicameral system with an appointed Senate and an entirely elected House of Representatives.

The delay in achieving independence was caused largely by the ongoing **dispute with Guatemala** as to its still unresolved claim to Belize. At least twice, in 1972 and 1977, Guatemala moved troops to the border and threatened to invade, but prompt British reinforcements were an effective dissuasion. The situation remained tense but international opinion gradually moved in favour of Belizean independence.

Independence and the border dispute

The most important demonstration of worldwide endorsement of Belize's right to self-determination was the **UN resolution** passed in 1980, which demanded secure independence, with all territory intact, before the next session. Further negotiations with Guatemala began but complete agreement could not be reached: Guatemala still insisted on some territorial concessions. On March 11, 1981, Britain, Guatemala and Belize released the "Heads of Agreement", a document which, they hoped, would eventually result in a peaceful solution to the dispute. Accordingly, on September 21, 1981, Belize became an independent country within the British Commonwealth, with Queen Elizabeth II as head of state. In a unique decision, British troops were to remain in Belize to ensure the territorial integrity of the new nation.

The new government of Belize, formed by the PUP with George Price as premier, continued in power until 1984, when the United Democratic Party (UDP), led by **Manuel Esquivel**, won Belize's first general election after independence. The new government encouraged private enterprise and foreign investment, and began a programme of neo-liberal economic reforms which meant privatizing much of the public sector. The next general election, in 1989, returned the PUP to power.

In 1988 Guatemala and Belize established a joint commission to work towards a "just and honourable" solution to the **border dispute**, and by August 1990 it was agreed in principle that Guatemala would accept the existing border with Belize. The only sticking point preventing full recognition by Guatemala was a geographical anomaly in the extreme south, where the territorial waters of Belize and Honduras formed a common boundary, making it theoretically possible for Guatemalan ships to be excluded from their own Caribbean ports. The PUP government's response was to draft the **Maritime Areas Bill** in August 1991, which would allow Guatemala access to the high seas by restricting Belize's territorial waters between the Sarstoon River and Ranguana Caye, 100km to the northeast. This measure proved acceptable to Guatemala's President Serrano, and on September 11, with just ten days to go before the celebrations for Belize's tenth anniversary of independence, Guatemala and Belize established full diplomatic relations for the first time.

The air of euphoria soured somewhat during 1992 as opposition to Serrano's controversial recognition of Belize became more vocal and was ultimately challenged in Guatemala's Constitutional Court. Eventually the court decided that the president had not actually violated the constitution, and in November 1992 Congress (albeit with thirteen abstentions) conditionally approved Serrano's actions. The Guatemalan president's remaining time in office was short, however: in May 1993 he attempted to rule without Congress, and by June was overthown and in exile. Belize's premier, George Price, hoped to gain from the confusion this caused and, with the opposition UDP deeply divided, called a snap general election in July 1993. To his astonishment the gamble failed, and Manuel Esquivel's UDP was allowed a second term of office.

Eventually negotiations between the two countries resumed, and in 2002 both governments agreed that the territorial dispute – now called the "**border differendum**" – could at long last be resolved by Belize ceding a tiny sliver of land in the far northwest (the result of an incorrectly positioned survey marker in 1931), and by establishing a joint-use area in the southern territorial waters. Almost everyone in Belize realized this was a golden opportunity: a few square kilometres of unoccupied land (which had never actually belonged to Belize in the first place) and joint use of sea lanes and seabed (together with the creation of an international protected area) and the Guatemalan claim would be over. The problem in implementing what was, on the face of it, a proposal where both parties had everything to gain and neither lost face, was that in order to ratify the agreement a referendum would have to be held in each country, with the electorate voting in favour. This would not be difficult to arrange in Belize, but holding a referendum in Guatemala, where most people have only a vague idea (if any) of the border dispute and of the attempts to resolve it, would require such a massive education programme to inform voters that the government is making no moves to hold one.

And so, despite agreement between the two governments, the border issue remains a stumbling block in relations between the two countries. The dispute simmers on as Guatemalan peasant farmers clear land just inside Belize and small groups of soldiers from each country stray across the other's border. One positive outcome of the 2002 agreement is the setting up of an **adjacency zone** a few kilometres either side of the border, where potentially inflammatory cross-border disputes can be referred to an impartial committee under the jurisdiction of the Organization of American States. Thus, despite the failure to reach a completely watertight agreement, the outlook is probably brighter than at any time in history; both countries continue to exchange ambassadors and are committed to resolving the dispute through **negotiation**.

Belize's **democratic credentials** are beyond dispute: at each general election since independence (until the most recent) the voters have kicked out the incumbent government and replaced it with the opposition. This has meant that the nominally left-of-centre **People's United Party (PUP)** has alternated with the more market-led **United Democratic Party (UDP)**. At the general election of March 2003, however, the PUP under the leadership of Prime Minister **Said Musa** won an unprecedented second term in a second consecutive landslide victory.

The booming **tourist industry**, bringing in over US$400 million a year out of Belize's US$2.31 billion GDP and employing almost a third of the country's workforce, is now the mainstay of Belize's **economy**, pushing agriculture and fisheries into a close second place. Annual growth is around 3.5 percent, with inflation at 4.5 percent, while unemployment hovers around 10 percent. Figures are obviously not available for Belize's income from the lucrative drug transshipment business, but this illicit economy is certainly a sizeable fraction of the official one. **Per capita** income is high for Central America, at about US$8400, boosted by the remittances many Belizeans receive from relatives abroad, mainly in the US. This apparent advantage is somewhat offset by the fact that many of the brightest and most highly trained citizens leave Belize, fitting in well in English-speaking North America, though increasingly many graduates do return as more skilled and managerial positions become available within Belize.

Though Belize's traditional links with Britain and the Commonwealth countries in the West Indies remain strong, the **United States** is by far its largest trading partner and supplies much of the **foreign aid** on which Belize still depends. Britain's position as the former colonial power and a major aid-provider following independence is gradually being replaced by aid channelled through multilateral organizations, including the EU.

Belize is currently participating in the negotiations for the **Free Trade Area of the Americas** (FTAA). This agreement would establish the largest free trade area in the world, an idea viewed with alarm by many Belizean workers, who fear that an end to all tariffs will further depress agricultural prices and drive the small manufacturing base into bankruptcy. Even worse in many eyes, such proposals might signal an end to the **fixed rate of exchange** with the US$, leading to a potentially catastrophic devaluation of the Belize dollar. A leading opponent of the FTAA describes it as "an economic onslaught on national sovereignty". Regardless of the populist rhetoric of the PUP government and domestic popular sentiment, however, Belize is firmly linked to the US-dominated international financial structures and will have to face increasing challenges from global competition in the future.

Chronology of the Maya

25,000 BC ▶ **Paleo-Indian** First waves of nomadic hunters from Siberia.

10,000 BC ▶ **Clovis culture** Worked stone tools found at many sites in North and Central America.

7500 BC ▶ **Archaic period** Beginnings of settled agricultural communities throughout Mesoamerica; maize and other food crops cultivated.

4500 BC ▶ **Proto-Maya period** First Maya-speaking groups settle in western Guatemala; Proto-Maya speakers probably spread throughout extent of Maya area.

2000 BC ▶ **Preclassic** or **Formative period** Divided into: Early: 2000–1000 BC; Middle: 1000–300 BC; Late: 300 BC–250 AD.

The Maya begin building centres which will develop into the great cities of the Classic period. Trade increases, and contact with the **Olmec** on the Gulf coast of Mexico brings many cultural developments, including the calendar and new gods. **Kaminaljuyú** dominates highland Guatemala, **El Mirador** is the most important city in Petén and by 1000 BC Lamanai is a large city.

200 BC ▶ Earliest carved stela found in Belize: Stela 9 at Cahal Pech.

250 AD ▶ **Classic period** Divided into: Early: 250–600 AD; Late: 600–850 AD; Terminal: 850–c.1000 AD.

During this period Maya culture reaches its height. Introduction of the **long count calendar**, used to mark dates of important events on stelae and monuments. The central lowlands are thickly populated, with almost all of the sites now known flourishing. The great monumental architecture associated with the Maya mainly dates from the Classic period. **Caracol** is the largest Classic Maya city in Belize.

800 AD ▶ **Terminal Classic period** Decline (some say collapse) of Classic Maya civilization for reasons that remain unclear. Population decline and abandonment of many Maya cities, though some in Belize – notably **Lamanai** – survive throughout the Terminal Classic period.

987 AD ▶ Yucatán sites show strong evidence of **Toltec culture**, possibly a result of invasion. Toltec culture grafted onto the region's Maya culture, possibly also extending into Belize.

1000 AD ▶ **Early Postclassic period**

Re-focus of populations. Some centres, such as **Xunantunich**, which survived the Terminal Classic, are now abandoned, but many centres in Belize continue to thrive. Toltec domination of the Guatemalan highlands.

c. 1250 ▶ Rivalry and trade among the city-states of Petén, Yucatán and Belize. New, competitive, power structures formed by centres along the trade routes. **Tayasal** (near Flores) rises to dominance in Petén. Cities in the river valleys of Belize grow rich controlling trade routes.

1511 ▶ First **Spanish contact with Maya** in Yucatán; Spanish sailors are captured.

1521 ▶ Aztec capital Tenochtitlán falls to Spanish troops commanded by **Cortés**.

1531 ▶ **Alonso Dávila** makes first attempt to capture and settle at Chetumal.

1543 & 1544 ▶ Gaspar and Melchor **Pacheco** brutally conquer southern Yucatán and northern Belize.

1570 **Spanish mission** established at Lamanai; eight others built in northern Belize.

1697 ▶ **Conquest of the Itzá Maya** of Noh Petén (present-day Flores), the last independent Maya kingdom.

Chronology of Belize

1618 ▶ Spanish priests Fuensalida and Orbita visit **Tipú**, on the Macal River, where they punish the Maya for worshipping "idols"; the Maya burn the church in defiance.

1630–1640 ▶ Led by Tipú, the **Maya revolt against Spanish rule**. First pirate attacks on Bacalar, just north of Hondo River.

1640s ▶ First **buccaneer** (pirate) settlements at mouth of Belize River.

1670 ▶ **Treaty of Madrid**, under which European powers begin to restrict piracy. Buccaneers start to cut logwood in the swamps of Belize. Spain claims sovereignty over Belize (but had never effectively colonized the area).

1716 ▶ First **Spanish attacks** on British woodcutters (**Baymen**) in Belize. These attacks continue until 1798; at times the whole population of the settlement is driven off or captured, but the Baymen always return. African slaves brought from Jamaica to cut wood.

1763 ▶ **Treaty of Paris** allows British to cut and export wood in Belize; Spanish continue to maintain sovereignty but Britain increasingly prepared to defend settlers' rights.

1786 ▶ **Convention of London** allows Baymen to cut wood, but not to establish plantations, fortifications or government. First **British superintendent** in Belize.

1798 ▶ **Battle of St George's Caye**: settlers and slaves under the command of British army and with support from the Royal Navy defeat a Spanish invasion fleet.

1821–1824 ▶ Mexico and the **Central American republics gain independence** from Spain. Both Mexico and Guatemala claim sovereignty over Belize.

1832 ▶ Main date of arrival of **Garifuna** from Honduras, though some were already in Belize.

1838 ▶ Emancipation of slaves (five years later than in Britain).

1847–1900 ▶ **Caste Wars of Yucatán** Maya refugees flee to northern Belize; other groups of Maya raid towns and settlements in Belize until 1880.

1859 ▶ **Anglo-Guatemalan Treaty** and other agreements aim to end dispute over sovereignty of Belize, but no real conclusion reached.

1862 ▶ Belize becomes part of the British empire as the colony of **British Honduras**.

1871 ▶ Status of British Honduras changed to **Crown Colony**.

1919 ▶ Belizean troops riot on return from World War I. Start of **nationalist sentiment** and beginning of calls for independence.

1931 ▶ **Hurricane** (unnamed) devastates Belize City and the entire coast.

1945 ▶ New Guatemalan constitution defines "Belice" as a department of Guatemala.

1950 ▶ **PUP** formed.

1954 ▶ New constitution introduces universal adult suffrage. PUP wins the **general election**.

1964 ▶ Belize gains **full internal self-government**. Independence delayed by Guatemala's claim to Belize. Guatemala threatens to invade in 1972 and 1977.

1979 ▶ First of 40,000 **refugees** from Guatemala and El Salvador arrive in Belize.

1981 ▶ Belize gains **independence** on September 21. **George Price** of PUP is prime minister.

1984 ▶ First general election after independence. UDP wins; **Manuel Esquivel** becomes prime minister.

1989 ▶ **PUP wins general election**; George Price is again prime minister.

1991–1993 ▶ Guatemala's President Serrano agrees to recognize Belize. Diplomatic relations are established but no final agreement signed. George Price and PUP lose the general election. Manuel Esquivel and **UDP are elected**.

1998 & 2003 ▶ PUP wins landslide general elections; **Said Musa** is prime minister.

2002 ▶ Organization of American States (OAS) sponsors agreement to settle border dispute agreed to by Belize and Guatemala, but neither likely to hold the necessary referendum leading to ratification.

2006 ▶ Belize celebrates the 25th anniversary of its independence from Britain.

The Maya achievement

For some three thousand years before the arrival of the Spanish, Maya civilization dominated Central America. The culture was complex and sophisticated, a fact made evident by the remains of the Maya's great centres: despite centuries of neglect and abuse they are still astounding, with temples towering above the forest roof. Stone monuments, however, leave much of the story untold, and there is still a great deal we have to learn about Maya civilization. What follows is a brief introduction to the subject, hopefully just enough to whet your appetite for the immense volumes that have been written on it.

Maya life and society

While the remains of the great Maya sites are a testament to the scale and sophistication of Maya civilization, they offer little insight into daily life in Maya times. To reconstruct the lives of ordinary people, archeologists have turned to the smaller **residential groups** that surround the main sites, littered with the remains of household utensils, pottery, bones and farming tools. These groups are made up of simple structures made of poles and wattle-and-daub, each of which was home to a single family. The groups as a whole probably housed an extended family, who would have farmed and hunted together and may well have specialized in some trade or craft. The people living in these groups were the commoners, their lives largely dependent on agriculture. Maize, beans, cacao, squash, chillies and fruit trees were cultivated in raised and irrigated fields, while wild fruits were harvested from the surrounding forest. Much of the land was communally owned and groups of around twenty men worked in the fields together.

Maya **agriculture** was continuously adapting to the needs of the developing society, and the early practice of slash-and-burn farming was soon replaced by more intensive and sophisticated methods to meet the needs of a growing population. Some of the land was terraced, drained or irrigated in order to improve its fertility and ensure that fields didn't have to lie fallow for long periods, and the capture of water became crucial to the success of a site. The large cities, today hemmed in by the forest, were once surrounded by open fields, canals and residential compounds, while slash-and-burn .agriculture probably continued in marginal and outlying areas. Agriculture became a specialized profession, and a large section of the population would have bought at least some of their food in markets, although all households still had a kitchen garden where they grew herbs and fruit.

Maize has always been the basis of the Maya **diet**, in ancient times as much as it is today. Once harvested it was made into *saka*, a corn-meal gruel, which was eaten with chilli as the first meal of the day. During the day labourers ate a mixture of corn dough and water, and we know that *tamales* were also a popular speciality. The main meal, eaten in the evenings, would have been similarly maize-based, although it may well have included vegetables, and occasionally meat. As a supplement to this simple diet, deer, peccary, wild turkey, duck, pigeon and quail were all hunted with bows and arrows or blowguns. The Maya also made use of dogs, both for **hunting** and eating. Fish were also eaten, and

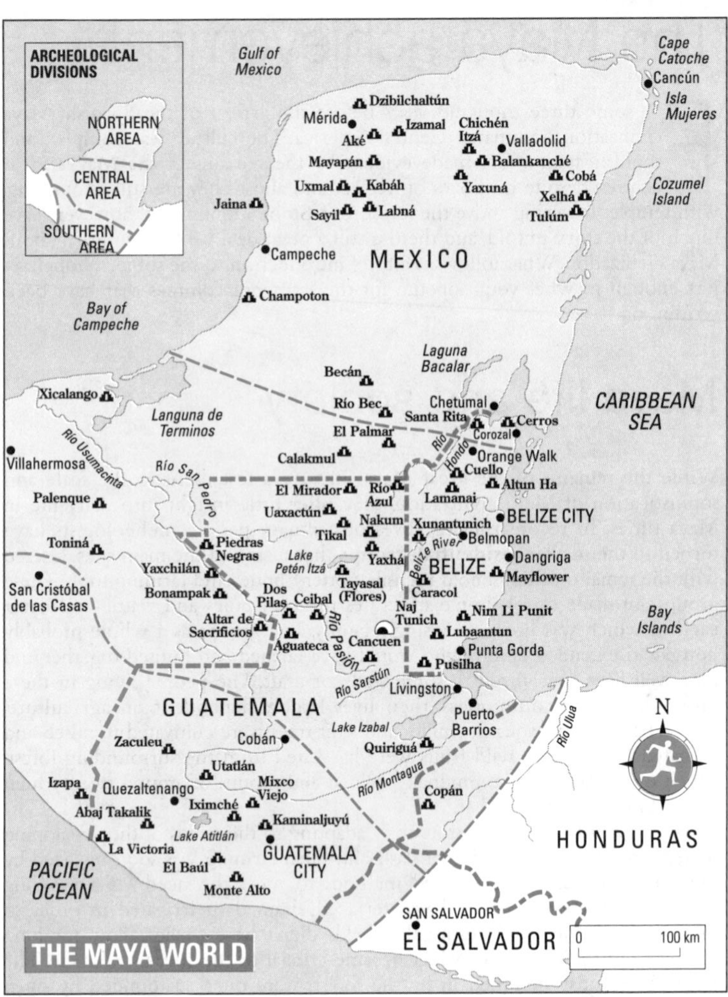

the remains of fish hooks and nets have been found in some sites, while there is evidence that those living on the coast traded dried fish far inland. As well as food, the forest provided firewood, and cotton was cultivated to be dyed with natural colours and then spun into cloth.

The main sites represent larger versions of the basic residential groups, housing the most powerful families and their assorted retainers. Beyond this these centres transcended the limits of family ties, taking on larger political, religious and administrative roles, and as Maya society developed they became large cities. The principal occupants were members of royal families and the nobility, but others included bureaucrats, merchants, warriors, architects and assorted craftsmen – an emerging **middle class**. At the highest level this hierarchy was controlled by a series of hereditary positions, with a **king** (occasionally a queen) at its head; these figures also occupied the role of religious leader. At certain times in the calendar cycle kings (and probably other members of the ruling class) communicated with gods and illustrious ancestors by performing acts of ritual **blood-letting** upon themselves, often accompanied by the sacrifice of important captives who may have been kept alive for years, awaiting the ceremonial celebrations.

The relationship between the cities and the land, drawn up along feudal lines, was at the heart of Maya life. The **peasant farmers** supported the ruling class by providing labour – building and maintaining the temples and palaces – food and other basic goods. In return the elite provided the peasantry with leadership, direction, protection and above all else the security of their knowledge of calendrics and supernatural prophecy. This knowledge was thought to be the basis of successful agriculture, and the ruler-priests were relied upon to divine the appropriate time to plant and harvest.

In turn, the cities themselves became organized into a hierarchy of power. At times a single city, such as El Mirador, Tikal or Calakmul dominated vast areas, controlling all of the smaller sites, while at other times smaller centres operated independently. The distance between the larger sites averaged around 30km, and between these were myriad smaller settlements, religious centres and residential groups. A complex, shifting structure of **alliances** (and rivalries) bound the various sites together in an endless round of competition and conflict, and there were frequent outbursts of **open warfare**. The structure of these alliances can be traced in the use of emblem-glyphs. Only those of the main centres are used in isolation, while the names of smaller sites are used in conjunction with those of their larger patrons.

The Maya calendar

For both practical and mystical reasons the Maya developed a highly sophisticated understanding of arithmetic, calendrics and astronomy, all of which they believed gave them the power to understand and predict events. All great occasions were interpreted on the basis of the **Maya calendar**, and it was this precise understanding of time that gave the ruling elite its authority. The majority of carving, on temples and stelae, records the exact date at which rulers were born, ascended to power, sacrificed captives and died.

The basis of all Maya **calculation** was the vigesimal counting system, which used multiples of twenty. All figures were written using a combination of three symbols – a shell to denote zero, a dot for one and a bar for five – which you can still see on many stelae. When calculating calendrical systems the Maya used

Maya time – the units

1 *kin* = 24 hours
20 *kins* = 1 *winal*, or 20 days
18 *winals* = 1 *tun*, or 360 days
20 *tuns* = 1 *katun*, or 7200 days
20 *katuns* = 1 *baktun*, or 144,000 days
20 *baktun* = 1 *pictun*, or 2,880,000 days
20 *pictuns* = 1 *calabtun*, or 57,600,000 days
20 *calabtuns* = 1 *kinchiltun*, or 1,152,000,000 days
20 *kinchiltuns* = 1 *alautun*, or 23,040,000,000 days

△ Maya calendar

a slightly different notation known as the head-variant system, in which each number from one to twenty was represented by a deity, whose head was used to represent the number.

When it comes to the Maya **calendar** things start to get more complicated, as a number of different counting systems were used, depending on the reason the date was being calculated. The basic unit of the Maya calendar was the day, or *kin*, followed by the *winal*, a group of twenty *kins* roughly equivalent to our month, but at the next level things start to get more complex, as the Maya marked the passing of time in three distinct ways. In an ideal vigesimal system (as the Maya arithmetic system was) the next level would be 400 *kins* – but for marking the passing of a period approximating a year the Maya used the *tun*, comprising 18 (rather than 20) *winals*, plus a closing month of five days, the *Uayeb*, a total of 365 days. This so-called "**vague year**", or *haab*, made it a very close approximation of the annual cycle, though of course the Maya elite knew that the solar year was a fraction over 365 days. Beyond this unit however, the passing of time was ordered in multiples of twenty, with the *katun* being twenty *tuns*.

The 260-day **sacred almanac** was used to calculate the timing of ceremonial events and as a basis for prophecy. Each day (*kin*) was associated with a particular deity that had strong influence over those born on that particular day. This calendar wasn't divided into months but had 260 distinct day names. (This system is still in use among the Cakchiquel in the highlands of Guatemala, who name their children according to its structure and celebrate fiestas according to its dictates.) These first two calendars weren't used in isolation but operated in parallel so that once every 52 years the new day of the solar year coincided with the same day in the 260-day almanac, a meeting that was regarded as very powerful and marked the end of one "**calendar round**" and the beginning of the next.

Finally, the Maya had another system for marking the passing of history, which is used on dedicatory monuments. The system, known as the **long count**, is based on the "great cycle" of 13 *baktuns* (a period of 5128 years). The dates in this system simply record the number of days that have elapsed since the start of the current great cycle – dating from 3114 BC and destined to come to an end on December 21, 2012 – a task that calls for ten different numbers, recording the equivalent of months, years, decades, centuries, etc. In later years the Maya sculptors obviously tired of this exhaustive process and opted instead for the **short count**, an abbreviated version.

Astronomy

Alongside their fascination with time, the Maya were interested in the sky and devoted much time and energy to unravelling its patterns. Several large sites such as Copán, Uaxactún and Chichén Itzá have **observatories** carefully aligned with solar and lunar sequences; in all probability, a building or buildings in each city was dedicated to this role.

The Maya showed a great understanding of **astronomy** and with their 365-day "vague year" were just a quarter of a day out in their calculations of the solar year, while at Copán, towards the end of the seventh century AD, Maya astronomers had calculated the lunar cycle at 29.53020 days, just slightly off from our current estimate of 29.53059. In the Dresden Codex their calculations extend to the 405 lunations over a period of 11,960 days, as part of a pattern that set out to predict eclipses. At the same time they had calculated with astonishing accuracy the movements of Venus, Mars and perhaps Mercury. Venus was of particular importance to the Maya as they linked its presence with success in war; there are several stelae that record the appearance of Venus prompting the decision to attack.

Religion

Maya **cosmology** is by no means straightforward, as at every stage an idea is balanced by its opposite and each part of the universe is made up of many layers. To the Maya, this is the third version of the earth, the previous two having been destroyed by deluges. The current version is a flat surface, with four corners, each associated with a certain colour; white for north, red for east, yellow for south and black for west, with green at the centre. Above this the sky is supported by four trees, each a different colour and species, which are also sometimes depicted as gods, known as *Bacabs*. At its centre the sky is supported by a ceiba tree. Above the sky is a heaven of thirteen layers, each of which has its own god, while the very top layer is overseen by an owl. Other attested models of the world include that of a turtle (the land) floating on the sea. However, it was the underworld, *Xibalba*, "the place of fright", which was of greater importance to most Maya, as it was in this direction that they passed after death, on their way to the place of rest. The nine layers of the Maya "hell" were guarded by the "lords of the night", and deep caves were thought to connect with the underworld.

Woven into this universe, the Maya recognized an incredible array of **gods**. Every divinity had four manifestations based upon colour and direction and many also had counterparts in the underworld and consorts of the opposite sex. In addition to this there was an extensive array of patron deities, each associated with a particular trade or particular class. Every activity from suicide to sex had its representative in the Maya pantheon.

Religious ritual

The combined complexity of the Maya pantheon and calendar gave every day a particular significance, and the ancient Maya were bound up in a demanding **cycle of religious ritual**. The main purpose of ritual was the procurement of success by appealing to the right god at the right time and in the right way. As every event, from planting to childbirth, was associated with a particular divinity, all of the main events in daily life demanded some kind of religious ritual and for the most important of these the Maya staged elaborate ceremonies.

While each ceremony had its own format, there is a certain pattern that binds them all. The correct day was carefully chosen by priestly divination, and for several days beforehand the participants fasted and remained abstinent. The main ceremony was dominated by the expulsion of all evil spirits, the burning of incense before the idols, a sacrifice (either animal or human) and blood-letting.

In divination rituals, used to foretell the pattern of future events or to account for the cause of past events, the elite used various **drugs** to achieve altered states of consciousness. Perhaps the most obvious of these was alcohol, made either from fermented maize or a combination of honey and the bark of the balche tree. Wild tobacco, which is considerably stronger than the modern domesticated version, was also smoked. The Maya also used a range of hallucinogenic mushrooms, all of which were appropriately named, but none more so than the *xibalbaj obox*, "underworld mushroom", and the *k'aizalah obox*, "lost judgement mushroom".

Archeology

Like almost everything in Belize, archeology has made leaps and bounds in the last couple of decades as researchers have unveiled a wealth of new material. The main text that follows was originally written by the late Winnel Branche, former Belize Museums Director, and illustrates the problems that faced Belizean archeology in the past, as it emerged into the limelight under siege from foreign expeditions and looters. At the beginning of the twenty-first century, Belize is taking control of its own archeological heritage; as such, this section has been written with help from Dr Jaime Awe and staff of the Belize Institute of Archaeology.

The ancient Maya sites of Belize have seen activity since the late nineteenth century. During these early times British amateur archeologists and both **British and American museums** kept up a lively interest in artefacts from these sites. Preservation of monuments was not yet "in", and techniques were far from subtle. In some cases dynamite was used to plunder the sites and Belizean artifacts often found their way, unmonitored, into museums and private collections worldwide.

Since 1894 the ancient monuments and antiquities of Belize have had loosely structured legislation to protect them, but it was not until 1957 that the **Belize Department of Archaeology** (now called, since 2003, the **Institute of Archaeology**) was formed to excavate, protect and preserve these remains. Since then, scientific excavation of hundreds of sites in Belize has been carried out by universities, museums and scientific institutions from the US, Canada and, to a lesser extent, Britain, always with prior agreement from the institute. The institute's main role is to monitor fieldwork and excavations carried out by foreign researchers in the country, though it has lately expanded into other areas: it now trains Belizeans to carry out archeological work in the country, still in conjunction with foreign researchers, and it also performs small-scale salvage excavations in emergencies.

With the wealth of Maya remains in the country, it is hardly surprising but most unfortunate that **looting** of sites and the sale of antiquities on the black market is still prevalent. Since any immovable manmade structure over 100 years old and any movable manmade item over 150 years old are considered ancient monuments and artifacts respectively, the institute is also in charge of all the **non-Maya historical and colonial remains**. The responsibility of maintaining archeological sites, especially those open to the public, falls to the institute, as does the safekeeping of the vast national collections.

In Belize, all ancient monuments and antiquities are owned by the state, whether on private or government land or under water. Residents are still allowed to keep registered collections under licence, but the sale, purchase, import or export of antiquities is illegal. Excavation and other scientific research can only be done with permission from the Commissioner of Archaeology, under agreed conditions. While intended to prevent looting and destruction, this law is also meant to keep the remains intact and within the country so that Belizeans and visitors can see the evidence of this splendid heritage.

Extensive **cave systems** form a vast network under much of inland Belize, and the Chiquibul Cave System (see p.186), the longest cave system in Central America, contains the largest cave room in the western hemisphere. All caves discovered so far in Belize contain Maya artifacts, making them archeological sites only visitable with prior permission from the Institute of Archaeology or with a licensed tour guide. Cave tourism in Belize increases every year, and the

Archeology field schools and projects in Belize

Many of the sites under investigation in Belize accept paying students (and often non-students): the average two- to four-week stint at a field school costs in the region of US$1100–2600. It's fascinating work, but be prepared for some pretty arduous conditions. In addition to the schools and projects listed below it's worth looking in the Archaeological Institute of America's website (Ⓦwww.archaeological.org) for details of fieldwork opportunities, or check out *Archaeology Magazine* (Ⓦwww.archaeology.org). Earthwatch (see p.52 for details) frequently has archeological projects in Belize and throughout the region. Check also *Lamanai Outpost Lodge* (see p.111) for details of their field study centre. Finally, the websites Ⓦwww.mesoweb.com and Ⓦwww.famsi.org (Foundation for the Advancement of Mesoamerican Studies, or FAMSI) have myriad useful links.

The Belize Fieldwork Program of Boston University undertakes research at a number of sites in Belize, including La Milpa, in the northwest (see p.112) and Xibun, in the Sibun River valley, Cayo. Directed by noted Maya scholars Norman Hammond and Patricia McAnany, these programmes are very highly regarded and places are in great demand. Contact the directors by visiting Ⓦwww.bu.edu/archaeology.

The Belize Postclassic Project of SUNY-Albany is a long-term regional programme of research to understand processes of social transformation of Maya populations living in northern Belize after the "collapse" of Classic period city-state civilizations, from 1000 AD until the Spanish colonial era. Research takes place at Progresso Lagoon, in northern Belize, an inland waterway surrounded by the Freshwater Creek Forest Reserve. Contact Robert Rosenswig, SUNY-Albany, New York (Ⓔrrosenswig@albany.edu, Ⓦwww.albany.edu/anthro/belize/belize.htm).

The Belize River Archaeological Settlement Survey (BRASS) has been working in the Belize River valley area since 1983 and at El Pilar since 1993. El Pilar, a major Maya centre straddling the Belize–Guatemala border (see p.196), forms the core of the new El Pilar Archaeological Reserve for Maya Flora and Fauna. Preference is given to those with experience in or enthusiasm for forest gardens, or skills in ceramics, drafting, computers and photography. Contact Dr Anabel Ford, MesoAmerican Research Center, University of California, Santa Barbara (Ⓔelpilar@btl.net, Ⓦwww.marc.ucsb.edu/elpilar).

The Belize Valley Archaeological Reconnaissance Project (BVAR) has been conducting long-term research at several sites in the Belize River valley, particularly at Baking Pot and also at *Pook's Hill* (see p.171). Students are involved in all aspects of archeological investigations, from the excavation of Maya architecture to the illustration of the artifacts recovered from the site. No previous experience is required,

caves visitation policy sets out regulations for both tourists and tour guides. Ancient Maya **maritime trade routes** are also a focus of recent research, with coastal sites and those on the cayes receiving more attention.

Since 2003 the Institute of Archaeology has become responsible for overseeing all archeological investigation in Belize, issuing site-excavation permits only to those scholars whose proposals conform to their policies and will be of demonstrable benefit to Belize. The Institute also carries out **educational programmes** including lectures, slide shows and travelling exhibitions in an attempt to interest the public in this part of their heritage. It also hosts the **Belize Archaeology Symposium**, held annually in July, where all the archeological teams excavating in Belize present their latest findings – a fascinating and well-organized event which anyone can attend; email Ⓔia@nichbelize.org for details.

though participants will need to be in good physical condition. Email Ⓔarchaeology @bvar.org, or visit Ⓦwww.bvar.org.

Blue Creek Archaeological Project of the Maya Research Program (MRP) has been conducting excavations at Blue Creek (see p.112) in northwestern Belize for fourteen years. Their research attempts to learn about the growth of Blue Creek and understand its role in the region. Contact Tom Guderjan (Ⓔguderjan@mrpmail.com, Ⓦwww.mayaresearchprogram.org).

Mayflower Archaeology Project in Stann Creek District covers three Late Classic sites: Mayflower, Maintzunun and T'au Witz (see p.252). The area was surveyed over twenty years ago but, until fairly recently, excavations have been virtually nonexistent; much of the site is still covered in tropical forest. Students stay in Hopkins (see p.252). Contact Wendy Brown, Social Sciences Division, College of Lake County, Grayslake, IL 60030 (Ⓣ847/543-2608, Ⓔwbrown@clcillinois.edu, Ⓦclcpages .clcillinois.edu).

Minanha Archaeology Project of the Social Archaeology Research Program (SARP) of Trent University, Canada, focuses on ancient Maya sociopolitical interaction, investigating how centres of different hierarchical rank interacted with one another, and what life was like on the borders of political units. Research is carried out at Minanha', on the Vaca plateau in Cayo District, a site located between two major Classic period cities, Caracol and Naranjo; students stay at *Martz Farm* (see p.201). Contact Dr Gyles Iannone, Dept of Anthropology, Trent University (Ⓣ705/748-1011 ext. 1453, Ⓔgiannone@trentu.ca, Ⓦwww.trentu.ca/academic/anthro/Belize/Belize1.html).

The University of Texas Archaeological Field School undertakes research at several Maya sites in the Rio Bravo Conservation and Management Area (see p.111), including La Milpa and Dos Hombres, where a royal tomb has been discovered. You can take part either as a volunteer for a minimum of one week (US$640) or enrol as a student. Contact Dr Fred Valdez, Dept of Anthropology, University of Texas at Austin (Ⓔfredv@mail.utexas.edu, Ⓦuts.cc.utexas.edu/~marl).

The Western Belize Regional Cave Project, under the direction of Dr Jaime Awe of the Belize Institute of Archaeology, has undertaken research at several caves in Cayo District (including Actun Tunichil Muknal; see p.173), collecting and analyzing data in order to understand the use of caves by the ancient Maya. Current investigations include Actun Chapat ("the cave of the centipede") and other recently discovered caves. Due to the strenuous and dangerous nature of cave reconnaissance, volunteers/students must be in excellent physical condition. Prior archeological field school or caving experience is preferred. Contact Cameron Griffith (Ⓔgwrobel@bvar .org, Ⓦwww.indiana.edu/~belize).

At least sixteen archeological research teams visit Belize annually (see box, above), illustrating the fact that the Maya of Belize were not on the fringe of Maya civilization, as was once thought, but were in fact a core area of the culture. Evidence has been found of extensive raised-field agriculture and irrigation canals in northern Belize, and the oldest known site so far found in the Maya world is at Cuello, near Orange Walk. Even Tikal in Guatemala, once thought to have been the centre of power of the lowland Maya, is now known to have been toppled by Caracol, the largest Maya city in Belize.

Landscape and wildlife

For its size, Belize has a diverse range of environments: from the coral reefs and atolls of the Caribbean coast, through lowland swamps and lagoons, up the valleys of pristine tropical rivers, to the exposed ridges of the Maya Mountains. Physically, the land increases in elevation as you head south and west; the main rivers rise in the west and flow north and east to the Caribbean.

Away from the coast, which is entirely low-lying and covered by marine sediments for 10–20km inland, the country can be roughly divided into three **geological regions**: the **northern lowlands**, a continuation of the Yucatán Platform, with Cretaceous limestone overlaid by deposits of alluvial sand; the **Maya Mountains**, where Santa Rosa quartz with granite intrusions rises to over 1000m to form the highest peaks in the country; and **southern Belize**, where more Cretaceous limestone hills with an impressive range of wonderfully developed **karst features** – including caverns, natural arches and sinkholes – give way to foothills and the coastal plain.

The **wildlife** is correspondingly varied; undisturbed forests provide a home to both temperate species from the north and tropical species from the south, as well as a number of indigenous species unique to Belize. In winter, the hundreds of native bird species are joined by dozens of migrant species from the eastern seaboard of North America. With its variety of tropical land and marine ecosystems Belize is increasingly a focus of scientific research.

The tropical forest

Belize still has over fifty percent of its **primary forest**, and across most of the country the natural vegetation is technically **tropical moist forest**, classified by average temperatures of 25°C and annual rainfall of 2000–4000mm; the only true **rainforest** lies in a small belt in the extreme southwest. More than four thousand flowering plant species can be found in Belize, including around seven hundred species of tree (about the same number as the whole of the US and Canada) and over two hundred varieties of orchid. So diverse is the forest that scientists have identified seventy different types, though these can be placed into three broad groups: 13 percent is fairly open **pine savannah** (known in Belize as "pine ridge", regardless of the elevation); 19 percent is **mangrove and coastal forest** (which includes the rarest habitat type in Belize, **caye littoral forest**); with the remaining 68 percent **broadleaf forest** and cohune palm forest – the type commonly referred to as rainforest.

While temperate forests tend to be dominated by a few species – for example, fir, oak or beech – it's **diversity** that characterizes the tropical forest, with each species specifically adapted to fit a particular ecological niche. This biological storehouse has yet to be fully explored, though it has already yielded some astonishing discoveries. Steroid hormones, such as cortisone, and diosgenin, the active ingredient in birth control pills, were developed from wild yams found in these forests, while tetrodoxin, derived from a species of Central American frog, is an anaesthetic 160,000 times stronger than cocaine.

But despite its size and diversity the forest is surprisingly **fragile**, forming a closed system in which nutrients are continuously recycled and decaying plant matter fuels new growth. The forest floor is a spongy mass of roots, fungi, mosses, bacteria and micro-organisms, in which nutrients are stored, broken down with the assistance of insects and chemical decay, and gradually released to the waiting roots and fresh seedlings. The thick canopy prevents much light from reaching the forest floor, ensuring that the soil remains damp but warm, a hotbed of chemical activity. The death of a large tree prompts a flurry of growth as new light reaches the forest floor and seedlings struggle towards the sunlight. However, once a number of trees are removed the soil is highly vulnerable – exposed to the harsh tropical sun and direct rainfall, an area of cleared forest soon becomes prone to flooding and drought. Recently cleared land will contain enough nutrients for three or four years of crop growth, but soon afterwards its usefulness declines rapidly and within twenty years it can become almost completely barren. If the trees are stripped from a large area soil erosion will silt the rivers and parched soils disrupt local rainfall patterns.

Belize's forests are home to abundant **birdlife** – 574 species at the last count, with several species "new" to the country discovered each year. In fact, birds are the most visible of the country's wildlife, and a big draw for many visitors. Even if you've never had much of an interest in them, you'll be astonished at the sheer numbers of birds you can see just by sitting by a cabin in any one of the jungle lodges in Belize. Parrots, such as the **Aztec** and **green parakeets**, are seen every day, and if you're an expert you'll be aware of a range of otherwise scarce species that you might catch a glimpse of here, from the tiny **orange-breasted falcon** to the massive **harpy eagle**, the largest of Belize's raptors. Watching a jewel-like **hummingbird** feed by dipping its long, delicate bill into a heliconia flower as it hovers just inches in front of your eyes is a wonderful experience. Hummingbird names are as fascinating as their colours: the rufous-tailed, the little hermit, the white-bellied emerald and the violet sabrewing, to mention just a few.

Although Belize has 60 species of **snakes**, many of which occur widely throughout the country, only nine are venomous and you're unlikely to see any snakes at all. One of the commonest is the **boa constrictor**, which is also the largest, growing up to 4m, though it poses no threat to humans. Others you might see are **coral snakes** (which are venomous) and **false coral snakes** (which are not); you'd need to be quite skilled to tell them apart. **Frogs and toads** (collectively anurans) are plentiful, and at night in the forest you'll hear the characteristic chorus of frog mating calls. You'll also frequently find the **red-eyed tree frog** – a beautiful, pale green creature about 2–3cm long – in your shower in any rustic cabin. Less appealing perhaps are the giant **marine toads**, the largest toad in the Americas, weighing in at up to 1kg and growing to 20cm. These are infamous as the "cane toad", which caused havoc with the native species when introduced into Australia; it eats anything it can get into its capacious mouth. Like most frogs and toads it has toxic glands and the toxin of the marine toad has hallucinogenic properties – a characteristic the ancient Maya employed in their ceremonies by licking these glands and interpreting the resultant visions.

Finally, one thing you'll realize pretty quickly is that you're never far from an **insect** in Belize. Mostly you'll be trying to avoid them or even destroy them, particularly the common (though by no means ever-present) mosquitoes and sandflies. But the **butterflies** are beautiful, and you'll frequently see clouds of them feeding at the edges of puddles on trails; the caterpillars are fascinating and sometimes enormous. The largest and most spectacular are the gorgeous, electric-blue **blue morpho** and the **owl butterfly**, and you can see many more on a visit to one of a number of **butterfly exhibits** around the country.

Ants are the most numerous insects on the planet – something you can easily believe here. Perhaps the most impressive are the **army ants**, called the "marchin' army" in Belize, as the whole colony ranges through the forest in a narrow column voraciously hunting for insects. Rest assured that, unlike their Hollywood movie counterparts, they can't overpower you and rip the flesh from your bones – though they will give you a nasty bite if you get too close. People in rural areas welcome a visit, as the ants clear pests from their houses. **Leafcutter ants** ("wee-wee ants" in Kriol) have regular trails through the forest along which they carry bits of leaves often much larger than themselves – which is how they get the name "parasol ants". The leaves themselves aren't for food, but they provide a growing medium for a unique type of fungus that the ants do eat.

Spiders are also very common: take a walk at night with a torch anywhere in the countryside and you'll see the beam reflected back by the eyes of dozens of **wolf spiders**. **Tarantulas**, too, are found everywhere – the sharp fangs may look dangerous but, despite their reputation, tarantulas won't bite unless they're severely provoked.

The Maya Mountains

The main range of the **Maya Mountains** runs southwest to northeast across the whole of south-central Belize and straddles the border with Guatemala. This wild region, covered in dense forest and riddled with caves and underground rivers, has few permanent residents. The mountains form part of the great swath of **national parks** and **forest reserves**, the most accessible of which are the **Mountain Pine Ridge** (see p.179) and the **Cockscomb Basin Wildlife Sanctuary** (see p.260), home to the world's only **jaguar reserve**.

The flora and fauna, though similar to those found in the tropical forests of Guatemala, are often more prolific here as there's much less pressure on the land. Though rarely seen, the **scarlet macaw** is occasionally found in large flocks in the southern Maya Mountains and the Cockscomb Basin. All of Belize's cat species are found here, too. **Jaguars** ("tigers") range widely over the whole country, but the densest population is found in the lower elevation forests of the west, while **pumas** ("red tigers") usually keep to remote ridges. The two smaller species of spotted cats – the **ocelot** and the smaller **margay** (both called "tiger cat" in Belize and slightly larger than a domestic cat) – are also found here, as is the **jaguarundi**, the smallest and commonest of Belize's cats – you might spot one on a trail since it hunts during the day. Belize's largest land animal, **Baird's tapir** ("mountain cow"), weighing up to 300kg, is usually found near water. Tapirs are endangered throughout most of their range, but are not that rare in Belize, though you're unlikely to see one without a guide.

On the northern flank of the Maya Mountains, the **Mountain Pine Ridge** is a granite massif intruded into the sedimentary quartz and resulting in a ring of metamorphic rock around the granite. Many of the rivers rising here fall away to the Macal and Belize river valleys below, in some of the most spectacular waterfalls in the country. On this nutrient-poor soil the dominant vegetation is the **Caribbean pine**, which covers sixty percent of the area in the largest stands anywhere in its range; bromeliads and orchids adorn the trunks and branches. It's a unique habitat in Belize, and home to several endemic species, including two frogs and a fish known only by their Latin names.

Currently, the forest is recovering from a very severe outbreak of **pine bark beetles** (see p.179).

Lowland Belize

The forests of Petén, Guatemala extend into northwestern Belize, where the generally low-lying topography is broken by a series of roughly parallel **limestone escarpments**. The main ones – the Booth's River and Rio Bravo escarpments – each have a river below that drain north to the Río Hondo. Here the **Rio Bravo Conservation and Management Area** (see p.111) protects a huge area of forest. Further east, the plain is more open; pine savannah is interspersed with slow-flowing rivers and lagoons, providing spectacular wetland habitats that continue to the coast. In the centre, **Crooked Tree Wildlife Sanctuary** (see p.100) covers several freshwater lagoons, protecting over three hundred bird species, including the nesting sites of the rare jabiru stork. The tiny village of Sarteneja is the only settlement between Belize City and Corozal on the northeast coast – an important wetland area for wading birds, crocodiles (Morelet's and American) and several species of turtles, protected in **Shipstern Nature Reserve** (see p.115). In addition, almost all of the mammals of Belize – with the exception of monkeys but including jaguar, ocelot and tapir – can be found in this mosaic of coastal lagoons, hardwood forest and mangrove swamp. Other forest mammals you might see signs of include the collared and the white-lipped peccaries ("warries"), brocket and white-tailed deer, opossums, weasels, porcupines and armadillos. At the **Community Baboon Sanctuary** in the lower Belize River valley (see p.96), visitors can be almost guaranteed views of troops of black howler monkeys ("baboons"); you'll certainly hear the deep-throated roar of the males.

In the south there's only a relatively narrow stretch of lowland between the Maya Mountains and the coast, but heavy rainfall ensures the growth of lush rainforest. Along the coast and navigable rivers much of the original forest has been selectively logged for mahogany and some is in varying stages of regrowth after hurricane damage; around human settlements the original forest has been replaced by patches of agricultural land and citrus plantations. A boat journey in **Burdon Canal Nature Reserve** (see p.238), which connects the Belize and Sibun rivers to the Northern and Southern lagoons, and on into **Gales Point Wildlife Sanctuary** (see p.238), where manatees congregate, is a good introduction to the wildlife to be found in the inland mangrove forests and lagoons.

Take a trip along almost any **river** and you'll see green iguanas, which, along with their very similar cousin the spiny-tailed iguana ("wish-willy"), are probably the most prominent of Belize's reptiles; despite protection these are still hunted for their meat and eggs. Rarer, but still fairly frequently seen in protected-area rivers, the Central American river otter is much larger than its European cousin. Along the New River and in many lagoons you'll see (or more likely be shown) Morelet's crocodiles, which can be found in almost any body of water, and are of no danger to humans unless they're very large – at least 3m long. Previously hunted to the brink of extinction, they've made a remarkable comeback since being protected, and are now frequently spotted in the mangroves of Haulover Creek, immediately west of Belize City. Rivers also offer great birding, with several species of kingfisher. One

△ Fish among mangrove roots

of the most common, the belted kingfisher, is also Belize's largest. You'll also see many species of herons and egrets, including the tri-coloured heron, the boat-billed heron, the great egret and occasionally the two-metre tall jabiru stork.

The Caribbean coast and the Barrier Reef

Belize's most exceptional environment is its **Caribbean coastline** and offshore barrier reef, dotted with hundreds of small islands and three atolls. Much of the shoreline is still largely covered with mangroves, which play an important role in the Belizean economy, not merely as nurseries for commercial fish species but also for their stabilization of the shoreline and their ability to absorb the force of hurricanes. The dominant species of the coastal fringe is the red mangrove, although in due course it undermines its own environment by consolidating the sea bed until it becomes more suitable for the less salt-tolerant black and white mangroves. The cutting down of mangroves, particularly on the cayes, exposes the land to the full force of the sea and can mean the end of a small and unstable island.

Just inland from the mangroves along the coast and on the cayes, the **littoral forest** occupies slightly higher ground. The vegetation here is salt-tolerant, and many plants are characterized by their tough, waxy leaves which help conserve water. Species include red and white gumbo limbo, black poisonwood, zericote, sea grape, palmetto and of course the coconut palm which typifies Caribbean beaches, though it's not actually a native and is now threatened by the lethal yellowing disease spreading down the coast from Mexico. The littoral forest supports a very high density of fauna, especially migrating birds, due to the succession of fruits and seeds, yet it also faces the highest development pressure in Belize due to its slightly higher coastal elevation; the limited extent of **caye littoral forest** is the most endangered habitat in the country.

The basis of the shoreline food chain is the nutrient-rich mud, held in place by the mangroves, while the roots themselves are home to mangrove oysters and sponges. Young stingrays cruise through the shallows adjacent to the tangle of mangrove roots, accompanied by juvenile snappers, bonefish and small barracudas; you'll see the adult versions on the reef and around the cayes. The tallest mangrove forests in Belize are found along the Temash River, in **Sarstoon-Temash National Park** (see p.292), where the black mangroves reach heights of over 30m. From a canoe among the mangrove cayes and lagoons you can easily spot the brown pelican, white ibis or roseate spoonbill. You might even see the American saltwater crocodile, rarer and much larger than the Morelet's crocodile.

The mangrove lagoons are also home to the West Indian manatee. Belize has the largest manatee population in the Caribbean, estimated to be somewhere between three hundred and seven hundred individuals. Several large areas have been set aside for their protection, including **Corozal Bay**, **Gales Point** and **Swallow Caye** wildlife sanctuaries. Manatees can grow up to 4m in length and 450kg in weight, but are placid and shy, moving between the freshwater lagoons and the open sea. Once hunted for their meat, they are now protected, and the places where they congregate are tourist attractions. In shallows offshore, "meadows" of seagrass beds provide nurseries for many fish and invertebrates and pasture for conch, manatees and turtles. The extensive root system of seagrasses also protects beaches from erosion by holding the fragments of sand and coral together.

The **Western Caribbean Barrier Reef** is the longest in the western hemisphere, an almost continuous chain of coral that stretches over 600km from northern Quintana Roo in Mexico to the far south of Belize. For centuries the reef has been harvested by fishermen. In the past they caught manatees (and they still take some turtles), but these days the spiny lobster and queen conch are the main catch, though numbers of both species have declined and are now protected during the breeding season.

East of the barrier reef are the **atolls**, roughly oval-shaped reefs rising from the seabed surrounding a central lagoon. **Glover's Reef** atoll is considered by the scientific community to be one of the most pristine and important coral reef sites in the Caribbean. Whale sharks, the largest fish in the world, are sometimes found here, gathering in large numbers to gorge on snapper eggs at **Gladden Spit**, offshore from Placencia. Beneath the water is a world of astounding beauty, with fish and coral in every imaginable colour. Resembling a brilliant underwater forest, each coral is in fact composed of colonies of individual polyps, feeding off plankton wafting past in the current. There are basically two types of coral: hard, calcareous, reef-building corals, such as brain coral and elkhorn coral (known scientifically as the hydrocorals), and soft corals such as sea fans and feather plumes (the ococorals). On the reefs you'll find the garish-pink chalice sponge, the appropriately-named fire coral, the delicate feather-star crinoid and the apartment sponge, a tall thin tube with lots of small holes in it.

Coral is extremely fragile and its habitats are very easily damaged; human interference and increasing toxic runoff and sediment from coastal development adversely affect the already slow growth of the coral. "Coral bleaching", a symptom of extensive damage, occurs when the polyp loses some or all of the symbiotic microalgae (zooxanthellae) that live in its cells, usually in response to stress. The most common cause of bleaching is a period of above-average sea temperatures – a major coral reef bleaching event occurred throughout the Caribbean in 1995, midway through what is reported to have been the hottest decade on record. Temperatures continue to be above the average of previous decades, almost certainly indicating that **global warming** is taking place. Recent discovery of oil and its imminent export though Belize's maze of marine protected waters only furthers the dilemma.

The reef teems with **fish**, including **angel** and **parrot fish**, several species of **stingrays** and **sharks** (the most common the relatively harmless **nurse shark**, frequently seen on reef trips), **conger** and **moray eels**, **spotted goatfish**, the striped **sergeant-major** and many, many more. The sea and islands are also home to **grouper**, **barracuda**, **marlin** and the magnificent **sailfish**. Dolphins are frequently seen just offshore, and will mostly be of the Atlantic **bottle-nosed** variety, though further out large schools of the smaller **spotted dolphin** are sometimes found.

Belize's three species of **marine turtles**, the loggerhead, the green and the hawksbill, occur throughout the reef, nesting on isolated beaches. These are infrequently seen as they are still hunted for food during a limited open season.

Above the water, the cayes are an ideal nesting ground for birds, providing protection from predators and surrounded by an inexhaustible food supply. At **Half Moon Caye**, right out on the eastern edge of the reef, there's a reserve designed to protect a breeding colony of over four thousand **red-footed boobies**. Here you'll also see magnificent frigate birds, ospreys and mangrove warblers, among a total of 98 species.

Conservation

Growing additions to Belize's already impressive network of national parks, nature reserves and wildlife sanctuaries bring over 42 percent of the land under some form of legal protection, a feat made possible in part by the country's low population density (one of the lowest in the world). It's an amazing accomplishment for a developing country, and with such enlightened strategies to safeguard its biodiversity, Belize has gained recognition as the most conservation-conscious country in the Americas. That said, the success of these protected areas is due as much to the efforts of local communities as it is to governmental decisions.

Conservation strategy

Following independence in 1981, the conservation of natural resources was the main plank in the government's declared policy to make "**eco-tourism**" a focus of development and marketing in the nation's tourism industry. Ideally, this is a community-based form of tourism, inspired primarily by the wildlife and landscape of an area and showing respect for local cultures. The theory is that by practising small-scale, nonconsumptive use of the country's natural resources, visitors will be contributing financially both to the conservation of protected areas and to local communities; it is hoped that this will aid sustainable development not only locally but in Belize as a whole. However, the recent and rapid growth of the **cruise ship industry**, creating massive visitor pressure on fragile sites, now threatens to undermine this policy. Calls from environmentalists within Belize to set limits to cruise ship visitor numbers and increase the head tax per individual have prompted only token responses from a government unwilling to halt the ever-increasing flow of dollars the industry generates.

Legislation

In 1928 the southern tip of Half Moon Caye was established as a Crown Reserve to offer protection to the rare red-footed booby (*Sula sula*); other bird sanctuaries were established in the 1960s and 1970s. The **Forestry Act** of 1960 focused on forest reserves established by the colonial government to provide areas for timber exploitation. This law was passed primarily as an instrument to protect the country's timber industry, and was not meant to be a tool for conservation. In the period since the country's independence, the government has taken numerous measures to increase the area of land and sea under protection. The passing of the **National Parks Systems Act** in 1981 provided the legal basis for establishing national parks, natural monuments, wildlife sanctuaries and nature reserves; and the **Wildlife Protection Act** of 1981 (amended in 1991) created closed seasons or total protection for various endangered species, including marine and freshwater turtles, dolphins and manatees.

Hunting, which has long been a means of supplementing diet and income, remains a real problem in almost all reserves and protected lands; the most popular species include iguana, armadillo, hicatee (freshwater turtle), deer and the gibnut, or tepescuintle, a large rodent sometimes seen on menus. Needless to say, you should avoid ordering these beasts in restaurants.

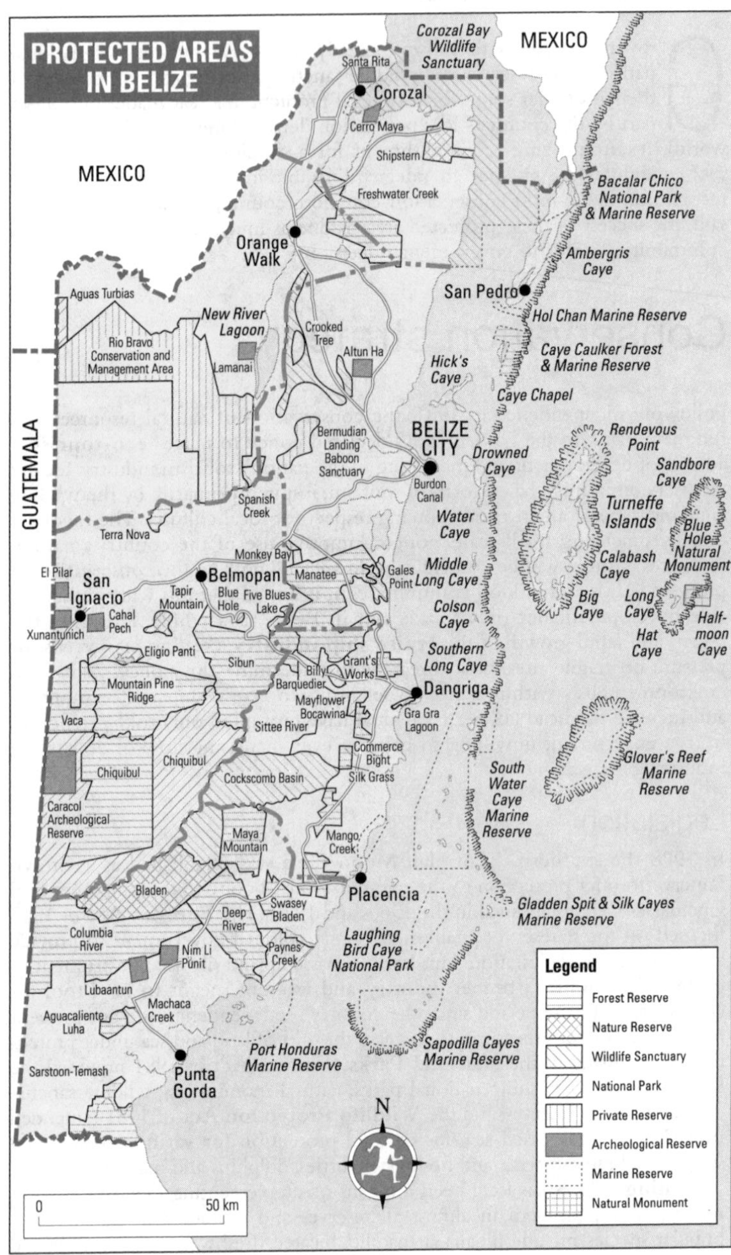

PROTECTED AREAS IN BELIZE
MEXICO
MEXICO
GUATEMALA
Corozal Bay Wildlife Sanctuary
Santa Rita
Corozal
Cerro Maya
Shipstern
Freshwater Creek
Bacalar Chico National Park & Marine Reserve
Orange Walk
Ambergris Caye
San Pedro
Hol Chan Marine Reserve
Aguas Turbias
Rio Bravo Conservation and Management Area
New River Lagoon
Lamanai
Crooked Tree
Altun Ha
Hick's Caye
Caye Caulker Forest & Marine Reserve
Caye Chapel
Bermudian Landing Baboon Sanctuary
BELIZE CITY
Burdon Canal
Drowned Caye
Rendevous Point
Sandbore Caye
Turneffe Islands
Blue Hole Natural Monument
Spanish Creek
Terra Nova
Water Caye
Monkey Bay
Manatee
Gales Point
Middle Long Caye
Calabash Caye
El Pilar
San Ignacio
Belmopan
Tapir Mountain
Blue Hole
Five Blues Lake
Xunantunich
Cahal Pech
Colson Caye
Big Caye
Long Caye
Hat Caye
Half-moon Caye
Eligio Panti
Sibun
Billy Barquedier
Grant's Works
Southern Long Caye
Dangriga
Mountain Pine Ridge
Mayflower Bocawina
Gra Gra Lagoon
Vaca
Sittee River
Commerce Bight
Chiquibul
Chiquibul
Cockscomb Basin
Silk Grass
South Water Caye Marine Reserve
Glover's Reef Marine Reserve
Caracol Archeological Reserve
Maya Mountain
Mango Creek
Placencia
Bladen
Swasey Bladen
Deep River
Gladden Spit & Silk Cayes Marine Reserve
Columbia River
Nim Li Punit
Paynes Creek
Laughing Bird Caye National Park
Lubaantun
Machaca Creek
Aguacaliente Luha
Punta Gorda
Port Honduras Marine Reserve
Sapodilla Cayes Marine Reserve
Sarstoon-Temash
N
0
50 km
Legend
Forest Reserve
Nature Reserve
Wildlife Sanctuary
National Park
Private Reserve
Archeological Reserve
Marine Reserve
Natural Monument

Another step in the right direction came with the 1992 **Environmental Protection Act** (EPA), intended to control pollution and promote environmental health by requiring companies to carry out an Environmental Impact Assessment (EIA) before undertaking any potentially polluting development. The law utilizes the "polluters pay principle" and recent amendments to the EPA increased penalties for contravention and have resulted in more stringent enforcement.

Belize has also signed and ratified and actively implements twenty important **international environmental agreements**, including the Ramsar Convention on Wetlands of International Importance, the UNESCO World Heritage Convention, the Convention on the International Trade in Endangered Species (CITES), the Convention on Biodiversity and the Cartagena Convention on the Protection of the Marine Environment. Seven reserves on the Belize Barrier Reef, totalling over ninety square kilometres, were declared World Heritage Sites in 1996: Bacalar Chico National Park and Marine Reserve, Blue Hole and Half Moon Caye Natural Monuments, South Water Caye Marine Reserve, Glover's Reef Marine Reserve, Sapodilla Cayes Marine Reserve and Laughing Bird Caye National Park. These and other protected areas form the **Belize Barrier Reef Reserve System**, which has the ultimate aim of forming a continuous corridor of marine reserves from Mexico to Honduras. An important step towards this was taken in 1997 when the leaders of Belize, Guatemala, Honduras and Mexico signed the **Mesoamerican Caribbean Coral Reef System Initiative** (the Tulum Declaration) to promote conservation and sustainable use of the coral reef system shared by these four nations.

These countries are also members of the **Central American Commission on Environment and Development** (CCAD), an organization that encompasses all seven Central American nations and is now planning the implementation of an even more ambitious project: the **Mesoamerican Biological Corridor** (Ⓦwww.biomeso.org), which aims for an unbroken corridor of parks and wildlife refuges stretching from southern Mexico to Panama. It is hoped that international cooperation in linking the reserves will create a network of protected areas spanning the isthmus and safeguarding the entire region's biodiversity.

The role of government

Three government ministries in Belize (and various departments within them) shoulder between them most of the responsibility for drafting and implementing legislation relating to conservation, and ensuring compliance with the relevant laws: the **Ministry of Agriculture and Fisheries**, the **Ministry of Natural Resources and the Environment**, the **Ministry of National Development, Investment and Culture** and the **Ministry of Tourism, Information and National Emergency**. They are staffed by very able, dedicated professionals, and Belize's reputation as a leader in protected areas management owes much to these government institutions.

The **Department of the Environment** has overall responsibility for management of the country's natural resources and control of pollution, and is tasked with identifying and developing solutions for environmental problems facing Belize. It implements and enforces the Environmental Protection Act.

The **Fisheries Authority** is charged with not only monitoring and enforcing fishing regulations, but also managing the country's increasing number of marine reserves and the responsible exploitation of commercially viable species. The Ecosystems Management Unit and Conservation Compliance Unit carry out these tasks. The **Coastal Zone Management Authority and Institute** is responsible for implementing and monitoring all policies that affect the use and development of the coastal zone in Belize and for fostering regional and international collaboration in marine conservation.

Belize's timber reserves (including all mangroves) have always been under the compass of the **Forest Department** (part of the Ministry of Natural Resources and the Environment), which now has a much greater role in forest conservation than simply the provision and regulation of hardwoods for export. The department's **Protected Areas Management Division** also has overall responsibility for the management of all terrestrial protected areas and the coordination of biodiversity management, including implementing plans to establish the Mesoamerican Biological Corridor (see p.347). Its **Wildlife Management Programme** is responsible for the enforcement of the Wildlife Protection Act, and conservation officers have been appointed to all the country's forest reserves.

Apart from attracting tourists to Belize and providing them with information, the **Ministry of Tourism**, together with the **Belize Tourism Board**, licenses and trains the country's tour guides; you'll find the guides in Belize are highly motivated guardians of the environment. The **National Institute of Culture and History** (NICH) manages all cultural and historical features, including all **archeological sites** (which are also reserves), and has responsibility for developing appropriate tourism packages for all historic sites.

In general, these government agencies have proved extremely successful in coordinating protection of the nation's reserves, almost always with the cooperation of the private sector and expert assistance from a range of local and international NGOs (see below). However, the dramatic increase in the amount of protected land has posed the question of how such protection is to be financed by a developing nation. Following years of discussion between the government and various NGOs on the best way to raise conservation funds, the **Protected Areas Conservation Trust (PACT)** was established in 1996 and has since become a model for other developing countries. The primary source of income is a **conservation exit fee** of Bz$7.50 per person, payable at all departure points. PACT also receives twenty percent of entrance fees to protected areas and fees from cruise ship passengers; a percentage of the money raised is invested in a trust fund to provide a long-term buffer against the vicissitudes of government funding. Other revenue generated is shared between the government departments and voluntary organizations responsible for conservation, according to a pre-arranged formula, but cannot be used for salaries or recurrent expenses. For more information visit PACT's superb website, ⓦwww.pactbelize.org.

A thorough overview of Belize's environmental and wildlife protection policies and legislation, undertaken by both government and conservation NGOs, the **National Protected Areas Systems Plan** identifies areas where critical habitat has not been protected and recommends a comprehensive yet practical system to protect viable examples of all Belize's ecosystems, whether on public or private land. Although the government has not yet approved or endorsed all the plan's recommendations, present progress on protected areas management has largely been enacted in accordance with them.

NGOs and voluntary organizations

Various national and international **nongovernmental organizations** (NGOs) have been active in conservation in Belize for many years, building up experience through practical work in the country and by attending and hosting environmental conferences. Most conservation organizations have been members of the **Belize Association of Conservation NGOs** (BACONGO), believing that a united front presents their cause to government more effectively. This unity was successfully demonstrated in the Lamanai Room Declaration (see below), which called into question the then-government's environmental and conservation policies. However, in recent years, member organizations' differing attitudes toward several controversial development proposals have opened a rift in BACONGO, resulting in the gradual and continual withdrawal of key players from the association.

Despite this setback, Belize continues to demonstrate innovative and successful methods in protected areas funding and management. PACT (see p.212) is one example, and **co-management agreements** between the relevant government departments, national NGOs and local conservation organizations play an increasingly important role in involving local communities in managing nearby protected areas. The **Belize Audubon Society** (see p.74) already manages several reserves, and other reserves, including the Sapodilla Cayes Marine Reserve, Port Honduras Marine Reserve, Gales Point Wildlife Sanctuary and Laughing Bird Caye National Park, have co-management agreements in place.

The tourism industry also plays a part in raising environmental awareness. The **Belize Eco-Tourism Association** (BETA, ⓦwww.bzecotourism.org) is a small but growing band of hotels and other tourism businesses whose members agree to a code of ethics promoting sustainable tourism management. One of the agreed aims is to reduce (and eliminate) the use of disposable products from their businesses. A longer-term goal is to develop an accredited "**Green Listing**" system, which will rate the environmental efforts and credentials of members on a sliding scale. If you're concerned about your hotel's impact on the environment, ask if they're a member of BETA.

If it sounds as if the Belize authorities and the NGOs are too closely linked to enable the latter to undertake proper scrutiny of proposals that might adversely affect the environment, the outcome of the **Lamanai Room Declaration** of August 1997 should put your mind at ease. Signed by over thirty NGOs, the declaration sent a strong message to the government of the time that it could not ignore their concerns, which, at that point, related to certain existing and proposed developments that they claimed indicated "disregard for the principles of sustainable development", and were "a possible violation of Belizean legislation…and international agreements relating to the environment". These included damage to the reef by cruise ships and the sale of logging concessions on Maya lands in Toledo District. But it was the proposal by a Mexican company to build a "dolphin park attraction" at Cangrejo Caye, southwest of San Pedro, that caused alarm nationwide. Dolphins (imported from Mexico, as they are a protected species in Belize) were to be held in "semi-captivity" – a term no one was able to define satisfactorily – and resort cabañas built around the enclosure. So vehement was the opposition that the government never issued the necessary licence and all other proposals that had triggered the protests were dropped.

Current conservation issues

One of the most vociferous and contentious "conservation or development" debates has focused on the **Chalillo Dam project**, where a hydro-electric

Conservation organizations in Belize

The following are some of the national and international organizations either directly involved in conservation projects in Belize or providing support and funding to various projects. Several of these organizations welcome **volunteers** to help carry out a huge range of conservation work, from constructing trails and camping facilities in national parks to undertaking wildlife surveys. If you're interested, contact the organizations directly, but have a look first at the general information on volunteering in Belize given on p.51.

The Belize Audubon Society (BAS), founded in 1969, is the country's pre-eminent conservation organization and extremely well-respected both in Belize and internationally. While the name might suggest birding as its main focus of activity, BAS is active in all aspects of nature conservation and manages nine of the country's protected areas. It also publishes a range of books, guides and fact sheets on the reserves it manages. Members receive an excellent quarterly newsletter about the progress of wildlife conservation in Belize. Call in at the office to find out how to get to the various nature reserves. For details write to BAS, 12 Fort St, Belize City, call Ⓣ223-5004 or visit Ⓦwww.belizeaudubon.org.

The Belize Foundation for Research and Environmental Education (Bfree) was formed in 1995 by professional biologists to assist the government of Belize in the management and conservation of the rainforests as well as to coordinate and facilitate scientific research in the Bladen Nature Reserve and other protected areas in the south. Bfree welcomes visitors interested in conservation, sustainable living and the study and appreciation of tropical rainforests. They also provide accommodation for researchers and run educational programmes on topics such as tropical watershed ecology. Contact Judy Dourson, General Manager, at Ⓣ614-3896 or Ⓔbfreemgr@xplornet.com.

The Belize Zoo and Tropical Education Center (see p.79; Ⓦwww.belizezoo.org) is renowned throughout the conservation world for the quality of its educational programmes. The zoo encourages Belizean schoolchildren to explore the natural environment by visits and the Outreach Programme. If you wish to support its aims, individual membership is available.

Friends of Nature (FoN) co-manages Laughing Bird Caye National Park and Gladden Spit and Silk Cayes Marine Reserve, off Placencia (see p.275), and provides an environmental education programme for students from the village and four other local communities. The FoN office is at the south end of The Sidewalk in Placencia; call Ⓣ523-3377 or visit Ⓦwww.friendsofnaturebelize.org for volunteer opportunities.

Green Reef is dedicated to the promotion of sustainable use and conservation of Belize's marine and coastal resources. It's actively involved in implementing management plans for bird sanctuaries on the leeward side of Ambergris Caye, and aims to incorporate these into new extensions to existing protected areas. The organization also provides educational programmes for schools in Belize, and can accept volunteers to help with many aspects of its work. Contact Mito Paz, 100 Coconut Drive, San Pedro, Ambergris Caye (Ⓣ226-2833, Ⓦwww.ambergriscaye.com/greenreef).

The Programme for Belize (PFB), initiated in 1988 by the Massachusetts Audubon Society and launched in Britain in 1989, manages over 260,000 acres in the Rio Bravo Conservation and Management Area (see p.111). The programme has bought land to be held in trust for the people of Belize, now managed entirely by Belizeans. For information on visiting the sites in Belize contact the PFB in Belize City (Ⓣ227-5616, Ⓦwww.pfbelize.org). In the UK, the former PFB is now the **World Land Trust** (Ⓦwww.worldlandtrust.org), which raises funds for conservation in Belize under the title Friends of Belize and has volunteer opportunities.

The Smithsonian Institute operates a marine research station on Carrie Bow Caye, in South Water Caye Marine Reserve. It is primarily a base for marine scientists and supports the institute's Caribbean Coral Reef Ecosystems (CCRE) program. Some of the ongoing research involves species interactions and behaviour and processes linking species and environment. If you are in Belize, you can contact the Pelican Beach Resort in Dangriga for a visit. Scientists can contact the institute at the Arts and Industries Building 1163, Washington, DC 20560 (Ⓔeducation@soe.si.edu, Ⓦwww.si.edu/marinescience/msn).

The Toledo Institute for Development and Environment (TIDE) was formed in 1997 to focus resources and attention on the conservation of a network of protected areas in southern Toledo District, linking the Maya Mountains to the Sapodilla Cayes. TIDE, with support from The Nature Conservancy (TNC), also promotes Integrated Conservation and Development Projects (ICDPs), providing alternative sources of income for local people through conservation-based tour-guiding activities such as fly-fishing and kayaking. TIDE co-manages Paynes Creek National Park and the Port Honduras Marine Reserve (see p.291). Visit Ⓦwww.tidetours.org for more information.

The Wildlife Care Center of Belize (WCCB), established in 1998, operates a holding facility for confiscated and rescued native wildlife, many of which have been kept illegally as pets. WCCB works in collaboration with the Forest Department's Conservation Division to raise public awareness of Belize's wildlife protection laws and to discourage the acquisition of wild animals as pets in the first place. The WCCB is not open to the public but there are opportunities for volunteers; you'll need zoo experience, be self-funded and be able to commit for at least three months. If you're interested, email the director, Robin Brockett, at Ⓔwildlifecarecenter@yahoo.com.

The Wildlife Conservation Society (WCS) works with all the countries involved in the Mesoamerican Biological Corridor project (see p.347) to strengthen and improve management of parks and conservation lands, and to restore degraded habitat for migratory wildlife. Instrumental in developing plans to establish marine reserves throughout the barrier reef, it maintains a research station on Middle Caye, Glover's Reef, working closely with the Belize government to develop a coordinated research and management programme for the whole atoll. Inland, in reserves in the Maya Mountains and at Gallon Jug (see p.113), researchers are developing guidelines to preserve biodiversity. Visit Ⓦwww.wcs.org for more information.

The World Wide Fund for Nature (WWF) works closely with the BAS (see opposite) and is also helping the Belize government to raise its capacity for environmental regulation and protected-area management. WWF has for many years provided initial support for a number of projects in Belize, from the Community Baboon Sanctuary at Bermudian Landing (see p.96) to the Cockscomb Basin Wildlife Sanctuary (see p.260) and Gladden Spit and Silk Cayes Marine Reserve (see p.275). One current project works with farmers in the buffer zones adjacent to the Maya Mountains to develop new technologies for profitable and sustainable agricultural systems. The excellent and well-organized website (Ⓦwww.panda.org) is packed with useful information.

The Ya'axché Conservation Trust (YCT), an NGO established in 1997 and based in Toledo District, aims to promote biodiversity and provide sustainable economic opportunities for the Maya communities bordering the Golden Stream watershed. These include making furniture using wood salvaged from trees felled by Hurricane Iris in 2001. With financial and technical support from Flora and Fauna International (Ⓦwww.fauna-flora.org), YCT co-manages the Golden Stream Corridor Preserve. For volunteer opportunities call Ⓣ722-0108, or email Ⓔyct_ffi@btl.net.

△ Cruise ship in Belize City harbour

dam on the upper Macal River has flooded a beautiful valley that's not only ideal habitat for Baird's tapirs and a threatened subspecies of the scarlet macaw but also contains unexcavated and undocumented Maya sites. The flooding has damaged legally designated protected areas and may also contravene international conservation conventions to which Belize is a signatory. After years of determined and often bitter opposition by environmentalists and activists, the dam proposal was given the go-ahead in 2004, despite the developers, Fortis, having been shown in court to have erased geological fault lines on a map submitted as part of the Environmental Impact Assessment (EIA). Recently, the dam that was built to save Belizeans money on their energy bills has done anything but: Fortis raised rates twelve percent in 2005 and another thirteen percent in 2006. The dam controversy highlights the perpetual problem in Belize of balancing conservation with improving infrastructure. For the latest news visit ⓦwww.stopfortis.org.

Today the hottest topic on the conservation agenda is the growing opposition to the meteoric rise in the number of **cruise ships** and their passengers to Belize's shores – described by one activist as "**mobile mass tourism**". The scale of increase in these arrivals is staggering: from just a few hundred passengers per year in the late 1990s to a peak of over 850,000 in 2004. Although the government's **Cruise Ship Policy Document** states a recommended upper limit of eight thousand cruise ship visitors per day, this limit (which was arbitrarily set by the BTB without reference to any scientific study) is regularly exceeded with impunity. Many Belizeans protest this number and are hoping that a change of government will mean a change of policy. Visitor pressure at many archeological sites and certain cayes already exceeds carrying capacity many times over, leading to destructive trampling and environmental degradation from the sheer numbers involved. Additionally, as word of the numbers of cruise ship visitors spreads, many overnight tourists are stating they do not want to visit sites scheduled for cruise ship tours. Despite having a very poor sewage and waste disposal plan, Belize accepts waste from the cruise ships, depositing much of it in landfills. The Belize Eco-tourism Association is strongly opposed to the unrestricted growth of the cruise ship industry, claiming that, in addition to the reasons outlined above, this growth undermines the very principles of eco-tourism. Along with many others, BETA is calling on the government to better limit, regulate and monitor the cruise ship industry.

Other current issues include the **de-reservation** of protected areas, an instance of which took place recently in Payne's Creek National Park to provide a cruise ship dock in Punta Negra village, and the proposal to build a large tourism facility on Tom Owen's Caye, a tiny outcrop of rock in the Sapodilla Cayes Marine Reserve. The government has also allowed **oil exploration** in several protected areas, such as Sarstoon-Temash National Park, which encompasses fourteen rare and diverse ecosystems and supports indigenous Maya communities. BETA, BACONGO and several other conservation and tourism organizations are joining forces to resist these and other potentially damaging and unsustainable developments which may hurt Belize's world-renowned record of sound environmental stewardship.

Further undermining its country's natural splendour, the government actively sells remote cayes and other lands to foreign investors and Belizeans returning from overseas. **Mangrove-cutting** by resort developers is technically illegal, though fines are rarely imposed, and construction continues at an unprecedented rate all over the country. One of many current sources of concern is a proposed development bordering Bacalar Chico National Park on Ambergris Caye, which, when finished, may flood the delicate ecosystem with up to a thousand visitors at a time. At the other end of the caye, dredging for a new barge facility is also prompting many Belizeans to action and protest. Though the development borders **Hol Chan Marine Reserve**, construction seems to have commenced without proper consultation. There is a significant risk that the reserve will suffer irreversible damage due to the kicking up of silt from barge operations.

Human rights and democracy

Despite the absence of the kind of political turmoil and mass human rights abuses that have characterized much of Latin America – and while tourists remain largely unaffected – there are nonetheless grounds to doubt the extent and depth of human rights protection and political participation in Belize.

On the face of it, this relaxed idyll of Latin America and the Caribbean – with a constitution and multi-party democracy built on the British system – might appear to be a model state as far as the protection of **fundamental human rights** is concerned. However, delving just below the surface reveals a majority with little knowledge of their rights and subject to a historical system of **political patronage** where local affiliation to one of the two political parties (PUP or UDP) can seriously undermine full **freedom of expression**. In other words, contesting the party line in your constituency could find you without land or services, or worse.

Awareness of potential victimization by higher authority is a concrete part of Belizean social life, and maintains a population careful not to speak out. **Freedom of the press**, too, has its problems. The only paper independent of political affiliation, the *Reporter*, regularly notes a lack of transparency across the media and the intimidation of journalists into withdrawing from publication articles against government or party favour.

In this respect, for the Belizean majority, human rights are hardly seen as universal, being viewed instead as being granted: the higher up the socio-economic ladder you are, the more rights you're deemed to have. Ask most Belizeans, and a regular reply perceives rights as belonging to the rich, powerful, white and male. At the opposite end of the scale you'll find the poor, black and female; and it's worth remembering that thirty percent of Belizeans live in abject poverty.

A contributing factor to the political climate may well be the **abuse of power by police**. For many years the Belize Defence Force (BDF) has joined the police on the streets in response to increased gang, often drug-related, violence. Tourists probably notice little difference between the two groups of law enforcers, and this increased **militarization** adds to a general atmosphere of intimidation and danger. The **checkpoints** on roads across the country have been a subject of further dispute, as have the increasing numbers of killings at them by police shooting, both on the mainland and the cayes.

Recent issues

A number of recent incidents remind us of the fragility of law enforcement – but perhaps most serious were the police shootings at a peaceful protest in **Benque Viejo** in 2003 against an increase in bus fares. PUP and UDP supporters were marching together on the streets of this small border town when police responded to a few youngsters throwing stones by opening fire on demonstrators. Over thirty were injured as police fired indiscriminately and used tear gas. Declaring it a riot so as to legitimize violent repression, police continued with **arbitrary arrests** and excessive beatings for three days after the event. The government's failure to condemn the police action further demonstrated its attitude towards protest and freedom of expression.

Another issue that has come to the fore in recent years is that of indigenous **Maya land rights**. In 1998, the Indian Law Resource Centre and the Toledo Maya Cultural Council issued a petition to the **Inter-American Commission of Human Rights**, alleging the state be responsible for violations of Mopan and Kekchí Maya rights to land and resources. This requested the suspension of licenses for logging and resource extraction in Maya areas, which are deemed to have adversely affected the local environment and culture. In response the government contends that petitioners have presented insufficient evidence, and that they failed to take advantage of domestic judicial processes when able to do so. In spite of this, it appears that some headway has been made on the issue, with a ten-point agreement signed by both government and Maya groups. Other **minorities** continue to suffer abuses of rights, including large numbers of **immigrants** from El Salvador, Nicaragua, Guatemala and Honduras, who are frequently denied the same rights as nationals and are very often referred to as aliens.

Many visitors will encounter Maya children from Guatemala and Belize selling their wares on the cayes and in the south of Belize, and should be aware that, despite financing their families in this way, they really should be in school. The immigrant issue increasingly manifests itself in the business of **people trafficking** – very often of women and children for the sex industry; a 2001 study commissioned by UNICEF reported that 35 percent of prostitutes in Belize were under 18 and the majority of them from Honduras, El Salvador and Guatemala.

The death penalty

Corporal punishment and the **death penalty** remain highly popular in Belize, despite the fact that no one has been executed since 1985. General disputes are often solved through violence – lashings in schools and at home are common for children, and flogging by tamarind whip was reintroduced around three years ago in the Hattieville prison, though there are no reports of recent floggings. The unknown level of **domestic abuse of women** is also cause for growing concern by human rights groups.

The popular campaign to replace the British-based **Privy Council** with a **Caribbean Court of Justice** as the highest court of appeal may owe itself largely to the perception that more executions would be approved. In 2002 the Belize government introduced a fifth amendment to the constitution, lowering the level of coherent justice through the prevention of the right of appeal to the Privy Council for capital punishment cases. If it had been passed, this bill would have built discrimination into the constitution; now, a move towards a regional court seems almost inevitable. While on the face of it removing that last bastion of direct colonial authority and replacing it with a regional court seems a positive step forward, the fear in some quarters is of a lower standard of justice. The Privy Council could well be in a better position to look at individual rights and representations; in the context of the region's growing **drug economy**, alongside the downsizing of the state through structural adjustment programmes and the high level of **external debt** (in Belize around US$1.2 billion), it may be harder to uphold democratic principles and fundamental freedoms at a state or regional level than ever before.

Ethnic Belize

Belize has a very mixed cultural background, with the two largest ethnic groups, Creoles and mestizos – forming 75 percent of the total population (currently around 295,000) – being the descendants of very different ancestors. In total, thirteen ethnic groups are recognized in Belize, the vast majority being members of one of the groups described below. There is also a great deal of ethnic mixing between the groups.

The largest ethnic group (just under fifty percent) are **mestizos**, descended from Amerindians and early Spanish settlers, many of whom speak Spanish as their first language. They are mainly located in the north and on Ambergris Caye and Caye Caulker, with a sizeable population in Cayo. Many of the ancestors of the present population fled to Belize during the Caste Wars of Yucatán (see p.319). In the 1980s many thousands of refugees (see p.328) from conflicts and repression in El Salvador, Guatemala and Honduras have settled in Belize, adding permanently to the numbers of Spanish-speaking mestizos – though many of these people refer to themselves as Ladinos.

Creoles, descended from Africans brought to the West Indies as slaves and early white settlers, comprise just under a quarter of the population. They make up a large proportion of the population of Belize City, with scattered settlements elsewhere. Creole is the common language in Belize, a form of English similar to that spoken in areas of the West Indies that were once part of the British empire. Belizean spoken Creole is undergoing a formalization similar to that taken by the Garifuna in the 1980s, with a more or less standardized written Creole (referred to as "Kriol") used in some academic writing, newspaper articles and published folklore tales; for more on this see Language, p.379. Occasionally, controversy rages in the press over whether or not Kriol should become the country's official language and be taught in schools alongside English.

The **Maya** in Belize are from three groups – the Yucatec, Mopan and Kekchí – and make up around eleven percent of the population. The Yucatecan Maya also entered Belize to escape the fighting in the Caste Wars, and most were soon acculturated into the mestizo way of life as small farmers. The Mopan Maya came to Belize in the 1880s and settled in the hills of Toledo and the area of Benque Viejo in the west. The last and largest group, the Kekchí, came from the area around Cobán in Guatemala to work in cacao plantations in southern Belize. Small numbers still arrive in Belize each year, founding new villages in the southern district of Toledo.

The **Garifuna** (see box, p.246) form just over six percent of the population and live mainly in Dangriga and the villages on the south coast. They are descended from shipwrecked and escaped African slaves who mingled with the last of the Caribs on the island of St Vincent and eventually settled in Belize. A Garifuna dictionary, published by the National Garifuna Council, is available in the country.

Another significant group is **East Indians**, with a relatively large population in southern Toledo District. These are the descendants of indentured labourers brought over in the late 1860s by a small number of Confederate refugees seeking to re-establish the plantocracy following their defeat in the American Civil War.

Though the white, German-speaking **Mennonites** (see box, p.105) form only around four percent of the total population, they contribute to Belizean agriculture out of all proportion to their actual numbers. Over the past several centuries their opposition to government interference in their religious beliefs – particularly their utter rejection of military service – has forced them to move on to other lands. In Belize, however, they appear to have found a secure and permanent home at last.

The **Chinese (and Taiwanese)** are one of Belize's smallest ethnic groups. In the nineteenth century, many arrived as labourers for the sugar estates in the south. Many more from Taiwan and Hong Kong arrived in the 1980s, and while they do contribute to the agricultural sector, their presence is most evident in the lottery, retail and restaurant industries. It's very likely that any grocery store you visit in Belize will be run by a Chinese family.

Without a doubt, the greatest shift in Belize's demography for centuries has been the recent Hispanic influence. During the 1980s, the arrival of an estimated 40,000 **Central American immigrants**, refugees from war and poverty, boosted Belize's population to more than 200,000. Those granted refugee status were settled in camps, mostly in Cayo, and allowed to farm small plots, though many, especially the undocumented refugees, provide convenient cheap labour in citrus and banana plantations. The immigrants are tolerated, if not exactly welcomed – few countries could absorb a sudden twenty percent increase in population without a certain amount of turmoil – and the official policy is to encourage them to integrate into Belizean society. Despite the signing of peace accords ending the civil wars in their countries of origin, there is no question of enforced repatriation for these former refugees. Their children born in Belize are Belizean citizens, and the vast majority of the original refugees have since received Belizean nationality.

The former refugees are industrious agriculturists providing a variety of crops for the domestic market. Nevertheless they are often referred to as aliens and blamed for crimes. Their presence means that Spanish is now the most widely spoken first language in Belize, causing some Creoles to feel marginalized. Additionally, Guatemalan peasant farmers continue to clear land just inside Belize's western border, but these are regarded as illegal immigrants and official policy is to remove them – creating tensions between the two governments.

An excellent TV **documentary series** entitled *Simply Belize*, which will eventually cover all thirteen ethnic groups, is currently in production, and the first three programmes, each featuring a different Maya group, have already been screened. This series is available on video in the Belize City Museum and some gift shops; for more information visit ⓦwww.simplybelize.org.

Music

For such a tiny country, Belize enjoys an exceptional range of musical styles and traditions. Whether your tastes run to the wind melodies and percussion of the Maya, the up-tempo punta rock of the Garifuna or to calypso, marimba, brukdown, soca or steel pan, Belize is sure to have something to suit. Some visitors still complain about the noisiness of Belizean society and the volume at which the music is played, but if you can get into it, it's one of the quickest ways to the heart of Belizeans and their culture.

Roots

Until the demise of the Maya civilization and the arrival of the Spanish, the indigenous **Maya** of Belize played a range of instruments drawn almost entirely from the flute and percussion families. Drums were usually made from hollowed logs covered in deerskin, with rattles, gourd drums and turtle shells providing further rhythmic accompaniment. Trumpets, bells, shells and whistles completed the instrumentation. However, as befits a nation of immigrants, each new group arriving – the Europeans, the Creoles, the mestizos and the Garifuna – brought with them new styles, vigour and variety which today inform and influence popular culture.

Mestizo music combined elements of its two constituent cultures: Maya ceremonial music and new instruments from Spain, such as the classical guitar and violin, and later brass band music. Mestizo communities (including the Mopan Maya) in the north and west of the country continue to favour **marimba** bands: half a dozen men playing two large, multi-keyed wooden xylophones, perhaps supported by a double bass and a drum kit. Up to half a

△ Musician in Belize City

Andy Palacio

For two decades **Andy Palacio** has influenced, dominated and even helped produce the modern Belizean sound. Although he performs less often than he did in the 1990s, he remains the country's only truly professional star and music ambassador to the rest of the world. Over the years Palacio has succeeded in incorporating an enormous diversity of national and regional styles into a unique popular sound that appeals to all sections of the music market.

Born in Barranco, he grew up in the rural cosmopolitanism of Garifuna, Maya and mestizo communities, integrating a diversity of linguistic and cultural influences from an early age. As a teenager in the 1970s he experienced first-hand the new Belizean cultural nationalism of the PUP party, which brought the country to independence, introducing a broader ideological dimension to his inevitable cultural affinity with the Garifuna musical tradition. The break came in 1987 when, on an exchange visit to London, he spent a year picking up the latest recording techniques and honing his compositional skills. He returned triumphantly to Belize a year later with enough equipment to open a studio, also bringing with him several London recordings of the songs that would become huge hits back home and transform the music scene.

The biggest song was undoubtedly the 1988 hit **Bikini Panti** – an English-Garifuna, punta-rock satire on Belize's burgeoning tourist business – which set a new musical and lyrical standard for the entire country. But if *Bikini Panti* was the dancefloor killer, it was **Me Goin' Back** that provided the clear ideological expression of the new national sensitivity, as the almost calypsonian lyrics demonstrate:

Set up the line for the Dangriga posse
Play a little rhythm for the Stann Creek posse
Mash up the place with the Cayo posse
Bruk down the house with the Belize posse
Control the area for the Orange Walk posse
Mek them know that me fresh and ready
Mek them know, me have the authority

Now don't burst your brains wondering what
I'm goin back to
So I'll mention just a few
Some old and some new

Rice n Beans and a Belikin
Friends FM and a dollar chicken
Pine Ridge and a Swing Bridge
Brukdown, Punta Rock
Sunshine and a cashew wine
Belize Times and Amandala
Maya, Creole and the Garifuna

Palacio's longstanding collaboration with Stonetree Records has seen three releases to date (see the discography box on p.360), and his project with the **Garifuna Collective** band from across Central America now tours around the world. More comfortable in his national superstar status, he has established an enviable reputation as a musician capable of producing catchy melodies accompanied by articulate, astute and entertaining lyrics, underpinned by unique Garifuna rhythms. For more information, visit ⓦ www.myspace.com/andypalacio.

dozen bands play regularly in Cayo District: famed healer Eligio Panti presided over the nation's pre-eminent marimba group, **Alma Beliceña**, and **Los Angeles Marimba Band** is another popular group. Leading marimba bands frequently pop over from Flores in Guatemala, and Mexican **mariachi** bands occasionally make an appearance, too. Nonetheless, traditional mestizo music remains under threat as the youth turn to rock, rap and punta.

Europeans introduced much of the hardware and software for playing music: "western" musical instruments and sheet music, and, much later, record players, compact discs and massive sound systems. From the mid-nineteenth century onwards, British colonial culture, through church music, military bands and the popular music of the time, was able to exert a dominant influence over what was acceptable music in Belize.

An exciting melange of **West African rhythms** and melodies, as well as drums and stringed instruments, arrived in Belize as a result of the slave trade during the eighteenth century. However, given that the Baymen purchased

Discography

For a current list of the best of Belize's recorded music, check out **Stonetree's website**, ⓦwww.stonetreerecords.com.

Andy Palacio *Keimoun* and *Til Da Mawnin* (Stonetree) Two great albums displaying a mastery of punta and a widening of scope to incorporate Latin and Anglophone Caribbean influences. Newest release *Watina* with the **Garifuna Collective** features *parranderos* **Aurelio** and **Paul Nabor**.

Aurelio Martinez *Garifuna Soul* (Stonetree) Honduran Aurelio's Belizean debut, demonstrating soulful vocals over a rich blend of Latin, punta and parranda rhythms.

Bredda David & Tribal Vibes *Raw* (Stonetree) Rock guitars overlaid on new-generation Belizean rhythm and lyrical wit combine to produce a satisfying run around the kungo kingdom.

Caribbean Pulse *Stand-Up* and *Unity* (Irie Records) Two albums from this US-based Belizean reggae group present well-produced conscious music. Visit ⓦwww.caribbeanpulse.com.

Florencio Mess *Maya K'ekchi' Strings* (Stonetree) An essential album. One of the few remaining harpists to maintain this centuries-old Maya tradition.

Leroy Young the Grandmaster *Just Like That* (Stonetree) Impressive musical debut from Belize's own dub-poet presents a powerful commentary and new Creole style, featuring a wide range of roots rhythms and strings.

Lugua and the Larubeya Drummers *Bumari* (Stonetree) Roots Garifuna music at its strongest, a new chapter in the history of Garifuna percussion.

Maria Reimer *Maria* (Digitrax/EMI) Belizean country/Latin singer demonstrates a powerful voice.

MKL and others *Three Generations Walking* (Spiritual Life Music) This project from Belizean MKL and others showcases a highly original blend of dub, jazz and modern electronic music.

Mr. Peters and his Boom and Chime *The King of Brukdown*, *Weh Mi Love Deh* and *Rub Mi Belly* (Stonetree) Three excellent releases from the undisputed king of brukdown. A musical journey through Creole culture and the ideal introduction to this genuine Belizean art form.

The Original Turtle Shell Band *Beginning* The first-ever punta rock recording from 1982 features Pen Cayetano, Mohubub and the band, remastered here in 2000. See ⓦwww.cayetano.de.

slaves from **Jamaica** rather than directly from Africa it should be remembered that African influences arrived indirectly.

A new, syncretic style, nurtured in the logging camps and combining Western instrumentation with specifically African musical inflections, emerged in the late nineteenth century to create a specifically Belizean musical tradition known as "**brukdown**". Featuring a modern line-up of guitar, banjo, accordion, drums and the jawbone of an ass (rattling a stick up and down the teeth!), brukdown remains a potent reminder of past **Creole** culture. Although the style is slowly fading, as Creole society itself changes, there are a few active practitioners. The style's most prominent figure, master accordionist **Wilfred Peters** (now in his seventies and still playing), is the founder of the nationally celebrated **Mr. Peters and his Boom and Chime**, and has composed countless classics and performed to audiences in festivals around the world. Generally, though, brukdown is recreational music best enjoyed in the Creole villages of Burrell Boom, Hattieville, Bermudian Landing and Isabella Bank.

Pablo Collado *Naturaleza Despierta* and *Amanecer* (Derechos Reservados, Guatemala) Two of the best from this Maya-mestizo master flautist/guitarist.

Super G *Unity* and *Unlock* (Love Entertainment) Two recent albums showcasing Spanish, English and Garifuna lyrics from this punta favourite, although often using backing tracks in preference to live drumming.

Titiman Flores *Fedu* (Stonetree) A punta rock party album from beginning to end. The recent *Stop Crime* (Love Entertainment) shows Titiman still controlling the dancefloor.

Various Artists *Belize City Boil Up* (Stonetree/Contemporary Electronic Systems /Numero Group) A sample of pre-Independence Belize, featuring remastered vintage recordings from the 50s, 60s and 70s – a time when the Belizean scene was alive with cool jazz, smooth rhythm and blues and even some psychedelic funk.

Various Artists *Celebration Belize* (Belize Arts Council) Includes contributions from Andy Palacio, Mr. Peters, Leela Vernon, Florencio Mess and many others in this colourful musical journey.

Various Artists *PARRANDA: Africa in Central America* (Stonetree/Warner Classics) Three generations of Garifuna together for the first time on this landmark recording. Imagine African drumming, American blues, Cuban son and West African guitar all wrapped into one.

Various Artists *The Rough Guide to Central America* (World Music Network) Covering music from six countries, the album includes five well-known Belizean artists from the cross-section of styles – an ideal introduction to the music of the whole region.

Other punta artists and recordings to look out for are **Aziatic** with *Most Wanted* (Stonetree), *The Re Birth* (Sta-tic Productions) and, together with **Griga Boyz**, *Crazy Fi We* (Stonetree); **Mohubub**'s self-titled album (Stonetree), with conscious lyrics; the **Punta Rebels** *Gial DePan Fiya*; and *Desire* (Love Entertainment), from former Rebels **Lloyd and Reckless**.

Forthcoming on Stonetree are *Garifuna Women Voices*, featuring songs from coastal villages in Belize, Guatemala and Honduras; and *The Creole Experience – Music from the Riverbanks*, based on traditional Creole songs with an eclectic mix of acoustic instruments.

Brad Patico, an accomplished guitarist and singer-songwriter, similarly does his best to keep the Creole folksong tradition alive from his base in Burrell Boom – his recordings can still be found in Belizean record stores. Originating from the same cultural roots, and equally conscious of a disappearing musical past, is Brother David Obi, better known as **Bredda David**, the creator of **kungo music**, a mixture of musical styles that includes the traditional Creole music of Belize and the pulsating drum rhythms of Africa. A skilful musician and songwriter, David still plays occasionally in Belize City with his **Tribal Vibes** band. Currently the best-known singer seen to preserve traditional Creole folksong is **Leela Vernon** from Punta Gorda, who plays to highly appreciative audiences at national festivals, often appearing with long-standing pop bands, including **Youth Connection**, **Gilharry 7** and **Santino's Messengers**. Her most famous song, "Who say Creole gat no culture?" is a national favourite amongst older people and a reminder of pride in Belizean society.

More recently, the African elements in Creole music have been expressed through wider **pan-Caribbean** styles like calypso, reggae, soca and rap. **Calypso** enjoyed a brief period of pre-eminence – Belize's most famous calypsonian **Lord Rhaburn** is still occasionally to be seen as a special guest at official functions, increasingly rare performances that shouldn't be missed.

Punta rock

If traditional Maya, mestizo and Creole styles retain only a fragile hold on popular musical consciousness, it is the Garifuna who have been catapulted to centre-stage over the last two decades with the invention and development of **punta rock**. The key musical developments that led to punta rock were the amplification of several traditional **drum rhythms** originally associated with courtship dances, while keeping faith with other traditional instruments such as the turtle shell – and initially the almost universal aversion to singing in anything but Garifuna. Although many master musicians and cultural nationalists (both from Belize and the other Garifuna communities across Central America) pushed Garifuna culture forward, particular recognition must go to master drummer and drum-maker **Isabel Flores** and the enigmatic singer, guitarist and artist **Pen Cayetano** in Dangriga. Pen pioneered popular Garifuna music, widening the scope of punta with the introduction of electric guitars and helping to spark a new cultural assertiveness that saw dozens of younger musicians take up the challenge. His **Turtle Shell Band** set the standard, and within a few years other electric bands – including **Sounds Incorporated**, **Black Coral**, **Jeff Zuniga**, **Titiman Flores**, **Mohubub** and, above all, **Andy Palacio** (see box, p.359) – consolidated punta's popularity. Palacio's brainchild, the seminal compilation *Punta Rockers* (1988) featured recordings by himself and several other punta rock pioneers. Credit should also be given to Dangriga-based **Al Obando** in the development of the punta rock sound. As Belize's pre-eminent sound engineer, Obando produced the hugely popular band the **Punta Rebels** through the 1990s and is still relied upon for studio recordings today.

Guardians of more orthodox arrangements, **Lugua and the Larubeya Drummers** marked their debut with the release of *Bumari* (1997). Covering the full range of Garifuna drumming styles alongside powerful call and response vocals, their music is a telling reminder of the African influence in Garifuna history; their live shows should on no account be missed. Recently there has also been a resurgence of the traditional Garifuna style of **parranda**, performed with acoustic guitars, drums and shakers. This was marked by the international release of the eponymous album, recorded by various *parranderos* living in Belize, Honduras and Guatemala. It is recognized as being one of the best collections to come out of Central America. This movement grows stronger with two recent releases – the first by Belize-produced Honduran **Aurelio Martínez**, who blends parranda with Latin influences and Spanish vocals, and the second by **Andy Palacio & The Garifuna Collective**, featuring other Garifuna stars such as **Paul Nabor**.

Additionally, several young Garifuna stars from Dangriga have emerged to take the nation by storm, combining fast infectious punta with reggae dancehall and soca in highly energized performances. This is punta for the young generation, relying largely on **sound systems**, often at the expense of live musicians. Former Punta Rebels **Super G** and **Lloyd & Reckless**, alongside favourites the **Griga Boyz**, are the main exponents and can be found performing regularly throughout the country. Showing an awareness of the wider market potential in Guatemala and Mexico, Super G now also sings in Spanish and includes **cumbia** numbers on his albums – a Latin style highly popular amongst young mestizos. Increasingly often these punta rock stars make the trip across the borders to rapturous audiences in Chetumal and Flores, demonstrating the position of Belize both as a major regional music producer and as a bridge between Caribbean and Latin American styles.

Special events

Perhaps the best times to hear and see the full panoply of Belizean musical culture are the various national events that regularly punctuate the social calendar. Biggest and best are **National Day/St George's Caye Day** (Sept 10) and **Independence Day** (Sept 21) – dates that mark almost two weeks of festivities as Belize City comes close to the spirit and atmosphere of Caribbean carnival. In fact, between these dates there's a genuine **Carnival**, established only since independence but a hugely popular event, with an enormous street parade, floats, a carnival queen attended by a bevy of princesses and of course bands and sound systems. Block parties, "jump-ups" and late-night revelry characterize what are popularly known as the "**September Celebrations**". On Independence Day, Eve Street (leading to the BTL Park) is closed to traffic and the country's top bands and sound systems line the parade route and perform on stages in the park.

The **Costa Maya Festival**, held in San Pedro during the third week of August, is a celebration of dance, music and culture that attracts performers from Mexico and throughout Central America. **Garifuna Settlement Day** (Nov 19) brings huge crowds to Dangriga, where **Puntafest** – a long weekend of late nights, rum and rhythm – is a must-attend event. The **National Agricultural Show**, held just outside Belmopan in May, gathers together up to 50,000 people over three days for all things agricultural and recreational. Almost all the country's top artists, bands and sound systems will appear at some stage during the weekend.

Mestizo communities celebrate with a number of Latin-type **fiestas**: bands, funfairs, sports and competitions, usually held around Easter. The week-long **Flores Fiesta**, held in mid-January across the border in Guatemala, is also great fun, with many Belizean artists performing alongside Guatemalan acts.

Belizean musicians abroad

No review of Belizean music would be complete without considering the impact of the Belizean diaspora on the national scene. A number of Belize-born bands and artists from a diversity of musical genres are now experiencing fame in their respective styles both in the US and back home.

The wider Garifuna community in the US, from both Belizean and Honduran origins, sustains a growing market for punta rock in North America and crosses over into the wider Latin music market. Artists such as **Aziatic**, **Garifuna Legacy**, punta-rap group **Garifuna Kidz**, **Punta Cartel** and the more traditional **Del and the Sensations** all make annual trips to Belize and are well worth a listen. On a different musical note, but nonetheless wholeheartedly Belizean, is country-Latin singer **Maria Reimer**, born in Cayo to Mennonite and mestizo parents, and recently having recorded for EMI in Nashville. You may well hear her melodic country tones while travelling in Cayo and the north, or catch her live performances at national festivals. California-based Belizean conscious-reggae outfit **Caribbean Pulse** is also making good headway with two albums to date and tracks featuring such reggae luminaries as Tony Rebel and Damian Marley.

Apart from traditional Caribbean and Latin musical territory – and proving that Belizean musicians are breaking boundaries beyond drums and roots – is Belize City-born **MKL**, alias Michael Lopez. Based in New York, his highly original musical project entitled *Three Generations Walking* (see box, p.360) encompasses soul, jazz, dub, laid-back electronics and female vocals, alongside live congas and guitars. Outside the studio, MKL occupies himself as a global touring DJ, and may yet find his niche in the Belize music scene.

Original text by Ronnie Graham. Fully revised by Rob Coates, with additional material from Ivan Duran, Hector Martinez and Daniel C. Chang.

Dance

Alongside the growth in music production since independence, Belize has witnessed the formation and development of an active dance scene. Most visitors will notice a vibrant dancing culture among the different ethnic groups – but since the inception of the Belize National Dance Company in 1990, a countrywide programme has been established.

Under the leadership of director-choreographers **Gregory Vernon** and **Althea Sealy**, and with initial assistance from Eduardo Rivero of the Caribbean Dance Theatre of Santiago de Cuba, the **Belize National Dance Company** was created in an effort both to promote a collective cultural identity and to preserve the traditional dances of the Belizean people. Amalgamating the various dances from across the country, the **Belize modern technique** draws from Afro-folkloric dances including traditional Garifuna movements and expression and Creole brukdown and bram dance, alongside Cuban technique and creative modern and contemporary styles. Traditional dances such as the punta, Jonkunnu (John Canoe) and chumba all still feature strongly. In addition to performance, the BNDC also includes the promotion of dance countrywide as part of its vision. Its members give regular dance workshops in schools, and a summer camp is held each year to bring together young dancers for training and skill development. The company's consistent choreographic works demonstrate national sensitivity through the use of entirely Belizean choreographers alongside the compositions of local musicians, touring Belize to popular acclaim from Punta Gorda to Corozal.

Another dance group that performs regularly – both in Belize and internationally – is the **Ugandani** ("happiness" in Garifuna) group led by **Charles Flores**, which encourages the promotion of traditional Garifuna dances, music and language.

Books

Belize under British rule didn't inspire much literature, but independence has prompted a handful of writers to publish works based on the transition to independence and the emergence of a national identity. There are a number of excellent wildlife guides and studies, and also several good travel accounts covering Belize. Books on the ancient Maya increase in number and quality of information every year.

Cubola Productions is Belize's pre-eminent specialist publisher, with a wide range of fiction and non-fiction on all subjects related to Belize, including many of the archeology and wildlife books listed below; check their website, ⓦwww.cubolabelize.com, for full details. The Angelus Press in Belize also publishes an impressive list of titles by Belizean authors and books about Belize, and they offer an online and mail order service; visit ⓦwww.angeluspress.com. Where possible we have given both the US and UK publishers (listed after the book title), with the US publisher first. Many books are published only in Belize; o/p means a book is out of print.

Travel

Thor Janson *Belize, Land of the Free by the Carib Sea* (Bowen and Bowen, Belize). Published by the company which produces Belikin beer, this lavishly illustrated coffee-table travelogue through modern Belize makes a perfect souvenir. Janson also authored *Maya Nature: An Introduction to the Ecosystems, Plants and Animals of the Mayan World*, showcasing a photographic safari of the region.

Aldous Huxley *Beyond the Mexique Bay* (Flamingo, UK; o/p). In 1934, Huxley's travels took him from Belize through Guatemala to Mexico, swept on by his fascination with history and religion, and sprouting bizarre theories on the basis of what he saw. There are some great descriptions of Maya sites and Indian culture, with superb one-liners summing up people and places, including the classic "If the world had any ends British Honduras would surely be one of them."

Jeremy Paxman *Through the Volcanoes* (Paladin, UK; o/p). A political travel account investigating the turmoil of Central America and finding solace in the calm of Costa Rica. Paxman's travels take him through all seven countries, including Belize, and he offers a good overview of the politics and history of the region in the mid-1980s.

John Lloyd Stephens *Incidents of Travel in Central America, Chiapas, and Yucatán* (Dover; Prentice Hall). Stephens was a classic nineteenth-century traveller. Acting as American ambassador to Central America, he indulged his own enthusiasm for archeology: while the republics fought it out among themselves he was wading through the jungle stumbling across ancient cities. In Belize he dines with high society and is given a naval gun salute from the superintendent, though he doesn't venture inland. His journals, written with superb Victorian pomposity, punctuated with sudden waves of enthusiasm, make great reading. Some editions include fantastic illustrations by Frederick Catherwood of Maya ruins overgrown with tropical rainforest.

Ronald Wright *Time Among the Maya* (Grove Press, US). A vivid and sympathetic account of Wright's travels in the late 1980s from Belize through Guatemala, Chiapas and Yucatán, meeting the Maya and exploring their obsession with time. The book's twin points of interest are the ancient Maya and the violence that occurred throughout the 1980s. Certainly one of the best travel books on the area, and the author's knowledge is evident in the superb historical insight he imparts throughout the book.

Literature

If Di Pin Neva Ben: Folktales and Legends of Belize (various authors; Cubola, Belize). A vibrant collection of traditional Belizean folklore. Includes a host of colourful characters, ranging from creatures who enforce the preservation of nature to figures who allow storytellers to explore otherwise taboo subjects. Gathered by folklorists during the late 1970s, these short tales capture the richness of a society that fluidly blends the cultures of its many ethnic groups. Other anthologies of Belizean literature published by Cubola include *Snapshots of Belize*, a collection of short stories by major Belizean writers, and *Ping Wing Juk Me*, six short plays reproduced in an attempt to revive the strong theatrical tradition which thrived prior to the advent of television; both of these contain some writing in Kriol (see Language, p.379).

Meg Craig *Characters and Caricatures In Belizean Folklore* (UNESCO Folklore Fund Committee, Belize). A compilation from oral sources and considered the most important work on Belizean folklore.

Zee Edgell *Beka Lamb* (Heinemann, UK). A young girl's account of growing up in Belize in the 1950s, in which the problems of adolescence are described alongside those of the Belizean independence movement. The book also explores everyday life in the colony, describing the powerful structure of matriarchal society and the influence of the Catholic Church. *In Times Like These*, also by Edgell, is a semi-autobiographical account of personal and political intrigue set in the months leading up to Belize's independence.

Zoila Ellis *On Heroes, Lizards and Passion* (Cubola, Belize). Seven short stories written by a Belizean woman with a deep understanding of her country's people and their culture.

Felicia Hernandez *Those Ridiculous Years* (Cubola, Belize). A short autobiographical book about growing up in Dangriga in the 1960s.

Emory King *Belize 1798, The Road to Glory* (Tropical Books, Belize). Rip-roaring historical novel peopled by the characters involved in the Battle of St George's Caye. King's enthusiasm for his country's history is supported by meticulous research in archives on both sides of the Atlantic. Wonderful holiday reading. King is something of a celebrity in Belize (see box on p.73): his first book *Hey Dad, This Is Belize*, a hilarious account of family life in Belize, became something of a minor classic and was followed up with *I Spent It All In Belize*, an anthology of witty, lightly satirical articles gently but effectively pricking the pomposity of officialdom. These and other books by King are usually only available in Belize, though you can order online from the Angelus Press.

Carlos Ledson Miller *Belize – A Novel* (Xlibris, US). Fast-paced historical saga of a Central American father and his two sons – one American and one Belizean – who struggle against a forbidding land, and often with each other. The story opens in 1961, on the eve of Hurricane Hattie, then transports the reader across forty years from the unrest of colonial British Honduras to the turbulence of present-day Belize. A good read.

History, politics and society

A History of Belize – A Nation in the Making (Cubola, Belize). Straightforward and simple historical accounts, written for use in schools but providing a good, accurate background; available within Belize.

The Maya Atlas (North Atlantic Books, US; o/p). As much a collection of personal accounts of contemporary Maya life as a geography book, this is a fascinating co-production between university researchers and the Maya of Toledo in southern Belize. Trained by Berkeley cartographers, teams of villagers surveyed their lands, completed a census and then wrote a history of each community. The regional maps accurately show the position of each village, and drawings and photographs show scenes from everyday life.

Readings in Belizean History (various authors; St John's College Press, Belize). Recently updated version of a highly acclaimed textbook, comprising essays by noted Belizean scholars on all aspects of Belize's history. Will interest anyone looking for a broader and deeper insight into Belize.

O. Nigel Bolland *Colonialism and Resistance in Belize: Essays in Historical Sociology* (Cubola, Belize/UWI Press) This revised (2003) edition of the 1988 text is the most comprehensive and academic study of Belizean history there is. Covering both the early colonization of the Maya, the growth of slavery and progress of Creole culture, through to the development of nationalism over divergent ethnic identities, Bolland places particular emphasis on labour control and resistance – providing a broadly Marxist analysis that is both compelling and convincingly argued.

Sebastian Cayetano *Garifuna History, Language & Culture of Belize, Central America & the Caribbean* (Angelus Press, Belize). A brief, simply written history of the Garifuna. Mainly aimed at children, it also mentions the great changes the Garifuna are experiencing as they adapt to modern life.

Byron Foster *Heart Drum* and *Spirit Possession in the Garifuna Community of Belize* (Cubola, Belize). These two slim volumes focus on the importance of spirituality in the lives of the Garifuna and the experience of spirit possession as described to Foster, an anthropologist. Another of Foster's books, *The Baymen's Legacy: A Portrait of Belize City* (Cubola), is a school text but offers an approachable and interesting history of the city.

Emory King *The Great Story of Belize* (Tropical Books, Belize). Four slim, large-format volumes from a master raconteur. The meticulously researched narrative, full of events great and small and packed with larger-than-life characters, presents a vivid account of Belize's history from the first Spanish contact to the 1990s.

Gerhard S. Koop *Pioneer Years in Belize* (self-published; available in Belize). A history of the Mennonites in Belize, written in a style as stolid and practical as the lives of the pioneers themselves. A good read nonetheless.

Ian Peedle *Belize in Focus* (Resource Center; LAB). A relatively up-to-date, easily digested overview of Belizean society and politics. Worth taking along if you're there for more than a few days.

Assad Shoman *Thirteen Chapters of a History of Belize* (Angelus Press, Belize). A treatment of the country's history written by a Belizean who's not afraid to examine colonial myths with a detailed and rational analysis. Primarily a school textbook, but the style will not alienate non-student readers. Shoman, active in politics both before and since independence, also wrote *Party Politics in Belize*, a short but highly detailed account of the development of party politics in the country.

Donald C. Simmons, Jr *Confederate Settlements in British Honduras* (McFarland & Company, US). Tells the fascinating story of the defeated Confederates who inadvertently shaped the cultural landscape of southern Belize.

Anne Sutherland *The Making of Belize: Globalization in the Margins* (Bergin and Garvey, US). A fairly recent study of cultural and economic changes in Belize, based on the author's experiences as a visitor and her observations as an anthropologist. The result is an enjoyable mixture of academic research, anecdotal insights and strong, even controversial, opinion; Sutherland reserves her strongest criticism for conservationists, whom she castigates as "ecocolonialists [who] totally disregard the interests of the Belizean people".

Colville Young *Creole Proverbs of Belize* (Cubola, Belize). A wonderful compilation of oral folk-wisdom from Belize, written by the present governor general, who's also a distinguished linguist. Each saying or proverb is written in Creole, translated into English, and then has its meaning explained. A primer for street life. Other books by Young include *Pataki Full*, a slim anthology of Belizean short stories and folk tales, and two volumes of poetry, *From One Caribbean Corner* and *Caribbean Corner Calling*, which bring Belize and its Creole language to life.

Archeology

The Popol Vuh (Touchstone; Scribner). The great creation myth poem of the K'iche' (Quiche) Maya of the Guatemalan highlands, written shortly after the conquest and intended to preserve the K'iche' people's knowledge of their history. Although not directly connected with Belize and strictly speaking a work of literature not archeology, the characters and images in the book are directly relevant to an understanding of the ancient Maya anywhere. It's an amazing swirl of fantastic gods and mortals who become gods, particularly the Hero Twins and their battle to overcome the Lords of Death in Xibalba. There are several versions on offer, though many of them are half-hearted and include only a few lines from the original. The best is translated by Dennis Tedlock (Simon & Schuster).

Jamie Awe *100 Questions and Answers about the Ancient Maya of Belize* (Factory Books, Belize). Written by Belize's Director of Archaeology and designed primarily for schoolchildren, this slim book is ideal for anyone interested in the basic facts about the Maya. Awe also authored *Maya Cities and Sacred Caves* (Cubola, Belize), which guides you through the Maya sites of Belize.

Michael Coe *The Maya* (Thames & Hudson, UK). Now in its seventh edition, this clear and comprehensive introduction to Maya archeology is the best on offer. Coe has also written several more weighty, academic volumes. His *Breaking the Maya Code* (Thames & Hudson), a very personal history of the decipherment of the glyphs, owes much to the fact that Coe was present at many of the most important meetings leading to the breakthrough. While his pointed criticism of J. Eric S. Thompson – much of whose work he describes as burdened with "irrelevant quotations", and his role in the decipherment of the Maya script as "entirely negative" – may provoke controversy, this book demonstrates that the glyphs did actually reproduce Maya speech.

William Coe *Tikal: A Handbook to the Ancient Maya Ruins* (University of Pennsylvania, US). Superbly detailed account of the site, usually available at the ruins. The detailed map of the main area is essential for in-depth exploration.

David Drew *The Lost Chronicles of the Maya Kings* (University of California Press; Weidenfeld and Nicolson). Superbly readable and engaging; the author draws on a wealth of material including some of the very latest findings to deliver an excellent account of ancient Maya political history. The alliances and rivalries between the main cities are skilfully unravelled, and there's a particularly revealing analysis of late Classic Maya power politics.

Anabel Ford *The Maya Forest Garden and El Pilar* (ISBER/Meso American Research Center). Perfect for visitors with children, this colouring book promotes awareness of Maya sites as well as medicinal plants and forest gardens.

Byron Foster (ed.) *Warlords and Maize Men – A Guide to the Maya Sites of Belize* (Cubola, Belize; o/p). An excellent handbook to fifteen of the most accessible sites in Belize, compiled by the Association for Belizean Archaeology and the Belize Department of Archaeology.

Thomas H. Guderjan *Ancient Maya Traders of Ambergris Caye* (Cubola, Belize). Interesting details about the original inhabitants of Belize's most popular tourist destination. Fifteen hundred years ago this was one of the busiest places in the Maya world, with even higher numbers of locals and visitors than there are today.

Peter D. Harrison *The Lords of Tikal* (Thames & Hudson, UK). Outstanding study of the great Maya metropolis, based on more than thirty years of research and the latest hieroglyphic readings. There's a tremendous amount of detail about the city's monuments and artifacts, and the rulers who commissioned them.

Grant D. Jones *The Conquest of the Last Maya Kingdom* (Stanford University Press, US). A massive academic tome that's also a fascinating history of the Itzá Maya and a gripping tale of how the Spanish entered and finally defeated the last independent Maya kingdom, at Tayasal, site of present-day Flores.

Joyce Kelly *An Archaeological Guide to Northern Central America* (University of Oklahoma, US). Detailed and practical guide to 38 Maya sites and 25 museums in four countries; an essential companion for anyone travelling purposefully through the Maya world. Kelly's "star" rating – based on a site's archeological importance, degree of restoration and accessibility – may affront purists but it does provide a valuable opinion on how worthwhile a particular visit might be. Still the most detailed single-edition guide available to the Maya sites of Belize, though recent developments make it somewhat dated in certain areas.

Diego de Landa *Yucatán Before and After the Conquest* (Dover, UK). A translation edited by William Gates of the work written in 1566 as *Relación de las Cosas de Yucatán*. De Landa's destruction of almost all original Maya books as "works of the devil" leaves his own account as the chief source on Maya life and society in the immediate post-conquest period. Written during his imprisonment in Spain on charges of cruelty to the Indians (remarkable in itself, given the institutional brutality of the time), the book provides a fascinating wealth of detail for historians. Although (as far as is known) Landa did not visit Belize, the vivid descriptions of Maya life and ceremony are applicable to the Maya of Chetumal, a province then extending into northern Belize.

Simon Martin and Nikolai Grube *Chronicle of the Maya Kings and Queens* (Thames & Hudson, UK). Highly acclaimed work based on exhaustive new epigraphic studies, and the re-reading of previously translated glyphic texts. The historical records of eleven key Maya cities – including Tikal and Caracol – complete with biographies of 152 kings and four queens, plus full dynastic sequences and all the key battles and dates. As Michael Coe, author of *The Maya* says, "There's nothing else like this book. It supersedes everything else ever written on Maya history."

Heather McKillop *Salt: White Gold of the Ancient Maya* (University Press of Florida, US). Salt, essential to life and a precious resource, was traded throughout the Maya world. This groundbreaking work overturns earlier theories, demonstrating that much of the salt consumed in the great lowland cities of Belize and Petén was produced on the coast of Belize. These previously unknown sites also show evidence of rising sea levels in the Postclassic Period, as many are now underwater. The author's latest book, *The Ancient Maya: New Perspectives* (ABC-CLIO, US) is a comprehensive account of the ancient Maya, incorporating the most recent findings and theories from current research.

John Montgomery *Tikal: An Illustrated History of the Ancient Maya Capital* (Hippocrene Books, US). Easily the most readable book on the subject and sure to become a classic. In addition to being a detailed history of Tikal, it's packed with fascinating information about the Maya in general, and the comprehensive chronology gives an overview of what was happening elsewhere in the Maya world. The author is a noted scholar and his other books (same publisher), including *A Dictionary of Maya Hieroglyphs* and *How to Read Maya Hieroglyphs*, are well worth reading.

Mary Ellen Miller *The Art of Mesoamerica: From Olmec to Aztec* (Thames & Hudson, UK). An excellent, wonderfully illustrated survey of the artisanship of the ancient cultures of Mexico, whose work reflects the sophistication of their civilizations. Miller is the acknowledged expert on Mayan and Mesoamerican art; her more recent *Maya Art and Architecture* (Thames & Hudson) provides fascinating and well-illustrated background reading, though little specifically on sites in Belize.

Mary Ellen Miller and Karl Taube *The Gods and Symbols of Ancient Mexico and the Maya: An Illustrated Dictionary of Mesoamerican Religion* (Thames & Hudson, UK). A superb modern reference on ancient Mesoamerica, written by two leading scholars. Taube's *Aztec and Maya*

Myths (British Museum Press, UK) is perfect as a short, accessible introduction to Mesoamerican mythology.

Jeremy A. Sabloff *The New Archaeology and the Ancient Maya* (Scientific American Library). Sabloff explains the "revolution" which has taken place in Maya archeology since the 1960s, overturning many firmly held beliefs and assumptions on the nature of Maya society, and stating how the study of archeology relates to current environmental problems.

Linda Schele and David Freidel (et al.) *A Forest of Kings: The Untold Story of the Ancient Maya* (Quill, US). The authors, at the forefront of the "new archeology", have been personally responsible for decoding many of the glyphs. Their writing style, which frequently includes "recreations" of scenes inspired by their discoveries, is controversial in some areas, but has nevertheless inspired a devoted following. This book, in conjunction with *The Blood of Kings* (Thames & Hudson, US; Braziller, UK), by Linda Schele and Mary Ellen Miller, shows that far from being governed by peaceful astronomer-priests, the ancient Maya were ruled by hereditary kings, lived in aggressive city-states and engaged in a continuous entanglement of alliances and war. *The Maya Cosmos* (Quill, US) by Schele, Freidel and Joy Parker is perhaps more difficult to read, dense with copious notes, but continues to examine Maya ritual and religion in a unique and far-reaching way. *The Code of Kings* (Scribner, US), written in collaboration with Peter Matthews and illustrated with Justin Kerr's famous "rollout" photography of Maya ceramics, examines in detail the significance of the monuments at selected Maya sites (Tikal is included, though none are in Belize). This, Schele's last book (she died in 1998), is a classic of epigraphic interpretation.

Robert Sharer *The Ancient Maya* (Stanford University Press, US). A comprehensive (and weighty) account of Maya civilization, now in a completely revised and much more readable fifth edition, yet as authoritative as ever. Required reading for archeology students, it also provides a fascinating reference for the non-expert.

J. Eric S. Thompson *The Rise and Fall of the Maya Civilization* (University of Oklahoma, US). A major authority on the ancient Maya, Thompson has produced many academic studies – this is one of the more approachable. *The Maya of Belize – Historical Chapters Since Columbus* (Cubola, Belize) is a very interesting book on the first two centuries of Spanish colonial rule —a little-studied area of Belizean history – and casts some light on the groups that weren't immediately conquered by the Spanish.

Wildlife and the environment

Belize has a range of superb wildlife books and pamphlets, written by specialists with visitors, teachers and students in mind. Unfortunately, many are difficult to obtain outside the country; the best ones might be available from Cubola or the Belize Audubon Society (BAS; see p.74), who offer a mail-order service.

Rosita Arvigo with Nadia Epstein *Sastun: My Apprenticeship with a Maya Healer* (HarperCollins, US). A rare glimpse into the life and work of a Maya *curandero*, the late Eligio Panti of San Antonio (see p.177). Dr Arvigo has ensured the survival of generations of healing knowledge, and this book is a testimony both to her perseverance in becoming accepted by Mr Panti and the cultural wisdom of the indigenous people. Arvigo has also written or collaborated on several other books on traditional medicine in Belize. *Rainforest Remedies: One Hundred Healing Herbs of Belize* (Lotus Books, US), co-authored with Michael Balick of the New York Botanical Garden, is a detailed account of some of Belize's commonest medicinal plants and their uses. Both books are widely available in Belize.

Les Beletsky *Belize and Northern Guatemala – The Ecotraveller's Wildlife Guide* (Academic Press, UK). Although other, specialist wildlife guides may cover their own subjects in more detail, this is the only reasonably comprehensive single-volume guide to the mammals, birds, reptiles, amphibians and marine life of the region. Helpfully, the illustration of each creature is given opposite its description, avoiding confusing page-flicking.

Louise H. Emmons *Neotropical Rainforest Mammals* (University of Chicago, US). Highly informative and very detailed, with colour illustrations by Francois Feer, a book written by experts for non-scientists. Local and scientific names are given, along with plenty of interesting snippets. Emmons is also the principal author of *The Cockscomb Basin Wildlife Sanctuary* (Producciones de la Hamaca, Belize; Orang-Utan Press, US), a comprehensive guide to the history, flora and fauna of Belize's Jaguar Reserve. Though aimed at teachers and students, it's incredibly useful to any visitor and is available from the sanctuary and the BAS.

Carol Farnetti Foster and John R. Meyer *A Guide to the Frogs and Toads of Belize* (Kreiger, US). Great book with plenty of photos and text to help you identify the many anurans you'll see – and hear – in Belize.

Tony Garel and Sharon Matola *A Field Guide to the Snakes of Belize* (Cubola, Belize). Slim guide to all 60 species of snakes in Belize, most illustrated with a colour photograph.

Idaz Greenberg *Guide to Corals and Fishes of Florida, the Bahamas and the Caribbean* (Seahawk Press, US). Great, easy-to-use guide to 260 species that you're most likely to encounter in Belize. Inexpensive and widely available on the cayes; it's waterproof, so you can take it with you on a snorkel trip.

Steve Howell and Sophie Webb *The Birds of Mexico and Northern Central America* (Oxford University Press, UK). The result of years of research, this tremendous work is the definitive book on the region's birds. Essential for all serious birders.

Paul Humann and Ned Loach *Reef Fish Identification: Florida, Caribbean and Bahamas* (New World, US). This guide is for real enthusiasts; it's the one the professionals use, with sturdy bindings, detailed drawings and 825 colour plates. *Reef Creatures* and *Reef Corals*, by the same publisher, are the definitive guides in their respective fields.

Kimo Jolly and Ellen McRae *The Environment of Belize* (Cubola, Belize). Intended as a high-school textbook, this is still an excellent introduction to the ecosystems of Belize. Clearly and intelligently covers all relevant issues from environmental laws to energy cycles.

H. Lee Jones *Birds of Belize* (University of Texas Press, US). A long-awaited, comprehensive guide to all 574 species so far recorded in Belize. Already receiving the highest praise from the experts, this excellent book is written by a biologist who's lived in the country for over ten years. At over three hundred pages it's a fairly weighty volume, but the text is very well organized, with 234 range maps, and the superb colour illustrations by Dana Gardner help you easily identify the birds you're looking at. The author, with A. C. Vallely, also has written the *Annotated Checklist of the Birds of Belize* (Lynx, US).

John C. Kricher *A Neotropical Companion* (Princeton University, US). Subtitled "An Introduction to the Animals, Plants and Ecosystems of the New World Tropics", this book contains an amazing amount of valuable information for nature lovers. Researched mainly in Central America and recently updated, there's plenty that's directly relevant to Belize.

Julian C. Lee *A Field Guide to the Amphibians and Reptiles of the Maya World* (Cornell UP, US). The definitive guide to the herpetology of Yucatán, northern Guatemala, with 180 photographs and 180 drawings covering all 188 species found in the region, with much of the research undertaken in Belize. Excellent range maps and there's even a guide to identifying tadpoles of different species of frogs and toads.

Alan Rabinowitz *Jaguar* (Anchor/Doubleday, US). A personal account of the author's experiences studying jaguars for the New York Zoological Society in the early 1980s, while living with a Maya family in the Cockscomb Basin. Rabinowitz was instrumental in the establishment of the Jaguar Reserve in 1984.

Stephen B. Reichling *Tarantulas of Belize* (Kreiger, US). The best guide to these fascinating and often falsely maligned creatures, telling you all you need to know about their habits and habitats, illustrated with plenty of photos and great anatomical drawings by Norma B. Reichling. A real gem for arachnophiles.

Fiona A. Reid *A Field Guide to the Mammals of Central America and Southeast Mexico* (Oxford University Press, UK). The first comprehensive guide to the mammals of the region, written by a truly dedicated researcher who also drew the colour illustrations based on live specimens she caught herself, many of them in Belize. Reid also has written and illustrated *Mammals of Belize* (Hopscotch Interactive, Canada), a booklet widely available in Belize.

Victoria Schlesinger *Animals and Plants of the Ancient Maya* (University of Texas, US). Part field guide, with illustrations by Juan C. Chab, and part author's observations and vignettes, this book covers around a hundred commonly seen species, giving for most of them their Maya name as well as their common and scientific name.

Peter J. Stafford and John R. Meyer *A Guide to the Reptiles of Belize* (Academic Press, UK). Superb, comprehensive and thoroughly detailed guide to the 120 species of crocodiles, turtles, lizards and snakes found in Belize; the colour photographs really help with identification.

Specialist guides

For field guides to plants, animals, birds, reptiles and the marine fish of Belize, look under Wildlife and the environment, p.372.

Emory King *Emory King's Driving Guide to Beautiful Belize* (Tropical Books, Belize). Worth a look if you're driving around the country. The maps are perhaps a little too sketchy for complete accuracy, but the book is typically Belizean: laid-back and easy-going.

Freya Rauscher *Cruising Guide to Belize & Mexico's Caribbean Coast* (Wescott Cove Publishing, US; o/p). Although aimed primarily at yachting visitors, this very detailed book offers fascinating insights into the cayes and the entire Belize Barrier Reef; you'll find it in some island resorts and on larger boats.

A single cookbook

Mmm... A Taste of Belizean Cooking (various authors; Cubola, Belize). A compilation of successful recipes and mixed drinks from chefs in restaurants and resorts all over Belize, illustrated by young artists from St John's College, Belize City. Everything from rice and beans with coconut milk from *Elvi's Kitchen* in San Pedro on Ambergris Caye to shrimp and feta pasta from Chef Whiz at *Tranquility Lodge*, Toledo District.

Language

Language

Kriol...379

Spanish 381

Language

English is the official language of Belize (the only English-speaking country in Central America) and naturally enough it's spoken everywhere. However, it's really the first language of only a small percentage of Belize's multilingual population, since seven main languages are spoken here, including the Mopan, Yucatec and Kekchí Maya dialects. For at least half the population, mainly the mestizos in the north and the west, **Spanish** is the language spoken at home and in the workplace. In fact, the last thirty years have seen a significant increase in the speaking of Spanish, largely due to immigration from neighbouring Central American countries. If you plan to cross the border into **Guatemala** to visit Tikal, some Spanish will be essential.

The first language of one third of the population – mainly the Creole people – is **Kriol** (the modern spelling favoured by linguists, though still usually spelt "Creole"), a language partly derived from English and similar to the languages spoken in other parts of the Caribbean colonized by the British. Uniting the different ethnic groups of Belize, it is the **most widely spoken** language. English and Kriol are the languages used in public or official situations and for speaking to outsiders. That said, listening to any conversation can be confusing, as people switch from, say, English to Kriol to Spanish to Garifuna and back – often in the same sentence.

Many **Garifuna** continue to speak their own tongue as their first language, although the only community where *everyone* does this is the village of Hopkins (see p.252). The Belizean **Mennonites** add to the linguistic cocktail with their old form of High German, spoken in many of their communities. The jigsaw puzzle is completed by recent immigrants from Asia speaking Chinese and south Asian languages.

Kriol

Kriol is the *lingua franca* of Belize: whether a local's first language is Maya, Spanish, Garifuna or English, they'll almost always be able to communicate in Kriol. It may sound like English from a distance and as you listen to a few words you'll think that their meaning is clear, but as things proceed you'll soon realize that complete comprehension is just out of reach; those familiar with other English Creole languages, however, may find understanding comes easily. It's a beautifully warm, expressive and relaxed language, typically Caribbean, with a vocabulary loosely based on English but with significant differences in pronunciation and a grammatical structure that is distinctly West African in origin. One characteristic is the heavy nasalization of some vowels, for example *waahn* (want) and *frahn* (from).

Written Kriol, which you'll see in some newspaper columns and booklets, is a little easier to come to grips with, though you'll need to study it hard at first to get the meaning. A booklet designed for use by Peace Corps volunteers explains the grammar; this is available from some bookstores. A dictionary is also available, though Kriol will always be much more of a spoken language than a written one.

Some history

Only in recent years has Kriol begun to be **recognized** as a distinct language, though there is still much debate among Belizeans as to whether it is just a dialect of English. In **colonial times** Kriol was not accepted as a legitimate language and its use was prohibited in schools, although in practice teachers often lapsed into it. But for all intents and purposes Kriol was (and remains) the language of the people both at home and work, clearly an integral part of their culture and identity. **Independence** brought a growing pride in the language and today a movement is underway to formalize Kriol and to recognize it as one of Belize's national languages, alongside English and Spanish.

For a long time Kriol was an **oral language** with no written form. However, by the 1970s some writers and poets were beginning to write it using ad hoc forms of spelling. In 1980 Sir Colville Young – at that time a school principal and today Governor General of Belize – published his *Creole Proverbs of Belize* (see p.269), and in 1993 a group of educators and enthusiasts started the **Belize Kriol Project** to work on developing Kriol into a written language. In 1995 the **National Kriol Council** was formed with the principal aim of promoting the culture and language of the Creole people of Belize. A standardized writing system using a phonemic structure has since been developed and, despite some controversy, is gradually gaining acceptance.

The Kriol Council's **website**, Ⓦwww.kriol.org.bz, has a great deal of useful information on the Kriol language, including a mini-dictionary and information on the history and culture of the Creole people.

Phrases and proverbs

To give a taste of Belizean Kriol, here are some useful phrases:

Excuse me, where is the post office?	Eksyooz mi, weh di poas aafis deh?
Where do I catch the bus to Dangriga?	Weh fu kech di bos tu Dangriga?
Do you have any rooms free?	Yu gat eni room fu rent?
How much is a single room?	How moch wahn singl room kaas?
I have some dirty laundry for washing.	Ah gat sohn doti kloaz fu wash.
Is there a restaurant near here serving Creole food?	Weh sel Kriol food kloas tu ya?

And some proverbs:

Proverb	Literal translation	Meaning
Mek di man weh loos taiga tai ahn bak.	*Let the man who loosed the tiger tie it back.*	Let the man who created a dangerous situation deal with it.
Fish geh kech bai ih own mowt.	*A fish gets caught by its own mouth.*	Guilt often gives itself away.
Kyaahn kech Hari, kech ih shot.	*If you can't catch Harry, catch his shirt.*	If you can't get what you want, get the next best thing.

Publications and media

For more of these fantastic **proverbs** arm yourself with a copy of *Creole Proverbs of Belize*, written by Sir Colville Young and available from bookstores and Angelus Press in Belize City. Several **publications** in Kriol have been produced, including *A Bileez Kriol Glassary an Spellin Gide* (a Kriol–English dictionary), *Rabbit Play Trik Pahn Hanaasi*, a traditional folktale, and *Kenti an Ih Pah Mek Wahn Doary*, a children's story about constructing a canoe.

Kriol is increasingly seen and heard in **radio and TV** advertising and on hoardings – for example, "*Dis da fu wi chikin*" ("This is our chicken") on delivery vans, and "*Da paynt yu waahn?*" ("You want paint?"). *The Reporter* newspaper has a weekly Kriol column, "*Weh Wi Gat fi Seh*" ("What we have to say"). An **anglicized Kriol** can often be heard on radio and TV, much easier for foreigners to understand.

The Kriol section was supplied by John Pirie.

Spanish

The **Spanish** spoken in both Guatemala and Belize has a strong Latin American flavour to it, and if you're used to the dainty intonation of Madrid or Granada then this may come as a surprise. Gone is the soft "s", replaced by a crisp and clear version. If you're new to Spanish it's a lot easier to pick up than the Iberian version.

The rules of **pronunciation** are pretty straightforward and, once you get to know them, strictly observed. Unless there's an accent, words ending in d, l, r and z are **stressed** on the last syllable, all others on the second last. All **vowels** are pure and short.

A somewhere between the "a" sound of back and that of father.

E as in get.

I as in police.

O as in hot.

U as in rule.

C is soft before "e" and "i", hard otherwise: *cerca* is pronounced serka.

G works the same way, a guttural "h" sound (like the *ch* in loch) before "e" or "i", a hard "g" elsewhere: *gigante* becomes higante.

H always silent.

J the same sound as a guttural "g": *jamón* is pronounced hamon.

LL sounds like an English "y": *tortilla* is pronounced torteeya.

N as in English unless it has a tilde (accent) over it, when it becomes "ny": *mañana* sounds like manyana.

QU is pronounced like an English "k".

R is rolled, RR doubly so.

V sounds more like "b", *vino* becoming beano.

X is slightly softer than in English – sometimes almost "s" – except between vowels in place names where it has an "h" sound – ie Mexico (Meh-hee-ko) or Oaxaca (Wa-ha-ka). Note: in Maya the English letter "x" is pronounced "*sh*", thus *Xunantunich* is Shunan-tun-eech.

Z is the same as a soft "c", so *cerveza* becomes servesa.

Although we've listed a few essential words and phrases, some kind of dictionary or **phrasebook** is a worthwhile investment: the *Rough Guide to Mexican Spanish* is the best practical guide, correct and colloquial, and certainly acceptable for most purposes when travelling in Guatemala. One of the best small Latin American Spanish dictionaries is the University of Chicago version (Pocket Books); the Collins series (published by HarperCollins) of pocket grammars and dictionaries is also excellent.

Basics

por favor, gracias	please, thank you
dónde, cuando	where, when
qué, cuanto	what, how much
aquí, allí	here, there
esto, eso	this, that
ahora, más tarde	now, later
abierto/a, cerrado/a	open, closed
con, sin	with, without
buen(o)/a, mal(o)/a	good, bad
gran(de), pequeño/a	big, small
más, menos	more, less
hoy, mañana	today, tomorrow
ayer	yesterday

Greetings and responses

hola, adios	hello, goodbye
Buenos días	Good morning
Buenas tardes/noches	Good afternoon/night
¿Qué tal?	How do you do?
Hasta luego	See you later
Lo siento/disculpeme	Sorry
Con permiso/perdón	Excuse me
¿Cómo está (usted)? (formal)	How are you?
¿Cómo estás? (to someone you know)	
De nada	Not at all/ You're welcome
(No) Entiendo	I (don't) understand
¿Habla (usted) inglés?	Do you speak English?
(No) Hablo español	I (don't) speak Spanish
¿Mande?	What (did you say)?
Me llamo...	My name is...
¿Cómo se llama usted?	What's your name?
Soy inglés(a)	I am English
americano(a)	...American
australiano(a)	...Australian
canadiense(a)	...Canadian
irlandés(a)	...Irish
escosés(a)	...Scottish
galés(a)	...Welsh
neozelandés(a)	...New Zealander

Needs, hotels and transport

Quiero	I want
¿Sabe…?	Do you know...?
Quisiera... por favor	I'd like....
No sé	I don't know
Hay (?)	There is (is there?)
Deme...	Give me...
(uno así)	(one like that)
¿Tiene...?	Do you have...?
...la hora	...the time
...un cuarto	...a room
...con dos camas	...with two beds
...con cama matrimonial	...with a double bed
Es para una persona	It's for one person
(dos personas)	(two people)
...para una noche	...for one night
(una semana)	(one week)
¿Está bien, cuánto es?	It's fine, how much is it?
Es demasiado caro	It's too expensive
¿No tiene algo más barato?	Don't you have anything cheaper?
¿Se puede...?	Can one...?
¿...acampar aquí (cerca)?	...camp (near) here?
¿Hay un hotel aquí cerca?	Is there a hotel nearby?
¿Por dónde se va a...?	How do I get to...?
Izquierda, derecha, derecho	Left, right, straight on
¿Dónde está...?	Where is...?
…el banco más cercano (*ATM is cajero automático*)	...the nearest bank
...el correo	...the post office
...el baño/sanitario	...the toilet
¿De dónde sale el camión para…?	Where does the bus to… leave from?
¿A qué hora sale llega en)...?	What time does it leave (arrive in)...?
¿Qué hay para comer?	What is there to eat?
¿Qué es eso?	What's that?
¿Cómo se llama esto en español?	What's this called in Spanish?

LANGUAGE | Spanish

Numbers and days

un/uno/una	1
dos	2
tres	3
cuatro	4
cinco	5
seis	6
siete	7
ocho	8
nueve	9
diez	10
once	11
doce	12
trece	13
catorce	14
quince	15
dieciséis	16
diecisiete	17
dieciocho	18
diecinueve	19
veinte	20
veintiuno	21
treinta	30
cuarenta	40
cincuenta	50
sesenta	60
setenta	70
ochenta	80
noventa	90
cien(to)	100
ciento uno/una	101
doscientos/as	200
quinientos/as	500
setecientos	700
mil	1000
mil novecientos noventa y nueve	1999
dos mil	2000
primero/a	first
segundo/a	second
tercero/a	third
quinto/a	fifth
décimo/a	tenth

Lunes	Monday
Martes	Tuesday
Miércoles	Wednesday
Jueves	Thursday
Viernes	Friday
Sábado	Saturday
Domingo	Sunday

Travel store

Kenya
Marrakesh **D**
Morocco
South Africa, Lesotho & Swaziland
Syria
Tanzania
Tunisia
West Africa
Zanzibar

Travel Specials
First-Time Africa
First-Time Around the World
First-Time Asia
First-Time Europe
First-Time Latin America
Travel Health
Travel Online
Travel Survival
Walks in London & SE England
Women Travel
World Party

Maps
Algarve
Amsterdam
Andalucia & Costa del Sol
Argentina
Athens
Australia
Barcelona
Berlin
Boston & Cambridge
Brittany
Brussels
California
Chicago
Chile
Corsica
Costa Rica & Panama
Crete
Croatia
Cuba
Cyprus
Czech Republic
Dominican Republic
Dubai & UAE
Dublin
Egypt
Florence & Siena
Florida
France
Frankfurt
Germany
Greece
Guatemala & Belize
Iceland
India
Ireland
Italy
Kenya & Northern Tanzania
Lisbon
London
Los Angeles
Madrid
Malaysia
Mallorca
Marrakesh
Mexico
Miami & Key West
Morocco
New England
New York City
New Zealand
Northern Spain
Paris
Peru
Portugal
Prague
Pyrenees & Andorra
Rome
San Francisco
Sicily
South Africa
South India
Spain & Portugal
Sri Lanka
Tenerife
Thailand
Toronto
Trinidad & Tobago
Tunisia
Turkey
Tuscany
Venice
Vietnam, Laos & Cambodia
Washington DC
Yucatán Peninsula

Dictionary Phrasebooks
Croatian
Czech
Dutch
Egyptian Arabic
French
German
Greek
Hindi & Urdu
Italian
Japanese
Latin American Spanish
Mandarin Chinese
Mexican Spanish
Polish
Portuguese
Russian
Spanish
Swahili
Thai
Turkish
Vietnamese

Computers
Blogging
eBay
iPhone
iPods, iTunes & music online
The Internet
Macs & OS X
MySpace
PCs and Windows
PlayStation Portable
Website Directory

Film & TV
American Independent Film
British Cult Comedy
Chick Flicks
Comedy Movies
Cult Movies
Film
Film Musicals
Film Noir
Gangster Movies
Horror Movies
Kids' Movies
Sci-Fi Movies
Westerns

Lifestyle
Babies
Ethical Living
Pregnancy & Birth
Running

Music Guides
The Beatles
Blues
Bob Dylan
Book of Playlists
Classical Music
Elvis
Frank Sinatra
Heavy Metal
Hip-Hop
Jazz
Led Zeppelin
Opera
Pink Floyd
Punk
Reggae
Rock
The Rolling Stones
Soul and R&B
Velvet Underground
World Music (2 vols)

Popular Culture
Books for Teenagers
Children's Books, 5-11
Conspiracy Theories
Crime Fiction
Cult Fiction
The Da Vinci Code
His Dark Materials
Lord of the Rings
Shakespeare
Superheroes
The Templars
Unexplained Phenomena

Science
The Brain
Climate Change
The Earth
Genes & Cloning
The Universe
Weather

NOTES

NOTES

NOTES

NOTES

NOTES

NOTES

Small print and

Index

A Rough Guide to Rough Guides

Published in 1982, the first Rough Guide – to Greece – was a student scheme that became a publishing phenomenon. Mark Ellingham, a recent graduate in English from Bristol University, had been traveling in Greece the previous summer and couldn't find the right guidebook. With a small group of friends he wrote his own guide, combining a highly contemporary, journalistic style with a thoroughly practical approach to travelers' needs.

The immediate success of the book spawned a series that rapidly covered dozens of destinations. And, in addition to impecunious backpackers, Rough Guides soon acquired a much broader and older readership that relished the guides' wit and inquisitiveness as much as their enthusiastic, critical approach and value-for-money ethos.

These days, Rough Guides include recommendations from shoestring to luxury and cover more than 200 destinations around the globe, including almost every country in the Americas and Europe, more than half of Africa and most of Asia and Australasia. Our ever-growing team of authors and photographers is spread all over the world, particularly in Europe, the USA and Australia.

In the early 1990s, Rough Guides branched out of travel, with the publication of Rough Guides to World Music, Classical Music and the Internet. All three have become benchmark titles in their fields, spearheading the publication of a wide range of books under the Rough Guide name.

Including the travel series, Rough Guides now number more than 350 titles, covering: phrasebooks, waterproof maps, music guides from Opera to Heavy Metal, reference works as diverse as Conspiracy Theories and Shakespeare, and popular culture books from iPods to Poker. Rough Guides also produce a series of more than 120 World Music CDs in partnership with World Music Network.

Visit www.roughguides.com to see our latest publications.

Rough Guide travel images are available for commercial licensing at www.roughguidespictures.com.

Rough Guide credits

Text editor: Seph Petta
Layout: Sachin Tanwar
Cartography: Alakananda Bhattacharya
Picture editor: Sarah Cummins
Production: Vicky Baldwin
Proofreader: Serena Stephenson
Cover design: Chloë Roberts
Editorial: London Kate Berens, Claire Saunders, Ruth Blackmore, Polly Thomas, Alison Murchie, Karoline Densley, Andy Turner, Keith Drew, Edward Aves, Nikki Birrell, Alice Park, Sarah Eno, Lucy White, Jo Kirby, Samantha Cook, James Smart, Natasha Foges, Roísín Cameron, Emma Traynor, Emma Gibbs, Joe Staines, Duncan Clark, Peter Buckley, Matthew Milton, Tracy Hopkins, Ruth Tidball; **New York** Andrew Rosenberg, Steven Horak, AnneLise Sorensen, Amy Hegarty, April Isaacs, Ella Steim, Anna Owens, Sean Mahoney; **Delhi** Madhavi Singh, Karen D'Souza
Design & Pictures: **London** Scott Stickland, Dan May, Diana Jarvis, Mark Thomas, Jj Luck, Chloë Roberts, Nicole Newman, **Delhi** Umesh Aggarwal, Ajay Verma, Jessica Subramanian, Ankur Guha, Pradeep Thapliyal, Anita Singh, Nikhil Agarwal
Production: Aimee Hampson
Cartography: London Maxine Repath, Ed Wright, Katie Lloyd-Jones; **Delhi** Jai Prakash Mishra, Rajesh Chhibber, Ashutosh Bharti, Rajesh Mishra, Animesh Pathak, Jasbir Sandhu, Karobi Gogoi, Amod Singh, Swati Handoo
Online: New York Jennifer Gold, Kristin Mingrone; **Delhi** Manik Chauhan, Narender Kumar, Rakesh Kumar, Amit Verma, Rahul Kumar, Ganesh Sharma, Debojit Borah
Marketing & Publicity: **London** Liz Statham, Niki Hanmer, Louise Maher, Jess Carter, Vanessa Godden, Vivienne Watton, Anna Paynton, Rachel Sprackett; **New York** Geoff Colquitt, Megan Kennedy, Katy Ball; **Delhi** Reem Khokhar
Manager India: Punita Singh
Series Editor: Mark Ellingham
Reference Director: Andrew Lockett
Publishing Coordinator: Helen Phillips
Publishing Director: Martin Dunford
Commercial Manager: Gino Magnotta
Managing Director: John Duhigg

Publishing information

This fourth edition published September 2007 by **Rough Guides Ltd**,
80 Strand, London WC2R 0RL
345 Hudson St, 4th Floor,
New York, NY 10014, USA
14 Local Shopping Centre, Panchsheel Park,
New Delhi 110017, India
Distributed by the Penguin Group
Penguin Books Ltd,
80 Strand, London WC2R 0RL
Penguin Group (USA)
375 Hudson Street, NY 10014, USA
Penguin Group (Australia)
250 Camberwell Road, Camberwell,
Victoria 3124, Australia
Penguin Books Canada Ltd,
10 Alcorn Avenue, Toronto, Ontario,
Canada M4V 1E4
Penguin Group (NZ)
67 Apollo Drive, Mairangi Bay, Auckland 1310,
New Zealand

Cover concept by Peter Dyer.

Typeset in Bembo and Helvetica to an original design by Henry Iles.

Printed in Italy by LegoPrint S.p.A

416 includes index

A catalogue record for this book is available from the British Library

ISBN: 978-1-84353-846-6

1 3 5 7 9 8 6 4 2

Help us update

We've gone to a lot of effort to ensure that the fourth edition of **The Rough Guide to Belize** is accurate and up to date. However, things change – places get "discovered", opening hours are notoriously fickle, restaurants and rooms raise prices or lower standards. If you feel we've got it wrong or left something out, we'd like to know, and if you can remember the address, the price, the time, the phone number, so much the better. We'll credit all contributions, and send a copy of the next edition (or any other Rough Guide if you prefer) for the best letters. Everyone who writes to us and isn't already a subscriber will receive a copy of our full-colour thrice-yearly newsletter. Please mark letters: "**Rough Guide Belize Update**" and send to: Rough Guides, 80 Strand, London WC2R 0RL, or Rough Guides, 345 Hudson St, 4th Floor, New York, NY 10014. Or send an email to **mail@roughguides.com.**

Have your questions answered and tell others about your trip at **www.roughguides.atinfopop.com.**

Acknowledgements

Peter Eltringham: This edition of the Rough Guide to Belize is the only one in the book's history that, due to illness, I've not been able to research myself. So, first of all I'd like to say a very big thank you to Daniel, Nadine and AnneLise for stepping in and travelling through this beautiful country for the update. Thanks also to the Rough Guides staff, including Seph, AnneLise and Andrew, for all their hard work. I've now made a full recovery but I couldn't have done so without the support of all my family and friends here in the UK, in Guatemala and throughout Belize – many, many thanks to all of you. I'll be seeing you all, with a copy of the new edition, very soon.

Nadine Pedoe: Completing the research and writing for this edition during a very sickly pregnancy has been a challenge and I thank all those in Belize who gave me extra assistance and kindness. Many of those are listed in the guide and special thanks should be given to Allison Morris, Renita Dellaca and Cindy Reinert in San Pedro, everyone in Sarteneja, Andrew and Janis in Corozal, Katie Valk in Belize City, Stefano Ragagnin in Placencia and Tropic Air for transporting me. Thanks also to the many generations that have protected Belize and allowed it to remain so close to nature. Thanks as well to the Rough Guides team, especially Joseph Petta and AnneLise Sorensen for their advice and patience. Thanks always to Peter Eltringham for all his help and advice, and, most of all, thanks to my husband for sharing his love and knowledge of and devotion to his country with me.

AnneLise Sorensen: In Belize: thanks to all who welcomed me in and shared information, advice, stories and lively evenings, including Emory King; Lorraine Herrera and Shakira Oxley at the Belize Tourism Board; the knowledgeable staff at the Museum of Belize; Françoise Boscardi; Lucy and Mick Fleming; Orlando and Cyndi at *Hotel de la Fuente*; the helpful folks at the *Mopan Hotel*, *The Great House*, *Black Orchid Resort*, *La Casa de Don David* in El Remate and *Casazul* in Flores; Jungle River Tours; Gaby and Oty at *D'Nest Inn*; Mark Usher at *Faiyah Haat*; Niall Gillett at Old River Adventures; Katie Valk; and Mo and Irene Miller at *Lazy Iguana* on Caye Caulker. *Gracias*, also, to friends and family for their cheery emails and phone calls, and to Kurt Sorensen, who was a splendid travel companion, as always. I'd also like to give special thanks to Nadine, Daniel and especially Peter Eltringham. And on the homefront: thanks to Sachin Tanwar, Umesh Aggarwal and the rest of the Delhi team; Alakananda Bhattacharya, Maxine Repath and Katie Lloyd-Jones for top-notch maps; and Sarah Cummins and the London team for photo research. And finally, a resounding thanks to Seph Petta for editing the book with enthusiasm, patience and aplomb, and to Andrew Rosenberg for his overall guidance and support.

Daniel C. Chang: First, a special thank you to Peter Eltringham, who can take credit for many of the wonderful adventures I've had in Belize. Many thanks to Seph Petta and the entire Rough Guides editorial team for your support and the opportunity to contribute to this guide. Also, thanks to Nadine and AnneLise for your help and collaboration – it was truly a pleasure to work with such a great team. A genuinely big thank you to everyone in Belize, who were all vital in helping me with this guide, including but not limited to: Matt Miller, Bruno Kuppinger, Wende Bryan, Yuko Ikeda, Anabel Ford, Sharon Matola, Juli Puryear, Ken Dart, Chena Galvez, Tony and Erica Chuc, Yoli Collins, Maria Preston, Martha August, Lisa Crawford, David Simpson, Elsie Alpuche, Therese Rath, Andrew Usher, Breeze Cabral, Marsha-Jo Lomont, Darius Avila, Brad Paumen, Marcos and Teodora Cucul and Mick and Lucy Fleming. And thanks to all those in Belize who speedily and accurately responded to my last-minute enquiries. Chet Schmidt and Wil Maheia – thanks for everything over the years, and I wish you both the best in your endeavours. A big thank you to Diana Tasher and the Belize Medical Associates for superb care and treatment, and I'd especially like to thank Carlos Santos for your tremendous support, enthusiasm and resourcefulness during the research. Back in the US, thanks to my mother, father and friends for your enduring support of my endeavours; Victoria Brown and Susanne Hackett for your encouragement and assistance; and to Brienne Collison, who has loved and supported me through my many pursuits.

The **editor** would like to thank AnneLise Sorensen, Daniel Chang, Nadine Pedoe, Andrew Rosenberg, Amy Hegarty, Sachin Tanwar, Sarah Cummins, Alakananda Bhattacharya, Maxine Repath and Katie Lloyd-Jones, Christina Markel and his family.

Readers' letters

Thanks to the readers who have taken the time to write in with comments and suggestions (and apologies if we've inadvertently omitted or misspelt anyone's name):

F. Antone Accuardi, Cindy Blount, Shaun Bollig, Claire Boobbyer, Jane Bryce, Dave Chadwick, Joe Clift, Eleanora Cunietti, Scott Enriquez, Roberto Fabbri, Roy Fontaine, Elisabeth Fox, Jerry Garfield, Allan M. Gathercoal, Abby and Javier Gomez, Richard Hahn, Louis Hellerman, Anja Huber, Reinhard Illner, Helga Itulah, Dawn Kaiser, Kevin Layton, Suzanne Lehr, Laura Leveson, Ann Llewellyn, David McIntosh, Sherawaye Pascual, Lola Reid, Peter S. Ross, Lea Schulman, Sarah E. Spencer, Justin Teerlinck, Janis Valdes, Mary Weerts, Peter J. Wright

Photo credits

All photos © Rough Guides except the following:

Title page

Palapa in Belize © Mark Lewis/Alamy

Full page

Glover's Reef © Stephen Frink Collection/Alamy

Introduction

Queen angelfish © Brandon Cole Marine Photography/Alamy
Maya pottery © David Sanger Photography/Alamy
Local art sign © Daniel C. Chang
Ambergris Caye © Brandon Cole Marine Photography/Alamy
Scarlet macaws © Paul Cannon/Alamy
Women at Garifuna festival © Robert Harding Picture Library Ltd/Alamy
Beach for sale on Caye Caulker © AnneLise Sorensen

Things not to miss

02 Path through the Mountain Pine Ridge © Robert Harding Picture Library Ltd/Alamy
03 Stone carving of Altar 12, Caracol © Danita Delimont/Alamy
04 Loggerhead turtle © Visual&Written SL/Alamy
05 Carnival © James Beveridge
07 Maya ruins at Lamanai © Jon Crwys-Williams/Alamy
08 Garifuna drumming © Bruno Morandi/Robert Harding Picture Library Ltd
09 Toucan © Visual&Written SL/Alamy
10 Blue Hole © Danita Delimont/Alamy
11 Museum of Belize © James Beveridge
12 Watersports off Caye Caulker © Nadine Pedoe
13 Cave canoeing near San Ignacio © James Caldwell/Alamy
14 Belize Zoo © Robert Harding Picture Library Ltd
15 San Ignacio © Corbis
16 Sea kayaking © Mark Lewis/Alamy
17 Grand Plaza ruin, Tikal © Robert Harding Picture Library Ltd/Alamy
19 Lobster-Fest © Nadine Pedoe

Colour section: Belize's reef and cayes

Diver at Barrier Reef © Brandon Cole Marine Photography/Alamy
Queen angelfish © Brandon Cole Marine Photography/Alamy
Lighthouse Reef © Danita Delimont/Alamy
Dolphins © Daniel C. Chang
Sea kayaking group at Tobacco Caye © Zach Holmes/Alamy
Windsurfers © Nadine Pedoe

Colour section: The Maya world

Grand Plaza ruin, Tikal © AM Corporation/Alamy
Carving detail in Plaza B, Caracol © Danita Delimont/Alamy
Temple of the Masonry Altars, Altun Ha © Robert Harding Picture Library Ltd/Alamy
Climbing a pyramid, Caracol © Danita Delimont/Alamy
Maya vessels in ATM cave © Steve Taylor/Alamy

Black and whites

p.62 Shoppers and vendors, Belize City © Central America/Alamy
p.67 Swing Bridge © Nadine Pedoe
p.76 Courthouse © Central America/Alamy
p.80 Coatimundi, Belize Zoo © Danita Delimont/Alamy
p.92 *Chan Chich Lodge*, Gallon Jug © Macduff Everton/Corbis
p.96 Black howler monkey © Kevin Schafer/Alamy
p.106 Mennonite boys © Jon Crwys-Williams/Alamy
p.118 Locals in Corozal © Jeff Greenberg/Alamy
p.124 Snorkeller at Half Moon Caye © Brandon Cole Marine Photography/Alamy
p.136 Chairs on Ambergris Caye © Donald Nausbaum/Alamy
p.147 Caye Caulker palm trees © Alamy
p.155 Fishing on Turneffe Islands © M. Timothy O'Keefe/Alamy
p.160 Caracol © Danita Delimont/Alamy
p.172 Hiking to ATM cave © Daniel C. Chang
p.182 Waterfall in Mountain Pine Ridge © Danita Delimont/Alamy
p.203 Xunantunich carving © Keith Douglas/Alamy
p.210 Girls in Flores © Thomas Lehne/Alamy
p.218 People climbing Tikal temple © Robert Fried/Alamy
p.226 Boat on Lago Peten Itzá © Danita Delimont/Alamy
p.234 Laughing Bird Caye © Jim West/Alamy
p.248 Dangriga boat man © Zach Holmes/Alamy
p.257 Hopkins drummer © Jim West/Alamy
p.264 Jaguar reserve © Ange/Alamy
p.277 Kayaks on Monkey River © Joel W. Rogers/Corbis
p.300 Houses near San Antonio © Alamy
p.310 Hernán Cortés © South American Pictures
p.332 Maya calendar stone © Sylvia Cordaiy Photo Library Ltd/Alamy
p.342 Fish among mangrove roots © Images&Stories/Alamy
p.352 Cruise ship in Belize City harbour © Bill Bachmann/Alamy
p.358 Local musician in Belize City © Barry Lewis/Alamy

Index

Map entries are in colour.

A

Abalone Caye 291
accommodation 31
Actun Loch Tunich 241
Actun Tunichil Muknal... 173
Aguacate 298
Aguada Hotel (Cayo Dist.) 176
Aguascalientes Lagoon....................... 297
airlines 19–25
- in Australia and New Zealand 21
- in Belize 27
- in North America 22
- in UK and Ireland 23

airpasses 23
Airport, Belize International................. 68
Altun Ha (Maya site) 98
Altun Ha 99
Ambergris Caye... 129–144
Ambergris Caye........... 131
- accommodation 134–136
- arrival and departure 130–132
- Bacalar Chico Marine Reserve............. 141
- diving and reef trips... 138–140
- drinking and nightlife 144
- eating 142–144
- Hol Chan Marine Reserve......................... 140
- information 132
- Maya sites 142
- sailing 140
- San Pedro *see* San Pedro
- shops and galleries 137
- snorkelling 139

Amigos Dive Camp (Turneffe Is.) 156
Andy Palacio 294, 359
Antelope Falls............... 252
ARCAS (Guatemala) 230
Archaeology Symposium................ 336
Archaeology, Belize Institute of................. 169
archeology.......... 108, 113, 169, 196, 198, 335–337, 369–372 & *The Maya world* colour section
Archives Department.... 169
Arenal 199
art galleries.......... 8, 72–75, 137, 266
arts 8, 45, 72, 206, 267
Arvigo, Rosita 202
atolls .... 126, 154–157, 343 & *Belize's reef and cayes* colour section
atolls and northern cayes 126
Audubon Society, Belize 74
Augustine/Douglas Silva 180

B

Bacalar Chico National Park and Marine Reserve 141
Banana Bank Lodge (Cayo Dist.) 166
bank cards...................... 54
banks............................. 53
Banquitas House of Culture.................. 106
Baron Bliss 77
Barranco....................... 293
Barrier Reef .... 125, 343 & *Belize's reef and cayes* colour section
Barrier Reef Reserve System....................... 125
Barton Creek Cave 174
Baymen 63, 313–318
Be Pukte Cultural Center....................... 195
beer 36
Belize 4–5
Belize, northern 94
Belize, southern... 236–237
Belize, western 162–163
Belize Agroforestry Research Center........ 297
Belize Association of Conservation NGOs (BACONGO)............... 349
Belize Botanic Gardens..................... 202
BELIZE CITY 61–90
Belize City............... 64–65
- accommodation 69
- airlines 95
- airports 68
- arrival 68
- Bliss Centre for the Performing Arts 76
- bookshops 98
- car rental 98
- drinking 94–95
- eating 81–84
- embassies 73
- hassle 68
- history 63
- House of Culture 75
- Image Factory 95
- immigration 98
- information 69
- moving on from 95–97
- Museum of Belize 75
- nightlife 94–95
- orientation 67
- tours 99
- travel agents 99

Belize Eco-Tourism Association (BETA) 349
Belize Foundation for Research and Environmental Education (Bfree) 279
Belize National Dance Company 365
Belize River Lodge (Belize Dist.)................. 95
Belize Tourism Board..................... 56, 69
Belize Tourism Industry Association............ 32, 56
Belize Zoo 15, 79, 350
Belmopan 167
Belmopan..................... 168
Ben Lomond's Cave 239
Ben's Bluff Trail............. 263
Benque House of Culture.................. 206
Benque Viejo del Carmen (Cayo Dist.)................ 206
Bermudian Landing........ 97
Big Falls........................ 283
biodiversity 345
Bird's Eye View Lodge (Crooked Tree) 102
birding......... 100–102, 111, 114, 129, 152, 164–166, 188–189, 240, 249, 263, 350

Black Rock River Lodge (Cayo Dist.)..............201
Blackbird Caye Resort (Turneffe Is.)..............156
Bladen Nature Reserve..............279
Blancaneaux Lodge (Cayo Dist.)..............182
Bliss Centre for the Performing Arts..............76
Blue Creek (Orange Walk Dist.)..............112–114
Blue Creek (Toledo Dist.)..............297
Blue Creek Rainforest Lodge (Toledo Dist.)...297
Blue Hole National Park..............240
Blue Hole Natural Monument (Lighthouse Reef)..............126, 129
Blue Marlin Lodge (South Water Caye)...251
Bluefield Range Cayes..............154
boat travel..............28
Boca del Rio (Ambergris Caye)..............137
Bocatura Bank (Sittee River)..............258
Boden Creek Ecological Reserve..............282
Bol's Camping and Tours (Cayo Dist.)..............180
boobies, red-footed.....129, 151, 157
books..............366–375
Botanic Garden, Green Hills..............175, 176
Botanic Gardens, Belize..............202
Branch Mouth..............194
British High Commission..............168
buccaneers..............127, 313
Buenavista del Cayo (Maya site)..............199
Bullet Tree Falls..............195
Burdon Canal Nature Reserve..............238
Burnaby, Admiral..............314
Burrell Boom..............95
buses..............21, 27, 86
butterfly exhibits..............116, 170, 175, 176, 202, 206, 262

C

Caana..............184
cacao..............290
Caesar's Place (Cayo Dist.)..............173
Cahal Pech (Maya site)..............194
camping..............34, 180, 263
Canning House Library...55
Canul, Marcos.....103, 104, 320
car rental..............30
Caracol (Maya site)....183
Caracol..............184
Caribbean Court of Justice..............355
Caribbean ecosystems..............342
Carnival..............63, 363
Carrie Bow Caye..............251
Casa Bonita Apartments (Punta Gorda)..............284
Casa Maya Eco-Resort (Cayo Dist.)..............200
Cashew Festival (Crooked Tree)..............101
casinos..............94
Caste Wars of Yucatán...93, 103, 127, 319
Cattle Landing..............284
caves and caving..............43
- Actun Loch Tunich..............241
- Actun Tunichil Muknal......173
- archeology..............335 & *The Maya world* colour section
- Barton Creek Cave..............174
- Ben Lomond's Cave..............239
- cave tubing...188 & *The Maya world* colour section
- Che Chem Ha Cave..............207
- Chiquibul Caves..............186
- Crystal Cave..............240
- Hokeb Ha Cave..............298
- Museum Cave..............180
- Rio Frio Cave..............181
- St Herman's Cave..............240
- San Ignacio area..............194

Caves Branch Jungle Lodge (Cayo Dist.).....241
Caves Branch River......241
Caye Bokel..............156
Caye Caulker..............144–153
Caye Caulker..............146
- accommodation..............147–149
- activities..............151, 152
- arrival and departure..............145
- drinking..............153
- eating..............152
- information..............147
- Marine Reserve..............149
- Mini Reserve..............145
- reef trips..............150–152

Caye Chapel..............154
cayes... 124–157, 257–278, 291, 292 & *Belize's reef and cayes* colour section
cayes, northern..............126
Cayo District..............161–207
Cayo and the west..............162–163
cenotes..............216
Cerro Cahuí, Biotopo...216
Cerros (Maya site)..............120
Chaa Creek Lodge and Camp (Cayo Dist.).....200
Chaa Creek Natural History Centre..............202
Chalillo Dam..............352
Chan Chich Lodge (Orange Walk Dist.)....113
Chau Hiix (Maya site)...102
Chetumal..............95, 107, 117, 121
Chiquibul Cave System..............186
Chiquibul Road..............174
chocolate, organic..............290 & *The Maya world* colour section
chultun..............113
CITES (Convention on International Trade in Endangered Species)...45
Clarissa Falls (Cayo Dist.)..............200
Clovis culture..............305
Coastal Road..............238
Cockscomb Basin Wildlife Sanctuary..............260–264
Cohune Palms (Bullet Tree Falls)..............196
Columbus Reef..............249
Columbus, Christopher..............127
communications..............54
Community Baboon Sanctuary (Bermudian Landing)..............96
Confederate settlements..............110, 286, 369
Consejo..............120
conservation..............128, 345–353 & *Belize's reef and cayes* colour section
Copper Bank..............121

Copper Bank Inn 121
coral reef ...6, 14, 128, 343
& *Belize's reef and cayes* colour section
Corozal 117
Corozal 116
Corozal Free Zone........ 121
Cortés, Hernán 309–311
Costa Maya Festival..... 137
costs 47, 53, 212
Cox Lagoon Crocodile Sanctuary 165
crafts ....45, 74, 137, 216, 222, 228, 285 & *The Maya world* colour section
credit and debit cards 54
Creole language 379
Creoles 63, 356
crime and safety............ 48
Cristo Rey..................... 177
Cristo Rey Road 176
crocodile sanctuary, Macanché (Guatemala) 216
Crooked Tree................ 101
Crooked Tree Wildlife Sanctuary 100
cruise ships 73–75, 353
Cruzob Maya........ 103, 320
Crystal Cave................. 240
Crystal Paradise Resort (Cayo Dist.) 177
Crystal Skull 10, 294
Cucul, Marcos 165, 169, 194, 240, 300
Cucumber Beach Wharf 78
Cuello (Maya site)......... 107
cuisine 34, 345
currency...........47, 53, 212
cycling 30

D

dance.............76, 243, 365
Dangriga 243–249
Dangriga 244
Dávila, Alonso.............. 311
disabled travellers 56
discography.................. 360
diving and snorkelling...43
& *Belize's reef and cayes* colour section
Ambergris Caye 138, 139
Blue Hole 139
Caye Caulker 150, 151
Glover's Reef.................... 259
Hol Chan Marine Reserve........................ 140
Hopkins 253
Lighthouse Reef.............. 151
Placencia......................... 274
St George's Caye............ 154
South Water Caye........... 250
technical diving 138
Turneffe Islands............... 156
Tobacco Caye 250
doctors 39
domestic flights 27
Doyle's Delight......261, 300
drink............................... 35
driving 29
drugs, illegal 47
drum-making 238
Dump junction (Toledo Dist.)............. 283
duPlooy's (Cayo Dist.) .. 200
Dzuluinicob.................. 188

E

Earthwatch 52, 336
East Indians..........285, 356
economy........................ 323
Ek Tun Cabañas (Cayo Dist.)............... 201
El Castillo (Xunantunich)............. 204
El Chiclero Hotel (Burrell Boom).............. 95
El Pilar (Maya site and reserve) 196–198
El Pilar 197
El Remate (Guatemala) 216
El Retiro, Santuario Ecológico (Guatemala) 215
El Sombrero (Guatemala) 214
electricity 49
Eligio Panti National Park 177
email 51
embassies 49, 50, 74
Enna's Guest House (Monkey River)........... 278
entry requirements 49
Environment, Department of the 347
environmental issues........ 128, 345–353
& *Belize's reef and cayes* colour section
ethnic groups 356
exit tax...................47, 212

F

False Sittee Point 255
festivals 42, 363
film...........................42, 73
Film Festival 42, 73
Five Blues Lake National Park............. 242
Five Sisters Lodge (Cayo Dist.)................ 183
flights 19–25
from Australia and New Zealand.......................... 21
from North America 19
from UK and Ireland.......... 19
shopping for...................... 19
within Belize...................... 27
Floral Park (Maya site)...174
Flores (Guatemala) 226–231
Flores 227
Flores and Tikal 211
accommodation 228
activities 230
arrival............................... 228
departure.......................... 231
eating and drinking 229
information 228
tours and guides.............. 230
food 34, 345
forest ecosystems 345
Frank's Caye................ 292
Free Trade Area of the Americas (FTAA) 324
French Louie Caye 276
Friends of Nature.......... 274

G

Gales Point.................. 238
Gales Point Wildlife Sanctuary 238
Gallon Jug 113
Garcia sisters............... 177
Garifuna 246
food................ 243, 247, 248, 255, 256, 266
history 78, 246, 356
music................. 14, 243, 253, 256, 266, 358, 362
religion........................ 10, 294
Settlement Day 10, 42, 243, 252
Garvey, Marcus 321
Gaviota Coral Reef Resort (Tobacco Caye).......... 250
gay and lesbian travel 50
Gentle's Cool Spot (Gales Point) 239

INDEX

geology 345
George Price Centre..... 169
Georgeville.... 170, 174, 190
Gladden Spit Marine
Reserve 275
Glover's Atoll Resort..... 259
Glover's Guest House
(Sittee River) 258
Glover's Reef....... 258–260
& *Belize's reef and cayes*
colour insert
Golf Club, Roaring
River 170
golf, frisbee.................. 206
Gracie Rock................. 164
Green Hills Butterfly
Ranch 175, 176
Green Reef (Ambergris
Caye) 138
Guacamallo Bridge....... 179
Guacamallo Jungle
Camp (Cayo Dist.) 200
Guanacaste National
Park 166
Guatemala 210–231
Guatemalan border
practicalities 212
Guerrero, Gonzalo 310

H

H'men Herbal Center ... 263
Half Moon Caye
(Lighthouse Reef) 157
Handicraft Center,
Belize City................... 74
handicrafts............... 45, 74,
137, 216, 222, 228, 285 &
The Maya world
colour section
harpy eagle............ 79, 195,
263, 339
Hasaw Chan K'awil 219
hassle 68
Hattieville..................... 164
Hawkesworth Bridge... 176,
194
health...................... 36–40
herbal medicine..... 39, 195,
196, 202, 370, 373
Hidden Valley Falls 181
Hidden Valley Inn
(Cayo Dist.) 181
Hill Bank Field Station... 113
history........ 305–333 & *The*
Maya world colour section
hitchhiking 30
Hokeb Ha Cave 298
Hol Chan Marine
Reserve 140
Hopkins 252–256
Hopkins 254
accommodation 253–255
activities 252, 253
arrival and departure 253
drinking and nightlife 256
eating 255, 256
Lebeha 253
tours and guides 253
hotel rates...................... 32
hotel tax......................... 32
howler monkey
("baboon") 97
human rights 354, 355
Hummingbird
Highway 239–243
Hunting Caye............... 291
Hurricane Hattie 66
hurricanes............. 11, 129,
235, 342

I

Icaiché Maya 103, 320
Iguana Junction
(Bullet Tree Falls) 196
Image Factory 72
immigrants................... 356
immigration
regulations 49, 88
Independence.............. 273
Indian Church 110
Indian Creek 280
Indian Creek Lodge 282
Indian Creek Trail ... 165, 242
Inn at Robert's Grove
(Placencia) 266
insurance 50
International Airport,
Belize 68
Internet 51, 56, 57
Isla Marisol Resort
(Glover's Reef) 260
Itzá Maya 312
Ix Chel Wellness
Center 176, 202
Ixlú (Guatemala)............ 216

J

Jacintoville.................. 284
Jaguar Reserve........... 10,
263, 264
Jalacte (Toledo Dist.) 302
Jonkunu dance 243

K

Kanantik Reef and Jungle
Resort (Stann
Creek Dist.) 264
Kekchí Maya 278
King, Emory 73, 74
Kinich Ahau 99
Kriol language 356, 379

L

La Milpa (Maya site) 112
La Milpa Field Station ... 112
La Ruta Maya
Canoe Race... 42, 77, 190
La Unión (Mexico) 112
Ladyville......................... 95
Lago Petén Itzá
(Guatemala) 226
Lago Petén Itzá 216
Laguna Tintal
(Guatemala) 216
Lamanai Field Research
Center 108
Lamanai
(Maya site) 108–111
Lamanai 109
Lamanai Outpost
Lodge 111
Lana's on the Reef
(Tobacco Caye).......... 250
landscape and
wildlife............. 338–344
& *Belize's reef and cayes*
colour section
language.......... 8, 379–383
Las Cuevas Research
Station 186
Last Resort, The (Copper
Bank) 121
Latin America Bureau..... 55
Latin American Information
Center 56
Laughing Bird Caye
National Park 275
laundry 51
Leslie Cottages (South
Water Caye) 251
Lighthouse Reef 14, 126,
156
Lime Caye 292

literature 366–375
Lívingston (Guatemala), boats to 287
Lobster-Fest 16, 42, 145, 267
Lodge at Big Falls (Toledo Dist.) 283
logwood 63, 127, 313
Long Caye (Glover's Reef) 259
long count calendar 325, 333
Lord Smoking Shell 109
Lubaantun (Maya site) 295
Lubaantun 296
Lucky Strike 100

M

Macal River... 161, 199–202
Macanché (Guatemala) 215
Machaca Hill Lodge (Toledo Dist.) 284
Mafredi 297
mahogany 314
Mai Gate 180
mail 52
malaria 37
Mama Noots Backabush (Stann Creek Dist.) 251
Manatee Lodge (Gales Point) 239
Manatee Road 238
Manatee Special Development Area 238
manatees ..... 115, 151, 157, 238, 343 & *Belize's reef and cayes* colour section
Man-O'-War Caye 249
Marco Gonzalez (Maya site) 137
marine ecosystems ...... 342 & *Belize's reef and cayes* colour section
Marine Terminal, Belize City 72
Mariposa Beach Suites (Placencia) 267
Maroon Creole Drum School 238
Martz Farm (Cayo Dist.) 201
Maruba Resort and Jungle Spa (Belize Dist.) 100
Maskall 100
Massachusetts Audubon Society 111
massage 33, 98, 136, 149, 152, 193, 200, 274
Maya *see* The Maya world colour section
Maya world, the 330
Archaic Period 306, 325
archeology 335
astronomy 333
calendar 306, 332
chronology 325, 326
Classic Period 307, 325
healing 176, 177, 196, 201, 263, 373
modern Maya ... 255, 266, 270, 329
Postclassic Period 308, 309, 325
Preclassic Period 306, 307
religion and ritual 333, 334
society 329
time units 332
Village Guest House Programme 289, 290
Maya Beach 265
Maya Centre 262
Maya Mountain Divide Trail 235, 300
Maya Mountain Lodge (Cayo Dist.) 176
Maya Mountains ... 171, 177, 183, 186, 199, 235, 239, 249, 340
Mayflower (Maya site and National Park) 251
media 41
medical information 39, 40
medicinal plants 39, 195, 196, 202, 370, 373
Mejen Tz'il Lodge (Maya Centre) 262
Melchor de Mencos 212
Mennonites 104–106, 112, 113, 171, 173, 356, 357
Mesoamerica 305
Mesoamerican Biological Corridor 347
mestizos 8, 206, 356
Metho's Coconut Camping (Gales Point) 239
Mexican border crossing 121
Middle Caye (Glover's Reef) 260
Miller's Landing (Placencia) 267
Moho River (Toledo Dist.) 298
money 47, 53, 212
Monkey Bay Wildlife Sanctuary 164
Monkey River 276–278
Mopan Maya 278
Mopan River 161, 186, 194, 195, 199–202
Mopan River Resort (Cayo Dist.) 207
Mountain Equestrian Trails (Cayo Dist.) 175
Mountain Pine Ridge ... 13, 170–186
Municipal Airport, Belize City 68
Musa, Said 323
Museo Tikal 223
Museum Cave 180
Museum of Belize (Belize City) 75
music 14, 238, 239, 294, 358–364
music venues ... 78, 94, 174

N

National Handicraft Center 74
National Kriol Council ... 380
Nature Resort (Bermudian Landing) ... 97
New River 93, 111, 117, 341
New River Lagoon 108
newspapers 41
Nicolas Caye 292
Nim Li Punit (Maya site) 281
Nim Li Punit 281
Noh Petén (Guatemala) 226
Nohmul (Maya site) 107
non-governmental organizations (NGOs) 348, 350
Northeast Caye (Glover's Reef) 259
Northeast Caye (Sapodilla Cayes) 292
Northern Caye (Lighthouse Reef) 157
Northern Highway 68, 94
Northern Lagoon (Gales Point) 238

Nu'uk Che'il Cottages (Maya Centre)............263
nurse shark..................140 & *Belize's reef and cayes* colour section

O

Off the Wall Resort (Glover's Reef)...........259
Old Belize Cultural and Historical Center....78, 79
Olmec civilization..........305–307
opening hours................54
Orange Walk.......103–107
Orange Walk................103
 accommodation...............104
 arrival and departure........104
 Banquitas House of Culture......................106
 eating and drinking..........106
 information......................104
 tours and guides.............110
Over the Top................242

P

Pacbitún (Maya site).....178
Palacio, Andy.......294, 359
Palacio's Mountain Retreat......................242
Panti, Don Eligio...177, 201
Paradise Inn (Crooked Tree)...........102
Parrot Nest Lodge (Bullet Tree Falls).................196
Passionflower Collection, Belize National...........176
Pelican Beach Resorts (South Water Caye)...251
People's United Party (PUP)................321
Petencito Zoo (Guatemala)...............230
pine bark beetle...179, 341
Pine Ridge Lodge (Cayo Dist.)................182
pirates..........................312
Placencia peninsula..........265–278
Placencia (village)...10, 16, 267–273
Placencia.....................268
 accommodation.......270, 271
 arrival and departure......267, 269, 273
 sailing, kayaking and fishing..................274, 275
 diving and snorkelling.......274
 eating and drinking................271, 272
 information.......................269
Plan Pueblo-Panamá....295
Planeta..........................56
police.......................48, 68
Pook's Hill Jungle Lodge (Cayo Dist.).....171
Port Honduras Marine Reserve......................291
Possum Point Biological Station.......................258
postal services...............52
Postclassic Period.........98, 107, 113, 120, 308
Poustinia Land-Sculpture Park.......................8, 206
Preclassic Period.........178, 195, 198, 301, 306
Price, George...............321
Privy Council................355
Programme for Belize..................74, 350
protected areas..........98, 108, 111, 125, 129, 141, 165, 170, 345–353 & *Belize's reef and cayes* colour section
protected areas...........346
Protected Areas Conservation Trust (PACT).......212, 349
public holidays...............54
public transport........28–30
Pueblo Escondido (Cayo Dist.)................100
Pueblo Viejo (Toledo Dist.).............301
Puente Natural.............186
Puerto Barrios (Guatemala), boats to...............28, 287
Puerto Cortés (Honduras), boats to.........28, 87, 249
Punta Gorda........284–289
Punta Gorda................285
 accommodation..............288
 arrival and departure.............286, 287
 eating, drinking and nightlife.................288, 289
 information..............286, 287
 tours and guides............286, 289–292
Punta Negra (Toledo Dist.).............290
punta rock....................358
Pusilhá (Maya site).................298

Q

quetzal (Guatemalan currency)...................213

R

radio..............................41
rainforest............292, 297, 298, 302, 345
Rainforest Medicine Trail............................201
Ramsar site..................101
Ranguana Caye............276
rappelling...241 & *The Maya world* colour section
Red Bank......................279
Reef's End Lodge (Tobacco Caye)..........250
refugees, Central American..................328
Rendezvous Caye........155
Ricardo's Beach Huts (Bluefield Range Cayes)........................154
Richardson Peak..........280
Rio Blanco National Park...........................301
Rio Bravo Conservation and Management Area..................111–114
Rio Frio Cave................181
Río Hondo............104, 121
Rio On Pools................181
river kayaking......161, 195, 199, 277
Riversdale.....................265
Riverside Lodge (Bullet Tree Falls).......196
Roaring Creek......166, 167
Roaring River Golf Club...................170
rock climbing................241
Ropewalk Caye (Turneffe Is.)...............156
Rum Point Inn (Placencia).................267

S

sailing.....15, 43, 128, 130, 140, 151, 239, 258, 264, 273–275
St George's Caye.........154

St George's Caye, Battle of.....315
St George's Lodge (St George's Caye)....154
St Herman's Cave........240
St Margaret's Village.....242
sales tax.........47
Sam Tillet's Hotel (Crooked Tree)..........102
San Antonio (Cayo Dist.)..........177
San Antonio (Toledo Dist.)..........299
San Benito Poité (Toledo Dist.)..........298
San Ignacio...16, 186–193
San Ignacio..........187
San Ignacio, around....178
- accommodation.......191, 192
- arrival..........190
- eating, drinking and nightlife..........192–194
- history..........187–190
- information..........190
- tours and guides..........188

San José (Toledo Dist.)..........300
San José Succotz........203
San Juan (Maya site)..........141,142
San Pablo..........108
San Pedro (Ambergris Caye)..........129–144
San Pedro..........133
- accommodation..........134–136
- activities..........130–132
- arrival and departure..........130–132
- diving and reef trips...138–140
- drinking and nightlife.......144
- eating..........142–144
- information..........132
- sailing..........140
- shops and galleries..........137
- snorkelling..........139

San Pedro Columbia....295
Santa Cruz (Toledo Dist.)..........300
Santa Elena (Cayo Dist.)..........176
Santa Elena (Guatemala)......226–231
Santa Elena..........227
- accommodation..........229
- activities..........230
- arrival..........228
- departure..........231
- eating and drinking..........230
- information..........228
- tours and guides..........230

Santa Elena (Mexican border).......121
Santa Rita (Maya site)..........119
Sapodilla Cayes Marine Reserve..........292
Sarstoon-Temash National Park..........292
Sarteneja..........114, 115
scarlet macaw..........9, 79, 263, 278, 279, 352
sea kayaking..........16, 22, 259, 260, 276, 291, 293
security..........48
Seine Bight..........266
September Celebrations........42, 363
Serenade Island Resort (Sapodilla Cayes).......292
serpentarium (Guatemala)..........215
Serpon Sugar Mill.........256
Shark-Ray Alley..........140
Shipstern Nature Reserve..........115, 116
shopping..........45
Sibun River..........164, 238
Silk Cayes Marine Reserve..........275
Silver Creek..........281
Sittee Branch River......261
Sittee River..........256
Siwa-Ban Foundation...350
Skyway Ixpanpajul (Guatemala)..........230
slate carvings..........45
Slate Creek Preserve....175
slavery..........246, 316
Snake Cayes..........291
snorkelling *see* diving and snorkelling
Soberanis, Antonio.......321
South Water Caye........250
Southern Highway.......235, 243, 251
Southern Lagoon (Gales Point)..........238
Southwest Caye (Glover's Reef)..........260
souvenirs..........45
Spanish language.........381
Spanish Lookout...173, 174
spas..........98, 100, 136, 152, 200, 274
sports..........43
Stann Creek valley.......242
study abroad..........51
Sun Creek Lodge (Toledo Dist.)..........283
Sunset Inn (Monkey River)..........278
Super Constellation (airliner)..........112
Swallow Caye Wildlife Sanctuary..........157

T

Tanah Museum..........177
Tapir Mountain Nature Reserve..........170
taxes..........47
taxis..........30
Tayasal..........311
Teakettle..........171
telephones..........54
televison..........41
Temash River..........292
The Last Resort (Copper Bank)..........121
Thompson, J. Eric S.....204
Thousand-foot Falls.....181
Tiger Fern Falls..........263
Tikal..........16, 218–226 & *The Maya world* colour section
Tikal..........220–221
Tikal and Flores..........211
- accommodation..........223
- history..........219
- information.......212, 213, 222
- museums..........223
- Tikal Canopy Tour..........223
- transport to......212, 213, 222

time..........55
tipping..........44
Tipú..........188
Tobacco Caye..........250
Tobacco Caye Lodge...250
Tobacco Caye Paradise..........250
toilets..........44, 46
Toledo Association for Sustainable Tourism and Empowerment (TASTE)..........292
Toledo District.....278–302
Toledo District, southern..........293
Toledo Ecotourism Association..........290
Toledo Institute for Development and Environment (TIDE)...290, 351
Toledo Visitors Information Center..........286
Toltec influence..........309
topographic maps..........53

Topoxté (Maya site)......214
toucans..........................14
Toucan Sittee
(Sittee River)..............256
tour operators.........43, 48
in Ambergris Caye ... 138, 139
in Australia and
New Zealand 25
in Belize............................ 29
in Belize City 69
in Caye Caulker.........150–152
in Flores
(Guatemala).......... 230, 231
in North America.......... 22, 23
in San Ignacio.................. 188
in UK and Ireland......... 23, 24
Tranquility Lodge
(Toledo Dist.)..............284
travel advice...................48
travel and guide
books................366, 367
travel essentials........ 47–57
travel health clinics... 36–40
travel insurance..............50
traveller's cheques 54
Trek Stop Cabins
(Cayo Dist.)................205
Tri-national Alliance for the
Conservation of the Gulf
of Honduras...............290
Tropical Education
Center..........................81
Tropical Update (The
Weather Channel)......129
Tropical Wings Butterfly
House........................205
Turneffe Island Lodge...156
Turneffe Islands............155
Turtle Inn (Placencia)....267
turtles, marine........13, 238,
258, 344
Tutzil Nah Cottages
(Maya Centre)............262

U

Uaxactún..............212, 219
United Democratic
Party (UDP)................323
United States Embassy...74
Upper Barton Creek.....175
Uxbenká (Maya site).....300
vaccinations 37

V

Victoria Peak Trail.........261
video.............................42
visas 49
voluntary organizations
(conservation).....51, 52,
348–351

W

Waight, Beatrice...........196
water purification...........38
water taxis.......87, 95, 121,
130, 145, 269, 287
websites 56
Wee Wee Caye.............258
whale shark.................258
& *Belize's reef and cayes*
colour section
Whipray Caye...............276
Wild Cane Caye............291
wildlife................... 338–344
wildlife books 372–374
Wildlife Care Center.....350
Wildlife Conservation
Society..............260, 351
windsurfing..........140, 255,
259 & *Belize's reef and*
cayes colour section
wine................................36
women travellers......30, 48
work.........51, 52, 348–351
World Challenge
Expeditions..................52
World Heritage Site 125
World Land Trust..........350
World Wide Fund for
Nature........................350

X

Xcalak Peninsula
(Mexico).....................129
Xunantunich
(Maya site)................204
Xunantunich.................205

Y

Ya'axché Conservation
Trust (YCT).................350
Yaxhá (Maya site) 214
Yucatán, Caste
Wars of 93, 103,
127, 319
Yucatec Maya...............177

Z

Zoo, Belize 15, 79
Zoo, Petencito
(Flores, Guatemala) ...230

Map symbols

maps are listed in the full index using coloured text

- International boundary
- Chapter boundary
- District boundary
- Major road
- Minor road
- Path
- River
- Reef
- Escarpment
- Mountain range
- Gorge
- Peak
- Cave
- Waterfall
- Place of interest
- One-way arrow
- Immigration post
- Maya ruin
- Lighthouse
- Bus stop
- Airport
- Parking
- Hospital
- Tree
- Internet
- Phone office
- Tourist office
- Restaurant/bar/café
- Accommodation
- Campsite
- Petrol station
- Post office
- Golf course
- Monument
- Building
- Church
- Stadium
- Cemetery
- Park
- Beach
- Jungle/forest